The Privacy Law Sourcebook 2020

United States Law, International Law and Recent Developments

MARC ROTENBERG

Electronic Privacy Information Center
WASHINGTON DC

Electronic Privacy Information Center
1519 Connecticut Ave. NW
Washington, DC 20036

Visit the EPIC Bookstore
http://www.epic.org/bookstore/

Edition 2020
Printed in the United States of America
All Rights Reserved

ISBN 13: 978-1-7326139-3-5
ISBN 10: 1-7326139-3-1

Preface to the 2020 Edition

The EPIC Privacy Law Sourcebook continues to provide a basic reference for those interested in privacy law. The **Sourcebook** highlights the major laws in the field, recent developments, and useful resources. The 2020 edition includes the complete text of California Consumer Privacy Act and the Illinois Biometric Information Privacy Act, two of the most influential privacy laws in the United States. Both laws show the vitality of the state legislative process and also caution against federal legislation that would make it more difficult for states to respond to emerging challenges. The **EPIC Privacy Law Sourcebook** also includes the Cybersecurity Law of China. The Chinese law increasingly frames the most consequential privacy developments in that country. As with the past editions, we have included the text of the GDPR, though with the EU law the focus has shifted from adoption to enforcement. We will follow developments on that front closely over the next year.

We have also included the declaration from The Public Voice proposing a moratorium on facial recognition. Few privacy issues have received more attention in the past few years. From a ban in the state of California concerning police-worn body cameras to the protests in the streets of Hong Kong, this particular technology has raised profound challenges for lawmakers and democratic societies. A new website, managed by EPIC, tracks developments in this field. (epic.org/banfacesurveillance/)

Over twenty years, we have seen the growing significance of case law from the high courts in North America, Europe, and Asia. **The Privacy Law Sourcebook** is limited to statutory materials and legal frameworks. A discussion of recent court decisions can be found in ALLEN AND ROTENBERG, PRIVACY LAW AND SOCIETY (West Academic) and the associated website privacylawandsociety.org, which includes links to significant opinions interpreting the laws included in the **Sourcebook**.

We are at an interesting moment in the development of privacy law in the United States. For the first time in many years, there is widespread support in Congress for comprehensive legislation and perhaps also the creation of a data protection agency. More than a dozen bills have been introduced. Democrats in the Senate have put forward a framework for data protection incorporating the major elements of a modern-day privacy law, with clear rights for individuals and clear responsibilities for companies that choose to collect and use personal data. There is also a provision on algorithmic transparency. Among the legislative proposals, the Online Privacy Act, introduced in the House, has received the top score from EPIC, based on a careful review of the Act's provisions and as compared with international norms for data protection. (The evaluation from EPIC is available here: epic.org/GradingOnACurve/.) The Online Privacy Act would establish a data protection agency and fill a gap in the structure of U.S. privacy law that has long concerned advocates, scholars, and also U.S. trading partners. The Online Privacy Act would be a welcome addition to the next edition of the **EPIC Privacy Law Sourcebook.**

The *2020 Privacy Law Sourcebook* was prepared with the expert assistance of EPIC International Counsel Eleni Kyriakides. Ms. Kyriakides' contributions to the efforts to establish stronger human rights safeguards for the cross-border transfer of personal data sought by law enforcement are also worth noting.

As always, we welcome your suggestions. Please send comments, corrections and additions to pls@epic.org. EPIC will continue to make *The Privacy Law Sourcebook* freely available to students, researchers, and policymakers. For more information visit: epic.org/bookstore/pls2020/

Marc Rotenberg
Washington, DC
November 2019

Preface to the 2018 Edition

Twenty years have now passed since we published the first collection of U.S. and international privacy laws. Our aim was to provide a useful reference to those interested in the text of basic privacy law, and to enable well informed policy proposals as new challenges emerged. With the 2018 edition of *The Privacy Law Sourcebook*, we continue to highlight most significant legal frameworks around the world, including most notably the GDPR. We have also expanded the listing of resources and included links to national legislation as well as a current Privacy Year in Review.

There have been institutional changes in the privacy world over the past year. The Article 29 Working Party, once the source of useful commentary on emerging privacy issues, has given way to the European Data Protection Board. We hope the EDPB will continue this important function as the public seeks to understand how legal frameworks apply to new circumstances.

The year 2018 is notable also because of the Privacy Shield review and the growing concern that Europe and the United States will not be able to maintain a legal basis for the processing of personal data. Twenty years ago, it appeared that the U.S. and Europe were heading toward convergence. Today, the world looks very different.

Over twenty years, we have also seen the growing significance of case law from the high courts in North America, Europe, and Asia. Although *The Privacy Law Sourcebook* is limited to statutory materials and legal frameworks, discussion of recent cases can be found in Allen and Rotenberg, Privacy Law and Society (West Academic 2015), and the associated web site privacylawandsociety.org, which includes also links to significant opinions.

The 2018 *Privacy Law Sourcebook* was prepared with the expert assistance of EPIC International Counsel Eleni Kyriakides and EPIC Policy Director Caitriona Fitzgerald.

As always, we welcome your suggestions. Please send comments, corrections and additions to pls@epic.org. EPIC will continue to make *The Privacy Law Sourcebook* freely available to students, researchers, and policymakers. For more information: epic.org/bookstore/pls2018/

Marc Rotenberg
Washington, DC
September 2018

Preface to the 2016 Edition

More than a decade has passed since the last publication of *The Privacy Law Sourcebook*. Although much has happened in the privacy world, we remain committed to providing an accurate and timely collection of the main legal instruments for privacy protection in the modern age, as well as useful resources to aid further research.

In the current version of *The Sourcebook*, we include the recently adopted General Data Protection Regulation of the European Union that will soon replace the EU Data Protection Directive. The GDPR is perhaps the most significant development in modern privacy law, reflecting the ongoing challenge of enabling new technology and new business practices while safeguarding a fundamental right.

Post Snowden, the United Nations has refocused its efforts on privacy and data protection, created a Special Rapporteur on the Right to Privacy, and passed several important resolutions. The 2014 resolution of the General Assembly on the Right to Privacy in the Modern Age is included, as are related texts from the UN. In this edition of *The Privacy Law Sourcebook*, as in previous editions, Article 12 of the UN Universal Declaration of Human Rights provides the starting point for the establishment of privacy as a fundamental right.

We also draw attention in this edition to regional frameworks for privacy protection, including the Cairo Declaration on Human Rights in Islam, the Declaration of Principles on Freedom of Expression in Africa, and the Declaration of Santa Cruz de la Sierra.

Over the past decade, there was not as much privacy activity in the United States as one might have hoped. The section on US materials, but for a few amendments (some favorable, some not) remains largely unchanged, though the passage of the USA Freedom Act in 2015 did bring about the end of the bulk record collection program in the United States. And recent legislation points to emerging privacy safeguards for automated vehicles and new techniques for deidentification.

NGOs and experts continue to play an important role shaping the contours of the modern right to privacy. We note both the Madrid Privacy Declaration and the Necessary and Proportionate Principles.

The *2016 Privacy Law Sourcebook* was prepared with the assistance of Caitriona Fitzgerald, John Tran, and Kimberly Miller. Please send comments, corrections, and suggestions to pls@epic.org. Related resources will be found also at privacy.org and privacylawandsociety.org.

Marc Rotenberg
Washington, DC
September 2016

Preface to 2004 Edition

The 2004 edition of the *Privacy Law Sourcebook* chronicles recent developments in the privacy and data protection world. New US legislation includes the Video Voyeurism Prevention Act, the Do-Not-Call Implementation Act, and the CAN-SPAM Act. New reports from the Article 29 Working Group examine the technology of Radio Frequency Identification (RFID), the impact on methods to protect intellectual property rights on data protection, and the application of European privacy law to unsolicited marketing communications. The APEC Privacy Framework, adopted in 2004, is a significant new development as is the new Mexican Information Law. We have updated the privacy resources section and added links to new laws for many countries, including the new member states of the European Union.

As we have noted in previous editions, our goal is to keep the *Privacy Law Sourcebook* to a single volume. As a result, we do not reprint certain materials that can be found in earlier editions. These include (from the *Privacy Law Sourcebook 2003*) the Argentina Data Protection Act and EU materials on the transfer of Passenger Name Record (PNR) Data; (from the *Privacy Law Sourcebook 2002*) the proposed consent decree between Microsoft and the US Federal Trade Commission; (from the *Privacy Law Sourcebook 2001*) materials on the Safe Harbor Arrangement, the Personal Data Protection Law for Latvia, the Protection of Personal Data Act for the Czech Republic; (from the *Privacy Law Sourcebook 2000)* the Italian Data Protection Act, the Council of European Guidelines for Internet Privacy, the Privacy Law of Chile, the Personal Information Protection Act of Canada, the UK Regulation of Investigative Powers Act; and (from the *Privacy Law Sourcebook 1999*) the Freedom of Information and Protection of Privacy Act for British Columbia, the German Law for Information and Communication, and the Hong Kong Personal Data (Privacy) Ordinance. Readers are encouraged to consult earlier editions of the Privacy Law Sourcebook for these materials. Significant reports from the Article 29 Working Group may also be found in earlier editions of the Privacy Law Sourcebook. The annual *Privacy and Human Rights* report contains extensive country reports and thematic materials. We have also removed the text of the US Freedom of Information Act from the *Privacy Law Sourcebook*. That law and detailed legal commentary will be found in the EPIC publication *Litigation Under the Federal Open Government Laws*.

The 2004 *Privacy Law Sourcebook* was prepared with the assistance of Charles Duan, Ula Galster, Cédric Laurant, Katitza Rodriguez Pereda, and Nerisha Singh. Please send comments, corrections, and suggestions to pls@epic.org.

Marc Rotenberg
Washington, DC
August 2005

Preface to First Edition

This collection provides a basic set of privacy materials for the United States and the international sphere. The materials are current as of the time of publication. Application of U.S. statutes and international instruments, such as the Council of Europe Convention, are subject to judicial interpretation and case decisions that are not included in this volume. Certain U.S. privacy laws, such as the Privacy Act of 1974, are qualified by federal regulations, which are also not included. The section on privacy resources provides information about how to locate additional legal material on privacy.

Several points should be made about the development of privacy laws. In the United States, privacy statutes have typically resulted from an effort by the legislative branch to address a matter left unresolved by the judicial branch or they have resulted from an attempt to codify a legal standard for privacy for commercial transactions in new technological services.

In the first category are such laws as the Right to Financial Privacy Act of 1978, the Privacy Protection Act of 1980, and to some extent, the Electronic Communication Privacy Act of 1986. These laws came about in response to decisions of the United States Supreme Court where the Court chose not establish a privacy right. Part of the development of privacy law in the United States is, therefore, the dialogue between the courts and the legislature on the proper scope of privacy as a legal claim.

In the second category are such laws as the Privacy Act of 1974, the Video Privacy Protection Act of 1988, the Employee Polygraph Protection Act of 1988, and the Telephone Consumer Protection Act of 1991. These statutes came about in direct response to new technologies that raised public concern and called for the establishment of legal standards to protect privacy.

The Electronic Communications Privacy Act is, in many respects, the most complex of US privacy laws. Its roots can be found in the dissent of Justice Brandeis in *Olmstead v. United States,* the first case in which the United States Supreme Court considered the Constitutionality of electronic surveillance. Title III of the Omnibus Crime Control Act of 1968, the precursor to ECPA, codified two decisions of the Supreme Court from the 1967 term and established the legislative framework for regulating electronic surveillance. In 1986 Title III was amended to include stored electronic mail and data in transit, and the name was changed to the "Electronic Communications Privacy Act." Then in 1994, the Act was once again amended to provide law enforcement access to electronic communications.

The Privacy Act of 1974 and the Freedom of Information Act, first enacted in 1966 and then significantly expanded in 1974, are a special case. These two laws were passed to give citizens rights of privacy and rights of access, two complimentary legal claims, in government record-keeping systems. They fall into a hybrid of the two categories described above: an attempt by Congress to establish legal rights in the absence of judicial decision-making and a response to new developments in technology.

The privacy materials provided here from the international sphere are of a different origin. In the first instance, they reflect a fundamental concern with human rights. This can be seen, for example, in Article 12 of the Universal Declaration of Human Rights that established privacy as a fundamental human right shortly after the end of World War II. Language similar to that found in Article 12 will be found in other international instruments on human rights, not included in this volume, such as the International Covenant on Civil and Political Rights (Article 17), the European Convention on Human Rights (Article 8), and the American Convention on Human Rights (Article 11). Many of these documents can be found at the web site of Privacy International.

In the second instance, international privacy law attempts to address the problem of privacy protection across national borders, what is sometimes called "transborder data flows." The Council of Europe Convention, for example, and the European Data Directive set out privacy standards so that personal information is protected when it moves between nations. Commentators on international privacy law have often noted that the paradox of privacy is found in this need to protect data so that it may be exchanged more freely.

The guidelines of the Organization for Economic Cooperation and Development do not of themselves have the force of law. However, OECD principles have played an important role in directing the development of national law and helping to establish international legal norms. By way of example, the subscriber privacy provisions of the Cable Communications Policy Act adopted in the United States in 1984 follow closely the OECD Privacy Guidelines of 1980.

The Data Protection Directive of the European Union is the most significant development in privacy law in many years. It draws together several of the traditions in privacy law. Based on the precept that privacy is a fundamental human right, it establishes a common standard for privacy protection for the benefit of European citizens among the member states of the European Union. It also seeks to extend privacy standards to the new, rapidly evolving commercial environment. The critical question of how the European Commission will determine whether data may be transferred to countries that lack similar privacy standards is taken up in the Recent Developments section in a short piece prepared by a working group of the European Commission on the problem of "adequacy."

The Recent Developments section also looks at several attempts to extend privacy principles in the age of the Internet. The German Telecommunications law is the first privacy law specifically tailored to recent on-line developments. It is noteworthy in that it both applies traditional Fair Information Practices to new commercial services and also encourages the use of anonymous payment techniques.

The OECD Cryptography Guidelines cover one of the most interesting and rapidly developing areas in privacy law and policy. The technique to encode digital data offers the possibility that technology could protect privacy, a belief that runs contrary to the premise supporting most privacy law to date. An appropriate role for public policy may be to encourage its adoption. Cryptography also raises some new privacy issues. Both dimensions were considered in the development of the OECD Cryptography Guidelines.

Also included in this section is the pledge of database firms concerning the protection of personal privacy. This might not generally be considered appropriate for a volume of legal materials. It is included here to show one approach to privacy protection.

The Freedom of Information and Protection of Privacy Act for British Columbia is one of the most recent privacy laws adopted in North America. Its structure and scope provides a helpful example of the role of privacy and access law in our modern society. Recent developments include the growing presence of the US Federal Trade Commission in the enforcement of privacy policies. Excerpts from the Federal Trade Commission Act are included.

I am grateful to the Georgetown University Law Center for the opportunity to develop my course on information privacy law over the last several years and to the Washington College of Law. Shauna Van Dongen, Lisa Harrinanan, and Dan Lin helped with the production of this volume. Privacy International and the Electronic Privacy Information Center provided excellent resources for privacy materials.

Marc Rotenberg
Washington, DC
August 1998

TABLE OF CONTENTS

DETAILED TABLE OF CONTENTS

United States Law

FEDERAL TRADE COMMISSION ACT
(1914) [EXCERPT]

Summary

In 1914 Congress passed the Federal Trade Commission Act (FTCA) to protect consumers from deceptive practices and unfair methods of competition. An unfair method of competition is defined under section 45(n) as "one that causes or is likely to cause substantial injury to consumers which is not reasonably avoidable by consumers themselves and not outweighed by countervailing benefits to consumers or to competition."

The Act created the Federal Trade Commission to regulate and enforce its provisions. It gave the FTC authority to investigate unfair practices, to pursue complaints, to issue reports, and to enforce orders. Thus, if the FTC finds that a practice violates the Act it may issue an order requiring the individual or entity to cease from using such method or practice. The individual or entity subject to the order may request to a court to review the order. If the court finds the practice to be unfair or deceptive it may impose preliminary/permanent injunctions or a penalty of no more than $10,000 for each violation of the FTC order.

References

Public Law 63-203. Codified as amended at 15 U.S.C. § 45 et seq.
[https://www.law.cornell.edu/uscode/text/15/45]

Federal Trade Commission, Privacy Initiatives
[https://www.ftc.gov/tips-advice/business-center/privacy-and-security]

EPIC, Federal Trade Commission
[https://www.epic.org/privacy/internet/ftc/]

* * *

§ 45. Unfair methods of competition unlawful; prevention by Commission

(a) Declaration of unlawfulness; power to prohibit unfair practices; inapplicability to foreign trade

(1) Unfair methods of competition in or affecting commerce, and unfair or deceptive acts or practices in or affecting commerce, are hereby declared unlawful.

(2) The Commission is hereby empowered and directed to prevent persons, partnerships, or corporations, except banks, savings and loan institutions described in section 57a(f)(3)

of this title, Federal credit unions described in section 57a(f)(4) of this title, common carriers subject to the Acts to regulate commerce, air carriers and foreign air carriers subject to part A of subtitle VII of title 49, and persons, partnerships, or corporations insofar as they are subject to the Packers and Stockyards Act, 1921, as amended [7 U.S.C. 181 et seq.], except as provided in section 406(b) of said Act [7 U.S.C. 227(b)], from using unfair methods of competition in or affecting commerce and unfair or deceptive acts or practices in or affecting commerce.

(3) This subsection shall not apply to unfair methods of competition involving commerce with foreign nations (other than import commerce) unless-

(A) such methods of competition have a direct, substantial, and reasonably foreseeable effect-

(i) on commerce which is not commerce with foreign nations, or on import commerce with foreign nations; or

(ii) on export commerce with foreign nations, of a person engaged in such commerce in the United States; and

(B) such effect gives rise to a claim under the provisions of this subsection, other than this paragraph.

If this subsection applies to such methods of competition only because of the operation of subparagraph (A)(ii), this subsection shall apply to such conduct only for injury to export business in the United States.

(4)

(A) For purposes of subsection (a), the term "unfair or deceptive acts or practices" includes such acts or practices involving foreign commerce that-

(i) cause or are likely to cause reasonably foreseeable injury within the United States; or

(ii) involve material conduct occurring within the United States.

(B) All remedies available to the Commission with respect to unfair and deceptive acts or practices shall be available for acts and practices described in this paragraph, including restitution to domestic or foreign victims.

(b) Proceeding by Commission; modifying and setting aside orders

Whenever the Commission shall have reason to believe that any such person, partnership, or corporation has been or is using any unfair method of competition or unfair or deceptive act or practice in or affecting commerce, and if it shall appear to the Commission that a proceeding by it in respect thereof would be to the interest of the public, it shall issue and serve upon such person, partnership, or corporation a complaint stating its charges in that respect and containing a notice of a hearing upon a day and at a place therein fixed at least thirty days after the service of said complaint. The person, partnership, or corporation so complained of shall have the right to appear at the place and time so fixed and show cause why an order should not be entered by the Commission requiring such person, partnership, or corporation to cease and desist from the violation of the law so charged in said complaint. Any person, partnership, or corporation may make application, and upon good cause shown may be allowed by the Commission to intervene and appear in said proceeding by counsel or in person. The testimony in any such proceeding shall be reduced to writing and filed in the office of the Commission. If upon such hearing the Commission shall be of the opinion that the method of competition or the act or practice in question is prohibited by this subchapter, it shall make a report in writing in which it shall state its findings as to the facts and shall issue and cause to be served on such person, partnership, or corporation an order requiring such person, partnership, or corporation to cease and desist from using such method of competition or such act or practice. Until the expiration of the time allowed for filing a petition for review, if no such petition has been duly filed within such time, or, if a petition for review has been filed within such time then until the record in the proceeding has been filed in a court of appeals of the United States, as hereinafter provided, the Commission may at any time, upon such notice and in such manner as it shall deem proper, modify or set aside, in whole or in part, any report or any order made or issued by it under this section. After the expiration of the time allowed for filing a petition for review, if no such petition has been duly filed within such time, the Commission may at any time, after notice and opportunity for hearing, reopen and alter, modify, or set aside, in whole or in part any report or order made or issued by it under this section, whenever in the opinion of the Commission conditions of fact or of law have so changed as to require such action or if the public interest shall so require, except that (1) the said person, partnership, or corporation may, within sixty days after service upon him or it of said report or order entered after such a reopening, obtain a review thereof in the appropriate court of appeals of the United States, in the manner provided in subsection (c) of this section; and (2) in the case of an order, the Commission shall reopen any such order to consider whether such order (including any affirmative relief provision contained in such order) should be altered, modified, or set aside, in whole or in part, if the person, partnership, or corporation involved files a request with the Commission which makes a satisfactory showing that changed conditions of law or fact require such order to be altered, modified, or set aside, in whole or in part. The Commission shall determine whether to alter, modify, or set aside any order of the Commission in response to a request made by a person, partnership, or corporation under paragraph [1] (2) not later than 120 days after the date of the filing of such request.

(c) Review of order; rehearing
Any person, partnership, or corporation required by an order of the Commission to cease and desist from using any method of competition or act or practice may obtain a review of such order in the court of appeals of the United States, within any circuit where the method of competition or the act or practice in question was used or where such person, partnership, or corporation resides or carries on business, by filing in the court, within sixty days from the date of the service of such order, a written petition praying that the order of the Commission be set aside. A copy of such petition shall be forthwith transmitted by the clerk of the court to the Commission, and thereupon the Commission shall file in the court the record in the proceeding, as provided in section 2112 of title 28. Upon such filing of the petition the court shall have jurisdiction of the proceeding and of the question determined therein concurrently with the Commission until the filing of the record and shall have power to make and enter a decree affirming, modifying, or setting aside the order of the Commission, and enforcing the same to the extent that such order is affirmed and to issue such writs as are ancillary to its jurisdiction

or are necessary in its judgement to prevent injury to the public or to competitors pendente lite. The findings of the Commission as to the facts, if supported by evidence, shall be conclusive. To the extent that the order of the Commission is affirmed, the court shall thereupon issue its own order commanding obedience to the terms of such order of the Commission. If either party shall apply to the court for leave to adduce additional evidence, and shall show to the satisfaction of the court that such additional evidence is material and that there were reasonable grounds for the failure to adduce such evidence in the proceeding before the Commission, the court may order such additional evidence to be taken before the Commission and to be adduced upon the hearing in such manner and upon such terms and conditions as to the court may seem proper. The Commission may modify its findings as to the facts, or make new findings, by reason of the additional evidence so taken, and it shall file such modified or new findings, which, if supported by evidence, shall be conclusive, and its recommendation, if any, for the modification or setting aside of its original order, with the return of such additional evidence. The judgment and decree of the court shall be final, except that the same shall be subject to review by the Supreme Court upon certiorari, as provided in section 1254 of title 28.

(d) Jurisdiction of court
Upon the filing of the record with it the jurisdiction of the court of appeals of the United States to affirm, enforce, modify, or set aside orders of the Commission shall be exclusive.

(e) Exemption from liability
No order of the Commission or judgement of court to enforce the same shall in anywise relieve or absolve any person, partnership, or corporation from any liability under the Antitrust Acts.

(f) Service of complaints, orders and other processes; return
Complaints, orders, and other processes of the Commission under this section may be served by anyone duly authorized by the Commission, either (a) by delivering a copy thereof to the person to be served, or to a member of the partnership to be served, or the president, secretary, or other executive officer or a director of the corporation to be served; or (b) by leaving a copy thereof at the residence or the principal office or place of business of such person, partnership, or corporation; or (c) by mailing a copy thereof by registered mail or by certified mail addressed to such person, partnership, or corporation at his or its residence or principal office or place of business. The verified return by the person so serving said complaint, order, or other process setting forth the manner of said service shall be proof of the same, and the return post office receipt for said complaint, order, or other process mailed by registered mail or by certified mail as aforesaid shall be proof of the service of the same.

(g) Finality of order
An order of the Commission to cease and desist shall become final-
> (1) Upon the expiration of the time allowed for filing a petition for review, if no such petition has been duly filed within such time; but the Commission may thereafter modify or set aside its order to the extent provided in the last sentence of subsection (b).

(2) Except as to any order provision subject to paragraph (4), upon the sixtieth day after such order is served, if a petition for review has been duly filed; except that any such order may be stayed, in whole or in part and subject to such conditions as may be appropriate, by-

(A) the Commission;

(B) an appropriate court of appeals of the United States, if (i) a petition for review of such order is pending in such court, and (ii) an application for such a stay was previously submitted to the Commission and the Commission, within the 30-day period beginning on the date the application was received by the Commission, either denied the application or did not grant or deny the application; or

(C) the Supreme Court, if an applicable petition for certiorari is pending.

(3) For purposes of subsection (m)(1)(B) and of section 57b(a)(2) of this title, if a petition for review of the order of the Commission has been filed-

(A) upon the expiration of the time allowed for filing a petition for certiorari, if the order of the Commission has been affirmed or the petition for review has been dismissed by the court of appeals and no petition for certiorari has been duly filed;

(B) upon the denial of a petition for certiorari, if the order of the Commission has been affirmed or the petition for review has been dismissed by the court of appeals; or

(C) upon the expiration of 30 days from the date of issuance of a mandate of the Supreme Court directing that the order of the Commission be affirmed or the petition for review be dismissed.

(4) In the case of an order provision requiring a person, partnership, or corporation to divest itself of stock, other share capital, or assets, if a petition for review of such order of the Commission has been filed-

(A) upon the expiration of the time allowed for filing a petition for certiorari, if the order of the Commission has been affirmed or the petition for review has been dismissed by the court of appeals and no petition for certiorari has been duly filed;

(B) upon the denial of a petition for certiorari, if the order of the Commission has been affirmed or the petition for review has been dismissed by the court of appeals; or

(C) upon the expiration of 30 days from the date of issuance of a mandate of the Supreme Court directing that the order of the Commission be affirmed or the petition for review be dismissed.

(h) Modification or setting aside of order by Supreme Court

If the Supreme Court directs that the order of the Commission be modified or set aside, the order of the Commission rendered in accordance with the mandate of the Supreme Court shall become final upon the expiration of thirty days from the time it was rendered, unless within such thirty days either party has instituted proceedings to have such order corrected to accord with the mandate, in which event the order of the Commission shall become final when so corrected.

United States
Federal Trade Commission Act

(i) Modification or setting aside of order by Court of Appeals

If the order of the Commission is modified or set aside by the court of appeals, and if (1) the time allowed for filing a petition for certiorari has expired and no such petition has been duly filed, or (2) the petition for certiorari has been denied, or (3) the decision of the court has been affirmed by the Supreme Court, then the order of the Commission rendered in accordance with the mandate of the court of appeals shall become final on the expiration of thirty days from the time such order of the Commission was rendered, unless within such thirty days either party has instituted proceedings to have such order corrected so that it will accord with the mandate, in which event the order of the Commission shall become final when so corrected.

(j) Rehearing upon order or remand

If the Supreme Court orders a rehearing; or if the case is remanded by the court of appeals to the Commission for a rehearing, and if (1) the time allowed for filing a petition for certiorari has expired, and no such petition has been duly filed, or (2) the petition for certiorari has been denied, or (3) the decision of the court has been affirmed by the Supreme Court, then the order of the Commission rendered upon such rehearing shall become final in the same manner as though no prior order of the Commission had been rendered.

(k) "Mandate" defined

As used in this section the term "mandate", in case a mandate has been recalled prior to the expiration of thirty days from the date of issuance thereof, means the final mandate.

(l) Penalty for violation of order; injunctions and other appropriate equitable relief

Any person, partnership, or corporation who violates an order of the Commission after it has become final, and while such order is in effect, shall forfeit and pay to the United States a civil penalty of not more than $10,000 for each violation, which shall accrue to the United States and may be recovered in a civil action brought by the Attorney General of the United States. Each separate violation of such an order shall be a separate offense, except that in a case of a violation through continuing failure to obey or neglect to obey a final order of the Commission, each day of continuance of such failure or neglect shall be deemed a separate offense. In such actions, the United States district courts are empowered to grant mandatory injunctions and such other and further equitable relief as they deem appropriate in the enforcement of such final orders of the Commission.

(m) Civil actions for recovery of penalties for knowing violations of rules and cease and desist orders respecting unfair or deceptive acts or practices; jurisdiction; maximum amount of penalties; continuing violations; de novo determinations; compromise or settlement procedure

(1)

(A) The Commission may commence a civil action to recover a civil penalty in a district court of the United States against any person, partnership, or corporation which violates any rule under this subchapter respecting unfair or deceptive acts or practices (other than an interpretive rule or a rule violation of which the Commission has provided is not an unfair or deceptive act or practice in violation of subsection (a)(1)) with actual knowledge or knowledge fairly implied on the basis of objective circumstances that such act is unfair or deceptive and is prohibited by such rule. In such action, such person, partnership, or corporation shall be liable for a civil penalty of not more than $10,000 for each violation.

(B) If the Commission determines in a proceeding under subsection (b) that any act or practice is unfair or deceptive, and issues a final cease and desist order, other than a consent order, with respect to such act or practice, then the Commission may commence a civil action to obtain a civil penalty in a district court of the United States against any person, partnership, or corporation which engages in such act or practice-

    (1) after such cease and desist order becomes final (whether or not such person, partnership, or corporation was subject to such cease and desist order), and

      (2) with actual knowledge that such act or practice is unfair or deceptive and is unlawful under subsection (a)(1) of this section.

In such action, such person, partnership, or corporation shall be liable for a civil penalty of not more than $10,000 for each violation.

(C) In the case of a violation through continuing failure to comply with a rule or with subsection (a)(1), each day of continuance of such failure shall be treated as a separate violation, for purposes of subparagraphs (A) and (B). In determining the amount of such a civil penalty, the court shall take into account the degree of culpability, any history of prior such conduct, ability to pay, effect on ability to continue to do business, and such other matters as justice may require.

(2) If the cease and desist order establishing that the act or practice is unfair or deceptive was not issued against the defendant in a civil penalty action under paragraph (1)(B) the issues of fact in such action against such defendant shall be tried de novo. Upon request of any party to such an action against such defendant, the court shall also review the determination of law made by the Commission in the proceeding under subsection (b) that the act or practice which was the subject of such proceeding constituted an unfair or deceptive act or practice in violation of subsection (a).

(3) The Commission may compromise or settle any action for a civil penalty if such compromise or settlement is accompanied by a public statement of its reasons and is approved by the court.

(n) Standard of proof; public policy considerations

The Commission shall have no authority under this section or section 57a of this title to declare unlawful an act or practice on the grounds that such act or practice is unfair unless the act or practice causes or is likely to cause substantial injury to consumers which is not reasonably avoidable by consumers themselves and not outweighed by countervailing benefits to consumers or to competition. In determining whether an act or practice is unfair, the Commission may consider established public policies as evidence to be considered with all other evidence. Such public policy considerations may not serve as a primary basis for such determination.

United States
Federal Trade Commission Act

* * *

§ 46. Additional powers of Commission

The Commission shall also have power -

(a) Investigation of persons, partnerships, or corporations

To gather and compile information concerning, and to investigate from time to time the organization, business, conduct, practices, and management of any person, partnership, or corporation engaged in or whose business affects commerce, excepting banks, savings and loan institutions described in section 57a(f)(3) of this title, Federal credit unions described in section 57a(f)(4) of this title, and common carriers subject to the Act to regulate commerce, and its relation to other persons, partnerships, and corporations.

(b) Reports of persons, partnerships, and corporations

To require, by general or special orders, persons, partnerships, and corporations, engaged in or whose business affects commerce, excepting banks, savings and loan institutions described in section 57a(f)(3) of this title, Federal credit unions described in section 57a(f)(4) of this title, and common carriers subject to the Act to regulate commerce, or any class of them, or any of them, respectively, to file with the Commission in such form as the Commission may prescribe annual or special, or both annual and special, reports or answers in writing to specific questions, furnishing to the Commission such information as it may require as to the organization, business, conduct, practices, management, and relation to other corporations, partnerships, and individuals of the respective persons, partnerships, and corporations filing such reports or answers in writing. Such reports and answers shall be made under oath, or otherwise, as the Commission may prescribe, and shall be filed with the Commission within such reasonable period as the Commission may prescribe, unless additional time be granted in any case by the Commission.

(c) Investigation of compliance with antitrust decrees

Whenever a final decree has been entered against any defendant corporation in any suit brought by the United States to prevent and restrain any violation of the antitrust Acts, to make investigation, upon its own initiative, of the manner in which the decree has been or is being carried out, and upon the application of the Attorney General it shall be its duty to make such investigation. It shall transmit to the Attorney General a report embodying its findings and recommendations as a result of any such investigation, and the report shall be made public in the discretion of the Commission.

(d) Investigations of violations of antitrust statutes
Upon the direction of the President or either House of Congress to investigate and report the facts relating to any alleged violations of the antitrust Acts by any corporation.

(e) Readjustment of business of corporations violating antitrust statutes
Upon the application of the Attorney General to investigate and make recommendations for the readjustment of the business of any corporation alleged to be violating the antitrust Acts in order that the corporation may thereafter maintain its organization, management, and conduct of business in accordance with law.

(f) Publication of information; reports
To make public from time to time such portions of the information obtained by it hereunder as are in the public interest; and to make annual and special reports to the Congress and to submit therewith recommendations for additional legislation; and to provide for the publication of its reports and decisions in such form and manner as may be best adapted for public information and use: Provided, That the Commission shall not have any authority to make public any trade secret or any commercial or financial information which is obtained from any person and which is privileged or confidential, except that the Commission may disclose such information (1) to officers and employees of appropriate Federal law enforcement agencies or to any officer or employee of any State law enforcement agency upon the prior certification of an officer of any such Federal or State law enforcement agency that such information will be maintained in confidence and will be used only for official law enforcement purposes, and (2) to any officer or employee of any foreign law enforcement agency under the same circumstances that making material available to foreign law enforcement agencies is permitted under section 57b–2(b) of this title.

(g) Classification of corporations; regulations
From time to time classify corporations and (except as provided in section 57a(a)(2) of this title) to make rules and regulations for the purpose of carrying out the provisions of this subchapter.

(h) Investigations of foreign trade conditions; reports
To investigate, from time to time, trade conditions in and with foreign countries where associations, combinations, or practices of manufacturers, merchants, or traders, or other conditions, may affect the foreign trade of the United States, and to report to Congress thereon, with such recommendations as it deems advisable.

United States
Federal Trade Commission Act

(i) Investigations of foreign antitrust law violations

With respect to the International Antitrust Enforcement Assistance Act of 1994 [15 U.S.C. 6201 et seq.], to conduct investigations of possible violations of foreign antitrust laws (as defined in section 12 of such Act [15 U.S.C. 6211]).

(j) Investigative assistance for foreign law enforcement agencies

(1) In general

Upon a written request from a foreign law enforcement agency to provide assistance in accordance with this subsection, if the requesting agency states that it is investigating, or engaging in enforcement proceedings against, possible violations of laws prohibiting fraudulent or deceptive commercial practices, or other practices substantially similar to practices prohibited by any provision of the laws administered by the Commission, other than Federal antitrust laws (as defined in section 12(5) of the International Antitrust Enforcement Assistance Act of 1994 (15 U.S.C. 6211(5))), to provide the assistance described in paragraph (2) without requiring that the conduct identified in the request constitute a violation of the laws of the United States.

(2) Type of assistance

In providing assistance to a foreign law enforcement agency under this subsection, the Commission may-

   (A) conduct such investigation as the Commission deems necessary to collect information and evidence pertinent to the request for assistance, using all investigative powers authorized by this subchapter; and

   (B) when the request is from an agency acting to investigate or pursue the enforcement of civil laws, or when the Attorney General refers a request to the Commission from an agency acting to investigate or pursue the enforcement of criminal laws, seek and accept appointment by a United States district court of Commission attorneys to provide assistance to foreign and international tribunals and to litigants before such tribunals on behalf of a foreign law enforcement agency pursuant to section 1782 of title 28.

(3) Criteria for determination

In deciding whether to provide such assistance, the Commission shall consider all relevant factors, including-

   (A) whether the requesting agency has agreed to provide or will provide reciprocal assistance to the Commission;

   (B) whether compliance with the request would prejudice the public interest of the United States; and

   (C) whether the requesting agency's investigation or enforcement proceeding concerns acts or practices that cause or are likely to cause injury to a significant number of persons.

(4) International agreements

If a foreign law enforcement agency has set forth a legal basis for requiring execution of an international agreement as a condition for reciprocal assistance, or as a condition for provision of materials or information to the Commission, the Commission, with prior approval and ongoing oversight of the Secretary of State, and with final approval of the agreement by the Secretary of State, may negotiate and conclude an international agreement, in the name of either the United States or the Commission, for the purpose of obtaining such assistance, materials, or information. The Commission may undertake in such an international agreement to-

(A) provide assistance using the powers set forth in this subsection;

(B) disclose materials and information in accordance with subsection (f) and section 57b–2(b) of this title; and

(C) engage in further cooperation, and protect materials and information received from disclosure, as authorized by this subchapter.

(5) Additional authority

The authority provided by this subsection is in addition to, and not in lieu of, any other authority vested in the Commission or any other officer of the United States.

(6) Limitation

The authority granted by this subsection shall not authorize the Commission to take any action or exercise any power with respect to a bank, a savings and loan institution described in section 57a(f)(3) of this title, a Federal credit union described in section 57a(f)(4) of this title, or a common carrier subject to the Act to regulate commerce, except in accordance with the undesignated proviso following the last designated subsection of this section.

(7) Assistance to certain countries

The Commission may not provide investigative assistance under this subsection to a foreign law enforcement agency from a foreign state that the Secretary of State has determined, in accordance with section 4605(j) [1] of title 50, has repeatedly provided support for acts of international terrorism, unless and until such determination is rescinded pursuant to section 4605(j)(4) [1] of title 50.

(k) Referral of evidence for criminal proceedings

(1) In general

Whenever the Commission obtains evidence that any person, partnership, or corporation, either domestic or foreign, has engaged in conduct that may constitute a violation of Federal criminal law, to transmit such evidence to the Attorney General, who may institute criminal proceedings under appropriate statutes. Nothing in this paragraph affects any other authority of the Commission to disclose information.

(2) International information

The Commission shall endeavor to ensure, with respect to memoranda of understanding and international agreements it may conclude, that material it has obtained from foreign law enforcement agencies acting to investigate or pursue the enforcement of foreign criminal laws may be used for the purpose of investigation, prosecution, or prevention of violations of United States criminal laws.

(l) Expenditures for cooperative arrangements

To expend appropriated funds for-

(1) operating expenses and other costs of bilateral and multilateral cooperative law enforcement groups conducting activities of interest to the Commission and in which the Commission participates; and

(2) expenses for consultations and meetings hosted by the Commission with foreign government agency officials, members of their delegations, appropriate representatives and staff to exchange views concerning developments relating to the Commission's mission, development and implementation of cooperation agreements, and provision of technical assistance for the development of foreign consumer protection or competition regimes, such expenses to include necessary administrative and logistic expenses and the expenses of Commission staff and foreign invitees in attendance at such consultations and meetings including-

(A) such incidental expenses as meals taken in the course of such attendance;

(B) any travel and transportation to or from such meetings; and

(C) any other related lodging or subsistence.

Provided, That the exception of "banks, savings and loan institutions described in section 57a(f)(3) of this title, Federal credit unions described in section 57a(f)(4) of this title, and common carriers subject to the Act to regulate commerce" from the Commission's powers defined in subsections (a), (b), and (j) of this section, shall not be construed to limit the Commission's authority to gather and compile information, to investigate, or to require reports or answers from, any person, partnership, or corporation to the extent that such action is necessary to the investigation of any person, partnership, or corporation, group of persons, partnerships, or corporations, or industry which is not engaged or is engaged only incidentally in banking, in business as a savings and loan institution, in business as a Federal credit union, or in business as a common carrier subject to the Act to regulate commerce.

The Commission shall establish a plan designed to substantially reduce burdens imposed upon small businesses as a result of requirements established by the Commission under clause (b) relating to the filing of quarterly financial reports. Such plan shall (1) be established after consultation with small businesses and persons who use the information contained in such quarterly financial reports; (2) provide for a reduction of the number of small businesses required to file such quarterly financial reports; and (3) make revisions in the forms used for such quarterly financial reports for the purpose of reducing the complexity of such forms. The Commission, not later than December 31, 1980, shall submit such plan to the Committee on Commerce, Science, and Transportation of the Senate and to the Committee on Energy and Commerce of the House of Representatives. Such plan shall take effect not later than October 31, 1981.

No officer or employee of the Commission or any Commissioner may publish or disclose information to the public, or to any Federal agency, whereby any line-of-business data furnished by a particular establishment or individual can be identified. No one other than designated sworn officers and employees of the Commission may examine the line-of-business reports from individual firms, and information provided in the line-of-business program administered by the Commission shall be used only for statistical purposes. Information for carrying out specific law enforcement responsibilities of the Commission shall be obtained under practices and procedures in effect on May 28, 1980, or as changed by law.

Nothing in this section (other than the provisions of clause (c) and clause (d)) shall apply to the business of insurance, except that the Commission shall have authority to conduct studies and prepare reports relating to the business of insurance. The Commission may exercise such authority only upon receiving a request which is agreed to by a majority of the members of the Committee on Commerce, Science, and Transportation of the Senate or the Committee on Energy and Commerce of the House of Representatives. The authority to conduct any such study shall expire at the end of the Congress during which the request for such study was made.

* * *

§ 57a. Unfair or deceptive acts or practices rulemaking proceedings

(a) Authority of Commission to prescribe rules and general statements of policy

(1) Except as provided in subsection (h), the Commission may prescribe-

(A) interpretive rules and general statements of policy with respect to unfair or deceptive acts or practices in or affecting commerce (within the meaning of section 45(a)(1) of this title), and

(B) rules which define with specificity acts or practices which are unfair or deceptive acts or practices in or affecting commerce (within the meaning of section 45(a)(1) of this title), except that the Commission shall not develop or promulgate any trade rule or regulation with regard to the regulation of the development and utilization of the standards and certification activities pursuant to this section. Rules under this subparagraph may include requirements prescribed for the purpose of preventing such acts or practices.

(2) The Commission shall have no authority under this subchapter, other than its authority under this section, to prescribe any rule with respect to unfair or deceptive acts or practices in or affecting commerce (within the meaning of section 45(a)(1) of this title). The preceding sentence shall not affect any authority of the Commission to prescribe rules (including interpretive rules), and general statements of policy, with respect to unfair methods of competition in or affecting commerce.

(b) Procedures applicable

(1) When prescribing a rule under subsection (a)(1)(B) of this section, the Commission shall proceed in accordance with section 553 of title 5 (without regard to any reference in such section to sections 556 and 557 of such title), and shall also

(A) publish a notice of proposed rulemaking stating with particularity the text of the rule, including any alternatives, which the Commission proposes to promulgate, and the reason for the proposed rule; (B) allow interested persons to submit written data, views, and arguments, and make all such submissions publicly available; (C) provide an opportunity for an informal hearing in accordance with subsection (c); and (D) promulgate, if appropriate, a final rule based on the matter in the rulemaking record (as defined in subsection (e)(1)(B)), together with a statement of basis and purpose.

(2)

(A) Prior to the publication of any notice of proposed rulemaking pursuant to paragraph (1)(A), the Commission shall publish an advance notice of proposed rulemaking in the Federal Register. Such advance notice shall-

(i) contain a brief description of the area of inquiry under consideration, the objectives which the Commission seeks to achieve, and possible regulatory alternatives under consideration by the Commission; and

(ii) invite the response of interested parties with respect to such proposed rulemaking, including any suggestions or alternative methods for achieving such objectives.

(B) The Commission shall submit such advance notice of proposed rulemaking to the Committee on Commerce, Science, and Transportation of the Senate and to the Committee on Energy and Commerce of the House of Representatives. The Commission may use such additional mechanisms as the Commission considers useful to obtain suggestions regarding the content of the area of inquiry before the publication of a general notice of proposed rulemaking under paragraph (1)(A).

(C) The Commission shall, 30 days before the publication of a notice of proposed rulemaking pursuant to paragraph (1)(A), submit such notice to the Committee on Commerce, Science, and Transportation of the Senate and to the Committee on Energy and Commerce of the House of Representatives.

(3) The Commission shall issue a notice of proposed rulemaking pursuant to paragraph (1)(A) only where it has reason to believe that the unfair or deceptive acts or practices which are the subject of the proposed rulemaking are prevalent. The Commission shall make a determination that unfair or deceptive acts or practices are prevalent under this paragraph only if-

(A) it has issued cease and desist orders regarding such acts or practices, or

(B) any other information available to the Commission indicates a widespread pattern of unfair or deceptive acts or practices.

(c) Informal hearing procedure

The Commission shall conduct any informal hearings required by subsection (b)(1)(C) of this section in accordance with the following procedure:

(1)

(A) The Commission shall provide for the conduct of proceedings under this subsection by hearing officers who shall perform their functions in accordance with the requirements of this subsection.

(B) The officer who presides over the rulemaking proceedings shall be responsible to a chief presiding officer who shall not be responsible to any other officer or employee of the Commission. The officer who presides over the rulemaking proceeding shall make a recommended decision based upon the findings and conclusions of such officer as to all relevant and material evidence, except that such recommended decision may be made by another officer if the officer who presided over the proceeding is no longer available to the Commission.

(C) Except as required for the disposition of ex parte matters as authorized by law, no presiding officer shall consult any person or party with respect to any fact in issue unless such officer gives notice and opportunity for all parties to participate.

(2) Subject to paragraph (3) of this subsection, an interested person is entitled-

(A) to present his position orally or by documentary submission (or both), and

(B) if the Commission determines that there are disputed issues of material fact it is necessary to resolve, to present such rebuttal submissions and to conduct (or have conducted under paragraph (3)(B)) such cross-examination of persons as the Commission determines (i) to be appropriate, and (ii) to be required for a full and true disclosure with respect to such issues.

(3) The Commission may prescribe such rules and make such rulings concerning proceedings in such hearings as may tend to avoid unnecessary costs or delay. Such rules or rulings may include (A) imposition of reasonable time limits on each interested person's oral presentations, and (B) requirements that any cross-examination to which a person may be entitled under paragraph (2) be conducted by the Commission on behalf of that person in such manner as the Commission determines (i) to be appropriate, and (ii) to be required for a full and true disclosure with respect to disputed issues of material fact.

(4)

(A) Except as provided in subparagraph (B), if a group of persons each of whom under paragraphs (2) and (3) would be entitled to conduct (or have conducted) cross-examination and who are determined by the Commission to have the same or similar interests in the proceeding cannot agree upon a single representative of such interests for purposes of cross-examination, the Commission may make rules and rulings (i) limiting the representation of such interest, for such purposes, and (ii) governing the manner in which such cross-examination shall be limited.

(B) When any person who is a member of a group with respect to which the Commission has made a determination under subparagraph (A) is unable to agree upon group representation with the other members of the group, then such person shall not be denied under the authority of subparagraph (A) the opportunity to conduct (or have conducted) cross-examination as to issues affecting his particular interests if (i) he satisfies the Commission that he has made a reasonable and good faith effort to reach agreement upon group representation with the other members of the group and (ii) the Commission determines that there are substantial and relevant issues which are not adequately presented by the group representative.

(5) A verbatim transcript shall be taken of any oral presentation, and cross-examination, in an informal hearing to which this subsection applies. Such transcript shall be available to the public.

(d) Statement of basis and purpose accompanying rule; "Commission" defined; judicial review of amendment or repeal of rule; violation of rule

(1) The Commission's statement of basis and purpose to accompany a rule promulgated under subsection (a)(1)(B) shall include (A) a statement as to the prevalence of the acts or practices treated by the rule; (B) a statement as to the manner and context in which such acts or practices are unfair or deceptive; and (C) a statement as to the economic effect of the rule, taking into account the effect on small business and consumers.

(2)

(A) The term "Commission" as used in this subsection and subsections (b) and (c) includes any person authorized to act in behalf of the Commission in any part of the rulemaking proceeding.

(B) A substantive amendment to, or repeal of, a rule promulgated under subsection (a)(1)(B) shall be prescribed, and subject to judicial review, in the same manner as a rule prescribed under such subsection. An exemption under subsection (g) shall not be treated as an amendment or repeal of a rule.

(3) When any rule under subsection (a)(1)(B) takes effect a subsequent violation thereof shall constitute an unfair or deceptive act or practice in violation of section 45(a)(1) of this title, unless the Commission otherwise expressly provides in such rule.

(e) Judicial review; petition; jurisdiction and venue; rulemaking record; additional submissions and presentations; scope of review and relief; review by Supreme Court; additional remedies

(1)

(A) Not later than 60 days after a rule is promulgated under subsection (a)(1)(B) by the Commission, any interested person (including a consumer or consumer organization) may file a petition, in the United States Court of Appeals for the

District of Columbia circuit or for the circuit in which such person resides or has his principal place of business, for judicial review of such rule. Copies of the petition shall be forthwith transmitted by the clerk of the court to the Commission or other officer designated by it for that purpose. The provisions of section 2112 of title 28 shall apply to the filing of the rulemaking record of proceedings on which the Commission based its rule and to the transfer of proceedings in the courts of appeals.

(B) For purposes of this section, the term "rulemaking record" means the rule, its statement of basis and purpose, the transcript required by subsection (c)(5), any written submissions, and any other information which the Commission considers relevant to such rule.

(2) If the petitioner or the Commission applies to the court for leave to make additional oral submissions or written presentations and shows to the satisfaction of the court that such submissions and presentations would be material and that there were reasonable grounds for the submissions and failure to make such submissions and presentations in the proceeding before the Commission, the court may order the Commission to provide additional opportunity to make such submissions and presentations. The Commission may modify or set aside its rule or make a new rule by reason of the additional submissions and presentations and shall file such modified or new rule, and the rule's statement of basis of [1] purpose, with the return of such submissions and presentations. The court shall thereafter review such new or modified rule.

(3) Upon the filing of the petition under paragraph (1) of this subsection, the court shall have jurisdiction to review the rule in accordance with chapter 7 of title 5 and to grant appropriate relief, including interim relief, as provided in such chapter. The court shall hold unlawful and set aside the rule on any ground specified in subparagraphs (A), (B), (C), or (D) of section 706(2) of title 5 (taking due account of the rule of prejudicial error), or if-

(A) the court finds that the Commission's action is not supported by substantial evidence in the rulemaking record (as defined in paragraph (1)(B) of this subsection) taken as a whole, or

(B) the court finds that-

(i) a Commission determination under subsection (c) that the petitioner is not entitled to conduct cross-examination or make rebuttal submissions, or

(ii) a Commission rule or ruling under subsection (c) limiting the petitioner's cross-examination or rebuttal submissions, has precluded disclosure of disputed material facts which was necessary for fair determination by the Commission of the rulemaking proceeding taken as a whole.

The term "evidence", as used in this paragraph, means any matter in the rulemaking record.

(4) The judgment of the court affirming or setting aside, in whole or in part, any such rule shall be final, subject to review by the Supreme Court of the United States upon certiorari or certification, as provided in section 1254 of title 28.

(5)

(A) Remedies under the preceding paragraphs of this subsection are in addition to and not in lieu of any other remedies provided by law.

(B) The United States Courts of Appeal shall have exclusive jurisdiction of any action to obtain judicial review (other than in an enforcement proceeding) of a rule prescribed under subsection (a)(1)(B), if any district court of the United States would have had jurisdiction of such action but for this subparagraph. Any such action shall be brought in the United States Court of Appeals for the District of Columbia circuit, or for any circuit which includes a judicial district in which the action could have been brought but for this subparagraph.

(C) A determination, rule, or ruling of the Commission described in paragraph (3)(B)(i) or (ii) may be reviewed only in a proceeding under this subsection and only in accordance with paragraph (3)(B). Section 706(2)(E) of title 5 shall not apply to any rule promulgated under subsection (a)(1)(B). The contents and adequacy of any statement required by subsection (b)(1)(D) shall not be subject to judicial review in any respect.

(f) Definitions of banks, savings and loan institutions, and Federal credit unions

(1) Repealed. Pub. L. 111–203, title X, §1092(2), July 21, 2010, 124 Stat. 2095

(2) Definition.-For purposes of this subchapter, the term "bank" means-

(A) national banks and Federal branches and Federal agencies of foreign banks;

(B) member banks of the Federal Reserve System (other than national banks), branches and agencies of foreign banks (other than Federal branches, Federal agencies, and insured State branches of foreign banks), commercial lending companies owned or controlled by foreign banks, and organizations operating under section 25 or 25A of the Federal Reserve Act [12 U.S.C. 601 et seq., 611 et seq.]; and

(C) banks insured by the Federal Deposit Insurance Corporation (other than banks referred to in subparagraph (A) or (B)) and insured State branches of foreign banks.

(3) For purposes of this subchapter, the term "savings and loan institution" has the same meaning as in section 1813 of title 12.

(4) For purposes of this subchapter, the term "Federal credit union" has the same meaning as in sections 1766 and 1786 of title 12.

The terms used in this paragraph that are not defined in this subchapter or otherwise defined in section 1813(s) of title 12 shall have the meaning given to them in section 3101 of title 12.

(g) Exemptions and stays from application of rules; procedures

(1) Any person to whom a rule under subsection (a)(1)(B) of this section applies may petition the Commission for an exemption from such rule.

(2) If, on its own motion or on the basis of a petition under paragraph (1), the Commission finds that the application of a rule prescribed under subsection (a)(1)(B) to any person or class or [3] persons is not necessary to prevent the unfair or deceptive act or practice to which the rule relates, the Commission may exempt such person or class from all or part of such rule. Section 553 of title 5 shall apply to action under this paragraph.

(3) Neither the pendency of a proceeding under this subsection respecting an exemption from a rule, nor the pendency of judicial proceedings to review the Commission's action or failure to act under this subsection, shall stay the applicability of such rule under subsection (a)(1)(B).

(h) Restriction on rulemaking authority of Commission respecting children's advertising proceedings pending on May 28, 1980

The Commission shall not have any authority to promulgate any rule in the children's advertising proceeding pending on May 28, 1980, or in any substantially similar proceeding on the basis of a determination by the Commission that such advertising constitutes an unfair act or practice in or affecting commerce.

(i) Meetings with outside parties

(1) For purposes of this subsection, the term "outside party" means any person other than (A) a Commissioner; (B) an officer or employee of the Commission; or (C) any person who has entered into a contract or any other agreement or arrangement with the Commission to provide any goods or services (including consulting services) to the Commission.

(2) Not later than 60 days after May 28, 1980, the Commission shall publish a proposed rule, and not later than 180 days after May 28, 1980, the Commission shall promulgate a final rule, which shall authorize the Commission or any Commissioner to meet with any outside party concerning any rulemaking proceeding of the Commission. Such rule shall provide that-

(A) notice of any such meeting shall be included in any weekly calendar prepared by the Commission; and

(B) a verbatim record or a summary of any such meeting, or of any communication relating to any such meeting, shall be kept, made available to the public, and included in the rulemaking record.

(j) Communications by investigative personnel with staff of Commission concerning matters outside rulemaking record prohibited

Not later than 60 days after May 28, 1980, the Commission shall publish a proposed rule, and not later than 180 days after May 28, 1980, the Commission shall promulgate a final rule, which shall prohibit any officer, employee, or agent of the Commission with any investigative responsibility or other responsibility relating to any rulemaking proceeding within any operating bureau of the Commission, from communicating or causing to be communicated to any Commissioner or to the personal staff of any Commissioner any fact which is relevant to the merits of such proceeding and which is not on the rulemaking record of such proceeding, unless such communication is made available to the public and is included in the rulemaking record. The provisions of this subsection shall not apply to any communication to the extent such communication is required for the disposition of ex parte matters as authorized by law.

* * *

§ 57b. Civil actions for violations of rules and cease and desist orders respecting unfair or deceptive acts or practices

(a) Suits by Commission against persons, partnerships, or corporations; jurisdiction; relief for dishonest or fraudulent acts

(1) If any person, partnership, or corporation violates any rule under this subchapter respecting unfair or deceptive acts or practices (other than an interpretive rule, or a rule violation of which the Commission has provided is not an unfair or deceptive act or practice in violation of section 45(a) of this title), then the Commission may commence a civil action against such person, partnership, or corporation for relief under subsection (b) of this section in a United States district court or in any court of competent jurisdiction of a State.

(2) If any person, partnership, or corporation engages in any unfair or deceptive act or practice (within the meaning of section 45(a)(1) of this title) with respect to which the Commission has issued a final cease and desist order which is applicable to such person, partnership, or corporation, then the Commission may commence a civil action against such person, partnership, or corporation in a United States district court or in any court of competent jurisdiction of a State. If the Commission satisfies the court that the act or practice to which the cease and desist order relates is one which a reasonable man would have known under the circumstances was dishonest or fraudulent, the court may grant relief under subsection (b) of this section.

(b) Nature of relief available The court in an action under subsection (a) of this section shall have jurisdiction to grant such relief as the court finds necessary to redress injury to consumers or other persons, partnerships, and corporations resulting from the rule violation or the unfair or deceptive act or practice, as the case may be. Such relief may include, but shall not be limited to, rescission or reformation of contracts, the refund of money or return of property, the payment of damages, and public notification respecting the rule violation or the unfair or deceptive act or practice, as the case may be; except that nothing in this subsection is intended to authorize the imposition of any exemplary or punitive damages.

(c) Conclusiveness of findings of Commission in cease and desist proceedings; notice of judicial proceedings to injured persons, etc.

(1) If

(A) a cease and desist order issued under section 45(b) of this title has become final under section 45(g) of this title with respect to any person's, partnership's, or corporation's rule violation or unfair or deceptive act or practice, and

(B) an action under this section is brought with respect to such person's, partnership's, or corporation's rule violation or act or practice, then the findings of the Commission as to the material facts in the proceeding under section 45(b) of this title with respect to such person's, partnership's, or corporation's rule violation or act or practice, shall be conclusive unless

(i) the terms of such cease and desist order expressly provide that the Commission's findings shall not be conclusive, or

(ii) the order became final by reason of section 45(g)(1) of this title, in which case such finding shall be conclusive if supported by evidence.

(2) The court shall cause notice of an action under this section to be given in a manner which is reasonably calculated, under all of the circumstances, to apprise the persons, partnerships, and corporations allegedly injured by the defendant's rule violation or act or practice of the pendency of such action. Such notice may, in the discretion of the court, be given by publication.

(d) Time for bringing of actions No action may be brought by the Commission under this section more than 3 years after the rule violation to which an action under subsection (a)(1) of this section relates, or the unfair or deceptive act or practice to which an action under subsection (a)(2) of this section relates; except that if a cease and desist order with respect to any person's, partnership's, or corporation's rule violation or unfair or deceptive act or practice has become final and such order was issued in a proceeding under section 45(b) of this title which was commenced not later than 3 years after the rule violation or act or practice occurred, a civil action may be commenced under this section against such person, partnership, or corporation at any time before the expiration of one year after such order becomes final.

(e) Availability of additional Federal or State remedies; other authority of Commission unaffected Remedies provided in this section are in addition to, and not in lieu of, any other remedy or right of action provided by State or Federal law. Nothing in this section shall be construed to affect any authority of the Commission under any other provision of law.

§ 57b-1. Civil investigative demands

(a) Definitions For purposes of this section:

(1) The terms "civil investigative demand" and "demand" mean any demand issued by the commission under subsection (c)(1) of this section.

(2) The term "Commission investigation" means any inquiry conducted by a Commission investigator for the purpose of ascertaining whether any person is or has been engaged in any unfair or deceptive acts or practices in or affecting commerce (within the meaning of section 45(a)(1) of this title) or in any antitrust violations.

(3) The term "Commission investigator" means any attorney or investigator employed by the Commission who is charged with the duty of enforcing or carrying into effect any provisions relating to unfair or deceptive acts or practices in or affecting commerce (within the meaning of section 45(a)(1) of this title) or any provisions relating to antitrust violations.

(4) The term "custodian" means the custodian or any deputy custodian designated under section 57b-2(b)(2)(A) of this title.

(5) The term "documentary material" includes the original or any copy of any book, record, report, memorandum, paper, communication, tabulation, chart, or other document.

(6) The term "person" means any natural person, partnership, corporation, association, or other legal entity, including any person acting under color or authority of State law.

(7) The term "violation" means any act or omission constituting an unfair or deceptive act or practice in or affecting commerce (within the meaning of section 45(a)(1) of this title) or any antitrust violation.

(8) The term "antitrust violation" means -

    (A) any unfair method of competition (within the meaning of section 45(a)(1) of this title);

    (B) any violation of the Clayton Act (15 U.S.C. 12 et seq.) or of any other Federal statute that prohibits, or makes available to the Commission a civil remedy with respect to, any restraint upon or monopolization of interstate or foreign trade or commerce;

    (C) with respect to the International Antitrust Enforcement Assistance Act of 1994 (15 U.S.C. 6201 et seq.), any violation of any of the foreign antitrust laws (as defined in section 12 of such Act (15 U.S.C. 6211)) with respect to which a request is made under section 3 of such Act (15 U.S.C. 6202); or

    (D) any activity in preparation for a merger, acquisition, joint venture, or similar transaction, which if consummated, may result in any such unfair method of competition or in any such violation.

(b) Actions conducted by Commission respecting unfair or deceptive acts or practices in or affecting commerce For the purpose of investigations performed pursuant to this section with respect to unfair or deceptive acts or practices in or affecting commerce (within the meaning of section 45(a)(1) of this title); all actions of the Commission taken under section 46 and section 49 of this title shall be conducted pursuant to subsection (c) of this section.

(c) Issuance of demand; contents; service; verified return; sworn certificate; answers; taking of oral testimony

(1) Whenever the Commission has reason to believe that any person may be in possession, custody, or control of any documentary material or tangible things, or may have any information, relevant to unfair or deceptive acts or practices in or affecting commerce (within the meaning of section 45(a)(1) of this title), or to antitrust violations, the Commission may, before the institution of any proceedings under this subchapter, issue in writing, and cause to be served upon such person, a civil investigative demand requiring such person to produce such documentary material for inspection and copying or reproduction, to submit such tangible things, to file written reports or answers to questions, to give oral testimony concerning documentary material or other information, or to furnish any combination of such material, answers, or testimony.

(2) Each civil investigative demand shall state the nature of the conduct constituting the alleged violation which is under investigation and the provision of law applicable to such violation.

(3) Each civil investigative demand for the production of documentary material shall -

(A) describe each class of documentary material to be produced under the demand with such definiteness and certainty as to permit such material to be fairly identified;

(B) prescribe a return date or dates which will provide a reasonable period of time within which the material so demanded may be assembled and made available for inspection and copying or reproduction; and

(C) identify the custodian to whom such material shall be made available.

(4) Each civil investigative demand for the submission of tangible things shall -

(A) describe each class of tangible things to be submitted under the demand with such definiteness and certainty as to permit such things to be fairly identified;

(B) prescribe a return date or dates which will provide a reasonable period of time within which the things so demanded may be assembled and submitted; and

(C) identify the custodian to whom such things shall be submitted.

(5) Each civil investigative demand for written reports or answers to questions shall -

(A) propound with definiteness and certainty the reports to be produced or the questions to be answered;

(B) prescribe a date or dates at which time written reports or answers to questions shall be submitted; and

(C) identify the custodian to whom such reports or answers shall be submitted.

(6) Each civil investigative demand for the giving of oral testimony shall -

(A) prescribe a date, time, and place at which oral testimony shall be commenced; and

(B) identify a Commission investigator who shall conduct the investigation and the custodian to whom the transcript of such investigation shall be submitted.

(7) (A) Any civil investigative demand may be served by any Commission investigator at any place within the territorial jurisdiction of any court of the United States.

(B) Any such demand or any enforcement petition filed under this section may be served upon any person who is not found within the territorial jurisdiction of any court of the United States, in such manner as the Federal Rules of Civil Procedure prescribe for service in a foreign nation.

(C) To the extent that the courts of the United States have authority to assert jurisdiction over such person consistent with due process, the United States District Court for the District of Columbia shall have the same jurisdiction to take any action respecting compliance with this section by such person that such district court would have if such person were personally within the jurisdiction of such district court.

(8) Service of any civil investigative demand or any enforcement petition filed under this section may be made upon a partnership, corporation, association, or other legal entity by -

(A) delivering a duly executed copy of such demand or petition to any partner, executive officer, managing agent, or general agent of such partnership, corporation, association, or other legal entity, or to any agent of such partnership, corporation, association, or other legal entity authorized by appointment or by law to receive service of process on behalf of such partnership, corporation, association, or other legal entity;

(B) delivering a duly executed copy of such demand or petition to the principal office or place of business of the partnership, corporation, association, or other legal entity to be served; or

(C) depositing a duly executed copy in the United States mails, by registered or certified mail, return receipt requested, duly addressed to such partnership, corporation, association, or other legal entity at its principal office or place of business.

(9) Service of any civil investigative demand or of any enforcement petition filed under this section may be made upon any natural person by -

(A) delivering a duly executed copy of such demand or petition to the person to be served; or

(B) depositing a duly executed copy in the United States mails by registered or certified mail, return receipt requested, duly addressed to such person at his residence or principal office or place of business.

(10) A verified return by the individual serving any civil investigative demand or any enforcement petition filed under this section setting forth the manner of such service shall be proof of such service. In the case of service by registered or certified mail, such return shall be accompanied by the return post office receipt of delivery of such demand or enforcement petition.

(11) The production of documentary material in response to a civil investigative demand shall be made under a sworn certificate, in such form as the demand designates, by the person, if a natural person, to whom the demand is directed or, if not a natural person, by any person having knowledge of the facts and circumstances relating to such production, to the effect that all of the documentary material required by the demand and in the possession, custody, or control of the person to whom the demand is directed has been produced and made available to the custodian.

(12) The submission of tangible things in response to a civil investigative demand shall be made under a sworn certificate, in such form as the demand designates, by the person to whom the demand is directed or, if not a natural person, by any person having knowledge of the facts and circumstances relating to such production, to the effect that all of the tangible things required by the demand and in the possession, custody, or control of the person to whom the demand is directed have been submitted to the custodian.

(13) Each reporting requirement or question in a civil investigative demand shall be answered separately and fully in writing under oath, unless it is objected to, in which event the reasons for the objection shall be stated in lieu of an answer, and it shall be submitted under a sworn certificate, in such form as the demand designates, by the person, if a natural person, to whom the demand is directed or, if not a natural person, by any person responsible for answering each reporting requirement or question, to the effect that all information required by the demand and in the possession, custody, control, or knowledge of the person to whom the demand is directed has been submitted.

(14) (A) Any Commission investigator before whom oral testimony is to be taken shall put the witness on oath or affirmation and shall personally, or by any individual acting under his direction and in his presence, record the testimony of the witness. The testimony shall be taken stenographically and transcribed. After the testimony is fully transcribed, the Commission investigator before whom the testimony is taken shall promptly transmit a copy of the transcript of the testimony to the custodian.

(B) Any Commission investigator before whom oral testimony is to be taken shall exclude from the place where the testimony is to be taken all other persons except the person giving the testimony, his attorney, the officer before whom the testimony is to be taken, and any stenographer taking such testimony.

(C) The oral testimony of any person taken pursuant to a civil investigative demand shall be taken in the judicial district of the United States in which such person resides, is found, or transacts business, or in such other place as may be agreed upon by the Commission investigator before whom the oral testimony of such person is to be taken and such person.

(D) (i) Any person compelled to appear under a civil investigative demand for oral testimony pursuant to this section may be accompanied, represented, and advised by an attorney. The attorney may advise such person, in confidence, either upon the request of such person or upon the initiative of the attorney, with respect to any question asked of such person.

(ii) Such person or attorney may object on the record to any question, in whole or in part, and shall briefly state for the record the reason for the objection. An objection may properly be made, received, and entered upon the record when it is claimed that such person is entitled to refuse to answer the question on grounds of any constitutional or other legal right or privilege, including the privilege against self-incrimination. Such person shall not otherwise object to or refuse to answer any question, and shall not himself or through his attorney otherwise interrupt the oral examination. If such person refuses to answer any question, the Commission may petition the district court of the United States pursuant to this section for an order compelling such person to answer such question.

(iii) If such person refuses to answer any question on grounds of the privilege against self-incrimination, the testimony of such person may be compelled in accordance with the provisions of section 6004 of title 18.

(E) (i) After the testimony of any witness is fully transcribed, the Commission investigator shall afford the witness (who may be accompanied by an attorney) a reasonable opportunity to examine the transcript. The transcript shall be read to or by the witness, unless such examination and reading are waived by the witness. Any changes in form or substance which the witness desires to make shall be entered and identified upon the transcript by the Commission investigator with a statement of the reasons given by the witness for making such changes. The transcript shall then be signed by the witness, unless the witness in writing waives the signing, is ill, cannot be found, or refuses to sign.

(ii) If the transcript is not signed by the witness during the 30-day period following the date upon which the witness is first afforded a reasonable opportunity to examine it, the Commission investigator shall sign the transcript and state on the record the fact of the waiver, illness, absence of the witness, or the refusal to sign, together with any reasons given for the failure to sign.

(F) The Commission investigator shall certify on the transcript that the witness was duly sworn by him and that the transcript is a true record of the testimony given by the witness, and the Commission investigator shall promptly deliver the transcript or send it by registered or certified mail to the custodian.

(G) The Commission investigator shall furnish a copy of the transcript (upon payment of reasonable charges for the transcription) to the witness only, except that the Commission may for good cause limit such witness to inspection of the official transcript of his testimony.

(H) Any witness appearing for the taking of oral testimony pursuant to a civil investigative demand shall be entitled to the same fees and mileage which are paid to witnesses in the district courts of the United States.

(d) Procedures for demand material Materials received as a result of a civil investigative demand shall be subject to the procedures established in section 57b-2 of this title.

(e) Petition for enforcement Whenever any person fails to comply with any civil investigative demand duly served upon him under this section, or whenever satisfactory copying or reproduction of material requested pursuant to the demand cannot be accomplished and such person refuses to surrender such material, the Commission, through such officers or attorneys as it may designate, may file, in the district court of the United States for any judicial district in which such person resides, is found, or transacts business, and serve upon such person, a petition for an order of such court for the enforcement of this section. All process of any court to which application may be made as provided in this subsection may be served in any judicial district.

(f) Petition for order modifying or setting aside demand

(1) Not later than 20 days after the service of any civil investigative demand upon any person under subsection (c) of this section, or at any time before the return date specified in the demand, whichever period is shorter, or within such period exceeding 20 days after service or in excess of such return date as may be prescribed in writing, subsequent to service, by any Commission investigator named in the demand, such person may file with the Commission a petition for an order by the Commission modifying or setting aside the demand.

(2) The time permitted for compliance with the demand in whole or in part, as deemed proper and ordered by the Commission, shall not run during the pendency of such petition at the Commission, except that such person shall comply with any portions of the demand not sought to be modified or set aside. Such petition shall specify each ground upon which the petitioner relies in seeking such relief, and may be based upon any failure of the demand to comply with the provisions of this section, or upon any constitutional or other legal right or privilege of such person.

(g) Custodial control of documentary material, tangible things, reports, etc. At any time during which any custodian is in custody or control of any documentary material, tangible things, reports, answers to questions, or transcripts of oral testimony given by any person in compliance with any civil investigative demand, such person may file, in the district court of the United States for the judicial district within which the office of such custodian is situated, and serve upon such custodian, a petition for an order of such court requiring the performance by such custodian of any duty imposed upon him by this section or section 57b-2 of this title.

(h) Jurisdiction of court Whenever any petition is filed in any district court of the United States under this section, such court shall have jurisdiction to hear and determine the matter so presented, and to enter such order or orders as may be required to carry into effect the provisions of this section. Any final order so entered shall be subject to appeal pursuant to section 1291 of title 28. Any disobedience of any final order entered under this section by any court shall be punished as a contempt of such court.

(i) Commission authority to issue subpoenas or make demand for information Notwithstanding any other provision of law, the Commission shall have no authority to issue a subpoena or make a demand for information, under authority of this subchapter or any other provision of law, unless such subpoena or demand for information is signed by a Commissioner acting pursuant to a Commission resolution. The Commission shall not delegate the power conferred by this section to sign subpoenas or demands for information to any other person.

(j) Applicability of this section The provisions of this section shall not -

(1) apply to any proceeding under section 45(b) of this title, any proceeding under section 11(b) of the Clayton Act (15 U.S.C. 21(b)), or any adjudicative proceeding under any other provision of law; or

(2) apply to or affect the jurisdiction, duties, or powers of any agency of the Federal Government, other than the Commission, regardless of whether such jurisdiction, duties, or powers are derived in whole or in part, by reference to this subchapter.

§ 57b-2. Confidentiality

(a) Definitions For purposes of this section:

(1) The term "material" means documentary material, tangible things, written reports or answers to questions, and transcripts of oral testimony.

(2) The term "Federal agency" has the meaning given it in section 552(e) of title 5.[1]

(b) Procedures respecting documents, tangible things, or transcripts of oral testimony received pursuant to compulsory process or investigation

(1) With respect to any document, tangible thing, or transcript of oral testimony received by the Commission pursuant to compulsory process in an investigation, a

---

[1] See References in Text note below.

purpose of which is to determine whether any person may have violated any provision of the laws administered by the Commission, the procedures established in paragraph (2) through paragraph (7) shall apply.

(2) (A) The Commission shall designate a duly authorized agent to serve as custodian of documentary material, tangible things, or written reports or answers to questions, and transcripts of oral testimony, and such additional duly authorized agents as the Commission shall determine from time to time to be necessary to serve as deputies to the custodian.

(B) Any person upon whom any demand for the production of documentary material has been duly served shall make such material available for inspection and copying or reproduction to the custodian designated in such demand at the principal place of business of such person (or at such other place as such custodian and such person thereafter may agree or prescribe in writing or as the court may direct pursuant to section 57b-1(h) of this title) on the return date specified in such demand (or on such later date as such custodian may prescribe in writing). Such person may upon written agreement between such person and the custodian substitute copies for originals of all or any part of such material.

(3) (A) The custodian to whom any documentary material, tangible things, written reports or answers to questions, and transcripts of oral testimony are delivered shall take physical possession of such material, reports or answers, and transcripts, and shall be responsible for the use made of such material, reports or answers, and transcripts, and for the return of material, pursuant to the requirements of this section.

(B) The custodian may prepare such copies of the documentary material, written reports or answers to questions, and transcripts of oral testimony, and may make tangible things available, as may be required for official use by any duly authorized officer or employee of the Commission under regulations which shall be promulgated by the Commission. Notwithstanding subparagraph (C), such material, things, and transcripts may be used by any such officer or employee in connection with the taking of oral testimony under this section.

(C) Except as otherwise provided in this section, while in the possession of the custodian, no documentary material, tangible things, reports or answers to questions, and transcripts of oral testimony shall be available for examination by any individual other than a duly authorized officer or employee of the Commission without the consent of the person who produced the material, things, or transcripts. Nothing in this section is intended to prevent disclosure to either House of the Congress or to any committee or subcommittee of the Congress, except that the Commission immediately shall notify the owner or provider of any such information of a request for information designated as confidential by the owner or provider.

(D) While in the possession of the custodian and under such reasonable terms and conditions as the Commission shall prescribe -

(i) documentary material, tangible things, or written reports shall be available for examination by the person who produced the material, or by any duly authorized representative of such person; and

(ii) answers to questions in writing and transcripts of oral testimony shall be available for examination by the person who produced the testimony or by his attorney.

(4) Whenever the Commission has instituted a proceeding against a person, partnership, or corporation, the custodian may deliver to any officer or employee of the Commission documentary material, tangible things, written reports or answers to questions, and transcripts of oral testimony for official use in connection with such proceeding. Upon the completion of the proceeding, the officer or employee shall return to the custodian any such material so delivered which has not been received into the record of the proceeding.

(5) If any documentary material, tangible things, written reports or answers to questions, and transcripts of oral testimony have been produced in the course of any investigation by any person pursuant to compulsory process and -

(A) any proceeding arising out of the investigation has been completed; or

(B) no proceeding in which the material may be used has been commenced within a reasonable time after completion of the examination and analysis of all such material and other information assembled in the course of the investigation; then the custodian shall, upon written request of the person who produced the material, return to the person any such material which has not been received into the record of any such proceeding (other than copies of such material made by the custodian pursuant to paragraph (3)(B)).

(6) The custodian of any documentary material, written reports or answers to questions, and transcripts of oral testimony may deliver to any officers or employees of appropriate Federal law enforcement agencies, in response to a written request, copies of such material for use in connection with an investigation or proceeding under the jurisdiction of any such agency. The custodian of any tangible things may make such things available for inspection to such persons on the same basis. Such materials shall not be made available to any such agency until the custodian received certification of any officer of such agency that such information will be maintained in confidence and will be used only for official law enforcement purposes. Such documentary material, results of inspections of tangible things, written reports or answers to questions, and transcripts of oral testimony may be used by any officer or employee of such agency only in such manner and subject to such conditions as apply to the Commission under this section. The custodian may make such materials available to any State law enforcement agency upon the prior certification of any

officer of such agency that such information will be maintained in confidence and will be used only for official law enforcement purposes.

(7) In the event of the death, disability, or separation from service in the Commission of the custodian of any documentary material, tangible things, written reports or answers to questions, and transcripts of oral testimony produced under any demand issued under this subchapter, or the official relief of the custodian from responsibility for the custody and control of such material, the Commission promptly shall -

(A) designate under paragraph (2)(A) another duly authorized agent to serve as custodian of such material; and

(B) transmit in writing to the person who produced the material or testimony notice as to the identity and address of the successor so designated. Any successor designated under paragraph (2)(A) as a result of the requirements of this paragraph shall have (with regard to the material involved) all duties and responsibilities imposed by this section upon his predecessor in office with regard to such material, except that he shall not be held responsible for any default or dereliction which occurred before his designation.

(c) Information considered confidential

(1) All information reported to or otherwise obtained by the Commission which is not subject to the requirements of subsection (b) of this section shall be considered confidential when so marked by the person supplying the information and shall not be disclosed, except in accordance with the procedures established in paragraph (2) and paragraph (3).

(2) If the Commission determines that a document marked confidential by the person supplying it may be disclosed because it is not a trade secret or commercial or financial information which is obtained from any person and which is privileged or confidential, within the meaning of section 46(f) of this title, then the Commission shall notify such person in writing that the Commission intends to disclose the document at a date not less than 10 days after the date of receipt of notification.

(3) Any person receiving such notification may, if he believes disclosure of the document would cause disclosure of a trade secret, or commercial or financial information which is obtained from any person and which is privileged or confidential, within the meaning of section 46(f) of this title, before the date set for release of the document, bring an action in the district court of the United States for the district within which the documents are located or in the United States District Court for the District of Columbia to restrain disclosure of the document. Any person receiving such notification may file with the appropriate district court or court of appeals of the United States, as appropriate, an application for a stay of disclosure. The documents shall not be disclosed until the court has ruled on the application for a stay.

(d) Particular disclosures allowed

(1) The provisions of subsection (c) of this section shall not be construed to prohibit
-

(A) the disclosure of information to either House of the Congress or to any committee or subcommittee of the Congress, except that the Commission immediately shall notify the owner or provider of any such information of a request for information designated as confidential by the owner or provider;

(B) the disclosure of the results of any investigation or study carried out or prepared by the Commission, except that no information shall be identified nor shall information be disclosed in such a manner as to disclose a trade secret of any person supplying the trade secret, or to disclose any commercial or financial information which is obtained from any person and which is privileged or confidential;

(C) the disclosure of relevant and material information in Commission adjudicative proceedings or in judicial proceedings to which the Commission is a party; or

(D) the disclosure to a Federal agency of disaggregated information obtained in accordance with section 3512[1] of title 44, except that the recipient agency shall use such disaggregated information for economic, statistical, or policymaking purposes only, and shall not disclose such information in an individually identifiable form.

(2) Any disclosure of relevant and material information in Commission adjudicative proceedings or in judicial proceedings to which the Commission is a party shall be governed by the rules of the Commission for adjudicative proceedings or by court rules or orders, except that the rules of the Commission shall not be amended in a manner inconsistent with the purposes of this section.

(e) Effect on other statutory provisions limiting disclosure

Nothing in this section shall supersede any statutory provision which expressly prohibits or limits particular disclosures by the Commission, or which authorizes disclosures to any other Federal agency.

(f) Exemption from disclosure

Any material which is received by the Commission in any investigation, a purpose of which is to determine whether any person may have violated any provision of the laws administered by the Commission, and which is provided pursuant to any compulsory process under this subchapter or which is provided voluntarily in place of such compulsory process shall be exempt from disclosure under section 552 of title 5.

* * *

§ 57b-3. Rulemaking process

(a) Definitions For purposes of this section:

(1) The term "rule" means any rule promulgated by the Commission under section 46 or section 57a of this title, except that such term does not include interpretive rules, rules involving Commission management or personnel, general statements of policy, or rules relating to Commission organization, procedure, or practice. Such term does not include any amendment to a rule unless the Commission -

(A) estimates that such amendment will have an annual effect on the national economy of $100,000,000 or more;

(B) estimates that such amendment will cause a substantial change in the cost or price of goods or services which are used extensively by particular industries, which are supplied extensively in particular geographic regions, or which are acquired in significant quantities by the Federal Government, or by State or local governments; or

(C) otherwise determines that such amendment will have a significant impact upon persons subject to regulation under such amendment and upon consumers.

(2) The term "rulemaking" means any Commission process for formulating or amending a rule.

(b) Notice of proposed rulemaking; regulatory analysis; contents; issuance

(1) In any case in which the Commission publishes notice of a proposed rulemaking, the Commission shall issue a preliminary regulatory analysis relating to the proposed rule involved. Each preliminary regulatory analysis shall contain -

(A) a concise statement of the need for, and the objectives of, the proposed rule;

(B) a description of any reasonable alternatives to the proposed rule which may accomplish the stated objective of the rule in a manner consistent with applicable law; and

(C) for the proposed rule, and for each of the alternatives described in the analysis, a preliminary analysis of the projected benefits and any adverse economic effects and any other effects, and of the effectiveness of the proposed rule and each alternative in meeting the stated objectives of the proposed rule.

(2) In any case in which the Commission promulgates a final rule, the Commission shall issue a final regulatory analysis relating to the final rule. Each final regulatory analysis shall contain -

(A) a concise statement of the need for, and the objectives of, the final rule;

(B) a description of any alternatives to the final rule which were considered by the Commission;

(C) an analysis of the projected benefits and any adverse economic effects and any other effects of the final rule;

(D) an explanation of the reasons for the determination of the Commission that the final rule will attain its objectives in a manner consistent with applicable law and the reasons the particular alternative was chosen; and

(E) a summary of any significant issues raised by the comments submitted during the public comment period in response to the preliminary regulatory analysis, and a summary of the assessment by the Commission of such issues.

(3) (A) In order to avoid duplication or waste, the Commission is authorized to - (i) consider a series of closely related rules as one rule for purposes of this subsection; and

(ii) whenever appropriate, incorporate any data or analysis contained in a regulatory analysis issued under this subsection in the statement of basis and purpose to accompany any rule promulgated under section 57a(a)(1)(B) of this title, and incorporate by reference in any preliminary or final regulatory analysis information contained in a notice of proposed rulemaking or a statement of basis and purpose.

(B) The Commission shall include, in each notice of proposed rulemaking and in each publication of a final rule, a statement of the manner in which the public may obtain copies of the preliminary and final regulatory analyses. The Commission may charge a reasonable fee for the copying and mailing of regulatory analyses. The regulatory analyses shall be furnished without charge or at a reduced charge if the Commission determines that waiver or reduction of the fee is in the public interest because furnishing the information primarily benefits the general public.

(4) The Commission is authorized to delay the completion of any of the requirements established in this subsection by publishing in the Federal Register, not later than the date of publication of the final rule involved, a finding that the final rule is being promulgated in response to an emergency which makes timely compliance with the provisions of this subsection impracticable. Such publication shall include a statement of the reasons for such finding.

(5) The requirements of this subsection shall not be construed to alter in any manner the substantive standards applicable to any action by the Commission, or the procedural standards otherwise applicable to such action.

(c) Judicial review

(1) The contents and adequacy of any regulatory analysis prepared or issued by the Commission under this section, including the adequacy of any procedure involved in such preparation or issuance, shall not be subject to any judicial review in any court, except that a court, upon review of a rule pursuant to section 57a(e) of this title, may set aside such rule if the Commission has failed entirely to prepare a regulatory analysis.

(2) Except as specified in paragraph (1), no Commission action may be invalidated, remanded, or otherwise affected by any court on account of any failure to comply with the requirements of this section.

(3) The provisions of this subsection do not alter the substantive or procedural standards otherwise applicable to judicial review of any action by the Commission.

(d) Regulatory agenda; contents; publication dates in Federal Register

(1) The Commission shall publish at least semiannually a regulatory agenda. Each regulatory agenda shall contain a list of rules which the Commission intends to propose or promulgate during the 12-month period following the publication of the agenda. On the first Monday in October of each year, the Commission shall publish in the Federal Register a schedule showing the dates during the current fiscal year on which the semiannual regulatory agenda of the Commission will be published.

(2) For each rule listed in a regulatory agenda, the Commission shall -

(A) describe the rule;

(B) state the objectives of and the legal basis for the rule; and

(C) specify any dates established or anticipated by the Commission for taking action, including dates for advance notice of proposed rulemaking, notices of proposed rulemaking, and final action by the Commission.

(3) Each regulatory agenda shall state the name, office address, and office telephone number of the Commission officer or employee responsible for responding to any inquiry relating to each rule listed.

(4) The Commission shall not propose or promulgate a rule which was not listed on a regulatory agenda unless the Commission publishes with the rule an explanation of the reasons the rule was omitted from such agenda.

* * *

COMMUNICATIONS ACT (1934)
[EXCERPT]

Summary

Section 605 of the Communications Act followed from the dissent of Justice Brandeis in Olmstead v. U.S. (1928). The provision established a clear prohibition against the interception and subsequent publication of a wire communication.

References

> Public Law 73-416. Codified as amended at 47 U.S.C. § 605.
> [https://www.law.cornell.edu/uscode/text/47/605]

§605. Unauthorized publication or use of communications

(a) Practices prohibited

Except as authorized by chapter 119, title 18, no person receiving, assisting in receiving, transmitting, or assisting in transmitting, any interstate or foreign communication by wire or radio shall divulge or publish the existence, contents, substance, purport, effect, or meaning thereof, except through authorized channels of transmission or reception, (1) to any person other than the addressee, his agent, or attorney, (2) to a person employed or authorized to forward such communication to its destination, (3) to proper accounting or distributing officers of the various communicating centers over which the communication may be passed, (4) to the master of a ship under whom he is serving, (5) in response to a subpena issued by a court of competent jurisdiction, or (6) on demand of other lawful authority. No person not being authorized by the sender shall intercept any radio communication and divulge or publish the existence, contents, substance, purport, effect, or meaning of such intercepted communication to any person. No person not being entitled thereto shall receive or assist in receiving any interstate or foreign communication by radio and use such communication (or any information therein contained) for his own benefit or for the benefit of another not entitled thereto. No person having received any intercepted radio communication or having become acquainted with the contents, substance, purport, effect, or meaning of such communication (or any part thereof) knowing that such communication was intercepted, shall divulge or publish the existence, contents, substance, purport, effect, or meaning of such communication (or any part thereof) or use such communication (or any information therein contained) for his own benefit or for the benefit of another not entitled thereto. This section shall not apply to the receiving, divulging, publishing, or utilizing the contents of any radio communication which is transmitted by any station for the use of the general public, which relates to ships, aircraft, vehicles, or persons in distress, or which is transmitted by an amateur radio station operator or by a citizens band radio operator.

(b) Exceptions

The provisions of subsection (a) shall not apply to the interception or receipt by any individual, or the assisting (including the manufacture or sale) of such interception or receipt, of any satellite cable programming for private viewing if-

(1) the programming involved is not encrypted; and

(2)(A) a marketing system is not established under which-

(i) an agent or agents have been lawfully designated for the purpose of authorizing private viewing by individuals, and

(ii) such authorization is available to the individual involved from the appropriate agent or agents; or

(B) a marketing system described in subparagraph (A) is established and the individuals receiving such programming has obtained authorization for private viewing under that system.

(c) Scrambling of Public Broadcasting Service programming

No person shall encrypt or continue to encrypt satellite delivered programs included in the National Program Service of the Public Broadcasting Service and intended for public viewing by retransmission by television broadcast stations; except that as long as at least one unencrypted satellite transmission of any program subject to this subsection is provided, this subsection shall not prohibit additional encrypted satellite transmissions of the same program.

(d) Definitions

For purposes of this section-

(1) the term "satellite cable programming" means video programming which is transmitted via satellite and which is primarily intended for the direct receipt by cable operators for their retransmission to cable subscribers;

(2) the term "agent", with respect to any person, includes an employee of such person;

(3) the term "encrypt", when used with respect to satellite cable programming, means to transmit such programming in a form whereby the aural and visual characteristics (or both) are modified or altered for the purpose of preventing the unauthorized receipt of such programming by persons without authorized equipment which is designed to eliminate the effects of such modification or alteration;

(4) the term "private viewing" means the viewing for private use in an individual's dwelling unit by means of equipment, owned or operated by such individual, capable of receiving satellite cable programming directly from a satellite;

(5) the term "private financial gain" shall not include the gain resulting to any individual for the private use in such individual's dwelling unit of any programming for which the individual has not obtained authorization for that use; and

(6) the term "any person aggrieved" shall include any person with proprietary rights in the intercepted communication by wire or radio, including wholesale or retail

distributors of satellite cable programming, and, in the case of a violation of paragraph (4) of subsection (e), shall also include any person engaged in the lawful manufacture, distribution, or sale of equipment necessary to authorize or receive satellite cable programming.

(e) Penalties; civil actions; remedies; attorney's fees and costs; computation of damages; regulation by State and local authorities

(1) Any person who willfully violates subsection (a) shall be fined not more than $2,000 or imprisoned for not more than 6 months, or both.

(2) Any person who violates subsection (a) willfully and for purposes of direct or indirect commercial advantage or private financial gain shall be fined not more than $50,000 or imprisoned for not more than 2 years, or both, for the first such conviction and shall be fined not more than $100,000 or imprisoned for not more than 5 years, or both, for any subsequent conviction.

(3)(A) Any person aggrieved by any violation of subsection (a) or paragraph (4) of this subsection may bring a civil action in a United States district court or in any other court of competent jurisdiction.

(B) The court-

(i) may grant temporary and final injunctions on such terms as it may deem reasonable to prevent or restrain violations of subsection (a);

(ii) may award damages as described in subparagraph (C); and

(iii) shall direct the recovery of full costs, including awarding reasonable attorneys' fees to an aggrieved party who prevails.

(C)(i) Damages awarded by any court under this section shall be computed, at the election of the aggrieved party, in accordance with either of the following subclauses;

(I) the party aggrieved may recover the actual damages suffered by him as a result of the violation and any profits of the violator that are attributable to the violation which are not taken into account in computing the actual damages; in determining the violator's profits, the party aggrieved shall be required to prove only the violator's gross revenue, and the violator shall be required to prove his deductible expenses and the elements of profit attributable to factors other than the violation; or

(II) the party aggrieved may recover an award of statutory damages for each violation of subsection (a) involved in the action in a sum of not less than $1,000 or more than $10,000, as the court considers just, and for each violation of paragraph (4) of this subsection involved in the action an aggrieved party may recover statutory damages in a sum not less than $10,000, or more than $100,000, as the court considers just.

(ii) In any case in which the court finds that the violation was committed willfully and for purposes of direct or indirect commercial advantage or private financial gain, the court in its discretion may increase the award of damages, whether actual or statutory, by an amount of not more than $100,000 for each violation of subsection (a).

(iii) In any case where the court finds that the violator was not aware and had no reason to believe that his acts constituted a violation of this section, the court in its discretion may reduce the award of damages to a sum of not less than $250.

(4) Any person who manufactures, assembles, modifies, imports, exports, sells, or distributes any electronic, mechanical, or other device or equipment, knowing or having reason to know that the device or equipment is primarily of assistance in the unauthorized decryption of satellite cable programming, or direct-to-home satellite services, or is intended for any other activity prohibited by subsection (a), shall be fined not more than $500,000 for each violation, or imprisoned for not more than 5 years for each violation, or both. For purposes of all penalties and remedies established for violations of this paragraph, the prohibited activity established herein as it applies to each such device shall be deemed a separate violation.

(5) The penalties under this subsection shall be in addition to those prescribed under any other provision of this subchapter.

(6) Nothing in this subsection shall prevent any State, or political subdivision thereof, from enacting or enforcing any laws with respect to the importation, sale, manufacture, or distribution of equipment by any person with the intent of its use to assist in the interception or receipt of radio communications prohibited by subsection (a).

(f) Rights, obligations, and liabilities under other laws unaffected

Nothing in this section shall affect any right, obligation, or liability under title 17, any rule, regulation, or order thereunder, or any other applicable Federal, State, or local law.

(g) Universal encryption standard

The Commission shall initiate an inquiry concerning the need for a universal encryption standard that permits decryption of satellite cable programming intended for private viewing. In conducting such inquiry, the Commission shall take into account-

(1) consumer costs and benefits of any such standard, including consumer investment in equipment in operation;

(2) incorporation of technological enhancements, including advanced television formats;

(3) whether any such standard would effectively prevent present and future unauthorized decryption of satellite cable programming;

(4) the costs and benefits of any such standard on other authorized users of encrypted satellite cable programming, including cable systems and satellite master antenna television systems;

(5) the effect of any such standard on competition in the manufacture of decryption equipment; and

(6) the impact of the time delay associated with the Commission procedures necessary for establishment of such standards.

(h) Rulemaking for encryption standard

If the Commission finds, based on the information gathered from the inquiry required by subsection (g), that a universal encryption standard is necessary and in the public interest, the Commission shall initiate a rulemaking to establish such a standard.

FAIR CREDIT REPORTING ACT (1970)

Summary

Congress passed the Fair Credit Reporting Act of 1970 to protect individuals from the misuse of personal information by Credit Reporting Agencies, or CRAs. Under the Act, CRAs may only disclose personal information to persons whom they have reason to believe intend to use the information to evaluate an application for credit, employment, insurance, license, or governmental benefit. Notice must be given to an individual when the CRA is asked to procure extensive information on the individual's character and habits, if this information is being procured to evaluate initial eligibility for a benefit. Individuals are entitled to a copy of their credit report, and if errors or discrepancies are found, the CRA must investigate and correct them.

The Act also provides guidelines for the information that can be gathered, and how long it may be maintained within a credit report. For example, bankruptcy can only be reported for ten years, and other negative information is removed from the report after seven. A private action may be brought for any violation of the act, regardless of damages. The Federal Trade Commission is charged with enforcement of the Act.

By the 1990s, many commentators believed the FCRA needed to be updated to bring it into line with new developments in banking and in technology. In 1996, Congress amended the FCRA, in the Consumer Credit Reporting Reform Act. The CCRRA allows for greater sharing of information between affiliate-entities without their becoming CRAs within the meaning of the Act. The CCRRA also tightens some loopholes in the pre-existing FCRA, imposes new obligations on businesses to ensure the accuracy of reports, and increases civil and criminal penalties. The CCRRA also provides for extensive preemption of state laws dealing with credit reporting; this preemption expires on January 1, 2004 unless the Congress renews those provisions.

In 2003 Congress enacted the Fair and Accurate Credit Transactions Act (FACTA), which substantially amended much of the FCRA. The Act establishes remedial rights for identity theft victims, but does little to actually prevent the crime. For example, the FACTA requires merchants to truncate credit and debit card numbers printed on receipts, it gives individuals the right to free annual credit reports, it requires credit agencies to block credit information that was recorded as a result of identity theft, and it creates new document destruction procedures for personal information. The FACTA also preempts state laws that would provide greater privacy safeguards. For example, the FACTA provides that credit agencies must disclose credit scores to individuals for a "reasonable fee"; the states would not be permitted to grant consumers the right to free credit score disclosures.

References

Public Law 91-508. Codified as amended at 15 U.S.C. § 1681.
[https://www.law.cornell.edu/uscode/text/15/1681]

United States
Fair Credit Reporting Act

[https://www.ftc.gov/enforcement/rules/rulemaking-regulatory-reform-proceedings/fair-credit-reporting-act]

FTC, Credit Reporting
[https://www.ftc.gov/news-events/media-resources/consumer-finance/credit-reporting]

FTC, Consumer's Brochure on the FCRA
[http://www.ftc.gov/bcp/conline/pubs/credit/fcra.htm]
EPIC, Fair Credit Reporting Act
[https://www.epic.org/privacy/fcra/]

§ 601. Short title

This title may be cited as the Fair Credit Reporting Act.

15 U.S.C. § 1681. Congressional findings and statement of purpose

(a) Accuracy and fairness of credit reporting. The Congress makes the following findings:

(1) The banking system is dependent upon fair and accurate credit reporting. Inaccurate credit reports directly impair the efficiency of the banking system, and unfair credit reporting methods undermine the public confidence which is essential to the continued functioning of the banking system.

(2) An elaborate mechanism has been developed for investigating and evaluating the credit worthiness, credit standing, credit capacity, character, and general reputation of consumers.

(3) Consumer reporting agencies have assumed a vital role in assembling and evaluating consumer credit and other information on consumers.

(4) There is a need to insure that consumer reporting agencies exercise their grave responsibilities with fairness, impartiality, and a respect for the consumer's right to privacy.

(b) Reasonable procedures. It is the purpose of this title to require that consumer reporting agencies adopt reasonable procedures for meeting the needs of commerce for consumer credit, personnel, insurance, and other information in a manner which is fair and equitable to the consumer, with regard to the confidentiality, accuracy, relevancy, and proper utilization of such information in accordance with the requirements of this title.

§ 1681a. Definitions; rules of construction

(a) Definitions and rules of construction set forth in this section are applicable for the purposes of this subchapter.

(b) The term "person" means any individual, partnership, corporation, trust, estate, cooperative, association, government or governmental subdivision or agency, or other entity.

(c) The term "consumer" means an individual.

(d) Consumer Report.-

(1) In general.-The term "consumer report" means any written, oral, or other communication of any information by a consumer reporting agency bearing on a consumer's credit worthiness, credit standing, credit capacity, character, general reputation, personal characteristics, or mode of living which is used or expected to be used or collected in whole or in part for the purpose of serving as a factor in establishing the consumer's eligibility for-

(A) credit or insurance to be used primarily for personal, family, or household purposes;

(B) employment purposes; or

(C) any other purpose authorized under section 1681b of this title.

(2) Exclusions.-Except as provided in paragraph (3), the term "consumer report" does not include-

(A) subject to section 1681s–3 of this title, any-

(i) report containing information solely as to transactions or experiences between the consumer and the person making the report;

(ii) communication of that information among persons related by common ownership or affiliated by corporate control; or

(iii) communication of other information among persons related by common ownership or affiliated by corporate control, if it is clearly and conspicuously disclosed to the consumer that the information may be communicated among such persons and the consumer is given the opportunity, before the time that the information is initially communicated, to direct that such information not be communicated among such persons;

(B) any authorization or approval of a specific extension of credit directly or indirectly by the issuer of a credit card or similar device;

(C) any report in which a person who has been requested by a third party to make a specific extension of credit directly or indirectly to a consumer conveys his or her decision with respect to such request, if the third party advises the consumer of the name and address of the person to whom the request was made, and such person makes the disclosures to the consumer required under section 1681m of this title; or

(D) a communication described in subsection (o) or (x).[1]

(3) Restriction on sharing of medical information.-Except for information or any communication of information disclosed as provided in section 1681b(g)(3) of this title, the exclusions in paragraph (2) shall not apply with respect to information

disclosed to any person related by common ownership or affiliated by corporate control, if the information is-

(A) medical information;

(B) an individualized list or description based on the payment transactions of the consumer for medical products or services; or

(C) an aggregate list of identified consumers based on payment transactions for medical products or services.

(e) The term "investigative consumer report" means a consumer report or portion thereof in which information on a consumer's character, general reputation, personal characteristics, or mode of living is obtained through personal interviews with neighbors, friends, or associates of the consumer reported on or with others with whom he is acquainted or who may have knowledge concerning any such items of information. However, such information shall not include specific factual information on a consumer's credit record obtained directly from a creditor of the consumer or from a consumer reporting agency when such information was obtained directly from a creditor of the consumer or from the consumer.

(f) The term "consumer reporting agency" means any person which, for monetary fees, dues, or on a cooperative nonprofit basis, regularly engages in whole or in part in the practice of assembling or evaluating consumer credit information or other information on consumers for the purpose of furnishing consumer reports to third parties, and which uses any means or facility of interstate commerce for the purpose of preparing or furnishing consumer reports.

(g) The term "file", when used in connection with information on any consumer, means all of the information on that consumer recorded and retained by a consumer reporting agency regardless of how the information is stored.

(h) The term "employment purposes" when used in connection with a consumer report means a report used for the purpose of evaluating a consumer for employment, promotion, reassignment or retention as an employee.

(i) Medical Information.-The term "medical information"-

(1) means information or data, whether oral or recorded, in any form or medium, created by or derived from a health care provider or the consumer, that relates to-

(A) the past, present, or future physical, mental, or behavioral health or condition of an individual;

(B) the provision of health care to an individual; or

(C) the payment for the provision of health care to an individual.[2]

(2) does not include the age or gender of a consumer, demographic information about the consumer, including a consumer's residence address or e-mail address, or any other information about a consumer that does not relate to the physical, mental,

or behavioral health or condition of a consumer, including the existence or value of any insurance policy.

(j) Definitions Relating to Child Support Obligations.-

(1) Overdue support.-The term "overdue support" has the meaning given to such term in section 666(e) of title 42.

(2) State or local child support enforcement agency.-The term "State or local child support enforcement agency" means a State or local agency which administers a State or local program for establishing and enforcing child support obligations.

(k) Adverse Action.-

(1) Actions included.-The term "adverse action"-

(A) has the same meaning as in section 1691(d)(6) of this title; and

(B) means-

(i) a denial or cancellation of, an increase in any charge for, or a reduction or other adverse or unfavorable change in the terms of coverage or amount of, any insurance, existing or applied for, in connection with the underwriting of insurance;

(ii) a denial of employment or any other decision for employment purposes that adversely affects any current or prospective employee;

(iii) a denial or cancellation of, an increase in any charge for, or any other adverse or unfavorable change in the terms of, any license or benefit described in section 1681b(a)(3)(D) of this title; and

(iv) an action taken or determination that is-

(I) made in connection with an application that was made by, or a transaction that was initiated by, any consumer, or in connection with a review of an account under section 1681b(a)(3)(F)(ii) of this title; and

(II) adverse to the interests of the consumer.

(2) Applicable findings, decisions, commentary, and orders.-For purposes of any determination of whether an action is an adverse action under paragraph (1)(A), all appropriate final findings, decisions, commentary, and orders issued under section 1691(d)(6) of this title by the Bureau or any court shall apply.

(l) Firm Offer of Credit or Insurance.-The term "firm offer of credit or insurance" means any offer of credit or insurance to a consumer that will be honored if the consumer is determined, based on information in a consumer report on the consumer, to meet the specific criteria used to select the consumer for the offer, except that the offer may be further conditioned on one or more of the following:

(1) The consumer being determined, based on information in the consumer's application for the credit or insurance, to meet specific criteria bearing on credit worthiness or insurability, as applicable, that are established-

(A) before selection of the consumer for the offer; and

(B) for the purpose of determining whether to extend credit or insurance pursuant to the offer.

(2) Verification-

(A) that the consumer continues to meet the specific criteria used to select the consumer for the offer, by using information in a consumer report on the consumer, information in the consumer's application for the credit or insurance, or other information bearing on the credit worthiness or insurability of the consumer; or

(B) of the information in the consumer's application for the credit or insurance, to determine that the consumer meets the specific criteria bearing on credit worthiness or insurability.

(3) The consumer furnishing any collateral that is a requirement for the extension of the credit or insurance that was-

(A) established before selection of the consumer for the offer of credit or insurance; and

(B) disclosed to the consumer in the offer of credit or insurance.

(m) Credit or Insurance Transaction That Is Not Initiated by the Consumer.-The term "credit or insurance transaction that is not initiated by the consumer" does not include the use of a consumer report by a person with which the consumer has an account or insurance policy, for purposes of-

(1) reviewing the account or insurance policy; or

(2) collecting the account.

(n) State.-The term "State" means any State, the Commonwealth of Puerto Rico, the District of Columbia, and any territory or possession of the United States.

(o) Excluded Communications.-A communication is described in this subsection if it is a communication-

(1) that, but for subsection (d)(2)(D), would be an investigative consumer report;

(2) that is made to a prospective employer for the purpose of-

(A) procuring an employee for the employer; or

(B) procuring an opportunity for a natural person to work for the employer;

(3) that is made by a person who regularly performs such procurement;

(4) that is not used by any person for any purpose other than a purpose described in subparagraph (A) or (B) of paragraph (2); and

(5) with respect to which-

(A) the consumer who is the subject of the communication-

(i) consents orally or in writing to the nature and scope of the communication, before the collection of any information for the purpose of making the communication;

(ii) consents orally or in writing to the making of the communication to a prospective employer, before the making of the communication; and

(iii) in the case of consent under clause (i) or (ii) given orally, is provided written confirmation of that consent by the person making the communication, not later than 3 business days after the receipt of the consent by that person;

(B) the person who makes the communication does not, for the purpose of making the communication, make any inquiry that if made by a prospective employer of the consumer who is the subject of the communication would violate any applicable Federal or State equal employment opportunity law or regulation; and

(C) the person who makes the communication-

(i) discloses in writing to the consumer who is the subject of the communication, not later than 5 business days after receiving any request from the consumer for such disclosure, the nature and substance of all information in the consumer's file at the time of the request, except that the sources of any information that is acquired solely for use in making the communication and is actually used for no other purpose, need not be disclosed other than under appropriate discovery procedures in any court of competent jurisdiction in which an action is brought; and

(ii) notifies the consumer who is the subject of the communication, in writing, of the consumer's right to request the information described in clause (i).

(p) Consumer Reporting Agency That Compiles and Maintains Files on Consumers on a Nationwide Basis.-The term "consumer reporting agency that compiles and maintains files on consumers on a nationwide basis" means a consumer reporting agency that regularly engages in the practice of assembling or evaluating, and maintaining, for the purpose of furnishing consumer reports to third parties bearing on a consumer's credit worthiness, credit standing, or credit capacity, each of the following regarding consumers residing nationwide:

(1) Public record information.

(2) Credit account information from persons who furnish that information regularly and in the ordinary course of business.

(q) Definitions Relating to Fraud Alerts.-

(1) Active duty military consumer.-The term "active duty military consumer" means a consumer in military service who-

(A) is on active duty (as defined in section 101(d)(1) of title 10) or is a reservist performing duty under a call or order to active duty under a provision of law referred to in section 101(a)(13) of title 10; and

(B) is assigned to service away from the usual duty station of the consumer.

(2) Fraud alert; active duty alert.-The terms "fraud alert" and "active duty alert" mean a statement in the file of a consumer that-

(A) notifies all prospective users of a consumer report relating to the consumer that the consumer may be a victim of fraud, including identity theft, or is an active duty military consumer, as applicable; and

(B) is presented in a manner that facilitates a clear and conspicuous view of the statement described in subparagraph (A) by any person requesting such consumer report.

(3) Identity theft.-The term "identity theft" means a fraud committed using the identifying information of another person, subject to such further definition as the Bureau may prescribe, by regulation.

(4) Identity theft report.-The term "identity theft report" has the meaning given that term by rule of the Bureau, and means, at a minimum, a report-

(A) that alleges an identity theft;

(B) that is a copy of an official, valid report filed by a consumer with an appropriate Federal, State, or local law enforcement agency, including the

United States Postal Inspection Service, or such other government agency deemed appropriate by the Bureau; and

(C) the filing of which subjects the person filing the report to criminal penalties relating to the filing of false information if, in fact, the information in the report is false.

(5) New credit plan.-The term "new credit plan" means a new account under an open end credit plan (as defined in section 1602(i)¹ of this title) or a new credit transaction not under an open end credit plan.

(r) Credit and Debit Related Terms-

(1) Card issuer.-The term "card issuer" means-

(A) a credit card issuer, in the case of a credit card; and

(B) a debit card issuer, in the case of a debit card.

(2) Credit card.-The term "credit card" has the same meaning as in section 1602 of this title.

(3) Debit card.-The term "debit card" means any card issued by a financial institution to a consumer for use in initiating an electronic fund transfer from the account of the consumer at such financial institution, for the purpose of transferring money between accounts or obtaining money, property, labor, or services.

(4) Account and electronic fund transfer.-The terms "account" and "electronic fund transfer" have the same meanings as in section 1693a of this title.

(5) Credit and creditor.-The terms "credit" and "creditor" have the same meanings as in section 1691a of this title.

(s) Federal Banking Agency.-The term "Federal banking agency" has the same meaning as in section 1813 of title 12.

(t) Financial Institution.-The term "financial institution" means a State or National bank, a State or Federal savings and loan association, a mutual savings bank, a State or Federal credit union, or any other person that, directly or indirectly, holds a transaction account (as defined in section 461(b) of title 12) belonging to a consumer.

(u) Reseller.-The term "reseller" means a consumer reporting agency that-

(1) assembles and merges information contained in the database of another consumer reporting agency or multiple consumer reporting agencies concerning any

consumer for purposes of furnishing such information to any third party, to the extent of such activities; and

(2) does not maintain a database of the assembled or merged information from which new consumer reports are produced.

(v) Commission.-The term "Commission" means the Bureau.[3]

(w) The term "Bureau" means the Bureau of Consumer Financial Protection.

(x) Nationwide Specialty Consumer Reporting Agency.-The term "nationwide specialty consumer reporting agency" means a consumer reporting agency that compiles and maintains files on consumers on a nationwide basis relating to-

(1) medical records or payments;

(2) residential or tenant history;

(3) check writing history;

(4) employment history; or

(5) insurance claims.

(y) Exclusion of Certain Communications for Employee Investigations.-

(1) Communications described in this subsection.-A communication is described in this subsection if-

(A) but for subsection (d)(2)(D), the communication would be a consumer report;

(B) the communication is made to an employer in connection with an investigation of-

(i) suspected misconduct relating to employment; or

(ii) compliance with Federal, State, or local laws and regulations, the rules of a self-regulatory organization, or any preexisting written policies of the employer;

(C) the communication is not made for the purpose of investigating a consumer's credit worthiness, credit standing, or credit capacity; and

(D) the communication is not provided to any person except-

(i) to the employer or an agent of the employer;

(ii) to any Federal or State officer, agency, or department, or any officer, agency, or department of a unit of general local government;

(iii) to any self-regulatory organization with regulatory authority over the activities of the employer or employee;

(iv) as otherwise required by law; or

(v) pursuant to section 1681f of this title.

(2) Subsequent disclosure.-After taking any adverse action based in whole or in part on a communication described in paragraph (1), the employer shall disclose to the consumer a summary containing the nature and substance of the communication upon which the adverse action is based, except that the sources of information acquired solely for use in preparing what would be but for subsection (d)(2)(D) an investigative consumer report need not be disclosed.

(3) Self-regulatory organization defined.-For purposes of this subsection, the term "self-regulatory organization" includes any self-regulatory organization (as defined

in section 78c(a)(26) of this title), any entity established under title I of the Sarbanes-Oxley Act of 2002 [15 U.S.C. 7211 et seq.], any board of trade designated by the Commodity Futures Trading Commission, and any futures association registered with such Commission.

(z) Veteran.-The term "veteran" has the meaning given the term in section 101 of title 38.

(aa) Veteran's Medical Debt.-The term "veteran's medical debt"-

(1) means a medical collection debt of a veteran owed to a non-Department of Veterans Affairs health care provider that was submitted to the Department for payment for health care authorized by the Department of Veterans Affairs; and

(2) includes medical collection debt that the Department of Veterans Affairs has wrongfully charged a veteran.

§ 1681b. Permissible purposes of consumer reports

(a) In general. Subject to subsection (c), any consumer reporting agency may furnish a consumer report under the following circumstances and no other:

(1) In response to the order of a court having jurisdiction to issue such an order, or a subpoena issued in connection with proceedings before a Federal grand jury.

(2) In accordance with the written instructions of the consumer to whom it relates.

(3) To a person which it has reason to believe-

(A) intends to use the information in connection with a credit transaction involving the consumer on whom the information is to be furnished and involving the extension of credit to, or review or collection of an account of, the consumer; or

(B) intends to use the information for employment purposes; or

(C) intends to use the information in connection with the underwriting of insurance involving the consumer; or

(D) intends to use the information in connection with a determination of the consumer's eligibility for a license or other benefit granted by a governmental instrumentality required by law to consider an applicant's financial responsibility or status; or

(E) intends to use the information, as a potential investor or servicer, or current insurer, in connection with a valuation of, or an assessment of the credit or prepayment risks associated with, an existing credit obligation; or

(F) otherwise has a legitimate business need for the information-

(i) in connection with a business transaction that is initiated by the consumer; or

(ii) to review an account to determine whether the consumer continues to meet the terms of the account.

(G) executive departments and agencies in connection with the issuance of government-sponsored individually-billed travel charge cards.

(4) In response to a request by the head of a State or local child support enforcement agency (or a State or local government official authorized by the head of such an agency), if the person making the request certifies to the consumer reporting agency that-

(A) the consumer report is needed for the purpose of establishing an individual's capacity to make child support payments, determining the appropriate level of such payments, or enforcing a child support order, award, agreement, or judgment;

(B) the parentage of the consumer for the child to which the obligation relates has been established or acknowledged by the consumer in accordance with State laws under which the obligation arises (if required by those laws); and

(C) the consumer report will be kept confidential, will be used solely for a purpose described in subparagraph (A), and will not be used in connection with any other civil, administrative, or criminal proceeding, or for any other purpose.

(5) To an agency administering a State plan under section 654 of title 42 for use to set an initial or modified child support award.

(6) To the Federal Deposit Insurance Corporation or the National Credit Union Administration as part of its preparation for its appointment or as part of its exercise of powers, as conservator, receiver, or liquidating agent for an insured depository institution or insured credit union under the Federal Deposit Insurance Act [12 U.S.C. 1811 et seq.] or the Federal Credit Union Act [12 U.S.C. 1751 et seq.], or other applicable Federal or State law, or in connection with the resolution or liquidation of a failed or failing insured depository institution or insured credit union, as applicable.

(b) Conditions for furnishing and using consumer reports for employment purposes

(1) Certification from user

A consumer reporting agency may furnish a consumer report for employment purposes only if-

(A) the person who obtains such report from the agency certifies to the agency that-

(i) the person has complied with paragraph (2) with respect to the consumer report, and the person will comply with paragraph (3) with respect to the consumer report if paragraph (3) becomes applicable; and

(ii) information from the consumer report will not be used in violation of any applicable Federal or State equal employment opportunity law or regulation; and

(B) the consumer reporting agency provides with the report, or has previously provided, a summary of the consumer's rights under this subchapter, as prescribed by the Bureau under section 1681g(c)(3) 1 of this title.

(2) Disclosure to consumer

(A) In general

Except as provided in subparagraph (B), a person may not procure a consumer report, or cause a consumer report to be procured, for employment purposes with respect to any consumer, unless-

>   (i) a clear and conspicuous disclosure has been made in writing to the consumer at any time before the report is procured or caused to be procured, in a document that consists solely of the disclosure, that a consumer report may be obtained for employment purposes; and

>   (ii) the consumer has authorized in writing (which authorization may be made on the document referred to in clause (i)) the procurement of the report by that person.

(B) Application by mail, telephone, computer, or other similar means

If a consumer described in subparagraph (C) applies for employment by mail, telephone, computer, or other similar means, at any time before a consumer report is procured or caused to be procured in connection with that application-

>   (i) the person who procures the consumer report on the consumer for employment purposes shall provide to the consumer, by oral, written, or electronic means, notice that a consumer report may be obtained for employment purposes, and a summary of the consumer's rights under section 1681m(a)(3) 1 of this title; and

>   (ii) the consumer shall have consented, orally, in writing, or electronically to the procurement of the report by that person.

(C) Scope

Subparagraph (B) shall apply to a person procuring a consumer report on a consumer in connection with the consumer's application for employment only if-

>   (i) the consumer is applying for a position over which the Secretary of Transportation has the power to establish qualifications and maximum hours of service pursuant to the provisions of section 31502 of title 49, or a position subject to safety regulation by a State transportation agency; and

>   (ii) as of the time at which the person procures the report or causes the report to be procured the only interaction between the consumer and the person in connection with that employment application has been by mail, telephone, computer, or other similar means.

(3) Conditions on use for adverse actions

(A) In general

Except as provided in subparagraph (B), in using a consumer report for employment purposes, before taking any adverse action based in whole or in part on the report, the person intending to take such adverse action shall provide to the consumer to whom the report relates -

(i) a copy of the report; and

(ii) a description in writing of the rights of the consumer under this subchapter, as prescribed by the Bureau under section 1681g(c)(3) 1 of this title.

(B) Application by mail, telephone, computer, or other similar means

(i) If a consumer described in subparagraph (C) applies for employment by mail, telephone, computer, or other similar means, and if a person who has procured a consumer report on the consumer for employment purposes takes adverse action on the employment application based in whole or in part on the report, then the person must provide to the consumer to whom the report relates, in lieu of the notices required under subparagraph (A) of this section and under section 1681m(a) of this title, within 3 business days of taking such action, an oral, written or electronic notification-

(I) that adverse action has been taken based in whole or in part on a consumer report received from a consumer reporting agency;

(II) of the name, address and telephone number of the consumer reporting agency that furnished the consumer report (including a toll-free telephone number established by the agency if the agency compiles and maintains files on consumers on a nationwide basis);

(III) that the consumer reporting agency did not make the decision to take the adverse action and is unable to provide to the consumer the specific reasons why the adverse action was taken; and

(IV) that the consumer may, upon providing proper identification, request a free copy of a report and may dispute with the consumer reporting agency the accuracy or completeness of any information in a report.

(ii) If, under clause (B)(i)(IV), the consumer requests a copy of a consumer report from the person who procured the report, then, within 3 business days of receiving the consumer's request, together with proper identification, the person must send or provide to the consumer a copy of a report and a copy of the consumer's rights as prescribed by the Bureau under section 1681g(c)(3) 1 of this title.

(C) Scope

Subparagraph (B) shall apply to a person procuring a consumer report on a consumer in connection with the consumer's application for employment only if-

(i) the consumer is applying for a position over which the Secretary of Transportation has the power to establish qualifications and maximum hours of service pursuant to the provisions of section 31502 of title 49, or a position subject to safety regulation by a State transportation agency; and

(ii) as of the time at which the person procures the report or causes the report to be procured the only interaction between the consumer and the person in connection with that employment application has been by mail, telephone, computer, or other similar means.

(4) Exception for national security investigations

(A) In general

In the case of an agency or department of the United States Government which seeks to obtain and use a consumer report for employment purposes, paragraph (3) shall not apply to any adverse action by such agency or department which is based in part on such consumer report, if the head of such agency or department makes a written finding that -

(i) the consumer report is relevant to a national security investigation of such agency or department;

(ii) the investigation is within the jurisdiction of such agency or department;

(iii) there is reason to believe that compliance with paragraph (3) will-

(I) endanger the life or physical safety of any person;

(II) result in flight from prosecution;

(III) result in the destruction of, or tampering with, evidence relevant to the investigation;

(IV) result in the intimidation of a potential witness relevant to the investigation;

(V) result in the compromise of classified information; or

(VI) otherwise seriously jeopardize or unduly delay the investigation or another official proceeding.

(B) Notification of consumer upon conclusion of investigation

Upon the conclusion of a national security investigation described in subparagraph (A), or upon the determination that the exception under subparagraph (A) is no longer required for the reasons set forth in such subparagraph, the official exercising the authority in such subparagraph shall provide to the consumer who is the subject of the consumer report with regard to which such finding was made-

(i) a copy of such consumer report with any classified information redacted as necessary;

(ii) notice of any adverse action which is based, in part, on the consumer report; and

(iii) the identification with reasonable specificity of the nature of the investigation for which the consumer report was sought.

(C) Delegation by head of agency or department

For purposes of subparagraphs (A) and (B), the head of any agency or department of the United States Government may delegate his or her authorities under this paragraph to an official of such agency or department who has personnel security responsibilities and is a member of the Senior Executive Service or equivalent civilian or military rank.

(D) Definitions

For purposes of this paragraph, the following definitions shall apply:

(i) Classified information

The term "classified information" means information that is protected from unauthorized disclosure under Executive Order No. 12958 or successor orders.

(ii) National security investigation

The term "national security investigation" means any official inquiry by an agency or department of the United States Government to determine the eligibility of a consumer to receive access or continued access to classified information or to determine whether classified information has been lost or compromised.

(c) Furnishing reports in connection with credit or insurance transactions that are not initiated by consumer

(1) In general

A consumer reporting agency may furnish a consumer report relating to any consumer pursuant to subparagraph (A) or (C) of subsection (a)(3) in connection with any credit or insurance transaction that is not initiated by the consumer only if-

(A) the consumer authorizes the agency to provide such report to such person; or

(B)(i) the transaction consists of a firm offer of credit or insurance;

(ii) the consumer reporting agency has complied with subsection (e);

(iii) there is not in effect an election by the consumer, made in accordance with subsection (e), to have the consumer's name and address excluded from lists of names provided by the agency pursuant to this paragraph; and

(iv) the consumer report does not contain a date of birth that shows that the consumer has not attained the age of 21, or, if the date of birth on the consumer report shows that the consumer has not attained the age of 21, such consumer consents to the consumer reporting agency to such furnishing.

(2) Limits on information received under paragraph (1)(B)

A person may receive pursuant to paragraph (1)(B) only-

(A) the name and address of a consumer;

(B) an identifier that is not unique to the consumer and that is used by the person solely for the purpose of verifying the identity of the consumer; and

(C) other information pertaining to a consumer that does not identify the relationship or experience of the consumer with respect to a particular creditor or other entity.

(3) Information regarding inquiries

Except as provided in section 1681g(a)(5) of this title, a consumer reporting agency shall not furnish to any person a record of inquiries in connection with a credit or insurance transaction that is not initiated by a consumer.

(d) Reserved

(e) Election of consumer to be excluded from lists

(1) In general

A consumer may elect to have the consumer's name and address excluded from any list provided by a consumer reporting agency under subsection (c)(1)(B) in connection with a credit or insurance transaction that is not initiated by the consumer, by notifying the agency in accordance with paragraph (2) that the consumer does not consent to any use of a consumer report relating to the consumer in connection with any credit or insurance transaction that is not initiated by the consumer.

(2) Manner of notification

A consumer shall notify a consumer reporting agency under paragraph (1)-

(A) through the notification system maintained by the agency under paragraph (5); or

(B) by submitting to the agency a signed notice of election form issued by the agency for purposes of this subparagraph.

(3) Response of agency after notification through system

Upon receipt of notification of the election of a consumer under paragraph (1) through the notification system maintained by the agency under paragraph (5), a consumer reporting agency shall-

(A) inform the consumer that the election is effective only for the 5-year period following the election if the consumer does not submit to the agency a signed notice of election form issued by the agency for purposes of paragraph (2)(B); and

(B) provide to the consumer a notice of election form, if requested by the consumer, not later than 5 business days after receipt of the notification of the election through the system established under paragraph (5), in the case of a request made at the time the consumer provides notification through the system.

(4) Effectiveness of election

An election of a consumer under paragraph (1)-

(A) shall be effective with respect to a consumer reporting agency beginning 5 business days after the date on which the consumer notifies the agency in accordance with paragraph (2);

(B) shall be effective with respect to a consumer reporting agency-

(i) subject to subparagraph (C), during the 5-year period beginning 5 business days after the date on which the consumer notifies the agency of the election, in the case of an election for which a consumer notifies the agency only in accordance with paragraph (2)(A); or

(ii) until the consumer notifies the agency under subparagraph (C), in the case of an election for which a consumer notifies the agency in accordance with paragraph (2)(B);

(C) shall not be effective after the date on which the consumer notifies the agency, through the notification system established by the agency under paragraph (5), that the election is no longer effective; and

(D) shall be effective with respect to each affiliate of the agency.

(5) Notification system

(A) In general

Each consumer reporting agency that, under subsection (c)(1)(B), furnishes a consumer report in connection with a credit or insurance transaction that is not initiated by a consumer, shall-

(i) establish and maintain a notification system, including a toll-free telephone number, which permits any consumer whose consumer report is maintained by the agency to notify the agency, with appropriate identification, of the consumer's election to have the consumer's name and address excluded from any such list of names and addresses provided by the agency for such a transaction; and

(ii) publish by not later than 365 days after September 30, 1996, and not less than annually thereafter, in a publication of general circulation in the area served by the agency-

(I) a notification that information in consumer files maintained by the agency may be used in connection with such transactions; and

(II) the address and toll-free telephone number for consumers to use to notify the agency of the consumer's election under clause (i).

(B) Establishment and maintenance as compliance

Establishment and maintenance of a notification system (including a toll-free telephone number) and publication by a consumer reporting agency on the agency's own behalf and on behalf of any of its affiliates in accordance with this paragraph is deemed to be compliance with this paragraph by each of those affiliates.

(6) Notification system by agencies that operate nationwide

Each consumer reporting agency that compiles and maintains files on consumers on a nationwide basis shall establish and maintain a notification system for purposes of paragraph (5) jointly with other such consumer reporting agencies.

(f) Certain use or obtaining of information prohibited

A person shall not use or obtain a consumer report for any purpose unless-

(1) the consumer report is obtained for a purpose for which the consumer report is authorized to be furnished under this section; and

(2) the purpose is certified in accordance with section 1681e of this title by a prospective user of the report through a general or specific certification.

(g) Protection of medical information

(1) Limitation on consumer reporting agencies

A consumer reporting agency shall not furnish for employment purposes, or in connection with a credit or insurance transaction, a consumer report that contains medical information (other than medical contact information treated in the manner required under section 1681c(a)(6) of this title) about a consumer, unless-

(A) if furnished in connection with an insurance transaction, the consumer affirmatively consents to the furnishing of the report;

(B) if furnished for employment purposes or in connection with a credit transaction-

(i) the information to be furnished is relevant to process or effect the employment or credit transaction; and

(ii) the consumer provides specific written consent for the furnishing of the report that describes in clear and conspicuous language the use for which the information will be furnished; or

(C) the information to be furnished pertains solely to transactions, accounts, or balances relating to debts arising from the receipt of medical services, products, or devises, where such information, other than account status or amounts, is restricted or reported using codes that do not identify, or do not provide information sufficient to infer, the specific provider or the nature of such services, products, or devices, as provided in section 1681c(a)(6) of this title.

(2) Limitation on creditors

Except as permitted pursuant to paragraph (3)(C) or regulations prescribed under paragraph (5)(A), a creditor shall not obtain or use medical information (other than medical information treated in the manner required under section 1681c(a)(6) of this title) pertaining to a consumer in connection with any determination of the consumer's eligibility, or continued eligibility, for credit.

(3) Actions authorized by Federal law, insurance activities and regulatory determinations

Section 1681a(d)(3) of this title shall not be construed so as to treat information or any communication of information as a consumer report if the information or communication is disclosed-

(A) in connection with the business of insurance or annuities, including the activities described in section 18B of the model Privacy of Consumer Financial and Health Information Regulation issued by the National Association of Insurance Commissioners (as in effect on January 1, 2003);

(B) for any purpose permitted without authorization under the Standards for Individually Identifiable Health Information promulgated by the Department of Health and Human Services pursuant to the Health Insurance Portability and Accountability Act of 1996, or referred to under section 1179 of such Act,1 or described in section 6802(e) of this title; or

(C) as otherwise determined to be necessary and appropriate, by regulation or order, by the Bureau or the applicable State insurance authority (with respect to any person engaged in providing insurance or annuities).

(4) Limitation on redisclosure of medical information

Any person that receives medical information pursuant to paragraph (1) or (3) shall not disclose such information to any other person, except as necessary to carry out the purpose for which the information was initially disclosed, or as otherwise permitted by statute, regulation, or order.

(5) Regulations and effective date for paragraph (2)

(A) Regulations required

The Bureau may, after notice and opportunity for comment, prescribe regulations that permit transactions under paragraph (2) that are determined to be necessary and appropriate to protect legitimate operational, transactional, risk, consumer, and other needs (and which shall include permitting actions necessary for administrative verification purposes), consistent with the intent of paragraph (2) to restrict the use of medical information for inappropriate purposes.

(6) Coordination with other laws

No provision of this subsection shall be construed as altering, affecting, or superseding the applicability of any other provision of Federal law relating to medical confidentiality.

§ 1681c. Requirements relating to information contained in consumer reports

(a) Information excluded from consumer reports

Except as authorized under subsection (b), no consumer reporting agency may make any consumer report containing any of the following items of information:

(1) Cases under title 11 or under the Bankruptcy Act that, from the date of entry of the order for relief or the date of adjudication, as the case may be, antedate the report by more than 10 years.

(2) Civil suits, civil judgments, and records of arrest that, from date of entry, antedate the report by more than seven years or until the governing statute of limitations has expired, whichever is the longer period.

(3) Paid tax liens which, from date of payment, antedate the report by more than seven years.

(4) Accounts placed for collection or charged to profit and loss which antedate the report by more than seven years.

(5) Any other adverse item of information, other than records of convictions of crimes which antedates the report by more than seven years.

(6) The name, address, and telephone number of any medical information furnisher that has notified the agency of its status, unless-

(A) such name, address, and telephone number are restricted or reported using codes that do not identify, or provide information sufficient to infer, the specific provider or the nature of such services, products, or devices to a person other than the consumer; or

(B) the report is being provided to an insurance company for a purpose relating to engaging in the business of insurance other than property and casualty insurance.

(7) With respect to a consumer reporting agency described in section 1681a(p) of this title, any information related to a veteran's medical debt if the date on which the hospital care, medical services, or extended care services was rendered relating to the debt antedates the report by less than 1 year if the consumer reporting agency has actual knowledge that the information is related to a veteran's medical debt and the consumer reporting agency is in compliance with its obligation under section 302(c)(5) of the Economic Growth, Regulatory Relief, and Consumer Protection Act.

(8) With respect to a consumer reporting agency described in section 1681a(p) of this title, any information related to a fully paid or settled veteran's medical debt that had been characterized as delinquent, charged off, or in collection if the consumer reporting agency has actual knowledge that the information is related to a veteran's medical debt and the consumer reporting agency is in compliance with

its obligation under section 302(c)(5) of the Economic Growth, Regulatory Relief, and Consumer Protection Act.

(b) Exempted cases

The provisions of paragraphs (1) through (5) of subsection (a) are not applicable in the case of any consumer credit report to be used in connection with-

(1) a credit transaction involving, or which may reasonably be expected to involve, a principal amount of $150,000 or more;

(2) the underwriting of life insurance involving, or which may reasonably be expected to involve, a face amount of $150,000 or more; or

(3) the employment of any individual at an annual salary which equals, or which may reasonably be expected to equal $75,000, or more.

(c) Running of reporting period

(1) In general

The 7-year period referred to in paragraphs (4) and (6) of subsection (a) shall begin, with respect to any delinquent account that is placed for collection (internally or by referral to a third party, whichever is earlier), charged to profit and loss, or subjected to any similar action, upon the expiration of the 180-day period beginning on the date of the commencement of the delinquency which immediately preceded the collection activity, charge to profit and loss, or similar action.

(2) Effective date

Paragraph (1) shall apply only to items of information added to the file of a consumer on or after the date that is 455 days after September 30, 1996.

(d) Information required to be disclosed

(1) Title 11 information

Any consumer reporting agency that furnishes a consumer report that contains information regarding any case involving the consumer that arises under title 11 shall include in the report an identification of the chapter of such title 11 under which such case arises if provided by the source of the information. If any case arising or filed under title 11 is withdrawn by the consumer before a final judgment, the consumer reporting agency shall include in the report that such case or filing was withdrawn upon receipt of documentation certifying such withdrawal.

(2) Key factor in credit score information

Any consumer reporting agency that furnishes a consumer report that contains any credit score or any other risk score or predictor on any consumer shall include in the report a clear and conspicuous statement that a key factor (as defined in section 1681g(f)(2)(B) of this title) that adversely affected such score or predictor was the number of enquiries, if such a predictor was in fact a key factor that adversely affected such score. This paragraph shall not apply to a check services company, acting as such, which issues authorizations for the purpose of approving or processing negotiable instruments, electronic fund transfers, or similar methods of payments, but only to the extent that such company is engaged in such activities.

(e) Indication of closure of account by consumer

If a consumer reporting agency is notified pursuant to section 1681s–2(a)(4) of this title that a credit account of a consumer was voluntarily closed by the consumer, the agency shall indicate that fact in any consumer report that includes information related to the account.

(f) Indication of dispute by consumer

If a consumer reporting agency is notified pursuant to section 1681s–2(a)(3) of this title that information regarding a consumer who [1] was furnished to the agency is disputed by the consumer, the agency shall indicate that fact in each consumer report that includes the disputed information.

(g) Truncation of credit card and debit card numbers

(1) In general

Except as otherwise provided in this subsection, no person that accepts credit cards or debit cards for the transaction of business shall print more than the last 5 digits of the card number or the expiration date upon any receipt provided to the cardholder at the point of the sale or transaction.

(2) Limitation

This subsection shall apply only to receipts that are electronically printed, and shall not apply to transactions in which the sole means of recording a credit card or debit card account number is by handwriting or by an imprint or copy of the card.

(3) Effective date

This subsection shall become effective-

(A) 3 years after December 4, 2003, with respect to any cash register or other machine or device that electronically prints receipts for credit card or debit card transactions that is in use before January 1, 2005; and

(B) 1 year after December 4, 2003, with respect to any cash register or other machine or device that electronically prints receipts for credit card or debit card transactions that is first put into use on or after January 1, 2005.

(h) Notice of discrepancy in address

(1) In general

If a person has requested a consumer report relating to a consumer from a consumer reporting agency described in section 1681a(p) of this title, the request includes an address for the consumer that substantially differs from the addresses in the file of the consumer, and the agency provides a consumer report in response to the request, the consumer reporting agency shall notify the requester of the existence of the discrepancy.

(2) Regulations

(A) Regulations required

The Bureau shall,[2] in consultation with the Federal banking agencies, the National Credit Union Administration, and the Federal Trade Commission,[2] prescribe regulations providing guidance regarding reasonable policies and procedures that a user of a consumer report should employ when such user has received a notice of discrepancy under paragraph (1).

(B) Policies and procedures to be included

The regulations prescribed under subparagraph (A) shall describe reasonable policies and procedures for use by a user of a consumer report-

>(i) to form a reasonable belief that the user knows the identity of the person to whom the consumer report pertains; and

>(ii) if the user establishes a continuing relationship with the consumer, and the user regularly and in the ordinary course of business furnishes information to the consumer reporting agency from which the notice of discrepancy pertaining to the consumer was obtained, to reconcile the address of the consumer with the consumer reporting agency by furnishing such address to such consumer reporting agency as part of information regularly furnished by the user for the period in which the relationship is established.

§ 1681c-1. Identity theft prevention; fraud alerts and active duty alerts

(a) One-call fraud alerts

(1) Initial alerts

Upon the direct request of a consumer, or an individual acting on behalf of or as a personal representative of a consumer, who asserts in good faith a suspicion that the consumer has been or is about to become a victim of fraud or related crime, including identity theft, a consumer reporting agency described in section 1681a(p) of this title that maintains a file on the consumer and has received appropriate proof of the identity of the requester shall-

>(A) include a fraud alert in the file of that consumer, and also provide that alert along with any credit score generated in using that file, for a period of not less than 1 year, beginning on the date of such request, unless the consumer or such representative requests that such fraud alert be removed before the end of such period, and the agency has received appropriate proof of the identity of the requester for such purpose; and

>(B) refer the information regarding the fraud alert under this paragraph to each of the other consumer reporting agencies described in section 1681a(p) of this

title, in accordance with procedures developed under section 1681s(f) of this title.

(2) Access to free reports

In any case in which a consumer reporting agency includes a fraud alert in the file of a consumer pursuant to this subsection, the consumer reporting agency shall-

(A) disclose to the consumer that the consumer may request a free copy of the file of the consumer pursuant to section 1681j(d) of this title; and

(B) provide to the consumer all disclosures required to be made under section 1681g of this title, without charge to the consumer, not later than 3 business days after any request described in subparagraph (A).

(b) Extended alerts

(1) In general

Upon the direct request of a consumer, or an individual acting on behalf of or as a personal representative of a consumer, who submits an identity theft report to a consumer reporting agency described in section 1681a(p) of this title that maintains a file on the consumer, if the agency has received appropriate proof of the identity of the requester, the agency shall-

(A) include a fraud alert in the file of that consumer, and also provide that alert along with any credit score generated in using that file, during the 7-year period beginning on the date of such request, unless the consumer or such representative requests that such fraud alert be removed before the end of such period and the agency has received appropriate proof of the identity of the requester for such purpose;

(B) during the 5-year period beginning on the date of such request, exclude the consumer from any list of consumers prepared by the consumer reporting agency and provided to any third party to offer credit or insurance to the consumer as part of a transaction that was not initiated by the consumer, unless the consumer or such representative requests that such exclusion be rescinded before the end of such period; and

(C) refer the information regarding the extended fraud alert under this paragraph to each of the other consumer reporting agencies described in section 1681a(p) of this title, in accordance with procedures developed under section 1681s(f) of this title.

(2) Access to free reports

In any case in which a consumer reporting agency includes a fraud alert in the file of a consumer pursuant to this subsection, the consumer reporting agency shall-

(A) disclose to the consumer that the consumer may request 2 free copies of the file of the consumer pursuant to section 1681j(d) of this title during the 12-

month period beginning on the date on which the fraud alert was included in the file; and

(B) provide to the consumer all disclosures required to be made under section 1681g of this title, without charge to the consumer, not later than 3 business days after any request described in subparagraph (A).

(c) Active duty alerts

Upon the direct request of an active duty military consumer, or an individual acting on behalf of or as a personal representative of an active duty military consumer, a consumer reporting agency described in section 1681a(p) of this title that maintains a file on the active duty military consumer and has received appropriate proof of the identity of the requester shall-

(1) include an active duty alert in the file of that active duty military consumer, and also provide that alert along with any credit score generated in using that file, during a period of not less than 12 months, or such longer period as the Bureau shall determine, by regulation, beginning on the date of the request, unless the active duty military consumer or such representative requests that such fraud alert be removed before the end of such period, and the agency has received appropriate proof of the identity of the requester for such purpose;

(2) during the 2-year period beginning on the date of such request, exclude the active duty military consumer from any list of consumers prepared by the consumer reporting agency and provided to any third party to offer credit or insurance to the consumer as part of a transaction that was not initiated by the consumer, unless the consumer requests that such exclusion be rescinded before the end of such period; and

(3) refer the information regarding the active duty alert to each of the other consumer reporting agencies described in section 1681a(p) of this title, in accordance with procedures developed under section 1681s(f) of this title.

(d) Procedures

Each consumer reporting agency described in section 1681a(p) of this title shall establish policies and procedures to comply with this section, including procedures that inform consumers of the availability of initial, extended, and active duty alerts and procedures that allow consumers and active duty military consumers to request initial, extended, or active duty alerts (as applicable) in a simple and easy manner, including by telephone.

(e) Referrals of alerts

Each consumer reporting agency described in section 1681a(p) of this title that receives a referral of a fraud alert or active duty alert from another consumer reporting agency pursuant to this section shall, as though the agency received the request from the consumer directly, follow the procedures required under-

(1) paragraphs (1)(A) and (2) of subsection (a), in the case of a referral under subsection (a)(1)(B);

(2) paragraphs (1)(A), (1)(B), and (2) of subsection (b), in the case of a referral under subsection (b)(1)(C); and

(3) paragraphs (1) and (2) of subsection (c), in the case of a referral under subsection (c)(3).

(f) Duty of reseller to reconvey alert

A reseller shall include in its report any fraud alert or active duty alert placed in the file of a consumer pursuant to this section by another consumer reporting agency.

(g) Duty of other consumer reporting agencies to provide contact information

If a consumer contacts any consumer reporting agency that is not described in section 1681a(p) of this title to communicate a suspicion that the consumer has been or is about to become a victim of fraud or related crime, including identity theft, the agency shall provide information to the consumer on how to contact the Bureau and the consumer reporting agencies described in section 1681a(p) of this title to obtain more detailed information and request alerts under this section.

(h) Limitations on use of information for credit extensions

(1) Requirements for initial and active duty alerts

(A) Notification

Each initial fraud alert and active duty alert under this section shall include information that notifies all prospective users of a consumer report on the consumer to which the alert relates that the consumer does not authorize the establishment of any new credit plan or extension of credit, other than under an open-end credit plan (as defined in section 1602(i) [1] of this title), in the name of the consumer, or issuance of an additional card on an existing credit account requested by a consumer, or any increase in credit limit on an existing credit account requested by a consumer, except in accordance with subparagraph (B).

(B) Limitation on users

(i) In general

No prospective user of a consumer report that includes an initial fraud alert or an active duty alert in accordance with this section may establish a new credit plan or extension of credit, other than under an open-end credit plan (as defined in section 1602(i) [1] of this title), in the name of the consumer, or issue an additional card on an existing credit account requested by a consumer, or grant any increase in credit limit on an existing credit account requested by a consumer, unless the user utilizes reasonable policies and procedures to form a reasonable belief that the user knows the identity of the person making the request.

(ii) Verification

If a consumer requesting the alert has specified a telephone number to be used for identity verification purposes, before authorizing any new credit plan or extension described in clause (i) in the name of such consumer, a user of such consumer report shall contact the consumer using that telephone number or take reasonable steps to verify the consumer's identity and confirm that the application for a new credit plan is not the result of identity theft.

(2) Requirements for extended alerts

(A) Notification

Each extended alert under this section shall include information that provides all prospective users of a consumer report relating to a consumer with-

(i) notification that the consumer does not authorize the establishment of any new credit plan or extension of credit described in clause (i), other than under an open-end credit plan (as defined in section 1602(i) [1] of this title), in the name of the consumer, or issuance of an additional card on an existing credit account requested by a consumer, or any increase in credit limit on an existing credit account requested by a consumer, except in accordance with subparagraph (B); and

(ii) a telephone number or other reasonable contact method designated by the consumer.

(B) Limitation on users

No prospective user of a consumer report or of a credit score generated using the information in the file of a consumer that includes an extended fraud alert in accordance with this section may establish a new credit plan or extension of credit, other than under an open-end credit plan (as defined in section 1602(i) of this title), in the name of the consumer, or issue an additional card on an existing credit account requested by a consumer, or any increase in credit limit on an existing credit account requested by a consumer, unless the user contacts the consumer in person or using the contact method described in subparagraph (A)(ii) to confirm that the application for a new credit plan or increase in credit limit, or request for an additional card is not the result of identity theft.

(i) National security freeze

(1) Definitions

For purposes of this subsection:

(A) The term "consumer reporting agency" means a consumer reporting agency described in section 1681a(p) of this title.

(B) The term "proper identification" has the meaning of such term as used under section 1681h of this title.

(C) The term "security freeze" means a restriction that prohibits a consumer reporting agency from disclosing the contents of a consumer report that is subject to such security freeze to any person requesting the consumer report.

(2) Placement of security freeze

(A) In general

Upon receiving a direct request from a consumer that a consumer reporting agency place a security freeze, and upon receiving proper identification from the consumer, the consumer reporting agency shall, free of charge, place the security freeze not later than-

(i) in the case of a request that is by toll-free telephone or secure electronic means, 1 business day after receiving the request directly from the consumer; or

(ii) in the case of a request that is by mail, 3 business days after receiving the request directly from the consumer.

(B) Confirmation and additional information

Not later than 5 business days after placing a security freeze under subparagraph (A), a consumer reporting agency shall-

(i) send confirmation of the placement to the consumer; and

(ii) inform the consumer of-

(I) the process by which the consumer may remove the security freeze, including a mechanism to authenticate the consumer; and

(II) the consumer's right described in section 1681m(d)(1)(D) of this title.

(C) Notice to third parties

A consumer reporting agency may advise a third party that a security freeze has been placed with respect to a consumer under subparagraph (A).

(3) Removal of security freeze

(A) In general

A consumer reporting agency shall remove a security freeze placed on the consumer report of a consumer only in the following cases:

(i) Upon the direct request of the consumer.

(ii) The security freeze was placed due to a material misrepresentation of fact by the consumer.

(B) Notice if removal not by request

If a consumer reporting agency removes a security freeze under subparagraph (A)(ii), the consumer reporting agency shall notify the consumer in writing prior to removing the security freeze.

(C) Removal of security freeze by consumer request

Except as provided in subparagraph (A)(ii), a security freeze shall remain in place until the consumer directly requests that the security freeze be removed. Upon receiving a direct request from a consumer that a consumer reporting agency remove a security freeze, and upon receiving proper identification from the consumer, the consumer reporting agency shall, free of charge, remove the security freeze not later than-

(i) in the case of a request that is by toll-free telephone or secure electronic means, 1 hour after receiving the request for removal; or

(ii) in the case of a request that is by mail, 3 business days after receiving the request for removal.

(D) Third-party requests

If a third party requests access to a consumer report of a consumer with respect to which a security freeze is in effect, where such request is in connection with an application for credit, and the consumer does not allow such consumer report to be accessed, the third party may treat the application as incomplete.

(E) Temporary removal of security freeze

Upon receiving a direct request from a consumer under subparagraph (A)(i), if the consumer requests a temporary removal of a security freeze, the consumer reporting agency shall, in accordance with subparagraph (C), remove the security freeze for the period of time specified by the consumer.

(4) Exceptions

A security freeze shall not apply to the making of a consumer report for use of the following:

(A) A person or entity, or a subsidiary, affiliate, or agent of that person or entity, or an assignee of a financial obligation owed by the consumer to that person or entity, or a prospective assignee of a financial obligation owed by the consumer to that person or entity in conjunction with the proposed purchase of the financial obligation, with which the consumer has or had prior to assignment an account or contract including a demand deposit account, or to whom the consumer issued a negotiable instrument, for the purposes of reviewing the account or collecting the financial obligation owed for the account, contract, or negotiable instrument. For purposes of this subparagraph, "reviewing the account" includes activities related to account maintenance, monitoring, credit line increases, and account upgrades and enhancements.

(B) Any Federal, State, or local agency, law enforcement agency, trial court, or private collection agency acting pursuant to a court order, warrant, or subpoena.

(C) A child support agency acting pursuant to part D of title IV of the Social Security Act (42 U.S.C. 651 et seq.).

(D) A Federal agency or a State or its agents or assigns acting to investigate fraud or acting to investigate or collect delinquent taxes or unpaid court orders or to fulfill any of its other statutory responsibilities, provided such responsibilities are consistent with a permissible purpose under section 1681b of this title.

(E) By a person using credit information for the purposes described under section 1681b(c) of this title.

(F) Any person or entity administering a credit file monitoring subscription or similar service to which the consumer has subscribed.

(G) Any person or entity for the purpose of providing a consumer with a copy of the consumer's consumer report or credit score, upon the request of the consumer.

(H) Any person using the information in connection with the underwriting of insurance.

(I) Any person using the information for employment, tenant, or background screening purposes.

(J) Any person using the information for assessing, verifying, or authenticating a consumer's identity for purposes other than the granting of credit, or for investigating or preventing actual or potential fraud.

(5) Notice of rights

At any time a consumer is required to receive a summary of rights required under section 1681g of this title, the following notice shall be included:

"Consumers Have the Right To Obtain a Security Freeze

"You have a right to place a 'security freeze' on your credit report, which will prohibit a consumer reporting agency from releasing information in your credit report without your express authorization. The security freeze is designed to prevent credit, loans, and services from being approved in your name without your consent. However, you should be aware that using a security freeze to take control over who gets access to the personal and financial information in your credit report may delay, interfere with, or prohibit the timely approval of any subsequent request or application you make regarding a new loan, credit, mortgage, or any other account involving the extension of credit.

"As an alternative to a security freeze, you have the right to place an initial or extended fraud alert on your credit file at no cost. An initial fraud alert is a 1-year alert that is placed on a consumer's credit file. Upon seeing a fraud alert display on a consumer's credit file, a business is required to take steps to verify the consumer's identity before extending new credit. If you are a victim of identity theft, you are entitled to an extended fraud alert, which is a fraud alert lasting 7 years.

"A security freeze does not apply to a person or entity, or its affiliates, or collection agencies acting on behalf of the person or entity, with which you have an existing account that requests information in your credit report for the purposes of reviewing or collecting the account. Reviewing the account includes activities related to account maintenance, monitoring, credit line increases, and account upgrades and enhancements.".

(6) Webpage

(A) Consumer reporting agencies

A consumer reporting agency shall establish a webpage that-

(i) allows a consumer to request a security freeze;

(ii) allows a consumer to request an initial fraud alert;

(iii) allows a consumer to request an extended fraud alert;

(iv) allows a consumer to request an active duty fraud alert;

(v) allows a consumer to opt-out of the use of information in a consumer report to send the consumer a solicitation of credit or insurance, in accordance with section 1681m(d) of this title; and

(vi) shall not be the only mechanism by which a consumer may request a security freeze.

(B) FTC

The Federal Trade Commission shall establish a single webpage that includes a link to each webpage established under subparagraph (A) within the Federal Trade Commission's website www.Identitytheft.gov, or a successor website.

(j) National protection for files and credit records of protected consumers

(1) Definitions

As used in this subsection:

(A) The term "consumer reporting agency" means a consumer reporting agency described in section 1681a(p) of this title.

(B) The term "protected consumer" means an individual who is-

(i) under the age of 16 years at the time a request for the placement of a security freeze is made; or

(ii) an incapacitated person or a protected person for whom a guardian or conservator has been appointed.

(C) The term "protected consumer's representative" means a person who provides to a consumer reporting agency sufficient proof of authority to act on behalf of a protected consumer.

(D) The term "record" means a compilation of information that-

(i) identifies a protected consumer;

(ii) is created by a consumer reporting agency solely for the purpose of complying with this subsection; and

(iii) may not be created or used to consider the protected consumer's credit worthiness, credit standing, credit capacity, character, general reputation, personal characteristics, or mode of living.

(E) The term "security freeze" means a restriction that prohibits a consumer reporting agency from disclosing the contents of a consumer report that is the subject of such security freeze or, in the case of a protected consumer for whom the consumer reporting agency does not have a file, a record that is subject to such security freeze to any person requesting the consumer report for the purpose of opening a new account involving the extension of credit.

(F) The term "sufficient proof of authority" means documentation that shows a protected consumer's representative has authority to act on behalf of a protected consumer and includes-

(i) an order issued by a court of law;

(ii) a lawfully executed and valid power of attorney;

(iii) a document issued by a Federal, State, or local government agency in the United States showing proof of parentage, including a birth certificate; or

(iv) with respect to a protected consumer who has been placed in a foster care setting, a written communication from a county welfare department or its agent or designee, or a county probation department or its agent or designee, certifying that the protected consumer is in a foster care setting under its jurisdiction.

(G) The term "sufficient proof of identification" means information or documentation that identifies a protected consumer and a protected consumer's representative and includes-

(i) a social security number or a copy of a social security card issued by the Social Security Administration;

(ii) a certified or official copy of a birth certificate issued by the entity authorized to issue the birth certificate; or

(iii) a copy of a driver's license, an identification card issued by the motor vehicle administration, or any other government issued identification.

(2) Placement of security freeze for a protected consumer

(A) In general

Upon receiving a direct request from a protected consumer's representative that a consumer reporting agency place a security freeze, and upon receiving sufficient proof of identification and sufficient proof of authority, the consumer reporting agency shall, free of charge, place the security freeze not later than-

(i) in the case of a request that is by toll-free telephone or secure electronic means, 1 business day after receiving the request directly from the protected consumer's representative; or

(ii) in the case of a request that is by mail, 3 business days after receiving the request directly from the protected consumer's representative.

(B) Confirmation and additional information

Not later than 5 business days after placing a security freeze under subparagraph (A), a consumer reporting agency shall-

(i) send confirmation of the placement to the protected consumer's representative; and

(ii) inform the protected consumer's representative of the process by which the protected consumer may remove the security freeze, including a mechanism to authenticate the protected consumer's representative.

(C) Creation of file

If a consumer reporting agency does not have a file pertaining to a protected consumer when the consumer reporting agency receives a direct request under subparagraph (A), the consumer reporting agency shall create a record for the protected consumer.

(3) Prohibition on release of record or file of protected consumer

After a security freeze has been placed under paragraph (2)(A), and unless the security freeze is removed in accordance with this subsection, a consumer reporting agency may not release the protected consumer's consumer report, any information derived from the protected consumer's consumer report, or any record created for the protected consumer.

(4) Removal of a protected consumer security freeze

   (A) In general

A consumer reporting agency shall remove a security freeze placed on the consumer report of a protected consumer only in the following cases:

      (i) Upon the direct request of the protected consumer's representative.

      (ii) Upon the direct request of the protected consumer, if the protected consumer is not under the age of 16 years at the time of the request.

      (iii) The security freeze was placed due to a material misrepresentation of fact by the protected consumer's representative.

   (B) Notice if removal not by request

If a consumer reporting agency removes a security freeze under subparagraph (A)(iii), the consumer reporting agency shall notify the protected consumer's representative in writing prior to removing the security freeze.

   (C) Removal of freeze by request

Except as provided in subparagraph (A)(iii), a security freeze shall remain in place until a protected consumer's representative or protected consumer described in subparagraph (A)(ii) directly requests that the security freeze be removed. Upon receiving a direct request from the protected consumer's representative or protected consumer described in subparagraph (A)(ii) that a consumer reporting agency remove a security freeze, and upon receiving sufficient proof of identification and sufficient proof of authority, the consumer reporting agency shall, free of charge, remove the security freeze not later than-

      (i) in the case of a request that is by toll-free telephone or secure electronic means, 1 hour after receiving the request for removal; or

      (ii) in the case of a request that is by mail, 3 business days after receiving the request for removal.

   (D) Temporary removal of security freeze

Upon receiving a direct request from a protected consumer or a protected consumer's representative under subparagraph (A)(i), if the protected consumer or protected consumer's representative requests a temporary removal of a security freeze, the consumer reporting agency shall, in accordance with subparagraph (C), remove the security freeze for the period of time specified by the protected consumer or protected consumer's representative.

(k) Credit monitoring

   (1) Definitions

In this subsection:

      (A) The term "active duty military consumer" includes a member of the National Guard.

      (B) The term "National Guard" has the meaning given the term in section 101(c) of title 10.

   (2) Credit monitoring

A consumer reporting agency described in section 1681a(p) of this title shall provide a free electronic credit monitoring service that, at a minimum, notifies a consumer of material additions or modifications to the file of the consumer at the consumer reporting agency to any consumer who provides to the consumer reporting agency-

> (A) appropriate proof that the consumer is an active duty military consumer; and
>
> (B) contact information of the consumer.

(3) Rulemaking

Not later than 1 year after May 24, 2018, the Federal Trade Commission shall promulgate regulations regarding the requirements of this subsection, which shall at a minimum include-

> (A) a definition of an electronic credit monitoring service and material additions or modifications to the file of a consumer; and
>
> (B) what constitutes appropriate proof.

(4) Applicability

> (A) Sections 1681n and 1681o of this title shall not apply to any violation of this subsection.
>
> (B) This subsection shall be enforced exclusively under section 1681s of this title by the Federal agencies and Federal and State officials identified in that section.

§ 1681c-2. Block of information resulting from identity theft

(a) Block

Except as otherwise provided in this section, a consumer reporting agency shall block the reporting of any information in the file of a consumer that the consumer identifies as information that resulted from an alleged identity theft, not later than 4 business days after the date of receipt by such agency of-

> (1) appropriate proof of the identity of the consumer;
>
> (2) a copy of an identity theft report;
>
> (3) the identification of such information by the consumer; and
>
> (4) a statement by the consumer that the information is not information relating to any transaction by the consumer.

(b) Notification

A consumer reporting agency shall promptly notify the furnisher of information identified by the consumer under subsection (a)-

> (1) that the information may be a result of identity theft;
>
> (2) that an identity theft report has been filed;
>
> (3) that a block has been requested under this section; and
>
> (4) of the effective dates of the block.

(c) Authority to decline or rescind

(1) In general

A consumer reporting agency may decline to block, or may rescind any block, of information relating to a consumer under this section, if the consumer reporting agency reasonably determines that-

(A) the information was blocked in error or a block was requested by the consumer in error;

(B) the information was blocked, or a block was requested by the consumer, on the basis of a material misrepresentation of fact by the consumer relevant to the request to block; or

(C) the consumer obtained possession of goods, services, or money as a result of the blocked transaction or transactions.

(2) Notification to consumer

If a block of information is declined or rescinded under this subsection, the affected consumer shall be notified promptly, in the same manner as consumers are notified of the reinsertion of information under section 1681i(a)(5)(B) of this title.

(3) Significance of block

For purposes of this subsection, if a consumer reporting agency rescinds a block, the presence of information in the file of a consumer prior to the blocking of such information is not evidence of whether the consumer knew or should have known that the consumer obtained possession of any goods, services, or money as a result of the block.

(d) Exception for resellers

(1) No reseller file

This section shall not apply to a consumer reporting agency, if the consumer reporting agency-

(A) is a reseller;

(B) is not, at the time of the request of the consumer under subsection (a), otherwise furnishing or reselling a consumer report concerning the information identified by the consumer; and

(C) informs the consumer, by any means, that the consumer may report the identity theft to the Bureau to obtain consumer information regarding identity theft.

(2) Reseller with file

The sole obligation of the consumer reporting agency under this section, with regard to any request of a consumer under this section, shall be to block the consumer report maintained by the consumer reporting agency from any subsequent use, if-

(A) the consumer, in accordance with the provisions of subsection (a), identifies, to a consumer reporting agency, information in the file of the consumer that resulted from identity theft; and

(B) the consumer reporting agency is a reseller of the identified information.

(3) Notice

In carrying out its obligation under paragraph (2), the reseller shall promptly provide a notice to the consumer of the decision to block the file. Such notice shall contain the name, address, and telephone number of each consumer reporting agency from which the consumer information was obtained for resale.

(e) Exception for verification companies

The provisions of this section do not apply to a check services company, acting as such, which issues authorizations for the purpose of approving or processing negotiable instruments, electronic fund transfers, or similar methods of payments, except that, beginning 4 business days after receipt of information described in paragraphs (1) through (3) of subsection (a), a check services company shall not report to a national consumer reporting agency described in section 1681a(p) of this title, any information identified in the subject identity theft report as resulting from identity theft.

(f) Access to blocked information by law enforcement agencies

No provision of this section shall be construed as requiring a consumer reporting agency to prevent a Federal, State, or local law enforcement agency from accessing blocked information in a consumer file to which the agency could otherwise obtain access under this subchapter.

§ 1681d. Disclosure of investigative consumer reports

(a) Disclosure of fact of preparation

A person may not procure or cause to be prepared an investigative consumer report on any consumer unless-

(1) it is clearly and accurately disclosed to the consumer that an investigative consumer report including information as to his character, general reputation, personal characteristics, and mode of living, whichever are applicable, may be made, and such disclosure (A) is made in a writing mailed, or otherwise delivered, to the consumer, not later than three days after the date on which the report was first requested, and (B) includes a statement informing the consumer of his right to request the additional disclosures provided for under subsection (b) of this section and the written summary of the rights of the consumer prepared pursuant to section 1681g(c) of this title; and

(2) the person certifies or has certified to the consumer reporting agency that-

(A) the person has made the disclosures to the consumer required by paragraph (1); and

(B) the person will comply with subsection (b).

(b) Disclosure on request of nature and scope of investigation

Any person who procures or causes to be prepared an investigative consumer report on any consumer shall, upon written request made by the consumer within a reasonable period of time after the receipt by him of the disclosure required by subsection (a)(1), make a complete and accurate disclosure of the nature and scope of the investigation requested. This disclosure shall be made in a writing mailed, or otherwise delivered, to the consumer not later than five days after the date on which the request for such disclosure was received from the consumer or such report was first requested, whichever is the later.

(c) Limitation on liability upon showing of reasonable procedures for compliance with provisions

No person may be held liable for any violation of subsection (a) or (b) of this section if he shows by a preponderance of the evidence that at the time of the violation he maintained reasonable procedures to assure compliance with subsection (a) or (b).

(d) Prohibitions

   (1) Certification

   A consumer reporting agency shall not prepare or furnish an investigative consumer report unless the agency has received a certification under subsection (a)(2) from the person who requested the report.

   (2) Inquiries

   A consumer reporting agency shall not make an inquiry for the purpose of preparing an investigative consumer report on a consumer for employment purposes if the making of the inquiry by an employer or prospective employer of the consumer would violate any applicable Federal or State equal employment opportunity law or regulation.

   (3) Certain public record information

   Except as otherwise provided in section 1681k of this title, a consumer reporting agency shall not furnish an investigative consumer report that includes information that is a matter of public record and that relates to an arrest, indictment, conviction, civil judicial action, tax lien, or outstanding judgment, unless the agency has verified the accuracy of the information during the 30-day period ending on the date on which the report is furnished.

   (4) Certain adverse information

   A consumer reporting agency shall not prepare or furnish an investigative consumer report on a consumer that contains information that is adverse to the interest of the consumer and that is obtained through a personal interview with a neighbor, friend, or associate of the consumer or with another person with whom the consumer is acquainted or who has knowledge of such item of information, unless-

      (A) the agency has followed reasonable procedures to obtain confirmation of the information, from an additional source that has independent and direct knowledge of the information; or

      (B) the person interviewed is the best possible source of the information.

United States
Fair Credit Reporting Act

§ 1681e. Compliance procedures

(a) Identity and purposes of credit users

Every consumer reporting agency shall maintain reasonable procedures designed to avoid violations of section 1681c of this title and to limit the furnishing of consumer reports to the purposes listed under section 1681b of this title. These procedures shall require that prospective users of the information identify themselves, certify the purposes for which the information is sought, and certify that the information will be used for no other purpose. Every consumer reporting agency shall make a reasonable effort to verify the identity of a new prospective user and the uses certified by such prospective user prior to furnishing such user a consumer report. No consumer reporting agency may furnish a consumer report to any person if it has reasonable grounds for believing that the consumer report will not be used for a purpose listed in section 1681b of this title.

(b) Accuracy of report

Whenever a consumer reporting agency prepares a consumer report it shall follow reasonable procedures to assure maximum possible accuracy of the information concerning the individual about whom the report relates.

(c) Disclosure of consumer reports by users allowed

A consumer reporting agency may not prohibit a user of a consumer report furnished by the agency on a consumer from disclosing the contents of the report to the consumer, if adverse action against the consumer has been taken by the user based in whole or in part on the report.

(d) Notice to users and furnishers of information

(1) Notice requirement

A consumer reporting agency shall provide to any person-

(A) who regularly and in the ordinary course of business furnishes information to the agency with respect to any consumer; or

(B) to whom a consumer report is provided by the agency;

a notice of such person's responsibilities under this subchapter.

(2) Content of notice

The Bureau shall prescribe the content of notices under paragraph (1), and a consumer reporting agency shall be in compliance with this subsection if it provides a notice under paragraph (1) that is substantially similar to the Bureau prescription under this paragraph.

(e) Procurement of consumer report for resale

(1) Disclosure

A person may not procure a consumer report for purposes of reselling the report (or any information in the report) unless the person discloses to the consumer reporting agency that originally furnishes the report-

(A) the identity of the end-user of the report (or information); and

(B) each permissible purpose under section 1681b of this title for which the report is furnished to the end-user of the report (or information).

(2) Responsibilities of procurers for resale

A person who procures a consumer report for purposes of reselling the report (or any information in the report) shall-

(A) establish and comply with reasonable procedures designed to ensure that the report (or information) is resold by the person only for a purpose for which the report may be furnished under section 1681b of this title, including by requiring that each person to which the report (or information) is resold and that resells or provides the report (or information) to any other person-

(i) identifies each end user of the resold report (or information);

(ii) certifies each purpose for which the report (or information) will be used; and

(iii) certifies that the report (or information) will be used for no other purpose; and

(B) before reselling the report, make reasonable efforts to verify the identifications and certifications made under subparagraph (A).

(3) Resale of consumer report to a Federal agency or department

Notwithstanding paragraph (1) or (2), a person who procures a consumer report for purposes of reselling the report (or any information in the report) shall not disclose the identity of the end-user of the report under paragraph (1) or (2) if-

(A) the end user is an agency or department of the United States Government which procures the report from the person for purposes of determining the eligibility of the consumer concerned to receive access or continued access to classified information (as defined in section 1681b(b)(4)(E)(i) of this title); and

(B) the agency or department certifies in writing to the person reselling the report that nondisclosure is necessary to protect classified information or the safety of persons employed by or contracting with, or undergoing investigation for work or contracting with the agency or department.

§ 1681f. Disclosures to governmental agencies

Notwithstanding the provisions of section 1681b of this title, a consumer reporting agency may furnish identifying information respecting any consumer, limited to his name, address, former addresses, places of employment, or former places of employment, to a governmental agency.

§ 1681g. Disclosures to consumers

(a) Information on file; sources; report recipients

Every consumer reporting agency shall, upon request, and subject to section 1681h(a)(1) of this title, clearly and accurately disclose to the consumer:

(1) All information in the consumer's file at the time of the request, except that-

(A) if the consumer to whom the file relates requests that the first 5 digits of the social security number (or similar identification number) of the consumer not be included in the disclosure and the consumer reporting agency has received appropriate proof of the identity of the requester, the consumer reporting agency shall so truncate such number in such disclosure; and

(B) nothing in this paragraph shall be construed to require a consumer reporting agency to disclose to a consumer any information concerning credit scores or any other risk scores or predictors relating to the consumer.

(2) The sources of the information; except that the sources of information acquired solely for use in preparing an investigative consumer report and actually used for no other purpose need not be disclosed: Provided, That in the event an action is brought under this subchapter, such sources shall be available to the plaintiff under appropriate discovery procedures in the court in which the action is brought.

(3)(A) Identification of each person (including each end-user identified under section 1681e(e)(1) of this title) that procured a consumer report-

(i) for employment purposes, during the 2-year period preceding the date on which the request is made; or

(ii) for any other purpose, during the 1-year period preceding the date on which the request is made.

(B) An identification of a person under subparagraph (A) shall include-

(i) the name of the person or, if applicable, the trade name (written in full) under which such person conducts business; and

(ii) upon request of the consumer, the address and telephone number of the person.

(C) Subparagraph (A) does not apply if-

(i) the end user is an agency or department of the United States Government that procures the report from the person for purposes of determining the eligibility of the consumer to whom the report relates to receive access or continued access to classified information (as defined in section 1681b(b)(4)(E)(i) of this title); and

(ii) the head of the agency or department makes a written finding as prescribed under section 1681b(b)(4)(A) of this title.

(4) The dates, original payees, and amounts of any checks upon which is based any adverse characterization of the consumer, included in the file at the time of the disclosure.

(5) A record of all inquiries received by the agency during the 1-year period preceding the request that identified the consumer in connection with a credit or insurance transaction that was not initiated by the consumer.

(6) If the consumer requests the credit file and not the credit score, a statement that the consumer may request and obtain a credit score.

(b) Exempt information

The requirements of subsection (a) respecting the disclosure of sources of information and the recipients of consumer reports do not apply to information received or consumer reports furnished prior to the effective date of this subchapter except to the extent that the matter involved is contained in the files of the consumer reporting agency on that date.

(c) Summary of rights to obtain and dispute information in consumer reports and to obtain credit scores

    (1) Commission summary of rights required

        (A) In general

The Commission shall prepare a model summary of the rights of consumers under this subchapter.

        (B) Content of summary

The summary of rights prepared under subparagraph (A) shall include a description of-

            (i) the right of a consumer to obtain a copy of a consumer report under subsection (a) from each consumer reporting agency;

            (ii) the frequency and circumstances under which a consumer is entitled to receive a consumer report without charge under section 1681j of this title;

            (iii) the right of a consumer to dispute information in the file of the consumer under section 1681i of this title;

            (iv) the right of a consumer to obtain a credit score from a consumer reporting agency, and a description of how to obtain a credit score;

            (v) the method by which a consumer can contact, and obtain a consumer report from, a consumer reporting agency without charge, as provided in the regulations of the Bureau prescribed under section 211(c) of the Fair and Accurate Credit Transactions Act of 2003; and

            (vi) the method by which a consumer can contact, and obtain a consumer report from, a consumer reporting agency described in section 1681a(w) of this title, as provided in the regulations of the Bureau prescribed under section 1681j(a)(1)(C) of this title.

        (C) Availability of summary of rights

The Commission shall-

            (i) actively publicize the availability of the summary of rights prepared under this paragraph;

            (ii) conspicuously post on its Internet website the availability of such summary of rights; and

            (iii) promptly make such summary of rights available to consumers, on request.

    (2) Summary of rights required to be included with agency disclosures

A consumer reporting agency shall provide to a consumer, with each written disclosure by the agency to the consumer under this section-

(A) the summary of rights prepared by the Bureau under paragraph (1);

(B) in the case of a consumer reporting agency described in section 1681a(p) of this title, a toll-free telephone number established by the agency, at which personnel are accessible to consumers during normal business hours;

(C) a list of all Federal agencies responsible for enforcing any provision of this subchapter, and the address and any appropriate phone number of each such agency, in a form that will assist the consumer in selecting the appropriate agency;

(D) a statement that the consumer may have additional rights under State law, and that the consumer may wish to contact a State or local consumer protection agency or a State attorney general (or the equivalent thereof) to learn of those rights; and

(E) a statement that a consumer reporting agency is not required to remove accurate derogatory information from the file of a consumer, unless the information is outdated under section 1681c of this title or cannot be verified.

(d) Summary of rights of identity theft victims

(1) In general

The Commission, in consultation with the Federal banking agencies and the National Credit Union Administration, shall prepare a model summary of the rights of consumers under this subchapter with respect to the procedures for remedying the effects of fraud or identity theft involving credit, an electronic fund transfer, or an account or transaction at or with a financial institution or other creditor.

(2) Summary of rights and contact information

Beginning 60 days after the date on which the model summary of rights is prescribed in final form by the Bureau pursuant to paragraph (1), if any consumer contacts a consumer reporting agency and expresses a belief that the consumer is a victim of fraud or identity theft involving credit, an electronic fund transfer, or an account or transaction at or with a financial institution or other creditor, the consumer reporting agency shall, in addition to any other action that the agency may take, provide the consumer with a summary of rights that contains all of the information required by the Bureau under paragraph (1), and information on how to contact the Bureau to obtain more detailed information.

(e) Information available to victims

(1) In general

For the purpose of documenting fraudulent transactions resulting from identity theft, not later than 30 days after the date of receipt of a request from a victim in accordance with paragraph (3), and subject to verification of the identity of the victim and the claim of identity theft in accordance with paragraph (2), a business entity that has provided credit to, provided for consideration products, goods, or services to, accepted payment from, or otherwise entered into a commercial transaction for consideration with, a person who has allegedly made unauthorized use of the means of identification of the victim, shall provide a copy of application and business transaction records in the control of the business entity, whether maintained by the business entity or by another person on behalf of the business entity, evidencing any transaction alleged to be a result of identity theft to-

(A) the victim;

(B) any Federal, State, or local government law enforcement agency or officer specified by the victim in such a request; or

(C) any law enforcement agency investigating the identity theft and authorized by the victim to take receipt of records provided under this subsection.

(2) Verification of identity and claim

Before a business entity provides any information under paragraph (1), unless the business entity, at its discretion, otherwise has a high degree of confidence that it knows the identity of the victim making a request under paragraph (1), the victim shall provide to the business entity-

(A) as proof of positive identification of the victim, at the election of the business entity-

(i) the presentation of a government-issued identification card;

(ii) personally identifying information of the same type as was provided to the business entity by the unauthorized person; or

(iii) personally identifying information that the business entity typically requests from new applicants or for new transactions, at the time of the victim's request for information, including any documentation described in clauses (i) and (ii); and

(B) as proof of a claim of identity theft, at the election of the business entity-

(i) a copy of a police report evidencing the claim of the victim of identity theft; and

(ii) a properly completed-

(I) copy of a standardized affidavit of identity theft developed and made available by the Bureau; or

(II) an affidavit of fact that is acceptable to the business entity for that purpose.

(3) Procedures

The request of a victim under paragraph (1) shall-

(A) be in writing;

(B) be mailed to an address specified by the business entity, if any; and

(C) if asked by the business entity, include relevant information about any transaction alleged to be a result of identity theft to facilitate compliance with this section including-

(i) if known by the victim (or if readily obtainable by the victim), the date of the application or transaction; and

(ii) if known by the victim (or if readily obtainable by the victim), any other identifying information such as an account or transaction number.

(4) No charge to victim

Information required to be provided under paragraph (1) shall be so provided without charge.

(5) Authority to decline to provide information

A business entity may decline to provide information under paragraph (1) if, in the exercise of good faith, the business entity determines that-

(A) this subsection does not require disclosure of the information;

(B) after reviewing the information provided pursuant to paragraph (2), the business entity does not have a high degree of confidence in knowing the true identity of the individual requesting the information;

(C) the request for the information is based on a misrepresentation of fact by the individual requesting the information relevant to the request for information; or

(D) the information requested is Internet navigational data or similar information about a person's visit to a website or online service.

(6) Limitation on liability

Except as provided in section 1681s of this title, sections 1681n and 1681o of this title do not apply to any violation of this subsection.

(7) Limitation on civil liability

No business entity may be held civilly liable under any provision of Federal, State, or other law for disclosure, made in good faith pursuant to this subsection.

(8) No new recordkeeping obligation

Nothing in this subsection creates an obligation on the part of a business entity to obtain, retain, or maintain information or records that are not otherwise required to be obtained, retained, or maintained in the ordinary course of its business or under other applicable law.

(9) Rule of construction

(A) In general

No provision of subtitle A of title V of Public Law 106–102 [15 U.S.C. 6801 et seq.], prohibiting the disclosure of financial information by a business entity to third parties shall be used to deny disclosure of information to the victim under this subsection.

(B) Limitation

Except as provided in subparagraph (A), nothing in this subsection permits a business entity to disclose information, including information to law enforcement under subparagraphs (B) and (C) of paragraph (1), that the business entity is otherwise prohibited from disclosing under any other applicable provision of Federal or State law.

(10) Affirmative defense

In any civil action brought to enforce this subsection, it is an affirmative defense (which the defendant must establish by a preponderance of the evidence) for a business entity to file an affidavit or answer stating that-

(A) the business entity has made a reasonably diligent search of its available business records; and

(B) the records requested under this subsection do not exist or are not reasonably available.

(11) Definition of victim

For purposes of this subsection, the term "victim" means a consumer whose means of identification or financial information has been used or transferred (or has been alleged to have been used or transferred) without the authority of that consumer, with the intent to commit, or to aid or abet, an identity theft or a similar crime.

(12) Effective date

This subsection shall become effective 180 days after December 4, 2003.

(13) Effectiveness study

Not later than 18 months after December 4, 2003, the Comptroller General of the United States shall submit a report to Congress assessing the effectiveness of this provision.

(f) Disclosure of credit scores

(1) In general

Upon the request of a consumer for a credit score, a consumer reporting agency shall supply to the consumer a statement indicating that the information and credit scoring model may be different than the credit score that may be used by the lender, and a notice which shall include-

(A) the current credit score of the consumer or the most recent credit score of the consumer that was previously calculated by the credit reporting agency for a purpose related to the extension of credit;

(B) the range of possible credit scores under the model used;

(C) all of the key factors that adversely affected the credit score of the consumer in the model used, the total number of which shall not exceed 4, subject to paragraph (9);

(D) the date on which the credit score was created; and

(E) the name of the person or entity that provided the credit score or credit file upon which the credit score was created.

(2) Definitions

For purposes of this subsection, the following definitions shall apply:

(A) Credit score

The term "credit score"-

(i) means a numerical value or a categorization derived from a statistical tool or modeling system used by a person who makes or arranges a loan to predict the likelihood of certain credit behaviors, including default (and the numerical value or the categorization derived from such analysis may also be referred to as a "risk predictor" or "risk score"); and

(ii) does not include-

(I) any mortgage score or rating of an automated underwriting system that considers one or more factors in addition to credit information, including the loan to value ratio, the amount of down payment, or the financial assets of a consumer; or

(II) any other elements of the underwriting process or underwriting decision.

(B) Key factors

The term "key factors" means all relevant elements or reasons adversely affecting the credit score for the particular individual, listed in the order of their importance based on their effect on the credit score.

(3) Timeframe and manner of disclosure

The information required by this subsection shall be provided in the same timeframe and manner as the information described in subsection (a).

(4) Applicability to certain uses

This subsection shall not be construed so as to compel a consumer reporting agency to develop or disclose a score if the agency does not-

(A) distribute scores that are used in connection with residential real property loans; or

(B) develop scores that assist credit providers in understanding the general credit behavior of a consumer and predicting the future credit behavior of the consumer.

(5) Applicability to credit scores developed by another person

(A) In general

This subsection shall not be construed to require a consumer reporting agency that distributes credit scores developed by another person or entity to provide a further explanation of them, or to process a dispute arising pursuant to section 1681i of this title, except that the consumer reporting agency shall provide the consumer with the name and address and website for contacting the person or entity who developed the score or developed the methodology of the score.

(B) Exception

This paragraph shall not apply to a consumer reporting agency that develops or modifies scores that are developed by another person or entity.

(6) Maintenance of credit scores not required

This subsection shall not be construed to require a consumer reporting agency to maintain credit scores in its files.

(7) Compliance in certain cases

In complying with this subsection, a consumer reporting agency shall-

(A) supply the consumer with a credit score that is derived from a credit scoring model that is widely distributed to users by that consumer reporting agency in connection with residential real property loans or with a credit score that assists the consumer in understanding the credit scoring assessment of the credit behavior of the consumer and predictions about the future credit behavior of the consumer; and

(B) a statement indicating that the information and credit scoring model may be different than that used by the lender.

(8) Fair and reasonable fee

A consumer reporting agency may charge a fair and reasonable fee, as determined by the Bureau, for providing the information required under this subsection.

(9) Use of enquiries as a key factor

If a key factor that adversely affects the credit score of a consumer consists of the number of enquiries made with respect to a consumer report, that factor shall be included in the disclosure pursuant to paragraph (1)(C) without regard to the numerical limitation in such paragraph.

(g) Disclosure of credit scores by certain mortgage lenders

(1) In general

Any person who makes or arranges loans and who uses a consumer credit score, as defined in subsection (f), in connection with an application initiated or sought by a consumer for a closed end loan or the establishment of an open end loan for a consumer purpose that is secured by 1 to 4 units of residential real property (hereafter in this subsection referred to as the "lender") shall provide the following to the consumer as soon as reasonably practicable:

(A) Information required under subsection (f)

(i) In general

A copy of the information identified in subsection (f) that was obtained from a consumer reporting agency or was developed and used by the user of the information.

(ii) Notice under subparagraph (D)

In addition to the information provided to it by a third party that provided the credit score or scores, a lender is only required to provide the notice contained in subparagraph (D).

(B) Disclosures in case of automated underwriting system
    (i) In general
    If a person that is subject to this subsection uses an automated underwriting system to underwrite a loan, that person may satisfy the obligation to provide a credit score by disclosing a credit score and associated key factors supplied by a consumer reporting agency.
    (ii) Numerical credit score
    However, if a numerical credit score is generated by an automated underwriting system used by an enterprise, and that score is disclosed to the person, the score shall be disclosed to the consumer consistent with subparagraph (C).
    (iii) Enterprise defined
    For purposes of this subparagraph, the term "enterprise" has the same meaning as in paragraph (6) of section 4502 of title 12.
(C) Disclosures of credit scores not obtained from a consumer reporting agency
A person that is subject to the provisions of this subsection and that uses a credit score, other than a credit score provided by a consumer reporting agency, may satisfy the obligation to provide a credit score by disclosing a credit score and associated key factors supplied by a consumer reporting agency.
(D) Notice to home loan applicants
A copy of the following notice, which shall include the name, address, and telephone number of each consumer reporting agency providing a credit score that was used:
"notice to the home loan applicant
"In connection with your application for a home loan, the lender must disclose to you the score that a consumer reporting agency distributed to users and the lender used in connection with your home loan, and the key factors affecting your credit scores.
"The credit score is a computer generated summary calculated at the time of the request and based on information that a consumer reporting agency or lender has on file. The scores are based on data about your credit history and payment patterns. Credit scores are important because they are used to assist the lender in determining whether you will obtain a loan. They may also be used to determine what interest rate you may be offered on the mortgage. Credit scores can change over time, depending on your conduct, how your credit history and payment patterns change, and how credit scoring technologies change.
"Because the score is based on information in your credit history, it is very important that you review the credit-related information that is being furnished to make sure it is accurate. Credit records may vary from one company to another.

"If you have questions about your credit score or the credit information that is furnished to you, contact the consumer reporting agency at the address and telephone number provided with this notice, or contact the lender, if the lender developed or generated the credit score. The consumer reporting agency plays no part in the decision to take any action on the loan application and is unable to provide you with specific reasons for the decision on a loan application.

"If you have questions concerning the terms of the loan, contact the lender.".

(E) Actions not required under this subsection

This subsection shall not require any person to-

 (i) explain the information provided pursuant to subsection (f);

 (ii) disclose any information other than a credit score or key factors, as defined in subsection (f);

 (iii) disclose any credit score or related information obtained by the user after a loan has closed;

 (iv) provide more than 1 disclosure per loan transaction; or

 (v) provide the disclosure required by this subsection when another person has made the disclosure to the consumer for that loan transaction.

(F) No obligation for content

 (i) In general

The obligation of any person pursuant to this subsection shall be limited solely to providing a copy of the information that was received from the consumer reporting agency.

 (ii) Limit on liability

(No person has liability under this subsection for the content of that information or for the omission of any information within the report provided by the consumer reporting agency.

(G) Person defined as excluding enterprise

As used in this subsection, the term "person" does not include an enterprise (as defined in paragraph (6) of section 4502 of title 12).

(2) Prohibition on disclosure clauses null and void

(A) In general

Any provision in a contract that prohibits the disclosure of a credit score by a person who makes or arranges loans or a consumer reporting agency is void.

(B) No liability for disclosure under this subsection

A lender shall not have liability under any contractual provision for disclosure of a credit score pursuant to this subsection.

§ 1681h. Conditions and form of disclosure to consumers

(a) In general

 (1) Proper identification

A consumer reporting agency shall require, as a condition of making the disclosures required under section 1681g of this title, that the consumer furnish proper identification.

(2) Disclosure in writing

Except as provided in subsection (b), the disclosures required to be made under section 1681g of this title shall be provided under that section in writing.

(b) Other forms of disclosure

(1) In general

If authorized by a consumer, a consumer reporting agency may make the disclosures required under 1681g of this title-

(A) other than in writing; and

(B) in such form as may be-

(i) specified by the consumer in accordance with paragraph (2); and

(ii) available from the agency.

(2) Form

A consumer may specify pursuant to paragraph (1) that disclosures under section 1681g of this title shall be made-

(A) in person, upon the appearance of the consumer at the place of business of the consumer reporting agency where disclosures are regularly provided, during normal business hours, and on reasonable notice;

(B) by telephone, if the consumer has made a written request for disclosure by telephone;

(C) by electronic means, if available from the agency; or

(D) by any other reasonable means that is available from the agency.

(c) Trained personnel

Any consumer reporting agency shall provide trained personnel to explain to the consumer any information furnished to him pursuant to section 1681g of this title.

(d) Persons accompanying consumer

The consumer shall be permitted to be accompanied by one other person of his choosing, who shall furnish reasonable identification. A consumer reporting agency may require the consumer to furnish a written statement granting permission to the consumer reporting agency to discuss the consumer's file in such person's presence.

(e) Limitation of liability

Except as provided in sections 1681n and 1681o of this title, no consumer may bring any action or proceeding in the nature of defamation, invasion of privacy, or negligence with respect to the reporting of information against any consumer reporting agency, any user of information, or any person who furnishes information to a consumer reporting agency, based on information disclosed pursuant to section 1681g, 1681h, or 1681m of this title, or based on information disclosed by a user of a consumer report to or for a consumer against whom the user has taken adverse action, based in whole or in part on the report except as to false information furnished with malice or willful intent to injure such consumer.

§ 1681i. Procedure in case of disputed accuracy

(a) Reinvestigations of disputed information

(1) Reinvestigation required

(A) In general

Subject to subsection (f) and except as provided in subsection (g), if the completeness or accuracy of any item of information contained in a consumer's file at a consumer reporting agency is disputed by the consumer and the consumer notifies the agency directly, or indirectly through a reseller, of such dispute, the agency shall, free of charge, conduct a reasonable reinvestigation to determine whether the disputed information is inaccurate and record the current status of the disputed information, or delete the item from the file in accordance with paragraph (5), before the end of the 30-day period beginning on the date on which the agency receives the notice of the dispute from the consumer or reseller.

(B) Extension of period to reinvestigate

Except as provided in subparagraph (C), the 30-day period described in subparagraph (A) may be extended for not more than 15 additional days if the consumer reporting agency receives information from the consumer during that 30-day period that is relevant to the reinvestigation.

(C) Limitations on extension of period to reinvestigate

Subparagraph (B) shall not apply to any reinvestigation in which, during the 30-day period described in subparagraph (A), the information that is the subject of the reinvestigation is found to be inaccurate or incomplete or the consumer reporting agency determines that the information cannot be verified.

(2) Prompt notice of dispute to furnisher of information

(A) In general

Before the expiration of the 5-business-day period beginning on the date on which a consumer reporting agency receives notice of a dispute from any consumer or a reseller in accordance with paragraph (1), the agency shall provide notification of the dispute to any person who provided any item of information in dispute, at the address and in the manner established with the person. The notice shall include all relevant information regarding the dispute that the agency has received from the consumer or reseller.

(B) Provision of other information

The consumer reporting agency shall promptly provide to the person who provided the information in dispute all relevant information regarding the dispute that is received by the agency from the consumer or the reseller after the period referred to in subparagraph (A) and before the end of the period referred to in paragraph (1)(A).

(3) Determination that dispute is frivolous or irrelevant

(A) In general

Notwithstanding paragraph (1), a consumer reporting agency may terminate a reinvestigation of information disputed by a consumer under that paragraph if the agency reasonably determines that the dispute by the consumer is frivolous or irrelevant, including by reason of a failure by a consumer to provide sufficient information to investigate the disputed information.

(B) Notice of determination

Upon making any determination in accordance with subparagraph (A) that a dispute is frivolous or irrelevant, a consumer reporting agency shall notify the consumer of such determination not later than 5 business days after making such determination, by mail or, if authorized by the consumer for that purpose, by any other means available to the agency.

(C) Contents of notice

A notice under subparagraph (B) shall include-

(i) the reasons for the determination under subparagraph (A); and

(ii) identification of any information required to investigate the disputed information, which may consist of a standardized form describing the general nature of such information.

(4) Consideration of consumer information

In conducting any reinvestigation under paragraph (1) with respect to disputed information in the file of any consumer, the consumer reporting agency shall review and consider all relevant information submitted by the consumer in the period described in paragraph (1)(A) with respect to such disputed information.

(5) Treatment of inaccurate or unverifiable information

(A) In general

If, after any reinvestigation under paragraph (1) of any information disputed by a consumer, an item of the information is found to be inaccurate or incomplete or cannot be verified, the consumer reporting agency shall-

(i) promptly delete that item of information from the file of the consumer, or modify that item of information, as appropriate, based on the results of the reinvestigation; and

(ii) promptly notify the furnisher of that information that the information has been modified or deleted from the file of the consumer.

(B) Requirements relating to reinsertion of previously deleted material

(i) Certification of accuracy of information

If any information is deleted from a consumer's file pursuant to subparagraph (A), the information may not be reinserted in the file by the consumer reporting agency unless the person who furnishes the information certifies that the information is complete and accurate.

(ii) Notice to consumer

If any information that has been deleted from a consumer's file pursuant to subparagraph (A) is reinserted in the file, the consumer reporting agency shall notify the consumer of the reinsertion in writing not later than 5 business days after the reinsertion or, if authorized by the consumer for that purpose, by any other means available to the agency.

(iii) Additional information

As part of, or in addition to, the notice under clause (ii), a consumer reporting agency shall provide to a consumer in writing not later than 5 business days after the date of the reinsertion-

(I) a statement that the disputed information has been reinserted;

(II) the business name and address of any furnisher of information contacted and the telephone number of such furnisher, if reasonably available, or of any furnisher of information that contacted the consumer reporting agency, in connection with the reinsertion of such information; and

(III) a notice that the consumer has the right to add a statement to the consumer's file disputing the accuracy or completeness of the disputed information.

(C) Procedures to prevent reappearance

A consumer reporting agency shall maintain reasonable procedures designed to prevent the reappearance in a consumer's file, and in consumer reports on the consumer, of information that is deleted pursuant to this paragraph (other than information that is reinserted in accordance with subparagraph (B)(i)).

(D) Automated reinvestigation system

Any consumer reporting agency that compiles and maintains files on consumers on a nationwide basis shall implement an automated system through which furnishers of information to that consumer reporting agency may report the results of a reinvestigation that finds incomplete or inaccurate information in a consumer's file to other such consumer reporting agencies.

(6) Notice of results of reinvestigation

(A) In general

A consumer reporting agency shall provide written notice to a consumer of the results of a reinvestigation under this subsection not later than 5 business days after the completion of the reinvestigation, by mail or, if authorized by the consumer for that purpose, by other means available to the agency.

(B) Contents

As part of, or in addition to, the notice under subparagraph (A), a consumer reporting agency shall provide to a consumer in writing before the expiration of the 5-day period referred to in subparagraph (A)-

(i) a statement that the reinvestigation is completed;

(ii) a consumer report that is based upon the consumer's file as that file is revised as a result of the reinvestigation;

(iii) a notice that, if requested by the consumer, a description of the procedure used to determine the accuracy and completeness of the information shall be provided to the consumer by the agency, including the business name and address of any furnisher of information contacted in connection with such information and the telephone number of such furnisher, if reasonably available;

(iv) a notice that the consumer has the right to add a statement to the consumer's file disputing the accuracy or completeness of the information; and

(v) a notice that the consumer has the right to request under subsection (d) that the consumer reporting agency furnish notifications under that subsection.

(7) Description of reinvestigation procedure

A consumer reporting agency shall provide to a consumer a description referred to in paragraph (6)(B)(iii) by not later than 15 days after receiving a request from the consumer for that description.

(8) Expedited dispute resolution

If a dispute regarding an item of information in a consumer's file at a consumer reporting agency is resolved in accordance with paragraph (5)(A) by the deletion of the disputed information by not later than 3 business days after the date on which the agency receives notice of the dispute from the consumer in accordance with paragraph (1)(A), then the agency shall not be required to comply with paragraphs (2), (6), and (7) with respect to that dispute if the agency-

(A) provides prompt notice of the deletion to the consumer by telephone;

(B) includes in that notice, or in a written notice that accompanies a confirmation and consumer report provided in accordance with subparagraph (C), a statement of the consumer's right to request under subsection (d) that the agency furnish notifications under that subsection; and

(C) provides written confirmation of the deletion and a copy of a consumer report on the consumer that is based on the consumer's file after the deletion, not later than 5 business days after making the deletion.

(b) Statement of dispute

If the reinvestigation does not resolve the dispute, the consumer may file a brief statement setting forth the nature of the dispute. The consumer reporting agency may limit such statements to not more than one hundred words if it provides the consumer with assistance in writing a clear summary of the dispute.

(c) Notification of consumer dispute in subsequent consumer reports

Whenever a statement of a dispute is filed, unless there is reasonable grounds to believe that it is frivolous or irrelevant, the consumer reporting agency shall, in any subsequent consumer report containing the information in question, clearly note that it is disputed by the consumer and provide either the consumer's statement or a clear and accurate codification or summary thereof.

(d) Notification of deletion of disputed information

Following any deletion of information which is found to be inaccurate or whose accuracy can no longer be verified or any notation as to disputed information, the consumer reporting agency shall, at the request of the consumer, furnish notification that the item has been deleted or the statement, codification or summary pursuant to subsection (b) or (c) to any person specifically designated by the consumer who has within two years prior thereto received a consumer report for employment purposes, or within six months prior thereto received a consumer report for any other purpose, which contained the deleted or disputed information.

(e) Treatment of complaints and report to Congress

    (1) In general

    The Commission [1] shall-

        (A) compile all complaints that it receives that a file of a consumer that is maintained by a consumer reporting agency described in section 1681a(p) of this title contains incomplete or inaccurate information, with respect to which, the consumer appears to have disputed the completeness or accuracy with the consumer reporting agency or otherwise utilized the procedures provided by subsection (a); and

        (B) transmit each such complaint to each consumer reporting agency involved.

    (2) Exclusion

    Complaints received or obtained by the Bureau pursuant to its investigative authority under the Consumer Financial Protection Act of 2010 shall not be subject to paragraph (1).

    (3) Agency responsibilities

    Each consumer reporting agency described in section 1681a(p) of this title that receives a complaint transmitted by the Bureau pursuant to paragraph (1) shall-

        (A) review each such complaint to determine whether all legal obligations imposed on the consumer reporting agency under this subchapter (including any obligation imposed by an applicable court or administrative order) have been met with respect to the subject matter of the complaint;

(B) provide reports on a regular basis to the Bureau regarding the determinations of and actions taken by the consumer reporting agency, if any, in connection with its review of such complaints; and

(C) maintain, for a reasonable time period, records regarding the disposition of each such complaint that is sufficient to demonstrate compliance with this subsection.

(4) Rulemaking authority

The Commission [1] may prescribe regulations, as appropriate to implement this subsection.

(5) Annual report

The Commission [1] shall submit to the Committee on Banking, Housing, and Urban Affairs of the Senate and the Committee on Financial Services of the House of Representatives an annual report regarding information gathered by the Bureau under this subsection.

(f) Reinvestigation requirement applicable to resellers

(1) Exemption from general reinvestigation requirement

Except as provided in paragraph (2), a reseller shall be exempt from the requirements of this section.

(2) Action required upon receiving notice of a dispute

If a reseller receives a notice from a consumer of a dispute concerning the completeness or accuracy of any item of information contained in a consumer report on such consumer produced by the reseller, the reseller shall, within 5 business days of receiving the notice, and free of charge-

(A) determine whether the item of information is incomplete or inaccurate as a result of an act or omission of the reseller; and

(B) if-

(i) the reseller determines that the item of information is incomplete or inaccurate as a result of an act or omission of the reseller, not later than 20 days after receiving the notice, correct the information in the consumer report or delete it; or

(ii) if the reseller determines that the item of information is not incomplete or inaccurate as a result of an act or omission of the reseller, convey the notice of the dispute, together with all relevant information provided by the consumer, to each consumer reporting agency that provided the reseller with the information that is the subject of the dispute, using an address or a notification mechanism specified by the consumer reporting agency for such notices.

(3) Responsibility of consumer reporting agency to notify consumer through reseller

Upon the completion of a reinvestigation under this section of a dispute concerning the completeness or accuracy of any information in the file of a consumer by a consumer reporting agency that received notice of the dispute from a reseller under paragraph (2)-

> (A) the notice by the consumer reporting agency under paragraph (6), (7), or (8) of subsection (a) shall be provided to the reseller in lieu of the consumer; and

> (B) the reseller shall immediately reconvey such notice to the consumer, including any notice of a deletion by telephone in the manner required under paragraph (8)(A).

(4) Reseller reinvestigations

No provision of this subsection shall be construed as prohibiting a reseller from conducting a reinvestigation of a consumer dispute directly.

(g) Dispute process for veteran's medical debt

(1) In general

With respect to a veteran's medical debt, the veteran may submit a notice described in paragraph (2), proof of liability of the Department of Veterans Affairs for payment of that debt, or documentation that the Department of Veterans Affairs is in the process of making payment for authorized hospital care, medical services, or extended care services rendered to a consumer reporting agency or a reseller to dispute the inclusion of that debt on a consumer report of the veteran.

(2) Notification to veteran

The Department of Veterans Affairs shall submit to a veteran a notice that the Department of Veterans Affairs has assumed liability for part or all of a veteran's medical debt.

(3) Deletion of information from file

If a consumer reporting agency receives notice, proof of liability, or documentation under paragraph (1), the consumer reporting agency shall delete all information relating to the veteran's medical debt from the file of the veteran and notify the furnisher and the veteran of that deletion.

§ 1681j. Charges for certain disclosures

(a) Free annual disclosure

(1) Nationwide consumer reporting agencies

(A) In general

All consumer reporting agencies described in subsections (p) and (w) of section 1681a of this title shall make all disclosures pursuant to section 1681g of this title once during any 12-month period upon request of the consumer and without charge to the consumer.

(B) Centralized source

Subparagraph (A) shall apply with respect to a consumer reporting agency described in section 1681a(p) of this title only if the request from the consumer is made using the centralized source established for such purpose in accordance with section 211(c) of the Fair and Accurate Credit Transactions Act of 2003.

(C) Nationwide specialty consumer reporting agency

(i) In general

The Commission shall prescribe regulations applicable to each consumer reporting agency described in section 1681a(w) of this title to require the establishment of a streamlined process for consumers to request consumer reports under subparagraph (A), which shall include, at a minimum, the establishment by each such agency of a toll-free telephone number for such requests.

(ii) Considerations

In prescribing regulations under clause (i), the Bureau shall consider-

(b) the significant demands that may be placed on consumer reporting agencies in providing such consumer reports;

(II) appropriate means to ensure that consumer reporting agencies can satisfactorily meet those demands, including the efficacy of a system of staggering the availability to consumers of such consumer reports; and

(III) the ease by which consumers should be able to contact consumer reporting agencies with respect to access to such consumer reports.

(iii) Date of issuance

The Commission shall issue the regulations required by this subparagraph in final form not later than 6 months after December 4, 2003.

(iv) Consideration of ability to comply

The regulations of the Bureau under this subparagraph shall establish an effective date by which each nationwide specialty consumer reporting agency (as defined in section 1681a(w) of this title) shall be required to comply with subsection (a), which effective date-

(b) shall be established after consideration of the ability of each nationwide specialty consumer reporting agency to comply with subsection (a); and

(II) shall be not later than 6 months after the date on which such regulations are issued in final form (or such additional period not to exceed 3 months, as the Bureau determines appropriate).

(2) Timing

A consumer reporting agency shall provide a consumer report under paragraph (1) not later than 15 days after the date on which the request is received under paragraph (1).

(3) Reinvestigations

Notwithstanding the time periods specified in section 1681i(a)(1) of this title, a reinvestigation under that section by a consumer reporting agency upon a request of a consumer that is made after receiving a consumer report under this subsection shall be completed not later than 45 days after the date on which the request is received.

(4) Exception for first 12 months of operation

This subsection shall not apply to a consumer reporting agency that has not been furnishing consumer reports to third parties on a continuing basis during the 12-month period preceding a request under paragraph (1), with respect to consumers residing nationwide.

(b) Free disclosure after adverse notice to consumer

Each consumer reporting agency that maintains a file on a consumer shall make all disclosures pursuant to section 1681g of this title without charge to the consumer if, not later than 60 days after receipt by such consumer of a notification pursuant to section 1681m of this title, or of a notification from a debt collection agency affiliated with that consumer reporting agency stating that the consumer's credit rating may be or has been adversely affected, the consumer makes a request under section 1681g of this title.

(c) Free disclosure under certain other circumstances

Upon the request of the consumer, a consumer reporting agency shall make all disclosures pursuant to section 1681g of this title once during any 12-month period without charge to that consumer if the consumer certifies in writing that the consumer-

> (1) is unemployed and intends to apply for employment in the 60-day period beginning on the date on which the certification is made;
>
> (2) is a recipient of public welfare assistance; or
>
> (3) has reason to believe that the file on the consumer at the agency contains inaccurate information due to fraud.

(d) Free disclosures in connection with fraud alerts

Upon the request of a consumer, a consumer reporting agency described in section 1681a(p) of this title shall make all disclosures pursuant to section 1681g of this title without charge to the consumer, as provided in subsections (a)(2) and (b)(2) of section 1681c-1 of this title, as applicable.

(e) Other charges prohibited

A consumer reporting agency shall not impose any charge on a consumer for providing any notification required by this subchapter or making any disclosure required by this subchapter, except as authorized by subsection (f).

(f) Reasonable charges allowed for certain disclosures

> (1) In general
>
> In the case of a request from a consumer other than a request that is covered by any of subsections (a) through (d), a consumer reporting agency may impose a reasonable charge on a consumer-
>
> > (A) for making a disclosure to the consumer pursuant to section 1681g of this title, which charge-
> >
> > > (i) shall not exceed $8; and

(ii) shall be indicated to the consumer before making the disclosure; and

(B) for furnishing, pursuant to section 1681i(d) of this title, following a reinvestigation under section 1681i(a) of this title, a statement, codification, or summary to a person designated by the consumer under that section after the 30-day period beginning on the date of notification of the consumer under paragraph (6) or (8) of section 1681i(a) of this title with respect to the reinvestigation, which charge-

(i) shall not exceed the charge that the agency would impose on each designated recipient for a consumer report; and

(ii) shall be indicated to the consumer before furnishing such information.

(2) Modification of amount

The Bureau shall increase the amount referred to in paragraph (1)(A)(i) on January 1 of each year, based proportionally on changes in the Consumer Price Index, with fractional changes rounded to the nearest fifty cents.

(g) Prevention of deceptive marketing of credit reports

(1) In general

Subject to rulemaking pursuant to section 205(b) of the Credit CARD Act of 2009, any advertisement for a free credit report in any medium shall prominently disclose in such advertisement that free credit reports are available under Federal law at: "AnnualCreditReport.com" (or such other source as may be authorized under Federal law).

(2) Television and radio advertisement

In the case of an advertisement broadcast by television, the disclosures required under paragraph (1) shall be included in the audio and visual part of such advertisement. In the case of an advertisement broadcast by televison or radio, the disclosure required under paragraph (1) shall consist only of the following: "This is not the free credit report provided for by Federal law".

§ 1681k. Public record information for employment purposes

(a) In general

A consumer reporting agency which furnishes a consumer report for employment purposes and which for that purpose compiles and reports items of information on consumers which are matters of public record and are likely to have an adverse effect upon a consumer's ability to obtain employment shall-

(1) at the time such public record information is reported to the user of such consumer report, notify the consumer of the fact that public record information is being reported by the consumer reporting agency, together with the name and address of the person to whom such information is being reported; or

(2) maintain strict procedures designed to insure that whenever public record information which is likely to have an adverse effect on a consumer's ability to

obtain employment is reported it is complete and up to date. For purposes of this paragraph, items of public record relating to arrests, indictments, convictions, suits, tax liens, and outstanding judgments shall be considered up to date if the current public record status of the item at the time of the report is reported.

(b) Exemption for national security investigations

Subsection (a) does not apply in the case of an agency or department of the United States Government that seeks to obtain and use a consumer report for employment purposes, if the head of the agency or department makes a written finding as prescribed under section 1681b(b)(4)(A) of this title.

§ 1681l. Restrictions on investigative consumer reports

Whenever a consumer reporting agency prepares an investigative consumer report, no adverse information in the consumer report (other than information which is a matter of public record) may be included in a subsequent consumer report unless such adverse information has been verified in the process of making such subsequent consumer report, or the adverse information was received within the three-month period preceding the date the subsequent report is furnished.

§ 1681m. Requirements on users of consumer reports

(a) Duties of users taking adverse actions on basis of information contained in consumer reports

If any person takes any adverse action with respect to any consumer that is based in whole or in part on any information contained in a consumer report, the person shall-

(1) provide oral, written, or electronic notice of the adverse action to the consumer;

(2) provide to the consumer written or electronic disclosure-

(A) of a numerical credit score as defined in section 1681g(f)(2)(A) of this title used by such person in taking any adverse action based in whole or in part on any information in a consumer report; and

(B) of the information set forth in subparagraphs (B) through (E) of section 1681g(f)(1) of this title;

(3) provide to the consumer orally, in writing, or electronically-

(A) the name, address, and telephone number of the consumer reporting agency (including a toll-free telephone number established by the agency if the agency compiles and maintains files on consumers on a nationwide basis) that furnished the report to the person; and

(B) a statement that the consumer reporting agency did not make the decision to take the adverse action and is unable to provide the consumer the specific reasons why the adverse action was taken; and

(4) provide to the consumer an oral, written, or electronic notice of the consumer's right-

(A) to obtain, under section 1681j of this title, a free copy of a consumer report on the consumer from the consumer reporting agency referred to in paragraph (3), which notice shall include an indication of the 60-day period under that section for obtaining such a copy; and

(B) to dispute, under section 1681i of this title, with a consumer reporting agency the accuracy or completeness of any information in a consumer report furnished by the agency.

(b) Adverse action based on information obtained from third parties other than consumer reporting agencies

(1) In general

Whenever credit for personal, family, or household purposes involving a consumer is denied or the charge for such credit is increased either wholly or partly because of information obtained from a person other than a consumer reporting agency bearing upon the consumer's credit worthiness, credit standing, credit capacity, character, general reputation, personal characteristics, or mode of living, the user of such information shall, within a reasonable period of time, upon the consumer's written request for the reasons for such adverse action received within sixty days after learning of such adverse action, disclose the nature of the information to the consumer. The user of such information shall clearly and accurately disclose to the consumer his right to make such written request at the time such adverse action is communicated to the consumer.

(2) Duties of person taking certain actions based on information provided by affiliate

(A) Duties, generally

If a person takes an action described in subparagraph (B) with respect to a consumer, based in whole or in part on information described in subparagraph (C), the person shall-

(i) notify the consumer of the action, including a statement that the consumer may obtain the information in accordance with clause (ii); and

(ii) upon a written request from the consumer received within 60 days after transmittal of the notice required by clause (i), disclose to the consumer the nature of the information upon which the action is based by not later than 30 days after receipt of the request.

(B) Action described

An action referred to in subparagraph (A) is an adverse action described in section 1681a(k)(1)(A) of this title, taken in connection with a transaction initiated by the consumer, or any adverse action described in clause (i) or (ii) of section 1681a(k)(1)(B) of this title.

(C) Information described

Information referred to in subparagraph (A)-

(i) except as provided in clause (ii), is information that-

(I) is furnished to the person taking the action by a person related by common ownership or affiliated by common corporate control to the person taking the action; and

(II) bears on the credit worthiness, credit standing, credit capacity, character, general reputation, personal characteristics, or mode of living of the consumer; and

(ii) does not include-

(I) information solely as to transactions or experiences between the consumer and the person furnishing the information; or

(II) information in a consumer report.

(c) Reasonable procedures to assure compliance

No person shall be held liable for any violation of this section if he shows by a preponderance of the evidence that at the time of the alleged violation he maintained reasonable procedures to assure compliance with the provisions of this section.

(d) Duties of users making written credit or insurance solicitations on basis of information contained in consumer files

(1) In general

Any person who uses a consumer report on any consumer in connection with any credit or insurance transaction that is not initiated by the consumer, that is provided to that person under section 1681b(c)(1)(B) of this title, shall provide with each written solicitation made to the consumer regarding the transaction a clear and conspicuous statement that-

(A) information contained in the consumer's consumer report was used in connection with the transaction;

(B) the consumer received the offer of credit or insurance because the consumer satisfied the criteria for credit worthiness or insurability under which the consumer was selected for the offer;

(C) if applicable, the credit or insurance may not be extended if, after the consumer responds to the offer, the consumer does not meet the criteria used to select the consumer for the offer or any applicable criteria bearing on credit worthiness or insurability or does not furnish any required collateral;

(D) the consumer has a right to prohibit information contained in the consumer's file with any consumer reporting agency from being used in connection with any credit or insurance transaction that is not initiated by the consumer; and

(E) the consumer may exercise the right referred to in subparagraph (D) by notifying a notification system established under section 1681b(e) of this title.

(2) Disclosure of address and telephone number; format

A statement under paragraph (1) shall-

(A) include the address and toll-free telephone number of the appropriate notification system established under section 1681b(e) of this title; and

(B) be presented in such format and in such type size and manner as to be simple and easy to understand, as established by the Bureau, by rule, in consultation with the Federal Trade Commission, the Federal banking agencies, and the National Credit Union Administration.

(3) Maintaining criteria on file

A person who makes an offer of credit or insurance to a consumer under a credit or insurance transaction described in paragraph (1) shall maintain on file the criteria used to select the consumer to receive the offer, all criteria bearing on credit worthiness or insurability, as applicable, that are the basis for determining whether or not to extend credit or insurance pursuant to the offer, and any requirement for the furnishing of collateral as a condition of the extension of credit or insurance, until the expiration of the 3-year period beginning on the date on which the offer is made to the consumer.

(4) Authority of Federal agencies regarding unfair or deceptive acts or practices not affected

This section is not intended to affect the authority of any Federal or State agency to enforce a prohibition against unfair or deceptive acts or practices, including the making of false or misleading statements in connection with a credit or insurance transaction that is not initiated by the consumer.

(e) Red flag guidelines and regulations required

(1) Guidelines

The Federal banking agencies, the National Credit Union Administration, the Federal Trade Commission, the Commodity Futures Trading Commission, and the Securities and Exchange Commission shall jointly, with respect to the entities that are subject to their respective enforcement authority under section 1681s of this title-

(A) establish and maintain guidelines for use by each financial institution and each creditor regarding identity theft with respect to account holders at, or customers of, such entities, and update such guidelines as often as necessary;

(B) prescribe regulations requiring each financial institution and each creditor to establish reasonable policies and procedures for implementing the guidelines established pursuant to subparagraph (A), to identify possible risks to account holders or customers or to the safety and soundness of the institution or customers; and

(C) prescribe regulations applicable to card issuers to ensure that, if a card issuer receives notification of a change of address for an existing account, and within a short period of time (during at least the first 30 days after such notification is received) receives a request for an additional or replacement card for the same account, the card issuer may not issue the additional or replacement card, unless the card issuer, in accordance with reasonable policies and procedures-

(i) notifies the cardholder of the request at the former address of the cardholder and provides to the cardholder a means of promptly reporting incorrect address changes;

(ii) notifies the cardholder of the request by such other means of communication as the cardholder and the card issuer previously agreed to; or

(iii) uses other means of assessing the validity of the change of address, in accordance with reasonable policies and procedures established by the card issuer in accordance with the regulations prescribed under subparagraph (B).

(2) Criteria

(A) In general

In developing the guidelines required by paragraph (1)(A), the agencies described in paragraph (1) shall identify patterns, practices, and specific forms of activity that indicate the possible existence of identity theft.

(B) Inactive accounts

In developing the guidelines required by paragraph (1)(A), the agencies described in paragraph (1) shall consider including reasonable guidelines providing that when a transaction occurs with respect to a credit or deposit account that has been inactive for more than 2 years, the creditor or financial institution shall follow reasonable policies and procedures that provide for notice to be given to a consumer in a manner reasonably designed to reduce the likelihood of identity theft with respect to such account.

(3) Consistency with verification requirements

Guidelines established pursuant to paragraph (1) shall not be inconsistent with the policies and procedures required under section 5318(l) of title 31.

(4) Definitions

As used in this subsection, the term "creditor"-

(A) means a creditor, as defined in section 1691a of this title, that regularly and in the ordinary course of business-

(i) obtains or uses consumer reports, directly or indirectly, in connection with a credit transaction;

(ii) furnishes information to consumer reporting agencies, as described in section 1681s–2 of this title, in connection with a credit transaction; or

(iii) advances funds to or on behalf of a person, based on an obligation of the person to repay the funds or repayable from specific property pledged by or on behalf of the person;

(B) does not include a creditor described in subparagraph (A)(iii) that advances funds on behalf of a person for expenses incidental to a service provided by the creditor to that person; and

(C) includes any other type of creditor, as defined in that section 1691a of this title, as the agency described in paragraph (1) having authority over that creditor may determine appropriate by rule promulgated by that agency, based on a determination that such creditor offers or maintains accounts that are subject to a reasonably foreseeable risk of identity theft.

(f) Prohibition on sale or transfer of debt caused by identity theft

(1) In general

No person shall sell, transfer for consideration, or place for collection a debt that such person has been notified under section 1681c–2 of this title has resulted from identity theft.

(2) Applicability

The prohibitions of this subsection shall apply to all persons collecting a debt described in paragraph (1) after the date of a notification under paragraph (1).

(3) Rule of construction

Nothing in this subsection shall be construed to prohibit-

(A) the repurchase of a debt in any case in which the assignee of the debt requires such repurchase because the debt has resulted from identity theft;

(B) the securitization of a debt or the pledging of a portfolio of debt as collateral in connection with a borrowing; or

(C) the transfer of debt as a result of a merger, acquisition, purchase and assumption transaction, or transfer of substantially all of the assets of an entity.

(g) Debt collector communications concerning identity theft

If a person acting as a debt collector (as that term is defined in subchapter V) on behalf of a third party that is a creditor or other user of a consumer report is notified that any information relating to a debt that the person is attempting to collect may be fraudulent or may be the result of identity theft, that person shall-

(1) notify the third party that the information may be fraudulent or may be the result of identity theft; and

(2) upon request of the consumer to whom the debt purportedly relates, provide to the consumer all information to which the consumer would otherwise be entitled if the consumer were not a victim of identity theft, but wished to dispute the debt under provisions of law applicable to that person.

(h) Duties of users in certain credit transactions

(1) In general

Subject to rules prescribed as provided in paragraph (6), if any person uses a consumer report in connection with an application for, or a grant, extension, or other provision of, credit on material terms that are materially less favorable than the most favorable terms available to a substantial proportion of consumers from or through that person, based in whole or in part on a consumer report, the person shall provide an oral, written, or electronic notice to the consumer in the form and manner required by regulations prescribed in accordance with this subsection.

(2) Timing

The notice required under paragraph (1) may be provided at the time of an application for, or a grant, extension, or other provision of, credit or the time of communication of an approval of an application for, or grant, extension, or other provision of, credit, except as provided in the regulations prescribed under paragraph (6).

(3) Exceptions

No notice shall be required from a person under this subsection if-

(A) the consumer applied for specific material terms and was granted those terms, unless those terms were initially specified by the person after the transaction was initiated by the consumer and after the person obtained a consumer report; or

(B) the person has provided or will provide a notice to the consumer under subsection (a) in connection with the transaction.

(4) Other notice not sufficient

A person that is required to provide a notice under subsection (a) cannot meet that requirement by providing a notice under this subsection.

(5) Content and delivery of notice

A notice under this subsection shall, at a minimum-

(A) include a statement informing the consumer that the terms offered to the consumer are set based on information from a consumer report;

(B) identify the consumer reporting agency furnishing the report;

(C) include a statement informing the consumer that the consumer may obtain a copy of a consumer report from that consumer reporting agency without charge;

(D) include the contact information specified by that consumer reporting agency for obtaining such consumer reports (including a toll-free telephone number established by the agency in the case of a consumer reporting agency described in section 1681a(p) of this title); and

(E) include a statement informing the consumer of-

(i) a numerical credit score as defined in section 1681g(f)(2)(A) of this title, used by such person in making the credit decision described in paragraph (1) based in whole or in part on any information in a consumer report; and

(ii) the information set forth in subparagraphs (B) through (E) of section 1681g(f)(1) of this title.

(6) Rulemaking

(A) Rules required

The Bureau shall prescribe rules to carry out this subsection.

(B) Content

Rules required by subparagraph (A) shall address, but are not limited to-

(i) the form, content, time, and manner of delivery of any notice under this subsection;

(ii) clarification of the meaning of terms used in this subsection, including what credit terms are material, and when credit terms are materially less favorable;

(iii) exceptions to the notice requirement under this subsection for classes of persons or transactions regarding which the agencies determine that notice would not significantly benefit consumers;

(iv) a model notice that may be used to comply with this subsection; and

(v) the timing of the notice required under paragraph (1), including the circumstances under which the notice must be provided after the terms offered to the consumer were set based on information from a consumer report.

(7) Compliance

A person shall not be liable for failure to perform the duties required by this section if, at the time of the failure, the person maintained reasonable policies and procedures to comply with this section.

(8) Enforcement

(A) No civil actions

Sections 1681n and 1681o of this title shall not apply to any failure by any person to comply with this section.

(B) Administrative enforcement

This section shall be enforced exclusively under section 1681s of this title by the Federal agencies and officials identified in that section.

§ 1681n. Civil liability for willful noncompliance

(a) In general

Any person who willfully fails to comply with any requirement imposed under this subchapter with respect to any consumer is liable to that consumer in an amount equal to the sum of-

(1)(A) any actual damages sustained by the consumer as a result of the failure or damages of not less than $100 and not more than $1,000; or

(B) in the case of liability of a natural person for obtaining a consumer report under false pretenses or knowingly without a permissible purpose, actual damages sustained by the consumer as a result of the failure or $1,000, whichever is greater;

(2) such amount of punitive damages as the court may allow; and

(3) in the case of any successful action to enforce any liability under this section, the costs of the action together with reasonable attorney's fees as determined by the court.

(b) Civil liability for knowing noncompliance

Any person who obtains a consumer report from a consumer reporting agency under false pretenses or knowingly without a permissible purpose shall be liable to the consumer reporting agency for actual damages sustained by the consumer reporting agency or $1,000, whichever is greater.

(c) Attorney's fees

Upon a finding by the court that an unsuccessful pleading, motion, or other paper filed in connection with an action under this section was filed in bad faith or for purposes of harassment, the court shall award to the prevailing party attorney's fees reasonable in relation to the work expended in responding to the pleading, motion, or other paper.

(d) Clarification of willful noncompliance

For the purposes of this section, any person who printed an expiration date on any receipt provided to a consumer cardholder at a point of sale or transaction between December 4, 2004, and June 3, 2008, but otherwise complied with the requirements of section 1681c(g) of this title for such receipt shall not be in willful noncompliance with section 1681c(g) of this title by reason of printing such expiration date on the receipt.

§ 1681o. Civil liability for negligent noncompliance

(a) In general

Any person who is negligent in failing to comply with any requirement imposed under this subchapter with respect to any consumer is liable to that consumer in an amount equal to the sum of-

(1) any actual damages sustained by the consumer as a result of the failure; and
(2) in the case of any successful action to enforce any liability under this section, the costs of the action together with reasonable attorney's fees as determined by the court.

(b) Attorney's fees

On a finding by the court that an unsuccessful pleading, motion, or other paper filed in connection with an action under this section was filed in bad faith or for purposes of harassment, the court shall award to the prevailing party attorney's fees reasonable in relation to the work expended in responding to the pleading, motion, or other paper.

§ 1681p. Jurisdiction of courts; limitation of actions

An action to enforce any liability created under this subchapter may be brought in any appropriate United States district court, without regard to the amount in controversy, or in any other court of competent jurisdiction, not later than the earlier of-

(1) 2 years after the date of discovery by the plaintiff of the violation that is the basis for such liability; or
(2) 5 years after the date on which the violation that is the basis for such liability occurs.

United States
Fair Credit Reporting Act

§ 1681q. Obtaining information under false pretenses

Any person who knowingly and willfully obtains information on a consumer from a consumer reporting agency under false pretenses shall be fined under title 18, imprisoned for not more than 2 years, or both.

§ 1681r. Unauthorized disclosures by officers or employees

Any officer or employee of a consumer reporting agency who knowingly and willfully provides information concerning an individual from the agency's files to a person not authorized to receive that information shall be fined under title 18, imprisoned for not more than 2 years, or both.

§ 1681s. Administrative enforcement

(a) Enforcement by Federal Trade Commission

(1) In general

The Federal Trade Commission shall be authorized to enforce compliance with the requirements imposed by this subchapter under the Federal Trade Commission Act (15 U.S.C. 41 et seq.), with respect to consumer reporting agencies and all other persons subject thereto, except to the extent that enforcement of the requirements imposed under this subchapter is specifically committed to some other Government agency under any of subparagraphs (A) through (G) of subsection (b)(1), and subject to subtitle B of the Consumer Financial Protection Act of 2010 [12 U.S.C. 5511 et seq.], subsection (b). For the purpose of the exercise by the Federal Trade Commission of its functions and powers under the Federal Trade Commission Act, a violation of any requirement or prohibition imposed under this subchapter shall constitute an unfair or deceptive act or practice in commerce, in violation of section 5(a) of the Federal Trade Commission Act (15 U.S.C. 45(a)), and shall be subject to enforcement by the Federal Trade Commission under section 5(b) of that Act [15 U.S.C. 45(b)] with respect to any consumer reporting agency or person that is subject to enforcement by the Federal Trade Commission pursuant to this subsection, irrespective of whether that person is engaged in commerce or meets any other jurisdictional tests under the Federal Trade Commission Act. The Federal Trade Commission shall have such procedural, investigative, and enforcement powers, including the power to issue procedural rules in enforcing compliance with the requirements imposed under this subchapter and to require the filing of reports, the production of documents, and the appearance of witnesses, as though the applicable terms and conditions of the Federal Trade Commission Act were part of this subchapter. Any person violating any of the provisions of this subchapter shall be subject to the penalties and entitled to the privileges and immunities provided in the Federal Trade Commission Act as though the applicable terms and provisions of such Act are part of this subchapter.

(2) Penalties

(A) Knowing violations

Except as otherwise provided by subtitle B of the Consumer Financial Protection Act of 2010, in the event of a knowing violation, which constitutes a pattern or practice of violations of this subchapter, the Federal Trade Commission may commence a civil action to recover a civil penalty in a district court of the United States against any person that violates this subchapter. In such action, such person shall be liable for a civil penalty of not more than $2,500 per violation.

(B) Determining penalty amount

In determining the amount of a civil penalty under subparagraph (A), the court shall take into account the degree of culpability, any history of such prior conduct, ability to pay, effect on ability to continue to do business, and such other matters as justice may require.

(C) Limitation

Notwithstanding paragraph (2), a court may not impose any civil penalty on a person for a violation of section 1681s–2(a)(1) of this title, unless the person has been enjoined from committing the violation, or ordered not to commit the violation, in an action or proceeding brought by or on behalf of the Federal Trade Commission, and has violated the injunction or order, and the court may not impose any civil penalty for any violation occurring before the date of the violation of the injunction or order.

(b) Enforcement by other agencies

(1) In general

Subject to subtitle B of the Consumer Financial Protection Act of 2010, compliance with the requirements imposed under this subchapter with respect to consumer reporting agencies, persons who use consumer reports from such agencies, persons who furnish information to such agencies, and users of information that are subject to section 1681m(d) of this title shall be enforced under-

(A) section 8 of the Federal Deposit Insurance Act (12 U.S.C. 1818), by the appropriate Federal banking agency, as defined in section 3(q) of the Federal Deposit Insurance Act (12 U.S.C. 1813(q)), with respect to-

(i) any national bank or State savings association, and any Federal branch or Federal agency of a foreign bank;

(ii) any member bank of the Federal Reserve System (other than a national bank), a branch or agency of a foreign bank (other than a Federal branch, Federal agency, or insured State branch of a foreign bank), a commercial lending company owned or controlled by a foreign bank, and any organization operating under section 25 or 25A of the Federal Reserve Act [12 U.S.C. 601 et seq., 611 et seq.]; and

(iii) any bank or Federal savings association insured by the Federal Deposit Insurance Corporation (other than a member of the Federal Reserve System) and any insured State branch of a foreign bank;

(B) the Federal Credit Union Act (12 U.S.C. 1751 et seq.), by the Administrator of the National Credit Union Administration with respect to any Federal credit union;

(C) subtitle IV of title 49, by the Secretary of Transportation, with respect to all carriers subject to the jurisdiction of the Surface Transportation Board;

(D) part A of subtitle VII of title 49, by the Secretary of Transportation, with respect to any air carrier or foreign air carrier subject to that part;

(E) the Packers and Stockyards Act, 1921 (7 U.S.C. 181 et seq.) (except as provided in section 406 of that Act [7 U.S.C. 226, 227]), by the Secretary of Agriculture, with respect to any activities subject to that Act;

(F) the Commodity Exchange Act [7 U.S.C. 1 et seq.], with respect to a person subject to the jurisdiction of the Commodity Futures Trading Commission;

(G) the Federal securities laws, and any other laws that are subject to the jurisdiction of the Securities and Exchange Commission, with respect to a person that is subject to the jurisdiction of the Securities and Exchange Commission; and

(H) subtitle E of the Consumer Financial Protection Act of 2010 [12 U.S.C. 5561 et seq.], by the Bureau, with respect to any person subject to this subchapter.

(2) Incorporated definitions

The terms used in paragraph (1) that are not defined in this subchapter or otherwise defined in section 3(s) of the Federal Deposit Insurance Act (12 U.S.C. 1813(s)) have the same meanings as in section 1(b) of the International Banking Act of 1978 (12 U.S.C. 3101).

(c) State action for violations

(1) Authority of States

In addition to such other remedies as are provided under State law, if the chief law enforcement officer of a State, or an official or agency designated by a State, has reason to believe that any person has violated or is violating this subchapter, the State-

(A) may bring an action to enjoin such violation in any appropriate United States district court or in any other court of competent jurisdiction;

(B) subject to paragraph (5), may bring an action on behalf of the residents of the State to recover-

(i) damages for which the person is liable to such residents under sections 1681n and 1681o of this title as a result of the violation;

(ii) in the case of a violation described in any of paragraphs (1) through (3) of section 1681s–2(c) of this title, damages for which the person would, but for section 1681s–2(c) of this title, be liable to such residents as a result of the violation; or

(iii) damages of not more than $1,000 for each willful or negligent violation; and

(C) in the case of any successful action under subparagraph (A) or (B), shall be awarded the costs of the action and reasonable attorney fees as determined by the court.

(2) Rights of Federal regulators

The State shall serve prior written notice of any action under paragraph (1) upon the Bureau and the Federal Trade Commission or the appropriate Federal regulator determined under subsection (b) and provide the Bureau and the Federal Trade Commission or appropriate Federal regulator with a copy of its complaint, except in any case in which such prior notice is not feasible, in which case the State shall serve such notice immediately upon instituting such action. The Bureau and the Federal Trade Commission or appropriate Federal regulator shall have the right-

(A) to intervene in the action;

(B) upon so intervening, to be heard on all matters arising therein;

(C) to remove the action to the appropriate United States district court; and

(D) to file petitions for appeal.

(3) Investigatory powers

For purposes of bringing any action under this subsection, nothing in this subsection shall prevent the chief law enforcement officer, or an official or agency designated by a State, from exercising the powers conferred on the chief law enforcement officer or such official by the laws of such State to conduct investigations or to administer oaths or affirmations or to compel the attendance of witnesses or the production of documentary and other evidence.

(4) Limitation on State action while Federal action pending

If the Bureau, the Federal Trade Commission, or the appropriate Federal regulator has instituted a civil action or an administrative action under section 8 of the Federal Deposit Insurance Act [12 U.S.C. 1818] for a violation of this subchapter, no State may, during the pendency of such action, bring an action under this section against any defendant named in the complaint of the Bureau, the Federal Trade Commission, or the appropriate Federal regulator for any violation of this subchapter that is alleged in that complaint.

(5) Limitations on State actions for certain violations

(A) Violation of injunction required

A State may not bring an action against a person under paragraph (1)(B) for a violation described in any of paragraphs (1) through (3) of section 1681s–2(c) of this title, unless-

(i) the person has been enjoined from committing the violation, in an action brought by the State under paragraph (1)(A); and

(ii) the person has violated the injunction.

(B) Limitation on damages recoverable

In an action against a person under paragraph (1)(B) for a violation described in any of paragraphs (1) through (3) of section 1681s–2(c) of this title, a State may not recover any damages incurred before the date of the violation of an injunction on which the action is based.

(d) Enforcement under other authority

For the purpose of the exercise by any agency referred to in subsection (b) of its powers under any Act referred to in that subsection, a violation of any requirement imposed under this subchapter shall be deemed to be a violation of a requirement imposed under that Act. In addition to its powers under any provision of law specifically referred to in subsection (b), each of the agencies referred to in that subsection may exercise, for the purpose of enforcing compliance with any requirement imposed under this subchapter any other authority conferred on it by law.

(e) Regulatory authority

(1) In general

The Bureau shall prescribe such regulations as are necessary to carry out the purposes of this subchapter, except with respect to sections 1681m(e) and 1681w of this title. The Bureau may prescribe regulations as may be necessary or appropriate to administer and carry out the purposes and objectives of this subchapter, and to prevent evasions thereof or to facilitate compliance therewith. Except as provided in section 1029(a) of the Consumer Financial Protection Act of 2010 [12 U.S.C. 5519(a)], the regulations prescribed by the Bureau under this subchapter shall apply to any person that is subject to this subchapter, notwithstanding the enforcement authorities granted to other agencies under this section.

(2) Deference

Notwithstanding any power granted to any Federal agency under this subchapter, the deference that a court affords to a Federal agency with respect to a determination made by such agency relating to the meaning or interpretation of any provision of this subchapter that is subject to the jurisdiction of such agency shall be applied as if that agency were the only agency authorized to apply, enforce, interpret, or administer the provisions of this subchapter. The regulations prescribed by the Bureau under this subchapter shall apply to any person that is subject to this subchapter, notwithstanding the enforcement authorities granted to other agencies under this section.

(f) Coordination of consumer complaint investigations

(1) In general

Each consumer reporting agency described in section 1681a(p) of this title shall develop and maintain procedures for the referral to each other such agency of any consumer complaint received by the agency alleging identity theft, or requesting a fraud alert under section 1681c–1 of this title or a block under section 1681c–2 of this title.

(2) Model form and procedure for reporting identity theft

The Commission, in consultation with the Federal Trade Commission, the Federal banking agencies, and the National Credit Union Administration, shall develop a model form and model procedures to be used by consumers who are victims of identity theft for contacting and informing creditors and consumer reporting agencies of the fraud.

(3) Annual summary reports

Each consumer reporting agency described in section 1681a(p) of this title shall submit an annual summary report to the Bureau on consumer complaints received by the agency on identity theft or fraud alerts.

(g) Bureau regulation of coding of trade names

If the Bureau determines that a person described in paragraph (9) of section 1681s–2(a) of this title has not met the requirements of such paragraph, the Bureau shall take action to ensure the person's compliance with such paragraph, which may include issuing model guidance or prescribing reasonable policies and procedures, as necessary to ensure that such person complies with such paragraph.

§ 1681s-1. Information on overdue child support obligations

Notwithstanding any other provision of this subchapter, a consumer reporting agency shall include in any consumer report furnished by the agency in accordance with section 1681b of this title, any information on the failure of the consumer to pay overdue support which-

(1) is provided-

(A) to the consumer reporting agency by a State or local child support enforcement agency; or

(B) to the consumer reporting agency and verified by any local, State, or Federal Government agency; and

(2) antedates the report by 7 years or less.

United States
Fair Credit Reporting Act

§ 1681s-2. Responsibilities of furnishers of information to consumer reporting agencies

(a) Duty of furnishers of information to provide accurate information

(1) Prohibition

(A) Reporting information with actual knowledge of errors

A person shall not furnish any information relating to a consumer to any consumer reporting agency if the person knows or has reasonable cause to believe that the information is inaccurate.

(B) Reporting information after notice and confirmation of errors

A person shall not furnish information relating to a consumer to any consumer reporting agency if-

(i) the person has been notified by the consumer, at the address specified by the person for such notices, that specific information is inaccurate; and

(ii) the information is, in fact, inaccurate.

(C) No address requirement

A person who clearly and conspicuously specifies to the consumer an address for notices referred to in subparagraph (B) shall not be subject to subparagraph (A); however, nothing in subparagraph (B) shall require a person to specify such an address.

(D) Definition

For purposes of subparagraph (A), the term "reasonable cause to believe that the information is inaccurate" means having specific knowledge, other than solely allegations by the consumer, that would cause a reasonable person to have substantial doubts about the accuracy of the information.

(E) Rehabilitation of private education loans

(i) In general

Notwithstanding any other provision of this section, a consumer may request a financial institution to remove from a consumer report a reported default regarding a private education loan, and such information shall not be considered inaccurate, if-

(I) the financial institution chooses to offer a loan rehabilitation program which includes, without limitation, a requirement of the consumer to make consecutive on-time monthly payments in a number that demonstrates, in the assessment of the financial institution offering the loan rehabilitation program, a renewed ability and willingness to repay the loan; and

(II) the requirements of the loan rehabilitation program described in subclause (I) are successfully met.

(ii) Banking agencies

(I) In general

If a financial institution is supervised by a Federal banking agency, the financial institution shall seek written approval concerning the terms and conditions of the loan rehabilitation program described in clause (i) from the appropriate Federal banking agency.

(II) Feedback

An appropriate Federal banking agency shall provide feedback to a financial institution within 120 days of a request for approval under subclause (I).

(iii) Limitation

(I) In general

A consumer may obtain the benefits available under this subsection with respect to rehabilitating a loan only 1 time per loan.

(II) Rule of construction

Nothing in this subparagraph may be construed to require a financial institution to offer a loan rehabilitation program or to remove any reported default from a consumer report as a consideration of a loan rehabilitation program, except as described in clause (i).

(iv) Definitions

For purposes of this subparagraph-

(I) the term "appropriate Federal banking agency" has the meaning given the term in section 1813 of title 12; and

(II) the term "private education loan" has the meaning given the term in section 1650(a) of this title.

(2) Duty to correct and update information

A person who-

(A) regularly and in the ordinary course of business furnishes information to one or more consumer reporting agencies about the person's transactions or experiences with any consumer; and

(B) has furnished to a consumer reporting agency information that the person determines is not complete or accurate, shall promptly notify the consumer reporting agency of that determination and provide to the agency any corrections to that information, or any additional information, that is necessary to make the information provided by the person to the agency complete and accurate, and shall not thereafter furnish to the agency any of the information that remains not complete or accurate.

(3) Duty to provide notice of dispute

If the completeness or accuracy of any information furnished by any person to any consumer reporting agency is disputed to such person by a consumer, the person may not furnish the information to any consumer reporting agency without notice that such information is disputed by the consumer.

(4) Duty to provide notice of closed accounts

A person who regularly and in the ordinary course of business furnishes information to a consumer reporting agency regarding a consumer who has a credit account with that person shall notify the agency of the voluntary closure of the account by the consumer, in information regularly furnished for the period in which the account is closed.

(5) Duty to provide notice of delinquency of accounts

(A) In general

A person who furnishes information to a consumer reporting agency regarding a delinquent account being placed for collection, charged to profit or loss, or subjected to any similar action shall, not later than 90 days after furnishing the information, notify the agency of the date of delinquency on the account, which shall be the month and year of the commencement of the delinquency on the account that immediately preceded the action.

(B) Rule of construction

For purposes of this paragraph only, and provided that the consumer does not dispute the information, a person that furnishes information on a delinquent account that is placed for collection, charged for profit or loss, or subjected to any similar action, complies with this paragraph, if-

(i) the person reports the same date of delinquency as that provided by the creditor to which the account was owed at the time at which the commencement of the delinquency occurred, if the creditor previously reported that date of delinquency to a consumer reporting agency;

(ii) the creditor did not previously report the date of delinquency to a consumer reporting agency, and the person establishes and follows reasonable procedures to obtain the date of delinquency from the creditor or another reliable source and reports that date to a consumer reporting agency as the date of delinquency; or

(iii) the creditor did not previously report the date of delinquency to a consumer reporting agency and the date of delinquency cannot be reasonably obtained as provided in clause (ii), the person establishes and follows reasonable procedures to ensure the date reported as the date of delinquency precedes the date on which the account is placed for collection, charged to profit or loss, or subjected to any similar action, and reports such date to the credit reporting agency.

(6) Duties of furnishers upon notice of identity theft-related information

(A) Reasonable procedures

A person that furnishes information to any consumer reporting agency shall have in place reasonable procedures to respond to any notification that it receives from a consumer reporting agency under section 1681c–2 of this title relating to information resulting from identity theft, to prevent that person from refurnishing such blocked information.

(B) Information alleged to result from identity theft

If a consumer submits an identity theft report to a person who furnishes information to a consumer reporting agency at the address specified by that person for receiving such reports stating that information maintained by such person that purports to relate to the consumer resulted from identity theft, the person may not furnish such information that purports to relate to the consumer to any consumer reporting agency, unless the person subsequently knows or is informed by the consumer that the information is correct.

(7) Negative information

(A) Notice to consumer required

(i) In general

If any financial institution that extends credit and regularly and in the ordinary course of business furnishes information to a consumer reporting agency described in section 1681a(p) of this title furnishes negative information to such an agency regarding credit extended to a customer, the financial institution shall provide a notice of such furnishing of negative information, in writing, to the customer.

(ii) Notice effective for subsequent submissions

After providing such notice, the financial institution may submit additional negative information to a consumer reporting agency described in section 1681a(p) of this title with respect to the same transaction, extension of credit, account, or customer without providing additional notice to the customer.

(B) Time of notice

(i) In general

The notice required under subparagraph (A) shall be provided to the customer prior to, or no later than 30 days after, furnishing the negative information to a consumer reporting agency described in section 1681a(p) of this title.

(ii) Coordination with new account disclosures

If the notice is provided to the customer prior to furnishing the negative information to a consumer reporting agency, the notice may not be included in the initial disclosures provided under section 1637(a) of this title.

(C) Coordination with other disclosures

The notice required under subparagraph (A)-

(i) may be included on or with any notice of default, any billing statement, or any other materials provided to the customer; and

(ii) must be clear and conspicuous.

(D) Model disclosure

(i) Duty of Bureau

The Bureau shall prescribe a brief model disclosure that a financial institution may use to comply with subparagraph (A), which shall not exceed 30 words.

(ii) Use of model not required

No provision of this paragraph may be construed to require a financial institution to use any such model form prescribed by the Bureau.

(iii) Compliance using model

A financial institution shall be deemed to be in compliance with subparagraph (A) if the financial institution uses any model form prescribed by the Bureau under this subparagraph, or the financial institution uses any such model form and rearranges its format.

(E) Use of notice without submitting negative information

No provision of this paragraph shall be construed as requiring a financial institution that has provided a customer with a notice described in subparagraph (A) to furnish negative information about the customer to a consumer reporting agency.

(F) Safe harbor

A financial institution shall not be liable for failure to perform the duties required by this paragraph if, at the time of the failure, the financial institution maintained reasonable policies and procedures to comply with this paragraph or the financial institution reasonably believed that the institution is prohibited, by law, from contacting the consumer.

(G) Definitions

For purposes of this paragraph, the following definitions shall apply:

(i) Negative information

The term "negative information" means information concerning a customer's delinquencies, late payments, insolvency, or any form of default.

(ii) Customer; financial institution

The terms "customer" and "financial institution" have the same meanings as in section 6809 of this title.

(8) Ability of consumer to dispute information directly with furnisher

(A) In general

The Bureau, in consultation with the Federal Trade Commission, the Federal banking agencies, and the National Credit Union Administration, shall prescribe regulations that shall identify the circumstances under which a furnisher shall be required to reinvestigate a dispute concerning the accuracy of information contained in a consumer report on the consumer, based on a direct request of a consumer.

(B) Considerations

In prescribing regulations under subparagraph (A), the agencies shall weigh-

(i) the benefits to consumers with the costs on furnishers and the credit reporting system;

(ii) the impact on the overall accuracy and integrity of consumer reports of any such requirements;

(iii) whether direct contact by the consumer with the furnisher would likely result in the most expeditious resolution of any such dispute; and

(iv) the potential impact on the credit reporting process if credit repair organizations, as defined in section 1679a(3) of this title, including entities that would be a credit repair organization, but for section 1679a(3)(B)(i) of this title, are able to circumvent the prohibition in subparagraph (G).

(C) Applicability

Subparagraphs (D) through (G) shall apply in any circumstance identified under the regulations promulgated under subparagraph (A).

(D) Submitting a notice of dispute

A consumer who seeks to dispute the accuracy of information shall provide a dispute notice directly to such person at the address specified by the person for such notices that-

   (i) identifies the specific information that is being disputed;

   (ii) explains the basis for the dispute; and

   (iii) includes all supporting documentation required by the furnisher to substantiate the basis of the dispute.

(E) Duty of person after receiving notice of dispute

After receiving a notice of dispute from a consumer pursuant to subparagraph (D), the person that provided the information in dispute to a consumer reporting agency shall-

   (i) conduct an investigation with respect to the disputed information;

   (ii) review all relevant information provided by the consumer with the notice;

   (iii) complete such person's investigation of the dispute and report the results of the investigation to the consumer before the expiration of the period under section 1681i(a)(1) of this title within which a consumer reporting agency would be required to complete its action if the consumer had elected to dispute the information under that section; and

   (iv) if the investigation finds that the information reported was inaccurate, promptly notify each consumer reporting agency to which the person furnished the inaccurate information of that determination and provide to the agency any correction to that information that is necessary to make the information provided by the person accurate.

(F) Frivolous or irrelevant dispute

   (i) In general

This paragraph shall not apply if the person receiving a notice of a dispute from a consumer reasonably determines that the dispute is frivolous or irrelevant, including-

      (I) by reason of the failure of a consumer to provide sufficient information to investigate the disputed information; or

      (II) the submission by a consumer of a dispute that is substantially the same as a dispute previously submitted by or for the consumer, either directly to the person or through a consumer reporting agency under subsection (b), with respect to which the person has already performed the person's duties under this paragraph or subsection (b), as applicable.

(ii) Notice of determination

Upon making any determination under clause (i) that a dispute is frivolous or irrelevant, the person shall notify the consumer of such determination not later than 5 business days after making such determination, by mail or, if authorized by the consumer for that purpose, by any other means available to the person.

(iii) Contents of notice

A notice under clause (ii) shall include-

(I) the reasons for the determination under clause (i); and

(II) identification of any information required to investigate the disputed information, which may consist of a standardized form describing the general nature of such information.

(G) Exclusion of credit repair organizations

This paragraph shall not apply if the notice of the dispute is submitted by, is prepared on behalf of the consumer by, or is submitted on a form supplied to the consumer by, a credit repair organization, as defined in section 1679a(3) of this title, or an entity that would be a credit repair organization, but for section 1679a(3)(B)(i) of this title.

(9) Duty to provide notice of status as medical information furnisher

A person whose primary business is providing medical services, products, or devices, or the person's agent or assignee, who furnishes information to a consumer reporting agency on a consumer shall be considered a medical information furnisher for purposes of this subchapter, and shall notify the agency of such status.

(b) Duties of furnishers of information upon notice of dispute

(1) In general

After receiving notice pursuant to section 1681i(a)(2) of this title of a dispute with regard to the completeness or accuracy of any information provided by a person to a consumer reporting agency, the person shall-

(A) conduct an investigation with respect to the disputed information;

(B) review all relevant information provided by the consumer reporting agency pursuant to section 1681i(a)(2) of this title;

(C) report the results of the investigation to the consumer reporting agency;

(D) if the investigation finds that the information is incomplete or inaccurate, report those results to all other consumer reporting agencies to which the person furnished the information and that compile and maintain files on consumers on a nationwide basis; and

(E) if an item of information disputed by a consumer is found to be inaccurate or incomplete or cannot be verified after any reinvestigation under paragraph

(1), for purposes of reporting to a consumer reporting agency only, as appropriate, based on the results of the reinvestigation promptly-

(i) modify that item of information;

(ii) delete that item of information; or

(iii) permanently block the reporting of that item of information.

(2) Deadline

A person shall complete all investigations, reviews, and reports required under paragraph (1) regarding information provided by the person to a consumer reporting agency, before the expiration of the period under section 1681i(a)(1) of this title within which the consumer reporting agency is required to complete actions required by that section regarding that information.

(c) Limitation on liability

Except as provided in section 1681s(c)(1)(B) of this title, sections 1681n and 1681o of this title do not apply to any violation of-

(1) subsection (a) of this section, including any regulations issued thereunder;

(2) subsection (e) of this section, except that nothing in this paragraph shall limit, expand, or otherwise affect liability under section 1681n or 1681o of this title, as applicable, for violations of subsection (b) of this section; or

(3) subsection (e) of section 1681m of this title.

(d) Limitation on enforcement

The provisions of law described in paragraphs (1) through (3) of subsection (c) (other than with respect to the exception described in paragraph (2) of subsection (c)) shall be enforced exclusively as provided under section 1681s of this title by the Federal agencies and officials and the State officials identified in section 1681s of this title.

(e) Accuracy guidelines and regulations required

(1) Guidelines

The Bureau shall, with respect to persons or entities that are subject to the enforcement authority of the Bureau under section 1681s of this title-

(A) establish and maintain guidelines for use by each person that furnishes information to a consumer reporting agency regarding the accuracy and integrity of the information relating to consumers that such entities furnish to consumer reporting agencies, and update such guidelines as often as necessary; and

(B) prescribe regulations requiring each person that furnishes information to a consumer reporting agency to establish reasonable policies and procedures for implementing the guidelines established pursuant to subparagraph (A).

(2) Criteria

In developing the guidelines required by paragraph (1)(A), the Bureau shall-

(A) identify patterns, practices, and specific forms of activity that can compromise the accuracy and integrity of information furnished to consumer reporting agencies;

(B) review the methods (including technological means) used to furnish information relating to consumers to consumer reporting agencies;

(C) determine whether persons that furnish information to consumer reporting agencies maintain and enforce policies to ensure the accuracy and integrity of information furnished to consumer reporting agencies; and

(D) examine the policies and processes that persons that furnish information to consumer reporting agencies employ to conduct reinvestigations and correct inaccurate information relating to consumers that has been furnished to consumer reporting agencies.

§ 1681s-3. Affiliate sharing

(a) Special rule for solicitation for purposes of marketing

(1) Notice

Any person that receives from another person related to it by common ownership or affiliated by corporate control a communication of information that would be a consumer report, but for clauses (i), (ii), and (iii) of section 1681a(d)(2)(A) of this title, may not use the information to make a solicitation for marketing purposes to a consumer about its products or services, unless-

(A) it is clearly and conspicuously disclosed to the consumer that the information may be communicated among such persons for purposes of making such solicitations to the consumer; and

(B) the consumer is provided an opportunity and a simple method to prohibit the making of such solicitations to the consumer by such person.

(2) Consumer choice

(A) In general

The notice required under paragraph (1) shall allow the consumer the opportunity to prohibit all solicitations referred to in such paragraph, and may allow the consumer to choose from different options when electing to prohibit the sending of such solicitations, including options regarding the types of entities and information covered, and which methods of delivering solicitations the consumer elects to prohibit.

(B) Format

Notwithstanding subparagraph (A), the notice required under paragraph (1) shall be clear, conspicuous, and concise, and any method provided under paragraph (1)(B) shall be simple. The regulations prescribed to implement this section shall provide specific guidance regarding how to comply with such standards.

(3) Duration

(A) In general

The election of a consumer pursuant to paragraph (1)(B) to prohibit the making of solicitations shall be effective for at least 5 years, beginning on the date on which the person receives the election of the consumer, unless the consumer requests that such election be revoked.

(B) Notice upon expiration of effective period

At such time as the election of a consumer pursuant to paragraph (1)(B) is no longer effective, a person may not use information that the person receives in the manner described in paragraph (1) to make any solicitation for marketing purposes to the consumer, unless the consumer receives a notice and an opportunity, using a simple method, to extend the opt-out for another period of at least 5 years, pursuant to the procedures described in paragraph (1).

(4) Scope

This section shall not apply to a person-

(A) using information to make a solicitation for marketing purposes to a consumer with whom the person has a pre-existing business relationship;

(B) using information to facilitate communications to an individual for whose benefit the person provides employee benefit or other services pursuant to a contract with an employer related to and arising out of the current employment relationship or status of the individual as a participant or beneficiary of an employee benefit plan;

(C) using information to perform services on behalf of another person related by common ownership or affiliated by corporate control, except that this subparagraph shall not be construed as permitting a person to send solicitations on behalf of another person, if such other person would not be permitted to send the solicitation on its own behalf as a result of the election of the consumer to prohibit solicitations under paragraph (1)(B);

(D) using information in response to a communication initiated by the consumer;

(E) using information in response to solicitations authorized or requested by the consumer; or

(F) if compliance with this section by that person would prevent compliance by that person with any provision of State insurance laws pertaining to unfair discrimination in any State in which the person is lawfully doing business.

(5) No retroactivity

This subsection shall not prohibit the use of information to send a solicitation to a consumer if such information was received prior to the date on which persons are required to comply with regulations implementing this subsection.

(b) Notice for other purposes permissible

A notice or other disclosure under this section may be coordinated and consolidated with any other notice required to be issued under any other provision of law by a person that is subject to this section, and a notice or other disclosure that is equivalent to the notice required by subsection (a), and that is provided by a person described in subsection (a) to a consumer together with disclosures required by any other provision of law, shall satisfy the requirements of subsection (a).

(c) User requirements

Requirements with respect to the use by a person of information received from another person related to it by common ownership or affiliated by corporate control, such as the requirements of this section, constitute requirements with respect to the exchange of information among persons affiliated by common ownership or common corporate control, within the meaning of section 1681t(b)(2) of this title.

(d) Definitions

For purposes of this section, the following definitions shall apply:

(1) Pre-existing business relationship

The term "pre-existing business relationship" means a relationship between a person, or a person's licensed agent, and a consumer, based on-

(A) a financial contract between a person and a consumer which is in force;

(B) the purchase, rental, or lease by the consumer of that person's goods or services, or a financial transaction (including holding an active account or a policy in force or having another continuing relationship) between the consumer and that person during the 18-month period immediately preceding the date on which the consumer is sent a solicitation covered by this section;

(C) an inquiry or application by the consumer regarding a product or service offered by that person, during the 3-month period immediately preceding the date on which the consumer is sent a solicitation covered by this section; or

(D) any other pre-existing customer relationship defined in the regulations implementing this section.

(2) Solicitation

The term "solicitation" means the marketing of a product or service initiated by a person to a particular consumer that is based on an exchange of information described in subsection (a), and is intended to encourage the consumer to purchase such product or service, but does not include communications that are directed at the general public or determined not to be a solicitation by the regulations prescribed under this section.

§ 1681t. Relation to State laws

(a) In general

Except as provided in subsections (b) and (c), this subchapter does not annul, alter, affect, or exempt any person subject to the provisions of this subchapter from complying with the laws of any State with respect to the collection, distribution, or use of any information on consumers, or for the prevention or mitigation of identity theft, except to the extent that those laws are inconsistent with any provision of this subchapter, and then only to the extent of the inconsistency.

(b) General exceptions

No requirement or prohibition may be imposed under the laws of any State--

(1) with respect to any subject matter regulated under--

(A) subsection (c) or (e) of section 1681b of this title, relating to the prescreening of consumer reports;

(B) section 1681i of this title, relating to the time by which a consumer reporting agency must take any action, including the provision of notification to a consumer or other person, in any procedure related to the disputed accuracy of information in a consumer's file, except that this subparagraph shall not apply to any State law in effect on September 30, 1996;

(C) subsections (a) and (b) of section 1681m of this title, relating to the duties of a person who takes any adverse action with respect to a consumer;

(D) section 1681m(d) of this title, relating to the duties of persons who use a consumer report of a consumer in connection with any credit or insurance transaction that is not initiated by the consumer and that consists of a firm offer of credit or insurance;

(E) section 1681c of this title, relating to information contained in consumer reports, except that this subparagraph shall not apply to any State law in effect on September 30, 1996;

(F) section 1681s-2 of this title, relating to the responsibilities of persons who furnish information to consumer reporting agencies, except that this paragraph shall not apply--

(i) with respect to section 54A(a) of chapter 93 of the Massachusetts Annotated Laws (as in effect on September 30, 1996); or

(ii) with respect to section 1785.25(a) of the California Civil Code (as in effect on September 30, 1996);

(G) section 1681g(e) of this title, relating to information available to victims under section 1681g(e) of this title;

(H) section 1681s-3 of this title, relating to the exchange and use of information to make a solicitation for marketing purposes;

(I) section 1681m(h) of this title, relating to the duties of users of consumer reports to provide notice with respect to terms in certain credit transactions;

(J) subsections (i) and (j) of section 1681c-1 of this title relating to security freezes; or

(K) subsection (k) of section 1681c-1 of this title, relating to credit monitoring for active duty military consumers, as defined in that subsection;

(2) with respect to the exchange of information among persons affiliated by common ownership or common corporate control, except that this paragraph shall not apply with respect to subsection (a) or (c)(1) of section 2480e of title 9, Vermont Statutes Annotated (as in effect on September 30, 1996);

(3) with respect to the disclosures required to be made under subsection (c), (d), (e), or (g) of section 1681g of this title, or subsection (f) of section 1681g of this title relating to the disclosure of credit scores for credit granting purposes, except that this paragraph--

(A) shall not apply with respect to sections 1785.10, 1785.16, and 1785.20.2 of the California Civil Code (as in effect on December 4, 2003) and section 1785.15 through section 1785.15.2 of such Code (as in effect on such date);

(B) shall not apply with respect to sections 5-3-106(2) and 212-14.3-104.3 of the Colorado Revised Statutes (as in effect on December 4, 2003); and

(C) shall not be construed as limiting, annulling, affecting, or superseding any provision of the laws of any State regulating the use in an insurance activity, or regulating disclosures concerning such use, of a credit-based insurance score of a consumer by any person engaged in the business of insurance;

(4) with respect to the frequency of any disclosure under section 1681j(a) of this title, except that this paragraph shall not apply--

(A) with respect to section 12-14.3-105(1)(d) of the Colorado Revised Statutes (as in effect on December 4, 2003);

(B) with respect to section 10-1-393(29)(C) of the Georgia Code (as in effect on December 4, 2003);

(C) with respect to section 1316.2 of title 10 of the Maine Revised Statutes (as in effect on December 4, 2003);

(D) with respect to sections 14-1209(a)(1) and 14-1209(b)(1)(i) of the Commercial Law Article of the Code of Maryland (as in effect on December 4, 2003);

(E) with respect to section 59(d) and section 59(e) of chapter 93 of the General Laws of Massachusetts (as in effect on December 4, 2003);

(F) with respect to section 56:11-37.10(a)(1) of the New Jersey Revised Statutes (as in effect on December 4, 2003); or

(G) with respect to section 2480c(a)(1) of title 9 of the Vermont Statutes Annotated (as in effect on December 4, 2003); or

(5) with respect to the conduct required by the specific provisions of--

(A) section 1681c(g) of this title;

(B) section 1681c-1 of this title;

(C) section 1681c-2 of this title;

(D) section 1681g(a)(1)(A) of this title;

(E) section 1681j(a) of this title;

(F) subsections (e), (f), and (g) of section 1681m of this title;

(G) section 1681s(f) of this title;

(H) section 1681s-2(a)(6) of this title; or

(I) section 1681w of this title.

(c) "Firm offer of credit or insurance" defined

Notwithstanding any definition of the term "firm offer of credit or insurance" (or any equivalent term) under the laws of any State, the definition of that term contained in section 1681a(l) of this title shall be construed to apply in the enforcement and interpretation of the laws of any State governing consumer reports.

(d) Limitations

Subsections (b) and (c) do not affect any settlement, agreement, or consent judgment between any State Attorney General and any consumer reporting agency in effect on September 30, 1996.

§ 1681u. Disclosures to FBI for counterintelligence purposes

(a) Identity of financial institutions

Notwithstanding section 1681b of this title or any other provision of this subchapter, a consumer reporting agency shall furnish to the Federal Bureau of Investigation the names and addresses of all financial institutions (as that term is defined in section 3401 of title 12) at which a consumer maintains or has maintained an account, to the extent that information is in the files of the agency, when presented with a written request for that information that includes a term that specifically identifies a consumer or account to be used as the basis for the production of that information, signed by the Director of the Federal Bureau of Investigation, or the Director's designee in a position not lower than Deputy Assistant Director at Bureau headquarters or a Special Agent in Charge of a Bureau field office designated by the Director, which certifies compliance with this section. The Director or the Director's designee may make such a certification only if the Director or the Director's designee has determined in writing, that such information is sought for the conduct of an authorized investigation to protect against international terrorism or clandestine intelligence activities, provided that such an investigation of a United States person is not conducted solely upon the basis of activities protected by the first amendment to the Constitution of the United States.

(b) Identifying information

Notwithstanding the provisions of section 1681b of this title or any other provision of this subchapter, a consumer reporting agency shall furnish identifying information respecting a consumer, limited to name, address, former addresses, places of employment, or former places of employment, to the Federal Bureau of Investigation when presented with a written request that includes a term that specifically identifies a consumer or account to be used as the basis for the production of that information, signed by the Director or the Director's designee in a position not lower than Deputy Assistant Director at Bureau headquarters or a Special Agent in Charge of a Bureau field office designated by the Director, which certifies compliance with this subsection. The Director or the Director's designee may make such a certification only if the Director or the Director's designee has determined in writing that such information is sought for the conduct of an authorized investigation to protect against international terrorism or clandestine intelligence activities, provided that such an investigation of a United States person is not conducted solely upon the basis of activities protected by the first amendment to the Constitution of the United States.

(c) Court order for disclosure of consumer reports

Notwithstanding section 1681b of this title or any other provision of this subchapter, if requested in writing by the Director of the Federal Bureau of Investigation, or a designee of the Director in a position not lower than Deputy Assistant Director at Bureau headquarters or a Special Agent in Charge in a Bureau field office designated by the Director, a court may issue an order ex parte, which shall include a term that specifically identifies a consumer or account to be used as the basis for the production of the information, directing a consumer reporting agency to furnish a consumer report to the Federal Bureau of Investigation, upon a showing in camera that the consumer report is sought for the conduct of an authorized investigation to protect against international terrorism or clandestine intelligence activities, provided that such an investigation of a United States person is not conducted solely upon the basis of activities protected by the first amendment to the Constitution of the United States. The terms of an order issued under this subsection shall not disclose that the order is issued for purposes of a counterintelligence investigation.

(d) Prohibition of certain disclosure

    (1) Prohibition

        (A) In general

        If a certification is issued under subparagraph (B) and notice of the right to judicial review under subsection (e) is provided, no consumer reporting agency that receives a request under subsection (a) or (b) or an order under subsection (c), or officer, employee, or agent thereof, shall disclose or specify in any consumer report, that the Federal Bureau of Investigation has sought or obtained access to information or records under subsection (a), (b), or (c).

        (B) Certification

        The requirements of subparagraph (A) shall apply if the Director of the Federal Bureau of Investigation, or a designee of the Director whose rank shall be no lower than Deputy Assistant Director at Bureau headquarters or a Special Agent in Charge of a Bureau field office, certifies that the absence of a prohibition of disclosure under this subsection may result in-

            (i) a danger to the national security of the United States;

            (ii) interference with a criminal, counterterrorism, or counterintelligence investigation;

            (iii) interference with diplomatic relations; or

(iv) danger to the life or physical safety of any person.

(2) Exception

(A) In general

A consumer reporting agency that receives a request under subsection (a) or (b) or an order under subsection (c), or officer, employee, or agent thereof, may disclose information otherwise subject to any applicable nondisclosure requirement to-

(i) those persons to whom disclosure is necessary in order to comply with the request;

(ii) an attorney in order to obtain legal advice or assistance regarding the request; or

(iii) other persons as permitted by the Director of the Federal Bureau of Investigation or the designee of the Director.

(B) Application

A person to whom disclosure is made under subparagraph (A) shall be subject to the nondisclosure requirements applicable to a person to whom a request under subsection (a) or (b) or an order under subsection (c) is issued in the same manner as the person to whom the request is issued.

(C) Notice

Any recipient that discloses to a person described in subparagraph (A) information otherwise subject to a nondisclosure requirement shall inform the person of the applicable nondisclosure requirement.

(D) Identification of disclosure recipients

At the request of the Director of the Federal Bureau of Investigation or the designee of the Director, any person making or intending to make a disclosure under clause (i) or (iii) of subparagraph (A) shall identify to the Director or such designee the person to whom such disclosure will be made or to whom such disclosure was made prior to the request.

(e) Judicial review

(1) In general

A request under subsection (a) or (b) or an order under subsection (c) or a non-disclosure requirement imposed in connection with such request under subsection (d) shall be subject to judicial review under section 3511 of title 18.

(2) Notice

A request under subsection (a) or (b) or an order under subsection (c) shall include notice of the availability of judicial review described in paragraph (1).

(f) Payment of fees

The Federal Bureau of Investigation shall, subject to the availability of appropriations, pay to the consumer reporting agency assembling or providing report or information in accordance with procedures established under this section a fee for reimbursement for

such costs as are reasonably necessary and which have been directly incurred in searching, reproducing, or transporting books, papers, records, or other data required or requested to be produced under this section.

(g) Limit on dissemination

The Federal Bureau of Investigation may not disseminate information obtained pursuant to this section outside of the Federal Bureau of Investigation, except to other Federal agencies as may be necessary for the approval or conduct of a foreign counterintelligence investigation, or, where the information concerns a person subject to the Uniform Code of Military Justice, to appropriate investigative authorities within the military department concerned as may be necessary for the conduct of a joint foreign counterintelligence investigation.

(h) Rules of construction

Nothing in this section shall be construed to prohibit information from being furnished by the Federal Bureau of Investigation pursuant to a subpoena or court order, in connection with a judicial or administrative proceeding to enforce the provisions of this subchapter. Nothing in this section shall be construed to authorize or permit the withholding of information from the Congress.

(i) Reports to Congress

(1) On a semiannual basis, the Attorney General shall fully inform the Permanent Select Committee on Intelligence and the Committee on Banking, Finance and Urban Affairs of the House of Representatives, and the Select Committee on Intelligence and the Committee on Banking, Housing, and Urban Affairs of the Senate concerning all requests made pursuant to subsections (a), (b), and (c).

(2) In the case of the semiannual reports required to be submitted under paragraph (1) to the Permanent Select Committee on Intelligence of the House of Representatives and the Select Committee on Intelligence of the Senate, the submittal dates for such reports shall be as provided in section 3106 of title 50.

(j) Damages

Any agency or department of the United States obtaining or disclosing any consumer reports, records, or information contained therein in violation of this section is liable to the consumer to whom such consumer reports, records, or information relate in an amount equal to the sum of-

(1) $100, without regard to the volume of consumer reports, records, or information involved;

(2) any actual damages sustained by the consumer as a result of the disclosure;

(3) if the violation is found to have been willful or intentional, such punitive damages as a court may allow; and

(4) in the case of any successful action to enforce liability under this subsection, the costs of the action, together with reasonable attorney fees, as determined by the court.

(k) Disciplinary actions for violations

If a court determines that any agency or department of the United States has violated any provision of this section and the court finds that the circumstances surrounding the violation raise questions of whether or not an officer or employee of the agency or department acted willfully or intentionally with respect to the violation, the agency or department shall promptly initiate a proceeding to determine whether or not disciplinary action is warranted against the officer or employee who was responsible for the violation.

(l) Good-faith exception

Notwithstanding any other provision of this subchapter, any consumer reporting agency or agent or employee thereof making disclosure of consumer reports or identifying information pursuant to this subsection in good-faith reliance upon a certification of the Federal Bureau of Investigation pursuant to provisions of this section shall not be liable to any person for such disclosure under this subchapter, the constitution of any State, or any law or regulation of any State or any political subdivision of any State.

(m) Limitation of remedies

Notwithstanding any other provision of this subchapter, the remedies and sanctions set forth in this section shall be the only judicial remedies and sanctions for violation of this section.

(n) Injunctive relief

In addition to any other remedy contained in this section, injunctive relief shall be available to require compliance with the procedures of this section. In the event of any successful action under this subsection, costs together with reasonable attorney fees, as determined by the court, may be recovered.

§ 1681v. Disclosures to governmental agencies for counterterrorism purposes

(a) Disclosure

Notwithstanding section 1681b of this title or any other provision of this subchapter, a consumer reporting agency shall furnish a consumer report of a consumer and all other information in a consumer's file to a government agency authorized to conduct investigations of, or intelligence or counterintelligence activities or analysis related to, international terrorism when presented with a written certification by such government agency that such information is necessary for the agency's conduct or such investigation, activity or analysis and that includes a term that specifically identifies a consumer or account to be used as the basis for the production of such information.

(b) Form of certification

The certification described in subsection (a) shall be signed by a supervisory official designated by the head of a Federal agency or an officer of a Federal agency whose appointment to office is required to be made by the President, by and with the advice and consent of the Senate.

(c) Prohibition of certain disclosure

United States
Fair Credit Reporting Act

(1) Prohibition

(A) In general

If a certification is issued under subparagraph (B) and notice of the right to judicial review under subsection (d) is provided, no consumer reporting agency that receives a request under subsection (a), or officer, employee, or agent thereof, shall disclose or specify in any consumer report, that a government agency described in subsection (a) has sought or obtained access to information or records under subsection (a).

(B) Certification

The requirements of subparagraph (A) shall apply if the head of the government agency described in subsection (a), or a designee, certifies that the absence of a prohibition of disclosure under this subsection may result in-

(i) a danger to the national security of the United States;

(ii) interference with a criminal, counterterrorism, or counterintelligence investigation;

(iii) interference with diplomatic relations; or

(iv) danger to the life or physical safety of any person.

(2) Exception

(A) In general

A consumer reporting agency that receives a request under subsection (a), or officer, employee, or agent thereof, may disclose information otherwise subject to any applicable nondisclosure requirement to-

(i) those persons to whom disclosure is necessary in order to comply with the request;

(ii) an attorney in order to obtain legal advice or assistance regarding the request; or

(iii) other persons as permitted by the head of the government agency described in subsection (a) or a designee.

(B) Application

A person to whom disclosure is made under subparagraph (A) shall be subject to the nondisclosure requirements applicable to a person to whom a request under subsection (a) is issued in the same manner as the person to whom the request is issued.

(C) Notice

Any recipient that discloses to a person described in subparagraph (A) information otherwise subject to a nondisclosure requirement shall inform the person of the applicable nondisclosure requirement.

(D) Identification of disclosure recipients

At the request of the head of the government agency described in subsection (a) or a designee, any person making or intending to make a disclosure under clause

(i) or (iii) of subparagraph (A) shall identify to the head or such designee the person to whom such disclosure will be made or to whom such disclosure was made prior to the request.

(d) Judicial review

(1) In general

A request under subsection (a) or a non-disclosure requirement imposed in connection with such request under subsection (c) shall be subject to judicial review under section 3511 of title 18.

(2) Notice

A request under subsection (a) shall include notice of the availability of judicial review described in paragraph (1).

(e) Rule of construction

Nothing in section 1681u of this title shall be construed to limit the authority of the Director of the Federal Bureau of Investigation under this section.

(f) Safe harbor

Notwithstanding any other provision of this subchapter, any consumer reporting agency or agent or employee thereof making disclosure of consumer reports or other information pursuant to this section in good-faith reliance upon a certification of a government agency pursuant to the provisions of this section shall not be liable to any person for such disclosure under this subchapter, the constitution of any State, or any law or regulation of any State or any political subdivision of any State.

(g) Reports to Congress

(1) On a semi-annual basis, the Attorney General shall fully inform the Committee on the Judiciary, the Committee on Financial Services, and the Permanent Select Committee on Intelligence of the House of Representatives and the Committee on the Judiciary, the Committee on Banking, Housing, and Urban Affairs, and the Select Committee on Intelligence of the Senate concerning all requests made pursuant to subsection (a).

(2) In the case of the semiannual reports required to be submitted under paragraph (1) to the Permanent Select Committee on Intelligence of the House of Representatives and the Select Committee on Intelligence of the Senate, the submittal dates for such reports shall be as provided in section 3106 of title 50.

§ 1681w. Disposal of records

(a) Regulations

(1) In general

The Federal Trade Commission, the Securities and Exchange Commission, the Commodity Futures Trading Commission, the Federal banking agencies, and the National Credit Union Administration, with respect to the entities that are subject to their respective enforcement authority under section 1681s of this title, and in coordination as described in paragraph (2), shall issue final regulations requiring any person that maintains or otherwise possesses consumer information, or any compilation of consumer information, derived from consumer reports for a business purpose to properly dispose of any such information or compilation.

(2) Coordination

Each agency required to prescribe regulations under paragraph (1) shall-

(A) consult and coordinate with each other such agency so that, to the extent possible, the regulations prescribed by each such agency are consistent and comparable with the regulations by each such other agency; and

(B) ensure that such regulations are consistent with the requirements and regulations issued pursuant to Public Law 106–102 and other provisions of Federal law.

(3) Exemption authority

In issuing regulations under this section, the agencies identified in paragraph (1) may exempt any person or class of persons from application of those regulations, as such agency deems appropriate to carry out the purpose of this section.

(b) Rule of construction

Nothing in this section shall be construed-

(1) to require a person to maintain or destroy any record pertaining to a consumer that is not imposed under other law; or

(2) to alter or affect any requirement imposed under any other provision of law to maintain or destroy such a record.

§ 1681x. Corporate and technological circumvention prohibited

The Commission shall prescribe regulations, to become effective not later than 90 days after December 4, 2003, to prevent a consumer reporting agency from circumventing or evading treatment as a consumer reporting agency described in section 1681a(p) of this title for purposes of this subchapter, including-

(1) by means of a corporate reorganization or restructuring, including a merger, acquisition, dissolution, divestiture, or asset sale of a consumer reporting agency; or

(2) by maintaining or merging public record and credit account information in a manner that is substantially equivalent to that described in paragraphs (1) and (2) of section 1681a(p) of this title, in the manner described in section 1681a(p) of this title.

PRIVACY ACT (1974)

Summary

In enacting the Privacy Act of 1974, Congress's stated purpose was to promote governmental respect for citizens' privacy by requiring federal agencies to observe certain guidelines in the use and disclosure of citizens' personal information. The Act was to promote accountability and legislative oversight with respect to the use of computer databases and other information systems in managing personal data files. The Act was also meant to strengthen review within agencies of criteria for the collection and retention of personal data.

The Act implements a set of privacy principles known as 'Fair Information Practices.' The Code of Fair Information Practices was first articulated by the Department of Health, Education and Welfare Special Advisory Commission in its 1973 report on "Records, Computers and the Rights of Citizens." It includes five core principles: that there should be no secret record keeping systems; that information collected for one purpose should not be used for another purpose without the consent of the individual; that individuals should be given access to information held about them and the opportunity to correct or amend that information; that information is kept relevant, accurate, and up to date; and that information is protected against unauthorized loss, alteration or disclosure.

Accordingly, the Act requires each Federal agency to publish a description of each system of records maintained by that agency. It requires that surrender of personal information is made with informed consent or with some guarantees of the uses and confidentiality of the information. It grants individuals the right of access including the right to review, copy and amend the record. It requires that information is maintained with "accuracy, relevance, timeliness and completeness." Finally, it requires agencies to protect against any security breaches which could result in "substantial harm, embarrassment, inconvenience, or unfairness to any individual on whom information is maintained." To aid in the enforcement of these legislative restraints, the Act provides administrative and judicial machinery for oversight and for civil remedy of violations. The Act also provides a private cause of action to individuals denied access to their information.

As originally drafted, the Privacy Act would have created a Federal Privacy Board to act as an oversight and enforcement mechanism. The final Act, however, created a far more limited body, the Privacy Protection Study Commission which issued a report in 1977 examining the problems with both private and public sector record keeping systems and making numerous recommendations for change. The Commission was dissolved following the release of its report. In 2016, the Act was amended to permit non-US citizens to bring suit in limited circumstances, against a subset of federal agencies, where the Attorney General has determined that the individual is from a country that (1) shares information with the United States for law enforcement purposes, (2) permits the transfer of personal information to the United States for commercial use, and (3) such policies do not impede the national security interests of the United States. The Attorney General may also subsequently revoke the designation.

United States
Privacy Act

References

Public Law 93-579. Codified as amended at 5 U.S.C. § 552a.
[https://www.law.cornell.edu/uscode/text/5/552a]

Senate Report No. 93-1183, September 26, 1974

U.S. Department of Health, Education & Welfare, Report of the Secretary's Advisory Committee on Automated Personal Data Systems, *Records Computers and the Rights of Citizens* (MIT 1973)
[https://www.epic.org/privacy/hew1973report/]

Privacy Protection Study Commission, *Personal Privacy in an Information Society* (GPO 1977)
[https://www.epic.org/privacy/ppsc1977report/]

EPIC, Privacy Act of 1974
[https://www.epic.org/privacy/1974act/]

Congressional findings and statement of purpose

(a) The Congress finds that--

(1) the privacy of an individual is directly affected by the collection, maintenance, use, and dissemination of personal information by Federal agencies;

(2) the increasing use of computers and sophisticated information technology, while essential to the efficient operations of the Government, has greatly magnified the harm to individual privacy that can occur from any collection, maintenance, use, or dissemination of personal information;

(3) the opportunities for an individual to secure employment, insurance, and credit, and his right to due process, and other legal protections are endangered by the misuse of certain information systems;

(4) the right to privacy is a personal and fundamental right protected by the Constitution of the United States; and

(5) in order to protect the privacy of individuals identified in information systems maintained by Federal agencies, it is necessary and proper for the Congress to regulate the collection, maintenance, use, and dissemination of information by such agencies.

(b) The purpose of this Act is to provide certain safeguards for an individual against an invasion of personal privacy by requiring Federal agencies, except as otherwise provided by law, to--

(1) permit an individual to determine what records pertaining to him are collected, maintained, used, or disseminated by such agencies;

(2) permit an individual to prevent records pertaining to him obtained by such agencies for a particular purpose from being used or made available for another purpose without his consent;

(3) permit an individual to gain access to information pertaining to him in Federal agency records, to have a copy made of all or any portion thereof, and to correct or amend such records;

(4) collect, maintain, use, or disseminate any record of identifiable personal information in a manner that assures that such action is for a necessary and lawful purpose, that the information is current and accurate for its intended use, and that adequate safeguards are provided to prevent misuse of such information;

(5) permit exemptions from the requirements with respect to records provided in this Act only in those cases where there is an important public policy need for such exemption as has been determined by specific statutory authority; and

(6) be subject to civil suit for any damages which occur as a result of willful or intentional action which violates any individual's rights under this Act.

5 U.S.C. § 552a Public information; agency rules, opinions, orders, records, and proceedings

(a) Definitions.-For purposes of this section-

(1) the term "agency" means agency as defined in section 552(e) of this title;

(2) the term "individual" means a citizen of the United States or an alien lawfully admitted for permanent residence;

(3) the term "maintain" includes maintain, collect, use, or disseminate;

(4) the term "record" means any item, collection, or grouping of information about an individual that is maintained by an agency, including, but not limited to, his education, financial transactions, medical history, and criminal or employment history and that contains his name, or the identifying number, symbol, or other identifying particular assigned to the individual, such as a finger or voice print or a photograph;

(5) the term "system of records" means a group of any records under the control of any agency from which information is retrieved by the name of the individual or by some identifying number, symbol, or other identifying particular assigned to the individual;

(6) the term "statistical record" means a record in a system of records maintained for statistical research or reporting purposes only and not used in whole or in part in making any determination about an identifiable individual, except as provided by section 8 of title 13;

(7) the term "routine use" means, with respect to the disclosure of a record, the use of such record for a purpose which is compatible with the purpose for which it was collected;

(8) the term "matching program"-

(A) means any computerized comparison of-

(i) two or more automated systems of records or a system of records with non-Federal records for the purpose of-

(I) establishing or verifying the eligibility of, or continuing compliance with statutory and regulatory requirements by, applicants for, recipients or beneficiaries of, participants in, or providers of services with respect to, cash or in-kind assistance or payments under Federal benefit programs, or

(II) recouping payments or delinquent debts under such Federal benefit programs, or

(ii) two or more automated Federal personnel or payroll systems of records or a system of Federal personnel or payroll records with non-Federal records,

(B) but does not include-

(i) matches performed to produce aggregate statistical data without any personal identifiers;

(ii) matches performed to support any research or statistical project, the specific data of which may not be used to make decisions concerning the rights, benefits, or privileges of specific individuals;

(iii) matches performed, by an agency (or component thereof) which performs as its principal function any activity pertaining to the enforcement of criminal laws, subsequent to the initiation of a specific criminal or civil law enforcement investigation of a named person or persons for the purpose of gathering evidence against such person or persons;

(iv) matches of tax information (I) pursuant to section 6103(d) of the Internal Revenue Code of 1986, (II) for purposes of tax administration as defined in section 6103(b)(4) of such Code, (III) for the purpose of intercepting a tax refund due an individual under authority granted by section 404(e), 464, or 1137 of the Social Security Act; or (IV) for the purpose of intercepting a tax refund due an individual under any other tax refund intercept program authorized by statute which has been determined by the Director of the Office of Management and Budget to contain verification, notice, and hearing requirements that are substantially similar to the procedures in section 1137 of the Social Security Act;

(v) matches-

(I) using records predominantly relating to Federal personnel, that are performed for routine administrative purposes (subject to guidance provided by the Director of the Office of Management and Budget pursuant to subsection (v)); or

(II) conducted by an agency using only records from systems of records maintained by that agency;

if the purpose of the match is not to take any adverse financial, personnel, disciplinary, or other adverse action against Federal personnel;

(vi) matches performed for foreign counterintelligence purposes or to produce background checks for security clearances of Federal personnel or Federal contractor personnel;

(vii) matches performed incident to a levy described in section 6103(k)(8) of the Internal Revenue Code of 1986;

(viii) matches performed pursuant to section 202(x)(3) or 1611(e)(1) of the Social Security Act (42 U.S.C. 402(x)(3), 1382(e)(1));

(ix) matches performed by the Secretary of Health and Human Services or the Inspector General of the Department of Health and Human Services with respect to potential fraud, waste, and abuse, including matches of a system of records with non-Federal records; or

(x) matches performed pursuant to section 3(d)(4) of the Achieving a Better Life Experience Act of 2014;

(9) the term "recipient agency" means any agency, or contractor thereof, receiving records contained in a system of records from a source agency for use in a matching program;

(10) the term "non-Federal agency" means any State or local government, or agency thereof, which receives records contained in a system of records from a source agency for use in a matching program;

(11) the term "source agency" means any agency which discloses records contained in a system of records to be used in a matching program, or any State or local government, or agency thereof, which discloses records to be used in a matching program;

(12) the term "Federal benefit program" means any program administered or funded by the Federal Government, or by any agent or State on behalf of the Federal Government, providing cash or in-kind assistance in the form of payments, grants, loans, or loan guarantees to individuals; and

(13) the term "Federal personnel" means officers and employees of the Government of the United States, members of the uniformed services (including members of the Reserve Components), individuals entitled to receive immediate or deferred retirement benefits under any retirement program of the Government of the United States (including survivor benefits).

(b) Conditions of Disclosure.-No agency shall disclose any record which is contained in a system of records by any means of communication to any person, or to another agency, except pursuant to a written request by, or with the prior written consent of, the individual to whom the record pertains, unless disclosure of the record would be-

> (1) to those officers and employees of the agency which maintains the record who have a need for the record in the performance of their duties;
>
> (2) required under section 552 of this title;
>
> (3) for a routine use as defined in subsection (a)(7) of this section and described under subsection (e)(4)(D) of this section;
>
> (4) to the Bureau of the Census for purposes of planning or carrying out a census or survey or related activity pursuant to the provisions of title 13;
>
> (5) to a recipient who has provided the agency with advance adequate written assurance that the record will be used solely as a statistical research or reporting record, and the record is to be transferred in a form that is not individually identifiable;
>
> (6) to the National Archives and Records Administration as a record which has sufficient historical or other value to warrant its continued preservation by the United States Government, or for evaluation by the Archivist of the United States or the designee of the Archivist to determine whether the record has such value;
>
> (7) to another agency or to an instrumentality of any governmental jurisdiction within or under the control of the United States for a civil or criminal law enforcement activity if the activity is authorized by law, and if the head of the agency or instrumentality has made a written request to the agency which maintains the record specifying the particular portion desired and the law enforcement activity for which the record is sought;
>
> (8) to a person pursuant to a showing of compelling circumstances affecting the health or safety of an individual if upon such disclosure notification is transmitted to the last known address of such individual;
>
> (9) to either House of Congress, or, to the extent of matter within its jurisdiction, any committee or subcommittee thereof, any joint committee of Congress or subcommittee of any such joint committee;
>
> (10) to the Comptroller General, or any of his authorized representatives, in the course of the performance of the duties of the Government Accountability Office;
>
> (11) pursuant to the order of a court of competent jurisdiction; or
>
> (12) to a consumer reporting agency in accordance with section 3711(e) of title 31.

(c) Accounting of Certain Disclosures.-Each agency, with respect to each system of records under its control, shall-

> (1) except for disclosures made under subsections (b)(1) or (b)(2) of this section, keep an accurate accounting of-

(A) the date, nature, and purpose of each disclosure of a record to any person or to another agency made under subsection (b) of this section; and

(B) the name and address of the person or agency to whom the disclosure is made;

(2) retain the accounting made under paragraph (1) of this subsection for at least five years or the life of the record, whichever is longer, after the disclosure for which the accounting is made;

(3) except for disclosures made under subsection (b)(7) of this section, make the accounting made under paragraph (1) of this subsection available to the individual named in the record at his request; and

(4) inform any person or other agency about any correction or notation of dispute made by the agency in accordance with subsection (d) of this section of any record that has been disclosed to the person or agency if an accounting of the disclosure was made.

(d) Access to Records.-Each agency that maintains a system of records shall-

(1) upon request by any individual to gain access to his record or to any information pertaining to him which is contained in the system, permit him and upon his request, a person of his own choosing to accompany him, to review the record and have a copy made of all or any portion thereof in a form comprehensible to him, except that the agency may require the individual to furnish a written statement authorizing discussion of that individual's record in the accompanying person's presence;

(2) permit the individual to request amendment of a record pertaining to him and-

(A) not later than 10 days (excluding Saturdays, Sundays, and legal public holidays) after the date of receipt of such request, acknowledge in writing such receipt; and

(B) promptly, either-

(i) make any correction of any portion thereof which the individual believes is not accurate, relevant, timely, or complete; or

(ii) inform the individual of its refusal to amend the record in accordance with his request, the reason for the refusal, the procedures established by the agency for the individual to request a review of that refusal by the head of the agency or an officer designated by the head of the agency, and the name and business address of that official;

(3) permit the individual who disagrees with the refusal of the agency to amend his record to request a review of such refusal, and not later than 30 days (excluding Saturdays, Sundays, and legal public holidays) from the date on which the individual requests such review, complete such review and make a final determination unless, for good cause shown, the head of the agency extends such 30-day period; and if, after his review, the reviewing official also refuses to amend the record in

accordance with the request, permit the individual to file with the agency a concise statement setting forth the reasons for his disagreement with the refusal of the agency, and notify the individual of the provisions for judicial review of the reviewing official's determination under subsection (g)(1)(A) of this section;

(4) in any disclosure, containing information about which the individual has filed a statement of disagreement, occurring after the filing of the statement under paragraph (3) of this subsection, clearly note any portion of the record which is disputed and provide copies of the statement and, if the agency deems it appropriate, copies of a concise statement of the reasons of the agency for not making the amendments requested, to persons or other agencies to whom the disputed record has been disclosed; and

(5) nothing in this section shall allow an individual access to any information compiled in reasonable anticipation of a civil action or proceeding.

(e) Agency Requirements.-Each agency that maintains a system of records shall-

(1) maintain in its records only such information about an individual as is relevant and necessary to accomplish a purpose of the agency required to be accomplished by statute or by executive order of the President;

(2) collect information to the greatest extent practicable directly from the subject individual when the information may result in adverse determinations about an individual's rights, benefits, and privileges under Federal programs;

(3) inform each individual whom it asks to supply information, on the form which it uses to collect the information or on a separate form that can be retained by the individual-

(A) the authority (whether granted by statute, or by executive order of the President) which authorizes the solicitation of the information and whether disclosure of such information is mandatory or voluntary;

(B) the principal purpose or purposes for which the information is intended to be used;

(C) the routine uses which may be made of the information, as published pursuant to paragraph (4)(D) of this subsection; and

(D) the effects on him, if any, of not providing all or any part of the requested information;

(4) subject to the provisions of paragraph (11) of this subsection, publish in the Federal Register upon establishment or revision a notice of the existence and character of the system of records, which notice shall include-

(A) the name and location of the system;

(B) the categories of individuals on whom records are maintained in the system;

(C) the categories of records maintained in the system;

(D) each routine use of the records contained in the system, including the categories of users and the purpose of such use;

(E) the policies and practices of the agency regarding storage, retrievability, access controls, retention, and disposal of the records;

(F) the title and business address of the agency official who is responsible for the system of records;

(G) the agency procedures whereby an individual can be notified at his request if the system of records contains a record pertaining to him;

(H) the agency procedures whereby an individual can be notified at his request how he can gain access to any record pertaining to him contained in the system of records, and how he can contest its content; and

(I) the categories of sources of records in the system;

(5) maintain all records which are used by the agency in making any determination about any individual with such accuracy, relevance, timeliness, and completeness as is reasonably necessary to assure fairness to the individual in the determination;

(6) prior to disseminating any record about an individual to any person other than an agency, unless the dissemination is made pursuant to subsection (b)(2) of this section, make reasonable efforts to assure that such records are accurate, complete, timely, and relevant for agency purposes;

(7) maintain no record describing how any individual exercises rights guaranteed by the First Amendment unless expressly authorized by statute or by the individual about whom the record is maintained or unless pertinent to and within the scope of an authorized law enforcement activity;

(8) make reasonable efforts to serve notice on an individual when any record on such individual is made available to any person under compulsory legal process when such process becomes a matter of public record;

(9) establish rules of conduct for persons involved in the design, development, operation, or maintenance of any system of records, or in maintaining any record, and instruct each such person with respect to such rules and the requirements of this section, including any other rules and procedures adopted pursuant to this section and the penalties for noncompliance;

(10) establish appropriate administrative, technical, and physical safeguards to insure the security and confidentiality of records and to protect against any anticipated threats or hazards to their security or integrity which could result in substantial harm, embarrassment, inconvenience, or unfairness to any individual on whom information is maintained;

(11) at least 30 days prior to publication of information under paragraph (4)(D) of this subsection, publish in the Federal Register notice of any new use or intended use of the information in the system, and provide an opportunity for interested persons to submit written data, views, or arguments to the agency; and

(12) if such agency is a recipient agency or a source agency in a matching program with a non-Federal agency, with respect to any establishment or revision of a matching program, at least 30 days prior to conducting such program, publish in the Federal Register notice of such establishment or revision.

(f) Agency Rules.-In order to carry out the provisions of this section, each agency that maintains a system of records shall promulgate rules, in accordance with the requirements (including general notice) of section 553 of this title, which shall-

(1) establish procedures whereby an individual can be notified in response to his request if any system of records named by the individual contains a record pertaining to him;

(2) define reasonable times, places, and requirements for identifying an individual who requests his record or information pertaining to him before the agency shall make the record or information available to the individual;

(3) establish procedures for the disclosure to an individual upon his request of his record or information pertaining to him, including special procedure, if deemed necessary, for the disclosure to an individual of medical records, including psychological records, pertaining to him;

(4) establish procedures for reviewing a request from an individual concerning the amendment of any record or information pertaining to the individual, for making a determination on the request, for an appeal within the agency of an initial adverse agency determination, and for whatever additional means may be necessary for each individual to be able to exercise fully his rights under this section; and

(5) establish fees to be charged, if any, to any individual for making copies of his record, excluding the cost of any search for and review of the record.

The Office of the Federal Register shall biennially compile and publish the rules promulgated under this subsection and agency notices published under subsection (e)(4) of this section in a form available to the public at low cost.

(g)(1) Civil Remedies.-Whenever any agency

(A) makes a determination under subsection (d)(3) of this section not to amend an individual's record in accordance with his request, or fails to make such review in conformity with that subsection;

(B) refuses to comply with an individual request under subsection (d)(1) of this section;

(C) fails to maintain any record concerning any individual with such accuracy, relevance, timeliness, and completeness as is necessary to assure fairness in any determination relating to the qualifications, character, rights, or opportunities of, or benefits to the individual that may be made on the basis of such record, and consequently a determination is made which is adverse to the individual; or

(D) fails to comply with any other provision of this section, or any rule promulgated thereunder, in such a way as to have an adverse effect on an individual, the individual may bring a civil action against the agency, and the district courts of the United States shall have jurisdiction in the matters under the provisions of this subsection.

(2)(A) In any suit brought under the provisions of subsection (g)(1)(A) of this section, the court may order the agency to amend the individual's record in accordance with his request or in such other way as the court may direct. In such a case the court shall determine the matter de novo.

(B) The court may assess against the United States reasonable attorney fees and other litigation costs reasonably incurred in any case under this paragraph in which the complainant has substantially prevailed.

(3)(A) In any suit brought under the provisions of subsection (g)(1)(B) of this section, the court may enjoin the agency from withholding the records and order the production to the complainant of any agency records improperly withheld from him. In such a case the court shall determine the matter de novo, and may examine the contents of any agency records in camera to determine whether the records or any portion thereof may be withheld under any of the exemptions set forth in subsection (k) of this section, and the burden is on the agency to sustain its action.

(B) The court may assess against the United States reasonable attorney fees and other litigation costs reasonably incurred in any case under this paragraph in which the complainant has substantially prevailed.

(4) In any suit brought under the provisions of subsection (g)(1)(C) or (D) of this section in which the court determines that the agency acted in a manner which was intentional or willful, the United States shall be liable to the individual in an amount equal to the sum of-

(A) actual damages sustained by the individual as a result of the refusal or failure, but in no case shall a person entitled to recovery receive less than the sum of $1,000; and

(B) the costs of the action together with reasonable attorney fees as determined by the court.

(5) An action to enforce any liability created under this section may be brought in the district court of the United States in the district in which the complainant resides, or has his principal place of business, or in which the agency records are situated, or in the District of Columbia, without regard to the amount in controversy, within two years from the date on which the cause of action arises, except that where an agency has materially and willfully misrepresented any information required under this section to be disclosed to an individual and the information so misrepresented is material to establishment of the liability of the agency to the individual under this

section, the action may be brought at any time within two years after discovery by the individual of the misrepresentation. Nothing in this section shall be construed to authorize any civil action by reason of any injury sustained as the result of a disclosure of a record prior to September 27, 1975.

(h) Rights of Legal Guardians.-For the purposes of this section, the parent of any minor, or the legal guardian of any individual who has been declared to be incompetent due to physical or mental incapacity or age by a court of competent jurisdiction, may act on behalf of the individual.

(i)(1) Criminal Penalties.-Any officer or employee of an agency, who by virtue of his employment or official position, has possession of, or access to, agency records which contain individually identifiable information the disclosure of which is prohibited by this section or by rules or regulations established thereunder, and who knowing that disclosure of the specific material is so prohibited, willfully discloses the material in any manner to any person or agency not entitled to receive it, shall be guilty of a misdemeanor and fined not more than $5,000.

(2) Any officer or employee of any agency who willfully maintains a system of records without meeting the notice requirements of subsection (e)(4) of this section shall be guilty of a misdemeanor and fined not more than $5,000.

(3) Any person who knowingly and willfully requests or obtains any record concerning an individual from an agency under false pretenses shall be guilty of a misdemeanor and fined not more than $5,000.

(j) General Exemptions.-The head of any agency may promulgate rules, in accordance with the requirements (including general notice) of sections 553(b)(1), (2), and (3), (c), and (e) of this title, to exempt any system of records within the agency from any part of this section except subsections (b), (c)(1) and (2), (e)(4)(A) through (F), (e)(6), (7), (9), (10), and (11), and (i) if the system of records is-
(1) maintained by the Central Intelligence Agency; or
(2) maintained by an agency or component thereof which performs as its principal function any activity pertaining to the enforcement of criminal laws, including police efforts to prevent, control, or reduce crime or to apprehend criminals, and the activities of prosecutors, courts, correctional, probation, pardon, or parole authorities, and which consists of (A) information compiled for the purpose of identifying individual criminal offenders and alleged offenders and consisting only of identifying data and notations of arrests, the nature and disposition of criminal charges, sentencing, confinement, release, and parole and probation status; (B) information compiled for the purpose of a criminal investigation, including reports of informants and investigators, and associated with an identifiable individual; or (C) reports identifiable to an individual compiled at any stage

of the process of enforcement of the criminal laws from arrest or indictment through release from supervision.

At the time rules are adopted under this subsection, the agency shall include in the statement required under section 553(c) of this title, the reasons why the system of records is to be exempted from a provision of this section.

(k) Specific Exemptions.-The head of any agency may promulgate rules, in accordance with the requirements (including general notice) of sections 553(b)(1), (2), and (3), (c), and (e) of this title, to exempt any system of records within the agency from subsections (c)(3), (d), (e)(1), (e)(4)(G), (H), and (I) and (f) of this section if the system of records is-

(1) subject to the provisions of section 552(b)(1) of this title;

(2) investigatory material compiled for law enforcement purposes, other than material within the scope of subsection (j)(2) of this section: Provided, however, That if any individual is denied any right, privilege, or benefit that he would otherwise be entitled by Federal law, or for which he would otherwise be eligible, as a result of the maintenance of such material, such material shall be provided to such individual, except to the extent that the disclosure of such material would reveal the identity of a source who furnished information to the Government under an express promise that the identity of the source would be held in confidence, or, prior to the effective date of this section, under an implied promise that the identity of the source would be held in confidence;

(3) maintained in connection with providing protective services to the President of the United States or other individuals pursuant to section 3056 of title 18;

(4) required by statute to be maintained and used solely as statistical records;

(5) investigatory material compiled solely for the purpose of determining suitability, eligibility, or qualifications for Federal civilian employment, military service, Federal contracts, or access to classified information, but only to the extent that the disclosure of such material would reveal the identity of a source who furnished information to the Government under an express promise that the identity of the source would be held in confidence, or, prior to the effective date of this section, under an implied promise that the identity of the source would be held in confidence;

(6) testing or examination material used solely to determine individual qualifications for appointment or promotion in the Federal service the disclosure of which would compromise the objectivity or fairness of the testing or examination process; or

(7) evaluation material used to determine potential for promotion in the armed services, but only to the extent that the disclosure of such material would reveal the identity of a source who furnished information to the Government under an express promise that the identity of the source would be held in confidence, or, prior to the

effective date of this section, under an implied promise that the identity of the source would be held in confidence.

At the time rules are adopted under this subsection, the agency shall include in the statement required under section 553(c) of this title, the reasons why the system of records is to be exempted from a provision of this section.

(l)(1) Archival Records.-Each agency record which is accepted by the Archivist of the United States for storage, processing, and servicing in accordance with section 3103 of title 44 shall, for the purposes of this section, be considered to be maintained by the agency which deposited the record and shall be subject to the provisions of this section. The Archivist of the United States shall not disclose the record except to the agency which maintains the record, or under rules established by that agency which are not inconsistent with the provisions of this section.

(2) Each agency record pertaining to an identifiable individual which was transferred to the National Archives of the United States as a record which has sufficient historical or other value to warrant its continued preservation by the United States Government, prior to the effective date of this section, shall, for the purposes of this section, be considered to be maintained by the National Archives and shall not be subject to the provisions of this section, except that a statement generally describing such records (modeled after the requirements relating to records subject to subsections (e)(4)(A) through (G) of this section) shall be published in the Federal Register.

(3) Each agency record pertaining to an identifiable individual which is transferred to the National Archives of the United States as a record which has sufficient historical or other value to warrant its continued preservation by the United States Government, on or after the effective date of this section, shall, for the purposes of this section, be considered to be maintained by the National Archives and shall be exempt from the requirements of this section except subsections (e)(4)(A) through (G) and (e)(9) of this section.

(m)(1) Government Contractors.-When an agency provides by a contract for the operation by or on behalf of the agency of a system of records to accomplish an agency function, the agency shall, consistent with its authority, cause the requirements of this section to be applied to such system. For purposes of subsection (i) of this section any such contractor and any employee of such contractor, if such contract is agreed to on or after the effective date of this section, shall be considered to be an employee of an agency.

(2) A consumer reporting agency to which a record is disclosed under section 3711(e) of title 31 shall not be considered a contractor for the purposes of this section.

(n) Mailing Lists.-An individual's name and address may not be sold or rented by an agency unless such action is specifically authorized by law. This provision shall not be construed to require the withholding of names and addresses otherwise permitted to be made public.

(o) Matching Agreements.-(1) No record which is contained in a system of records may be disclosed to a recipient agency or non-Federal agency for use in a computer matching program except pursuant to a written agreement between the source agency and the recipient agency or non-Federal agency specifying-
    (A) the purpose and legal authority for conducting the program;
    (B) the justification for the program and the anticipated results, including a specific estimate of any savings;
    (C) a description of the records that will be matched, including each data element that will be used, the approximate number of records that will be matched, and the projected starting and completion dates of the matching program;
    (D) procedures for providing individualized notice at the time of application, and notice periodically thereafter as directed by the Data Integrity Board of such agency (subject to guidance provided by the Director of the Office of Management and Budget pursuant to subsection (v)), to-
        (i) applicants for and recipients of financial assistance or payments under Federal benefit programs, and
        (ii) applicants for and holders of positions as Federal personnel, that any information provided by such applicants, recipients, holders, and individuals may be subject to verification through matching programs;
    (E) procedures for verifying information produced in such matching program as required by subsection (p);
    (F) procedures for the retention and timely destruction of identifiable records created by a recipient agency or non-Federal agency in such matching program;
    (G) procedures for ensuring the administrative, technical, and physical security of the records matched and the results of such programs;
    (H) prohibitions on duplication and redisclosure of records provided by the source agency within or outside the recipient agency or the non-Federal agency, except where required by law or essential to the conduct of the matching program;
    (I) procedures governing the use by a recipient agency or non-Federal agency of records provided in a matching program by a source agency, including procedures governing return of the records to the source agency or destruction of records used in such program;
    (J) information on assessments that have been made on the accuracy of the records that will be used in such matching program; and

(K) that the Comptroller General may have access to all records of a recipient agency or a non-Federal agency that the Comptroller General deems necessary in order to monitor or verify compliance with the agreement.

(2)(A) A copy of each agreement entered into pursuant to paragraph (1) shall-

(i) be transmitted to the Committee on Governmental Affairs of the Senate and the Committee on Government Operations of the House of Representatives; and

(ii) be available upon request to the public.

(B) No such agreement shall be effective until 30 days after the date on which such a copy is transmitted pursuant to subparagraph (A)(i).

(C) Such an agreement shall remain in effect only for such period, not to exceed 18 months, as the Data Integrity Board of the agency determines is appropriate in light of the purposes, and length of time necessary for the conduct, of the matching program.

(D) Within 3 months prior to the expiration of such an agreement pursuant to subparagraph (C), the Data Integrity Board of the agency may, without additional review, renew the matching agreement for a current, ongoing matching program for not more than one additional year if-

(i) such program will be conducted without any change; and

(ii) each party to the agreement certifies to the Board in writing that the program has been conducted in compliance with the agreement.

(p) Verification and Opportunity to Contest Findings.-(1) In order to protect any individual whose records are used in a matching program, no recipient agency, non-Federal agency, or source agency may suspend, terminate, reduce, or make a final denial of any financial assistance or payment under a Federal benefit program to such individual, or take other adverse action against such individual, as a result of information produced by such matching program, until-

(A)(i) the agency has independently verified the information; or

(ii) the Data Integrity Board of the agency, or in the case of a non-Federal agency the Data Integrity Board of the source agency, determines in accordance with guidance issued by the Director of the Office of Management and Budget that-

(I) the information is limited to identification and amount of benefits paid by the source agency under a Federal benefit program; and

(II) there is a high degree of confidence that the information provided to the recipient agency is accurate;

(B) the individual receives a notice from the agency containing a statement of its findings and informing the individual of the opportunity to contest such findings; and

(C)(i) the expiration of any time period established for the program by statute or regulation for the individual to respond to that notice; or

(ii) in the case of a program for which no such period is established, the end of the 30-day period beginning on the date on which notice under subparagraph (B) is mailed or otherwise provided to the individual.

(2) Independent verification referred to in paragraph (1) requires investigation and confirmation of specific information relating to an individual that is used as a basis for an adverse action against the individual, including where applicable investigation and confirmation of-

(A) the amount of any asset or income involved;

(B) whether such individual actually has or had access to such asset or income for such individual's own use; and

(C) the period or periods when the individual actually had such asset or income.

(3) Notwithstanding paragraph (1), an agency may take any appropriate action otherwise prohibited by such paragraph if the agency determines that the public health or public safety may be adversely affected or significantly threatened during any notice period required by such paragraph.

(q) Sanctions.-(1) Notwithstanding any other provision of law, no source agency may disclose any record which is contained in a system of records to a recipient agency or non-Federal agency for a matching program if such source agency has reason to believe that the requirements of subsection (p), or any matching agreement entered into pursuant to subsection (o), or both, are not being met by such recipient agency.

(2) No source agency may renew a matching agreement unless-

(A) the recipient agency or non-Federal agency has certified that it has complied with the provisions of that agreement; and

(B) the source agency has no reason to believe that the certification is inaccurate.

(r) Report on New Systems and Matching Programs.-Each agency that proposes to establish or make a significant change in a system of records or a matching program shall provide adequate advance notice of any such proposal (in duplicate) to the Committee on Government Operations of the House of Representatives, the Committee on Governmental Affairs of the Senate, and the Office of Management and Budget in order to permit an evaluation of the probable or potential effect of such proposal on the privacy or other rights of individuals.

(s) Biennial Report.-The President shall biennially submit to the Speaker of the House of Representatives and the President pro tempore of the Senate a report-

(1) describing the actions of the Director of the Office of Management and Budget pursuant to section 6 of the Privacy Act of 1974 during the preceding 2 years;

(2) describing the exercise of individual rights of access and amendment under this section during such years;

(3) identifying changes in or additions to systems of records;

(4) containing such other information concerning administration of this section as may be necessary or useful to the Congress in reviewing the effectiveness of this section in carrying out the purposes of the Privacy Act of 1974.

(t)(1) Effect of Other Laws.-No agency shall rely on any exemption contained in section 552 of this title to withhold from an individual any record which is otherwise accessible to such individual under the provisions of this section.

(2) No agency shall rely on any exemption in this section to withhold from an individual any record which is otherwise accessible to such individual under the provisions of section 552 of this title.

(u) Data Integrity Boards.-(1) Every agency conducting or participating in a matching program shall establish a Data Integrity Board to oversee and coordinate among the various components of such agency the agency's implementation of this section.

(2) Each Data Integrity Board shall consist of senior officials designated by the head of the agency, and shall include any senior official designated by the head of the agency as responsible for implementation of this section, and the inspector general of the agency, if any. The inspector general shall not serve as chairman of the Data Integrity Board.

(3) Each Data Integrity Board-

(A) shall review, approve, and maintain all written agreements for receipt or disclosure of agency records for matching programs to ensure compliance with subsection (o), and all relevant statutes, regulations, and guidelines;

(B) shall review all matching programs in which the agency has participated during the year, either as a source agency or recipient agency, determine compliance with applicable laws, regulations, guidelines, and agency agreements, and assess the costs and benefits of such programs;

(C) shall review all recurring matching programs in which the agency has participated during the year, either as a source agency or recipient agency, for continued justification for such disclosures;

(D) shall compile an annual report, which shall be submitted to the head of the agency and the Office of Management and Budget and made available to the public on request, describing the matching activities of the agency, including-

(i) matching programs in which the agency has participated as a source agency or recipient agency;

(ii) matching agreements proposed under subsection (o) that were disapproved by the Board;

(iii) any changes in membership or structure of the Board in the preceding year;

(iv) the reasons for any waiver of the requirement in paragraph (4) of this section for completion and submission of a cost-benefit analysis prior to the approval of a matching program;

(v) any violations of matching agreements that have been alleged or identified and any corrective action taken; and

(vi) any other information required by the Director of the Office of Management and Budget to be included in such report;

(E) shall serve as a clearinghouse for receiving and providing information on the accuracy, completeness, and reliability of records used in matching programs;

(F) shall provide interpretation and guidance to agency components and personnel on the requirements of this section for matching programs;

(G) shall review agency recordkeeping and disposal policies and practices for matching programs to assure compliance with this section; and

(H) may review and report on any agency matching activities that are not matching programs.

(4)(A) Except as provided in subparagraphs (B) and (C), a Data Integrity Board shall not approve any written agreement for a matching program unless the agency has completed and submitted to such Board a cost-benefit analysis of the proposed program and such analysis demonstrates that the program is likely to be cost effective.2

(B) The Board may waive the requirements of subparagraph (A) of this paragraph if it determines in writing, in accordance with guidelines prescribed by the Director of the Office of Management and Budget, that a cost-benefit analysis is not required.

(C) A cost-benefit analysis shall not be required under subparagraph (A) prior to the initial approval of a written agreement for a matching program that is specifically required by statute. Any subsequent written agreement for such a program shall not be approved by the Data Integrity Board unless the agency has submitted a cost-benefit analysis of the program as conducted under the preceding approval of such agreement.

(5)(A) If a matching agreement is disapproved by a Data Integrity Board, any party to such agreement may appeal the disapproval to the Director of the Office of Management and Budget. Timely notice of the filing of such an appeal shall be provided by the Director of the Office of Management and Budget to the Committee on Governmental Affairs of the Senate and the Committee on Government Operations of the House of Representatives.

(B) The Director of the Office of Management and Budget may approve a matching agreement notwithstanding the disapproval of a Data Integrity Board if the Director determines that-

(i) the matching program will be consistent with all applicable legal, regulatory, and policy requirements;

(ii) there is adequate evidence that the matching agreement will be cost-effective; and

(iii) the matching program is in the public interest.

(C) The decision of the Director to approve a matching agreement shall not take effect until 30 days after it is reported to committees described in subparagraph (A).

(D) If the Data Integrity Board and the Director of the Office of Management and Budget disapprove a matching program proposed by the inspector general of an agency, the inspector general may report the disapproval to the head of the agency and to the Congress.

(6) In the reports required by paragraph (3)(D), agency matching activities that are not matching programs may be reported on an aggregate basis, if and to the extent necessary to protect ongoing law enforcement or counterintelligence investigations.

(v) Office of Management and Budget Responsibilities.-The Director of the Office of Management and Budget shall-

(1) develop and, after notice and opportunity for public comment, prescribe guidelines and regulations for the use of agencies in implementing the provisions of this section; and

(2) provide continuing assistance to and oversight of the implementation of this section by agencies.

(w) Applicability to Bureau of Consumer Financial Protection.-Except as provided in the Consumer Financial Protection Act of 2010, this section shall apply with respect to the Bureau of Consumer Financial Protection.

Pub. L. 114–126, Feb. 24, 2016, 130 Stat. 282 , provided that:

SECTION 1. SHORT TITLE.

This Act may be cited as the 'Judicial Redress Act of 2015'.

SEC. 2. EXTENSION OF PRIVACY ACT REMEDIES TO CITIZENS OF DESIGNATED COUNTRIES.

(a) Civil Action; Civil Remedies.-With respect to covered records, a covered person may bring a civil action against an agency and obtain civil remedies, in the same manner, to the same extent, and subject to the same limitations, including exemptions and exceptions, as an individual may bring and obtain with respect to records under-

(1) section 552a(g)(1)(D) of title 5, United States Code, but only with respect to disclosures intentionally or willfully made in violation of section 552a(b) of such title; and

(2) subparagraphs (A) and (B) of section 552a(g)(1) of title 5, United States Code, but such an action may only be brought against a designated Federal agency or component.

(b) Exclusive Remedies.-The remedies set forth in subsection (a) are the exclusive remedies available to a covered person under this section.

(c) Application of the Privacy Act With Respect to a Covered Person.-For purposes of a civil action described in subsection (a), a covered person shall have the same rights, and be subject to the same limitations, including exemptions and exceptions, as an individual has and is subject to under section 552a of title 5, United States Code, when pursuing the civil remedies described in paragraphs (1) and (2) of subsection (a).

(d) Designation of Covered Country.-

(1) In general.-The Attorney General may, with the concurrence of the Secretary of State, the Secretary of the Treasury, and the Secretary of Homeland Security, designate a foreign country or regional economic integration organization, or member country of such organization, as a 'covered country' for purposes of this section if-

(A)(i) the country or regional economic integration organization, or member country of such organization, has entered into an agreement with the United States that provides for appropriate privacy protections for information shared for the purpose of preventing, investigating, detecting, or prosecuting criminal offenses; or

(ii) the Attorney General has determined that the country or regional economic integration organization, or member country of such organization, has effectively shared information with the United States for the purpose of preventing, investigating, detecting, or prosecuting criminal offenses and has appropriate privacy protections for such shared information;

(B) the country or regional economic integration organization, or member country of such organization, permits the transfer of personal data for commercial purposes between the territory of that country or regional economic organization and the territory of the United States, through an agreement with the United States or otherwise; and

(C) the Attorney General has certified that the policies regarding the transfer of personal data for commercial purposes and related actions of the country or regional economic integration organization, or member country of such organization, do not materially impede the national security interests of the United States.

(2) Removal of designation.-The Attorney General may, with the concurrence of the Secretary of State, the Secretary of the Treasury, and the Secretary of Homeland Security, revoke the designation of a foreign country or regional economic integration organization, or member country of such organization, as a 'covered country' if the Attorney General determines that such designated 'covered country'-

(A) is not complying with the agreement described under paragraph (1)(A)(i);

(B) no longer meets the requirements for designation under paragraph (1)(A)(ii);

(C) fails to meet the requirements under paragraph (1)(B);

(D) no longer meets the requirements for certification under paragraph (1)(C); or

(E) impedes the transfer of information (for purposes of reporting or preventing unlawful activity) to the United States by a private entity or person.

(e) Designation of Designated Federal Agency or Component.-

(1) In general.-The Attorney General shall determine whether an agency or component thereof is a 'designated Federal agency or component' for purposes of this section. The Attorney General shall not designate any agency or component thereof other than the Department of Justice or a component of the Department of Justice without the concurrence of the head of the relevant agency, or of the agency to which the component belongs.

(2) Requirements for designation.-The Attorney General may determine that an agency or component of an agency is a 'designated Federal agency or component' for purposes of this section, if-

(A) the Attorney General determines that information exchanged by such agency with a covered country is within the scope of an agreement referred to in subsection (d)(1)(A); or

(B) with respect to a country or regional economic integration organization, or member country of such organization, that has been designated as a 'covered country' under subsection (d)(1)(B), the Attorney General determines that designating such agency or component thereof is in the law enforcement interests of the United States.

(f) Federal Register Requirement; Nonreviewable Determination.-The Attorney General shall publish each determination made under subsections (d) and (e). Such determination shall not be subject to judicial or administrative review.

(g) Jurisdiction.-The United States District Court for the District of Columbia shall have exclusive jurisdiction over any claim arising under this section.

(h) Definitions.-In this Act:

(1) Agency.-The term 'agency' has the meaning given that term in section 552(f) of title 5, United States Code.

(2) Covered country.-The term 'covered country' means a country or regional economic integration organization, or member country of such organization, designated in accordance with subsection (d).

(3) Covered person.-The term 'covered person' means a natural person (other than an individual) who is a citizen of a covered country.

(4) Covered record.-The term 'covered record' has the same meaning for a covered person as a record has for an individual under section 552a of title 5, United States Code, once the covered record is transferred-

(A) by a public authority of, or private entity within, a country or regional economic organization, or member country of such organization, which at the time the record is transferred is a covered country; and

(B) to a designated Federal agency or component for purposes of preventing, investigating, detecting, or prosecuting criminal offenses.

(5) Designated federal agency or component.-The term 'designated Federal agency or component' means a Federal agency or component of an agency designated in accordance with subsection (e).

(6) Individual.-The term 'individual' has the meaning given that term in section 552a(a)(2) of title 5, United States Code.

(i) Preservation of Privileges.-Nothing in this section shall be construed to waive any applicable privilege or require the disclosure of classified information. Upon an agency's request, the district court shall review in camera and ex parte any submission by the agency in connection with this subsection.

(j) Effective Date.-This Act shall take effect 90 days after the date of the enactment of this Act [Feb. 24, 2016]."

FAMILY EDUCATIONAL RIGHTS AND PRIVACY ACT (1974)

Summary

The Family Educational Rights and Privacy Act (FERPA) protects the confidentiality of student educational records. It states that educational institutions shall not disclose any information from those records without the written consent of the student, or, if the student is a minor, without the written consent of his or her parents. Under the Act, students have the right to inspect and review their own educational records, request corrections, stop the release of personally identifiable information, and obtain a copy of the institutional policy concerning access to educational records. The Act applies to primary, secondary, and post-secondary educational institutions.

Federal funding will be denied to any institution that discloses information without the student's prior written consent, or without his or her parent's consent if the student is under eighteen years of age. There are exceptions to allow certain personnel within the institution to see the records and to allow certain information to be disclosed to the public and to the parents. There are also certain exceptions allowing disclosure to aid in development, validation, and administration of standardized tests, to administer student aid programs, and to improve instruction. However, such information may be released only when it protects the personal identification of students. Written consent is needed for any disclosure of personally identifiable information.

Individuals who have grievances under the Act must petition the head of the educational institution for redress. If unsatisfied, they may petition the Secretary of Education, who is the only person authorized to limit federal funding for non-complying institutions.

In 2002, the Supreme Court decided two cases involving FERPA claims. In Owasso Independent School District, the Court held that the practice of "peer grading" did not violate the FERPA because the student papers in question had not yet been collected by the teacher and thus were not "maintained" by the school under § 1232(a)(4)(A). Furthermore, the Court concluded that a student grader is not a "person acting for" an educational institution under § 1232g(a)(4)(A). In Gonzaga University v. Doe, the Court reversed an award for damages, holding that the FERPA created no new private cause of action enforceable under 42 U.S.C. § 1983. Under Gonzaga, the FERPA is enforced through administrative review procedures under the Secretary of Education.

References

Public Law 90-247. Codified as amended at 20 U.S.C. § 1232g.
[https://www.law.cornell.edu/uscode/text/20/1232g]

Owasso Independent School District v. Falvo, 534 U.S. 426 (2002)
[http://supct.law.cornell.edu/supct/html/00-1073.ZO.html]

Gonzaga Univ. v. Doe, 122 S. Ct. 2268 (2002)
[http://supct.law.cornell.edu/supct/html/01-679.ZS.html]

EPIC, EPIC Student Privacy Project
[http://www.epic.org/privacy/student/]

20 U.S.C. § 1232g. Family educational and privacy rights

a) Conditions for availability of funds to educational agencies or institutions; inspection and review of education records; specific information to be made available; procedure for access to education records; reasonableness of time for such access; hearings; written explanations by parents; definitions

(1)(A) No funds shall be made available under any applicable program to any educational agency or institution which has a policy of denying, or which effectively prevents, the parents of students who are or have been in attendance at a school of such agency or at such institution, as the case may be, the right to inspect and review the education records of their children. If any material or document in the education record of a student includes information on more than one student, the parents of one of such students shall have the right to inspect and review only such part of such material or document as relates to such student or to be informed of the specific information contained in such part of such material. Each educational agency or institution shall establish appropriate procedures for the granting of a request by parents for access to the education records of their children within a reasonable period of time, but in no case more than forty-five days after the request has been made.

(B) No funds under any applicable program shall be made available to any State educational agency (whether or not that agency is an educational agency or institution under this section) that has a policy of denying, or effectively prevents, the parents of students the right to inspect and review the education records maintained by the State educational agency on their children who are or have been in attendance at any school of an educational agency or institution that is subject to the provisions of this section.

(C) The first sentence of subparagraph (A) shall not operate to make available to students in institutions of postsecondary education the following materials:

(i) financial records of the parents of the student or any information contained therein;

(ii) confidential letters and statements of recommendation, which were placed in the education records prior to January 1, 1975, if such letters or statements are not used for purposes other than those for which they were specifically intended;

(iii) if the student has signed a waiver of the student's right of access under this subsection in accordance with subparagraph (D), confidential recommendations-

(I) respecting admission to any educational agency or institution,

(II) respecting an application for employment, and

(III) respecting the receipt of an honor or honorary recognition.

(D) A student or a person applying for admission may waive his right of access to confidential statements described in clause (iii) of subparagraph (C), except that such waiver shall apply to recommendations only if (i) the student is, upon request, notified of the names of all persons making confidential recommendations and (ii) such recommendations are used solely for the purpose for which they were specifically intended. Such waivers may not be required as a condition for admission to, receipt of financial aid from, or receipt of any other services or benefits from such agency or institution.

(2) No funds shall be made available under any applicable program to any educational agency or institution unless the parents of students who are or have been in attendance at a school of such agency or at such institution are provided an opportunity for a hearing by such agency or institution, in accordance with regulations of the Secretary, to challenge the content of such student's education records, in order to insure that the records are not inaccurate, misleading, or otherwise in violation of the privacy rights of students, and to provide an opportunity for the correction or deletion of any such inaccurate, misleading or otherwise inappropriate data contained therein and to insert into such records a written explanation of the parents respecting the content of such records.

(3) For the purposes of this section the term "educational agency or institution" means any public or private agency or institution which is the recipient of funds under any applicable program.

(4)(A) For the purposes of this section, the term "education records" means, except as may be provided otherwise in subparagraph (B), those records, files, documents, and other materials which-

(i) contain information directly related to a student; and

(ii) are maintained by an educational agency or institution or by a person acting for such agency or institution.

(B) The term "education records" does not include-

(i) records of instructional, supervisory, and administrative personnel and educational personnel ancillary thereto which are in the sole possession of the maker thereof and which are not accessible or revealed to any other person except a substitute;

(ii) records maintained by a law enforcement unit of the educational agency or institution that were created by that law enforcement unit for the purpose of law enforcement;

(iii) in the case of persons who are employed by an educational agency or institution but who are not in attendance at such agency or institution, records made and maintained in the normal course of business which relate exclusively to such person in that person's capacity as an employee and are not available for use for any other purpose; or

(iv) records on a student who is eighteen years of age or older, or is attending an institution of postsecondary education, which are made or maintained by a physician, psychiatrist, psychologist, or other recognized professional or paraprofessional acting in his professional or paraprofessional capacity, or assisting in that capacity, and which are made, maintained, or used only in connection with the provision of treatment to the student, and are not available to anyone other than persons providing such treatment, except that such records can be personally reviewed by a physician or other appropriate professional of the student's choice.

(5)(A) For the purposes of this section the term "directory information" relating to a student includes the following: the student's name, address, telephone listing, date and place of birth, major field of study, participation in officially recognized activities and sports, weight and height of members of athletic teams, dates of attendance, degrees and awards received, and the most recent previous educational agency or institution attended by the student.

(B) Any educational agency or institution making public directory information shall give public notice of the categories of information which it has designated as such information with respect to each student attending the institution or agency and shall allow a reasonable period of time after such notice has been given for a parent to inform the institution or agency that any or all of the information designated should not be released without the parent's prior consent.

(6) For the purposes of this section, the term "student" includes any person with respect to whom an educational agency or institution maintains education records or personally identifiable information, but does not include a person who has not been in attendance at such agency or institution.

(b) Release of education records; parental consent requirement; exceptions; compliance with judicial orders and subpoenas; audit and evaluation of federally-supported education programs; recordkeeping

(1) No funds shall be made available under any applicable program to any educational agency or institution which has a policy or practice of permitting the release of education records (or personally identifiable information contained therein other than directory information, as defined in paragraph (5) of subsection (a)) of students without the written consent of their parents to any individual, agency, or organization, other than to the following-

(A) other school officials, including teachers within the educational institution or local educational agency, who have been determined by such agency or institution to have legitimate educational interests, including the educational interests of the child for whom consent would otherwise be required;

(B) officials of other schools or school systems in which the student seeks or intends to enroll, upon condition that the student's parents be notified of the transfer, receive a copy of the record if desired, and have an opportunity for a hearing to challenge the content of the record;

(C)(i) authorized representatives of (I) the Comptroller General of the United States, (II) the Secretary, or (III) State educational authorities, under the conditions set forth in paragraph (3), or (ii) authorized representatives of the Attorney General for law enforcement purposes under the same conditions as apply to the Secretary under paragraph (3);

(D) in connection with a student's application for, or receipt of, financial aid;

(E) State and local officials or authorities to whom such information is specifically allowed to be reported or disclosed pursuant to State statute adopted-

> (i) before November 19, 1974, if the allowed reporting or disclosure concerns the juvenile justice system and such system's ability to effectively serve the student whose records are released, or

> (ii) after November 19, 1974, if-

>> (I) the allowed reporting or disclosure concerns the juvenile justice system and such system's ability to effectively serve, prior to adjudication, the student whose records are released; and

>> (II) the officials and authorities to whom such information is disclosed certify in writing to the educational agency or institution that the information will not be disclosed to any other party except as provided under State law without the prior written consent of the parent of the student.

(F) organizations conducting studies for, or on behalf of, educational agencies or institutions for the purpose of developing, validating, or administering predictive tests, administering student aid programs, and improving instruction, if such studies are conducted in such a manner as will not permit the personal identification of students and their parents by persons other than representatives of such organizations and such information will be destroyed when no longer needed for the purpose for which it is conducted;

(G) accrediting organizations in order to carry out their accrediting functions;

(H) parents of a dependent student of such parents, as defined in section 152 of title 26;

(I) subject to regulations of the Secretary, in connection with an emergency, appropriate persons if the knowledge of such information is necessary to protect the health or safety of the student or other persons;

(J)(i) the entity or persons designated in a Federal grand jury subpoena, in which case the court shall order, for good cause shown, the educational agency or institution (and any officer, director, employee, agent, or attorney for such agency or institution) on which the subpoena is served, to not disclose to any person the existence or contents of the subpoena or any information furnished to the grand jury in response to the subpoena; and

(ii) the entity or persons designated in any other subpoena issued for a law enforcement purpose, in which case the court or other issuing agency may order, for good cause shown, the educational agency or institution (and any officer, director, employee, agent, or attorney for such agency or institution) on which the subpoena is served, to not disclose to any person the existence or contents of the subpoena or any information furnished in response to the subpoena;

(K) the Secretary of Agriculture, or authorized representative from the Food and Nutrition Service or contractors acting on behalf of the Food and Nutrition Service, for the purposes of conducting program monitoring, evaluations, and performance measurements of State and local educational and other agencies and institutions receiving funding or providing benefits of 1 or more programs authorized under the Richard B. Russell National School Lunch Act (42 U.S.C. 1751 et seq.) or the Child Nutrition Act of 1966 (42 U.S.C. 1771 et seq.) for which the results will be reported in an aggregate form that does not identify any individual, on the conditions that-

(i) any data collected under this subparagraph shall be protected in a manner that will not permit the personal identification of students and their parents by other than the authorized representatives of the Secretary; and

(ii) any personally identifiable data shall be destroyed when the data are no longer needed for program monitoring, evaluations, and performance measurements; and

(L) an agency caseworker or other representative of a State or local child welfare agency, or tribal organization (as defined in section 5304 of title 25), who has the right to access a student's case plan, as defined and determined by the State or tribal organization, when such agency or organization is legally responsible, in accordance with State or tribal law, for the care and protection of the student, provided that the education records, or the personally identifiable information contained in such records, of the student will not be disclosed by such agency or organization, except to an individual or entity engaged in addressing the student's education needs and authorized by such agency or organization to receive such disclosure and such disclosure is consistent with the State or tribal laws applicable to protecting the confidentiality of a student's education records.

Nothing in subparagraph (E) of this paragraph shall prevent a State from further limiting the number or type of State or local officials who will continue to have access thereunder.
(2) No funds shall be made available under any applicable program to any educational agency or institution which has a policy or practice of releasing, or providing access to, any personally identifiable information in education records other than directory information, or as is permitted under paragraph (1) of this subsection, unless-

(A) there is written consent from the student's parents specifying records to be released, the reasons for such release, and to whom, and with a copy of the records to be released to the student's parents and the student if desired by the parents, or

(B) except as provided in paragraph (1)(J), such information is furnished in compliance with judicial order, or pursuant to any lawfully issued subpoena, upon condition that parents and the students are notified of all such orders or subpoenas in advance of the compliance therewith by the educational institution or agency, except when a parent is a party to a court proceeding involving child abuse and neglect (as defined in section 3 of the Child Abuse Prevention and Treatment Act (42 U.S.C. 5101 note)) or dependency matters, and the order is issued in the context of that proceeding, additional notice to the parent by the educational agency or institution is not required.

(3) Nothing contained in this section shall preclude authorized representatives of (A) the Comptroller General of the United States, (B) the Secretary, or (C) State educational authorities from having access to student or other records which may be necessary in connection with the audit and evaluation of Federally-supported education programs, or in connection with the enforcement of the Federal legal requirements which relate to such programs: Provided, That except when collection of personally identifiable information is specifically authorized by Federal law, any data collected by such officials shall be protected in a manner which will not permit the personal identification of students and their parents by other than those officials, and such personally identifiable data shall be destroyed when no longer needed for such audit, evaluation, and enforcement of Federal legal requirements.

(4)(A) Each educational agency or institution shall maintain a record, kept with the education records of each student, which will indicate all individuals (other than those specified in paragraph (1)(A) of this subsection), agencies, or organizations which have requested or obtained access to a student's education records maintained by such educational agency or institution, and which will indicate specifically the legitimate interest that each such person, agency, or organization has in obtaining this information. Such record of access shall be available only to parents, to the school official and his assistants who are responsible for the custody of such records, and to persons or organizations authorized in, and under the conditions of, clauses (A) and (C) of paragraph (1) as a means of auditing the operation of the system.

(B) With respect to this subsection, personal information shall only be transferred to a third party on the condition that such party will not permit any other party to have access to such information without the written consent of the parents of the student. If a third party outside the educational agency or institution permits access to information in violation of paragraph (2)(A), or fails to destroy information in violation of paragraph (1)(F), the educational agency or institution shall be prohibited from permitting access to information from education records to that third party for a period of not less than five years.

(5) Nothing in this section shall be construed to prohibit State and local educational officials from having access to student or other records which may be necessary in connection with the audit and evaluation of any federally or State supported education program or in connection with the enforcement of the Federal legal requirements which relate to any such program, subject to the conditions specified in the proviso in paragraph (3).

(6)(A) Nothing in this section shall be construed to prohibit an institution of postsecondary education from disclosing, to an alleged victim of any crime of violence (as that term is defined in section 16 of title 18), or a nonforcible sex offense, the final results of any disciplinary proceeding conducted by such institution against the alleged perpetrator of such crime or offense with respect to such crime or offense.

(B) Nothing in this section shall be construed to prohibit an institution of postsecondary education from disclosing the final results of any disciplinary proceeding conducted by such institution against a student who is an alleged perpetrator of any crime of violence (as that term is defined in section 16 of title 18), or a nonforcible sex offense, if the institution determines as a result of that disciplinary proceeding that the student committed a violation of the institution's rules or policies with respect to such crime or offense.

(C) For the purpose of this paragraph, the final results of any disciplinary proceeding-

(i) shall include only the name of the student, the violation committed, and any sanction imposed by the institution on that student; and

(ii) may include the name of any other student, such as a victim or witness, only with the written consent of that other student.

(7)(A) Nothing in this section may be construed to prohibit an educational institution from disclosing information provided to the institution under section 14071 of title 42 concerning registered sex offenders who are required to register under such section.

(B) The Secretary shall take appropriate steps to notify educational institutions that disclosure of information described in subparagraph (A) is permitted.

(c) Surveys or data-gathering activities; regulations

Not later than 240 days after October 20, 1994, the Secretary shall adopt appropriate regulations or procedures, or identify existing regulations or procedures, which protect the rights of privacy of students and their families in connection with any surveys or data-gathering activities conducted, assisted, or authorized by the Secretary or an administrative head of an education agency. Regulations established under this subsection shall include provisions controlling the use, dissemination, and protection of such data. No survey or data-gathering activities shall be conducted by the Secretary, or an administrative head of an education agency under an applicable program, unless such activities are authorized by law.

(d) Students' rather than parents' permission or consent

For the purposes of this section, whenever a student has attained eighteen years of age, or is attending an institution of postsecondary education, the permission or consent required of and the rights accorded to the parents of the student shall thereafter only be required of and accorded to the student.

(e) Informing parents or students of rights under this section

No funds shall be made available under any applicable program to any educational agency or institution unless such agency or institution effectively informs the parents of students, or the students, if they are eighteen years of age or older, or are attending an institution of postsecondary education, of the rights accorded them by this section.

(f) Enforcement; termination of assistance

The Secretary shall take appropriate actions to enforce this section and to deal with violations of this section, in accordance with this chapter, except that action to terminate assistance may be taken only if the Secretary finds there has been a failure to comply with this section, and he has determined that compliance cannot be secured by voluntary means.

(g) Office and review board; creation; functions

The Secretary shall establish or designate an office and review board within the Department for the purpose of investigating, processing, reviewing, and adjudicating violations of this section and complaints which may be filed concerning alleged violations of this section. Except for the conduct of hearings, none of the functions of the Secretary under this section shall be carried out in any of the regional offices of such Department.

(h) Disciplinary records; disclosure

Nothing in this section shall prohibit an educational agency or institution from-
(1) including appropriate information in the education record of any student concerning disciplinary action taken against such student for conduct that posed a significant risk to the safety or well-being of that student, other students, or other members of the school community; or
(2) disclosing such information to teachers and school officials, including teachers and school officials in other schools, who have legitimate educational interests in the behavior of the student.

(i) Drug and alcohol violation disclosures

(1) In general

Nothing in this Act or the Higher Education Act of 1965 [20 U.S.C. 1001 et seq., 42 U.S.C. 2751 et seq.] shall be construed to prohibit an institution of higher education from disclosing, to a parent or legal guardian of a student, information regarding any violation of any Federal, State, or local law, or of any rule or policy of the institution, governing the use or possession of alcohol or a controlled substance, regardless of whether that information is contained in the student's education records, if-

(A) the student is under the age of 21; and

(B) the institution determines that the student has committed a disciplinary violation with respect to such use or possession.

(2) State law regarding disclosure

Nothing in paragraph (1) shall be construed to supersede any provision of State law that prohibits an institution of higher education from making the disclosure described in subsection (a).

(j) Investigation and prosecution of terrorism

(1) In general

Notwithstanding subsections (a) through (i) or any provision of State law, the Attorney General (or any Federal officer or employee, in a position not lower than an Assistant Attorney General, designated by the Attorney General) may submit a written application to a court of competent jurisdiction for an ex parte order requiring an educational agency or institution to permit the Attorney General (or his designee) to-

(A) collect education records in the possession of the educational agency or institution that are relevant to an authorized investigation or prosecution of an offense listed in section 2332b(g)(5)(B) of title 18, or an act of domestic or international terrorism as defined in section 2331 of that title; and

(B) for official purposes related to the investigation or prosecution of an offense described in paragraph (1)(A), retain, disseminate, and use (including as evidence at trial or in other administrative or judicial proceedings) such records, consistent with such guidelines as the Attorney General, after consultation with the Secretary, shall issue to protect confidentiality.

(2) Application and approval

(A) In general.-An application under paragraph (1) shall certify that there are specific and articulable facts giving reason to believe that the education records are likely to contain information described in paragraph (1)(A).

(B) The court shall issue an order described in paragraph (1) if the court finds that the application for the order includes the certification described in subparagraph (A).

(3) Protection of educational agency or institution

United States
Family Educational Rights and Privacy Act

An educational agency or institution that, in good faith, produces education records in accordance with an order issued under this subsection shall not be liable to any person for that production.

(4) Record-keeping

Subsection (b)(4) does not apply to education records subject to a court order under this subsection.

FOREIGN INTELLIGENCE
SURVEILLANCE ACT (1978)

Summary

Congress enacted the Foreign Intelligence Surveillance Act (FISA) in 1978 to establish a legal regime for "foreign intelligence" information gathering in the United States, independent from the rules that govern surveillance for ordinary law enforcement. The Supreme Court invited Congress to establish a separate regime for foreign intelligence surveillance in United States v. U.S District Court, 407 U.S. 297 (1972), stating: "Given these potential distinctions between Title III criminal surveillances and those involving the domestic security, Congress may wish to consider protective standards for the latter which differ from those already prescribed for specific crimes in Title III. Different standards may be compatible with the Fourth Amendment if they are reasonable both in relation to the legitimate needs of Government for intelligence information and the protected rights of our citizens."

Although ordinarily under the Fourth Amendment a search warrant will only be issued upon showing of probable cause to believe that a crime has been or is being committed, FISA requires only a showing of probable cause that the target is a foreign power or an agent of a foreign power. FISA also applies differently to "U.S. persons" and aliens; in order to be used against a U.S. person, there must be probable cause to believe that person's activities involve a violation of the criminal statutes of the United States. Furthermore, the information sought must be "necessary to" U.S. self-protective ability or U.S. national defense, national security, or foreign affairs. No such restrictions apply when the target or surveillance is not a U.S. person as defined in 50 U.S.C. § 1801(i).

FISA's reach was continually expanded over its history. The USA Patriot Act in particular represented a significant shift in U.S. foreign intelligence, 107 PL 56 (2001). Prior to the amending Act, FISA could only be used when foreign intelligence information gathering was the primary or sole purpose of an investigation. Under the USA Patriot Act, however, surveillance can be conducted under FISA when foreign counterintelligence is merely a "significant" purpose of the investigation. 50 U.S.C. §§ 1804(a)(7)(B), 1823(a)(7)(B). The Patriot Act also amended FISA to bar certain investigations of U.S. persons conducted solely on the basis of activities protected by the First Amendment. 50 U.S.C. §§ 1842, 1843, 1861. Importantly, the FISA Amendments Act of 2008 expanded FISA to allow the Attorney General and Director of National Intelligence to jointly authorize a program of surveillance, rather than individualized orders, that targets non-U.S. persons located abroad, 110 PL 261 (2008). Congress extended this authority in 2018, 115 PL 118 (2018).

However, in 2015, the USA Freedom Act was passed, rolling back some FISA surveillance for the first time. limited the bulk collection of telephone metadata of domestic communications, enhanced judicial oversight, narrows the scope of National Security Letters, promotes established amicus curiae for the Foreign Intelligence Surveillance Court ("FISC"), established declassification procedures for the FISC, and creates new reporting requirements.

United States
Foreign Intelligence Surveillance Act

References

> Public Law 95-511. Codified as amended at 50 U.S.C. § 1801 et seq.
> [https://www.law.cornell.edu/uscode/text/50/1801]

> EPIC, Foreign Intelligence Surveillance Act (FISA)
> [https://epic.org/privacy/terrorism/fisa/]

50 U.S.C. § 1801. Definitions

As used in this subchapter:

(a) "Foreign power" means-

(1) a foreign government or any component thereof, whether or not recognized by the United States;

(2) a faction of a foreign nation or nations, not substantially composed of United States persons;

(3) an entity that is openly acknowledged by a foreign government or governments to be directed and controlled by such foreign government or governments;

(4) a group engaged in international terrorism or activities in preparation therefor;

(5) a foreign-based political organization, not substantially composed of United States persons;

(6) an entity that is directed and controlled by a foreign government or governments; or

(7) an entity not substantially composed of United States persons that is engaged in the international proliferation of weapons of mass destruction.

(b) "Agent of a foreign power" means-

(1) any person other than a United States person, who-

(A) acts in the United States as an officer or employee of a foreign power, or as a member of a foreign power as defined in subsection (a)(4), irrespective of whether the person is inside the United States;

(B) acts for or on behalf of a foreign power which engages in clandestine intelligence activities in the United States contrary to the interests of the United States, when the circumstances indicate that such person may engage in such activities, or when such person knowingly aids or abets any person in the conduct of such activities or knowingly conspires with any person to engage in such activities;

(C) engages in international terrorism or activities in preparation therefore;

(D) engages in the international proliferation of weapons of mass destruction, or activities in preparation therefor; or

(E) engages in the international proliferation of weapons of mass destruction, or activities in preparation therefor, for or on behalf of a foreign power, or knowingly aids or abets any person in the conduct of such proliferation or activities in preparation therefor, or knowingly conspires with any person to engage in such proliferation or activities in preparation therefor; or

(2) any person who-

(A) knowingly engages in clandestine intelligence gathering activities for or on behalf of a foreign power, which activities involve or may involve a violation of the criminal statutes of the United States;

(B) pursuant to the direction of an intelligence service or network of a foreign power, knowingly engages in any other clandestine intelligence activities for or on behalf of such foreign power, which activities involve or are about to involve a violation of the criminal statutes of the United States;

(C) knowingly engages in sabotage or international terrorism, or activities that are in preparation therefor, for or on behalf of a foreign power;

(D) knowingly enters the United States under a false or fraudulent identity for or on behalf of a foreign power or, while in the United States, knowingly assumes a false or fraudulent identity for or on behalf of a foreign power; or

(E) knowingly aids or abets any person in the conduct of activities described in subparagraph (A), (B), or (C) or knowingly conspires with any person to engage in activities described in subparagraph (A), (B), or (C).

(c) "International terrorism" means activities that-

(1) involve violent acts or acts dangerous to human life that are a violation of the criminal laws of the United States or of any State, or that would be a criminal violation if committed within the jurisdiction of the United States or any State;

(2) appear to be intended-

(A) to intimidate or coerce a civilian population;

(B) to influence the policy of a government by intimidation or coercion; or

(C) to affect the conduct of a government by assassination or kidnapping; and

(3) occur totally outside the United States, or transcend national boundaries in terms of the means by which they are accomplished, the persons they appear intended to coerce or intimidate, or the locale in which their perpetrators operate or seek asylum.

(d) "Sabotage" means activities that involve a violation of chapter 105 of title 18, or that would involve such a violation if committed against the United States.

(e) "Foreign intelligence information" means-

(1) information that relates to, and if concerning a United States person is necessary to, the ability of the United States to protect against-

(A) actual or potential attack or other grave hostile acts of a foreign power or an agent of a foreign power;

(B) sabotage, international terrorism, or the international proliferation of weapons of mass destruction by a foreign power or an agent of a foreign power; or

(C) clandestine intelligence activities by an intelligence service or network of a foreign power or by an agent of a foreign power; or

(2) information with respect to a foreign power or foreign territory that relates to, and if concerning a United States person is necessary to-

(A) the national defense or the security of the United States; or

(B) the conduct of the foreign affairs of the United States.

(f) "Electronic surveillance" means-

(1) the acquisition by an electronic, mechanical, or other surveillance device of the contents of any wire or radio communication sent by or intended to be received by a particular, known United States person who is in the United States, if the contents are acquired by intentionally targeting that United States person, under circumstances in which a person has a reasonable expectation of privacy and a warrant would be required for law enforcement purposes;

(2) the acquisition by an electronic, mechanical, or other surveillance device of the contents of any wire communication to or from a person in the United States, without the consent of any party thereto, if such acquisition occurs in the United States, but does not include the acquisition of those communications of computer trespassers that would be permissible under section 2511(2)(i) of title 18;

(3) the intentional acquisition by an electronic, mechanical, or other surveillance device of the contents of any radio communication, under circumstances in which a person has a reasonable expectation of privacy and a warrant would be required for law enforcement purposes, and if both the sender and all intended recipients are located within the United States; or

(4) the installation or use of an electronic, mechanical, or other surveillance device in the United States for monitoring to acquire information, other than from a wire or radio communication, under circumstances in which a person has a reasonable expectation of privacy and a warrant would be required for law enforcement purposes.

(g) "Attorney General" means the Attorney General of the United States (or Acting Attorney General), the Deputy Attorney General, or, upon the designation of the Attorney General, the Assistant Attorney General designated as the Assistant Attorney General for National Security under section 507A of title 28.

(h) "Minimization procedures", with respect to electronic surveillance, means-

(1) specific procedures, which shall be adopted by the Attorney General, that are reasonably designed in light of the purpose and technique of the particular surveillance, to minimize the acquisition and retention, and prohibit the dissemination, of nonpublicly available information concerning unconsenting United States persons consistent with the need of the United States to obtain, produce, and disseminate foreign intelligence information;

(2) procedures that require that nonpublicly available information, which is not foreign intelligence information, as defined in subsection (e)(1), shall not be disseminated in a manner that identifies any United States person, without such person's consent, unless such person's identity is necessary to understand foreign intelligence information or assess its importance;

(3) notwithstanding paragraphs (1) and (2), procedures that allow for the retention and dissemination of information that is evidence of a crime which has been, is being, or is about to be committed and that is to be retained or disseminated for law enforcement purposes; and

(4) notwithstanding paragraphs (1), (2), and (3), with respect to any electronic surveillance approved pursuant to section 1802(a) of this title, procedures that require that no contents of any communication to which a United States person is a party shall be disclosed, disseminated, or used for any purpose or retained for longer than 72 hours unless a court order under section 1805 of this title is obtained or unless the Attorney General determines that the information indicates a threat of death or serious bodily harm to any person.

(i) "United States person" means a citizen of the United States, an alien lawfully admitted for permanent residence (as defined in section 1101(a)(20) of title 8), an unincorporated association a substantial number of members of which are citizens of the United States or aliens lawfully admitted for permanent residence, or a corporation which is incorporated in the United States, but does not include a corporation or an association which is a foreign power, as defined in subsection (a)(1), (2), or (3).

(j) "United States", when used in a geographic sense, means all areas under the territorial sovereignty of the United States and the Trust Territory of the Pacific Islands.

(k) "Aggrieved person" means a person who is the target of an electronic surveillance or any other person whose communications or activities were subject to electronic surveillance.

(l) "Wire communication" means any communication while it is being carried by a wire, cable, or other like connection furnished or operated by any person engaged as a common carrier in providing or operating such facilities for the transmission of interstate or foreign communications.

(m) "Person" means any individual, including any officer or employee of the Federal Government, or any group, entity, association, corporation, or foreign power.

(n) "Contents", when used with respect to a communication, includes any information concerning the identity of the parties to such communication or the existence, substance, purport, or meaning of that communication.

(o) "State" means any State of the United States, the District of Columbia, the Commonwealth of Puerto Rico, the Trust Territory of the Pacific Islands, and any territory or possession of the United States.

(p) "Weapon of mass destruction" means-

(1) any explosive, incendiary, or poison gas device that is designed, intended, or has the capability to cause a mass casualty incident;

(2) any weapon that is designed, intended, or has the capability to cause death or serious bodily injury to a significant number of persons through the release, dissemination, or impact of toxic or poisonous chemicals or their precursors;

(3) any weapon involving a biological agent, toxin, or vector (as such terms are defined in section 178 of title 18) that is designed, intended, or has the capability to cause death, illness, or serious bodily injury to a significant number of persons; or

(4) any weapon that is designed, intended, or has the capability to release radiation or radioactivity causing death, illness, or serious bodily injury to a significant number of persons.

50 U.S.C. § 1802. Electronic surveillance authorization without court order; certification by Attorney General; reports to Congressional committees; transmittal under seal; duties and compensation of communication common carrier; applications; jurisdiction of court

a)(1) Notwithstanding any other law, the President, through the Attorney General, may authorize electronic surveillance without a court order under this subchapter to acquire foreign intelligence information for periods of up to one year if the Attorney General certifies in writing under oath that-

(A) the electronic surveillance is solely directed at-

(i) the acquisition of the contents of communications transmitted by means of communications used exclusively between or among foreign powers, as defined in section 1801(a)(1), (2), or (3) of this title; or

(ii) the acquisition of technical intelligence, other than the spoken communications of individuals, from property or premises under the open and exclusive control of a foreign power, as defined in section 1801(a)(1), (2), or (3) of this title;

(B) there is no substantial likelihood that the surveillance will acquire the contents of any communication to which a United States person is a party; and

(C) the proposed minimization procedures with respect to such surveillance meet the definition of minimization procedures under section 1801(h) of this title; and if the Attorney General reports such minimization procedures and any changes thereto to the House Permanent Select Committee on Intelligence and the Senate Select Committee on Intelligence at least thirty days prior to their effective date, unless the Attorney General determines immediate action is required and notifies the committees immediately of such minimization procedures and the reason for their becoming effective immediately.

(2) An electronic surveillance authorized by this subsection may be conducted only in accordance with the Attorney General's certification and the minimization procedures adopted by him. The Attorney General shall assess compliance with such procedures and

shall report such assessments to the House Permanent Select Committee on Intelligence and the Senate Select Committee on Intelligence under the provisions of section 1808(a) of this title.

(3) The Attorney General shall immediately transmit under seal to the court established under section 1803(a) of this title a copy of his certification. Such certification shall be maintained under security measures established by the Chief Justice with the concurrence of the Attorney General, in consultation with the Director of National Intelligence, and shall remain sealed unless-

> (A) an application for a court order with respect to the surveillance is made under sections 1801(h)(4) and 1804 of this title; or
>
> (B) the certification is necessary to determine the legality of the surveillance under section 1806(f) of this title.

(4) With respect to electronic surveillance authorized by this subsection, the Attorney General may direct a specified communication common carrier to-

> (A) furnish all information, facilities, or technical assistance necessary to accomplish the electronic surveillance in such a manner as will protect its secrecy and produce a minimum of interference with the services that such carrier is providing its customers; and
>
> (B) maintain under security procedures approved by the Attorney General and the Director of National Intelligence any records concerning the surveillance or the aid furnished which such carrier wishes to retain.

The Government shall compensate, at the prevailing rate, such carrier for furnishing such aid.

(b) Applications for a court order under this subchapter are authorized if the President has, by written authorization, empowered the Attorney General to approve applications to the court having jurisdiction under section 1803 of this title, and a judge to whom an application is made may, notwithstanding any other law, grant an order, in conformity with section 1805 of this title, approving electronic surveillance of a foreign power or an agent of a foreign power for the purpose of obtaining foreign intelligence information, except that the court shall not have jurisdiction to grant any order approving electronic surveillance directed solely as described in paragraph (1)(A) of subsection (a) unless such surveillance may involve the acquisition of communications of any United States person.

50 U.S.C. § 1803. Designation of judges

> (a) Court to hear applications and grant orders; record of denial; transmittal to court of review
>
> > (1) The Chief Justice of the United States shall publicly designate 11 district court judges from at least seven of the United States judicial circuits of whom no fewer than 3 shall reside within 20 miles of the District of Columbia who shall constitute

a court which shall have jurisdiction to hear applications for and grant orders approving electronic surveillance anywhere within the United States under the procedures set forth in this chapter, except that no judge designated under this subsection (except when sitting en banc under paragraph (2)) shall hear the same application for electronic surveillance under this chapter which has been denied previously by another judge designated under this subsection. If any judge so designated denies an application for an order authorizing electronic surveillance under this chapter, such judge shall provide immediately for the record a written statement of each reason for his decision and, on motion of the United States, the record shall be transmitted, under seal, to the court of review established in subsection (b).

(2)(A) The court established under this subsection may, on its own initiative, or upon the request of the Government in any proceeding or a party under section 1861(f) of this title or paragraph (4) or (5) of section 1881a(h) of this title, hold a hearing or rehearing, en banc, when ordered by a majority of the judges that constitute such court upon a determination that-

(i) en banc consideration is necessary to secure or maintain uniformity of the court's decisions; or

(ii) the proceeding involves a question of exceptional importance.

(B) Any authority granted by this chapter to a judge of the court established under this subsection may be exercised by the court en banc. When exercising such authority, the court en banc shall comply with any requirements of this chapter on the exercise of such authority.

(C) For purposes of this paragraph, the court en banc shall consist of all judges who constitute the court established under this subsection.

(b) Court of review; record, transmittal to Supreme Court

The Chief Justice shall publicly designate three judges, one of whom shall be publicly designated as the presiding judge, from the United States district courts or courts of appeals who together shall comprise a court of review which shall have jurisdiction to review the denial of any application made under this chapter. If such court determines that the application was properly denied, the court shall immediately provide for the record a written statement of each reason for its decision and, on petition of the United States for a writ of certiorari, the record shall be transmitted under seal to the Supreme Court, which shall have jurisdiction to review such decision.

(c) Expeditious conduct of proceedings; security measures for maintenance of records

Proceedings under this chapter shall be conducted as expeditiously as possible. The record of proceedings under this chapter, including applications made and orders granted, shall be maintained under security measures established by the Chief Justice in consultation with the Attorney General and the Director of National Intelligence.

(d) Tenure

Each judge designated under this section shall so serve for a maximum of seven years and shall not be eligible for redesignation, except that the judges first designated under subsection (a) shall be designated for terms of from one to seven years so that one term expires each year, and that judges first designated under subsection (b) shall be designated for terms of three, five, and seven years.

(e) Jurisdiction and procedures for review of petitions

(1) Three judges designated under subsection (a) who reside within 20 miles of the District of Columbia, or, if all of such judges are unavailable, other judges of the court established under subsection (a) as may be designated by the presiding judge of such court, shall comprise a petition review pool which shall have jurisdiction to review petitions filed pursuant to section 1861(f)(1) or 1881a(h)(4) of this title.

(2) Not later than 60 days after March 9, 2006, the court established under subsection (a) shall adopt and, consistent with the protection of national security, publish procedures for the review of petitions filed pursuant to section 1861(f)(1) or 1881a(h)(4) of this title by the panel established under paragraph (1). Such procedures shall provide that review of a petition shall be conducted in camera and shall also provide for the designation of an acting presiding judge.

(f) Stay of order

(1) A judge of the court established under subsection (a), the court established under subsection (b) or a judge of that court, or the Supreme Court of the United States or a justice of that court, may, in accordance with the rules of their respective courts, enter a stay of an order or an order modifying an order of the court established under subsection (a) or the court established under subsection (b) entered under any subchapter of this chapter, while the court established under subsection (a) conducts a rehearing, while an appeal is pending to the court established under subsection (b), or while a petition of certiorari is pending in the Supreme Court of the United States, or during the pendency of any review by that court.

(2) The authority described in paragraph (1) shall apply to an order entered under any provision of this chapter.

(g) Establishment and transmittal of rules and procedures

(1) The courts established pursuant to subsections (a) and (b) may establish such rules and procedures, and take such actions, as are reasonably necessary to administer their responsibilities under this chapter.

(2) The rules and procedures established under paragraph (1), and any modifications of such rules and procedures, shall be recorded, and shall be transmitted to the following:

(A) All of the judges on the court established pursuant to subsection (a).

(B) All of the judges on the court of review established pursuant to subsection (b).

(C) The Chief Justice of the United States.

(D) The Committee on the Judiciary of the Senate.

(E) The Select Committee on Intelligence of the Senate.

(F) The Committee on the Judiciary of the House of Representatives.

(G) The Permanent Select Committee on Intelligence of the House of Representatives.

(3) The transmissions required by paragraph (2) shall be submitted in unclassified form, but may include a classified annex.

(h) Compliance with orders, rules, and procedures

Nothing in this chapter shall be construed to reduce or contravene the inherent authority of the court established under subsection (a) to determine or enforce compliance with an order or a rule of such court or with a procedure approved by such court.

(i) Amicus curiae

(1) Designation

The presiding judges of the courts established under subsections (a) and (b) shall, not later than 180 days after June 2, 2015, jointly designate not fewer than 5 individuals to be eligible to serve as amicus curiae, who shall serve pursuant to rules the presiding judges may establish. In designating such individuals, the presiding judges may consider individuals recommended by any source, including members of the Privacy and Civil Liberties Oversight Board, the judges determine appropriate.

(2) Authorization

A court established under subsection (a) or (b), consistent with the requirement of subsection (c) and any other statutory requirement that the court act expeditiously or within a stated time-

(A) shall appoint an individual who has been designated under paragraph (1) to serve as amicus curiae to assist such court in the consideration of any application for an order or review that, in the opinion of the court, presents a novel or significant interpretation of the law, unless the court issues a finding that such appointment is not appropriate; and

(B) may appoint an individual or organization to serve as amicus curiae, including to provide technical expertise, in any instance as such court deems appropriate or, upon motion, permit an individual or organization leave to file an amicus curiae brief.

(3) Qualifications of amicus curiae

(A) Expertise

Individuals designated under paragraph (1) shall be persons who possess expertise in privacy and civil liberties, intelligence collection, communications technology, or any other area that may lend legal or technical expertise to a court established under subsection (a) or (b).

(B) Security clearance

Individuals designated pursuant to paragraph (1) shall be persons who are determined to be eligible for access to classified information necessary to participate in matters before the courts. Amicus curiae appointed by the court pursuant to paragraph (2) shall be persons who are determined to be eligible for access to classified information, if such access is necessary to participate in the matters in which they may be appointed.

(4) Duties

If a court established under subsection (a) or (b) appoints an amicus curiae under paragraph (2)(A), the amicus curiae shall provide to the court, as appropriate-

(A) legal arguments that advance the protection of individual privacy and civil liberties;

(B) information related to intelligence collection or communications technology; or

(C) legal arguments or information regarding any other area relevant to the issue presented to the court.

(5) Assistance

An amicus curiae appointed under paragraph (2)(A) may request that the court designate or appoint additional amici curiae pursuant to paragraph (1) or paragraph (2), to be available to assist the amicus curiae.

(6) Access to information

(A) In general

If a court established under subsection (a) or (b) appoints an amicus curiae under paragraph (2), the amicus curiae-

(i) shall have access to any legal precedent, application, certification, petition, motion, or such other materials that the court determines are relevant to the duties of the amicus curiae; and

(ii) may, if the court determines that it is relevant to the duties of the amicus curiae, consult with any other individuals designated pursuant to paragraph (1) regarding information relevant to any assigned proceeding.

(B) Briefings

The Attorney General may periodically brief or provide relevant materials to individuals designated pursuant to paragraph (1) regarding constructions and interpretations of this chapter and legal, technological, and other issues related to actions authorized by this chapter.

(C) Classified information

An amicus curiae designated or appointed by the court may have access to classified documents, information, and other materials or proceedings only if that individual is eligible for access to classified information and to the extent consistent with the national security of the United States.

(D) Rule of construction

Nothing in this section shall be construed to require the Government to provide information to an amicus curiae appointed by the court that is privileged from disclosure.

(7) Notification

A presiding judge of a court established under subsection (a) or (b) shall notify the Attorney General of each exercise of the authority to appoint an individual to serve as amicus curiae under paragraph (2).

(8) Assistance

A court established under subsection (a) or (b) may request and receive (including on a nonreimbursable basis) the assistance of the executive branch in the implementation of this subsection.

(9) Administration

A court established under subsection (a) or (b) may provide for the designation, appointment, removal, training, or other support for an individual designated to serve as amicus curiae under paragraph (1) or appointed to serve as amicus curiae under paragraph (2) in a manner that is not inconsistent with this subsection.

(10) Receipt of information

Nothing in this subsection shall limit the ability of a court established under subsection (a) or (b) to request or receive information or materials from, or otherwise communicate with, the Government or amicus curiae appointed under paragraph (2) on an ex parte basis, nor limit any special or heightened obligation in any ex parte communication or proceeding.

(j) Review of FISA court decisions

Following issuance of an order under this chapter, a court established under subsection (a) shall certify for review to the court established under subsection (b) any question of law that may affect resolution of the matter in controversy that the court determines warrants such review because of a need for uniformity or because consideration by the court established under subsection (b) would serve the interests of justice. Upon certification of a question of law under this subsection, the court established under subsection (b) may give binding instructions or require the entire record to be sent up for decision of the entire matter in controversy.

(k) Review of FISA court of review decisions

(1) Certification

For purposes of section 1254(2) of title 28, the court of review established under subsection (b) shall be considered to be a court of appeals.

(2) Amicus curiae briefing

Upon certification of an application under paragraph (1), the Supreme Court of the United States may appoint an amicus curiae designated under subsection (i)(1), or any other person, to provide briefing or other assistance.

50 U.S.C. § 1804. Applications for court orders

(a) Submission by Federal officer; approval of Attorney General; contents

Each application for an order approving electronic surveillance under this subchapter shall be made by a Federal officer in writing upon oath or affirmation to a judge having jurisdiction under section 1803 of this title. Each application shall require the approval of the Attorney General based upon his finding that it satisfies the criteria and requirements of such application as set forth in this subchapter. It shall include-

(1) the identity of the Federal officer making the application;

(2) the identity, if known, or a description of the specific target of the electronic surveillance;

(3) a statement of the facts and circumstances relied upon by the applicant to justify his belief that-

(A) the target of the electronic surveillance is a foreign power or an agent of a foreign power; and

(B) each of the facilities or places at which the electronic surveillance is directed is being used, or is about to be used, by a foreign power or an agent of a foreign power;

(4) a statement of the proposed minimization procedures;

(5) a description of the nature of the information sought and the type of communications or activities to be subjected to the surveillance;

(6) a certification or certifications by the Assistant to the President for National Security Affairs, an executive branch official or officials designated by the President from among those executive officers employed in the area of national security or defense and appointed by the President with the advice and consent of the Senate, or the Deputy Director of the Federal Bureau of Investigation, if designated by the President as a certifying official-

(A) that the certifying official deems the information sought to be foreign intelligence information;

(B) that a significant purpose of the surveillance is to obtain foreign intelligence information;

(C) that such information cannot reasonably be obtained by normal investigative techniques;

(D) that designates the type of foreign intelligence information being sought according to the categories described in section 1801(e) of this title; and

(E) including a statement of the basis for the certification that-

(i) the information sought is the type of foreign intelligence information designated; and

(ii) such information cannot reasonably be obtained by normal investigative techniques;

(7) a summary statement of the means by which the surveillance will be effected and a statement whether physical entry is required to effect the surveillance;

(8) a statement of the facts concerning all previous applications that have been made to any judge under this subchapter involving any of the persons, facilities, or places specified in the application, and the action taken on each previous application; and

(9) a statement of the period of time for which the electronic surveillance is required to be maintained, and if the nature of the intelligence gathering is such that the approval of the use of electronic surveillance under this subchapter should not automatically terminate when the described type of information has first been obtained, a description of facts supporting the belief that additional information of the same type will be obtained thereafter.

(b) Additional affidavits or certifications

The Attorney General may require any other affidavit or certification from any other officer in connection with the application.

(c) Additional information

The judge may require the applicant to furnish such other information as may be necessary to make the determinations required by section 1805 of this title.

(d) Personal review by Attorney General

(1)(A) Upon written request of the Director of the Federal Bureau of Investigation, the Secretary of Defense, the Secretary of State, the Director of National Intelligence, or the Director of the Central Intelligence Agency, the Attorney General shall personally review under subsection (a) an application under that subsection for a target described in section 1801(b)(2) of this title.

(B) Except when disabled or otherwise unavailable to make a request referred to in subparagraph (A), an official referred to in that subparagraph may not delegate the authority to make a request referred to in that subparagraph.

(C) Each official referred to in subparagraph (A) with authority to make a request under that subparagraph shall take appropriate actions in advance to ensure that delegation of such authority is clearly established in the event such official is disabled or otherwise unavailable to make such request.

(2)(A) If as a result of a request under paragraph (1) the Attorney General determines not to approve an application under the second sentence of subsection (a) for purposes of making the application under this section, the Attorney General shall provide written notice of the determination to the official making the request for the review of the application under that paragraph. Except when disabled or otherwise unavailable to make a determination under the preceding sentence, the Attorney General may not delegate the responsibility to make a determination under that sentence. The Attorney General shall take appropriate actions in advance to ensure that delegation of such responsibility is clearly established in the event the Attorney General is disabled or otherwise unavailable to make such determination.

(B) Notice with respect to an application under subparagraph (A) shall set forth the modifications, if any, of the application that are necessary in order for the Attorney General to approve the application under the second sentence of subsection (a) for purposes of making the application under this section.

(C) Upon review of any modifications of an application set forth under subparagraph (B), the official notified of the modifications under this paragraph shall modify the application if such official determines that such modification is warranted. Such official shall supervise the making of any modification under this subparagraph. Except when disabled or otherwise unavailable to supervise the making of any modification under the preceding sentence, such official may not delegate the responsibility to supervise the making of any modification under that preceding sentence. Each such official shall take appropriate actions in advance to ensure that delegation of such responsibility is clearly established in the event such official is disabled or otherwise unavailable to supervise the making of such modification.

50 U.S.C. § 1805. Issuance of order

(a) Necessary findings

Upon an application made pursuant to section 1804 of this title, the judge shall enter an ex parte order as requested or as modified approving the electronic surveillance if he finds that-

(1) the application has been made by a Federal officer and approved by the Attorney General;

(2) on the basis of the facts submitted by the applicant there is probable cause to believe that-

(A) the target of the electronic surveillance is a foreign power or an agent of a foreign power: Provided, That no United States person may be considered a foreign power or an agent of a foreign power solely upon the basis of activities protected by the first amendment to the Constitution of the United States; and

(B) each of the facilities or places at which the electronic surveillance is directed is being used, or is about to be used, by a foreign power or an agent of a foreign power;

(3) the proposed minimization procedures meet the definition of minimization procedures under section 1801(h) of this title; and

(4) the application which has been filed contains all statements and certifications required by section 1804 of this title and, if the target is a United States person, the certification or certifications are not clearly erroneous on the basis of the statement made under section 1804(a)(7)(E) of this title and any other information furnished under section 1804(d) of this title.

(b) Determination of probable cause

In determining whether or not probable cause exists for purposes of an order under subsection (a)(2), a judge may consider past activities of the target, as well as facts and circumstances relating to current or future activities of the target.

(c) Specifications and directions of orders

 (1) Specifications

An order approving an electronic surveillance under this section shall specify-

 (A) the identity, if known, or a description of the specific target of the electronic surveillance identified or described in the application pursuant to section 1804(a)(3) of this title;

 (B) the nature and location of each of the facilities or places at which the electronic surveillance will be directed, if known;

 (C) the type of information sought to be acquired and the type of communications or activities to be subjected to the surveillance;

 (D) the means by which the electronic surveillance will be effected and whether physical entry will be used to effect the surveillance; and

 (E) the period of time during which the electronic surveillance is approved.

 (2) Directions

An order approving an electronic surveillance under this section shall direct-

 (A) that the minimization procedures be followed;

 (B) that, upon the request of the applicant, a specified communication or other common carrier, landlord, custodian, or other specified person, or in circumstances where the Court finds, based upon specific facts provided in the application, that the actions of the target of the application may have the effect of thwarting the identification of a specified person, such other persons, furnish the applicant forthwith all information, facilities, or technical assistance necessary to accomplish the electronic surveillance in such a manner as will protect its secrecy and produce a minimum of interference with the services that such carrier, landlord, custodian, or other person is providing that target of electronic surveillance;

 (C) that such carrier, landlord, custodian, or other person maintain under security procedures approved by the Attorney General and the Director of National Intelligence any records concerning the surveillance or the aid furnished that such person wishes to retain; and

 (D) that the applicant compensate, at the prevailing rate, such carrier, landlord, custodian, or other person for furnishing such aid.

 (3) Special directions for certain orders

An order approving an electronic surveillance under this section in circumstances where the nature and location of each of the facilities or places at which the surveillance will be directed is unknown shall direct the applicant to provide notice to the court within ten days after the date on which surveillance begins to be directed at any new facility or place, unless the court finds good cause to justify a longer period of up to 60 days, of-

(A) the nature and location of each new facility or place at which the electronic surveillance is directed;

(B) the facts and circumstances relied upon by the applicant to justify the applicant's belief that each new facility or place at which the electronic surveillance is directed is or was being used, or is about to be used, by the target of the surveillance;

(C) a statement of any proposed minimization procedures that differ from those contained in the original application or order, that may be necessitated by a change in the facility or place at which the electronic surveillance is directed; and

(D) the total number of electronic surveillances that have been or are being conducted under the authority of the order.

(d) Duration of order; extensions; review of circumstances under which information was acquired, retained or disseminated

(1) An order issued under this section may approve an electronic surveillance for the period necessary to achieve its purpose, or for ninety days, whichever is less, except that (A) an order under this section shall approve an electronic surveillance targeted against a foreign power, as defined in section 1801(a)(1), (2), or (3) of this title, for the period specified in the application or for one year, whichever is less, and (B) an order under this chapter for a surveillance targeted against an agent of a foreign power who is not a United States person may be for the period specified in the application or for 120 days, whichever is less.

(2) Extensions of an order issued under this subchapter may be granted on the same basis as an original order upon an application for an extension and new findings made in the same manner as required for an original order, except that (A) an extension of an order under this chapter for a surveillance targeted against a foreign power, as defined in paragraph (5), (6), or (7) of section 1801(a) of this title, or against a foreign power as defined in section 1801(a)(4) of this title that is not a United States person, may be for a period not to exceed one year if the judge finds probable cause to believe that no communication of any individual United States person will be acquired during the period, and (B) an extension of an order under this chapter for a surveillance targeted against an agent of a foreign power who is not a United States person may be for a period not to exceed 1 year.

(3) At or before the end of the period of time for which electronic surveillance is approved by an order or an extension, the judge may assess compliance with the minimization procedures by reviewing the circumstances under which information concerning United States persons was acquired, retained, or disseminated.

(e) Emergency orders

(1) Notwithstanding any other provision of this subchapter, the Attorney General may authorize the emergency employment of electronic surveillance if the Attorney General-

    (A) reasonably determines that an emergency situation exists with respect to the employment of electronic surveillance to obtain foreign intelligence information before an order authorizing such surveillance can with due diligence be obtained;

    (B) reasonably determines that the factual basis for the issuance of an order under this subchapter to approve such electronic surveillance exists;

    (C) informs, either personally or through a designee, a judge having jurisdiction under section 1803 of this title at the time of such authorization that the decision has been made to employ emergency electronic surveillance; and

    (D) makes an application in accordance with this subchapter to a judge having jurisdiction under section 1803 of this title as soon as practicable, but not later than 7 days after the Attorney General authorizes such surveillance.

(2) If the Attorney General authorizes the emergency employment of electronic surveillance under paragraph (1), the Attorney General shall require that the minimization procedures required by this subchapter for the issuance of a judicial order be followed.

(3) In the absence of a judicial order approving such electronic surveillance, the surveillance shall terminate when the information sought is obtained, when the application for the order is denied, or after the expiration of 7 days from the time of authorization by the Attorney General, whichever is earliest.

(4) A denial of the application made under this subsection may be reviewed as provided in section 1803 of this title.

(5) In the event that such application for approval is denied, or in any other case where the electronic surveillance is terminated and no order is issued approving the surveillance, no information obtained or evidence derived from such surveillance shall be received in evidence or otherwise disclosed in any trial, hearing, or other proceeding in or before any court, grand jury, department, office, agency, regulatory body, legislative committee, or other authority of the United States, a State, or political subdivision thereof, and no information concerning any United States person acquired from such surveillance shall subsequently be used or disclosed in any other manner by Federal officers or employees without the consent of such person, except with the approval of the Attorney General if the information indicates a threat of death or serious bodily harm to any person.

(6) The Attorney General shall assess compliance with the requirements of paragraph (5).

(f) Emergencies involving non-United States persons

    (1) Notwithstanding any other provision of this chapter, the lawfully authorized targeting of a non-United States person previously believed to be located outside the

United States for the acquisition of foreign intelligence information may continue for a period not to exceed 72 hours from the time that the non-United States person is reasonably believed to be located inside the United States and the acquisition is subject to this subchapter or to subchapter II of this chapter, provided that the head of an element of the intelligence community-

(A) reasonably determines that a lapse in the targeting of such non-United States person poses a threat of death or serious bodily harm to any person;

(B) promptly notifies the Attorney General of a determination under subparagraph (A); and

(C) requests, as soon as practicable, the employment of emergency electronic surveillance under subsection (e) or the employment of an emergency physical search pursuant to section 1824(e) of this title, as warranted.

(2) The authority under this subsection to continue the acquisition of foreign intelligence information is limited to a period not to exceed 72 hours and shall cease upon the earlier of the following:

(A) The employment of emergency electronic surveillance under subsection (e) or the employment of an emergency physical search pursuant to section 1824(e) of this title.

(B) An issuance of a court order under this subchapter or subchapter II of this chapter.

(C) The Attorney General provides direction that the acquisition be terminated.

(D) The head of the element of the intelligence community conducting the acquisition determines that a request under paragraph (1)(C) is not warranted.

(E) When the threat of death or serious bodily harm to any person is no longer reasonably believed to exist.

(3) Nonpublicly available information concerning unconsenting United States persons acquired under this subsection shall not be disseminated during the 72 hour time period under paragraph (1) unless necessary to investigate, reduce, or eliminate the threat of death or serious bodily harm to any person.

(4) If the Attorney General declines to authorize the employment of emergency electronic surveillance under subsection (e) or the employment of an emergency physical search pursuant to section 1824(e) of this title, or a court order is not obtained under this subchapter or subchapter II of this chapter, information obtained during the 72 hour acquisition time period under paragraph (1) shall not be retained, except with the approval of the Attorney General if the information indicates a threat of death or serious bodily harm to any person.

(5) Paragraphs (5) and (6) of subsection (e) shall apply to this subsection.

(g) Testing of electronic equipment; discovering unauthorized electronic surveillance; training of intelligence personnel

Notwithstanding any other provision of this subchapter, officers, employees, or agents of the United States are authorized in the normal course of their official duties to conduct electronic surveillance not targeted against the communications of any particular person or persons, under procedures approved by the Attorney General, solely to-

(1) test the capability of electronic equipment, if-

(A) it is not reasonable to obtain the consent of the persons incidentally subjected to the surveillance;

(B) the test is limited in extent and duration to that necessary to determine the capability of the equipment;

(C) the contents of any communication acquired are retained and used only for the purpose of determining the capability of the equipment, are disclosed only to test personnel, and are destroyed before or immediately upon completion of the test; and:

(D) Provided, That the test may exceed ninety days only with the prior approval of the Attorney General;

(2) determine the existence and capability of electronic surveillance equipment being used by persons not authorized to conduct electronic surveillance, if-

(A) it is not reasonable to obtain the consent of persons incidentally subjected to the surveillance;

(B) such electronic surveillance is limited in extent and duration to that necessary to determine the existence and capability of such equipment; and

(C) any information acquired by such surveillance is used only to enforce chapter 119 of title 18, or section 605 of title 47, or to protect information from unauthorized surveillance; or

(3) train intelligence personnel in the use of electronic surveillance equipment, if-

(A) it is not reasonable to-

(i) obtain the consent of the persons incidentally subjected to the surveillance;

(ii) train persons in the course of surveillances otherwise authorized by this subchapter; or

(iii) train persons in the use of such equipment without engaging in electronic surveillance;

(B) such electronic surveillance is limited in extent and duration to that necessary to train the personnel in the use of the equipment; and

(C) no contents of any communication acquired are retained or disseminated for any purpose, but are destroyed as soon as reasonably possible.

(h) Retention of certifications, applications and orders

Certifications made by the Attorney General pursuant to section 1802(a) of this title and applications made and orders granted under this subchapter shall be retained for a period of at least ten years from the date of the certification or application.

(i) Bar to legal action

No cause of action shall lie in any court against any provider of a wire or electronic communication service, landlord, custodian, or other person (including any officer, employee, agent, or other specified person thereof) that furnishes any information, facilities, or technical assistance in accordance with a court order or request for emergency assistance under this chapter for electronic surveillance or physical search.

(j) Pen registers and trap and trace devices

In any case in which the Government makes an application to a judge under this subchapter to conduct electronic surveillance involving communications and the judge grants such application, upon the request of the applicant, the judge shall also authorize the installation and use of pen registers and trap and trace devices, and direct the disclosure of the information set forth in section 1842(d)(2) of this title.

50 U.S.C. § 1806. Use of information

(a) Compliance with minimization procedures; privileged communications; lawful purposes

Information acquired from an electronic surveillance conducted pursuant to this subchapter concerning any United States person may be used and disclosed by Federal officers and employees without the consent of the United States person only in accordance with the minimization procedures required by this subchapter. No otherwise privileged communication obtained in accordance with, or in violation of, the provisions of this subchapter shall lose its privileged character. No information acquired from an electronic surveillance pursuant to this subchapter may be used or disclosed by Federal officers or employees except for lawful purposes.

(b) Statement for disclosure

No information acquired pursuant to this subchapter shall be disclosed for law enforcement purposes unless such disclosure is accompanied by a statement that such information, or any information derived therefrom, may only be used in a criminal proceeding with the advance authorization of the Attorney General.

(c) Notification by United States

Whenever the Government intends to enter into evidence or otherwise use or disclose in any trial, hearing, or other proceeding in or before any court, department, officer, agency, regulatory body, or other authority of the United States, against an aggrieved person, any information obtained or derived from an electronic surveillance of that aggrieved person pursuant to the authority of this subchapter, the Government shall, prior to the trial, hearing, or other proceeding or at a reasonable time prior to an effort to so disclose or so use that information or submit it in evidence, notify the aggrieved person and the court or other authority in which the information is to be disclosed or used that the Government intends to so disclose or so use such information.

(d) Notification by States or political subdivisions

Whenever any State or political subdivision thereof intends to enter into evidence or otherwise use or disclose in any trial, hearing, or other proceeding in or before any court, department, officer, agency, regulatory body, or other authority of a State or a political subdivision thereof, against an aggrieved person any information obtained or derived from an electronic surveillance of that aggrieved person pursuant to the authority of this subchapter, the State or political subdivision thereof shall notify the aggrieved person, the court or other authority in which the information is to be disclosed or used, and the Attorney General that the State or political subdivision thereof intends to so disclose or so use such information.

(e) Motion to suppress

Any person against whom evidence obtained or derived from an electronic surveillance to which he is an aggrieved person is to be, or has been, introduced or otherwise used or disclosed in any trial, hearing, or other proceeding in or before any court, department, officer, agency, regulatory body, or other authority of the United States, a State, or a political subdivision thereof, may move to suppress the evidence obtained or derived from such electronic surveillance on the grounds that-

(1) the information was unlawfully acquired; or

(2) the surveillance was not made in conformity with an order of authorization or approval.

Such a motion shall be made before the trial, hearing, or other proceeding unless there was no opportunity to make such a motion or the person was not aware of the grounds of the motion.

(f) In camera and ex parte review by district court

Whenever a court or other authority is notified pursuant to subsection (c) or (d), or whenever a motion is made pursuant to subsection (e), or whenever any motion or request is made by an aggrieved person pursuant to any other statute or rule of the United States or any State before any court or other authority of the United States or any State to discover or obtain applications or orders or other materials relating to electronic surveillance or to discover, obtain, or suppress evidence or information obtained or derived from electronic surveillance under this chapter, the United States district court or, where the motion is made before another authority, the United States district court in the same district as the authority, shall, notwithstanding any other law, if the Attorney General files an affidavit under oath that disclosure or an adversary hearing would harm the national security of the United States, review in camera and ex parte the application, order, and such other materials relating to the surveillance as may be necessary to determine whether the surveillance of the aggrieved person was lawfully authorized and conducted. In making this determination, the court may disclose to the aggrieved person, under appropriate security procedures and protective orders, portions of the application, order, or other materials relating to the surveillance only where such disclosure is necessary to make an accurate determination of the legality of the surveillance.

(g) Suppression of evidence; denial of motion

If the United States district court pursuant to subsection (f) determines that the surveillance was not lawfully authorized or conducted, it shall, in accordance with the requirements of law, suppress the evidence which was unlawfully obtained or derived from electronic surveillance of the aggrieved person or otherwise grant the motion of the aggrieved person. If the court determines that the surveillance was lawfully authorized and conducted, it shall deny the motion of the aggrieved person except to the extent that due process requires discovery or disclosure.

(h) Finality of orders

Orders granting motions or requests under subsection (g), decisions under this section that electronic surveillance was not lawfully authorized or conducted, and orders of the United States district court requiring review or granting disclosure of applications, orders, or other materials relating to a surveillance shall be final orders and binding upon all courts of the United States and the several States except a United States court of appeals and the Supreme Court.

(i) Destruction of unintentionally acquired information

In circumstances involving the unintentional acquisition by an electronic, mechanical, or other surveillance device of the contents of any communication, under circumstances in which a person has a reasonable expectation of privacy and a warrant would be required for law enforcement purposes, and if both the sender and all intended recipients are located within the United States, such contents shall be destroyed upon recognition, unless the Attorney General determines that the contents indicate a threat of death or serious bodily harm to any person.

(j) Notification of emergency employment of electronic surveillance; contents; postponement, suspension or elimination

If an emergency employment of electronic surveillance is authorized under subsection (e) or (f) of section 1805 of this title and a subsequent order approving the surveillance is not obtained, the judge shall cause to be served on any United States person named in the application and on such other United States persons subject to electronic surveillance as the judge may determine in his discretion it is in the interest of justice to serve, notice of-

 (1) the fact of the application;

 (2) the period of the surveillance; and

 (3) the fact that during the period information was or was not obtained.

On an ex parte showing of good cause to the judge the serving of the notice required by this subsection may be postponed or suspended for a period not to exceed ninety days. Thereafter, on a further ex parte showing of good cause, the court shall forego ordering the serving of the notice required under this subsection.

(k) Coordination with law enforcement on national security matters

(1) Federal officers who conduct electronic surveillance to acquire foreign intelligence information under this subchapter may consult with Federal law enforcement officers or law enforcement personnel of a State or political subdivision of a State (including the chief executive officer of that State or political subdivision who has the authority to appoint or direct the chief law enforcement officer of that State or political subdivision) to coordinate efforts to investigate or protect against-

(A) actual or potential attack or other grave hostile acts of a foreign power or an agent of a foreign power;

(B) sabotage, international terrorism, or the international proliferation of weapons of mass destruction by a foreign power or an agent of a foreign power; or

(C) clandestine intelligence activities by an intelligence service or network of a foreign power or by an agent of a foreign power.

(2) Coordination authorized under paragraph (1) shall not preclude the certification required by section 1804(a)(7)(B) of this title or the entry of an order under section 1805 of this title.

50 U.S.C. § 1807. Report to Administrative Office of the United States Court and to Congress

In April of each year, the Attorney General shall transmit to the Administrative Office of the United States Court and to Congress a report setting forth with respect to the preceding calendar year -

(a) the total number of applications made for orders and extensions of orders approving electronic surveillance under this subchapter; and

(b) the total number of such orders and extensions either granted, modified, or denied.

50 U.S.C. § 1808. Report of Attorney General to Congressional committees; limitation on authority or responsibility of information gathering activities of Congressional committees; report of Congressional committees to Congress

(a)(1) On a semiannual basis the Attorney General shall fully inform the Permanent Select Committee on Intelligence and the Committee on the Judiciary of the House of Representatives and the Select Committee on Intelligence and the Committee on the Judiciary of the Senate concerning all electronic surveillance under this subchapter. Nothing in this subchapter shall be deemed to limit the authority and responsibility of the appropriate committees of each House of Congress to obtain such information as they may need to carry out their respective functions and duties.

(2) Each report under the first sentence of paragraph (1) shall include a description of-

(A) the total number of applications made for orders and extensions of orders approving electronic surveillance under this subchapter where the nature and location of each facility or place at which the electronic surveillance will be directed is unknown;

(B) each criminal case in which information acquired under this chapter has been authorized for use at trial during the period covered by such report;

(C) the total number of emergency employments of electronic surveillance under section 1805(e) of this title and the total number of subsequent orders approving or denying such electronic surveillance; and

(D) the total number of authorizations under section 1805(f) of this title and the total number of subsequent emergency employments of electronic surveillance under section 1805(e) of this title or emergency physical searches pursuant to section 301(e).

(b) On or before one year after October 25, 1978, and on the same day each year for four years thereafter, the Permanent Select Committee on Intelligence and the Senate Select Committee on Intelligence shall report respectively to the House of Representatives and the Senate, concerning the implementation of this chapter. Said reports shall include but not be limited to an analysis and recommendations concerning whether this chapter should be (1) amended, (2) repealed, or (3) permitted to continue in effect without amendment.

50 U.S.C. § 1809. Criminal sanctions

(a) Prohibited activities

A person is guilty of an offense if he intentionally-

(1) engages in electronic surveillance under color of law except as authorized by this chapter, chapter 119, 121, or 206 of title 18, or any express statutory authorization that is an additional exclusive means for conducting electronic surveillance under section 1812 of this title;

(2) discloses or uses information obtained under color of law by electronic surveillance, knowing or having reason to know that the information was obtained through electronic surveillance not authorized by this chapter, chapter 119, 121, or 206 of title 18, or any express statutory authorization that is an additional exclusive means for conducting electronic surveillance under section 1812 of this title.

(b) Defense

It is a defense to a prosecution under subsection (a) that the defendant was a law enforcement or investigative officer engaged in the course of his official duties and the electronic surveillance was authorized by and conducted pursuant to a search warrant or court order of a court of competent jurisdiction.

(c) Penalties

An offense described in this section is punishable by a fine of not more than $10,000 or imprisonment for not more than five years, or both.

(d) Federal jurisdiction

There is Federal jurisdiction over an offense under this section if the person committing the offense was an officer or employee of the United States at the time the offense was committed.

50 U.S.C. § 1810. Civil liability

An aggrieved person, other than a foreign power or an agent of a foreign power, as defined in section 1801(a) or (b)(1)(A) of this title, respectively, who has been subjected to an electronic surveillance or about whom information obtained by electronic surveillance of such person has been disclosed or used in violation of section 1809 of this title shall have a cause of action against any person who committed such violation and shall be entitled to recover -

(a) actual damages, but not less than liquidated damages of $1,000 or $100 per day for each day of violation, whichever is greater;

(b) punitive damages; and

(c) reasonable attorney's fees and other investigation and litigation costs reasonably incurred.

50 U.S.C. § 1811. Authorization during time of war

Notwithstanding any other law, the President, through the Attorney General, may authorize electronic surveillance without a court order under this subchapter to acquire foreign intelligence information for a period not to exceed fifteen calendar days following a declaration of war by the Congress.

50 U.S.C. § 1821. Definitions

As used in this subchapter:

(1) The terms "foreign power", "agent of a foreign power", "international terrorism", "sabotage", "foreign intelligence information", "Attorney General", "United States person", "United States", "person", "weapon of mass destruction", and "State" shall have the same meanings as in section 1801 of this title, except as specifically provided by this subchapter.

(2) "Aggrieved person" means a person whose premises, property, information, or material is the target of physical search or any other person whose premises, property, information, or material was subject to physical search.

(3) "Foreign Intelligence Surveillance Court" means the court established by section 1803(a) of this title.

(4) "Minimization procedures" with respect to physical search, means-

(A) specific procedures, which shall be adopted by the Attorney General, that are reasonably designed in light of the purposes and technique of the particular physical search, to minimize the acquisition and retention, and prohibit the dissemination, of nonpublicly available information concerning unconsenting United States persons consistent with the need of the United States to obtain, produce, and disseminate foreign intelligence information;

(B) procedures that require that nonpublicly available information, which is not foreign intelligence information, as defined in section 1801(e)(1) of this title, shall not be disseminated in a manner that identifies any United States person, without such person's consent, unless such person's identity is necessary to understand such foreign intelligence information or assess its importance;

(C) notwithstanding subparagraphs (A) and (B), procedures that allow for the retention and dissemination of information that is evidence of a crime which has been, is being, or is about to be committed and that is to be retained or disseminated for law enforcement purposes; and

(D) notwithstanding subparagraphs (A), (B), and (C), with respect to any physical search approved pursuant to section 1822(a) of this title, procedures that require that no information, material, or property of a United States person shall be disclosed, disseminated, or used for any purpose or retained for longer than 72 hours unless a court order under section 1824 of this title is obtained or unless the Attorney General determines that the information indicates a threat of death or serious bodily harm to any person.

(5) "Physical search" means any physical intrusion within the United States into premises or property (including examination of the interior of property by technical means) that is intended to result in a seizure, reproduction, inspection, or alteration of information, material, or property, under circumstances in which a person has a reasonable expectation of privacy and a warrant would be required for law enforcement purposes, but does not include (A) "electronic surveillance", as defined in section 1801(f) of this title, or (B) the acquisition by the United States Government of foreign intelligence information from international or foreign communications, or foreign intelligence activities conducted in accordance with otherwise applicable Federal law involving a foreign electronic communications system, utilizing a means other than electronic surveillance as defined in section 1801(f) of this title.

50 U.S.C. § 1822. Authorization of physical searches for foreign intelligence purposes

(a) Presidential authorization

(1) Notwithstanding any other provision of law, the President, acting through the Attorney General, may authorize physical searches without a court order under this subchapter to acquire foreign intelligence information for periods of up to one year if-

(A) the Attorney General certifies in writing under oath that-

(i) the physical search is solely directed at premises, information, material, or property used exclusively by, or under the open and exclusive control of, a foreign power or powers (as defined in section 1801(a)(1), (2), or (3) of this title);

(ii) there is no substantial likelihood that the physical search will involve the premises, information, material, or property of a United States person; and

(iii) the proposed minimization procedures with respect to such physical search meet the definition of minimization procedures under paragraphs (1) through (4) of section 1821(4) of this title; and

(B) the Attorney General reports such minimization procedures and any changes thereto to the Permanent Select Committee on Intelligence of the House of Representatives and the Select Committee on Intelligence of the Senate at least 30 days before their effective date, unless the Attorney General determines that immediate action is required and notifies the committees immediately of such minimization procedures and the reason for their becoming effective immediately.

(2) A physical search authorized by this subsection may be conducted only in accordance with the certification and minimization procedures adopted by the Attorney General. The Attorney General shall assess compliance with such procedures and shall report such assessments to the Permanent Select Committee on Intelligence of the House of Representatives and the Select Committee on Intelligence of the Senate under the provisions of section 1826 of this title.

(3) The Attorney General shall immediately transmit under seal to the Foreign Intelligence Surveillance Court a copy of the certification. Such certification shall be maintained under security measures established by the Chief Justice of the United States with the concurrence of the Attorney General, in consultation with the Director of National Intelligence, and shall remain sealed unless-

(A) an application for a court order with respect to the physical search is made under section 1821(4) of this title and section 1823 of this title; or

(B) the certification is necessary to determine the legality of the physical search under section 1825(g) of this title.

(4)(A) With respect to physical searches authorized by this subsection, the Attorney General may direct a specified landlord, custodian, or other specified person to-

(i) furnish all information, facilities, or assistance necessary to accomplish the physical search in such a manner as will protect its secrecy and produce a minimum of interference with the services that such landlord, custodian, or other person is providing the target of the physical search; and

(ii) maintain under security procedures approved by the Attorney General and the Director of National Intelligence any records concerning the search or the aid furnished that such person wishes to retain.

(B) The Government shall compensate, at the prevailing rate, such landlord, custodian, or other person for furnishing such aid.

(b) Application for order; authorization

Applications for a court order under this subchapter are authorized if the President has, by written authorization, empowered the Attorney General to approve applications to the Foreign Intelligence Surveillance Court. Notwithstanding any other provision of law, a judge of the court to whom application is made may grant an order in accordance with section 1824 of this title approving a physical search in the United States of the premises, property, information, or material of a foreign power or an agent of a foreign power for the purpose of collecting foreign intelligence information.

(c) Jurisdiction of Foreign Intelligence Surveillance Court

The Foreign Intelligence Surveillance Court shall have jurisdiction to hear applications for and grant orders approving a physical search for the purpose of obtaining foreign intelligence information anywhere within the United States under the procedures set forth in this subchapter, except that no judge (except when sitting en banc) shall hear the same application which has been denied previously by another judge designated under section 1803(a) of this title. If any judge so designated denies an application for an order authorizing a physical search under this subchapter, such judge shall provide immediately for the record a written statement of each reason for such decision and, on motion of the United States, the record shall be transmitted, under seal, to the court of review established under section 1803(b) of this title.

(d) Court of review; record; transmittal to Supreme Court

The court of review established under section 1803(b) of this title shall have jurisdiction to review the denial of any application made under this subchapter. If such court determines that the application was properly denied, the court shall immediately provide for the record a written statement of each reason for its decision and, on petition of the United States for a writ of certiorari, the record shall be transmitted under seal to the Supreme Court, which shall have jurisdiction to review such decision.

(e) Expeditious conduct of proceedings; security measures for maintenance of records

Judicial proceedings under this subchapter shall be concluded as expeditiously as possible. The record of proceedings under this subchapter, including applications made and orders granted, shall be maintained under security measures established by the Chief Justice of the United States in consultation with the Attorney General and the Director of National Intelligence.

50 U.S.C. § 1823. Application for order

(a) Submission by Federal officer; approval of Attorney General; contents

Each application for an order approving a physical search under this subchapter shall be made by a Federal officer in writing upon oath or affirmation to a judge of the Foreign Intelligence Surveillance Court. Each application shall require the approval of the Attorney General based upon the Attorney General's finding that it satisfies the criteria and requirements for such application as set forth in this subchapter. Each application shall include-

(1) the identity of the Federal officer making the application;

(2) the identity, if known, or a description of the target of the search, and a description of the premises or property to be searched and of the information, material, or property to be seized, reproduced, or altered;

(3) a statement of the facts and circumstances relied upon by the applicant to justify the applicant's belief that-

> (A) the target of the physical search is a foreign power or an agent of a foreign power;

> (B) the premises or property to be searched contains foreign intelligence information; and

> (C) the premises or property to be searched is or is about to be owned, used, possessed by, or is in transit to or from a foreign power or an agent of a foreign power;

(4) a statement of the proposed minimization procedures;

(5) a statement of the nature of the foreign intelligence sought and the manner in which the physical search is to be conducted;

(6) a certification or certifications by the Assistant to the President for National Security Affairs, an executive branch official or officials designated by the President from among those executive branch officers employed in the area of national security or defense and appointed by the President, by and with the advice and consent of the Senate, or the Deputy Director of the Federal Bureau of Investigation, if designated by the President as a certifying official-

> (A) that the certifying official deems the information sought to be foreign intelligence information;

> (B) that a significant purpose of the search is to obtain foreign intelligence information;

> (C) that such information cannot reasonably be obtained by normal investigative techniques;

> (D) that designates the type of foreign intelligence information being sought according to the categories described in section 1801(e) of this title; and

> (E) includes a statement explaining the basis for the certifications required by subparagraphs (C) and (D);

(7) where the physical search involves a search of the residence of a United States person, the Attorney General shall state what investigative techniques have previously been utilized to obtain the foreign intelligence information concerned and the degree to which these techniques resulted in acquiring such information; and

(8) a statement of the facts concerning all previous applications that have been made to any judge under this subchapter involving any of the persons, premises, or property specified in the application, and the action taken on each previous application.

(b) Additional affidavits or certifications

The Attorney General may require any other affidavit or certification from any other officer in connection with the application.

(c) Additional information

The judge may require the applicant to furnish such other information as may be necessary to make the determinations required by section 1824 of this title.

(d) Personal review by Attorney General

(1)(A) Upon written request of the Director of the Federal Bureau of Investigation, the Secretary of Defense, the Secretary of State, the Director of National Intelligence, or the Director of the Central Intelligence Agency, the Attorney General shall personally review under subsection (a) an application under that subsection for a target described in section 1801(b)(2) of this title.

(B) Except when disabled or otherwise unavailable to make a request referred to in subparagraph (A), an official referred to in that subparagraph may not delegate the authority to make a request referred to in that subparagraph.

(C) Each official referred to in subparagraph (A) with authority to make a request under that subparagraph shall take appropriate actions in advance to ensure that delegation of such authority is clearly established in the event such official is disabled or otherwise unavailable to make such request.

(2)(A) If as a result of a request under paragraph (1) the Attorney General determines not to approve an application under the second sentence of subsection (a) for purposes of making the application under this section, the Attorney General shall provide written notice of the determination to the official making the request for the review of the application under that paragraph. Except when disabled or otherwise unavailable to make a determination under the preceding sentence, the Attorney General may not delegate the responsibility to make a determination under that sentence. The Attorney General shall take appropriate actions in advance to ensure that delegation of such responsibility is clearly established in the event the Attorney General is disabled or otherwise unavailable to make such determination.

(B) Notice with respect to an application under subparagraph (A) shall set forth the modifications, if any, of the application that are necessary in order for the Attorney General to approve the application under the second sentence of subsection (a) for purposes of making the application under this section.

(C) Upon review of any modifications of an application set forth under subparagraph (B), the official notified of the modifications under this paragraph shall modify the application if such official determines that such modification is warranted. Such official shall supervise the making of any modification under this subparagraph. Except when disabled or otherwise unavailable to supervise the making of any modification under the preceding sentence, such official may not delegate the responsibility to supervise the making of any modification under that preceding sentence. Each such official shall take appropriate actions in advance to ensure that delegation of such responsibility is clearly established in the event such official is disabled or otherwise unavailable to supervise the making of such modification.

50 U.S.C. § 1824. Issuance of order

(a) Necessary findings

Upon an application made pursuant to section 1823 of this title, the judge shall enter an ex parte order as requested or as modified approving the physical search if the judge finds that-

(1) the application has been made by a Federal officer and approved by the Attorney General;

(2) on the basis of the facts submitted by the applicant there is probable cause to believe that-

(A) the target of the physical search is a foreign power or an agent of a foreign power, except that no United States person may be considered an agent of a foreign power solely upon the basis of activities protected by the first amendment to the Constitution of the United States; and

(B) the premises or property to be searched is or is about to be owned, used, possessed by, or is in transit to or from an agent of a foreign power or a foreign power;

(3) the proposed minimization procedures meet the definition of minimization contained in this subchapter; and

(4) the application which has been filed contains all statements and certifications required by section 1823 of this title, and, if the target is a United States person, the certification or certifications are not clearly erroneous on the basis of the statement made under section 1823(a)(6)(E) of this title and any other information furnished under section 1823(c) of this title.

(b) Determination of probable cause

In determining whether or not probable cause exists for purposes of an order under subsection (a)(2), a judge may consider past activities of the target, as well as facts and circumstances relating to current or future activities of the target.

(c) Specifications and directions of orders

An order approving a physical search under this section shall-

(1) specify-

(A) the identity, if known, or a description of the target of the physical search;

(B) the nature and location of each of the premises or property to be searched;

(C) the type of information, material, or property to be seized, altered, or reproduced;

(D) a statement of the manner in which the physical search is to be conducted and, whenever more than one physical search is authorized under the order, the authorized scope of each search and what minimization procedures shall apply to the information acquired by each search; and

(E) the period of time during which physical searches are approved; and

(2) direct-

(A) that the minimization procedures be followed;

(B) that, upon the request of the applicant, a specified landlord, custodian, or other specified person furnish the applicant forthwith all information, facilities, or assistance necessary to accomplish the physical search in such a manner as will protect its secrecy and produce a minimum of interference with the services that such landlord, custodian, or other person is providing the target of the physical search;

(C) that such landlord, custodian, or other person maintain under security procedures approved by the Attorney General and the Director of National Intelligence any records concerning the search or the aid furnished that such person wishes to retain;

(D) that the applicant compensate, at the prevailing rate, such landlord, custodian, or other person for furnishing such aid; and

(E) that the Federal officer conducting the physical search promptly report to the court the circumstances and results of the physical search.

(d) Duration of order; extensions; assessment of compliance

(1) An order issued under this section may approve a physical search for the period necessary to achieve its purpose, or for 90 days, whichever is less, except that (A) an order under this section shall approve a physical search targeted against a foreign power, as defined in paragraph (1), (2), or (3) of section 1801(a) of this title, for the period specified in the application or for one year, whichever is less, and (B) an order under this section for a physical search targeted against an agent of a foreign power who is not a United States person may be for the period specified in the application or for 120 days, whichever is less.

(2) Extensions of an order issued under this subchapter may be granted on the same basis as the original order upon an application for an extension and new findings made in the same manner as required for the original order, except that an extension of an order under this chapter for a physical search targeted against a foreign power, as defined in paragraph (5), (6), or (7) of section 1801(a) of this title, or against a foreign power, as defined in section 1801(a)(4) of this title, that is not a United States person, or against an agent of a foreign power who is not a United States person, may be for a period not to exceed one year if the judge finds probable cause to

believe that no property of any individual United States person will be acquired during the period.

(3) At or before the end of the period of time for which a physical search is approved by an order or an extension, or at any time after a physical search is carried out, the judge may assess compliance with the minimization procedures by reviewing the circumstances under which information concerning United States persons was acquired, retained, or disseminated.

(e) Emergency orders

(1) Notwithstanding any other provision of this subchapter, the Attorney General may authorize the emergency employment of a physical search if the Attorney General-

(A) reasonably determines that an emergency situation exists with respect to the employment of a physical search to obtain foreign intelligence information before an order authorizing such physical search can with due diligence be obtained;

(B) reasonably determines that the factual basis for issuance of an order under this subchapter to approve such physical search exists;

(C) informs, either personally or through a designee, a judge of the Foreign Intelligence Surveillance Court at the time of such authorization that the decision has been made to employ an emergency physical search; and

(D) makes an application in accordance with this subchapter to a judge of the Foreign Intelligence Surveillance Court as soon as practicable, but not more than 7 days after the Attorney General authorizes such physical search.

(2) If the Attorney General authorizes the emergency employment of a physical search under paragraph (1), the Attorney General shall require that the minimization procedures required by this subchapter for the issuance of a judicial order be followed.

(3) In the absence of a judicial order approving such physical search, the physical search shall terminate when the information sought is obtained, when the application for the order is denied, or after the expiration of 7 days from the time of authorization by the Attorney General, whichever is earliest.

(4) A denial of the application made under this subsection may be reviewed as provided in section 1803 of this title.

(5) In the event that such application for approval is denied, or in any other case where the physical search is terminated and no order is issued approving the physical search, no information obtained or evidence derived from such physical search shall be received in evidence or otherwise disclosed in any trial, hearing, or other proceeding in or before any court, grand jury, department, office, agency, regulatory body, legislative committee, or other authority of the United States, a State, or political subdivision thereof, and no information concerning any United States

person acquired from such physical search shall subsequently be used or disclosed in any other manner by Federal officers or employees without the consent of such person, except with the approval of the Attorney General if the information indicates a threat of death or serious bodily harm to any person.

(6) The Attorney General shall assess compliance with the requirements of paragraph (5).

(f) Retention of applications and orders

Applications made and orders granted under this subchapter shall be retained for a period of at least 10 years from the date of the application.

50 U.S.C. § 1825. Use of information

(a) Compliance with minimization procedures; lawful purposes

Information acquired from a physical search conducted pursuant to this subchapter concerning any United States person may be used and disclosed by Federal officers and employees without the consent of the United States person only in accordance with the minimization procedures required by this subchapter. No information acquired from a physical search pursuant to this subchapter may be used or disclosed by Federal officers or employees except for lawful purposes.

(b) Notice of search and identification of property seized, altered, or reproduced

Where a physical search authorized and conducted pursuant to section 1824 of this title involves the residence of a United States person, and, at any time after the search the Attorney General determines there is no national security interest in continuing to maintain the secrecy of the search, the Attorney General shall provide notice to the United States person whose residence was searched of the fact of the search conducted pursuant to this chapter and shall identify any property of such person seized, altered, or reproduced during such search.

(c) Statement for disclosure

No information acquired pursuant to this subchapter shall be disclosed for law enforcement purposes unless such disclosure is accompanied by a statement that such information, or any information derived therefrom, may only be used in a criminal proceeding with the advance authorization of the Attorney General.

(d) Notification by United States

Whenever the United States intends to enter into evidence or otherwise use or disclose in any trial, hearing, or other proceeding in or before any court, department, officer, agency, regulatory body, or other authority of the United States, against an aggrieved person, any information obtained or derived from a physical search pursuant to the authority of this subchapter, the United States shall, prior to the trial, hearing, or the other proceeding or at a reasonable time prior to an effort to so disclose or so use that information or submit it in evidence, notify the aggrieved person and the court or other authority in which the information is to be disclosed or used that the United States intends to so disclose or so use such information.

(e) Notification by States or political subdivisions

Whenever any State or political subdivision thereof intends to enter into evidence or otherwise use or disclose in any trial, hearing, or other proceeding in or before any court, department, officer, agency, regulatory body, or other authority of a State or a political subdivision thereof against an aggrieved person any information obtained or derived from a physical search pursuant to the authority of this subchapter, the State or political subdivision thereof shall notify the aggrieved person, the court or other authority in which the information is to be disclosed or used, and the Attorney General that the State or political subdivision thereof intends to so disclose or so use such information.

(f) Motion to suppress

> (1) Any person against whom evidence obtained or derived from a physical search to which he is an aggrieved person is to be, or has been, introduced or otherwise used or disclosed in any trial, hearing, or other proceeding in or before any court, department, officer, agency, regulatory body, or other authority of the United States, a State, or a political subdivision thereof, may move to suppress the evidence obtained or derived from such search on the grounds that-
>
> > (A) the information was unlawfully acquired; or
> >
> > (B) the physical search was not made in conformity with an order of authorization or approval.
>
> (2) Such a motion shall be made before the trial, hearing, or other proceeding unless there was no opportunity to make such a motion or the person was not aware of the grounds of the motion.

(g) In camera and ex parte review by district court

Whenever a court or other authority is notified pursuant to subsection (d) or (e), or whenever a motion is made pursuant to subsection (f), or whenever any motion or request is made by an aggrieved person pursuant to any other statute or rule of the United States or any State before any court or other authority of the United States or any State to discover or obtain applications or orders or other materials relating to a physical search authorized by this subchapter or to discover, obtain, or suppress evidence or information obtained or derived from a physical search authorized by this subchapter, the United States district court or, where the motion is made before another authority, the United States district court in the same district as the authority shall, notwithstanding any other provision of law, if the Attorney General files an affidavit under oath that disclosure or any adversary hearing would harm the national security of the United States, review in camera and ex parte the application, order, and such other materials relating to the physical search as may be necessary to determine whether the physical search of the aggrieved person was lawfully authorized and conducted. In making this determination, the court may disclose to the aggrieved person, under appropriate security procedures and protective orders, portions of the application, order, or other materials relating to the physical search, or may require the Attorney General to provide to the aggrieved person a summary of such materials, only where such disclosure is necessary to make an accurate determination of the legality of the physical search.

(h) Suppression of evidence; denial of motion

If the United States district court pursuant to subsection (g) determines that the physical search was not lawfully authorized or conducted, it shall, in accordance with the requirements of law, suppress the evidence which was unlawfully obtained or derived from the physical search of the aggrieved person or otherwise grant the motion of the aggrieved person. If the court determines that the physical search was lawfully authorized or conducted, it shall deny the motion of the aggrieved person except to the extent that due process requires discovery or disclosure.

(i) Finality of orders

Orders granting motions or requests under subsection (h), decisions under this section that a physical search was not lawfully authorized or conducted, and orders of the United States district court requiring review or granting disclosure of applications, orders, or other materials relating to the physical search shall be final orders and binding upon all courts of the United States and the several States except a United States Court of Appeals or the Supreme Court.

(j) Notification of emergency execution of physical search; contents; postponement, suspension, or elimination

(1) If an emergency execution of a physical search is authorized under section 1824(d) of this title and a subsequent order approving the search is not obtained, the judge shall cause to be served on any United States person named in the application and on such other United States persons subject to the search as the judge may determine in his discretion it is in the interests of justice to serve, notice of-

(A) the fact of the application;

(B) the period of the search; and

(C) the fact that during the period information was or was not obtained.

(2) On an ex parte showing of good cause to the judge, the serving of the notice required by this subsection may be postponed or suspended for a period not to exceed 90 days. Thereafter, on a further ex parte showing of good cause, the court shall forego ordering the serving of the notice required under this subsection.

(k) Coordination with law enforcement on national security matters

(1) Federal officers who conduct physical searches to acquire foreign intelligence information under this subchapter may consult with Federal law enforcement officers or law enforcement personnel of a State or political subdivision of a State (including the chief executive officer of that State or political subdivision who has the authority to appoint or direct the chief law enforcement officer of that State or political subdivision) to coordinate efforts to investigate or protect against-

(A) actual or potential attack or other grave hostile acts of a foreign power or an agent of a foreign power;

(B) sabotage, international terrorism, or the international proliferation of weapons of mass destruction by a foreign power or an agent of a foreign power; or

(C) clandestine intelligence activities by an intelligence service or network of a foreign power or by an agent of a foreign power.

(2) Coordination authorized under paragraph (1) shall not preclude the certification required by section 1823(a)(6) of this title or the entry of an order under section 1824 of this title.

50 U.S.C. § 1826. Congressional oversight

On a semiannual basis the Attorney General shall fully inform the Permanent Select Committee on Intelligence and the Committee on the Judiciary of the House of Representatives and the Select Committee on Intelligence and the Committee on the Judiciary of the Senate concerning all physical searches conducted pursuant to this subchapter. On a semiannual basis the Attorney General shall also provide to those committees a report setting forth with respect to the preceding six-month period-

(1) the total number of applications made for orders approving physical searches under this subchapter;

(2) the total number of such orders either granted, modified, or denied;

(3) the number of physical searches which involved searches of the residences, offices, or personal property of United States persons, and the number of occasions, if any, where the Attorney General provided notice pursuant to section 1825(b) of this title; and

(4) the total number of emergency physical searches authorized by the Attorney General under section 1824(e) of this title and the total number of subsequent orders approving or denying such physical searches.

50 U.S.C. § 1827. Penalties

(a) Prohibited activities

A person is guilty of an offense if he intentionally -

(1) under color of law for the purpose of obtaining foreign intelligence information, executes a physical search within the United States except as authorized by statute; or

(2) discloses or uses information obtained under color of law by physical search within the United States, knowing or having reason to know that the information was obtained through physical search not authorized by statute, for the purpose of obtaining intelligence information.

(b) Defense

It is a defense to a prosecution under subsection (a) of this section that the defendant was a law enforcement or investigative officer engaged in the course of his official duties and the physical search was authorized by and conducted pursuant to a search warrant or court order of a court of competent jurisdiction.

(c) Fine or imprisonment

An offense described in this section is punishable by a fine of not more than $10,000 or imprisonment for not more than five years, or both.

(d) Federal jurisdiction

There is Federal jurisdiction over an offense under this section if the person committing the offense was an officer or employee of the United States at the time the offense was committed.

50 U.S.C. § 1828. Civil liability

An aggrieved person, other than a foreign power or an agent of a foreign power, as defined in section 1801(a) or (b)(1)(A), respectively, of this title, whose premises, property, information, or material has been subjected to a physical search within the United States or about whom information obtained by such a physical search has been disclosed or used in violation of section 1827 of this title shall have a cause of action against any person who committed such violation and shall be entitled to recover -

> (1) actual damages, but not less than liquidated damages of $1,000 or $100 per day for each day of violation, whichever is greater;
>
> (2) punitive damages; and
>
> (3) reasonable attorney's fees and other investigative and litigation costs reasonably incurred.

50 U.S.C. § 1829. Authorization during time of war

Notwithstanding any other provision of law, the President, through the Attorney General, may authorize physical searches without a court order under this subchapter to acquire foreign intelligence information for a period not to exceed 15 calendar days following a declaration of war by the Congress.

50 U.S.C. § 1841. Definitions

As used in this subchapter:

> (1) The terms "foreign power", "agent of a foreign power", "international terrorism", "foreign intelligence information", "Attorney General", "United States person", "United States", "person", and "State" shall have the same meanings as in section 1801 of this title.
>
> (2) The terms "pen register" and "trap and trace device" have the meanings given such terms in section 3127 of title 18.
>
> (3) The term "aggrieved person" means any person-

(A) whose telephone line was subject to the installation or use of a pen register or trap and trace device authorized by this subchapter; or

(B) whose communication instrument or device was subject to the use of a pen register or trap and trace device authorized by this subchapter to capture incoming electronic or other communications impulses.

(4)(A) The term "specific selection term"-

(i) is a term that specifically identifies a person, account, address, or personal device, or any other specific identifier; and

(ii) is used to limit, to the greatest extent reasonably practicable, the scope of information sought, consistent with the purpose for seeking the use of the pen register or trap and trace device.

(B) A specific selection term under subparagraph (A) does not include an identifier that does not limit, to the greatest extent reasonably practicable, the scope of information sought, consistent with the purpose for seeking the use of the pen register or trap and trace device, such as an identifier that-

(i) identifies an electronic communication service provider (as that term is defined in section 1881 of this title) or a provider of remote computing service (as that term is defined in section 2711 of title 18), when not used as part of a specific identifier as described in subparagraph (A), unless the provider is itself a subject of an authorized investigation for which the specific selection term is used as the basis for the use; or

(ii) identifies a broad geographic region, including the United States, a city, a county, a State, a zip code, or an area code, when not used as part of a specific identifier as described in subparagraph (A).

(C) For purposes of subparagraph (A), the term "address" means a physical address or electronic address, such as an electronic mail address or temporarily assigned network address (including an Internet protocol address).

(D) Nothing in this paragraph shall be construed to preclude the use of multiple terms or identifiers to meet the requirements of subparagraph (A).

50 U.S.C. § 1842. Pen registers and trap and trace devices for foreign intelligence and international terrorism investigations

(a) Application for authorization or approval

(1) Notwithstanding any other provision of law, the Attorney General or a designated attorney for the Government may make an application for an order or an extension of an order authorizing or approving the installation and use of a pen register or trap and trace device for any investigation to obtain foreign intelligence information not concerning a United States person or to protect against international terrorism or clandestine intelligence activities, provided that such investigation of a United States person is not conducted solely upon the basis of activities protected

by the first amendment to the Constitution which is being conducted by the Federal Bureau of Investigation under such guidelines as the Attorney General approves pursuant to Executive Order No. 12333, or a successor order.

(2) The authority under paragraph (1) is in addition to the authority under subchapter I of this chapter to conduct the electronic surveillance referred to in that paragraph.

(b) Form of application; recipient

Each application under this section shall be in writing under oath or affirmation to-

(1) a judge of the court established by section 1803(a) of this title; or

(2) a United States Magistrate Judge under chapter 43 of title 28 who is publicly designated by the Chief Justice of the United States to have the power to hear applications for and grant orders approving the installation and use of a pen register or trap and trace device on behalf of a judge of that court.

(c) Executive approval; contents of application

Each application under this section shall require the approval of the Attorney General, or a designated attorney for the Government, and shall include-

(1) the identity of the Federal officer seeking to use the pen register or trap and trace device covered by the application;

(2) a certification by the applicant that the information likely to be obtained is foreign intelligence information not concerning a United States person or is relevant to an ongoing investigation to protect against international terrorism or clandestine intelligence activities, provided that such investigation of a United States person is not conducted solely upon the basis of activities protected by the first amendment to the Constitution; and

(3) a specific selection term to be used as the basis for the use of the pen register or trap and trace device.

(d) Ex parte judicial order of approval

(1) Upon an application made pursuant to this section, the judge shall enter an ex parte order as requested, or as modified, approving the installation and use of a pen register or trap and trace device if the judge finds that the application satisfies the requirements of this section.

(2) An order issued under this section-

(A) shall specify-

(i) the identity, if known, of the person who is the subject of the investigation;

(ii) the identity, if known, of the person to whom is leased or in whose name is listed the telephone line or other facility to which the pen register or trap and trace device is to be attached or applied; and

(iii) the attributes of the communications to which the order applies, such as the number or other identifier, and, if known, the location of the telephone line or other facility to which the pen register or trap and trace device is to be attached or applied and, in the case of a trap and trace device, the geographic limits of the trap and trace order;

(B) shall direct that-

(i) upon request of the applicant, the provider of a wire or electronic communication service, landlord, custodian, or other person shall furnish any information, facilities, or technical assistance necessary to accomplish the installation and operation of the pen register or trap and trace device in such a manner as will protect its secrecy and produce a minimum amount of interference with the services that such provider, landlord, custodian, or other person is providing the person concerned;

(ii) such provider, landlord, custodian, or other person-

(I) shall not disclose the existence of the investigation or of the pen register or trap and trace device to any person unless or until ordered by the court; and

(II) shall maintain, under security procedures approved by the Attorney General and the Director of National Intelligence pursuant to section 1805(b)(2)(C) of this title, any records concerning the pen register or trap and trace device or the aid furnished; and

(iii) the applicant shall compensate such provider, landlord, custodian, or other person for reasonable expenses incurred by such provider, landlord, custodian, or other person in providing such information, facilities, or technical assistance; and

(C) shall direct that, upon the request of the applicant, the provider of a wire or electronic communication service shall disclose to the Federal officer using the pen register or trap and trace device covered by the order-

(i) in the case of the customer or subscriber using the service covered by the order (for the period specified by the order)-

(I) the name of the customer or subscriber;

(II) the address of the customer or subscriber;

(III) the telephone or instrument number, or other subscriber number or identifier, of the customer or subscriber, including any temporarily assigned network address or associated routing or transmission information;

(IV) the length of the provision of service by such provider to the customer or subscriber and the types of services utilized by the customer or subscriber;

(V) in the case of a provider of local or long distance telephone service, any local or long distance telephone records of the customer or subscriber;

(VI) if applicable, any records reflecting period of usage (or sessions) by the customer or subscriber; and

(VII) any mechanisms and sources of payment for such service, including the number of any credit card or bank account utilized for payment for such service; and

(ii) if available, with respect to any customer or subscriber of incoming or outgoing communications to or from the service covered by the order-

(I) the name of such customer or subscriber;

(II) the address of such customer or subscriber;

(III) the telephone or instrument number, or other subscriber number or identifier, of such customer or subscriber, including any temporarily assigned network address or associated routing or transmission information; and

(IV) the length of the provision of service by such provider to such customer or subscriber and the types of services utilized by such customer or subscriber.

(e) Time limitation

(1) Except as provided in paragraph (2), an order issued under this section shall authorize the installation and use of a pen register or trap and trace device for a period not to exceed 90 days. Extensions of such an order may be granted, but only upon an application for an order under this section and upon the judicial finding required by subsection (d). The period of extension shall be for a period not to exceed 90 days.

(2) In the case of an application under subsection (c) where the applicant has certified that the information likely to be obtained is foreign intelligence information not concerning a United States person, an order, or an extension of an order, under this section may be for a period not to exceed one year.

(f) Cause of action barred

No cause of action shall lie in any court against any provider of a wire or electronic communication service, landlord, custodian, or other person (including any officer, employee, agent, or other specified person thereof) that furnishes any information, facilities, or technical assistance under subsection (d) in accordance with the terms of an order issued under this section.

(g) Furnishing of results

Unless otherwise ordered by the judge, the results of a pen register or trap and trace device shall be furnished at reasonable intervals during regular business hours for the duration of the order to the authorized Government official or officials.

(h) Privacy procedures

(1) In general

The Attorney General shall ensure that appropriate policies and procedures are in place to safeguard nonpublicly available information concerning United States persons that is collected through the use of a pen register or trap and trace device installed under this section. Such policies and procedures shall, to the maximum extent practicable and consistent with the need to protect national security, include privacy protections that apply to the collection, retention, and use of information concerning United States persons.

(2) Rule of construction

Nothing in this subsection limits the authority of the court established under section 1803(a) of this title or of the Attorney General to impose additional privacy or minimization procedures with regard to the installation or use of a pen register or trap and trace device.

50 U.S.C. § 1843. Authorization during emergencies

(a) Requirements for authorization

Notwithstanding any other provision of this subchapter, when the Attorney General makes a determination described in subsection (b), the Attorney General may authorize the installation and use of a pen register or trap and trace device on an emergency basis to gather foreign intelligence information not concerning a United States person or information to protect against international terrorism or clandestine intelligence activities, provided that such investigation of a United States person is not conducted solely upon the basis of activities protected by the first amendment to the Constitution if-

(1) a judge referred to in section 1842(b) of this title is informed by the Attorney General or his designee at the time of such authorization that the decision has been made to install and use the pen register or trap and trace device, as the case may be, on an emergency basis; and

(2) an application in accordance with section 1842 of this title is made to such judge as soon as practicable, but not more than 7 days, after the Attorney General authorizes the installation and use of the pen register or trap and trace device, as the case may be, under this section.

(b) Determination of emergency and factual basis

A determination under this subsection is a reasonable determination by the Attorney General that-

(1) an emergency requires the installation and use of a pen register or trap and trace device to obtain foreign intelligence information not concerning a United States person or information to protect against international terrorism or clandestine intelligence activities, provided that such investigation of a United States person is not conducted solely upon the basis of activities protected by the first amendment to the Constitution before an order authorizing the installation and use of the pen

register or trap and trace device, as the case may be, can with due diligence be obtained under section 1842 of this title; and

(2) the factual basis for issuance of an order under such section 1842 of this title to approve the installation and use of the pen register or trap and trace device, as the case may be, exists.

(c) Effect of absence of order

(1) In the absence of an order applied for under subsection (a)(2) approving the installation and use of a pen register or trap and trace device authorized under this section, the installation and use of the pen register or trap and trace device, as the case may be, shall terminate at the earlier of-

(A) when the information sought is obtained;

(B) when the application for the order is denied under section 1842 of this title; or

(C) 7 days after the time of the authorization by the Attorney General.

(2) In the event that an application for an order applied for under subsection (a)(2) is denied, or in any other case where the installation and use of a pen register or trap and trace device under this section is terminated and no order under section 1842 of this title is issued approving the installation and use of the pen register or trap and trace device, as the case may be, no information obtained or evidence derived from the use of the pen register or trap and trace device, as the case may be, shall be received in evidence or otherwise disclosed in any trial, hearing, or other proceeding in or before any court, grand jury, department, office, agency, regulatory body, legislative committee, or other authority of the United States, a State, or political subdivision thereof, and no information concerning any United States person acquired from the use of the pen register or trap and trace device, as the case may be, shall subsequently be used or disclosed in any other manner by Federal officers or employees without the consent of such person, except with the approval of the Attorney General if the information indicates a threat of death or serious bodily harm to any person.

(d) Privacy procedures

Information collected through the use of a pen register or trap and trace device installed under this section shall be subject to the policies and procedures required under section 1842(h) of this title.

50 U.S.C. § 1844. Authorization during time of war

Notwithstanding any other provision of law, the President, through the Attorney General, may authorize the use of a pen register or trap and trace device without a court order under this subchapter to acquire foreign intelligence information for a period not to exceed 15 calendar days following a declaration of war by Congress.

United States
Foreign Intelligence Surveillance Act

50 U.S.C. § 1845. Use of information

(a) In general

(1) Information acquired from the use of a pen register or trap and trace device installed pursuant to this subchapter concerning any United States person may be used and disclosed by Federal officers and employees without the consent of the United States person only in accordance with the provisions of this section.

(2) No information acquired from a pen register or trap and trace device installed and used pursuant to this subchapter may be used or disclosed by Federal officers or employees except for lawful purposes.

(b) Disclosure for law enforcement purposes No information acquired pursuant to this subchapter shall be disclosed for law enforcement purposes unless such disclosure is accompanied by a statement that such information, or any information derived therefrom, may only be used in a criminal proceeding with the advance authorization of the Attorney General.

(c) Notification of intended disclosure by United States Whenever the United States intends to enter into evidence or otherwise use or disclose in any trial, hearing, or other proceeding in or before any court, department, officer, agency, regulatory body, or other authority of the United States against an aggrieved person any information obtained or derived from the use of a pen register or trap and trace device pursuant to this subchapter, the United States shall, before the trial, hearing, or the other proceeding or at a reasonable time before an effort to so disclose or so use that information or submit it in evidence, notify the aggrieved person and the court or other authority in which the information is to be disclosed or used that the United States intends to so disclose or so use such information.

(d) Notification of intended disclosure by State or political subdivision Whenever any State or political subdivision thereof intends to enter into evidence or otherwise use or disclose in any trial, hearing, or other proceeding in or before any court, department, officer, agency, regulatory body, or other authority of the State or political subdivision thereof against an aggrieved person any information obtained or derived from the use of a pen register or trap and trace device pursuant to this subchapter, the State or political subdivision thereof shall notify the aggrieved person, the court or other authority in which the information is to be disclosed or used, and the Attorney General that the State or political subdivision thereof intends to so disclose or so use such information.

(e) Motion to suppress

(1) Any aggrieved person against whom evidence obtained or derived from the use of a pen register or trap and trace device is to be, or has been, introduced or otherwise used or disclosed in any trial, hearing, or other proceeding in or before any court, department, officer, agency, regulatory body, or other authority of the United States, or a State or political subdivision thereof, may move to suppress the evidence

obtained or derived from the use of the pen register or trap and trace device, as the case may be, on the grounds that -

    (A) the information was unlawfully acquired; or

    (B) the use of the pen register or trap and trace device, as the case may be, was not made in conformity with an order of authorization or approval under this subchapter.

(2) A motion under paragraph (1) shall be made before the trial, hearing, or other proceeding unless there was no opportunity to make such a motion or the aggrieved person concerned was not aware of the grounds of the motion.

(f) In camera and ex parte review

(1) Whenever a court or other authority is notified pursuant to subsection (c) or (d) of this section, whenever a motion is made pursuant to subsection (e) of this section, or whenever any motion or request is made by an aggrieved person pursuant to any other statute or rule of the United States or any State before any court or other authority of the United States or any State to discover or obtain applications or orders or other materials relating to the use of a pen register or trap and trace device authorized by this subchapter or to discover, obtain, or suppress evidence or information obtained or derived from the use of a pen register or trap and trace device authorized by this subchapter, the United States district court or, where the motion is made before another authority, the United States district court in the same district as the authority shall, notwithstanding any other provision of law and if the Attorney General files an affidavit under oath that disclosure or any adversary hearing would harm the national security of the United States, review in camera and ex parte the application, order, and such other materials relating to the use of the pen register or trap and trace device, as the case may be, as may be necessary to determine whether the use of the pen register or trap and trace device, as the case may be, was lawfully authorized and conducted.

(2) In making a determination under paragraph (1), the court may disclose to the aggrieved person, under appropriate security procedures and protective orders, portions of the application, order, or other materials relating to the use of the pen register or trap and trace device, as the case may be, or may require the Attorney General to provide to the aggrieved person a summary of such materials, only where such disclosure is necessary to make an accurate determination of the legality of the use of the pen register or trap and trace device, as the case may be.

(g) Effect of determination of lawfulness

(1) If the United States district court determines pursuant to subsection (f) of this section that the use of a pen register or trap and trace device was not lawfully authorized or conducted, the court may, in accordance with the requirements of law, suppress the evidence which was unlawfully obtained or derived from the use of the

pen register or trap and trace device, as the case may be, or otherwise grant the motion of the aggrieved person.

(2) If the court determines that the use of the pen register or trap and trace device, as the case may be, was lawfully authorized or conducted, it may deny the motion of the aggrieved person except to the extent that due process requires discovery or disclosure.

(h) Binding final orders

Orders granting motions or requests under subsection (g) of this section, decisions under this section that the use of a pen register or trap and trace device was not lawfully authorized or conducted, and orders of the United States district court requiring review or granting disclosure of applications, orders, or other materials relating to the installation and use of a pen register or trap and trace device shall be final orders and binding upon all courts of the United States and the several States except a United States Court of Appeals or the Supreme Court.

50 U.S.C. § 1846. Congressional oversight

(a) On a semiannual basis, the Attorney General shall fully inform the Permanent Select Committee on Intelligence of the House of Representatives and the Select Committee on Intelligence of the Senate, and the Committee on the Judiciary of the House of Representatives and the Committee on the Judiciary of the Senate, concerning all uses of pen registers and trap and trace devices pursuant to this subchapter.

(b) On a semiannual basis, the Attorney General shall also provide to the committees referred to in subsection (a) and to the Committees on the Judiciary of the House of Representatives and the Senate a report setting forth with respect to the preceding 6-month period-

(1) the total number of applications made for orders approving the use of pen registers or trap and trace devices under this subchapter;

(2) the total number of such orders either granted, modified, or denied;

(3) the total number of pen registers and trap and trace devices whose installation and use was authorized by the Attorney General on an emergency basis under section 1843 of this title, and the total number of subsequent orders approving or denying the installation and use of such pen registers and trap and trace devices;

(4) each department or agency on behalf of which the Attorney General or a designated attorney for the Government has made an application for an order authorizing or approving the installation and use of a pen register or trap and trace device under this subchapter; and

(5) for each department or agency described in paragraph (4), each number described in paragraphs (1), (2), and (3).

50 U.S.C. § 1861. Access to Certain Business Records for Foreign Intelligence and International Terrorism Investigations

(a) Application for order; conduct of investigation generally

(1) Subject to paragraph (3), the Director of the Federal Bureau of Investigation or a designee of the Director (whose rank shall be no lower than Assistant Special Agent in Charge) may make an application for an order requiring the production of any tangible things (including books, records, papers, documents, and other items) for an investigation to obtain foreign intelligence information not concerning a United States person or to protect against international terrorism or clandestine intelligence activities, provided that such investigation of a United States person is not conducted solely upon the basis of activities protected by the first amendment to the Constitution.

(2) An investigation conducted under this section shall-

(A) be conducted under guidelines approved by the Attorney General under Executive Order 12333 (or a successor order); and

(B) not be conducted of a United States person solely upon the basis of activities protected by the first amendment to the Constitution of the United States.

(3) In the case of an application for an order requiring the production of library circulation records, library patron lists, book sales records, book customer lists, firearms sales records, tax return records, educational records, or medical records containing information that would identify a person, the Director of the Federal Bureau of Investigation may delegate the authority to make such application to either the Deputy Director of the Federal Bureau of Investigation or the Executive Assistant Director for National Security (or any successor position). The Deputy Director or the Executive Assistant Director may not further delegate such authority.

(b) Recipient and contents of application

Each application under this section-

(1) shall be made to-

(A) a judge of the court established by section 1803(a) of this title; or

(B) a United States Magistrate Judge under chapter 43 of title 28, who is publicly designated by the Chief Justice of the United States to have the power to hear applications and grant orders for the production of tangible things under this section on behalf of a judge of that court; and

(2) shall include-

(A) a specific selection term to be used as the basis for the production of the tangible things sought;

(B) in the case of an application other than an application described in subparagraph (C) (including an application for the production of call detail records other than in the manner described in subparagraph (C)), a statement of facts showing that there are reasonable grounds to believe that the tangible things sought are relevant to an authorized investigation (other than a threat assessment) conducted in accordance with subsection (a)(2) to obtain foreign intelligence information not concerning a United States person or to protect against international terrorism or clandestine intelligence activities, such things being presumptively relevant to an authorized investigation if the applicant shows in the statement of the facts that they pertain to-

(i) a foreign power or an agent of a foreign power;

(ii) the activities of a suspected agent of a foreign power who is the subject of such authorized investigation; or

(iii) an individual in contact with, or known to, a suspected agent of a foreign power who is the subject of such authorized investigation;

(C) in the case of an application for the production on an ongoing basis of call detail records created before, on, or after the date of the application relating to an authorized investigation (other than a threat assessment) conducted in accordance with subsection (a)(2) to protect against international terrorism, a statement of facts showing that-

(i) there are reasonable grounds to believe that the call detail records sought to be produced based on the specific selection term required under subparagraph (A) are relevant to such investigation; and

(ii) there is a reasonable, articulable suspicion that such specific selection term is associated with a foreign power engaged in international terrorism or activities in preparation therefor, or an agent of a foreign power engaged in international terrorism or activities in preparation therefor; and

(D) an enumeration of the minimization procedures adopted by the Attorney General under subsection (g) that are applicable to the retention and dissemination by the Federal Bureau of Investigation of any tangible things to be made available to the Federal Bureau of Investigation based on the order requested in such application.

(c) Ex parte judicial order of approval

(1) Upon an application made pursuant to this section, if the judge finds that the application meets the requirements of subsections (a) and (b) and that the minimization procedures submitted in accordance with subsection (b)(2)(D) meet the definition of minimization procedures under subsection (g), the judge shall enter an ex parte order as requested, or as modified, approving the release of tangible things. Such order shall direct that minimization procedures adopted pursuant to subsection (g) be followed.

(2) An order under this subsection-

(A) shall describe the tangible things that are ordered to be produced with sufficient particularity to permit them to be fairly identified, including each specific selection term to be used as the basis for the production;

(B) shall include the date on which the tangible things must be provided, which shall allow a reasonable period of time within which the tangible things can be assembled and made available;

(C) shall provide clear and conspicuous notice of the principles and procedures described in subsection (d);

(D) may only require the production of a tangible thing if such thing can be obtained with a subpoena duces tecum issued by a court of the United States in aid of a grand jury investigation or with any other order issued by a court of the United States directing the production of records or tangible things;

(E) shall not disclose that such order is issued for purposes of an investigation described in subsection (a); and

(F) in the case of an application described in subsection (b)(2)(C), shall-

    (i) authorize the production on a daily basis of call detail records for a period not to exceed 180 days;

    (ii) provide that an order for such production may be extended upon application under subsection (b) and the judicial finding under paragraph (1) of this subsection;

    (iii) provide that the Government may require the prompt production of a first set of call detail records using the specific selection term that satisfies the standard required under subsection (b)(2)(C)(ii);

    (iv) provide that the Government may require the prompt production of a second set of call detail records using session-identifying information or a telephone calling card number identified by the specific selection term used to produce call detail records under clause (iii);

    (v) provide that, when produced, such records be in a form that will be useful to the Government;

    (vi) direct each person the Government directs to produce call detail records under the order to furnish the Government forthwith all information, facilities, or technical assistance necessary to accomplish the production in such a manner as will protect the secrecy of the production and produce a minimum of interference with the services that such person is providing to each subject of the production; and

    (vii) direct the Government to-

        (I) adopt minimization procedures that require the prompt destruction of all call detail records produced under the order that the Government determines are not foreign intelligence information; and

        (II) destroy all call detail records produced under the order as prescribed by such procedures.

(3) No order issued under this subsection may authorize the collection of tangible things without the use of a specific selection term that meets the requirements of subsection (b)(2).

(d) Nondisclosure

(1) No person shall disclose to any other person that the Federal Bureau of Investigation has sought or obtained tangible things pursuant to an order issued or an emergency production required under this section, other than to-

(A) those persons to whom disclosure is necessary to comply with such order or such emergency production;

(B) an attorney to obtain legal advice or assistance with respect to the production of things in response to the order or the emergency production; or

(C) other persons as permitted by the Director of the Federal Bureau of Investigation or the designee of the Director.

(2)

(A) A person to whom disclosure is made pursuant to paragraph (1) shall be subject to the nondisclosure requirements applicable to a person to whom an order or emergency production is directed under this section in the same manner as such person.

(B) Any person who discloses to a person described in subparagraph (A), (B), or (C) of paragraph (1) that the Federal Bureau of Investigation has sought or obtained tangible things pursuant to an order or emergency production under this section shall notify such person of the nondisclosure requirements of this subsection.

(C) At the request of the Director of the Federal Bureau of Investigation or the designee of the Director, any person making or intending to make a disclosure under subparagraph (A) or (C) of paragraph (1) shall identify to the Director or such designee the person to whom such disclosure will be made or to whom such disclosure was made prior to the request.

(e) Liability for good faith disclosure; waiver

(1) No cause of action shall lie in any court against a person who-

(A) produces tangible things or provides information, facilities, or technical assistance in accordance with an order issued or an emergency production required under this section; or

(B) otherwise provides technical assistance to the Government under this section or to implement the amendments made to this section by the USA FREEDOM Act of 2015.

(2) A production or provision of information, facilities, or technical assistance described in paragraph (1) shall not be deemed to constitute a waiver of any privilege in any other proceeding or context.

(f) Judicial review of FISA orders

(1) In this subsection-

    (A) the term "production order" means an order to produce any tangible thing under this section; and

    (B) the term "nondisclosure order" means an order imposed under subsection (d).

(2)

    (A)(i) A person receiving a production order may challenge the legality of the production order or any nondisclosure order imposed in connection with the production order by filing a petition with the pool established by section 1803(e)(1) of this title.

    (ii) The presiding judge shall immediately assign a petition under clause (i) to 1 of the judges serving in the pool established by section 1803(e)(1) of this title. Not later than 72 hours after the assignment of such petition, the assigned judge shall conduct an initial review of the petition. If the assigned judge determines that the petition is frivolous, the assigned judge shall immediately deny the petition and affirm the production order or nondisclosure order. If the assigned judge determines the petition is not frivolous, the assigned judge shall promptly consider the petition in accordance with the procedures established under section 1803(e)(2) of this title.

    (iii) The assigned judge shall promptly provide a written statement for the record of the reasons for any determination under this subsection. Upon the request of the Government, any order setting aside a nondisclosure order shall be stayed pending review pursuant to paragraph (3).

    (B) A judge considering a petition to modify or set aside a production order may grant such petition only if the judge finds that such order does not meet the requirements of this section or is otherwise unlawful. If the judge does not modify or set aside the production order, the judge shall immediately affirm such order, and order the recipient to comply therewith.

    (C)(i) A judge considering a petition to modify or set aside a nondisclosure order may grant such petition only if the judge finds that there is no reason to believe that disclosure may endanger the national security of the United States, interfere with a criminal, counterterrorism, or counterintelligence investigation, interfere with diplomatic relations, or endanger the life or physical safety of any person.

    (ii) If the judge denies a petition to modify or set aside a nondisclosure order, the recipient of such order shall be precluded for a period of 1 year from filing another such petition with respect to such nondisclosure order.

    (D) Any production or nondisclosure order not explicitly modified or set aside consistent with this subsection shall remain in full effect.

(3) A petition for review of a decision under paragraph (2) to affirm, modify, or set aside an order by the Government or any person receiving such order shall be made

to the court of review established under section 1803(b) of this title, which shall have jurisdiction to consider such petitions. The court of review shall provide for the record a written statement of the reasons for its decision and, on petition by the Government or any person receiving such order for writ of certiorari, the record shall be transmitted under seal to the Supreme Court of the United States, which shall have jurisdiction to review such decision.

(4) Judicial proceedings under this subsection shall be concluded as expeditiously as possible. The record of proceedings, including petitions filed, orders granted, and statements of reasons for decision, shall be maintained under security measures established by the Chief Justice of the United States, in consultation with the Attorney General and the Director of National Intelligence.

(5) All petitions under this subsection shall be filed under seal. In any proceedings under this subsection, the court shall, upon request of the Government, review ex parte and in camera any Government submission, or portions thereof, which may include classified information.

(g) Minimization procedures

(1) In general

The Attorney General shall adopt, and update as appropriate, specific minimization procedures governing the retention and dissemination by the Federal Bureau of Investigation of any tangible things, or information therein, received by the Federal Bureau of Investigation in response to an order under this subchapter.

(2) Defined

In this section, the term "minimization procedures" means-

(A) specific procedures that are reasonably designed in light of the purpose and technique of an order for the production of tangible things, to minimize the retention, and prohibit the dissemination, of nonpublicly available information concerning unconsenting United States persons consistent with the need of the United States to obtain, produce, and disseminate foreign intelligence information;

(B) procedures that require that nonpublicly available information, which is not foreign intelligence information, as defined in section 1801(e)(1) of this title, shall not be disseminated in a manner that identifies any United States person, without such person's consent, unless such person's identity is necessary to understand foreign intelligence information or assess its importance; and

(C) notwithstanding subparagraphs (A) and (B), procedures that allow for the retention and dissemination of information that is evidence of a crime which has been, is being, or is about to be committed and that is to be retained or disseminated for law enforcement purposes.

(3) Rule of construction

Nothing in this subsection shall limit the authority of the court established under section 1803(a) of this title to impose additional, particularized minimization procedures with regard to the production, retention, or dissemination of nonpublicly available information concerning unconsenting United States persons, including additional, particularized procedures related to the destruction of information within a reasonable time period.

(h) Use of information

Information acquired from tangible things received by the Federal Bureau of Investigation in response to an order under this subchapter concerning any United States person may be used and disclosed by Federal officers and employees without the consent of the United States person only in accordance with the minimization procedures adopted pursuant to subsection (g). No otherwise privileged information acquired from tangible things received by the Federal Bureau of Investigation in accordance with the provisions of this subchapter shall lose its privileged character. No information acquired from tangible things received by the Federal Bureau of Investigation in response to an order under this subchapter may be used or disclosed by Federal officers or employees except for lawful purposes.

(i) Emergency authority for production of tangible things

(1) Notwithstanding any other provision of this section, the Attorney General may require the emergency production of tangible things if the Attorney General-

(A) reasonably determines that an emergency situation requires the production of tangible things before an order authorizing such production can with due diligence be obtained;

(B) reasonably determines that the factual basis for the issuance of an order under this section to approve such production of tangible things exists;

(C) informs, either personally or through a designee, a judge having jurisdiction under this section at the time the Attorney General requires the emergency production of tangible things that the decision has been made to employ the authority under this subsection; and

(D) makes an application in accordance with this section to a judge having jurisdiction under this section as soon as practicable, but not later than 7 days after the Attorney General requires the emergency production of tangible things under this subsection.

(2) If the Attorney General requires the emergency production of tangible things under paragraph (1), the Attorney General shall require that the minimization procedures required by this section for the issuance of a judicial order be followed.

(3) In the absence of a judicial order approving the production of tangible things under this subsection, the production shall terminate when the information sought is obtained, when the application for the order is denied, or after the expiration of 7

days from the time the Attorney General begins requiring the emergency production of such tangible things, whichever is earliest.

(4) A denial of the application made under this subsection may be reviewed as provided in section 1803 of this title.

(5) If such application for approval is denied, or in any other case where the production of tangible things is terminated and no order is issued approving the production, no information obtained or evidence derived from such production shall be received in evidence or otherwise disclosed in any trial, hearing, or other proceeding in or before any court, grand jury, department, office, agency, regulatory body, legislative committee, or other authority of the United States, a State, or a political subdivision thereof, and no information concerning any United States person acquired from such production shall subsequently be used or disclosed in any other manner by Federal officers or employees without the consent of such person, except with the approval of the Attorney General if the information indicates a threat of death or serious bodily harm to any person.

(6) The Attorney General shall assess compliance with the requirements of paragraph (5).

(j) Compensation

The Government shall compensate a person for reasonable expenses incurred for-

(1) producing tangible things or providing information, facilities, or assistance in accordance with an order issued with respect to an application described in subsection (b)(2)(C) or an emergency production under subsection (i) that, to comply with subsection (i)(1)(D), requires an application described in subsection (b)(2)(C); or

(2) otherwise providing technical assistance to the Government under this section or to implement the amendments made to this section by the USA FREEDOM Act of 2015.

(k) Definitions

In this section:

(1) In general

The terms "foreign power", "agent of a foreign power", "international terrorism", "foreign intelligence information", "Attorney General", "United States person", "United States", "person", and "State" have the meanings provided those terms in section 1801 of this title.

(2) Address

The term "address" means a physical address or electronic address, such as an electronic mail address or temporarily assigned network address (including an Internet protocol address).

(3) Call detail record

The term "call detail record"-

(A) means session-identifying information (including an originating or terminating telephone number, an International Mobile Subscriber Identity number, or an International Mobile Station Equipment Identity number), a telephone calling card number, or the time or duration of a call; and

(B) does not include-

    (i) the contents (as defined in section 2510(8) of title 18) of any communication;

    (ii) the name, address, or financial information of a subscriber or customer; or

    (iii) cell site location or global positioning system information.

(4) Specific selection term

    (A) Tangible things

        (i) In general

Except as provided in subparagraph (B), a "specific selection term"-

        (I) is a term that specifically identifies a person, account, address, or personal device, or any other specific identifier; and

        (II) is used to limit, to the greatest extent reasonably practicable, the scope of tangible things sought consistent with the purpose for seeking the tangible things.

        (ii) Limitation

A specific selection term under clause (i) does not include an identifier that does not limit, to the greatest extent reasonably practicable, the scope of tangible things sought consistent with the purpose for seeking the tangible things, such as an identifier that-

        (I) identifies an electronic communication service provider (as that term is defined in section 1881 of this title) or a provider of remote computing service (as that term is defined in section 2711 of title 18), when not used as part of a specific identifier as described in clause (i), unless the provider is itself a subject of an authorized investigation for which the specific selection term is used as the basis for the production; or

        (II) identifies a broad geographic region, including the United States, a city, a county, a State, a zip code, or an area code, when not used as part of a specific identifier as described in clause (i).

        (iii) Rule of construction

Nothing in this paragraph shall be construed to preclude the use of multiple terms or identifiers to meet the requirements of clause (i).

    (B) Call detail record applications

For purposes of an application submitted under subsection (b)(2)(C), the term "specific selection term" means a term that specifically identifies an individual, account, or personal device.

50 U.S.C. § 1862. Congressional Oversight

(a) On an annual basis, the Attorney General shall fully inform the Permanent Select Committee on Intelligence and the Committee on the Judiciary of the House of Representatives and the Select Committee on Intelligence and the Committee on the Judiciary of the Senate concerning all requests for the production of tangible things under section 1861 of this title.

(b) In April of each year, the Attorney General shall submit to the House and Senate Committees on the Judiciary and the House Permanent Select Committee on Intelligence and the Senate Select Committee on Intelligence a report setting forth with respect to the preceding calendar year-

> (1) a summary of all compliance reviews conducted by the Government for the production of tangible things under section 1861 of this title;
> (2) the total number of applications described in section 1861(b)(2)(B) of this title made for orders approving requests for the production of tangible things;
> (3) the total number of such orders either granted, modified, or denied;
> (4) the total number of applications described in section 1861(b)(2)(C) of this title made for orders approving requests for the production of call detail records;
> (5) the total number of such orders either granted, modified, or denied;
> (6) the total number of applications made for orders approving requests for the production of tangible things under section 1861 of this title;
> (7) the total number of such orders either granted, modified, or denied; and
> (8) the number of such orders either granted, modified, or denied for the production of each of the following:
>> (A) Library circulation records, library patron lists, book sales records, or book customer lists.
>> (B) Firearms sales records.
>> (C) Tax return records.
>> (D) Educational records.
>> (E) Medical records containing information that would identify a person.

(c)(1) In April of each year, the Attorney General shall submit to Congress a report setting forth with respect to the preceding year-

> (A) the total number of applications made for orders approving requests for the production of tangible things under section 1861 of this title;
> (B) the total number of such orders either granted, modified, or denied;
> (C) the total number of applications made for orders approving requests for the production of tangible things under section 1861 of this title in which the specific

selection term does not specifically identify an individual, account, or personal device;

(D) the total number of orders described in subparagraph (C) either granted, modified, or denied; and

(E) with respect to orders described in subparagraph (D) that have been granted or modified, whether the court established under section 1803 of this title has directed additional, particularized minimization procedures beyond those adopted pursuant to section 1861(g) of this title.

(2) Each report under this subsection shall be submitted in unclassified form.

50 U.S.C. § 1863. [Repealed]

50 U.S.C. § 1864. Notification of changes to retention of call detail record policies

(a) Requirement to retain

(1) In general

Not later than 15 days after learning that an electronic communication service provider that generates call detail records in the ordinary course of business has changed the policy of the provider on the retention of such call detail records to result in a retention period of less than 18 months, the Director of National Intelligence shall notify, in writing, the congressional intelligence committees of such change.

(2) Report

Not later than 30 days after December 18, 2015, the Director shall submit to the congressional intelligence committees a report identifying each electronic communication service provider that has, as of the date of the report, a policy to retain call detail records for a period of 18 months or less.

(b) Definitions

In this section:

(1) Call detail record

The term "call detail record" has the meaning given that term in section 1861(k) of this title.

(2) Electronic communication service provider

The term "electronic communication service provider" has the meaning given that term in section 1881(b)(4) of this title.

50 U.S.C. § 1871. Semmiannual report of the Attorney General

(a) Report

On a semiannual basis, the Attorney General shall submit to the Permanent Select Committee on Intelligence of the House of Representatives, the Select Committee on Intelligence of the Senate, and the Committees on the Judiciary of the House of

Representatives and the Senate, in a manner consistent with the protection of the national security, a report setting forth with respect to the preceding 6-month period—

(1) the aggregate number of persons targeted for orders issued under this chapter, including a breakdown of those targeted for—

(A) electronic surveillance under section 1805 of this title;

(B) physical searches under section 1824 of this title;

(C) pen registers under section 1842 of this title;

(D) access to records under section 1861 of this title;

(E) acquisitions under section 1881b of this title; and

(F) acquisitions under section 1881c of this title;

(2) the number of individuals covered by an order issued pursuant to section 1801(b)(1)(C) of this title;

(3) the number of times that the Attorney General has authorized that information obtained under this chapter may be used in a criminal proceeding or any information derived therefrom may be used in a criminal proceeding;

(4) a summary of significant legal interpretations of this chapter involving matters before the Foreign Intelligence Surveillance Court or the Foreign Intelligence Surveillance Court of Review, including interpretations presented in applications or pleadings filed with the Foreign Intelligence Surveillance Court or the Foreign Intelligence Surveillance Court of Review by the Department of Justice; and

(5) copies of all decisions, orders, or opinions of the Foreign Intelligence Surveillance Court or Foreign Intelligence Surveillance Court of Review that include significant construction or interpretation of the provisions of this chapter.

(b) Frequency

The first report under this section shall be submitted not later than 6 months after December 17, 2004. Subsequent reports under this section shall be submitted semi-annually thereafter.

(c) Submissions to Congress

The Attorney General shall submit to the committees of Congress referred to in subsection (a)—

(1) not later than 45 days after the date on which the Foreign Intelligence Surveillance Court or the Foreign Intelligence Surveillance Court of Review issues a decision, order, or opinion, including any denial or modification of an application under this chapter, that includes significant construction or interpretation of any provision of law or results in a change of application of any provision of this chapter or a novel application of any provision of this chapter, a copy of such decision, order, or opinion and any pleadings, applications, or memoranda of law associated with such decision, order, or opinion; and

(2) a copy of each such decision, order, or opinion, and any pleadings, applications, or memoranda of law associated with such decision, order, or opinion, that was

issued during the 5-year period ending on July 10, 2008, and not previously submitted in a report under subsection (a).

(d) Protection of national security

The Attorney General, in consultation with the Director of National Intelligence, may authorize redactions of materials described in subsection (c) that are provided to the committees of Congress referred to in subsection (a), if such redactions are necessary to protect the national security of the United States and are limited to sensitive sources and methods information or the identities of targets.

(e) Definitions

In this section:

(1) Foreign Intelligence Surveillance Court

The term "Foreign Intelligence Surveillance Court" means the court established under section 1803(a) of this title.

(2) Foreign Intelligence Surveillance Court of Review

The term "Foreign Intelligence Surveillance Court of Review" means the court established under section 1803(b) of this title.

50 U.S.C. § 1872. Declassification of significant decisions, orders, and opinions

(a) Declassification required

Subject to subsection (b), the Director of National Intelligence, in consultation with the Attorney General, shall conduct a declassification review of each decision, order, or opinion issued by the Foreign Intelligence Surveillance Court or the Foreign Intelligence Surveillance Court of Review (as defined in section 1871(e) of this title) that includes a significant construction or interpretation of any provision of law, including any novel or significant construction or interpretation of the term "specific selection term", and, consistent with that review, make publicly available to the greatest extent practicable each such decision, order, or opinion.

(b) Redacted form

The Director of National Intelligence, in consultation with the Attorney General, may satisfy the requirement under subsection (a) to make a decision, order, or opinion described in such subsection publicly available to the greatest extent practicable by making such decision, order, or opinion publicly available in redacted form.

(c) National security waiver

The Director of National Intelligence, in consultation with the Attorney General, may waive the requirement to declassify and make publicly available a particular decision, order, or opinion under subsection (a), if—

(1) the Director of National Intelligence, in consultation with the Attorney General, determines that a waiver of such requirement is necessary to protect the national security of the United States or properly classified intelligence sources or methods; and

(2) the Director of National Intelligence makes publicly available an unclassified statement prepared by the Attorney General, in consultation with the Director of National Intelligence—

(A) summarizing the significant construction or interpretation of any provision of law, which shall include, to the extent consistent with national security, a description of the context in which the matter arises and any significant construction or interpretation of any statute, constitutional provision, or other legal authority relied on by the decision; and

(B) that specifies that the statement has been prepared by the Attorney General and constitutes no part of the opinion of the Foreign Intelligence Surveillance Court or the Foreign Intelligence Surveillance Court of Review.

50 U.S.C. § 1873. Annual reports

(a) Report by Director of the Administrative Office of the United States Courts

(1) Report required

The Director of the Administrative Office of the United States Courts shall annually submit to the Permanent Select Committee on Intelligence and the Committee on the Judiciary of the House of Representatives and the Select Committee on Intelligence and the Committee on the Judiciary of the Senate, subject to a declassification review by the Attorney General and the Director of National Intelligence, a report that includes—

(A) the number of applications or certifications for orders submitted under each of sections 1805, 1824, 1842, 1861, 1881a, 1881b, and 1881c of this title;

(B) the number of such orders granted under each of those sections;

(C) the number of orders modified under each of those sections;

(D) the number of applications or certifications denied under each of those sections;

(E) the number of appointments of an individual to serve as amicus curiae under section 1803 of this title, including the name of each individual appointed to serve as amicus curiae; and

(F) the number of findings issued under section 1803(i) of this title that such appointment is not appropriate and the text of any such findings.

(2) Publication

The Director shall make the report required under paragraph (1) publicly available on an Internet Web site, except that the Director shall not make publicly available on an Internet Web site the findings described in subparagraph (F) of paragraph (1).

(b) Mandatory reporting by Director of National Intelligence

Except as provided in subsection (d), the Director of National Intelligence shall annually make publicly available on an Internet Web site a report that identifies, for the preceding 12 month period—

(1) the total number of orders issued pursuant to subchapters I and II and sections 1881b and 1881c of this title and a good faith estimate of—

(A) the number of targets of such orders;

(B) the number of targets of such orders who are known to not be United States persons; and

(C) the number of targets of such orders who are known to be United States persons;

(2) the total number of orders issued pursuant to section 1881a of this title, including pursuant to subsection (f)(2) of such section, and a good faith estimate of —

(A) the number of targets of such orders;

(B) the number of search terms concerning a known United States person used to retrieve the unminimized contents of electronic communications or wire communications obtained through acquisitions authorized under such section, excluding the number of search terms used to prevent the return of information concerning a United States person;

(C) the number of queries concerning a known United States person of unminimized noncontents information relating to electronic communications or wire communications obtained through acquisitions authorized under such section, excluding the number of queries containing information used to prevent the return of information concerning a United States person;

(D) the number of instances in which the Federal Bureau of Investigation opened, under the Criminal Investigative Division or any successor division, an investigation of a United States person (who is not considered a threat to national security) based wholly or in part on an acquisition authorized under such section;

(3) the total number of orders issued pursuant to subchapter III and a good faith estimate of —

(A) the number of targets of such orders, including —

(i) the number of targets of such orders who are known to not be United States persons;

And

(ii) the number of targets of such orders who are known to be United States persons; and

(B) the number of unique identifiers used to communicate information collected pursuant to such orders;

(4) the number of criminal proceedings in which the United States or a State or political subdivision thereof provided notice pursuant to subsection (c) or (d) of section 1806 of this title (including with respect to information acquired from an acquisition conducted under section 1881a of this title) or subsection (d) or (e) of section 1825 of this title of the intent of the government to enter into evidence or otherwise use or disclose any information obtained or derived from electronic surveillance, physical search, or an acquisition conducted pursuant to this chapter;

(5) the total number of orders issued pursuant to applications made under section 1861(b)(2)(B) of this title and a good faith estimate of —

(A) the number of targets of such orders; and

(B) the number of unique identifiers used to communicate information collected pursuant to such orders;

(6) the total number of orders issued pursuant to applications made under section 1861(b)(2)(C) of this title and a good faith estimate of—

(A) the number of targets of such orders;

(B) the number of unique identifiers used to communicate information collected pursuant to such orders; and

(C) the number of search terms that included information concerning a United States person that were used to query any database of call detail records obtained through the use of such orders; and

(7) the total number of national security letters issued and the number of requests for information contained within such national security letters.

(c) Timing

The annual reports required by subsections (a) and (b) shall be made publicly available during April of each year and include information relating to the previous calendar year.

(d) Exceptions

(1) Statement of numerical range

If a good faith estimate required to be reported under subparagraph (B) of any of paragraphs (3), (5), or (6) of subsection (b) is fewer than 500, it shall be expressed as a numerical range of "fewer than 500" and shall not be expressed as an individual number.

(2) Nonapplicability to certain information

(A) Federal Bureau of Investigation

Paragraphs (2)(B), (2)(C), and (6)(C) of subsection (b) shall not apply to information or records held by, or queries conducted by, the Federal Bureau of Investigation, except with respect to information required under paragraph (2) relating to orders issued under section 1881a(f)(2) of this title.

(B) Electronic mail address and telephone numbers

Paragraph (3)(B) of subsection (b) shall not apply to orders resulting in the acquisition of information by the Federal Bureau of Investigation that does not include electronic mail addresses or telephone numbers.

(3) Certification

(A) In general

If the Director of National Intelligence concludes that a good faith estimate required to be reported under subsection (b)(2)(C) cannot be determined accurately because some but not all of the relevant elements of the intelligence community are able to provide such good faith estimate, the Director shall—

(i) certify that conclusion in writing to the Select Committee on Intelligence and the Committee on the Judiciary of the Senate and the Permanent Select Committee on Intelligence and the Committee on the Judiciary of the House of Representatives;

(ii) report the good faith estimate for those relevant elements able to provide such good faith estimate;

(iii) explain when it is reasonably anticipated that such an estimate will be able to be determined fully and accurately; and

(iv) make such certification publicly available on an Internet Web site.

(B) Form

A certification described in subparagraph (A) shall be prepared in unclassified form, but may contain a classified annex.

(C) Timing

If the Director of National Intelligence continues to conclude that the good faith estimates described in this paragraph cannot be determined accurately, the Director shall annually submit a certification in accordance with this paragraph.

(e) Definitions

In this section:

(1) Contents

The term "contents" has the meaning given that term under section 2510 of title 18.

(2) Electronic communication

The term "electronic communication" has the meaning given that term under section 2510 of title 18.

(3) National security letter

The term "national security letter" means a request for a report, records, or other information under—

(A) section 2709 of title 18;

(B) section 3414(a)(5)(A) of title 12;

(C) subsection (a) or (b) of section 1681u of title 15; or

(D) section 1681v(a) of title 15.

(4) United States person

The term "United States person" means a citizen of the United States or an alien lawfully admitted for permanent residence (as defined in section 1101(a) of title 8).

(5) Wire communication

The term "wire communication" has the meaning given that term under section 2510 of title 18.

50 U.S.C. § 1874. Public reporting by persons subject to orders

(a) Reporting

A person subject to a nondisclosure requirement accompanying an order or directive under this chapter or a national security letter may, with respect to such order, directive, or national security letter, publicly report the following information using one of the following structures:

(1) A semiannual report that aggregates the number of orders, directives, or national security letters with which the person was required to comply into separate categories of—

  (A) the number of national security letters received, reported in bands of 1000 starting with 0–999;

  (B) the number of customer selectors targeted by national security letters, reported in bands of 1000 starting with 0–999;

  (C) the number of orders or directives received, combined, under this chapter for contents, reported in bands of 1000 starting with 0–999;

  (D) the number of customer selectors targeted under orders or directives received, combined, under this chapter for contents, reported in bands of 1000 starting with 0–999;

  (E) the number of orders received under this chapter for noncontents, reported in bands of 1000 starting with 0–999; and

  (F) the number of customer selectors targeted under orders under this chapter for noncontents, reported in bands of 1000 starting with 0–999, pursuant to—

    (i) subchapter III;

    (ii) subchapter IV with respect to applications described in section 1861(b)(2)(B) of this title; and

    (iii) subchapter IV with respect to applications described in section 1861(b)(2)(C) of this title.

(2) A semiannual report that aggregates the number of orders, directives, or national security letters with which the person was required to comply into separate categories of—

  (A) the number of national security letters received, reported in bands of 500 starting with 0–499;

  (B) the number of customer selectors targeted by national security letters, reported in bands of 500 starting with 0–499;

  (C) the number of orders or directives received, combined, under this chapter for contents, reported in bands of 500 starting with 0–499;

  (D) the number of customer selectors targeted under orders or directives received, combined, under this chapter for contents, reported in bands of 500 starting with 0–499;

  (E) the number of orders received under this chapter for noncontents, reported in bands of 500 starting with 0–499; and

  (F) the number of customer selectors targeted under orders received under this chapter for noncontents, reported in bands of 500 starting with 0–499.

(3) A semiannual report that aggregates the number of orders, directives, or national security letters with which the person was required to comply into separate categories of—

  (A) the total number of all national security process received, including all national security letters, and orders or directives under this chapter, combined, reported in bands of 250 starting with 0–249; and

(B) the total number of customer selectors targeted under all national security process received, including all national security letters, and orders or directives under this chapter, combined, reported in bands of 250 starting with 0–249.

(4) An annual report that aggregates the number of orders, directives, and national security letters the person was required to comply with into separate categories of—

(A) the total number of all national security process received, including all national security letters, and orders or directives under this chapter, combined, reported in bands of 100 starting with 0–99; and

(B) the total number of customer selectors targeted under all national security process received, including all national security letters, and orders or directives under this chapter, combined, reported in bands of 100 starting with 0–99.

(b) Period of time covered by reports

(1) A report described in paragraph (1) or (2) of subsection (a) shall include only information—

(A) relating to national security letters for the previous 180 days; and

(B) relating to authorities under this chapter for the 180-day period of time ending on the date that is not less than 180 days prior to the date of the publication of such report, except that with respect to a platform, product, or service for which a person did not previously receive an order or directive (not including an enhancement to or iteration of an existing publicly available platform, product, or service) such report shall not include any information relating to such new order or directive until 540 days after the date on which such new order or directive is received.

(2) A report described in paragraph (3) of subsection (a) shall include only information relating to the previous 180 days.

(3) A report described in paragraph (4) of subsection (a) shall include only information for the 1-year period of time ending on the date that is not less than 1 year prior to the date of the publication of such report.

(c) Other forms of agreed to publication

Nothing in this section prohibits the Government and any person from jointly agreeing to the publication of information referred to in this subsection in a time, form, or manner other than as described in this section.

(d) Definitions

In this section:

(1) Contents

The term "contents" has the meaning given that term under section 2510 of title 18.

(2) National security letter

The term "national security letter" has the meaning given that term under section 1873 of this title.

50 U.S.C. § 1881. Definitions

(a) In general

In this subchapter, the terms "agent of a foreign power", "Attorney General", "contents", "electronic surveillance", "foreign intelligence information", "foreign power", "person", "United States", and "United States person" have the meanings given such terms in section 1801 of this title, except as specifically provided in this subchapter.

(b) Additional definitions

In this subchapter:

(1) Congressional intelligence committees

The term "congressional intelligence committees" means—

(A) the Select Committee on Intelligence of the Senate; and

(B) the Permanent Select Committee on Intelligence of the House of Representatives.

(2) Foreign Intelligence Surveillance Court; Court

The terms "Foreign Intelligence Surveillance Court" and "Court" mean the court established under section 1803(a) of this title.

(3) Foreign Intelligence Surveillance Court of Review; Court of Review

The terms "Foreign Intelligence Surveillance Court of Review" and "Court of Review" mean the court established under section 1803(b) of this title.

(4) Electronic communication service provider

The term "electronic communication service provider" means—

(A) a telecommunications carrier, as that term is defined in section 153 of title 47;

(B) a provider of electronic communication service, as that term is defined in section 2510 of title 18;

(C) a provider of a remote computing service, as that term is defined in section 2711 of title 18;

(D) any other communication service provider who has access to wire or electronic communications either as such communications are transmitted or as such communications are stored; or

(E) an officer, employee, or agent of an entity described in subparagraph (A), (B), (C), or (D).

(5) Intelligence community

The term "intelligence community" has the meaning given the term in section 3003(4) of this title.

50 U.S.C. § 1881a. Procedures for targeting certain persons outside the United States other than United States persons

(a) Authorization

Notwithstanding any other provision of law, upon the issuance of an order in accordance with subsection (j)(3) or a determination under subsection (c)(2), the Attorney General and the Director of National Intelligence may authorize jointly, for a period of up to 1 year from the effective date of the authorization, the targeting of persons reasonably believed to be located outside the United States to acquire foreign intelligence information.

(b) Limitations

An acquisition authorized under subsection (a)—

(1) may not intentionally target any person known at the time of acquisition to be located in the United States;

(2) may not intentionally target a person reasonably believed to be located outside the United States if the purpose of such acquisition is to target a particular, known person reasonably believed to be in the United States;

(3) may not intentionally target a United States person reasonably believed to be located outside the United States;

(4) may not intentionally acquire any communication as to which the sender and all intended recipients are known at the time of the acquisition to be located in the United States;

(5) may not intentionally acquire communications that contain a reference to, but are not to or from, a target of an acquisition authorized under subsection (a), except as provided under section 103(b) of the FISA Amendments Reauthorization Act of 2017; and

(6) shall be conducted in a manner consistent with the fourth amendment to the Constitution of the United States.

(c) Conduct of acquisition

(1) In general

An acquisition authorized under subsection (a) shall be conducted only in accordance with—

(A) the targeting and minimization procedures adopted in accordance with subsections (d) and (e); and

(B) upon submission of a certification in accordance with subsection (h), such certification.

(2) Determination

A determination under this paragraph and for purposes of subsection (a) is a determination by the Attorney General and the Director of National Intelligence that exigent circumstances exist because, without immediate implementation of an authorization under subsection (a), intelligence important to the national security of the United States may be lost or not timely acquired and time does not permit the issuance of an order pursuant to subsection (j)(3) prior to the implementation of such authorization.

(3) Timing of determination

The Attorney General and the Director of National Intelligence may make the determination under paragraph (2)—

(A) before the submission of a certification in accordance with subsection (h); or

(B) by amending a certification pursuant to subsection (j)(1)(C) at any time during which judicial review under subsection (j) of such certification is pending.

(4) Construction

Nothing in subchapter I shall be construed to require an application for a court order under such subchapter for an acquisition that is targeted in accordance with this section at a person reasonably believed to be located outside the United States.

(d) Targeting procedures

(1) Requirement to adopt

The Attorney General, in consultation with the Director of National Intelligence, shall adopt targeting procedures that are reasonably designed to —

(A) ensure that any acquisition authorized under subsection (a) is limited to targeting persons reasonably believed to be located outside the United States; and

(B) prevent the intentional acquisition of any communication as to which the sender and all intended recipients are known at the time of the acquisition to be located in the United States.

(2) Judicial review

The procedures adopted in accordance with paragraph (1) shall be subject to judicial review pursuant to subsection (j).

(e) Minimization procedures

(1) Requirement to adopt

The Attorney General, in consultation with the Director of National Intelligence, shall adopt minimization procedures that meet the definition of minimization procedures under section 1801(h) of this title or section 1821(4) of this title, as appropriate, for acquisitions authorized under subsection (a).

(2) Judicial review

The minimization procedures adopted in accordance with paragraph (1) shall be subject to judicial review pursuant to subsection (j).

(3) Publication

The Director of National Intelligence, in consultation with the Attorney General, shall —

(A) conduct a declassification review of any minimization procedures adopted or amended in accordance with paragraph (1); and

(B) consistent with such review, and not later than 180 days after conducting such review, make such minimization procedures publicly available to the greatest extent practicable, which may be in redacted form.

(f) Queries

(1) Procedures required

(A) Requirement to adopt

The Attorney General, in consultation with the Director of National Intelligence, shall adopt querying procedures consistent with the requirements of the fourth amendment to the Constitution of the United States for information collected pursuant to an authorization under subsection (a).

(B) Record of United States person query terms

The Attorney General, in consultation with the Director of National Intelligence, shall ensure that the procedures adopted under subparagraph (A) include a technical procedure whereby a record is kept of each United States person query term used for a query.

(C) Judicial review

The procedures adopted in accordance with subparagraph (A) shall be subject to judicial review pursuant to subsection (j).

(2) Access to results of certain queries conducted by FBI

(A) Court order required for fbi review of certain query results in criminal investigations unrelated to national security

Except as provided by subparagraph (E), in connection with a predicated criminal investigation opened by the Federal Bureau of Investigation that does not relate to the national security of the United States, the Federal Bureau of Investigation may not access the contents of communications acquired under subsection (a) that were retrieved pursuant to a query foreign intelligence information unless—

> (i) the Federal Bureau of Investigation applies for an order of the Court under subparagraph (C); and
>
> (ii) the Court enters an order under subparagraph (D) approving such application.

(B) Jurisdiction

The Court shall have jurisdiction to review an application and to enter an order approving the access described in subparagraph (A).

(C) Application

Each application for an order under this paragraph shall be made by a Federal officer in writing upon oath or affirmation to a judge having jurisdiction under subparagraph (B). Each application shall require the approval of the Attorney General based upon the finding of the Attorney General that the application satisfies the criteria and requirements of such application, as set forth in this paragraph, and shall include—

> (i) the identity of the Federal officer making the application; and
>
> (ii) an affidavit or other information containing a statement of the facts and circumstances relied upon by the applicant to justify the belief of the applicant that the contents of communications described in subparagraph (A) covered by the application would provide evidence of—
>
> (I) criminal activity;
>
> (II) contraband, fruits of a crime, or other items illegally possessed by a third party; or
>
> (III) property designed for use, intended for use, or used in committing a crime.

(D) Order

Upon an application made pursuant to subparagraph (C), the Court shall enter an order approving the accessing of the contents of communications described in subparagraph (A) covered by the application if the Court finds probable cause to believe that such contents would provide any of the evidence described in subparagraph (C)(ii).

(E) Exception

The requirement for an order of the Court under subparagraph (A) to access the contents of communications described in such subparagraph shall not apply with respect to a query if the Federal Bureau of Investigation determines there is a reasonable belief that such contents could assist in mitigating or eliminating a threat to life or serious bodily harm.

(F) Rule of construction

Nothing in this paragraph may be construed as —

(i) limiting the authority of the Federal Bureau of Investigation to conduct lawful queries of information acquired under subsection (a);

(ii) limiting the authority of the Federal Bureau of Investigation to review, without a court order, the results of any query of information acquired under subsection (a) that was reasonably designed to find and extract foreign intelligence information, regardless of whether such foreign intelligence information could also be considered evidence of a crime; or

(iii) prohibiting or otherwise limiting the ability of the Federal Bureau of Investigation to access the results of queries conducted when evaluating whether to open an assessment or predicated investigation relating to the national security of the United States.

(3) Definitions

In this subsection:

(A) The term "contents" has the meaning given that term in section 2510(8) of title 18.

(B) The term "query" means the use of one or more terms to retrieve the unminimized contents or noncontents located in electronic and data storage systems of communications of or concerning United States persons obtained through acquisitions authorized under subsection (a).

(g) Guidelines for compliance with limitations

(1) Requirement to adopt

The Attorney General, in consultation with the Director of National Intelligence, shall adopt guidelines to ensure —

(A) compliance with the limitations in subsection (b); and

(B) that an application for a court order is filed as required by this chapter.

(2) Submission of guidelines

The Attorney General shall provide the guidelines adopted in accordance with paragraph (1) to —

(A) the congressional intelligence committees;

(B) the Committees on the Judiciary of the Senate and the House of Representatives; and

(C) the Foreign Intelligence Surveillance Court.

(h) Certification

(1) In general

(A) Requirement

Subject to subparagraph (B), prior to the implementation of an authorization under subsection (a), the Attorney General and the Director of National Intelligence shall provide to the Foreign Intelligence Surveillance Court a written certification and any supporting affidavit, under oath and under seal, in accordance with this subsection.

(B) Exception

If the Attorney General and the Director of National Intelligence make a determination under subsection (c)(2) and time does not permit the submission of a certification under this subsection prior to the implementation of an authorization under subsection (a), the Attorney General and the Director of National Intelligence shall submit to the Court a certification for such authorization as soon as practicable but in no event later than 7 days after such determination is made.

(2) Requirements

A certification made under this subsection shall—

(A) attest that—

(i) there are targeting procedures in place that have been approved, have been submitted for approval, or will be submitted with the certification for approval by the Foreign Intelligence Surveillance Court that are reasonably designed to—

(I) ensure that an acquisition authorized under subsection (a) is limited to targeting persons reasonably believed to be located outside the United States; and

(II) prevent the intentional acquisition of any communication as to which the sender and all intended recipients are known at the time of the acquisition to be located in the United States;

(ii) the minimization procedures to be used with respect to such acquisition—

(I) meet the definition of minimization procedures under section 1801(h) or 1821(4) of this title, as appropriate; and

(II) have been approved, have been submitted for approval, or will be submitted with the certification for approval by the Foreign Intelligence Surveillance Court;

(iii) guidelines have been adopted in accordance with subsection (g) to ensure compliance with the limitations in subsection (b) and to ensure that an application for a court order is filed as required by this chapter;

(iv) the procedures and guidelines referred to in clauses (i), (ii), and (iii) are consistent with the requirements of the fourth amendment to the Constitution of the United States;

(v) a significant purpose of the acquisition is to obtain foreign intelligence information;

(vi) the acquisition involves obtaining foreign intelligence information from or with the assistance of an electronic communication service provider; and

(vii) the acquisition complies with the limitations in subsection (b);

(B) include the procedures adopted in accordance with subsections (d) and (e);

(C) be supported, as appropriate, by the affidavit of any appropriate official in the area of national security who is—

(i) appointed by the President, by and with the advice and consent of the Senate; or

(ii) the head of an element of the intelligence community;

(D) include—

(i) an effective date for the authorization that is at least 30 days after the submission of the written certification to the court; or

(ii) if the acquisition has begun or the effective date is less than 30 days after the submission of the written certification to the court, the date the acquisition began or the effective date for the acquisition; and

(E) if the Attorney General and the Director of National Intelligence make a determination under subsection (c)(2), include a statement that such determination has been made.

(3) Change in effective date

The Attorney General and the Director of National Intelligence may advance or delay the effective date referred to in paragraph (2)(D) by submitting an amended certification in accordance with subsection (j)(1)(C) to the Foreign Intelligence Surveillance Court for review pursuant to subsection (i).1

(4) Limitation

A certification made under this subsection is not required to identify the specific facilities, places, premises, or property at which an acquisition authorized under subsection (a) will be directed or conducted.

(5) Maintenance of certification

The Attorney General or a designee of the Attorney General shall maintain a copy of a certification made under this subsection.

(6) Review

A certification submitted in accordance with this subsection shall be subject to judicial review pursuant to subsection (j).

(i) Directives and judicial review of directives

(1) Authority

With respect to an acquisition authorized under subsection (a), the Attorney General and the Director of National Intelligence may direct, in writing, an electronic communication service provider to—

(A) immediately provide the Government with all information, facilities, or assistance necessary to accomplish the acquisition in a manner that will protect the secrecy of the acquisition and produce a minimum of interference with the services that such electronic communication service provider is providing to the target of the acquisition; and

(B) maintain under security procedures approved by the Attorney General and the Director o National Intelligence any records concerning the acquisition or the aid furnished that such electronic communication service provider wishes to maintain.

(2) Compensation

The Government shall compensate, at the prevailing rate, an electronic communication service provider for providing information, facilities, or assistance in accordance with a directive issued pursuant to paragraph (1).

(3) Release from liability

No cause of action shall lie in any court against any electronic communication service provider for providing any information, facilities, or assistance in accordance with a directive issued pursuant to paragraph (1).

(4) Challenging of directives

(A) Authority to challenge

An electronic communication service provider receiving a directive issued pursuant to paragraph (1) may file a petition to modify or set aside such directive with the Foreign Intelligence Surveillance Court, which shall have jurisdiction to review such petition.

(B) Assignment

The presiding judge of the Court shall assign a petition filed under subparagraph (A) to 1 of the judges serving in the pool established under section 1803(e)(1) of this title not later than 24 hours after the filing of such petition.

(C) Standards for review

A judge considering a petition filed under subparagraph (A) may grant such petition only if the judge finds that the directive does not meet the requirements of this section, or is otherwise unlawful.

(D) Procedures for initial review

A judge shall conduct an initial review of a petition filed under subparagraph (A) not later than 5 days after being assigned such petition. If the judge determines that such petition does not consist of claims, defenses, or other legal contentions that are warranted by existing law or by a nonfrivolous argument for extending, modifying, or reversing existing law or for establishing new law, the judge shall immediately deny such petition and affirm the directive or any part of the directive that is the subject of such petition and order the recipient to comply with the directive or any part of it. Upon making a determination under this subparagraph or promptly thereafter, the judge shall provide a written statement for the record of the reasons for such determination.

(E) Procedures for plenary review

If a judge determines that a petition filed under subparagraph (A) requires plenary review, the judge shall affirm, modify, or set aside the directive that is the subject of such petition not later than 30 days after being assigned such petition. If the judge does not set aside the directive, the judge shall immediately affirm or affirm with modifications the directive, and order the recipient to comply with the directive in its entirety or as modified. The judge shall provide a written statement for the record of the reasons for a determination under this subparagraph.

(F) Continued effect

Any directive not explicitly modified or set aside under this paragraph shall remain in full effect.

(G) Contempt of Court

Failure to obey an order issued under this paragraph may be punished by the Court as contempt of court.

(5) Enforcement of directives

(A) Order to compel

If an electronic communication service provider fails to comply with a directive issued pursuant to paragraph (1), the Attorney General may file a petition for an order to compel the electronic communication service provider to comply with the directive with the Foreign Intelligence Surveillance Court, which shall have jurisdiction to review such petition.

(B) Assignment

The presiding judge of the Court shall assign a petition filed under subparagraph (A) to 1 of the judges serving in the pool established under section 1803(e)(1) of this title not later than 24 hours after the filing of such petition.

(C) Procedures for review

A judge considering a petition filed under subparagraph (A) shall, not later than 30 days after being assigned such petition, issue an order requiring the electronic communication service provider to comply with the directive or any part of it, as issued or as modified, if the judge finds that the directive meets the requirements of this section and is otherwise lawful. The judge shall provide a written statement for the record of the reasons for a determination under this paragraph.

(D) Contempt of Court

Failure to obey an order issued under this paragraph may be punished by the Court as contempt of court.

(E) Process

Any process under this paragraph may be served in any judicial district in which the electronic communication service provider may be found.

(6) Appeal

(A) Appeal to the Court of Review

The Government or an electronic communication service provider receiving a directive issued pursuant to paragraph (1) may file a petition with the Foreign Intelligence Surveillance Court of Review for review of a decision issued pursuant to paragraph (4) or (5). The Court of Review shall have jurisdiction to consider such petition and shall provide a written statement for the record of the reasons for a decision under this subparagraph.

(B) Certiorari to the Supreme Court

The Government or an electronic communication service provider receiving a directive issued pursuant to paragraph (1) may file a petition for a writ of certiorari for review of a decision of the Court of Review issued under subparagraph (A). The record for such review shall be transmitted under seal to the Supreme Court of the United States, which shall have jurisdiction to review such decision.

(j) Judicial review of certifications and procedures

(1) In general

(A) Review by the Foreign Intelligence Surveillance Court

The Foreign Intelligence Surveillance Court shall have jurisdiction to review a certification submitted in accordance with subsection (g) 1 and the targeting, minimization, and querying procedures adopted in accordance with subsections (d), (e), and (f)(1), and amendments to such certification or such procedures.

(B) Time period for review

The Court shall review a certification submitted in accordance with subsection (g) 1 and the targeting, minimization, and querying procedures adopted in accordance with subsections (d), (e), and (f)(1) and shall complete such review and issue an order under paragraph (3) not later than 30 days after the date on which such certification and such procedures are submitted.

(C) Amendments

The Attorney General and the Director of National Intelligence may amend a certification submitted in accordance with subsection (g) 1 or the targeting, minimization, and querying procedures adopted in accordance with subsections (d), (e), and (f)(1) as necessary at any time, including if the Court is conducting or has completed review of such certification or such procedures, and shall submit the amended certification or amended procedures to the Court not later than 7 days after amending such certification or such procedures. The Court shall review any amendment under this subparagraph under the procedures set forth in this subsection. The Attorney General and the Director of National Intelligence may authorize the use of an amended certification or amended procedures pending the Court's review of such amended certification or amended procedures.

(2) Review

The Court shall review the following:

(A) Certification

A certification submitted in accordance with subsection (h) to determine whether the certification contains all the required elements.

(B) Targeting procedures

The targeting procedures adopted in accordance with subsection (d) to assess whether the procedures are reasonably designed to—

(i) ensure that an acquisition authorized under subsection (a) is limited to targeting persons reasonably believed to be located outside the United States; and

(ii) prevent the intentional acquisition of any communication as to which the sender and all intended recipients are known at the time of the acquisition to be located in the United States.

(C) Minimization procedures

The minimization procedures adopted in accordance with subsection (e) to assess whether such procedures meet the definition of minimization procedures under section 1801(h) of this title or section 1821(4) of this title, as appropriate.

(D) Querying procedures

The querying procedures adopted in accordance with subsection (f)(1) to assess whether such procedures comply with the requirements of such subsection.

(3) Orders

(A) Approval

If the Court finds that a certification submitted in accordance with subsection (h) contains all the required elements and that the targeting, minimization, and querying procedures adopted in accordance with subsections (d), (e), and (f)(1) are consistent with the requirements of those subsections and with the fourth amendment to the Constitution of the United States, the Court shall enter an order approving the certification and the use, or continued use in the case of an acquisition authorized pursuant to a determination under subsection (c)(2), of the procedures for the acquisition.

(B) Correction of deficiencies

If the Court finds that a certification submitted in accordance with subsection (h) does not contain all the required elements, or that the procedures adopted in accordance with subsections (d), (e), and (f)(1) are not consistent with the requirements of those subsections or the fourth amendment to the Constitution of the United States, the Court shall issue an order directing the Government to, at the Government's election and to the extent required by the Court's order—

(i) correct any deficiency identified by the Court's order not later than 30 days after the date on which the Court issues the order; or

(ii) cease, or not begin, the implementation of the authorization for which such certification was submitted.

(C) Requirement for written statement

In support of an order under this subsection, the Court shall provide, simultaneously with the order, for the record a written statement of the reasons for the order.

(D) Limitation on use of information

(i) In general

Except as provided in clause (ii), if the Court orders a correction of a deficiency in a certification or procedures under subparagraph (B), no information obtained or evidence derived pursuant to the part of the certification or procedures that has been identified by the Court as deficient concerning any United States person shall be received in evidence or otherwise disclosed in any trial, hearing, or other proceeding in or before any court, grand jury, department, office, agency, regulatory body, legislative committee, or other authority of the United States, a State, or political subdivision thereof, and no information concerning any United States person acquired pursuant to such part of such certification or procedures shall subsequently be used or disclosed in any other manner by Federal officers or employees without the consent of the United States person, except with the approval of the Attorney General if the information indicates a threat of death or serious bodily harm to any person.

(ii) Exception

If the Government corrects any deficiency identified by the order of the Court under subparagraph (B), the Court may permit the use or disclosure of information obtained before the date of the correction under such minimization procedures as the Court may approve for purposes of this clause.

(4) Appeal

(A) Appeal to the Court of Review

The Government may file a petition with the Foreign Intelligence Surveillance Court of Review for review of an order under this subsection. The Court of Review shall have jurisdiction to consider such petition. For any decision under this subparagraph affirming, reversing, or modifying an order of the Foreign Intelligence Surveillance Court, the Court of Review shall provide for the record a written statement of the reasons for the decision.

(B) Continuation of acquisition pending rehearing or appeal

Any acquisition affected by an order under paragraph (3)(B) may continue—

(i) during the pendency of any rehearing of the order by the Court en banc; and

(ii) if the Government files a petition for review of an order under this section, until the Court of Review enters an order under subparagraph (C).

(C) Implementation pending appeal

Not later than 60 days after the filing of a petition for review of an order under paragraph (3)(B) directing the correction of a deficiency, the Court of Review shall determine, and enter a corresponding order regarding, whether all or any part of the correction order, as issued or

modified, shall be implemented during the pendency of the review.

(D) Certiorari to the Supreme Court

The Government may file a petition for a writ of certiorari for review of a decision of the Court of Review issued under subparagraph (A). The record for such review shall be transmitted under seal to the Supreme Court of the United States, which shall have jurisdiction to review such decision.

(5) Schedule

(A) Reauthorization of authorizations in effect

If the Attorney General and the Director of National Intelligence seek to reauthorize or replace an authorization issued under subsection (a), the Attorney General and the Director of National Intelligence shall, to the extent practicable, submit to the Court the certification prepared in accordance with subsection (h) and the procedures adopted in accordance with subsections (d), (e), and (f)(1) at least 30 days prior to the expiration of such authorization.

(B) Reauthorization of orders, authorizations, and directives

If the Attorney General and the Director of National Intelligence seek to reauthorize or replace an authorization issued under subsection (a) by filing a certification pursuant to subparagraph (A), that authorization, and any directives issued thereunder and any order related thereto, shall remain in effect, notwithstanding the expiration provided for in subsection (a), until the Court issues an order with respect to such certification under paragraph (3) at which time the provisions of that paragraph and paragraph (4) shall apply with respect to such
certification.

(k) Judicial proceedings

(1) Expedited judicial proceedings

Judicial proceedings under this section shall be conducted as expeditiously as possible.

(2) Time limits

A time limit for a judicial decision in this section shall apply unless the Court, the Court of Review, or any judge of either the Court or the Court of Review, by order for reasons stated, extends that time as necessary for good cause in a manner consistent with national security.

(l) Maintenance and security of records and proceedings

(1) Standards

The Foreign Intelligence Surveillance Court shall maintain a record of a proceeding under this section, including petitions, appeals, orders, and statements of reasons for a decision, under security measures adopted by the Chief Justice of the United States, in consultation with the Attorney General and the Director of National Intelligence.

(2) Filing and review

All petitions under this section shall be filed under seal. In any proceedings under this section, the Court shall, upon request of the Government, review ex parte and in camera any Government submission, or portions of a submission, which may include classified information.

(3) Retention of records

The Attorney General and the Director of National Intelligence shall retain a directive or an order issued under this section for a period of not less than 10 years from the date on which such directive or such order is issued.

(m) Assessments 2 reviews, and reporting

(1) Semiannual assessment

Not less frequently than once every 6 months, the Attorney General and Director of National Intelligence shall assess compliance with the targeting, minimization, and querying procedures adopted in accordance with subsections (d), (e), and (f)(1) and the guidelines adopted in accordance with subsection (g) and shall submit each assessment to—

(A) the Foreign Intelligence Surveillance Court; and

(B) consistent with the Rules of the House of Representatives, the Standing Rules of the Senate, and Senate Resolution 400 of the 94th Congress or any successor Senate resolution—

(i) the congressional intelligence committees; and

(ii) the Committees on the Judiciary of the House of Representatives and the Senate.

(2) Agency assessment

The Inspector General of the Department of Justice and the Inspector General of each element of the intelligence community authorized to acquire foreign intelligence information under subsection (a), with respect to the department or element of such Inspector General—

(A) are authorized to review compliance with the targeting, minimization, and querying procedures adopted in accordance with subsections (d), (e), and (f)(1) and the guidelines adopted in accordance with with subsection (g);

(B) with respect to acquisitions authorized under subsection (a), shall review the number of disseminated intelligence reports containing a reference to a United States-person identity and the number of United States-person identities subsequently disseminated by the element concerned in response to requests for identities that were not referred to by name or title in the original reporting;

(C) with respect to acquisitions authorized under subsection (a), shall review the number of targets that were later determined to be located in the United States and, to the extent possible, whether communications of such targets were reviewed; and

(D) shall provide each such review to—

(i) the Attorney General;

(ii) the Director of National Intelligence; and

(iii) consistent with the Rules of the House of Representatives, the Standing Rules of the Senate, and Senate Resolution 400 of the 94th Congress or any successor Senate resolution—

(I) the congressional intelligence committees; and

(II) the Committees on the Judiciary of the House of Representatives and the Senate.

(3) Annual review

(A) Requirement to conduct

The head of each element of the intelligence community conducting an acquisition authorized under subsection (a) shall conduct an annual review to determine whether there is reason to believe that foreign intelligence information has been or will be obtained from the acquisition. The annual review shall provide, with respect to acquisitions authorized under subsection (a)—

(i) an accounting of the number of disseminated intelligence reports containing a reference to a United States-person identity;

(ii) an accounting of the number of United States-person identities subsequently disseminated by that element in response to requests for identities that were not referred to by name or title in the original reporting;

(iii) the number of targets that were later determined to be located in the United States and, to the extent possible, whether communications of such targets were reviewed; and

(iv) a description of any procedures developed by the head of such element of the intelligence community and approved by the Director of National Intelligence to assess, in a manner consistent with national security, operational requirements and the privacy interests of United States persons, the extent to which the acquisitions authorized under subsection (a) acquire the communications of United States persons, and the results of any such assessment.

(B) Use of review

The head of each element of the intelligence community that conducts an annual review under subparagraph (A) shall use each such review to evaluate the adequacy of the minimization procedures utilized by such element and, as appropriate, the application of the minimization procedures to a particular acquisition authorized under subsection (a).

(C) Provision of review

The head of each element of the intelligence community that conducts an annual review under subparagraph (A) shall provide such review to—

(i) the Foreign Intelligence Surveillance Court;

(ii) the Attorney General;

(iii) the Director of National Intelligence; and

(iv) consistent with the Rules of the House of Representatives, the Standing Rules of the Senate, and Senate Resolution 400 of the 94th Congress or any successor Senate resolution—

(I) the congressional intelligence committees; and

(II) the Committees on the Judiciary of the House of Representatives and the Senate.

(4) Reporting of material breach

(A) In general

The head of each element of the intelligence community involved in the acquisition of abouts communications shall fully and currently inform the Committees on the Judiciary of the House of Representatives and the Senate and the congressional intelligence committees of a material breach.

(B) Definitions

In this paragraph:

(i) The term "abouts communication" means a communication that contains a reference to, but is not to or from, a target of an acquisition authorized under subsection (a).

(ii) The term "material breach" means significant noncompliance with applicable law or an order of the Foreign Intelligence Surveillance Court concerning any acquisition of abouts communications.

50 U.S.C. § 1881b. Certain acquisitions inside the United States targeting United States persons outside the United States

(a) Jurisdiction of the Foreign Intelligence Surveillance Court

(1) In general

The Foreign Intelligence Surveillance Court shall have jurisdiction to review an application and to enter an order approving the targeting of a United States person reasonably believed to be located outside the United States to acquire foreign intelligence information, if the acquisition constitutes electronic surveillance or the acquisition of stored electronic communications or stored electronic data that requires an order under this chapter, and such acquisition is conducted within the United States.

(2) Limitation

If a United States person targeted under this subsection is reasonably believed to be located in the United States during the effective period of an order issued pursuant to subsection (c), an acquisition targeting such United States person under this section shall cease unless the targeted United States person is again reasonably believed to be located outside the United States while an order issued pursuant to subsection (c) is in effect. Nothing in this section shall be construed to limit the authority of the Government to seek an order or authorization under, or otherwise engage in any activity that is authorized under, any other subchapter of this chapter.

(b) Application

(1) In general

Each application for an order under this section shall be made by a Federal officer in writing upon oath or affirmation to a judge having jurisdiction under subsection (a)(1). Each application shall require the approval of the Attorney General based upon the Attorney General's finding that it satisfies the criteria and requirements of such application, as set forth in this section, and shall include—

(A) the identity of the Federal officer making the application;

(B) the identity, if known, or a description of the United States person who is the target of the acquisition;

(C) a statement of the facts and circumstances relied upon to justify the applicant's belief that the United States person who is the target of the acquisition is—

(i) a person reasonably believed to be located outside the United States; and

(ii) a foreign power, an agent of a foreign power, or an officer or employee of a foreign power;

(D) a statement of proposed minimization procedures that meet the definition of minimization procedures under section 1801(h) or 1821(4) of this title, as appropriate;

(E) a description of the nature of the information sought and the type of communications or activities to be subjected to acquisition;

(F) a certification made by the Attorney General or an official specified in section 1804(a)(6) of this title that—

(i) the certifying official deems the information sought to be foreign intelligence information;

(ii) a significant purpose of the acquisition is to obtain foreign intelligence information;

(iii) such information cannot reasonably be obtained by normal investigative techniques;

(iv) designates the type of foreign intelligence information being sought according to the categories described in section 1801(e) of this title; and

(v) includes a statement of the basis for the certification that—

(I) the information sought is the type of foreign intelligence information designated; and

(II) such information cannot reasonably be obtained by normal investigative techniques;

(G) a summary statement of the means by which the acquisition will be conducted and whether physical entry is required to effect the acquisition;

(H) the identity of any electronic communication service provider necessary to effect the acquisition, provided that the application is not required to identify the specific facilities, places, premises, or property at which the acquisition authorized under this section will be directed or conducted;

(I) a statement of the facts concerning any previous applications that have been made to any judge of the Foreign Intelligence Surveillance Court involving the United States person specified in the application and the action taken on each previous application; and

(J) a statement of the period of time for which the acquisition is required to be maintained, provided that such period of time shall not exceed 90 days per application.

(2) Other requirements of the Attorney General

The Attorney General may require any other affidavit or certification from any other officer in connection with the application.

(3) Other requirements of the judge

The judge may require the applicant to furnish such other information as may be necessary to make the findings required by subsection (c)(1).

(c) Order

(1) Findings

Upon an application made pursuant to subsection (b), the Foreign Intelligence Surveillance Court shall enter an ex parte order as requested or as modified by the Court approving the acquisition if the Court finds that—

(A) the application has been made by a Federal officer and approved by the Attorney General;

(B) on the basis of the facts submitted by the applicant, for the United States person who is the target of the acquisition, there is probable cause to believe that the target is—

(i) a person reasonably believed to be located outside the United States; and

(ii) a foreign power, an agent of a foreign power, or an officer or employee of a foreign power;

(C) the proposed minimization procedures meet the definition of minimization procedures under section 1801(h) or 1821(4) of this title, as appropriate; and

(D) the application that has been filed contains all statements and certifications required by subsection (b) and the certification or certifications are not clearly erroneous on the basis of the statement made under subsection (b)(1)(F)(v) and any other information furnished under subsection (b)(3).

(2) Probable cause

In determining whether or not probable cause exists for purposes of paragraph (1)(B), a judge having jurisdiction under subsection (a)(1) may consider past activities of the target and facts and circumstances relating to current or future activities of the target. No United States person may be considered a foreign power, agent of a foreign power, or officer or employee of a foreign power solely upon the basis of activities protected by the first amendment to the Constitution of the United States.

(3) Review

(A) Limitation on review

Review by a judge having jurisdiction under subsection (a)(1) shall be limited to that required to make the findings described in paragraph (1).

(B) Review of probable cause

If the judge determines that the facts submitted under subsection (b) are insufficient to establish probable cause under paragraph (1)(B), the judge shall enter an order so stating and provide a written statement for the record of the reasons for the determination. The Government may appeal an order under this subparagraph pursuant to subsection (f).

(C) Review of minimization procedures

If the judge determines that the proposed minimization procedures referred to in paragraph (1)(C) do not meet the definition of minimization procedures under section 1801(h) or 1821(4) of this title, as appropriate, the judge shall enter an order so stating and provide a written statement for the record of the reasons for the determination. The Government may appeal an order under this subparagraph pursuant to subsection (f).

(D) Review of certification

If the judge determines that an application pursuant to subsection (b) does not contain all of the required elements, or that the certification or certifications are clearly erroneous on the basis of the statement made under subsection (b)(1)(F)(v) and any other information furnished under subsection (b)(3), the judge shall enter an order so stating and provide a written statement for the record of the reasons for the determination. The Government may appeal an order under this subparagraph pursuant to subsection (f).

(4) Specifications

An order approving an acquisition under this subsection shall specify—

(A) the identity, if known, or a description of the United States person who is the target of the acquisition identified or described in the application pursuant to subsection (b)(1)(B);

(B) if provided in the application pursuant to subsection (b)(1)(H), the nature and location of each of the facilities or places at which the acquisition will be directed;

(C) the nature of the information sought to be acquired and the type of communications or activities to be subjected to acquisition;

(D) a summary of the means by which the acquisition will be conducted and whether physical entry is required to effect the acquisition; and

(E) the period of time during which the acquisition is approved.

(5) Directives

An order approving an acquisition under this subsection shall direct—

(A) that the minimization procedures referred to in paragraph (1)(C), as approved or modified by the Court, be followed;

(B) if applicable, an electronic communication service provider to provide to the Government forthwith all information, facilities, or assistance necessary to accomplish the acquisition authorized under such order in a manner that will protect the secrecy of the acquisition and produce a minimum of interference with the services that such electronic communication service provider is providing to the target of the acquisition;

(C) if applicable, an electronic communication service provider to maintain under security procedures approved by the Attorney General any records concerning the acquisition or the aid furnished that such electronic communication service provider wishes to maintain; and

(D) if applicable, that the Government compensate, at the prevailing rate, such electronic communication service provider for providing such information, facilities, or assistance.

(6) Duration

An order approved under this subsection shall be effective for a period not to exceed 90 days and such order may be renewed for additional 90-day periods upon submission of renewal applications meeting the requirements of subsection (b).

(7) Compliance

At or prior to the end of the period of time for which an acquisition is approved by an order or extension under this section, the judge may assess compliance with the minimization procedures referred to in paragraph (1)(C) by reviewing the circumstances under which information concerning United States persons was acquired, retained, or disseminated.

(d) Emergency authorization

(1) Authority for emergency authorization

Notwithstanding any other provision of this chapter, if the Attorney General reasonably

determines that—

(A) an emergency situation exists with respect to the acquisition of foreign intelligence information for which an order may be obtained under subsection (c) before an order authorizing such acquisition can with due diligence be obtained, and

(B) the factual basis for issuance of an order under this subsection to approve such acquisition exists, the Attorney General may authorize such acquisition if a judge having jurisdiction under subsection (a)(1) is informed by the Attorney General, or a designee of the Attorney General, at the time of such authorization that the decision has been made to conduct such acquisition and if an application in accordance with this section is made to a judge of the Foreign Intelligence Surveillance Court as soon as practicable, but not more than 7 days after the Attorney General authorizes such acquisition.

(2) Minimization procedures

If the Attorney General authorizes an acquisition under paragraph (1), the Attorney General shall require that the minimization procedures referred to in subsection (c)(1)(C) for the issuance of a judicial order be followed.

(3) Termination of emergency authorization

In the absence of a judicial order approving an acquisition under paragraph (1), such acquisition shall terminate when the information sought is obtained, when the application for the order is denied, or after the expiration of 7 days from the time of authorization by the Attorney General, whichever is earliest.

(4) Use of information

If an application for approval submitted pursuant to paragraph (1) is denied, or in any other case where the acquisition is terminated and no order is issued approving the acquisition, no information obtained or evidence derived from such acquisition, except under circumstances in which the target of the acquisition is determined not to be a United States person, shall be received in evidence or otherwise disclosed in any trial, hearing, or other proceeding in or before any court, grand jury, department, office, agency, regulatory body, legislative committee, or other authority of the United States, a State, or political subdivision thereof, and no information concerning any United States person acquired from such acquisition shall subsequently be used or disclosed in any other manner by Federal officers or employees without the consent of such person, except with the approval of the Attorney General if the information indicates a threat of death or serious bodily harm to any person.

(e) Release from liability

No cause of action shall lie in any court against any electronic communication service provider for providing any information, facilities, or assistance in accordance with an order or request for emergency assistance issued pursuant to subsection (c) or (d), respectively.

(f) Appeal

(1) Appeal to the Foreign Intelligence Surveillance Court of Review

The Government may file a petition with the Foreign Intelligence Surveillance Court of Review for review of an order issued pursuant to subsection (c). The Court of Review shall have jurisdiction to consider such petition and shall provide a written statement for the record of the reasons for a decision under this paragraph.

(2) Certiorari to the Supreme Court

The Government may file a petition for a writ of certiorari for review of a decision of the Court of Review issued under paragraph (1). The record for such review shall be transmitted under seal to the Supreme Court of the United States, which shall have jurisdiction to review such decision.

(g) Construction

Except as provided in this section, nothing in this chapter shall be construed to require an application for a court order for an acquisition that is targeted in accordance with this section at a United States person reasonably believed to be located outside the United States.

50 U.S.C. § 1881c. Other acquisitions targeting United States persons outside the United States

(a) Jurisdiction and scope

(1) Jurisdiction

The Foreign Intelligence Surveillance Court shall have jurisdiction to enter an order pursuant to subsection (c).

(2) Scope

No element of the intelligence community may intentionally target, for the purpose of acquiring foreign intelligence information, a United States person reasonably believed to be located outside the United States under circumstances in which the targeted United States person has a reasonable expectation of privacy and a warrant would be required if the acquisition were conducted inside the United States for law enforcement purposes, unless a judge of the Foreign Intelligence Surveillance Court has entered an order with respect to such targeted United States person or the Attorney General has authorized an emergency acquisition pursuant to subsection (c) or (d), respectively, or any other provision of this chapter.

(3) Limitations

(A) Moving or misidentified targets

If a United States person targeted under this subsection is reasonably believed to be located in the United States during the effective period of an order issued pursuant to subsection (c), an acquisition targeting such United States person under this section shall cease unless the targeted United States person is again reasonably believed to be located outside the United States during the effective period of such order.

(B) Applicability

If an acquisition for foreign intelligence purposes is to be conducted inside the United States and could be authorized under section 1881b of this title, the acquisition may only be conducted if authorized under section 1881b of this title or in accordance with another provision of this chapter other than this section.

(C) Construction

Nothing in this paragraph shall be construed to limit the authority of the Government to seek an order or authorization under, or otherwise engage in any activity that is authorized under, any other subchapter of this chapter.

(b) Application

Each application for an order under this section shall be made by a Federal officer in writing upon oath or affirmation to a judge having jurisdiction under subsection (a)(1). Each application shall require the approval of the Attorney General based upon the Attorney General's finding that it satisfies the criteria and requirements of such application as set forth in this section and shall include—

(1) the identity of the Federal officer making the application;

(2) the identity, if known, or a description of the specific United States person who is the target of the acquisition;

(3) a statement of the facts and circumstances relied upon to justify the applicant's belief that the United States person who is the target of the acquisition is—

(A) a person reasonably believed to be located outside the United States; and

(B) a foreign power, an agent of a foreign power, or an officer or employee of a foreign power;

(4) a statement of proposed minimization procedures that meet the definition of minimization procedures under section 1801(h) or 1821(4) of this title, as appropriate;

(5) a certification made by the Attorney General, an official specified in section 1804(a)(6) of this title, or the head of an element of the intelligence community that—

(A) the certifying official deems the information sought to be foreign intelligence information; and

(B) a significant purpose of the acquisition is to obtain foreign intelligence information;

(6) a statement of the facts concerning any previous applications that have been made to any judge of the Foreign Intelligence Surveillance Court involving the United States person specified in the application and the action taken on each previous application; and

(7) a statement of the period of time for which the acquisition is required to be maintained, provided that such period of time shall not exceed 90 days per application.

(c) Order

(1) Findings

Upon an application made pursuant to subsection (b), the Foreign Intelligence Surveillance Court shall enter an ex parte order as requested or as modified by the Court if the Court finds that—

(A) the application has been made by a Federal officer and approved by the Attorney General;

(B) on the basis of the facts submitted by the applicant, for the United States person who is the target of the acquisition, there is probable cause to believe that the target is—

(i) a person reasonably believed to be located outside the United States; and

(ii) a foreign power, an agent of a foreign power, or an officer or employee of a foreign power;

(C) the proposed minimization procedures, with respect to their dissemination provisions, meet the definition of minimization procedures under section 1801(h) or 1821(4) of this title, as appropriate; and

(D) the application that has been filed contains all statements and certifications required by subsection (b) and the certification provided under subsection (b)(5) is not clearly erroneous on the basis of the information furnished under subsection (b).

(2) Probable cause

In determining whether or not probable cause exists for purposes of paragraph (1)(B), a judge having jurisdiction under subsection (a)(1) may consider past activities of the target and facts and circumstances relating to current or future activities of the target. No United States person may be considered a foreign power, agent of a foreign power, or officer or employee of a foreign power solely upon the basis of activities protected by the first amendment to the Constitution of the United States.

(3) Review

(A) Limitations on review

Review by a judge having jurisdiction under subsection (a)(1) shall be limited to that required to make the findings described in paragraph (1). The judge shall not have jurisdiction to review the means by which an acquisition under this section may be conducted.

(B) Review of probable cause

If the judge determines that the facts submitted under subsection (b) are insufficient to establish probable cause to issue an order under this subsection, the judge shall enter an order so stating and provide a written statement for the record of the reasons for such determination. The Government may appeal an order under this subparagraph pursuant to subsection (e).

(C) Review of minimization procedures

If the judge determines that the minimization procedures applicable to dissemination of information obtained through an acquisition under this subsection do not meet the definition of minimization procedures under section 1801(h) or 1821(4) of this title, as appropriate, the judge shall enter an order so stating and provide a written statement for the record of the reasons for such determination. The Government may appeal an order under this subparagraph pursuant to subsection (e).

(D) Scope of review of certification

If the judge determines that an application under subsection (b) does not contain all the required elements, or that the certification provided under subsection (b)(5) is clearly erroneous on the basis of the information furnished under subsection (b), the judge shall enter an order so stating and provide a written statement for the record of the reasons for such determination. The Government may appeal an order under this subparagraph pursuant to subsection (e).

(4) Duration

An order under this paragraph shall be effective for a period not to exceed 90 days and such order may be renewed for additional 90-day periods upon submission of renewal applications meeting the requirements of subsection (b).

(5) Compliance

At or prior to the end of the period of time for which an order or extension is granted under this section, the judge may assess compliance with the minimization procedures referred to in paragraph (1)(C) by reviewing the circumstances under which information concerning United States persons was disseminated, provided that the judge may not inquire into the circumstances relating to the conduct of the acquisition.

(d) Emergency authorization

(1) Authority for emergency authorization

Notwithstanding any other provision of this section, if the Attorney General reasonably determines that—

(A) an emergency situation exists with respect to the acquisition of foreign intelligence information for which an order may be obtained under subsection (c) before an order under that subsection can, with due diligence, be obtained, and

(B) the factual basis for the issuance of an order under this section exists, the Attorney General may authorize the emergency acquisition if a judge having jurisdiction under subsection (a)(1) is informed by the Attorney General or a designee of the Attorney General at the time of such authorization that the decision has been made to conduct such acquisition and if an application in accordance with this section is made to a judge of the Foreign Intelligence Surveillance Court as soon as practicable, but not more than 7 days after the Attorney General authorizes such acquisition.

(2) Minimization procedures

If the Attorney General authorizes an emergency acquisition under paragraph (1), the Attorney General shall require that the minimization procedures referred to in subsection (c)(1)(C) be followed.

(3) Termination of emergency authorization

In the absence of an order under subsection (c), an emergency acquisition under paragraph (1) shall terminate when the information sought is obtained, if the application for the order is denied, or after the expiration of 7 days from the time of authorization by the Attorney General, whichever is earliest.

(4) Use of information

If an application submitted to the Court pursuant to paragraph (1) is denied, or in any other case where the acquisition is terminated and no order with respect to the target of the acquisition is issued under subsection (c), no information obtained or evidence derived from such acquisition, except under circumstances in which the target of the acquisition is determined not to be a United States person, shall be received in evidence or otherwise disclosed in any trial, hearing, or other proceeding in or before any court, grand jury, department, office, agency, regulatory body, legislative committee, or other authority of the United States, a State, or political subdivision thereof, and no information concerning any United States person acquired from such acquisition shall subsequently be used or disclosed in any other manner by Federal officers or employees without the consent of such person, except with the approval of the Attorney General if the information indicates a threat of death or serious bodily harm to any person.

(e) Appeal

(1) Appeal to the Court of Review

The Government may file a petition with the Foreign Intelligence Surveillance Court of Review for review of an order issued pursuant to subsection (c). The Court of Review shall have jurisdiction to consider such petition and shall provide a written statement for the record of the reasons for a decision under this paragraph.

(2) Certiorari to the Supreme Court

The Government may file a petition for a writ of certiorari for review of a decision of the Court of Review issued under paragraph (1). The record for such review shall be transmitted under seal to the Supreme Court of the United States, which shall have jurisdiction to review such decision.

50 U.S.C. § 1881d. Joint applications and concurrent authorizations

(a) Joint applications and orders

If an acquisition targeting a United States person under section 1881b or 1881c of this title is proposed to be conducted both inside and outside the United States, a judge having jurisdiction under section 1881b(a)(1) or 1881c(a)(1) of this title may issue simultaneously, upon the request of the Government in a joint application complying with the requirements of sections 1881b(b) and 1881c(b) of this title, orders under sections 1881b(c) and 1881c(c) of this title, as appropriate.

(b) Concurrent authorization

If an order authorizing electronic surveillance or physical search has been obtained under section 1805 or 1824 of this title, the Attorney General may authorize, for the effective period of that order, without an order under section 1881b or 1881c of this title, the targeting of that United States person for the purpose of acquiring foreign intelligence information while such person is reasonably believed to be located outside the United States.

(c) Emergency authorization

(1) Concurrent authorization

If the Attorney General authorized the emergency employment of electronic surveillance or a physical search pursuant to section 1805 or 1824 of this title, the Attorney General may authorize, for the effective period of the emergency authorization and subsequent order pursuant to section 1805 or 1824 of this title, without a separate order under section 1881b or 1881c of this title, the targeting of a United States person subject to such emergency employment for the purpose of acquiring foreign intelligence information while such United States person is reasonably believed to be located outside the United States.

(2) Use of information

If an application submitted to the Court pursuant to section 1804 or 1823 of this title is denied, or in any other case in which the acquisition pursuant to paragraph (1) is terminated and no order with respect to the target of the acquisition is issued under section 1805 or 1824 of this title, all information obtained or evidence derived from such acquisition shall be handled in accordance with section 1881c(d)(4) of this title.

50 U.S.C. § 1881e. Use of information acquired under this subchapter

(a) Information acquired under section 1881a

(1) In general

Information acquired from an acquisition conducted under section 1881a of this title shall be deemed to be information acquired from an electronic surveillance pursuant to subchapter I for purposes of section 1806 of this title, except for the purposes of subsection (j) of such section.

(2) United States persons

(A) In general

Any information concerning a United States person acquired under section 1881a of this title shall not be used in evidence against that United States person pursuant to paragraph (1) in any criminal proceeding unless —

(i) the Federal Bureau of Investigation obtained an order of the Foreign Intelligence Surveillance Court to access such information pursuant to section 1881a(f)(2) of this title; or

(ii) the Attorney General determines that —

(I) the criminal proceeding affects, involves, or is related to the national security of the United States; or

(II) the criminal proceeding involves —

(aa) death;

(bb) kidnapping;

(cc) serious bodily injury, as defined in section 1365 of title 18;

(dd) conduct that constitutes a criminal offense that is a specified offense against a minor, as defined in section 20911 of title 34;

(ee) incapacitation or destruction of critical infrastructure, as defined in section 5195c(e) of title 42;

(ff) cybersecurity, including conduct described in section 5195c(e) of title 42 or section 1029, 1030, or 2511 of title 18;

(gg) transnational crime, including transnational narcotics trafficking and transnational organized crime; or

(hh) human trafficking.

(B) No judicial review

A determination by the Attorney General under subparagraph (A)(ii) is not subject to judicial review.

(b) Information acquired under section 1881b

Information acquired from an acquisition conducted under section 1881b of this title shall be deemed to be information acquired from an electronic surveillance pursuant to subchapter I for purposes of section 1806 of this title.

50 U.S.C. § 1881f. Congressional oversight

(a) Semiannual report

Not less frequently than once every 6 months, the Attorney General shall fully inform, in a manner consistent with national security, the congressional intelligence committees and the Committees on the Judiciary of the Senate and the House of Representatives, consistent with the Rules of the House of Representatives, the Standing Rules of the

Senate, and Senate Resolution 400 of the 94th Congress or any successor Senate resolution, concerning the implementation of this subchapter.

(b) Content

Each report under subsection (a) shall include—

(1) with respect to section 1881a of this title—

(A) any certifications submitted in accordance with section 1881a(h) of this title during the reporting period;

(B) with respect to each determination under section 1881a(c)(2) of this title, the reasons for exercising the authority under such section;

(C) any directives issued under section 1881a(i) of this title during the reporting period;

(D) a description of the judicial review during the reporting period of such certifications and targeting and minimization procedures adopted in accordance with subsections (d) and (e) of section 1881a of this title and utilized with respect to an acquisition under such section, including a copy of an order or pleading in connection with such review that contains a significant legal interpretation of the provisions of section 1881a of this title;

(E) any actions taken to challenge or enforce a directive under paragraph (4) or (5) of section 1881a(i) of this title;

(F) any compliance reviews conducted by the Attorney General or the Director of National Intelligence of acquisitions authorized under section 1881a(a) of this title;

(G) a description of any incidents of noncompliance—

(i) with a directive issued by the Attorney General and the Director of National Intelligence under section 1881a(i) of this title, including incidents of noncompliance by a specified person to whom the Attorney General and Director of National Intelligence issued a directive under section 1881a(i) of this title; and

(ii) by an element of the intelligence community with procedures and guidelines adopted in accordance with subsections (d), (e), (f)(1), and (g) of section 1881a of this title; and

(H) any procedures implementing section 1881a of this title;

(2) with respect to section 1881b of this title—

(A) the total number of applications made for orders under section 1881b(b) of this title;

(B) the total number of such orders—

(i) granted;

(ii) modified; and

(iii) denied; and

(C) the total number of emergency acquisitions authorized by the Attorney General under section 1881b(d) of this title and the total number of subsequent orders approving or denying such acquisitions; and

(3) with respect to section 1881c of this title—

(A) the total number of applications made for orders under section 1881c(b) of this title;

(B) the total number of such orders—

    (i) granted;

    (ii) modified; and

    (iii) denied; and

(C) the total number of emergency acquisitions authorized by the Attorney General under section 1881c(d) of this title and the total number of subsequent orders approving or denying such applications.

50 U.S.C. § 1881g. Savings provision

Nothing in this subchapter shall be construed to limit the authority of the Government to seek an order or authorization under, or otherwise engage in any activity that is authorized under, any other subchapter of this chapter.

50 U.S.C. § 1885. Definitions

In this subchapter:

(1) Assistance

The term "assistance" means the provision of, or the provision of access to, information (including communication contents, communications records, or other information relating to a customer or communication), facilities, or another form of assistance.

(2) Civil action

The term "civil action" includes a covered civil action.

(3) Congressional intelligence committees

The term "congressional intelligence committees" means—

    (A) the Select Committee on Intelligence of the Senate; and

    (B) the Permanent Select Committee on Intelligence of the House of Representatives.

(4) Contents

The term "contents" has the meaning given that term in section 1801(n) of this title.

(5) Covered civil action

The term "covered civil action" means a civil action filed in a Federal or State court that—

    (A) alleges that an electronic communication service provider furnished assistance to an element of the intelligence community; and

    (B) seeks monetary or other relief from the electronic communication service provider related to the provision of such assistance.

(6) Electronic communication service provider

The term "electronic communication service provider" means—

    (A) a telecommunications carrier, as that term is defined in section 153 of title 47;

    (B) a provider of electronic communication service, as that term is defined in section 2510 of title 18;

(C) a provider of a remote computing service, as that term is defined in section 2711 of title 18;

(D) any other communication service provider who has access to wire or electronic communications either as such communications are transmitted or as such communications are stored;

(E) a parent, subsidiary, affiliate, successor, or assignee of an entity described in subparagraph (A), (B), (C), or (D); or

(F) an officer, employee, or agent of an entity described in subparagraph (A), (B), (C), (D), or (E).

(7) Intelligence community

The term "intelligence community" has the meaning given the term in section 3003(4) of this title.

(8) Person

The term "person" means—

(A) an electronic communication service provider; or

(B) a landlord, custodian, or other person who may be authorized or required to furnish assistance pursuant to—

(i) an order of the court established under section 1803(a) of this title directing such assistance;

(ii) a certification in writing under section 2511(2)(a)(ii)(B) or 2709(b) of title 18; or

(iii) a directive under section 1802(a)(4), 1805b(e), as added by section 2 of the Protect America Act of 2007 (Public Law 110–55), or 1881a(i) of this title.

(9) State

The term "State" means any State, political subdivision of a State, the Commonwealth of Puerto Rico, the District of Columbia, and any territory or possession of the United States, and includes any officer, public utility commission, or other body authorized to regulate an electronic communication service provider.

50 U.S.C. § 1885a. *Procedures for implementing statutory defenses*

(a) Requirement for certification

Notwithstanding any other provision of law, a civil action may not lie or be maintained in a Federal or State court against any person for providing assistance to an element of the intelligence community, and shall be promptly dismissed, if the Attorney General certifies to the district court of the United States in which such action is pending that—

(1) any assistance by that person was provided pursuant to an order of the court established under section 1803(a) of this title directing such assistance;

(2) any assistance by that person was provided pursuant to a certification in writing under section 2511(2)(a)(ii)(B) or 2709(b) of title 18;

(3) any assistance by that person was provided pursuant to a directive under section 1802(a)(4), 1805b(e), as added by section 2 of the Protect America Act of 2007 (Public Law 110–55), or 1881a(i) of this title directing such assistance;

(4) in the case of a covered civil action, the assistance alleged to have been provided by the electronic communication service provider was—

    (A) in connection with an intelligence activity involving communications that was—

        (i) authorized by the President during the period beginning on September 11, 2001, and ending on January 17, 2007; and

        (ii) designed to detect or prevent a terrorist attack, or activities in preparation for a terrorist attack, against the United States; and

    (B) the subject of a written request or directive, or a series of written requests or directives, from the Attorney General or the head of an element of the intelligence community (or the deputy of such person) to the electronic communication service provider indicating that the activity was—

        (i) authorized by the President; and

        (ii) determined to be lawful; or

(5) the person did not provide the alleged assistance.

(b) Judicial review

    (1) Review of certifications

A certification under subsection (a) shall be given effect unless the court finds that such certification is not supported by substantial evidence provided to the court pursuant to this section.

    (2) Supplemental materials

In its review of a certification under subsection (a), the court may examine the court order, certification, written request, or directive described in subsection (a) and any relevant court order, certification, written request, or directive submitted pursuant to subsection (d).

(c) Limitations on disclosure

If the Attorney General files a declaration under section 1746 of title 28 that disclosure of a certification made pursuant to subsection (a) or the supplemental materials provided pursuant to subsection (b) or (d) would harm the national security of the United States, the court shall—

    (1) review such certification and the supplemental materials in camera and ex parte; and

    (2) limit any public disclosure concerning such certification and the supplemental materials, including any public order following such in camera and ex parte review, to a statement as to whether the case is dismissed and a description of the legal standards that govern the order, without disclosing the paragraph of subsection (a) that is the basis for the certification.

(d) Role of the parties

Any plaintiff or defendant in a civil action may submit any relevant court order, certification, written request, or directive to the district court referred to in subsection (a) for review and shall be permitted to participate in the briefing or argument of any legal issue in a judicial proceeding conducted pursuant to this section, but only to the extent that such participation does not require the disclosure of classified information to such party. To the extent that classified information is relevant to the proceeding or would be revealed in the determination of an issue, the court shall review such information in camera and ex parte, and shall issue any part of the court's written order that would reveal classified information in camera and ex parte and maintain such part under seal.

(e) Nondelegation

The authority and duties of the Attorney General under this section shall be performed by the Attorney General (or Acting Attorney General) or the Deputy Attorney General.

(f) Appeal

The courts of appeals shall have jurisdiction of appeals from interlocutory orders of the district courts of the United States granting or denying a motion to dismiss or for summary judgment under this section.

(g) Removal

A civil action against a person for providing assistance to an element of the intelligence community that is brought in a State court shall be deemed to arise under th Constitution and laws of the United States and shall be removable under section 1441 of title 28.

(h) Relationship to other laws

Nothing in this section shall be construed to limit any otherwise available immunity, privilege, or defense under any other provision of law.

(i) Applicability

This section shall apply to a civil action pending on or filed after July 10, 2008.

50 U.S.C. § 1885b. Preemption

(a) In general

No State shall have authority to—

(1) conduct an investigation into an electronic communication service provider's alleged assistance to an element of the intelligence community;

(2) require through regulation or any other means the disclosure of information about an electronic communication service provider's alleged assistance to an element of the intelligence community;

(3) impose any administrative sanction on an electronic communication service provider for assistance to an element of the intelligence community; or

(4) commence or maintain a civil action or other proceeding to enforce a requirement that an electronic communication service provider disclose information concerning alleged assistance to an element of the intelligence community.

(b) Suits by the United States

The United States may bring suit to enforce the provisions of this section.

(c) Jurisdiction

The district courts of the United States shall have jurisdiction over any civil action brought by the United States to enforce the provisions of this section.

(d) Application

This section shall apply to any investigation, action, or proceeding that is pending on or commenced after July 10, 2008.

United States
Foreign Intelligence Surveillance Act

50 U.S.C. § 1885c. Reporting

(a) Semiannual report

Not less frequently than once every 6 months, the Attorney General shall, in a manner consistent with national security, the Rules of the House of Representatives, the Standing Rules of the Senate, and Senate Resolution 400 of the 94th Congress or any successor Senate resolution, fully inform the congressional intelligence committees, the Committee on the Judiciary of the Senate, and the Committee on the Judiciary of the House of Representatives concerning the implementation of this subchapter.

(b) Content

Each report made under subsection (a) shall include—

(1) any certifications made under section 1885a of this title;

(2) a description of the judicial review of the certifications made under section 1885a of this

title; and

(3) any actions taken to enforce the provisions of section 1885b of this title.

RIGHT TO FINANCIAL PRIVACY ACT
(1978)

Summary

The Right to Financial Privacy Act was precipitated by the Supreme Court's decision in United States v Miller, 425 U.S. 435 (1976) in which a customer challenged the disclosure of his personal financial information by his bank. The Court held that the records were the property of the bank and, therefore, that the customer did not have standing under the Fourth Amendment to challenge the disclosure. Furthermore, the Court ruled that the customer did not have a reasonable expectation of privacy regarding records of his checking account because in writing a check, the customer knew that the bank employees would see the information on it. The Right to Financial Privacy Act sought to regulate disclosure of personal financial information to federal agencies, to recognize individuals' privacy interest in their bank records, and to give them rights regarding the disclosure of those records. The Act does not prohibit the disclosure of financial information to federal agencies. Instead it puts strict guidelines into place regarding such disclosures, and mandates a procedure for notice and challenge. The Act only applies to the federal government; it does not regulate disclosure of financial information to private parties or businesses.

The Right to Financial Privacy Act prohibits any Government authority from obtaining copies of, access to, or the information contained in, the financial records of any customer from a financial institution unless such records are reasonably described and: (1) such customer has authorized such disclosure in accordance with this Act; (2) such records are disclosed in response to an administrative subpoena or summons; (3) such records are disclosed in response to a court order; (4) such records are disclosed in response to a judicial subpoena; or (5) such financial records are disclosed in response to a formal written request meeting specified requirements. Requires in all cases that the customer be notified of the agency seeking such records, the purpose for which such records are sought, and the rights of customers under this Act.

The Act establishes specific conditions and procedures for the delay of notice to a customer. It states that no financial institution may provide to a Government authority copies of or the information contained in the financial records of any customer except in accordance with the requirements of this Act. It sets forth provisions governing customer authorization, administrative subpoenas and summons, judicial subpoenas, and search warrants. It establishes procedures for a customer to challenge the disclosure of financial records. It provides exceptions to the provisions of this Act and special procedures for the disclosure of records to the Secret Service and government authorities acting in the field of foreign intelligence.

The Act establishes civil penalties and the right to injunctive relief without regard to the amount in controversy for violation of the provisions of this Title. Actions may be brought within three years of a customer's discovery of violation. Injunctive relief and compensatory and punitive damages are available under the Act.

References

> Public Law 95-630. Codified as amended at 12 U.S.C. § 3401 et seq.
> [https://www.law.cornell.edu/uscode/text/12/3401]

> L. Richard Fischer, *The Law of Financial Privacy* (A.S. Pratt & Sons 2000)

> EPIC, Right to Financial Privacy Act
> [https://www.epic.org/privacy/rfpa/]

12 U.S.C. § 3401. Definitions

For the purpose of this chapter, the term-

(1) "financial institution", except as provided in section 3414 of this title, means any office of a bank, savings bank, card issuer as defined in section 1602(n) [1] of title 15, industrial loan company, trust company, savings association, building and loan, or homestead association (including cooperative banks), credit union, or consumer finance institution, located in any State or territory of the United States, the District of Columbia, Puerto Rico, Guam, American Samoa, or the Virgin Islands;

(2) "financial record" means an original of, a copy of, or information known to have been derived from, any record held by a financial institution pertaining to a customer's relationship with the financial institution;

(3) "Government authority" means any agency or department of the United States, or any officer, employee, or agent thereof;

(4) "person" means an individual or a partnership of five or fewer individuals;

(5) "customer" means any person or authorized representative of that person who utilized or is utilizing any service of a financial institution, or for whom a financial institution is acting or has acted as a fiduciary, in relation to an account maintained in the person's name;

(6) "holding company" means-

   (A) any bank holding company (as defined in section 1841 of this title); and

   (B) any company described in section 1843(f)(1) of this title;

(7) "supervisory agency" means with respect to any particular financial institution, holding company, or any subsidiary of a financial institution or holding company, any of the following which has statutory authority to examine the financial condition, business operations, or records or transactions of that institution, holding company, or subsidiary-

   (A) the Federal Deposit Insurance Corporation;

   (B) the Bureau of Consumer Financial Protection;

(C) the National Credit Union Administration;

(D) the Board of Governors of the Federal Reserve System;

(E) the Comptroller of the Currency;

(F) the Securities and Exchange Commission;

(G) the Commodity Futures Trading Commission;

(H) the Secretary of the Treasury, with respect to the Bank Secrecy Act (Public Law 91–508, title I) [12 U.S.C. 1951 et seq.] and subchapter II of chapter 53 of title 31; or

(I) any State banking or securities department or agency; and

(8) "law enforcement inquiry" means a lawful investigation or official proceeding inquiring into a violation of, or failure to comply with, any criminal or civil statute or any regulation, rule, or order issued pursuant thereto.

Sec. 3402. Access to financial records by Government authorities prohibited; exceptions

Except as provided by section 3403(c) or (d), 3413, or 3414 of this title, no Government authority may have access to or obtain copies of, or the information contained in the financial records of any customer from a financial institution unless the financial records are reasonably described and -

(1) such customer has authorized such disclosure in accordance with section 3404 of this title;

(2) such financial records are disclosed in response to an administrative subpoena or summons which meets the requirements of section 3405 of this title;

(3) such financial records are disclosed in response to a search warrant which meets the requirements of section 3406 of this title;

(4) such financial records are disclosed in response to a judicial subpoena which meets the requirements of section 3407 of this title; or

(5) such financial records are disclosed in response to a formal written request which meets the requirements of section 3408 of this title.

Sec. 3403. Confidentiality of financial records

(a) Release of records by financial institutions prohibited

No financial institution, or officer, employees, or agent of a financial institution, may provide to any Government authority access to or copies of, or the information contained in, the financial records of any customer except in accordance with the provisions of this chapter.

(b) Release of records upon certification of compliance with chapter

A financial institution shall not release the financial records of a customer until the Government authority seeking such records certifies in writing to the financial institution that it has complied with the applicable provisions of this chapter.

(c) Notification to Government authority of existence of relevant information in records

Nothing in this chapter shall preclude any financial institution, or any officer, employee, or agent of a financial institution, from notifying a Government authority that such institution, or officer, employee, or agent has information which may be relevant to a possible violation of any statute or regulation. Such information may include only the name or other identifying information concerning any individual, corporation, or account involved in and the nature of any suspected illegal activity. Such information may be disclosed notwithstanding any constitution, law, or regulation of any State or political subdivision thereof to the contrary. Any financial institution, or officer, employee, or agent thereof, making a disclosure of information pursuant to this subsection, shall not be liable to the customer under any law or regulation of the United States or any constitution, law, or regulation of any State or political subdivision thereof, for such disclosure or for any failure to notify the customer of such disclosure.

(d) Release of records as incident to perfection of security interest, proving a claim in bankruptcy, collecting a debt, or processing an application with regard to a Government loan, loan guarantee, etc.

(1) Nothing in this chapter shall preclude a financial institution, as an incident to perfecting a security interest, proving a claim in bankruptcy, or otherwise collecting on a debt owing either to the financial institution itself or in its role as a fiduciary, from providing copies of any financial record to any court or Government authority.

(2) Nothing in this chapter shall preclude a financial institution, as an incident to processing an application for assistance to a customer in the form of a Government loan, loan guaranty, or loan insurance agreement, or as an incident to processing a default on, or administering, a Government guaranteed or insured loan, from initiating contact with an appropriate Government authority for the purpose of providing any financial record necessary to permit such authority to carry out its responsibilities under a loan, loan guaranty, or loan insurance agreement.

Sec. 3404. Customer authorizations

(a) Statement furnished by customer to financial institution and Government authority; contents

A customer may authorize disclosure under section 3402(1) of this title if he furnishes to the financial institution and to the Government authority seeking to obtain such disclosure a signed and dated statement which -

(1) authorizes such disclosure for a period not in excess of three months;

(2) states that the customer may revoke such authorization at any time before the financial records are disclosed;

(3) identifies the financial records which are authorized to be disclosed;

(4) specifies the purposes for which, and the Government authority to which, such records may be disclosed; and

(5) states the customer's rights under this chapter.

(b) Authorization as condition of doing business prohibited

No such authorization shall be required as a condition of doing business with any financial institution.

(c) Right of customer to access to financial institution's record of disclosures

The customer has the right, unless the Government authority obtains a court order as provided in section 3409 of this title, to obtain a copy of the record which the financial institution shall keep of all instances in which the customer's record is disclosed to a Government authority pursuant to this section, including the identity of the Government authority to which such disclosure is made.

Sec. 3405. Administrative subpoena and summons

A Government authority may obtain financial records under section 3402(2) of this title pursuant to an administrative subpoena or summons otherwise authorized by law only if -

(1) there is reason to believe that the records sought are relevant to a legitimate law enforcement inquiry;

(2) a copy of the subpoena or summons has been served upon the customer or mailed to his last known address on or before the date on which the subpoena or summons was served on the financial institution together with the following notice which shall state with reasonable specificity the nature of the law enforcement inquiry:

"Records or information concerning your transactions held by the financial institution named in the attached subpoena or summons are being sought by this (agency or department) in accordance with the Right to Financial Privacy Act of 1978 (12 U.S.C. 3401 et seq.) for the following purpose: If you desire that such records or information not be made available, you must:

"1. Fill out the accompanying motion paper and sworn statement or write one of your own, stating that you are the customer whose records are being requested by the Government and either giving the reasons you believe that the records are not relevant to the legitimate law enforcement inquiry stated in this notice or any other legal basis for objecting to the release of the records.

"2. File the motion and statement by mailing or delivering them to the clerk of any one of the following United States district courts:

"3. Serve the Government authority requesting the records by mailing or delivering a copy of your motion and statement to .

"4. Be prepared to come to court and present your position in further detail.

"5. You do not need to have a lawyer, although you may wish to employ one to represent you and protect your rights.

If you do not follow the above procedures, upon the expiration of ten days from the date of service or fourteen days from the date of mailing of this notice, the records or information requested therein will be made available. These records may be transferred to other Government authorities for legitimate law enforcement inquiries, in which event you will be notified after the transfer."; and

(3) ten days have expired from the date of service of the notice or fourteen days have expired from the date of mailing the notice to the customer and within such time period the customer has not filed a sworn statement and motion to quash in an appropriate court, or the customer challenge provisions of section 3410 of this title have been complied with.

Sec. 3406. Search warrants

(a) Applicability of Federal Rules of Criminal Procedure

A Government authority may obtain financial records under section 3402(3) of this title only if it obtains a search warrant pursuant to the Federal Rules of Criminal Procedure.

(b) Mailing of copy and notice to customer

No later than ninety days after the Government authority serves the search warrant, it shall mail to the customer's last known address a copy of the search warrant together with the following notice:

> "Records or information concerning your transactions held by the financial institution named in the attached search warrant were obtained by this (agency or department) on (date) for the following purpose: . You may have rights under the Right to Financial Privacy Act of 1978 (12 U.S.C. 3401 et seq.).".

(c) Court-ordered delays in mailing

Upon application of the Government authority, a court may grant a delay in the mailing of the notice required in subsection (b) of this section, which delay shall not exceed one hundred and eighty days following the service of the warrant, if the court makes the findings required in section 3409(a) of this title. If the court so finds, it shall enter an ex parte order granting the requested delay and an order prohibiting the financial institution from disclosing that records have been obtained or that a search warrant for such records has been executed. Additional delays of up to ninety days may be granted by the court upon application, but only in accordance with this subsection. Upon expiration of the period of delay of notification of the customer, the following notice shall be mailed to the customer along with a copy of the search warrant:

> "Records or information concerning your transactions held by the financial institution named in the attached search warrant were obtained by this (agency or department) on (date). Notification was delayed beyond the statutory ninety-day delay period pursuant to a determination by the court that such notice would seriously jeopardize an investigation concerning . You may have rights under the Right to Financial Privacy Act of 1978 (12 U.S.C. 3401 et seq.).".

Sec. 3407. Judicial subpoena

A Government authority may obtain financial records under section 3402(4) of this title pursuant to judicial subpoena only if -

(1) such subpoena is authorized by law and there is reason to believe that the records sought are relevant to a legitimate law enforcement inquiry;

(2) a copy of the subpoena has been served upon the customer or mailed to his last known address on or before the date on which the subpoena was served on the financial institution together with the following notice which shall state with reasonable specificity the nature of the law enforcement inquiry:

"Records or information concerning your transactions which are held by the financial institution named in the attached subpoena are being sought by this (agency or department or authority) in accordance with the Right to Financial Privacy Act of 1978 (12 U.S.C. 3401 et seq.) for the following purpose: If you desire that such records or information not be made available, you must:

"1. Fill out the accompanying motion paper and sworn statement or write one of your own, stating that you are the customer whose records are being requested by the Government and either giving the reasons you believe that the records are not relevant to the legitimate law enforcement inquiry stated in this notice or any other legal basis for objecting to the release of the records.

"2. File the motion and statement by mailing or delivering them to the clerk of the Court.

"3. Serve the Government authority requesting the records by mailing or delivering a copy of your motion and statement to .

"4. Be prepared to come to court and present your position in further detail.

"5. You do not need to have a lawyer, although you may wish to employ one to represent you and protect your rights. If you do not follow the above procedures, upon the expiration of ten days from the date of service or fourteen days from the date of mailing of this notice, the records or information requested therein will be made available. These records may be transferred to other government authorities for legitimate law enforcement inquiries, in which event you will be notified after the transfer;" and

(3) ten days have expired from the date of service or fourteen days from the date of mailing of the notice to the customer and within such time period the customer has not filed a sworn statement and motion to quash in an appropriate court, or the customer challenge provisions of section 3410 of this title have been complied with.

Sec. 3408. Formal written request

A Government authority may request financial records under section 3402(5) of this title pursuant to a formal written request only if -

(1) no administrative summons or subpoena authority reasonably appears to be available to that Government authority to obtain financial records for the purpose for which such records are sought;

(2) the request is authorized by regulations promulgated by the head of the agency or department;

(3) there is reason to believe that the records sought are relevant to a legitimate law enforcement inquiry; and

(4)(A) a copy of the request has been served upon the customer or mailed to his last known address on or before the date on which the request was made to the financial institution together with the following notice which shall state with reasonable specificity the nature of the law enforcement inquiry:

"Records or information concerning your transactions held by the financial institution named in the attached request are being sought by this (agency or department) in accordance with the Right to Financial Privacy Act of 1978 (12 U.S.C. 3401 et seq.) for the following purpose:

"If you desire that such records or information not be made available, you must:

"1. Fill out the accompanying motion paper and sworn statement or write one of your own, stating that you are the customer whose records are being requested by the Government and either giving the reasons you believe that the records are not relevant to the legitimate law enforcement inquiry stated in this notice or any other legal basis for objecting to the release of the records.

"2. File the motion and statement by mailing or delivering them to the clerk of any one of the following United States District Courts:

"3. Serve the Government authority requesting the records by mailing or delivering a copy of your motion and statement to .

"4. Be prepared to come to court and present your position in further detail.

"5. You do not need to have a lawyer, although you may wish to employ one to represent you and protect your rights. If you do not follow the above procedures, upon the expiration of ten days from the date of service or fourteen days from the date of mailing of this notice, the records or information requested therein may be made available. These records may be transferred to other Government authorities for legitimate law enforcement inquiries, in which event you will be notified after the transfer;" and

(B) ten days have expired from the date of service or fourteen days from the date of mailing of the notice by the customer and within such time period the customer has not filed a sworn statement and an application to enjoin the Government authority in an appropriate court, or the customer challenge provisions of section 3410 of this title have been complied with.

Sec. 3409. Delayed notice

(a) Application by Government authority; findings

Upon application of the Government authority, the customer notice required under section 3404(c), 3405(2), 3406(c), 3407(2), 3408(4), or 3412(b) of this title may be delayed by order of an appropriate court if the presiding judge or magistrate judge finds that -

(1) the investigation being conducted is within the lawful jurisdiction of the Government authority seeking the financial records;

(2) there is reason to believe that the records being sought are relevant to a legitimate law enforcement inquiry; and

(3) there is reason to believe that such notice will result in

(A) endangering life or physical safety of any person;

(B) flight from prosecution;

(C) destruction of or tampering with evidence;

(D) intimidation of potential witnesses; or

(E) otherwise seriously jeopardizing an investigation or official proceeding or unduly delaying a trial or ongoing official proceeding to the same extent as the circumstances in the preceding subparagraphs.

An application for delay must be made with reasonable specificity.

(b) Grant of delay order; duration and specifications; extensions; copy of request and notice to customer

(1) If the court makes the findings required in paragraphs (1), (2), and (3) of subsection (a) of this section, it shall enter an ex parte order granting the requested delay for a period not to exceed ninety days and an order prohibiting the financial institution from disclosing that records have been obtained or that a request for records has been made, except that, if the records have been sought by a Government authority exercising financial controls over foreign accounts in the United States under section 5(b) of the Trading with the Enemy Act (12 U.S.C. 95a, 50 App. U.S.C. 5(b)), the International Emergency Economic Powers Act (title II, Public Law 95-223) (50 U.S.C. 1701 et seq.), or section 287c of title 22, and the court finds that there is reason to believe that such notice may endanger the lives or physical safety of a customer or group of customers, or any person or group of persons associated with a customer, the court may specify that the delay be indefinite.

(2) Extensions of the delay of notice provided in paragraph (1) of up to ninety days each may be granted by the court upon application, but only in accordance with this subsection.

(3) Upon expiration of the period of delay of notification under paragraph (1) or (2), the customer shall be served with or mailed a copy of the process or request together with the following notice which shall state with reasonable specificity the nature of the law enforcement inquiry:

"Records or information concerning your transactions which are held by the financial institution named in the attached process or request were supplied to or requested by the Government authority named in the process or request on (date). Notification was withheld pursuant to a determination by the (title of court so ordering) under the Right to Financial Privacy Act of 1978 (12 U.S.C. 3401 et seq.) that such notice might (state reason). The purpose of the investigation or official proceeding was .".

(c) Notice requirement respecting emergency access to financial records

When access to financial records is obtained pursuant to section 3414(b) of this title (emergency access), the Government authority shall, unless a court has authorized delay of notice pursuant to subsections (a) and (b) of this section, as soon as practicable after such records are obtained serve upon the customer, or mail by registered or certified mail to his last known address, a copy of the request to the financial institution together with the following notice which shall state with reasonable specificity the nature of the law enforcement inquiry:

"Records concerning your transactions held by the financial institution named in the attached request were obtained by (agency or department) under the Right to Financial Privacy Act of 1978 (12 U.S.C. 3401 et seq.) on (date) for the following purpose: Emergency access to such records was obtained on the grounds that (state grounds).".

(d) Preservation of memorandums, affidavits, or other papers

Any memorandum, affidavit, or other paper filed in connection with a request for delay in notification shall be preserved by the court. Upon petition by the customer to whom such records pertain, the court may order disclosure of such papers to the petitioner unless the court makes the findings required in subsection (a) of this section.

Sec. 3410. Customer challenges

(a) Filing of motion to quash or application to enjoin; proper court; contents

Within ten days of service or within fourteen days of mailing of a subpoena, summons, or formal written request, a customer may file a motion to quash an administrative summons or judicial subpoena, or an application to enjoin a Government authority from obtaining financial records pursuant to a formal written request, with copies served upon the Government authority. A motion to quash a judicial subpoena shall be filed in the court which issued the subpoena. A motion to quash an administrative summons or an application to enjoin a Government authority from obtaining records pursuant to a formal written request shall be filed in the appropriate United States district court. Such motion or application shall contain an affidavit or sworn statement -

(1) stating that the applicant is a customer of the financial institution from which financial records pertaining to him have been sought; and

(2) stating the applicant's reasons for believing that the financial records sought are not relevant to the legitimate law enforcement inquiry stated by the Government authority in its notice, or that there has not been substantial compliance with the provisions of this chapter.

Service shall be made under this section upon a Government authority by delivering or mailing by registered or certified mail a copy of the papers to the person, office, or department specified in the notice which the customer has received pursuant to this chapter. For the purposes of this section, "delivery" has the meaning stated in rule 5(b) of the Federal Rules of Civil Procedure.

(b) Filing of response; additional proceedings

If the court finds that the customer has complied with subsection (a) of this section, it shall order the Government authority to file a sworn response, which may be filed in camera if the Government includes in its response the reasons which make in camera review appropriate. If the court is unable to determine the motion or application on the basis of the parties' initial allegations and response, the court may conduct such additional proceedings as it deems appropriate. All such proceedings shall be completed and the motion or application decided within seven calendar days of the filing of the Government's response.

(c) Decision of court

If the court finds that the applicant is not the customer to whom the financial records sought by the Government authority pertain, or that there is a demonstrable reason to believe that the law enforcement inquiry is legitimate and a reasonable belief that the records sought are relevant to that inquiry, it shall deny the motion or application, and, in the case of an administrative summons or court order other than a search warrant, order such process enforced. If the court finds that the applicant is the customer to whom the records sought by the Government authority pertain, and that there is not a demonstrable reason to believe that the law enforcement inquiry is legitimate and a reasonable belief that the records sought are relevant to that inquiry, or that there has not been substantial compliance with the provisions of this chapter, it shall order the process quashed or shall enjoin the Government authority's formal written request.

(d) Appeals

A court ruling denying a motion or application under this section shall not be deemed a final order and no interlocutory appeal may be taken therefrom by the customer. An appeal of a ruling denying a motion or application under this section may be taken by the customer

(1) within such period of time as provided by law as part of any appeal from a final order in any legal proceeding initiated against him arising out of or based upon the financial records, or

(2) within thirty days after a notification that no legal proceeding is contemplated against him. The Government authority obtaining the financial records shall

promptly notify a customer when a determination has been made that no legal proceeding against him is contemplated. After one hundred and eighty days from the denial of the motion or application, if the Government authority obtaining the records has not initiated such a proceeding, a supervisory official of the Government authority shall certify to the appropriate court that no such determination has been made. The court may require that such certifications be made, at reasonable intervals thereafter, until either notification to the customer has occurred or a legal proceeding is initiated as described in clause (A).

(e) Sole judicial remedy available to customer

The challenge procedures of this chapter constitute the sole judicial remedy available to a customer to oppose disclosure of financial records pursuant to this chapter.

(f) Affect on challenges by financial institutions

Nothing in this chapter shall enlarge or restrict any rights of a financial institution to challenge requests for records made by a Government authority under existing law. Nothing in this chapter shall entitle a customer to assert the rights of a financial institution.

Sec. 3411. Duty of financial institutions

Upon receipt of a request for financial records made by a Government authority under section 3405 or 3407 of this title, the financial institution shall, unless otherwise provided by law, proceed to assemble the records requested and must be prepared to deliver the records to the Government authority upon receipt of the certificate required under section 3403(b) of this title.

Sec. 3412. Use of information

(a) Transfer of financial records to other agencies or departments; certification

Financial records originally obtained pursuant to this chapter shall not be transferred to another agency or department unless the transferring agency or department certifies in writing that there is reason to believe that the records are relevant to a legitimate law enforcement inquiry, or intelligence or counterintelligence activity, investigation or analysis related to international terrorism within the jurisdiction of the receiving agency or department.

(b) Mailing of copy of certification and notice to customer

When financial records subject to this chapter are transferred pursuant to subsection (a), the transferring agency or department shall, within fourteen days, send to the customer a copy of the certification made pursuant to subsection (a) and the following notice, which shall state the nature of the law enforcement inquiry with reasonable specificity: "Copies of, or information contained in, your financial records lawfully in possession of _____ have been furnished to _____ pursuant to the Right of Financial Privacy Act of 1978 [12 U.S.C. 3401 et seq.] for the following purpose: _____. If you believe that this transfer has not been made to further a legitimate law enforcement inquiry, you may have legal rights under the Financial Privacy Act of 1978 or the Privacy Act of 1974 [5 U.S.C. 552a]."

(c) Court-ordered delays in mailing

Notwithstanding subsection (b), notice to the customer may be delayed if the transferring agency or department has obtained a court order delaying notice pursuant to section 3409(a) and (b) of this title and that order is still in effect, or if the receiving agency or department obtains a court order authorizing a delay in notice pursuant to section 3409(a) and (b) of this title. Upon the expiration of any such period of delay, the transferring agency or department shall serve to the customer the notice specified in subsection (b) and the agency or department that obtained the court order authorizing a delay in notice pursuant to section 3409(a) and (b) of this title shall serve to the customer the notice specified in section 3409(b) of this title.

(d) Exchanges of examination reports by supervisory agencies; transfer of financial records to defend customer action; withholding of information

Nothing in this chapter prohibits any supervisory agency from exchanging examination reports or other information with another supervisory agency. Nothing in this chapter prohibits the transfer of a customer's financial records needed by counsel for a Government authority to defend an action brought by the customer. Nothing in this chapter shall authorize the withholding of information by any officer or employee of a supervisory agency from a duly authorized committee or subcommittee of the Congress.

(e) Exchange of records, reports, or other information

Notwithstanding section 3401(6) of this title or any other provision of law, the exchange of financial records, examination reports or other information with respect to a financial institution, holding company, or any subsidiary of a depository institution or holding company, among and between the five member supervisory agencies of the Federal Financial Institutions Examination Council, the Securities and Exchange Commission, the Federal Trade Commission, the Commodity Futures Trading Commission, and the Bureau of Consumer Financial Protection is permitted.

(f) Transfer to Attorney General or Secretary of the Treasury

    (1) In general

Nothing in this chapter shall apply when financial records obtained by an agency or department of the United States are disclosed or transferred to the Attorney General or the Secretary of the Treasury upon the certification by a supervisory level official of the transferring agency or department that-

        (A) there is reason to believe that the records may be relevant to a violation of Federal criminal law; and

        (B) the records were obtained in the exercise of the agency's or department's supervisory or regulatory functions.

    (2) Limitation on use

Records so transferred shall be used only for criminal investigative or prosecutive purposes, for civil actions under section 1833a of this title, or for forfeiture under sections 981 or 982 of title 18 by the Department of Justice and only for criminal investigative purposes relating to money laundering and other financial crimes by the Department of the Treasury and shall, upon completion of the investigation or prosecution (including any appeal), be returned only to the transferring agency or department. No agency or department so transferring such records shall be deemed to have waived any privilege applicable to those records under law.

Sec. 3413. Exceptions

(a) Disclosure of financial records not identified with particular customers
Nothing in this chapter prohibits the disclosure of any financial records or information which is not identified with or identifiable as being derived from the financial records of a particular customer.

(b) Disclosure to, or examination by, supervisory agency pursuant to exercise of supervisory, regulatory, or monetary functions with respect to financial institutions, holding companies, subsidiaries, institution-affiliated parties, or other persons
This chapter shall not apply to the examination by or disclosure to any supervisory agency of financial records or information in the exercise of its supervisory, regulatory, or monetary functions, including conservatorship or receivership functions, with respect to any financial institution, holding company, subsidiary of a financial institution or holding company, institution-affiliated party (within the meaning of section 1813(u) of this title) with respect to a financial institution, holding company, or subsidiary, or other person participating in the conduct of the affairs thereof.

(c) Disclosure pursuant to title 26
Nothing in this chapter prohibits the disclosure of financial records in accordance with procedures authorized by title 26.

(d) Disclosure pursuant to Federal statute or rule promulgated thereunder
Nothing in this chapter shall authorize the withholding of financial records or information required to be reported in accordance with any Federal statute or rule promulgated thereunder.

(e) Disclosure pursuant to Federal Rules of Criminal Procedure or comparable rules of other courts
Nothing in this chapter shall apply when financial records are sought by a Government authority under the Federal Rules of Civil or Criminal Procedure or comparable rules of other courts in connection with litigation to which the Government authority and the customer are parties.

(f) Disclosure pursuant to administrative subpena issued by administrative law judge
Nothing in this chapter shall apply when financial records are sought by a Government authority pursuant to an administrative subpena issued by an administrative law judge in

an adjudicatory proceeding subject to section 554 of title 5 and to which the Government authority and the customer are parties.

(g) Disclosure pursuant to legitimate law enforcement inquiry respecting name, address, account number, and type of account of particular customers

The notice requirements of this chapter and sections 3410 and 3412 of this title shall not apply when a Government authority by a means described in section 3402 of this title and for a legitimate law enforcement inquiry is seeking only the name, address, account number, and type of account of any customer or ascertainable group of customers associated (1) with a financial transaction or class of financial transactions, or (2) with a foreign country or subdivision thereof in the case of a Government authority exercising financial controls over foreign accounts in the United States under section 5(b) of the Trading with the Enemy Act [50 U.S.C. 4305(b)]; the International Emergency Economic Powers Act (title II, Public Law 95–223) [50 U.S.C. 1701 et seq.]; or section 287c of title 22.

(h) Disclosure pursuant to lawful proceeding, investigation, etc., directed at financial institution or legal entity or consideration or administration respecting Government loans, loan guarantees, etc.

(1) Nothing in this chapter (except sections 3403, 3417 and 3418 of this title) shall apply when financial records are sought by a Government authority-

(A) in connection with a lawful proceeding, investigation, examination, or inspection directed at a financial institution (whether or not such proceeding, investigation, examination, or inspection is also directed at a customer) or at a legal entity which is not a customer; or

(B) in connection with the authority's consideration or administration of assistance to the customer in the form of a Government loan, loan guaranty, or loan insurance program.

(2) When financial records are sought pursuant to this subsection, the Government authority shall submit to the financial institution the certificate required by section 3403(b) of this title. For access pursuant to paragraph (1)(B), no further certification shall be required for subsequent access by the certifying Government authority during the term of the loan, loan guaranty, or loan insurance agreement.

(3) After the effective date of this chapter, whenever a customer applies for participation in a Government loan, loan guaranty, or loan insurance program, the Government authority administering such program shall give the customer written notice of the authority's access rights under this subsection. No further notification shall be required for subsequent access by that authority during the term of the loan, loan guaranty, or loan insurance agreement.

(4) Financial records obtained pursuant to this subsection may be used only for the purpose for which they were originally obtained, and may be transferred to another agency or department only when the transfer is to facilitate a lawful proceeding,

investigation, examination, or inspection directed at a financial institution (whether or not such proceeding, investigation, examination, or inspection is also directed at a customer), or at a legal entity which is not a customer, except that-

(A) nothing in this paragraph prohibits the use or transfer of a customer's financial records needed by counsel representing a Government authority in a civil action arising from a Government loan, loan guaranty, or loan insurance agreement; and

(B) nothing in this paragraph prohibits a Government authority providing assistance to a customer in the form of a loan, loan guaranty, or loan insurance agreement from using or transferring financial records necessary to process, service or foreclose a loan, or to collect on an indebtedness to the Government resulting from a customer's default.

(5) Notification that financial records obtained pursuant to this subsection may relate to a potential civil, criminal, or regulatory violation by a customer may be given to an agency or department with jurisdiction over that violation, and such agency or department may then seek access to the records pursuant to the provisions of this chapter.

(6) Each financial institution shall keep a notation of each disclosure made pursuant to paragraph (1)(B) of this subsection, including the date of such disclosure and the Government authority to which it was made. The customer shall be entitled to inspect this information.

(i) Disclosure pursuant to issuance of subpena or court order respecting grand jury proceeding

Nothing in this chapter (except sections 3415 and 3420 of this title) shall apply to any subpena or court order issued in connection with proceedings before a grand jury, except that a court shall have authority to order a financial institution, on which a grand jury subpoena for customer records has been served, not to notify the customer of the existence of the subpoena or information that has been furnished to the grand jury, under the circumstances and for the period specified and pursuant to the procedures established in section 3409 of this title.

(j) Disclosure pursuant to proceeding, investigation, etc., instituted by Government Accountability Office and directed at a government authority

This chapter shall not apply when financial records are sought by the Government Accountability Office pursuant to an authorized proceeding, investigation, examination or audit directed at a government authority.

(k) Disclosure necessary for proper administration of programs of certain Government authorities

(1) Nothing in this chapter shall apply to the disclosure by the financial institution of the name and address of any customer to the Department of the Treasury, the Social Security Administration, or the Railroad Retirement Board, where the

disclosure of such information is necessary to, and such information is used solely for the purpose of, the proper administration of section 1441 of title 26, title II of the Social Security Act [42 U.S.C. 401 et seq.], or the Railroad Retirement Act of 1974 [45 U.S.C. 231 et seq.].

(2) Nothing in this chapter shall apply to the disclosure by the financial institution of information contained in the financial records of any customer to any Government authority that certifies, disburses, or collects payments, where the disclosure of such information is necessary to, and such information is used solely for the purpose of-

> (A) verification of the identity of any person or proper routing and delivery of funds in connection with the issuance of a Federal payment or collection of funds by a Government authority; or
>
> (B) the investigation or recovery of an improper Federal payment or collection of funds or an improperly negotiated Treasury check.

(3) Notwithstanding any other provision of law, a request authorized by paragraph (1) or (2) (and the information contained therein) may be used by the financial institution or its agents solely for the purpose of providing information contained in the financial records of the customer to the Government authority requesting the information, and the financial institution and its agents shall be barred from redisclosure of such information. Any Government authority receiving information pursuant to paragraph (1) or (2) may not disclose or use the information, except for the purposes set forth in such paragraph.

(l) Crimes against financial institutions by insiders

Nothing in this chapter shall apply when any financial institution or supervisory agency provides any financial record of any officer, director, employee, or controlling shareholder (within the meaning of subparagraph (A) or (B) of section 1841(a)(2) of this title or subparagraph (A) or (B) of section 1730a(a)(2) of this title) of such institution, or of any major borrower from such institution who there is reason to believe may be acting in concert with any such officer, director, employee, or controlling shareholder, to the Attorney General of the United States, to a State law enforcement agency, or, in the case of a possible violation of subchapter II of chapter 53 of title 31, to the Secretary of the Treasury if there is reason to believe that such record is relevant to a possible violation by such person of-

> (1) any law relating to crimes against financial institutions or supervisory agencies by directors, officers, employees, or controlling shareholders of, or by borrowers from, financial institutions; or
>
> (2) any provision of subchapter II of chapter 53 of title 31 or of section 1956 or 1957 of title 18.

No supervisory agency which transfers any such record under this subsection shall be deemed to have waived any privilege applicable to that record under law.

(m) Disclosure to, or examination by, employees or agents of Board of Governors of Federal Reserve System or Federal Reserve Bank

This chapter shall not apply to the examination by or disclosure to employees or agents of the Board of Governors of the Federal Reserve System or any Federal Reserve Bank of financial records or information in the exercise of the Federal Reserve System's authority to extend credit to the financial institutions or others.

(n) Disclosure to, or examination by, Resolution Trust Corporation or its employees or agents

This chapter shall not apply to the examination by or disclosure to the Resolution Trust Corporation or its employees or agents of financial records or information in the exercise of its conservatorship, receivership, or liquidation functions with respect to a financial institution.

(o) Disclosure to, or examination by, Federal Housing Finance Agency or Federal home loan banks

This chapter shall not apply to the examination by or disclosure to the Federal Housing Finance Agency or any of the Federal home loan banks of financial records or information in the exercise of the Federal Housing Finance Agency's authority to extend credit (either directly or through a Federal home loan bank) to financial institutions or others.

(p) Access to information necessary for administration of certain veteran benefits laws

(1) Nothing in this chapter shall apply to the disclosure by the financial institution of the name and address of any customer to the Department of Veterans Affairs where the disclosure of such information is necessary to, and such information is used solely for the purposes of, the proper administration of benefits programs under laws administered by the Secretary.

(2) Notwithstanding any other provision of law, any request authorized by paragraph (1) (and the information contained therein) may be used by the financial institution or its agents solely for the purpose of providing the customer's name and address to the Department of Veterans Affairs and shall be barred from redisclosure by the financial institution or its agents.

(q) Disclosure pursuant to Federal contractor-issued travel charge card

Nothing in this chapter shall apply to the disclosure of any financial record or information to a Government authority in conjunction with a Federal contractor-issued travel charge card issued for official Government travel.

(r) Disclosure to the Bureau of Consumer Financial Protection

Nothing in this chapter shall apply to the examination by or disclosure to the Bureau of Consumer Financial Protection of financial records or information in the exercise of its authority with respect to a financial institution.

Sec. 3414. Special procedures

(a) Access to financial records for certain intelligence and protective purposes

(1) Nothing in this chapter (except sections 3415, 3417, 3418, and 3421 of this title) shall apply to the production and disclosure of financial records pursuant to requests from--

(A) a Government authority authorized to conduct foreign counter- or foreign positive-intelligence activities for purposes of conducting such activities;

(B) the Secret Service for the purpose of conducting its protective functions (18 U.S.C. 3056; 18 U.S.C. 3056A, Public Law 90-331, as amended); or

(C) a Government authority authorized to conduct investigations of, or intelligence or counterintelligence analyses related to, international terrorism for the purpose of conducting such investigations or analyses.

(2) In the instances specified in paragraph (1), the Government authority shall submit to the financial institution the certificate required in section 3403(b) of this title signed by a supervisory official of a rank designated by the head of the Government authority and a term that specifically identifies a customer, entity, or account to be used as the basis for the production and disclosure of financial records.

(3)

(A) If the Government authority described in paragraph (1) or the Secret Service, as the case may be, certifies that otherwise there may result a danger to the national security of the United States, interference with a criminal, counterterrorism, or counterintelligence investigation, interference with diplomatic relations, or danger to the life or physical safety of any person, no financial institution, or officer, employee, or agent of such institution, shall disclose to any person (other than those to whom such disclosure is necessary to comply with the request or an attorney to obtain legal advice or legal assistance with respect to the request) that the Government authority or the Secret Service has sought or obtained access to a customer's financial records.

(B) The request shall notify the person or entity to whom the request is directed of the nondisclosure requirement under subparagraph (A).

(C) Any recipient disclosing to those persons necessary to comply with the request or to an attorney to obtain legal advice or legal assistance with respect to the request shall inform such persons of any applicable nondisclosure requirement. Any person who receives a disclosure under this subsection shall be subject to the same prohibitions on disclosure under subparagraph (A).

(D) At the request of the authorized Government authority or the Secret Service, any person making or intending to make a disclosure under this section shall identify to the requesting official of the authorized Government authority or the Secret Service the person to whom such disclosure will be made or to whom such disclosure was made prior to the request, except that nothing in this section shall require a person to inform the requesting official of the authorized Government authority or the Secret Service of the identity of an attorney to whom disclosure was made or will be made to obtain legal advice or legal assistance with respect to the request for financial records under this subsection.

(4) The Government authority specified in paragraph (1) shall compile an annual tabulation of the occasions in which this section was used.

(5)

(A) Financial institutions, and officers, employees, and agents thereof, shall comply with a request for a customer's or entity's financial records made pursuant to this subsection by the Federal Bureau of Investigation when the Director of the Federal Bureau of Investigation (or the Director's designee in a position not lower than Deputy Assistant Director at Bureau headquarters or a Special Agent in Charge in a Bureau field office designated by the Director) certifies in writing to the financial institution that such records are sought for foreign counter intelligence[2]purposes to protect against international terrorism or clandestine intelligence activities, provided that such an investigation of a United States person is not conducted solely upon the basis of activities protected by the first amendment to the Constitution of the United States.

(B) The Federal Bureau of Investigation may disseminate information obtained pursuant to this paragraph only as provided in guidelines approved by the Attorney General for foreign intelligence collection and foreign counterintelligence investigations conducted by the Federal Bureau of Investigation, and, with respect to dissemination to an agency of the United States, only if such information is clearly relevant to the authorized responsibilities of such agency.

(C) On the dates provided in section 3106 of Title 50, the Attorney General shall fully inform the congressional intelligence committees (as defined in section 3003 of Title 50) concerning all requests made pursuant to this paragraph.

(D) Repealed. Pub.L. 114-23, Title V, § 502(b)(1), June 2, 2015, 129 Stat. 284

(b) Emergency access to financial records

(1) Nothing in this chapter shall prohibit a Government authority from obtaining financial records from a financial institution if the Government authority determines that delay in obtaining access to such records would create imminent danger of--

(A) physical injury to any person;

(B) serious property damage; or

(C) flight to avoid prosecution.

(2) In the instances specified in paragraph (1), the Government shall submit to the financial institution the certificate required in section 3403(b) of this title signed by a supervisory official of a rank designated by the head of the Government authority.

(3) Within five days of obtaining access to financial records under this subsection, the Government authority shall file with the appropriate court a signed, sworn statement of a supervisory official of a rank designated by the head of the Government authority setting forth the grounds for the emergency access. The Government authority shall thereafter comply with the notice provisions of section 3409(c) of this title.

(4) The Government authority specified in paragraph (1) shall compile an annual tabulation of the occasions in which this section was used.

(c) Prohibition of certain disclosure

    (1) Prohibition

        (A) In general

        If a certification is issued under subparagraph (B) and notice of the right to judicial review under subsection (d) is provided, no financial institution that receives a request under subsection (a), or officer, employee, or agent thereof, shall disclose to any person that the Federal Bureau of Investigation has sought or obtained access to information or records under subsection (a).

        (B) Certification

        The requirements of subparagraph (A) shall apply if the Director of the Federal Bureau of Investigation, or a designee of the Director whose rank shall be no lower than Deputy Assistant Director at Bureau headquarters or a Special Agent in Charge of a Bureau field office, certifies that the absence of a prohibition of disclosure under this subsection may result in--

            (i) a danger to the national security of the United States;

            (ii) interference with a criminal, counterterrorism, or counterintelligence investigation;

            (iii) interference with diplomatic relations; or

            (iv) danger to the life or physical safety of any person.

    (2) Exception

        (A) In general

        A financial institution that receives a request under subsection (a), or officer, employee, or agent thereof, may disclose information otherwise subject to any applicable nondisclosure requirement to--

            (i) those persons to whom disclosure is necessary in order to comply with the request;

            (ii) an attorney in order to obtain legal advice or assistance regarding the request; or

            (iii) other persons as permitted by the Director of the Federal Bureau of Investigation or the designee of the Director.

        (B) Application

A person to whom disclosure is made under subparagraph (A) shall be subject to the nondisclosure requirements applicable to a person to whom a request is issued under subsection (a) in the same manner as the person to whom the request is issued.

(C) Notice

Any recipient that discloses to a person described in subparagraph (A) information otherwise subject to a nondisclosure requirement shall inform the person of the applicable nondisclosure requirement.

(D) Identification of disclosure recipients

At the request of the Director of the Federal Bureau of Investigation or the designee of the Director, any person making or intending to make a disclosure under clause (i) or (iii) of subparagraph (A) shall identify to the Director or such designee the person to whom such disclosure will be made or to whom such disclosure was made prior to the request.

(d) Judicial review

(1) In general

A request under subsection (a) or a nondisclosure requirement imposed in connection with such request under subsection (c) shall be subject to judicial review under section 3511 of Title 18.

(2) Notice

A request under subsection (a) shall include notice of the availability of judicial review described in paragraph (1).

(e) Definition of "financial institution"

For purposes of this section, and sections 3415 and 3417 of this title insofar as they relate to the operation of this section, the term "financial institution" has the same meaning as in subsections (a)(2) and (c)(1) of section 5312 of Title 31, except that, for purposes of this section, such term shall include only such a financial institution any part of which is located inside any State or territory of the United States, the District of Columbia, Puerto Rico, Guam, American Samoa, the Commonwealth of the Northern Mariana Islands, or the United States Virgin Islands.

Sec. 3415. Cost reimbursement

Except for records obtained pursuant to section 3403(d) or 3413(a) through (h) of this title, or as otherwise provided by law, a Government authority shall pay to the financial institution assembling or providing financial records pertaining to a customer and in accordance with procedures established by this chapter a fee for reimbursement for such costs as are reasonably necessary and which have been directly incurred in searching for, reproducing, or transporting books, papers, records, or other data required or requested to be produced. The Board of Governors of the Federal Reserve System shall, by regulation, establish the rates and conditions under which such payment may be made.

Sec. 3416. Jurisdiction

An action to enforce any provision of this chapter may be brought in any appropriate United States district court without regard to the amount in controversy within three years from the date on which the violation occurs or the date of discovery of such violation, whichever is later.

Sec. 3417. Civil penalties

(a) Liability of agencies or departments of United States or financial institutions

Any agency or department of the United States or financial institution obtaining or disclosing financial records or information contained therein in violation of this chapter is liable to the customer to whom such records relate in an amount equal to the sum of -

(1) $100 without regard to the volume of records involved;

(2) any actual damages sustained by the customer as a result of the disclosure;

(3) such punitive damages as the court may allow, where the violation is found to have been willful or intentional; and

(4) in the case of any successful action to enforce liability under this section, the costs of the action together with reasonable attorney's fees as determined by the court.

(b) Disciplinary action for willful or intentional violation of chapter by agents or employees of department or agency

Whenever the court determines that any agency or department of the United States has violated any provision of this chapter and the court finds that the circumstances surrounding the violation raise questions of whether an officer or employee of the department or agency acted willfully or intentionally with respect to the violation, the Director of the Office of Personnel Management shall promptly initiate a proceeding to determine whether disciplinary action is warranted against the agent or employee who was primarily responsible for the violation. The Director after investigation and consideration of the evidence submitted, shall submit his findings and recommendations to the administrative authority of the agency concerned and shall send copies of the findings and recommendations to the officer or employee or his representative. The administrative authority shall take the corrective action that the Director recommends.

(c) Good faith defense

Any financial institution or agent or employee thereof making a disclosure of financial records pursuant to this chapter in good-faith reliance upon a certificate by any Government authority or pursuant to the provisions of section 3413(l) of this title shall not be liable to the customer for such disclosure under this chapter, the constitution of any State, or any law or regulation of any State or any political subdivision of any State.

(d) Exclusive judicial remedies and sanctions

The remedies and sanctions described in this chapter shall be the only authorized judicial remedies and sanctions for violations of this chapter.

United States
Right to Financial Privacy Act

Sec. 3418. Injunctive relief

In addition to any other remedy contained in this chapter, injunctive relief shall be available to require that the procedures of this chapter are complied with. In the event of any successful action, costs together with reasonable attorney's fees as determined by the court may be recovered.

Sec. 3419. Suspension of limitations

If any individual files a motion or application under this chapter which has the effect of delaying the access of a Government authority to financial records pertaining to such individual, any applicable statute of limitations shall be deemed to be tolled for the period extending from the date such motion or application was filed until the date upon which the motion or application is decided.

Sec. 3420. Grand jury information; notification of certain persons prohibited

(a) Financial records about a customer obtained from a financial institution pursuant to a subpoena issued under the authority of a Federal grand jury -

(1) shall be returned and actually presented to the grand jury unless the volume of such records makes such return and actual presentation impractical in which case the grand jury shall be provided with a description of the contents of the records.;

(2) shall be used only for the purpose of considering whether to issue an indictment or presentment by that grand jury, or of prosecuting a crime for which that indictment or presentment is issued, or for a purpose authorized by rule 6(e) of the Federal Rules of Criminal Procedure or for a purpose authorized by section 1112(a);

(3) shall be destroyed or returned to the financial institution if not used for one of the purposes specified in paragraph (2); and

(4) shall not be maintained, or a description of the contents of such records shall not be maintained by any Government authority other than in the sealed records of the grand jury, unless such record has been used in the prosecution of a crime for which the grand jury issued an indictment or presentment or for a purpose authorized by rule 6(e) of the Federal Rules of Criminal Procedure.

(b)

(1) No officer, director, partner, employee, or shareholder of, or agent or attorney for, a financial institution shall, directly or indirectly, notify any person named in a grand jury subpoena served on such institution in connection with an investigation relating to a possible -

(A) crime against any financial institution or supervisory agency or crime involving a violation of the Controlled Substance Act (21 U.S.C. 801 et seq.), the Controlled Substances Import and Export Act (21 U.S.C. 951 et seq.), section 1956 or 1957 of title 18, sections 5313, 5316 and 5324 of title 31, or section 6050I of title 26; or

(B) conspiracy to commit such a crime, about the existence or contents of such subpoena, or information that has been furnished to the grand jury in response to such subpoena.

(2) Section 1818 of this title and section 1786(k)(2) of this title shall apply to any violation of this subsection.

Sec. 3421. [Repealed]

Sec. 3422. Applicability to Securities and Exchange Commission

Except as provided in the Securities Exchange Act of 1934 (15 U.S.C. 78a et seq.), this chapter shall apply with respect to the Securities and Exchange Commission.

Sec. 3423. Immunity from suit for disclosure of financial exploitation of senior citizens

(a) Immunity

(1) Definitions

In this section--

(A) the term "Bank Secrecy Act officer" means an individual responsible for ensuring compliance with the requirements mandated by subchapter II of chapter 53 of Title 31 (commonly known as the "Bank Secrecy Act");

(B) the term "broker-dealer" means a broker and a dealer, as those terms are defined in section 78c(a) of Title 15;

(C) the term "covered agency" means--

(i) a State financial regulatory agency, including a State securities or law enforcement authority and a State insurance regulator;

(ii) each of the Federal agencies represented in the membership of the Financial Institutions Examination Council established under section 3303 of this title;

(iii) a securities association registered under section 78o-3 of Title 15;

(iv) the Securities and Exchange Commission;

(v) a law enforcement agency; or

(vi) a State or local agency responsible for administering adult protective service laws;

(D) the term "covered financial institution" means--

(i) a credit union;

(ii) a depository institution;

(iii) an investment adviser;

(iv) a broker-dealer;

(v) an insurance company;

(vi) an insurance agency; or

(vii) a transfer agent;

(E) the term "credit union" has the meaning given the term in section 5301 of this title;

(F) the term "depository institution" has the meaning given the term in section 1813(c) of this title;

(G) the term "exploitation" means the fraudulent or otherwise illegal, unauthorized, or improper act or process of an individual, including a caregiver or a fiduciary, that--

(i) uses the resources of a senior citizen for monetary or personal benefit, profit, or gain; or

(ii) results in depriving a senior citizen of rightful access to or use of benefits, resources, belongings, or assets;

(H) the term "insurance agency" means any business entity that sells, solicits, or negotiates insurance coverage;

(I) the term "insurance company" has the meaning given the term in section 80a-2(a) of Title 15;

(J) the term "insurance producer" means an individual who is required under State law to be licensed in order to sell, solicit, or negotiate insurance coverage;

(K) the term "investment adviser" has the meaning given the term in section 80b-2(a) of Title 15;

(L) the term "investment adviser representative" means an individual who--

(i) is employed by, or associated with, an investment adviser; and

(ii) does not perform solely clerical or ministerial acts;

(M) the term "registered representative" means an individual who represents a broker-dealer in effecting or attempting to effect a purchase or sale of securities;

(N) the term "senior citizen" means an individual who is not younger than 65 years of age;

(O) the term "State" means each of the several States, the District of Columbia, and any territory or possession of the United States;

(P) the term "State insurance regulator" has the meaning given the term in section 6735 of Title 15;

(Q) the term "State securities or law enforcement authority" has the meaning given the term in section 78x(f)(4) of Title 15; and

(R) the term "transfer agent" has the meaning given the term in section 78c(a) of Title 15.

(2) Immunity from suit

(A) Immunity for individuals

An individual who has received the training described in subsection (b) shall not be liable, including in any civil or administrative proceeding, for disclosing the suspected exploitation of a senior citizen to a covered agency if the individual, at the time of the disclosure--

(i) served as a supervisor or in a compliance or legal function (including as a Bank Secrecy Act officer) for, or, in the case of a registered representative, investment adviser representative, or insurance producer, was affiliated or associated with, a covered financial institution; and

(ii) made the disclosure--

(I) in good faith; and

(II) with reasonable care.

(B) Immunity for covered financial institutions

A covered financial institution shall not be liable, including in any civil or administrative proceeding, for a disclosure made by an individual described in subparagraph (A) if--

(i) the individual was employed by, or, in the case of a registered representative, insurance producer, or investment adviser representative, affiliated or associated with, the covered financial institution at the time of the disclosure; and

(ii) before the time of the disclosure, each individual described in subsection (b)(1) received the training described in subsection (b).

(C) Rule of construction

Nothing in subparagraph (A) or (B) shall be construed to limit the liability of an individual or a covered financial institution in a civil action for any act, omission, or fraud that is not a disclosure described in subparagraph (A).

(b) Training

(1) In general

A covered financial institution or a third party selected by a covered financial institution may provide the training described in paragraph (2)(A) to each officer or employee of, or registered representative, insurance producer, or investment adviser representative affiliated or associated with, the covered financial institution who--

(A) is described in subsection (a)(2)(A)(i);

(B) may come into contact with a senior citizen as a regular part of the professional duties of the individual; or

(C) may review or approve the financial documents, records, or transactions of a senior citizen in connection with providing financial services to a senior citizen.

(2) Content

(A) In general

The content of the training that a covered financial institution or a third party selected by the covered financial institution may provide under paragraph (1) shall--

(i) be maintained by the covered financial institution and made available to a covered agency with examination authority over the covered financial institution, upon request, except that a covered financial institution shall not be required to maintain or make available such content with respect to any individual who is no longer employed by, or affiliated or associated with, the covered financial institution;

(ii) instruct any individual attending the training on how to identify and report the suspected exploitation of a senior citizen internally and, as appropriate, to government officials or law enforcement authorities, including common signs that indicate the financial exploitation of a senior citizen;

(iii) discuss the need to protect the privacy and respect the integrity of each individual customer of the covered financial institution; and

(iv) be appropriate to the job responsibilities of the individual attending the training.

(B) Timing

The training under paragraph (1) shall be provided--

(i) as soon as reasonably practicable; and

(ii) with respect to an individual who begins employment, or becomes affiliated or associated, with a covered financial institution after May 24, 2018, not later than 1 year after the date on which the individual becomes employed by, or affiliated or associated with, the covered financial institution in a position described in subparagraph (A), (B), or (C) of paragraph (1).

(C) Records

A covered financial institution shall--

(i) maintain a record of each individual who--

(I) is employed by, or affiliated or associated with, the covered financial institution in a position described in subparagraph (A), (B), or (C) of paragraph (1); and

(II) has completed the training under paragraph (1), regardless of whether the training was--

(aa) provided by the covered financial institution or a third party selected by the covered financial institution;

(bb) completed before the individual was employed by, or affiliated or associated with, the covered financial institution; and

(cc) completed before, on, or after May 24, 2018; and

(ii) upon request, provide a record described in clause (i) to a covered agency with examination authority over the covered financial institution.

(c) Relationship to State law

Nothing in this section shall be construed to preempt or limit any provision of State law, except only to the extent that subsection (a) provides a greater level of protection against liability to an individual described in subsection (a)(2)(A) or to a covered financial institution described in subsection (a)(2)(B) than is provided under State law.

PRIVACY PROTECTION ACT (1980)

Summary

The Privacy Protection Act of 1980 was passed in response to Zurcher v. Stanford Daily, 436 U.S. 547 (1978), which upheld broad law enforcement access to a newspaper's files. The Act establishes procedures for law enforcement seeking access to records and other information from the offices and employees of a media organization. In general, the Act prohibits both federal and state officers and employees from searching or seizing journalists' "work product" or the "documentary materials" in their possession. Under the Act, in order to gain access to journalists' information, law enforcement must obtain a court subpoena, rather than a simple search warrant.

The Act provides limited exceptions that allow the government to use a warrant, rather than a subpoena, to search for certain types of national security information, child pornography, evidence that the journalists themselves have committed a crime, or materials that must be immediately seized to prevent death or serious bodily injury. "Documentary materials" may also be seized if there is reason to believe that they would be destroyed in the time it took to obtain them using a subpoena, or if a court has ordered disclosure, the news organization has refused to release the materials, and all other remedies have been exhausted.

A search may be conducted only when there is probable cause to believe that an individual is involved in a crime. Also, only those who are involved with a particular investigation can do the searching. Although the statute specifically provides that its violation is not grounds to suppress evidence, it does provide a civil remedy in Federal court against either the government entity or individual officers involved in the search where a search warrant, rather than a subpoena, is used contrary to the Act's provisions.

References

Public Law 96-440. Codified as amended at 42 U.S.C. § 2000aa et seq.
[https://www.law.cornell.edu/uscode/text/42/2000aa]

EPIC, Privacy Protection Act of 1980
[https://www.epic.org/privacy/ppa/]

42 U.S.C. 2000aa. Searches and seizures by government officers and employees in connection with investigation or prosecution of criminal offenses

(a) Work product materials

Notwithstanding any other law, it shall be unlawful for a government officer or employee, in connection with the investigation or prosecution of a criminal offense, to search for or seize any work product materials possessed by a person reasonably believed to have a purpose to disseminate to the public a newspaper, book, broadcast, or other similar form of public communication, in or affecting interstate or foreign commerce;

but this provision shall not impair or affect the ability of any government officer or employee, pursuant to otherwise applicable law, to search for or seize such materials, if -

(1) there is probable cause to believe that the person possessing such materials has committed or is committing the criminal offense to which the materials relate: Provided, however, That a government officer or employee may not search for or seize such materials under the provisions of this paragraph if the offense to which the materials relate consists of the receipt, possession, communication, or withholding of such materials or the information contained therein (but such a search or seizure may be conducted under the provisions of this paragraph if the offense consists of the receipt, possession, or communication of information relating to the national defense, classified information, or restricted data under the provisions of section 793, 794, 797, or 798 of title 18, or section 2274, 2275, or 2277 of this title, or section 783 of title 50; or if the offense involves the production, possession, receipt, mailing, sale, distribution, shipment, or transportation of child pornography, the sexual exploitation of children, or the sale or purchase of children under section 2251, 2251A, 2252, or 2252A of title 18); or

(2) there is reason to believe that the immediate seizure of such materials is necessary to prevent the death of, or serious bodily injury to, a human being.

(b) Other documents

Notwithstanding any other law, it shall be unlawful for a government officer or employee, in connection with the investigation or prosecution of a criminal offense, to search for or seize documentary materials, other than work product materials, possessed by a person in connection with a purpose to disseminate to the public a newspaper, book, broadcast, or other similar form of public communication, in or affecting interstate or foreign commerce; but this provision shall not impair or affect the ability of any government officer or employee, pursuant to otherwise applicable law, to search for or seize such materials, if -

(1) there is probable cause to believe that the person possessing such materials has committed or is committing the criminal offense to which the materials relate: Provided, however, That a government officer or employee may not search for or seize such materials under the provisions of this paragraph if the offense to which the materials relate consists of the receipt, possession, communication, or withholding of such materials or the information contained therein (but such a search or seizure may be conducted under the provisions of this paragraph if the offense consists of the receipt, possession, or communication of information relating to the national defense, classified information, or restricted data under the provisions of section 793, 794, 797, or 798 of title 18, or section 2274, 2275, or 2277 of this title, or section 783 of title 50, or if the offense involves the production, possession, receipt, mailing, sale, distribution, shipment, or transportation of child pornography,

the sexual exploitation of children, or the sale or purchase of children under section 2251, 2251A, 2252, or 2252A of title 18);

(2) there is reason to believe that the immediate seizure of such materials is necessary to prevent the death of, or serious bodily injury to, a human being;

(3) there is reason to believe that the giving of notice pursuant to a subpoena duces tecum would result in the destruction, alteration, or concealment of such materials; or

(4) such materials have not been produced in response to a court order directing compliance with a subpoena duces tecum, and-

    (A) all appellate remedies have been exhausted; or

    (B) there is reason to believe that the delay in an investigation or trial occasioned by further proceedings relating to the subpoena would threaten the interests of justice.

(c) Objections to court ordered subpoenas; affidavits

In the event a search warrant is sought pursuant to paragraph (4)(B) of subsection (b) of this section, the person possessing the materials shall be afforded adequate opportunity to submit an affidavit setting forth the basis for any contention that the materials sought are not subject to seizure.

Sec. 2000aa-5. Border and customs searches

This chapter shall not impair or affect the ability of a government officer or employee, pursuant to otherwise applicable law, to conduct searches and seizures at the borders of, or at international points of entry into the United States in order to enforce the customs laws of the United States.

Sec. 2000aa-6. Civil actions by aggrieved persons

(a) Right of action

A person aggrieved by a search for or seizure of materials in violation of this chapter shall have a civil cause of action for damages for such search or seizure -

    (1) against the United States, against a State which has waived its sovereign immunity under the Constitution to a claim for damages resulting from a violation of this chapter, or against any other governmental unit, all of which shall be liable for violations of this chapter by their officers or employees while acting within the scope or under color of their office or employment; and

    (2) against an officer or employee of a State who has violated this chapter while acting within the scope or under color of his office or employment, if such State has not waived its sovereign immunity as provided in paragraph (1).

(b) Good faith defense

It shall be a complete defense to a civil action brought under paragraph (2) of subsection (a) of this section that the officer or employee had a reasonable good faith belief in the lawfulness of his conduct.

(c) Official immunity

The United States, a State, or any other governmental unit liable for violations of this chapter under subsection (a)(1) of this section, may not assert as a defense to a claim arising under this chapter the immunity of the officer or employee whose violation is complained of or his reasonable good faith belief in the lawfulness of his conduct, except that such a defense may be asserted if the violation complained of is that of a judicial officer.

(d) Exclusive nature of remedy

The remedy provided by subsection (a)(1) of this section against the United States, a State, or any other governmental unit is exclusive of any other civil action or proceeding for conduct constituting a violation of this chapter, against the officer or employee whose violation gave rise to the claim, or against the estate of such officer or employee.

(e) Admissibility of evidence

Evidence otherwise admissible in a proceeding shall not be excluded on the basis of a violation of this chapter.

(f) Damages; costs and attorneys' fees

A person having a cause of action under this section shall be entitled to recover actual damages but not less than liquidated damages of $1,000, and such reasonable attorneys' fees and other litigation costs reasonably incurred as the court, in its discretion, may award: Provided, however, That the United States, a State, or any other governmental unit shall not be liable for interest prior to judgment.

(g) Attorney General; claims settlement; regulations

The Attorney General may settle a claim for damages brought against the United States under this section, and shall promulgate regulations to provide for the commencement of an administrative inquiry following a determination of a violation of this chapter by an officer or employee of the United States and for the imposition of administrative sanctions against such officer or employee, if warranted.

(h) Jurisdiction

The district courts shall have original jurisdiction of all civil actions arising under this section.

Sec. 2000aa-7. Definitions

(a) "Documentary materials", as used in this chapter, means materials upon which information is recorded, and includes, but is not limited to, written or printed materials, photographs, motion picture films, negatives, video tapes, audio tapes, and other mechanically, magnetically[1] or electronically recorded cards, tapes, or discs, but does not include contraband or the fruits of a crime or things otherwise criminally possessed, or property designed or intended for use, or which is or has been used as, the means of committing a criminal offense.

(b) "Work product materials", as used in this chapter, means materials, other than contraband or the fruits of a crime or things otherwise criminally possessed, or property designed or intended for use, or which is or has been used, as the means of committing a criminal offense, and -

> (1) in anticipation of communicating such materials to the public, are prepared, produced, authored, or created, whether by the person in possession of the materials or by any other person;

> (2) are possessed for the purposes of communicating such materials to the public; and

> (3) include mental impressions, conclusions, opinions, or theories of the person who prepared, produced, authored, or created such material.

(c) "Any other governmental unit", as used in this chapter, includes the District of Columbia, the Commonwealth of Puerto Rico, any territory or possession of the United States, and any local government, unit of local government, or any unit of State government.

Sec. 2000aa-11. Guidelines for Federal officers and employees

(a) Procedures to obtain documentary evidence; protection of certain privacy interests

The Attorney General shall, within six months of October 13, 1980, issue guidelines for the procedures to be employed by any Federal officer or employee, in connection with the investigation or prosecution of an offense, to obtain documentary materials in the private possession of a person when the person is not reasonably believed to be a suspect in such offense or related by blood or marriage to such a suspect, and when the materials sought are not contraband or the fruits or instrumentalities of an offense. The Attorney General shall incorporate in such guidelines

> (1) a recognition of the personal privacy interests of the person in possession of such documentary materials;

> (2) a requirement that the least intrusive method or means of obtaining such materials be used which do not substantially jeopardize the availability or usefulness of the materials sought to be obtained;

> (3) a recognition of special concern for privacy interests in cases in which a search or seizure for such documents would intrude upon a known confidential relationship such as that which may exist between clergyman and parishioner; lawyer and client; or doctor and patient; and

---

[1] So in original. Probably should be "magnetically".

(4) a requirement that an application for a warrant to conduct a search governed by this subchapter be approved by an attorney for the government, except that in an emergency situation the application may be approved by another appropriate supervisory official if within 24 hours of such emergency the appropriate United States Attorney is notified.

(b) Use of search warrants; reports to Congress

The Attorney General shall collect and compile information on, and report annually to the Committees on the Judiciary of the Senate and the House of Representatives on the use of search warrants by Federal officers and employees for documentary materials described in subsection (a)(3) of this section.

Sec. 2000aa-12. Binding nature of guidelines; disciplinary actions for violations; legal proceedings for non-compliance prohibited

Guidelines issued by the Attorney General under this subchapter shall have the full force and effect of Department of Justice regulations and any violation of these guidelines shall make the employee or officer involved subject to appropriate administrative disciplinary action. However, an issue relating to the compliance, or the failure to comply, with guidelines issued pursuant to this subchapter may not be litigated, and a court may not entertain such an issue as the basis for the suppression or exclusion of evidence.

CABLE COMMUNICATIONS POLICY ACT (1984) [EXCERPT]

Summary

The Cable Communications Policy Act of 1984 provides a strong statutory framework for the protection of cable subscribers' personal information and incorporates the privacy principles set out in the OECD Privacy Guidelines of 1980.

Under the Act, cable providers must provide written notice to subscribers of their privacy rights at the time they first subscribe to the cable service and, thereafter, at least once a year. These notices must specify the kind of information that may be collected, how it will be used, to whom and how often it may be disclosed, how long it will be stored, how a subscriber may access this information and the liability imposed by the Act on providers.

Subject to limited exceptions, the Act requires providers to obtain the prior written or electronic consent of the cable subscriber before collecting or disclosing personally identifiable information. Cable providers do not need consent to collect personally identifiable information needed to offer or render cable service to a subscriber, or to detect cable piracy. Furthermore, they do not need consent to disclose subscriber information where disclosure is necessary to rendering a legitimate business activity related to a cable service or pursuant to a court order. The Act grants cable subscribers the right to access the data collected about them and to correct any errors. It also provides for the destruction of personally identifiable information if that information is no longer necessary. Finally, it sets out a private right of action including actual and punitive damages, attorney's fees and litigation costs for violations of any of its provisions. State and local cable privacy laws are not preempted by the Act.

References

Public Law 98-549. Codified as amended at 47 U.S.C. § 551 et seq. [https://www.law.cornell.edu/uscode/text/47/551]

David H. Flaherty, *Protecting Privacy in Two-Way Electronic Services (1985)*

47 U.S.C. § 551. Protection of subscriber privacy

(a) Notice to subscriber regarding personally identifiable information; definitions

(1) At the time of entering into an agreement to provide any cable service or other service to a subscriber and at least once a year thereafter, a cable operator shall provide notice in the form of a separate, written statement to such subscriber which clearly and conspicuously informs the subscriber of -

(A) the nature of personally identifiable information collected or to be collected with respect to the subscriber and the nature of the use of such information;

(B) the nature, frequency, and purpose of any disclosure which may be made of such information, including an identification of the types of persons to whom the disclosure may be made;

(C) the period during which such information will be maintained by the cable operator;

(D) the times and place at which the subscriber may have access to such information in accordance with subsection (d) of this section; and

(E) the limitations provided by this section with respect to the collection and disclosure of information by a cable operator and the right of the subscriber under subsections (f) and (h) of this section to enforce such limitations.

In the case of subscribers who have entered into such an agreement before the effective date of this section, such notice shall be provided within 180 days of such date and at least once a year thereafter.

(2) For purposes of this section, other than subsection (h) of this section -

(A) the term "personally identifiable information" does not include any record of aggregate data which does not identify particular persons;

B) the term "other service" includes any wire or radio communications service provided using any of the facilities of a cable operator that are used in the provision of cable service; and

(C) the term "cable operator" includes, in addition to persons within the definition of cable operator in section 522 of this title, any person who

(i) is owned or controlled by, or under common ownership or control with, a cable operator, and

(ii) provides any wire or radio communications service.

(b) Collection of personally identifiable information using cable system

(1) Except as provided in paragraph (2), a cable operator shall not use the cable system to collect personally identifiable information concerning any subscriber without the prior written or electronic consent of the subscriber concerned.

(2) A cable operator may use the cable system to collect such information in order to -

(A) obtain information necessary to render a cable service or other service provided by the cable operator to the subscriber; or

(B) detect unauthorized reception of cable communications.

(c) Disclosure of personally identifiable information

(1) Except as provided in paragraph (2), a cable operator shall not disclose personally identifiable information concerning any subscriber without the prior written or electronic consent of the subscriber concerned and shall take such actions as are necessary to prevent unauthorized access to such information by a person other than the subscriber or cable operator.

(2) A cable operator may disclose such information if the disclosure is -

(A) necessary to render, or conduct a legitimate business activity related to, a cable service or other service provided by the cable operator to the subscriber;

(B) subject to subsection (h) of this section, made pursuant to a court order authorizing such disclosure, if the subscriber is notified of such order by the person to whom the order is directed;

(C) a disclosure of the names and addresses of subscribers to any cable service or other service, if -

    (i) the cable operator has provided the subscriber the opportunity to prohibit or limit such disclosure, and

    (ii) the disclosure does not reveal, directly or indirectly, the -

        (I) extent of any viewing or other use by the subscriber of a cable service or other service provided by the cable operator, or

        (II) the nature of any transaction made by the subscriber over the cable system of the cable operator; or

(D) to a government entity as authorized under chapters 119, 121, or 206 of title 18, United States Code, except that such disclosure shall not include records revealing cable subscriber selection of video programming from a cable operator.

(d) Subscriber access to information

A cable subscriber shall be provided access to all personally identifiable information regarding that subscriber which is collected and maintained by a cable operator. Such information shall be made available to the subscriber at reasonable times and at a convenient place designated by such cable operator. A cable subscriber shall be provided reasonable opportunity to correct any error in such information.

(e) Destruction of information

A cable operator shall destroy personally identifiable information if the information is no longer necessary for the purpose for which it was collected and there are no pending requests or orders for access to such information under subsection (d) of this section or pursuant to a court order.

(f) Civil action in United States district court; damages; attorney's fees and costs; nonexclusive nature of remedy

(1) Any person aggrieved by any act of a cable operator in violation of this section may bring a civil action in a United States district court.

(2) The court may award -

    (A) actual damages but not less than liquidated damages computed at the rate of $100 a day for each day of violation or $1,000, whichever is higher;

    (B) punitive damages; and

    (C) reasonable attorneys' fees and other litigation costs reasonably incurred.

(3) The remedy provided by this section shall be in addition to any other lawful remedy available to a cable subscriber.

(g) Regulation by States or franchising authorities

Nothing in this subchapter shall be construed to prohibit any State or any franchising authority from enacting or enforcing laws consistent with this section for the protection of subscriber privacy.

(h) Disclosure of information to governmental entity pursuant to court order

Except as provided in subsection (c)(2)(D), a governmental entity may obtain personally identifiable information concerning a cable subscriber pursuant to a court order only if, in the court proceeding relevant to such court order -

> (1) such entity offers clear and convincing evidence that the subject of the information is reasonably suspected of engaging in criminal activity and that the information sought would be material evidence in the case; and

> (2) the subject of the information is afforded the opportunity to appear and contest such entity's claim.

ELECTRONIC COMMUNICATIONS PRIVACY ACT (1986)

Summary

The Electronic Communications Privacy Act (ECPA) was enacted in 1986, as an amendment to the Omnibus Crime Control Act of 1968, to address technological advancements in communication networks and to bring "electronic communication" within the purview of federal law regarding wiretapping and bugging. ECPA covers wireless communication, email, and digitally transmitted conversations. ECPA criminalizes the interception of such communication, and provides civil remedies for violations. It also prevents government entities from requiring disclosure of electronic communications from a provider without proper procedure.

Title I of the Act protects electronic communications from unauthorized interception during transmission. In this way it mirrors the wiretap statute under the Omnibus Crime Control Act. Title II protects electronic data and messages in storage from unauthorized access and disclosure. Title II protects two kinds of data. First, it protects email and similar substantive electronic communications. Second, it protects data transfers between businesses and customers, such as fund transfers and computerized transfer of medical records.

It is useful to note that while the ECPA prohibits operators of electronic communications services from disclosing the content of messages in storage, this does not apply to purely internal email systems.

Both Title I and Title II mirror the principle of one-party consent found in the Omnibus Crime Control Act. Anyone may access electronic information if authorized by the user. Anyone may divulge such information with the consent of either the sender or recipient of the information. Sanctions under Title I include criminal penalties, a special injunction procedure, and a civil right of action. Penalties for Title II violations vary, but can include fines of up to $250,000 and prison sentences of no more than two years.

References

Public Law 99-508, Codified as amended at 18 U.S.C. § 2510 et seq.
[https://www.law.cornell.edu/uscode/text/18/2701]

James G. Carr, *The Law of Electronic Surveillance* (Clark, Boardman & Callaghan 2001)

Clifford S. Fishman & Anne T. McKenna, *Wiretapping and Eavesdropping* (Clark, Boardman & Callaghan 1995)

EPIC, Electronic Communications Privacy Act (ECPA)
[https://www.epic.org/privacy/ecpa/]

United States
Electronic Communications Privacy Act

Congressional Findings (1968)

Section 801 of Pub. L. 90-351 provided that: "On the basis of its own investigations and of published studies, the Congress makes the following findings:

"(a) Wire communications are normally conducted through the use of facilities which form part of an interstate network. The same facilities are used for interstate and intrastate communications. There has been extensive wiretapping carried on without legal sanctions, and without the consent of any of the parties to the conversation. Electronic, mechanical, and other intercepting devices are being used to overhear oral conversations made in private, without the consent of any of the parties to such communications. The contents of these communications and evidence derived therefrom are being used by public and private parties as evidence in court and administrative proceedings, and by persons whose activities affect interstate commerce. The possession, manufacture, distribution, advertising, and use of these devices are facilitated by interstate commerce.

"(b) In order to protect effectively the privacy of wire and oral communications, to protect the integrity of court and administrative proceedings, and to prevent the obstruction of interstate commerce, it is necessary for Congress to define on a uniform basis the circumstances and conditions under which the interception of wire and oral communications may be authorized, to prohibit any unauthorized interception of such communications, and the use of the contents thereof in evidence in courts and administrative proceedings.

"(c) Organized criminals make extensive use of wire and oral communications in their criminal activities. The interception of such communications to obtain evidence of the commission of crimes or to prevent their commission is an indispensable aid to law enforcement and the administration of justice.

"(d) To safeguard the privacy of innocent persons, the interception of wire or oral communications where none of the parties to the communication has consented to the interception should be allowed only when authorized by a court of competent jurisdiction and should remain under the control and supervision of the authorizing court. Interception of wire and oral communications should further be limited to certain major types of offenses and specific categories of crime with assurances that the interception is justified and that the information obtained thereby will not be misused."

18 U.S.C. § 2510. Definitions

As used in this chapter -

(1) "wire communication" means any aural transfer made in whole or in part through the use of facilities for the transmission of communications by the aid of wire, cable, or other like connection between the point of origin and the point of reception (including the use of such connection in a switching station) furnished or operated by any person engaged

in providing or operating such facilities for the transmission of interstate or foreign communications or communications affecting interstate or foreign commerce;

(2) "oral communication" means any oral communication uttered by a person exhibiting an expectation that such communication is not subject to interception under circumstances justifying such expectation, but such term does not include any electronic communication;

(3) "State" means any State of the United States, the District of Columbia, the Commonwealth of Puerto Rico, and any territory or possession of the United States;

(4) "intercept" means the aural or other acquisition of the contents of any wire, electronic, or oral communication through the use of any electronic, mechanical, or other device.

(5) "electronic, mechanical, or other device" means any device or apparatus which can be used to intercept a wire, oral, or electronic communication other than -

　(a) any telephone or telegraph instrument, equipment or facility, or any component thereof,

　　(i) furnished to the subscriber or user by a provider of wire or electronic communication service in the ordinary course of its business and being used by the subscriber or user in the ordinary course of its business or furnished by such subscriber or user for connection to the facilities of such service and used in the ordinary course of its business; or

　　(ii) being used by a provider of wire or electronic communication service in the ordinary course of its business, or by an investigative or law enforcement officer in the ordinary course of his duties;

　(b) a hearing aid or similar device being used to correct subnormal hearing to not better than normal;

(6) "person" means any employee, or agent of the United States or any State or political subdivision thereof, and any individual, partnership, association, joint stock company, trust, or corporation;

(7) "Investigative or law enforcement officer" means any officer of the United States or of a State or political subdivision thereof, who is empowered by law to conduct investigations of or to make arrests for offenses enumerated in this chapter, and any attorney authorized by law to prosecute or participate in the prosecution of such offenses;

(8) "contents", when used with respect to any wire, oral, or electronic communication, includes any information concerning the substance, purport, or meaning of that communication;

(9) "Judge of competent jurisdiction" means -

　(a) a judge of a United States district court or a United States court of appeals; and

　(b) a judge of any court of general criminal jurisdiction of a State who is authorized by a statute of that State to enter orders authorizing interceptions of wire, oral, or electronic communications;

(10) "communication common carrier" has the meaning given that term in section 3 of the Communications Act of 1934;

(11) "aggrieved person" means a person who was a party to any intercepted wire, oral, or electronic communication or a person against whom the interception was directed;

(12) "electronic communication" means any transfer of signs, signals, writing, images, sounds, data, or intelligence of any nature transmitted in whole or in part by a wire, radio, electromagnetic, photoelectronic or photooptical system that affects interstate or foreign commerce, but does not include -

(A) any wire or oral communication;

(B) any communication made through a tone-only paging device;

(C) any communication from a tracking device (as defined in section 3117 of this title); or

(D) electronic funds transfer information stored by a financial institution in a communications system used for the electronic storage and transfer of funds;

(13) "user" means any person or entity who -

(A) uses an electronic communication service; and

(B) is duly authorized by the provider of such service to engage in such use;

(14) "electronic communications system" means any wire, radio, electromagnetic, photooptical or photoelectronic facilities for the transmission of wire or electronic communications, and any computer facilities or related electronic equipment for the electronic storage of such communications;

(15) "electronic communication service" means any service which provides to users thereof the ability to send or receive wire or electronic communications;

(16) "readily accessible to the general public" means, with respect to a radio communication, that such communication is not

(A) scrambled or encrypted;

(B) transmitted using modulation techniques whose essential parameters have been withheld from the public with the intention of preserving the privacy of such communication;

(C) carried on a subcarrier or other signal subsidiary to a radio transmission;

(D) transmitted over a communication system provided by a common carrier, unless the communication is a tone only paging system communication; or

(E) transmitted on frequencies allocated under part 25, subpart D, E, or F of part 74, or part 94 of the Rules of the Federal Communications Commission, unless, in the case of a communication transmitted on a frequency allocated under part 74 that is not exclusively allocated to broadcast auxiliary services, the communication is a two-way voice communication by radio;

(17) "electronic storage" means -

(A) any temporary, intermediate storage of a wire or electronic communication incidental to the electronic transmission thereof; and

(B) any storage of such communication by an electronic communication service for purposes of backup protection of such communication;

(18) "aural transfer" means a transfer containing the human voice at any point between and including the point of origin and the point of reception;

(19) "foreign intelligence information", for purposes of section 2517(6) of this title, means –

(A) information, whether or not concerning a United States person, that relates to the ability of the United States to protect against –

(i) actual or potential attack or other grave hostile acts of a foreign power or an agent of a foreign power;

(ii) sabotage or international terrorism by a foreign power or an agent of a foreign power; or

(iii) clandestine intelligence activities by an intelligence service or network of a foreign power or by an agent of a foreign power; or

(B) information, whether or not concerning a United States person, with respect to a foreign power or foreign territory that relates to –

(i) the national defense or the security of the United States; or

(ii) the conduct of the foreign affairs of the United States;

(20) "protected computer" has the meaning set forth in section 1030; and

(21) "computer trespasser" –

(A) means a person who accesses a protected computer without authorization and thus has no reasonable expectation of privacy in any communication transmitted to, through, or from the protected computer; and

(b) does not include a person known by the owner or operator of the protected computer to have an existing contractual relationship with the owner or operator of the protected computer for access to all or part of the protected computer.

Sec. 2511. Interception and disclosure of wire, oral, or electronic communications prohibited

(1) Except as otherwise specifically provided in this chapter any person who-

(a) intentionally intercepts, endeavors to intercept, or procures any other person to intercept or endeavor to intercept, any wire, oral, or electronic communication;

(b) intentionally uses, endeavors to use, or procures any other person to use or endeavor to use any electronic, mechanical, or other device to intercept any oral communication when-

(i) such device is affixed to, or otherwise transmits a signal through, a wire, cable, or other like connection used in wire communication; or

(ii) such device transmits communications by radio, or interferes with the transmission of such communication; or

(iii) such person knows, or has reason to know, that such device or any component thereof has been sent through the mail or transported in interstate or foreign commerce; or

(iv) such use or endeavor to use (A) takes place on the premises of any business or other commercial establishment the operations of which affect interstate or foreign commerce; or (B) obtains or is for the purpose of obtaining information relating to the operations of any business or other commercial establishment the operations of which affect interstate or foreign commerce; or

(v) such person acts in the District of Columbia, the Commonwealth of Puerto Rico, or any territory or possession of the United States;

(c) intentionally discloses, or endeavors to disclose, to any other person the contents of any wire, oral, or electronic communication, knowing or having reason to know that the information was obtained through the interception of a wire, oral, or electronic communication in violation of this subsection;

(d) intentionally uses, or endeavors to use, the contents of any wire, oral, or electronic communication, knowing or having reason to know that the information was obtained through the interception of a wire, oral, or electronic communication in violation of this subsection; or

(e)(i) intentionally discloses, or endeavors to disclose, to any other person the contents of any wire, oral, or electronic communication, intercepted by means authorized by sections 2511(2)(a)(ii), 2511(2)(b)–(c), 2511(2)(e), 2516, and 2518 of this chapter, (ii) knowing or having reason to know that the information was obtained through the interception of such a communication in connection with a criminal investigation, (iii) having obtained or received the information in connection with a criminal investigation, and (iv) with intent to improperly obstruct, impede, or interfere with a duly authorized criminal investigation, shall be punished as provided in subsection (4) or shall be subject to suit as provided in subsection (5).

(2)(a)(i) It shall not be unlawful under this chapter for an operator of a switchboard, or an officer, employee, or agent of a provider of wire or electronic communication service, whose facilities are used in the transmission of a wire or electronic communication, to intercept, disclose, or use that communication in the normal course of his employment while engaged in any activity which is a necessary incident to the rendition of his service or to the protection of the rights or property of the provider of that service, except that a provider of wire communication service to the public shall not utilize service observing or random monitoring except for mechanical or service quality control checks.

(ii) Notwithstanding any other law, providers of wire or electronic communication service, their officers, employees, and agents, landlords, custodians, or other persons, are authorized to provide information, facilities, or technical assistance to persons authorized by law to intercept wire, oral, or electronic communications or to conduct electronic surveillance, as defined in section 101 of the Foreign Intelligence Surveillance Act of

1978, if such provider, its officers, employees, or agents, landlord, custodian, or other specified person, has been provided with-

(A) a court order directing such assistance or a court order pursuant to section 704 of the Foreign Intelligence Surveillance Act of 1978 signed by the authorizing judge, or

(B) a certification in writing by a person specified in section 2518(7) of this title or the Attorney General of the United States that no warrant or court order is required by law, that all statutory requirements have been met, and that the specified assistance is required, setting forth the period of time during which the provision of the information, facilities, or technical assistance is authorized and specifying the information, facilities, or technical assistance required. No provider of wire or electronic communication service, officer, employee, or agent thereof, or landlord, custodian, or other specified person shall disclose the existence of any interception or surveillance or the device used to accomplish the interception or surveillance with respect to which the person has been furnished a court order or certification under this chapter, except as may otherwise be required by legal process and then only after prior notification to the Attorney General or to the principal prosecuting attorney of a State or any political subdivision of a State, as may be appropriate. Any such disclosure, shall render such person liable for the civil damages provided for in section 2520. No cause of action shall lie in any court against any provider of wire or electronic communication service, its officers, employees, or agents, landlord, custodian, or other specified person for providing information, facilities, or assistance in accordance with the terms of a court order, statutory authorization, or certification under this chapter.

(iii) If a certification under subparagraph (ii)(B) for assistance to obtain foreign intelligence information is based on statutory authority, the certification shall identify the specific statutory provision and shall certify that the statutory requirements have been met.

(b) It shall not be unlawful under this chapter for an officer, employee, or agent of the Federal Communications Commission, in the normal course of his employment and in discharge of the monitoring responsibilities exercised by the Commission in the enforcement of chapter 5 of title 47 of the United States Code, to intercept a wire or electronic communication, or oral communication transmitted by radio, or to disclose or use the information thereby obtained.

(c) It shall not be unlawful under this chapter for a person acting under color of law to intercept a wire, oral, or electronic communication, where such person is a party to the communication or one of the parties to the communication has given prior consent to such interception.

(d) It shall not be unlawful under this chapter for a person not acting under color of law to intercept a wire, oral, or electronic communication where such person is a party to the communication or where one of the parties to the communication has given prior consent to such interception unless such communication is intercepted for the purpose of committing any criminal or tortious act in violation of the Constitution or laws of the United States or of any State.

(e) Notwithstanding any other provision of this title or section 705 or 706 of the Communications Act of 1934, it shall not be unlawful for an officer, employee, or agent of the United States in the normal course of his official duty to conduct electronic surveillance, as defined in section 101 of the Foreign Intelligence Surveillance Act of 1978, as authorized by that Act.

(f) Nothing contained in this chapter or chapter 121 or 206 of this title, or section 705 of the Communications Act of 1934, shall be deemed to affect the acquisition by the United States Government of foreign intelligence information from international or foreign communications, or foreign intelligence activities conducted in accordance with otherwise applicable Federal law involving a foreign electronic communications system, utilizing a means other than electronic surveillance as defined in section 101 of the Foreign Intelligence Surveillance Act of 1978, and procedures in this chapter or chapter 121 and the Foreign Intelligence Surveillance Act of 1978 shall be the exclusive means by which electronic surveillance, as defined in section 101 of such Act, and the interception of domestic wire, oral, and electronic communications may be conducted.

(g) It shall not be unlawful under this chapter or chapter 121 of this title for any person-

(i) to intercept or access an electronic communication made through an electronic communication system that is configured so that such electronic communication is readily accessible to the general public;

(ii) to intercept any radio communication which is transmitted-

(I) by any station for the use of the general public, or that relates to ships, aircraft, vehicles, or persons in distress;

(II) by any governmental, law enforcement, civil defense, private land mobile, or public safety communications system, including police and fire, readily accessible to the general public;

(III) by a station operating on an authorized frequency within the bands allocated to the amateur, citizens band, or general mobile radio services; or

(IV) by any marine or aeronautical communications system;

(iii) to engage in any conduct which-

(I) is prohibited by section 633 of the Communications Act of 1934; or

(II) is excepted from the application of section 705(a) of the Communications Act of 1934 by section 705(b) of that Act;

(iv) to intercept any wire or electronic communication the transmission of which is causing harmful interference to any lawfully operating station or consumer electronic equipment, to the extent necessary to identify the source of such interference; or

(v) for other users of the same frequency to intercept any radio communication made through a system that utilizes frequencies monitored by individuals engaged in the provision or the use of such system, if such communication is not scrambled or encrypted.

(h) It shall not be unlawful under this chapter-

(i) to use a pen register or a trap and trace device (as those terms are defined for the purposes of chapter 206 (relating to pen registers and trap and trace devices) of this title); or

(ii) for a provider of electronic communication service to record the fact that a wire or electronic communication was initiated or completed in order to protect such provider, another provider furnishing service toward the completion of the wire or electronic communication, or a user of that service, from fraudulent, unlawful or abusive use of such service.

(i) It shall not be unlawful under this chapter for a person acting under color of law to intercept the wire or electronic communications of a computer trespasser transmitted to, through, or from the protected computer, if-

(I) the owner or operator of the protected computer authorizes the interception of the computer trespasser's communications on the protected computer;

(II) the person acting under color of law is lawfully engaged in an investigation;

(III) the person acting under color of law has reasonable grounds to believe that the contents of the computer trespasser's communications will be relevant to the investigation; and

(IV) such interception does not acquire communications other than those transmitted to or from the computer trespasser.

(j) It shall not be unlawful under this chapter for a provider of electronic communication service to the public or remote computing service to intercept or disclose the contents of a wire or electronic communication in response to an order from a foreign government that is subject to an executive agreement that the Attorney General has determined and certified to Congress satisfies section 2523.

(3)(a) Except as provided in paragraph (b) of this subsection, a person or entity providing an electronic communication service to the public shall not intentionally divulge the contents of any communication (other than one to such person or entity, or an agent thereof) while in transmission on that service to any person or entity other than an addressee or intended recipient of such communication or an agent of such addressee or intended recipient.

(b) A person or entity providing electronic communication service to the public may divulge the contents of any such communication-

(i) as otherwise authorized in section 2511(2)(a) or 2517 of this title;

(ii) with the lawful consent of the originator or any addressee or intended recipient of such communication;

(iii) to a person employed or authorized, or whose facilities are used, to forward such communication to its destination; or

(iv) which were inadvertently obtained by the service provider and which appear to pertain to the commission of a crime, if such divulgence is made to a law enforcement agency.

(4)(a) Except as provided in paragraph (b) of this subsection or in subsection (5), whoever violates subsection (1) of this section shall be fined under this title or imprisoned not more than five years, or both.

(b) Conduct otherwise an offense under this subsection that consists of or relates to the interception of a satellite transmission that is not encrypted or scrambled and that is transmitted-

(i) to a broadcasting station for purposes of retransmission to the general public; or

(ii) as an audio subcarrier intended for redistribution to facilities open to the public, but not including data transmissions or telephone calls, is not an offense under this subsection unless the conduct is for the purposes of direct or indirect commercial advantage or private financial gain.

(5)(a)(i) If the communication is-

(A) a private satellite video communication that is not scrambled or encrypted and the conduct in violation of this chapter is the private viewing of that communication and is not for a tortious or illegal purpose or for purposes of direct or indirect commercial advantage or private commercial gain; or

(B) a radio communication that is transmitted on frequencies allocated under subpart D of part 74 of the rules of the Federal Communications Commission that is not scrambled or encrypted and the conduct in violation of this chapter is not for a tortious or illegal purpose or for purposes of direct or indirect commercial advantage or private commercial gain, then the person who engages in such conduct shall be subject to suit by the Federal Government in a court of competent jurisdiction.

(ii) In an action under this subsection-

(A) if the violation of this chapter is a first offense for the person under paragraph (a) of subsection (4) and such person has not been found liable in a civil action under section 2520 of this title, the Federal Government shall be entitled to appropriate injunctive relief; and

(B) if the violation of this chapter is a second or subsequent offense under paragraph (a) of subsection (4) or such person has been found liable in any prior civil action under section 2520, the person shall be subject to a mandatory $500 civil fine.

(b) The court may use any means within its authority to enforce an injunction issued under paragraph (ii)(A), and shall impose a civil fine of not less than $500 for each violation of such an injunction.

Sec. 2512. Manufacture, distribution, possession, and advertising of wire, oral, or electronic communication intercepting devices prohibited

(1) Except as otherwise specifically provided in this chapter, any person who intentionally

(a) sends through the mail, or sends or carries in interstate or foreign commerce, any electronic, mechanical, or other device, knowing or having reason to know that the design of such device renders it primarily useful for the purpose of the surreptitious interception of wire, oral, or electronic communications;

(b) manufactures, assembles, possesses, or sells any electronic, mechanical, or other device, knowing or having reason to know that the design of such device renders it primarily useful for the purpose of the surreptitious interception of wire, oral, or electronic communications, and that such device or any component thereof has been or will be sent through the mail or transported in interstate or foreign commerce; or

(c) places in any newspaper, magazine, handbill, or other publication or disseminates by electronic means any advertisement of

(i) any electronic, mechanical, or other device knowing or having reason to know that the design of such device renders it primarily useful for the purpose of the surreptitious interception of wire, oral, or electronic communications; or

(ii) any other electronic, mechanical, or other device, where such advertisement promotes the use of such device for the purpose of the surreptitious interception of wire, oral, or electronic communications

knowing the content of the advertisement and knowing or having reason to know that such advertisement will be sent through the mail or transported in interstate or foreign commerce, shall be fined under this title or imprisoned not more than five years, or both.

(2) It shall not be unlawful under this section for

(a) a provider of wire or electronic communication service or an officer, agent, or employee of, or a person under contract with, such a provider, in the normal course of the business of providing that wire or electronic communication service, or

(b) an officer, agent, or employee of, or a person under contract with, the United States, a State, or a political subdivision thereof, in the normal course of the activities of the United States, a State, or a political subdivision thereof,

to send through the mail, send or carry in interstate or foreign commerce, or manufacture, assemble, possess, or sell any electronic, mechanical, or other device knowing or having reason to know that the design of such device renders it primarily useful for the purpose of the surreptitious interception of wire, oral, or electronic communications.

(3) It shall not be unlawful under this section to advertise for sale a device described in subsection (1) of this section if the advertisement is mailed, sent, or carried in interstate or foreign commerce solely to a domestic provider of wire or electronic communication

service or to an agency of the United States, a State, or a political subdivision thereof which is duly authorized to use such device.

Sec. 2513. Confiscation of wire, oral, or electronic communication intercepting devices

Any electronic, mechanical, or other device used, sent, carried, manufactured, assembled, possessed, sold, or advertised in violation of section 2511 or section 2512 of this chapter may be seized and forfeited to the United States. All provisions of law relating to (1) the seizure, summary and judicial forfeiture, and condemnation of vessels, vehicles, merchandise, and baggage for violations of the customs laws contained in title 19 of the United States Code, (2) the disposition of such vessels, vehicles, merchandise, and baggage or the proceeds from the sale thereof, (3) the remission or mitigation of such forfeiture, (4) the compromise of claims, and (5) the award of compensation to informers in respect of such forfeitures, shall apply to seizures and forfeitures incurred, or alleged to have been incurred, under the provisions of this section, insofar as applicable and not inconsistent with the provisions of this section; except that such duties as are imposed upon the collector of customs or any other person with respect to the seizure and forfeiture of vessels, vehicles, merchandise, and baggage under the provisions of the customs laws contained in title 19 of the United States Code shall be performed with respect to seizure and forfeiture of electronic, mechanical, or other intercepting devices under this section by such officers, agents, or other persons as may be authorized or designated for that purpose by the Attorney General.

Sec. 2514. [Repealed]

Sec. 2515. Prohibition of use as evidence of intercepted wire or oral communications

Whenever any wire or oral communication has been intercepted, no part of the contents of such communication and no evidence derived therefrom may be received in evidence in any trial, hearing, or other proceeding in or before any court, grand jury, department, officer, agency, regulatory body, legislative committee, or other authority of the United States, a State, or a political subdivision thereof if the disclosure of that information would be in violation of this chapter.

Sec. 2516. Authorization for interception of wire, oral, or electronic communications

(1) The Attorney General, Deputy Attorney General, Associate Attorney General,[1] or any Assistant Attorney General, any acting Assistant Attorney General, or any Deputy Assistant Attorney General or acting Deputy Assistant Attorney General in the Criminal Division or National Security Division specially designated by the Attorney General, may authorize an application to a Federal judge of competent jurisdiction for, and such judge may grant in conformity with section 2518 of this chapter an order authorizing or approving the interception of wire or oral communications by the Federal Bureau of Investigation, or a Federal agency having responsibility for the investigation of the

offense as to which the application is made, when such interception may provide or has provided evidence of-

(a) any offense punishable by death or by imprisonment for more than one year under sections 2122 and 2274 through 2277 of title 42 of the United States Code (relating to the enforcement of the Atomic Energy Act of 1954), section 2284 of title 42 of the United States Code (relating to sabotage of nuclear facilities or fuel), or under the following chapters of this title: chapter 10 (relating to biological weapons), chapter 37 (relating to espionage), chapter 55 (relating to kidnapping), chapter 90 (relating to protection of trade secrets), chapter 105 (relating to sabotage), chapter 115 (relating to treason), chapter 102 (relating to riots), chapter 65 (relating to malicious mischief), chapter 111 (relating to destruction of vessels), or chapter 81 (relating to piracy);

(b) a violation of section 186 or section 501(c) of title 29, United States Code (dealing with restrictions on payments and loans to labor organizations), or any offense which involves murder, kidnapping, robbery, or extortion, and which is punishable under this title;

(c) any offense which is punishable under the following sections of this title: section 37 (relating to violence at international airports), section 43 (relating to animal enterprise terrorism), section 81 (arson within special maritime and territorial jurisdiction), section 201 (bribery of public officials and witnesses), section 215 (relating to bribery of bank officials), section 224 (bribery in sporting contests), subsection (d), (e), (f), (g), (h), or (i) of section 844 (unlawful use of explosives), section 1032 (relating to concealment of assets), section 1084 (transmission of wagering information), section 751 (relating to escape), section 832 (relating to nuclear and weapons of mass destruction threats), section 842 (relating to explosive materials), section 930 (relating to possession of weapons in Federal facilities), section 1014 (relating to loans and credit applications generally; renewals and discounts), section 1114 (relating to officers and employees of the United States), section 1116 (relating to protection of foreign officials), sections 1503, 1512, and 1513 (influencing or injuring an officer, juror, or witness generally), section 1510 (obstruction of criminal investigations), section 1511 (obstruction of State or local law enforcement), section 1581 (peonage), section 1582 (vessels for slave trade), section 1583 (enticement into slavery), section 1584 (involuntary servitude), section 1585 (seizure, detention, transportation or sale of slaves), section 1586 (service on vessels in slave trade), section 1587 (possession of slaves aboard vessel), section 1588 (transportation of slaves from United States), section 1589 (forced labor), section 1590 (trafficking with respect to peonage, slavery, involuntary servitude, or forced labor), section 1591 (sex trafficking of children by force, fraud, or coercion), section 1592 (unlawful conduct with respect to documents in furtherance of trafficking, peonage, slavery, involuntary servitude, or forced labor), section 1751 (Presidential and Presidential staff assassination, kidnapping, and assault), section 1951 (interference with commerce by threats or violence), section 1952 (interstate and foreign travel or transportation in aid of racketeering enterprises), section 1958 (relating to use of interstate commerce facilities in the commission of murder for hire), section 1959 (relating to violent crimes in aid of racketeering activity), section 1954 (offer, acceptance, or solicitation to influence operations of employee benefit plan), section 1955 (prohibition of business enterprises of gambling), section 1956 (laundering of monetary instruments), section 1957 (relating to engaging in monetary transactions in property derived from specified unlawful activity), section 659 (theft from interstate shipment), section 664 (embezzlement from pension and welfare funds), section 1343 (fraud by wire, radio, or television), section 1344 (relating to bank fraud), section 1992 (relating to terrorist attacks against mass transportation), sections 2251 and 2252 (sexual exploitation of children), section 2251A (selling or buying of children), section 2252A (relating to material constituting or containing child pornography), section 1466A (relating to child obscenity), section 2260 (production of sexually explicit depictions of a minor for importation into the United States), sections 2421, 2422, 2423, and 2425 (relating to transportation for illegal sexual activity and related crimes), sections 2312, 2313, 2314, and 2315 (interstate transportation of stolen property), section 2321 (relating to trafficking in certain motor vehicles or motor vehicle parts), section 2340A (relating to torture), section 1203 (relating to hostage taking), section 1029 (relating to fraud and related activity in connection with access devices), section 3146 (relating to penalty for failure to appear), section 3521(b)(3) (relating to witness relocation and assistance), section 32 (relating to destruction of aircraft or aircraft facilities), section 38 (relating to aircraft parts fraud), section 1963 (violations with respect to racketeer influenced and corrupt organizations), section 115 (relating to threatening or retaliating against a Federal official), section 1341 (relating to mail fraud), a felony violation of section 1030 (relating to computer fraud and abuse), section 351 (violations with respect to congressional, Cabinet, or Supreme Court assassinations, kidnapping, and assault), section 831 (relating to prohibited transactions involving nuclear materials), section 33 (relating to destruction of motor vehicles or motor vehicle facilities), section 175 (relating to biological weapons), section 175c (relating to variola virus), section 956 (conspiracy to harm persons or property overseas), a felony violation of section 1028 (relating to production of false identification documentation), section 1425 (relating to the procurement of citizenship or nationalization unlawfully), section 1426 (relating to the reproduction of naturalization or citizenship papers), section 1427 (relating to the sale of naturalization or citizenship papers), section 1541 (relating to passport issuance without authority), section 1542 (relating to false statements in passport applications), section 1543 (relating to forgery or false use of passports), section 1544 (relating to misuse of passports), section 1546 (relating to fraud and misuse of visas, permits, and other documents), or section 555 (relating to construction or use of international border tunnels);

(d) any offense involving counterfeiting punishable under section 471, 472, or 473 of this title;

(e) any offense involving fraud connected with a case under title 11 or the manufacture, importation, receiving, concealment, buying, selling, or otherwise dealing in narcotic drugs, marihuana, or other dangerous drugs, punishable under any law of the United States;

(f) any offense including extortionate credit transactions under sections 892, 893, or 894 of this title;

(g) a violation of section 5322 of title 31, United States Code (dealing with the reporting of currency transactions), or section 5324 of title 31, United States Code (relating to structuring transactions to evade reporting requirement prohibited);

(h) any felony violation of sections 2511 and 2512 (relating to interception and disclosure of certain communications and to certain intercepting devices) of this title;

(i) any felony violation of chapter 71 (relating to obscenity) of this title;

(j) any violation of section 60123(b) (relating to destruction of a natural gas pipeline), section 46502 (relating to aircraft piracy), the second sentence of section 46504 (relating to assault on a flight crew with dangerous weapon), or section 46505(b)(3) or (c) (relating to explosive or incendiary devices, or endangerment of human life, by means of weapons on aircraft) of title 49;

(k) any criminal violation of section 2778 of title 22 (relating to the Arms Export Control Act);

(l) the location of any fugitive from justice from an offense described in this section;

(m) a violation of section 274, 277, or 278 of the Immigration and Nationality Act (8 U.S.C. 1324, 1327, or 1328) (relating to the smuggling of aliens);

(n) any felony violation of sections 922 and 924 of title 18, United States Code (relating to firearms);

(o) any violation of section 5861 of the Internal Revenue Code of 1986 (relating to firearms);

(p) a felony violation of section 1028 (relating to production of false identification documents), section 1542 (relating to false statements in passport applications), section 1546 (relating to fraud and misuse of visas, permits, and other documents), section 1028A (relating to aggravated identity theft) of this title or a violation of section 274, 277, or 278 of the Immigration and Nationality Act (relating to the smuggling of aliens); or [2]

(q) any criminal violation of section 229 (relating to chemical weapons) or section 2332, 2332a, 2332b, 2332d, 2332f, 2332g, 2332h [3] 2339, 2339A, 2339B, 2339C, or 2339D of this title (relating to terrorism);

(r) any criminal violation of section 1 (relating to illegal restraints of trade or commerce), 2 (relating to illegal monopolizing of trade or commerce), or 3 (relating to illegal restraints of trade or commerce in territories or the District of Columbia) of the Sherman Act (15 U.S.C. 1, 2, 3);

(s) any violation of section 670 (relating to theft of medical products);

(t) any violation of the Export Control Reform Act of 2018; or

(u) any conspiracy to commit any offense described in any subparagraph of this paragraph.

(2) The principal prosecuting attorney of any State, or the principal prosecuting attorney of any political subdivision thereof, if such attorney is authorized by a statute of that State to make application to a State court judge of competent jurisdiction for an order authorizing or approving the interception of wire, oral, or electronic communications, may apply to such judge for, and such judge may grant in conformity with section 2518 of this chapter and with the applicable State statute an order authorizing, or approving the interception of wire, oral, or electronic communications by investigative or law enforcement officers having responsibility for the investigation of the offense as to which the application is made, when such interception may provide or has provided evidence of the commission of the offense of murder, kidnapping, human trafficking, child sexual exploitation, child pornography production, prostitution, gambling, robbery, bribery, extortion, or dealing in narcotic drugs, marihuana or other dangerous drugs, or other crime dangerous to life, limb, or property, and punishable by imprisonment for more than one year, designated in any applicable State statute authorizing such interception, or any conspiracy to commit any of the foregoing offenses.

(3) Any attorney for the Government (as such term is defined for the purposes of the Federal Rules of Criminal Procedure) may authorize an application to a Federal judge of competent jurisdiction for, and such judge may grant, in conformity with section 2518 of this title, an order authorizing or approving the interception of electronic communications by an investigative or law enforcement officer having responsibility for the investigation of the offense as to which the application is made, when such interception may provide or has provided evidence of any Federal felony.

Sec. 2517. Authorization for disclosure and use of intercepted wire, oral, or electronic communications

(1) Any investigative or law enforcement officer who, by any means authorized by this chapter, has obtained knowledge of the contents of any wire, oral, or electronic communication, or evidence derived therefrom, may disclose such contents to another investigative or law enforcement officer to the extent that such disclosure is appropriate to the proper performance of the official duties of the officer making or receiving the disclosure.

(2) Any investigative or law enforcement officer who, by any means authorized by this chapter, has obtained knowledge of the contents of any wire, oral, or electronic communication or evidence derived therefrom may use such contents to the extent such use is appropriate to the proper performance of his official duties.

(3) Any person who has received, by any means authorized by this chapter, any information concerning a wire, oral, or electronic communication, or evidence derived therefrom intercepted in accordance with the provisions of this chapter may disclose the contents of that communication or such derivative evidence while giving testimony under oath or affirmation in any proceeding held under the authority of the United States or of any State or political subdivision thereof.

(4) No otherwise privileged wire, oral, or electronic communication intercepted in accordance with, or in violation of, the provisions of this chapter shall lose its privileged character.

(5) When an investigative or law enforcement officer, while engaged in intercepting wire, oral, or electronic communications in the manner authorized herein, intercepts wire, oral, or electronic communications relating to offenses other than those specified in the order of authorization or approval, the contents thereof, and evidence derived therefrom, may be disclosed or used as provided in subsections (1) and (2) of this section. Such contents and any evidence derived therefrom may be used under subsection (3) of this section when authorized or approved by a judge of competent jurisdiction where such judge finds on subsequent application that the contents were otherwise intercepted in accordance with the provisions of this chapter. Such application shall be made as soon as practicable.

(6) Any investigative or law enforcement officer, or attorney for the Government, who by any means authorized by this chapter, has obtained knowledge of the contents of any wire, oral, or electronic communication, or evidence derived therefrom, may disclose such contents to any other Federal law enforcement, intelligence, protective, immigration, national defense, or national security official to the extent that such contents include foreign intelligence or counterintelligence (as defined in section 3 of the National Security Act of 1947 (50 U.S.C. 401a), or foreign intelligence information (as defined in subsection (19) of section 2510 of this title), to assist the official who is to receive that information in the performance of his official duties. Any Federal official who receives information pursuant to this provision may use that information only as necessary in the conduct of that person's official duties subject to any limitations on the unauthorized disclosure of such information.

(7) Any investigative or law enforcement officer, or other Federal official in carrying out official duties as such Federal official, who by any means authorized by this chapter, has obtained knowledge of the contents of any wire, oral, or electronic communication, or evidence derived therefrom, may disclose such contents or derivative evidence to a foreign investigative or law enforcement officer to the extent that such disclosure is appropriate to the proper performance of the official duties of the officer making or receiving the disclosure, and foreign investigative or law enforcement officers may use or disclose such contents or derivative evidence to the extent such use or disclosure is appropriate to the proper performance of their official duties.

(8) Any investigative or law enforcement officer, or other Federal official in carrying out official duties as such Federal official, who by any means authorized by this chapter, has obtained knowledge of the contents of any wire, oral, or electronic communication, or evidence derived therefrom, may disclose such contents or derivative evidence to any appropriate Federal, State, local, or foreign government official to the extent that such contents or derivative evidence reveals a threat of actual or potential attack or other grave hostile acts of a foreign power or an agent of a foreign power, domestic or international sabotage, domestic or international terrorism, or clandestine intelligence gathering activities by an intelligence service or network of a foreign power or by an agent of a foreign power, within the United States or elsewhere, for the purpose of preventing or responding to such a threat. Any official who receives information pursuant to this provision may use that information only as necessary in the conduct of that person's official duties subject to any limitations on the unauthorized disclosure of such information, and any State, local, or foreign official who receives information pursuant to this provision may use that information only consistent with such guidelines as the Attorney General and Director of National Intelligence shall jointly issue.

Sec. 2518. Procedure for interception of wire, oral, or electronic communications

(1) Each application for an order authorizing or approving the interception of a wire, oral, or electronic communication under this chapter shall be made in writing upon oath or affirmation to a judge of competent jurisdiction and shall state the applicant's authority to make such application. Each application shall include the following information:

(a) the identity of the investigative or law enforcement officer making the application, and the officer authorizing the application;

(b) a full and complete statement of the facts and circumstances relied upon by the applicant, to justify his belief that an order should be issued, including

(i) details as to the particular offense that has been, is being, or is about to be committed,

(ii) except as provided in subsection (11), a particular description of the nature and location of the facilities from which or the place where the communication is to be intercepted,

(iii) a particular description of the type of communications sought to be intercepted,

(iv) the identity of the person, if known, committing the offense and whose communications are to be intercepted;

(c) a full and complete statement as to whether or not other investigative procedures have been tried and failed or why they reasonably appear to be unlikely to succeed if tried or to be too dangerous;

(d) a statement of the period of time for which the interception is required to be maintained. If the nature of the investigation is such that the authorization for interception should not automatically terminate when the described type of communication has been first obtained, a particular description of facts establishing probable cause to believe that additional communications of the same type will occur thereafter;

(e) a full and complete statement of the facts concerning all previous applications known to the individual authorizing and making the application, made to any judge for authorization to intercept, or for approval of interceptions of, wire, oral, or electronic communications involving any of the same persons, facilities or places specified in the application, and the action taken by the judge on each such application; and

(f) where the application is for the extension of an order, a statement setting forth the results thus far obtained from the interception, or a reasonable explanation of the failure to obtain such results.

(2) The judge may require the applicant to furnish additional testimony or documentary evidence in support of the application.

(3) Upon such application the judge may enter an ex parte order, as requested or as modified, authorizing or approving interception of wire, oral, or electronic communications within the territorial jurisdiction of the court in which the judge is sitting (and outside that jurisdiction but within the United States in the case of a mobile interception device authorized by a Federal court within such jurisdiction), if the judge determines on the basis of the facts submitted by the applicant that -

(a) there is probable cause for belief that an individual is committing, has committed, or is about to commit a particular offense enumerated in section 2516 of this chapter;

(b) there is probable cause for belief that particular communications concerning that offense will be obtained through such interception;

(c) normal investigative procedures have been tried and have failed or reasonably appear to be unlikely to succeed if tried or to be too dangerous;

(d) except as provided in subsection (11), there is probable cause for belief that the facilities from which, or the place where, the wire, oral, or electronic communications are to be intercepted are being used, or are about to be used, in connection with the commission of such offense, or are leased to, listed in the name of, or commonly used by such person.

(4) Each order authorizing or approving the interception of any wire, oral, or electronic communication under this chapter shall specify -

(a) the identity of the person, if known, whose communications are to be intercepted;

(b) the nature and location of the communications facilities as to which, or the place where, authority to intercept is granted;

(c) a particular description of the type of communication sought to be intercepted, and a statement of the particular offense to which it relates;

(d) the identity of the agency authorized to intercept the communications, and of the person authorizing the application; and

(e) the period of time during which such interception is authorized, including a statement as to whether or not the interception shall automatically terminate when the described communication has been first obtained.

An order authorizing the interception of a wire, oral, or electronic communication under this chapter shall, upon request of the applicant, direct that a provider of wire or electronic communication service, landlord, custodian or other person shall furnish the applicant forthwith all information, facilities, and technical assistance necessary to accomplish the interception unobtrusively and with a minimum of interference with the services that such service provider, landlord, custodian, or person is according the person whose communications are to be intercepted. Any provider of wire or electronic communication service, landlord, custodian or other person furnishing such facilities or technical assistance shall be compensated therefor by the applicant for reasonable expenses incurred in providing such facilities or assistance. Pursuant to section 2522 of this chapter, an order may also be issued to enforce the assistance capability and capacity requirements under the Communications Assistance for Law Enforcement Act.

(5) No order entered under this section may authorize or approve the interception of any wire, oral, or electronic communication for any period longer than is necessary to achieve the objective of the authorization, nor in any event longer than thirty days. Such thirty-day period begins on the earlier of the day on which the investigative or law enforcement officer first begins to conduct an interception under the order or ten days after the order is entered. Extensions of an order may be granted, but only upon application for an extension made in accordance with subsection (1) of this section and the court making the findings required by subsection (3) of this section. The period of extension shall be no longer than the authorizing judge deems necessary to achieve the purposes for which it was granted and in no event for longer than thirty days. Every order and extension thereof shall contain a provision that the authorization to intercept shall be executed as soon as practicable, shall be conducted in such a way as to minimize the interception of communications not otherwise subject to interception under this chapter, and must terminate upon attainment of the authorized objective, or in any event in thirty days. In the event the intercepted communication is in a code or foreign language, and an expert in that foreign language or code is not reasonably available during the interception period, minimization may be accomplished as soon as practicable after such interception. An interception under this chapter may be conducted in whole or in part by Government personnel, or by an individual operating under a contract with the Government, acting under the supervision of an investigative or law enforcement officer authorized to conduct the interception.

(6) Whenever an order authorizing interception is entered pursuant to this chapter, the order may require reports to be made to the judge who issued the order showing what progress has been made toward achievement of the authorized objective and the need for continued interception. Such reports shall be made at such intervals as the judge may require.

(7) Notwithstanding any other provision of this chapter, any investigative or law enforcement officer, specially designated by the Attorney General, the Deputy Attorney General, the Associate Attorney General, or by the principal prosecuting attorney of any State or subdivision thereof acting pursuant to a statute of that State, who reasonably determines that -

    (a) an emergency situation exists that involves -

        (i) immediate danger of death or serious physical injury to any person,

        (ii) conspiratorial activities threatening the national security interest, or

        (iii) conspiratorial activities characteristic of organized crime, that requires a wire, oral, or electronic communication to be intercepted before an order authorizing such interception can, with due diligence, be obtained, and

    (b) there are grounds upon which an order could be entered under this chapter to authorize such interception, may intercept such wire, oral, or electronic communication if an application for an order approving the interception is made in accordance with this section within forty-eight hours after the interception has occurred, or begins to occur. In the absence of an order, such interception shall immediately terminate when the communication sought is obtained or when the application for the order is denied, whichever is earlier. In the event such application for approval is denied, or in any other case where the interception is terminated without an order having been issued, the contents of any wire, oral, or electronic communication intercepted shall be treated as having been obtained in violation of this chapter, and an inventory shall be served as provided for in subsection (d) of this section on the person named in the application.

(8)

    (a) The contents of any wire, oral, or electronic communication intercepted by any means authorized by this chapter shall, if possible, be recorded on tape or wire or other comparable device. The recording of the contents of any wire, oral, or electronic communication under this subsection shall be done in such way as will protect the recording from editing or other alterations. Immediately upon the expiration of the period of the order, or extensions thereof, such recordings shall be made available to the judge issuing such order and sealed under his directions. Custody of the recordings shall be wherever the judge orders. They shall not be destroyed except upon an order of the issuing or denying judge and in any event shall be kept for ten years. Duplicate recordings may be made for use or disclosure pursuant to the provisions of subsections (1) and (2) of section 2517 of this chapter for investigations. The presence of the seal provided for by this subsection, or a satisfactory explanation for the absence thereof, shall be a prerequisite for the use or disclosure of the contents of any wire, oral, or electronic communication or evidence derived therefrom under subsection (3) of section 2517.

(b) Applications made and orders granted under this chapter shall be sealed by the judge. Custody of the applications and orders shall be wherever the judge directs. Such applications and orders shall be disclosed only upon a showing of good cause before a judge of competent jurisdiction and shall not be destroyed except on order of the issuing or denying judge, and in any event shall be kept for ten years.

(c) Any violation of the provisions of this subsection may be punished as contempt of the issuing or denying judge.

(d) Within a reasonable time but not later than ninety days after the filing of an application for an order of approval under section 2518(7)(b) which is denied or the termination of the period of an order or extensions thereof, the issuing or denying judge shall cause to be served, on the persons named in the order or the application, and such other parties to intercepted communications as the judge may determine in his discretion that is in the interest of justice, an inventory which shall include notice of -

(1) the fact of the entry of the order or the application;

(2) the date of the entry and the period of authorized, approved or disapproved interception, or the denial of the application; and

(3) the fact that during the period wire, oral, or electronic communications were or were not intercepted.

The judge, upon the filing of a motion, may in his discretion make available to such person or his counsel for inspection such portions of the intercepted communications, applications and orders as the judge determines to be in the interest of justice. On an ex parte showing of good cause to a judge of competent jurisdiction the serving of the inventory required by this subsection may be postponed.

(9) The contents of any wire, oral, or electronic communication intercepted pursuant to this chapter or evidence derived therefrom shall not be received in evidence or otherwise disclosed in any trial, hearing, or other proceeding in a Federal or State court unless each party, not less than ten days before the trial, hearing, or proceeding, has been furnished with a copy of the court order, and accompanying application, under which the interception was authorized or approved. This ten-day period may be waived by the judge if he finds that it was not possible to furnish the party with the above information ten days before the trial, hearing, or proceeding and that the party will not be prejudiced by the delay in receiving such information.

(10)

(a) Any aggrieved person in any trial, hearing, or proceeding in or before any court, department, officer, agency, regulatory body, or other authority of the United States, a State, or a political subdivision thereof, may move to suppress the contents of any wire or oral communication intercepted pursuant to this chapter, or evidence derived therefrom, on the grounds that -

(i) the communication was unlawfully intercepted;

(ii) the order of authorization or approval under which it was intercepted is insufficient on its face; or

(iii) the interception was not made in conformity with the order of authorization or approval.

Such motion shall be made before the trial, hearing, or proceeding unless there was no opportunity to make such motion or the person was not aware of the grounds of the motion. If the motion is granted, the contents of the intercepted wire or oral communication, or evidence derived therefrom, shall be treated as having been obtained in violation of this chapter. The judge, upon the filing of such motion by the aggrieved person, may in his discretion make available to the aggrieved person or his counsel for inspection such portions of the intercepted communication or evidence derived therefrom as the judge determines to be in the interests of justice.

(b) In addition to any other right to appeal, the United States shall have the right to appeal from an order granting a motion to suppress made under paragraph (a) of this subsection, or the denial of an application for an order of approval, if the United States attorney shall certify to the judge or other official granting such motion or denying such application that the appeal is not taken for purposes of delay. Such appeal shall be taken within thirty days after the date the order was entered and shall be diligently prosecuted.

(c) The remedies and sanctions described in this chapter with respect to the interception of electronic communications are the only judicial remedies and sanctions for nonconstitutional violations of this chapter involving such communications.

(11) The requirements of subsections (1)(b)(ii) and (3)(d) of this section relating to the specification of the facilities from which, or the place where, the communication is to be intercepted do not apply if -

(a) in the case of an application with respect to the interception of an oral communication -

(i) the application is by a Federal investigative or law enforcement officer and is approved by the Attorney General, the Deputy Attorney General, the Associate Attorney General, an Assistant Attorney General, or an acting Assistant Attorney General;

(ii) the application contains a full and complete statement as to why such specification is not practical and identifies the person committing the offense and whose communications are to be intercepted; and

(iii) the judge finds that such specification is not practical; and

(b) in the case of an application with respect to a wire or electronic communication -

(i) the application is by a Federal investigative or law enforcement officer and is approved by the Attorney General, the Deputy Attorney General, the Associate Attorney General, an Assistant Attorney General, or an acting Assistant Attorney General;

(ii) the application identifies the person believed to be committing the offense and whose communications are to be intercepted and the applicant makes a showing that there is probable cause to believe that the person's actions could have the effect of thwarting interception from a specified facility;

(iii) the judge finds that such showing has been adequately made; and

(iv) the order authorizing or approving the interception is limited to interception only for such time as it is reasonable to presume that the person identified in the application is or was reasonably proximate to the instrument through which such communication will be or was transmitted.

(12) An interception of a communication under an order with respect to which the requirements of subsections (1)(b)(ii) and (3)(d) of this section do not apply by reason of subsection (11)(a) shall not begin until the place where the communication is to be intercepted is ascertained by the person implementing the interception order. A provider of wire or electronic communications service that has received an order as provided for in subsection (11)(b) may move the court to modify or quash the order on the ground that its assistance with respect to the interception cannot be performed in a timely or reasonable fashion. The court, upon notice to the government, shall decide such a motion expeditiously.

Sec. 2519. Reports concerning intercepted wire, oral, or electronic communications

(1) In January of each year, any judge who has issued an order (or an extension thereof) under section 2518 that expired during the preceding year, or who has denied approval of an interception during that year, shall report to the Administrative Office of the United States Courts-

(a) the fact that an order or extension was applied for;

(b) the kind of order or extension applied for (including whether or not the order was an order with respect to which the requirements of sections 2518(1)(b)(ii) and 2518(3)(d) of this title did not apply by reason of section 2518(11) of this title);

(c) the fact that the order or extension was granted as applied for, was modified, or was denied;

(d) the period of interceptions authorized by the order, and the number and duration of any extensions of the order;

(e) the offense specified in the order or application, or extension of an order;

(f) the identity of the applying investigative or law enforcement officer and agency making the application and the person authorizing the application; and

(g) the nature of the facilities from which or the place where communications were to be intercepted.

(2) In March of each year the Attorney General, an Assistant Attorney General specially designated by the Attorney General, or the principal prosecuting attorney of a State, or the principal prosecuting attorney for any political subdivision of a State, shall report to the Administrative Office of the United States Courts-

(a) the information required by paragraphs (a) through (g) of subsection (1) of this section with respect to each application for an order or extension made during the preceding calendar year;

(b) a general description of the interceptions made under such order or extension, including (i) the approximate nature and frequency of incriminating communications intercepted, (ii) the approximate nature and frequency of other communications intercepted, (iii) the approximate number of persons whose communications were intercepted, (iv) the number of orders in which encryption was encountered and whether such encryption prevented law enforcement from obtaining the plain text of communications intercepted pursuant to such order, and (v) the approximate nature, amount, and cost of the manpower and other resources used in the interceptions;

(c) the number of arrests resulting from interceptions made under such order or extension, and the offenses for which arrests were made;

(d) the number of trials resulting from such interceptions;

(e) the number of motions to suppress made with respect to such interceptions, and the number granted or denied;

(f) the number of convictions resulting from such interceptions and the offenses for which the convictions were obtained and a general assessment of the importance of the interceptions; and

(g) the information required by paragraphs (b) through (f) of this subsection with respect to orders or extensions obtained in a preceding calendar year.

(3) In June of each year the Director of the Administrative Office of the United States Courts shall transmit to the Congress a full and complete report concerning the number of applications for orders authorizing or approving the interception of wire, oral, or electronic communications pursuant to this chapter and the number of orders and extensions granted or denied pursuant to this chapter during the preceding calendar year. Such report shall include a summary and analysis of the data required to be filed with the Administrative Office by subsections (1) and (2) of this section. The Director of the Administrative Office of the United States Courts is authorized to issue binding regulations dealing with the content and form of the reports required to be filed by subsections (1) and (2) of this section.

United States
Electronic Communications Privacy Act

Sec. 2520. Recovery of civil damages authorized

(a) In General. - Except as provided in section 2511(2)(a)(ii), any person whose wire, oral, or electronic communication is intercepted, disclosed, or intentionally used in violation of this chapter may in a civil action recover from the person or entity, other than the United States, which engaged in that violation such relief as may be appropriate.

(b) Relief. - In an action under this section, appropriate relief includes -

(1) such preliminary and other equitable or declaratory relief as may be appropriate;

(2) damages under subsection (c) and punitive damages in appropriate cases; and

(3) a reasonable attorney's fee and other litigation costs reasonably incurred.

(c) Computation of Damages. -

(1) In an action under this section, if the conduct in violation of this chapter is the private viewing of a private satellite video communication that is not scrambled or encrypted or if the communication is a radio communication that is transmitted on frequencies allocated under subpart D of part 74 of the rules of the Federal Communications Commission that is not scrambled or encrypted and the conduct is not for a tortious or illegal purpose or for purposes of direct or indirect commercial advantage or private commercial gain, then the court shall assess damages as follows:

(A) If the person who engaged in that conduct has not previously been enjoined under section 2511(5) and has not been found liable in a prior civil action under this section, the court shall assess the greater of the sum of actual damages suffered by the plaintiff, or statutory damages of not less than $50 and not more than $500.

(B) If, on one prior occasion, the person who engaged in that conduct has been enjoined under section 2511(5) or has been found liable in a civil action under this section, the court shall assess the greater of the sum of actual damages suffered by the plaintiff, or statutory damages of not less than $100 and not more than $1000.

(2) In any other action under this section, the court may assess as damages whichever is the greater of -

(A) the sum of the actual damages suffered by the plaintiff and any profits made by the violator as a result of the violation; or

(B) statutory damages of whichever is the greater of $100 a day for each day of violation or $10,000.

(d) Defense. - A good faith reliance on -

(1) a court warrant or order, a grand jury subpoena, a legislative authorization, or a statutory authorization;

(2) a request of an investigative or law enforcement officer under section 2518(7) of this title; or

(3) a good faith determination that section 2511(3), 2511(2)(i), or 2511(2)(j) of this title permitted the conduct complained of;

is a complete defense against any civil or criminal action brought under this chapter or any other law.

(e) Limitation. - A civil action under this section may not be commenced later than two years after the date upon which the claimant first has a reasonable opportunity to discover the violation.

(f) Administrative Discipline. - If a court or appropriate department or agency determines that the United States or any of its departments or agencies has violated any provision of this chapter, and the court or appropriate department or agency finds that the circumstances surrounding the violation raise serious questions about whether or not an officer or employee of the United States acted willfully or intentionally with respect to the violation, the department or agency shall, upon receipt of a true and correct copy of the decision and findings of the court or appropriate department or agency promptly initiate a proceeding to determine whether disciplinary action against the officer or employee is warranted. If the head of the department or agency involved determines that disciplinary action is not warranted, he or she shall notify the Inspector General with jurisdiction over the department or agency concerned and shall provide the Inspector General with the reasons for such determination.

(g) Improper Disclosure is Violation. - Any willful disclosure or use by an investigative or law enforcement officer or governmental entity of information beyond the extent permitted by section 2517 is a violation of this chapter for purposes of section 2520(a).

Sec. 2521. Injunction against illegal interception

Whenever it shall appear that any person is engaged or is about to engage in any act which constitutes or will constitute a felony violation of this chapter, the Attorney General may initiate a civil action in a district court of the United States to enjoin such violation. The court shall proceed as soon as practicable to the hearing and determination of such an action, and may, at any time before final determination, enter such a restraining order or prohibition, or take such other action, as is warranted to prevent a continuing and substantial injury to the United States or to any person or class of persons for whose protection the action is brought. A proceeding under this section is governed by the Federal Rules of Civil Procedure, except that, if an indictment has been returned against the respondent, discovery is governed by the Federal Rules of Criminal Procedure.

Sec. 2522. Enforcement of the Communications Assistance for Law Enforcement Act

(a) Enforcement by Court Issuing Surveillance Order. - If a court authorizing an interception under this chapter, a State statute, or the Foreign Intelligence Surveillance Act of 1978 (50 U.S.C. 1801 et seq.) or authorizing use of a pen register or a trap and trace device under chapter 206 or a State statute finds that a telecommunications carrier has failed to comply with the requirements of the Communications Assistance for Law Enforcement Act, the court may, in accordance with section 108 of such Act, direct that the carrier comply forthwith and may direct that a provider of support services to the carrier or the manufacturer of the carrier's transmission or switching equipment furnish forthwith modifications necessary for the carrier to comply.

(b) Enforcement Upon Application by Attorney General. - The Attorney General may, in a civil action in the appropriate United States district court, obtain an order, in accordance with section 108 of the Communications Assistance for Law Enforcement Act, directing that a telecommunications carrier, a manufacturer of telecommunications transmission or switching equipment, or a provider of telecommunications support services comply with such Act.

(c) Civil Penalty. -

(1) In general. - A court issuing an order under this section against a telecommunications carrier, a manufacturer of telecommunications transmission or switching equipment, or a provider of telecommunications support services may impose a civil penalty of up to $10,000 per day for each day in violation after the issuance of the order or after such future date as the court may specify.

(2) Considerations. - In determining whether to impose a civil penalty and in determining its amount, the court shall take into account -

(A) the nature, circumstances, and extent of the violation;

(B) the violator's ability to pay, the violator's good faith efforts to comply in a timely manner, any effect on the violator's ability to continue to do business, the degree of culpability, and the length of any delay in undertaking efforts to comply; and

(C) such other matters as justice may require.

(d) Definitions. - As used in this section, the terms defined in section 102 of the Communications Assistance for Law Enforcement Act have the meanings provided, respectively, in such section.

Sec. 2523. Executive agreements on access to data by foreign governments

(a) Definitions.—In this section—

(1) the term "lawfully admitted for permanent residence" has the meaning given the term in section 101(a) of the Immigration and Nationality Act (8 U.S.C. 1101(a)); and

(2) the term "United States person" means a citizen or national of the United States, an alien lawfully admitted for permanent residence, an unincorporated association a substantial number of members of which are citizens of the United States or aliens lawfully admitted for permanent residence, or a corporation that is incorporated in the United States.

(b) Executive agreement requirements.—For purposes of this chapter, chapter 121, and chapter 206, an executive agreement governing access by a foreign government to data subject to this chapter, chapter 121, or chapter 206 shall be considered to satisfy the requirements of this section if the Attorney General, with the concurrence of the Secretary of State, determines, and submits a written certification of such determination to Congress, including a written certification and explanation of each consideration in paragraphs (1), (2), (3), and (4), that—

(1) the domestic law of the foreign government, including the implementation of that law, affords robust substantive and procedural protections for privacy and civil liberties in light of the data collection and activities of the foreign government that will be subject to the agreement, if—

(A) such a determination under this section takes into account, as appropriate, credible information and expert input; and

(B) the factors to be met in making such a determination include whether the foreign government—

(i) has adequate substantive and procedural laws on cybercrime and electronic evidence, as demonstrated by being a party to the Convention on Cybercrime, done at Budapest November 23, 2001, and entered into force January 7, 2004, or through domestic laws that are consistent with definitions and the requirements set forth in chapters I and II of that Convention;

(ii) demonstrates respect for the rule of law and principles of nondiscrimination;

(iii) adheres to applicable international human rights obligations and commitments or demonstrates respect for international universal human rights, including—

(I) protection from arbitrary and unlawful interference with privacy;

(II) fair trial rights;

(III) freedom of expression, association, and peaceful assembly;

(IV) prohibitions on arbitrary arrest and detention; and

(V) prohibitions against torture and cruel, inhuman, or degrading treatment or punishment;

(iv) has clear legal mandates and procedures governing those entities of the foreign government that are authorized to seek data under the executive agreement, including procedures through which those authorities collect, retain, use, and share data, and effective oversight of these activities;

(v) has sufficient mechanisms to provide accountability and appropriate transparency regarding the collection and use of electronic data by the foreign government; and

(vi) demonstrates a commitment to promote and protect the global free flow of information and the open, distributed, and interconnected nature of the Internet;

(2) the foreign government has adopted appropriate procedures to minimize the acquisition, retention, and dissemination of information concerning United States persons subject to the agreement;

(3) the terms of the agreement shall not create any obligation that providers be capable of decrypting data or limitation that prevents providers from decrypting data; and

(4) the agreement requires that, with respect to any order that is subject to the agreement—

(A) the foreign government may not intentionally target a United States person or a person located in the United States, and shall adopt targeting procedures designed to meet this requirement;

(B) the foreign government may not target a non-United States person located outside the United States if the purpose is to obtain information concerning a United States person or a person located in the United States;

(C) the foreign government may not issue an order at the request of or to obtain information to provide to the United States Government or a third-party government, nor shall the foreign government be required to share any information produced with the United States Government or a third-party government;

(D) an order issued by the foreign government—

(i) shall be for the purpose of obtaining information relating to the prevention, detection, investigation, or prosecution of serious crime, including terrorism;

(ii) shall identify a specific person, account, address, or personal device, or any other specific identifier as the object of the order;

(iii) shall be in compliance with the domestic law of that country, and any obligation for a provider of an electronic communications service or a remote computing service to produce data shall derive solely from that law;

(iv) shall be based on requirements for a reasonable justification based on articulable and credible facts, particularity, legality, and severity regarding the conduct under investigation;

(v) shall be subject to review or oversight by a court, judge, magistrate, or other independent authority prior to, or in proceedings regarding, enforcement of the order; and

(vi) in the case of an order for the interception of wire or electronic communications, and any extensions thereof, shall require that the interception order—

(I) be for a fixed, limited duration; and

(II) may not last longer than is reasonably necessary to accomplish the approved purposes of the order; and

(III) be issued only if the same information could not reasonably be obtained by another less intrusive method;

(E) an order issued by the foreign government may not be used to infringe freedom of speech;

(F) the foreign government shall promptly review material collected pursuant to the agreement and store any unreviewed communications on a secure system accessible only to those persons trained in applicable procedures;

(G) the foreign government shall, using procedures that, to the maximum extent possible, meet the definition of minimization procedures in section 101 of the Foreign Intelligence Surveillance Act of 1978 (50 U.S.C. 1801), segregate, seal, or delete, and not disseminate material found not to be information that is, or is necessary to understand or assess the importance of information that is, relevant to the prevention, detection, investigation, or prosecution of serious crime, including terrorism, or necessary to protect against a threat of death or serious bodily harm to any person;

(H) the foreign government may not disseminate the content of a communication of a United States person to United States authorities unless the communication may be disseminated pursuant to subparagraph (G) and relates to significant harm, or the threat thereof, to the United States or United States persons, including crimes involving national security such as terrorism, significant violent crime, child exploitation, transnational organized crime, or significant financial fraud;

(I) the foreign government shall afford reciprocal rights of data access, to include, where applicable, removing restrictions on communications service providers, including providers subject to United States jurisdiction, and thereby allow them to respond to valid legal process sought by a governmental entity (as defined in section 2711) if foreign law would otherwise prohibit communications-service providers from disclosing the data;

(J) the foreign government shall agree to periodic review of compliance by the foreign government with the terms of the agreement to be conducted by the United States Government; and

(K) the United States Government shall reserve the right to render the agreement inapplicable as to any order for which the United States Government concludes the agreement may not properly be invoked.

(c) Limitation on judicial review.—A determination or certification made by the Attorney General under subsection (b) shall not be subject to judicial or administrative review.

(d) Effective date of certification.—

(1) Notice.—Not later than 7 days after the date on which the Attorney General certifies an executive agreement under subsection (b), the Attorney General shall provide notice of the determination under subsection (b) and a copy of the executive agreement to Congress, including—

(A) the Committee on the Judiciary and the Committee on Foreign Relations of the Senate; and

(B) the Committee on the Judiciary and the Committee on Foreign Affairs of the House of Representatives.

(2) Entry into force.—An executive agreement that is determined and certified by the Attorney General to satisfy the requirements of this section shall enter into force not earlier than the date that is 180 days after the date on which notice is provided under paragraph (1), unless Congress enacts a joint resolution of disapproval in accordance with paragraph (4).

(3) Requests for information.—Upon request by the Chairman or Ranking Member of a congressional committee described in paragraph (1), the head of an agency shall promptly furnish a summary of factors considered in determining that the foreign government satisfies the requirements of this section.

(4) Congressional review.—

(A) Joint resolution defined.—In this paragraph, the term "joint resolution" means only a joint resolution—

(i) introduced during the 180-day period described in paragraph (2);

(ii) which does not have a preamble;

(iii) the title of which is as follows: "Joint resolution disapproving the executive agreement signed by the United States and _____.", the blank space being appropriately filled in; and

(iv) the matter after the resolving clause of which is as follows: "That Congress disapproves the executive agreement governing access by _____ to certain electronic data as submitted by the Attorney General on _____", the blank spaces being appropriately filled in.

(B) Joint resolution enacted.—Notwithstanding any other provision of this section, if not later than 180 days after the date on which notice is provided to Congress under paragraph (1), there is enacted into law a joint resolution disapproving of an executive agreement under this section, the executive agreement shall not enter into force.

(C) Introduction.—During the 180-day period described in subparagraph (B), a joint resolution of disapproval may be introduced—

(i) in the House of Representatives, by the majority leader or the minority leader; and

(ii) in the Senate, by the majority leader (or the majority leader's designee) or the minority leader (or the minority leader's designee).

(5) Floor consideration in house of representatives.—If a committee of the House of Representatives to which a joint resolution of disapproval has been referred has not reported the joint resolution within 120 days after the date of referral, that committee shall be discharged from further consideration of the joint resolution.

(6) Consideration in the Senate.—

(A) Committee Referral.—A joint resolution of disapproval introduced in the Senate shall be referred jointly—

(i) to the Committee on the Judiciary; and

(ii) to the Committee on Foreign Relations.

(B) Reporting and discharge.—If a committee to which a joint resolution of disapproval was referred has not reported the joint resolution within 120 days after the date of referral of the joint resolution, that committee shall be discharged from further consideration of the joint resolution and the joint resolution shall be placed on the appropriate calendar.

(C) Proceeding to consideration.—It is in order at any time after both the Committee on the Judiciary and the Committee on Foreign Relations report a joint resolution of disapproval to the Senate or have been discharged from consideration of such a joint resolution (even though a previous motion to the same effect has been disagreed to) to move to proceed to the consideration of the joint resolution, and all points of order against the joint resolution (and against consideration of the joint resolution) are waived. The motion is not debatable or subject to a motion to postpone. A motion to reconsider the vote by which the motion is agreed to or disagreed to shall not be in order.

(D) Consideration in the Senate.—In the Senate, consideration of the joint resolution, and on all debatable motions and appeals in connection therewith, shall be limited to not more than 10 hours, which shall be divided equally between those favoring and those opposing the joint resolution. A motion further to limit debate is in order and not debatable. An amendment to, or a motion to postpone, or a motion to proceed to the consideration of other business, or a motion to recommit the joint resolution is not in order.

(E) Consideration of veto messages.—Debate in the Senate of any veto message with respect to a joint resolution of disapproval, including all debatable motions and appeals in connection with the joint resolution, shall be limited to 10 hours, to be equally divided between, and controlled by, the majority leader and the minority leader or their designees.

(7) Rules relating to Senate and House of Representatives.—

(A) Treatment of Senate joint resolution in House.—In the House of Representatives, the following procedures shall apply to a joint resolution of disapproval received from the Senate (unless the House has already passed a joint resolution relating to the same proposed action):

(i) The joint resolution shall be referred to the appropriate committees.

(ii) If a committee to which a joint resolution has been referred has not reported the joint resolution within 7 days after the date of referral, that committee shall be discharged from further consideration of the joint resolution

(iii) Beginning on the third legislative day after each committee to which a joint resolution has been referred reports the joint resolution to the House or has been discharged from further consideration thereof, it shall be in order to move to proceed to consider the joint resolution in the House. All points of order against the motion are waived. Such a motion shall not be in order after the House has disposed of a motion to proceed on the joint resolution. The previous question shall be considered as ordered on the motion to its adoption without intervening motion. The motion shall not be debatable. A motion to reconsider the vote by which the motion is disposed of shall not be in order.

(iv) The joint resolution shall be considered as read. All points of order against the joint resolution and against its consideration are waived. The previous question shall be considered as ordered on the joint resolution to final passage without intervening motion except 2 hours of debate equally divided and controlled by the sponsor of the joint resolution (or a designee) and an opponent. A motion to reconsider the vote on passage of the joint resolution shall not be in order.

(B) Treatment of House joint resolution in Senate.—

(i) If, before the passage by the Senate of a joint resolution of disapproval, the Senate receives an identical joint resolution from the House of Representatives, the following procedures shall apply:

(I) That joint resolution shall not be referred to a committee.

(II) With respect to that joint resolution—

(aa) the procedure in the Senate shall be the same as if no joint resolution had been received from the House of Representatives; but

(bb) the vote on passage shall be on the joint resolution from the House of

(ii) If, following passage of a joint resolution of disapproval in the Senate, the Senate receives an identical joint resolution from the House of

Representatives, that joint resolution shall be placed on the appropriate Senate calendar.

(iii) If a joint resolution of disapproval is received from the House, and no companion joint resolution has been introduced in the Senate, the Senate procedures under this subsection shall apply to the House joint resolution.

(C) Application to revenue measures.—The provisions of this paragraph shall not apply in the House of Representatives to a joint resolution of disapproval that is a revenue measure.

(8) Rules of House of Representatives and Senate.—This subsection is enacted by Congress—

(A) as an exercise of the rulemaking power of the Senate and the House of Representatives, respectively, and as such is deemed a part of the rules of each House, respectively, and supersedes other rules only to the extent that it is inconsistent with such rules; and

(B) with full recognition of the constitutional right of either House to change the rules (so far as relating to the procedure of that House) at any time, in the same manner, and to the same extent as in the case of any other rule of that House.

(e) Renewal of determination.—

(1) In general.—The Attorney General, with the concurrence of the Secretary of State, shall review and may renew a determination under subsection (b) every 5 years.

(2) Report.—Upon renewing a determination under subsection (b), the Attorney General shall file a report with the Committee on the Judiciary and the Committee on Foreign Relations of the Senate and the Committee on the Judiciary and the Committee on Foreign Affairs of the House of Representatives describing—

(A) the reasons for the renewal;

(B) any substantive changes to the agreement or to the relevant laws or procedures of the foreign government since the original determination or, in the case of a second or subsequent renewal, since the last renewal; and

(C) how the agreement has been implemented and what problems or controversies, if any, have arisen as a result of the agreement or its implementation.

(3) Nonrenewal.—If a determination is not renewed under paragraph (1), the agreement shall no longer be considered to satisfy the requirements of this section.

(f) Revisions to agreement.—A revision to an agreement under this section shall be treated as a new agreement for purposes of this section and shall be subject to the certification requirement under subsection (b), and to the procedures under subsection (d), except that for purposes of a revision to an agreement—

(1) the applicable time period under paragraphs (2), (4)(A)(i), (4)(B), and (4)(C) of subsection (d) shall be 90 days after the date notice is provided under subsection (d)(1); and

(2) the applicable time period under paragraphs (5) and (6)(B) of subsection (d) shall be 60 days after the date notice is provided under subsection (d)(1).

(g) Publication.—Any determination or certification under subsection (b) regarding an executive agreement under this section, including any termination or renewal of such an agreement, shall be published in the Federal Register as soon as is reasonably practicable.

(h) Minimization procedures.—A United States authority that receives the content of a communication described in subsection (b)(4)(H) from a foreign government in accordance with an executive agreement under this section shall use procedures that, to the maximum extent possible, meet the definition of minimization procedures in section 101 of the Foreign Intelligence Surveillance Act of 1978 (50 U.S.C. 1801) to appropriately protect nonpublicly available information concerning United States persons.

Sec. 2701. Unlawful access to stored communications

(a) Offense. - Except as provided in subsection (c) of this section whoever -

(1) intentionally accesses without authorization a facility through which an electronic communication service is provided; or

(2) intentionally exceeds an authorization to access that facility; and thereby obtains, alters, or prevents authorized access to a wire or electronic communication while it is in electronic storage in such system shall be punished as provided in subsection (b) of this section.

(b) Punishment. - The punishment for an offense under subsection (a) of this section is-

(1) if the offense is committed for purposes of commercial advantage, malicious destruction or damage, or private commercial gain, or in furtherance of any criminal or tortious act in violation of the Constitution or laws of the United States or any State -

(A) a fine under this title or imprisonment for not more than 5 years, or both, in the case of a first offense under this subparagraph; and

(B) a fine under this title or imprisonment for not more than 10 years, or both, for any subsequent offense under this subparagraph; and

(2) in any other case -

(A) a fine under this title or imprisonment for not more than 1 year or both, in the case of a first offense under this paragraph; and

(B) a fine under this title or imprisonment for not more than 5 years, or both, in the case of an offense under this subparagraph that occurs after a conviction of another offense under this section.

(c) Exceptions. - Subsection (a) of this section does not apply with respect to conduct authorized

(1) by the person or entity providing a wire or electronic communications service;

(2) by a user of that service with respect to a communication of or intended for that user; or

(3) in section 2703, 2704 or 2518 of this title.

Sec. 2702. Voluntary Disclosure of Customer Communications or Records

(a) Prohibitions.-Except as provided in subsection (b) or (c)-

(1) a person or entity providing an electronic communication service to the public shall not knowingly divulge to any person or entity the contents of a communication while in electronic storage by that service; and

(2) a person or entity providing remote computing service to the public shall not knowingly divulge to any person or entity the contents of any communication which is carried or maintained on that service-

(A) on behalf of, and received by means of electronic transmission from (or created by means of computer processing of communications received by means of electronic transmission from), a subscriber or customer of such service;

(B) solely for the purpose of providing storage or computer processing services to such subscriber or customer, if the provider is not authorized to access the contents of any such communications for purposes of providing any services other than storage or computer processing; and

(3) a provider of remote computing service or electronic communication service to the public shall not knowingly divulge a record or other information pertaining to a subscriber to or customer of such service (not including the contents of communications covered by paragraph (1) or (2)) to any governmental entity.

(b) Exceptions for disclosure of communications.-A provider described in subsection (a) may divulge the contents of a communication-

(1) to an addressee or intended recipient of such communication or an agent of such addressee or intended recipient;

(2) as otherwise authorized in section 2517, 2511(2)(a), or 2703 of this title;

(3) with the lawful consent of the originator or an addressee or intended recipient of such communication, or the subscriber in the case of remote computing service;

(4) to a person employed or authorized or whose facilities are used to forward such communication to its destination;

(5) as may be necessarily incident to the rendition of the service or to the protection of the rights or property of the provider of that service;

(6) to the National Center for Missing and Exploited Children, in connection with a report submitted thereto under section 2258A;

(7) to a law enforcement agency-

(A) if the contents-
    (i) were inadvertently obtained by the service provider; and
    (ii) appear to pertain to the commission of a crime; or

[(B) Repealed. Pub. L. 108–21, title V, §508(b)(1)(A), Apr. 30, 2003, 117 Stat. 684]

(8) to a governmental entity, if the provider, in good faith, believes that an emergency involving danger of death or serious physical injury to any person requires disclosure without delay of communications relating to the emergency; or

(9) to a foreign government pursuant to an order from a foreign government that is subject to an executive agreement that the Attorney General has determined and certified to Congress satisfies section 2523.

(c) Exceptions for Disclosure of Customer Records.-A provider described in subsection (a) may divulge a record or other information pertaining to a subscriber to or customer of such service (not including the contents of communications covered by subsection (a)(1) or (a)(2))-

(1) as otherwise authorized in section 2703;

(2) with the lawful consent of the customer or subscriber;

(3) as may be necessarily incident to the rendition of the service or to the protection of the rights or property of the provider of that service;

(4) to a governmental entity, if the provider, in good faith, believes that an emergency involving danger of death or serious physical injury to any person requires disclosure without delay of information relating to the emergency;

(5) to the National Center for Missing and Exploited Children, in connection with a report submitted thereto under section 2258A;

(6) to any person other than a governmental entity; or

(7) to a foreign government pursuant to an order from a foreign government that is subject to an executive agreement that the Attorney General has determined and certified to Congress satisfies section 2523.

(d) Reporting of Emergency Disclosures.-On an annual basis, the Attorney General shall submit to the Committee on the Judiciary of the House of Representatives and the Committee on the Judiciary of the Senate a report containing-

(1) the number of accounts from which the Department of Justice has received voluntary disclosures under subsection (b)(8);

(2) a summary of the basis for disclosure in those instances where-

    (A) voluntary disclosures under subsection (b)(8) were made to the Department of Justice; and

    (B) the investigation pertaining to those disclosures was closed without the filing of criminal charges; and

(3) the number of accounts from which the Department of Justice has received voluntary disclosures under subsection (c)(4).

Sec. 2703. Required Disclosure of Customer Communications or Records

(a) Contents of Wire or Electronic Communications in Electronic Storage.-A governmental entity may require the disclosure by a provider of electronic communication service of the contents of a wire or electronic communication, that is in electronic storage in an electronic communications system for one hundred and eighty days or less, only pursuant to a warrant issued using the procedures described in the Federal Rules of Criminal Procedure (or, in the case of a State court, issued using State warrant procedures and, in the case of a court-martial or other proceeding under chapter 47 of title 10 (the Uniform Code of Military Justice), issued under section 846 of that title, in accordance with regulations prescribed by the President) by a court of competent jurisdiction. A governmental entity may require the disclosure by a provider of electronic communications services of the contents of a wire or electronic communication that has been in electronic storage in an electronic communications system for more than one hundred and eighty days by the means available under subsection (b) of this section.

(b) Contents of Wire or Electronic Communications in a Remote Computing Service.-

(1) A governmental entity may require a provider of remote computing service to disclose the contents of any wire or electronic communication to which this paragraph is made applicable by paragraph (2) of this subsection-

(A) without required notice to the subscriber or customer, if the governmental entity obtains a warrant issued using the procedures described in the Federal Rules of Criminal Procedure (or, in the case of a State court, issued using State warrant procedures and, in the case of a court-martial or other proceeding under chapter 47 of title 10 (the Uniform Code of Military Justice), issued under section 846 of that title, in accordance with regulations prescribed by the President) by a court of competent jurisdiction; or

(B) with prior notice from the governmental entity to the subscriber or customer if the governmental entity-

(i) uses an administrative subpoena authorized by a Federal or State statute or a Federal or State grand jury or trial subpoena; or

(ii) obtains a court order for such disclosure under subsection (d) of this section;

except that delayed notice may be given pursuant to section 2705 of this title.

(2) Paragraph (1) is applicable with respect to any wire or electronic communication that is held or maintained on that service-

(A) on behalf of, and received by means of electronic transmission from (or created by means of computer processing of communications received by means of electronic transmission from), a subscriber or customer of such remote computing service; and

(B) solely for the purpose of providing storage or computer processing services to such subscriber or customer, if the provider is not authorized to access the contents of any such communications for purposes of providing any services other than storage or computer processing.

(c) Records Concerning Electronic Communication Service or Remote Computing Service.-

(1) A governmental entity may require a provider of electronic communication service or remote computing service to disclose a record or other information pertaining to a subscriber to or customer of such service (not including the contents of communications) only when the governmental entity-

(A) obtains a warrant issued using the procedures described in the Federal Rules of Criminal Procedure (or, in the case of a State court, issued using State warrant procedures and, in the case of a court-martial or other proceeding under chapter 47 of title 10 (the Uniform Code of Military Justice), issued under section 846 of that title, in accordance with regulations prescribed by the President) by a court of competent jurisdiction;

(B) obtains a court order for such disclosure under subsection (d) of this section;

(C) has the consent of the subscriber or customer to such disclosure;

(D) submits a formal written request relevant to a law enforcement investigation concerning telemarketing fraud for the name, address, and place of business of a subscriber or customer of such provider, which subscriber or customer is engaged in telemarketing (as such term is defined in section 2325 of this title); or

(E) seeks information under paragraph (2).

(2) A provider of electronic communication service or remote computing service shall disclose to a governmental entity the-

(A) name;

(B) address;

(C) local and long distance telephone connection records, or records of session times and durations;

(D) length of service (including start date) and types of service utilized;

(E) telephone or instrument number or other subscriber number or identity, including any temporarily assigned network address; and

(F) means and source of payment for such service (including any credit card or bank account number),

of a subscriber to or customer of such service when the governmental entity uses an administrative subpoena authorized by a Federal or State statute or a Federal or State grand jury or trial subpoena or any means available under paragraph (1).

(3) A governmental entity receiving records or information under this subsection is not required to provide notice to a subscriber or customer.

(d) Requirements for Court Order.-A court order for disclosure under subsection (b) or (c) may be issued by any court that is a court of competent jurisdiction and shall issue only if the governmental entity offers specific and articulable facts showing that there are reasonable grounds to believe that the contents of a wire or electronic communication, or the records or other information sought, are relevant and material to an ongoing criminal investigation. In the case of a State governmental authority, such a court order shall not issue if prohibited by the law of such State. A court issuing an order pursuant to this section, on a motion made promptly by the service provider, may quash or modify such order, if the information or records requested are unusually voluminous in nature or compliance with such order otherwise would cause an undue burden on such provider.

(e) No Cause of Action Against a Provider Disclosing Information Under This Chapter.-No cause of action shall lie in any court against any provider of wire or electronic communication service, its officers, employees, agents, or other specified persons for providing information, facilities, or assistance in accordance with the terms of a court order, warrant, subpoena, statutory authorization, or certification under this chapter.

(f) Requirement To Preserve Evidence.-

(1) In general.-A provider of wire or electronic communication services or a remote computing service, upon the request of a governmental entity, shall take all necessary steps to preserve records and other evidence in its possession pending the issuance of a court order or other process.

(2) Period of retention.-Records referred to in paragraph (1) shall be retained for a period of 90 days, which shall be extended for an additional 90-day period upon a renewed request by the governmental entity.

(g) Presence of Officer Not Required.-Notwithstanding section 3105 of this title, the presence of an officer shall not be required for service or execution of a search warrant issued in accordance with this chapter requiring disclosure by a provider of electronic communications service or remote computing service of the contents of communications or records or other information pertaining to a subscriber to or customer of such service.

(h) Comity Analysis and Disclosure of Information Regarding Legal Process Seeking Contents of Wire or Electronic Communication.-

(1) Definitions.-In this subsection-

(A) the term "qualifying foreign government" means a foreign government-

(i) with which the United States has an executive agreement that has entered into force under section 2523; and

(ii) the laws of which provide to electronic communication service providers and remote computing service providers substantive and procedural opportunities similar to those provided under paragraphs (2) and (5); and

(B) the term "United States person" has the meaning given the term in section 2523.

(2) Motions to quash or modify.-

(A) A provider of electronic communication service to the public or remote computing service, including a foreign electronic communication service or remote computing service, that is being required to disclose pursuant to legal process issued under this section the contents of a wire or electronic communication of a subscriber or customer, may file a motion to modify or quash the legal process where the provider reasonably believes-

(i) that the customer or subscriber is not a United States person and does not reside in the United States; and

(ii) that the required disclosure would create a material risk that the provider would violate the laws of a qualifying foreign government.

Such a motion shall be filed not later than 14 days after the date on which the provider was served with the legal process, absent agreement with the government or permission from the court to extend the deadline based on an application made within the 14 days. The right to move to quash is without prejudice to any other grounds to move to quash or defenses thereto, but it shall be the sole basis for moving to quash on the grounds of a conflict of law related to a qualifying foreign government.

(B) Upon receipt of a motion filed pursuant to subparagraph (A), the court shall afford the governmental entity that applied for or issued the legal process under this section the opportunity to respond. The court may modify or quash the legal process, as appropriate, only if the court finds that-

(i) the required disclosure would cause the provider to violate the laws of a qualifying foreign government;

(ii) based on the totality of the circumstances, the interests of justice dictate that the legal process should be modified or quashed; and

(iii) the customer or subscriber is not a United States person and does not reside in the United States.

(3) Comity analysis.-For purposes of making a determination under paragraph (2)(B)(ii), the court shall take into account, as appropriate-

(A) the interests of the United States, including the investigative interests of the governmental entity seeking to require the disclosure;

(B) the interests of the qualifying foreign government in preventing any prohibited disclosure;

(C) the likelihood, extent, and nature of penalties to the provider or any employees of the provider as a result of inconsistent legal requirements imposed on the provider;

(D) the location and nationality of the subscriber or customer whose communications are being sought, if known, and the nature and extent of the subscriber or customer's connection to the United States, or if the legal process has been sought on behalf of a foreign authority pursuant to section 3512, the nature and extent of the subscriber or customer's connection to the foreign authority's country;

(E) the nature and extent of the provider's ties to and presence in the United States;

(F) the importance to the investigation of the information required to be disclosed;

(G) the likelihood of timely and effective access to the information required to be disclosed through means that would cause less serious negative consequences; and

(H) if the legal process has been sought on behalf of a foreign authority pursuant to section 3512, the investigative interests of the foreign authority making the request for assistance.

(4) Disclosure obligations during pendency of challenge.-A service provider shall preserve, but not be obligated to produce, information sought during the pendency of a motion brought under this subsection, unless the court finds that immediate production is necessary to prevent an adverse result identified in section 2705(a)(2).

(5) Disclosure to qualifying foreign government.-

(A) It shall not constitute a violation of a protective order issued under section 2705 for a provider of electronic communication service to the public or remote computing service to disclose to the entity within a qualifying foreign government, designated in an executive agreement under section 2523, the fact of the existence of legal process issued under this section seeking the contents of a wire or electronic communication of a customer or subscriber who is a national or resident of the qualifying foreign government.

(B) Nothing in this paragraph shall be construed to modify or otherwise affect any other authority to make a motion to modify or quash a protective order issued under section 2705.

Sec. 2704. Backup preservation

(a) Backup Preservation. -

(1) A governmental entity acting under section 2703(b)(2) may include in its subpoena or court order a requirement that the service provider to whom the request is directed create a backup copy of the contents of the electronic communications sought in order to preserve those communications. Without notifying the subscriber or customer of such subpoena or court order, such service provider shall create such backup copy as soon as practicable consistent with its regular business practices and shall confirm to the governmental entity that such backup copy has been made. Such backup copy shall be created within two business days after receipt by the service provider of the subpoena or court order.

(2) Notice to the subscriber or customer shall be made by the governmental entity within three days after receipt of such confirmation, unless such notice is delayed pursuant to section 2705(a).

(3) The service provider shall not destroy such backup copy until the later of -

(A) the delivery of the information; or

(B) the resolution of any proceedings (including appeals of any proceeding) concerning the government's subpoena or court order.

(4) The service provider shall release such backup copy to the requesting governmental entity no sooner than fourteen days after the governmental entity's notice to the subscriber or customer if such service provider -

(A) has not received notice from the subscriber or customer that the subscriber or customer has challenged the governmental entity's request; and

(B) has not initiated proceedings to challenge the request of the governmental entity.

(5) A governmental entity may seek to require the creation of a backup copy under subsection (a)(1) of this section if in its sole discretion such entity determines that there is reason to believe that notification under section 2703 of this title of the existence of the subpoena or court order may result in destruction of or tampering with evidence. This determination is not subject to challenge by the subscriber or customer or service provider.

(b) Customer Challenges. -

(1) Within fourteen days after notice by the governmental entity to the subscriber or customer under subsection (a)(2) of this section, such subscriber or customer may file a motion to quash such subpoena or vacate such court order, with copies served upon the governmental entity and with written notice of such challenge to the service provider. A motion to vacate a court order shall be filed in the court which issued such order. A motion to quash a subpoena shall be filed in the appropriate United States district court or State court. Such motion or application shall contain an affidavit or sworn statement-

(A) stating that the applicant is a customer or subscriber to the service from which the contents of electronic communications maintained for him have been sought; and

(B) stating the applicant's reasons for believing that the records sought are not relevant to a legitimate law enforcement inquiry or that there has not been substantial compliance with the provisions of this chapter in some other respect.

(2) Service shall be made under this section upon a governmental entity by delivering or mailing by registered or certified mail a copy of the papers to the person, office, or department specified in the notice which the customer has received pursuant to this chapter. For the purposes of this section, the term "delivery" has the meaning given that term in the Federal Rules of Civil Procedure.

(3) If the court finds that the customer has complied with paragraphs (1) and (2) of this subsection, the court shall order the governmental entity to file a sworn response, which may be filed in camera if the governmental entity includes in its response the reasons which make in camera review appropriate. If the court is unable to determine the motion or application on the basis of the parties' initial allegations and response, the court may conduct such additional proceedings as it deems

appropriate. All such proceedings shall be completed and the motion or application decided as soon as practicable after the filing of the governmental entity's response.

(4) If the court finds that the applicant is not the subscriber or customer for whom the communications sought by the governmental entity are maintained, or that there is a reason to believe that the law enforcement inquiry is legitimate and that the communications sought are relevant to that inquiry, it shall deny the motion or application and order such process enforced. If the court finds that the applicant is the subscriber or customer for whom the communications sought by the governmental entity are maintained, and that there is not a reason to believe that the communications sought are relevant to a legitimate law enforcement inquiry, or that there has not been substantial compliance with the provisions of this chapter, it shall order the process quashed.

(5) A court order denying a motion or application under this section shall not be deemed a final order and no interlocutory appeal may be taken therefrom by the customer.

Sec. 2705. Delayed notice

(a) Delay of Notification. -

    (1) A governmental entity acting under section 2703(b) of this title may -

        (A) where a court order is sought, include in the application a request, which the court shall grant, for an order delaying the notification required under section 2703(b) of this title for a period not to exceed ninety days, if the court determines that there is reason to believe that notification of the existence of the court order may have an adverse result described in paragraph (2) of this subsection; or

        (B) where an administrative subpoena authorized by a Federal or State statute or a Federal or State grand jury subpoena is obtained, delay the notification required under section 2703(b) of this title for a period not to exceed ninety days upon the execution of a written certification of a supervisory official that there is reason to believe that notification of the existence of the subpoena may have an adverse result described in paragraph (2) of this subsection.

    (2) An adverse result for the purposes of paragraph (1) of this subsection is -

        (A) endangering the life or physical safety of an individual;

        (B) flight from prosecution;

        (C) destruction of or tampering with evidence;

        (D) intimidation of potential witnesses; or

        (E) otherwise seriously jeopardizing an investigation or unduly delaying a trial.

    (3) The governmental entity shall maintain a true copy of certification under paragraph (1)(B).

(4) Extensions of the delay of notification provided in section 2703 of up to ninety days each may be granted by the court upon application, or by certification by a governmental entity, but only in accordance with subsection (b) of this section.

(5) Upon expiration of the period of delay of notification under paragraph (1) or (4) of this subsection, the governmental entity shall serve upon, or deliver by registered or first-class mail to, the customer or subscriber a copy of the process or request together with notice that -

> (A) states with reasonable specificity the nature of the law enforcement inquiry; and

> (B) informs such customer or subscriber -

>> (i) that information maintained for such customer or subscriber by the service provider named in such process or request was supplied to or requested by that governmental authority and the date on which the supplying or request took place;

>> (ii) that notification of such customer or subscriber was delayed;

>> (iii) what governmental entity or court made the certification or determination pursuant to which that delay was made; and

>> (iv) which provision of this chapter allowed such delay.

(6) As used in this subsection, the term "supervisory official" means the investigative agent in charge or assistant investigative agent in charge or an equivalent of an investigating agency's headquarters or regional office, or the chief prosecuting attorney or the first assistant prosecuting attorney or an equivalent of a prosecuting attorney's headquarters or regional office.

(b) Preclusion of Notice to Subject of Governmental Access. -

A governmental entity acting under section 2703, when it is not required to notify the subscriber or customer under section 2703(b)(1), or to the extent that it may delay such notice pursuant to subsection (a) of this section, may apply to a court for an order commanding a provider of electronic communications service or remote computing service to whom a warrant, subpoena, or court order is directed, for such period as the court deems appropriate, not to notify any other person of the existence of the warrant, subpoena, or court order. The court shall enter such an order if it determines that there is reason to believe that notification of the existence of the warrant, subpoena, or court order will result in -

> (1) endangering the life or physical safety of an individual;

> (2) flight from prosecution;

> (3) destruction of or tampering with evidence;

> (4) intimidation of potential witnesses; or

> (5) otherwise seriously jeopardizing an investigation or unduly delaying a trial.

Sec. 2706. Cost reimbursement

(a) Payment. -

Except as otherwise provided in subsection (c), a governmental entity obtaining the contents of communications, records, or other information under section 2702, 2703, or 2704 of this title shall pay to the person or entity assembling or providing such information a fee for reimbursement for such costs as are reasonably necessary and which have been directly incurred in searching for, assembling, reproducing, or otherwise providing such information. Such reimbursable costs shall include any costs due to necessary disruption of normal operations of any electronic communication service or remote computing service in which such information may be stored.

(b) Amount. -

The amount of the fee provided by subsection (a) shall be as mutually agreed by the governmental entity and the person or entity providing the information, or, in the absence of agreement, shall be as determined by the court which issued the order for production of such information (or the court before which a criminal prosecution relating to such information would be brought, if no court order was issued for production of the information).

(c) Exception. -

The requirement of subsection (a) of this section does not apply with respect to records or other information maintained by a communications common carrier that relate to telephone toll records and telephone listings obtained under section 2703 of this title. The court may, however, order a payment as described in subsection (a) if the court determines the information required is unusually voluminous in nature or otherwise caused an undue burden on the provider.

Sec. 2707. Civil action

(a) Cause of Action. -

Except as provided in section 2703(e), any provider of electronic communication service, subscriber, or other person aggrieved by any violation of this chapter in which the conduct constituting the violation is engaged in with a knowing or intentional state of mind may, in a civil action, recover from the person or entity, other than the United States, which engaged in that violation such relief as may be appropriate.

(b) Relief. - In a civil action under this section, appropriate relief includes -

(1) such preliminary and other equitable or declaratory relief as may be appropriate;

(2) damages under subsection (c); and

(3) a reasonable attorney's fee and other litigation costs reasonably incurred.

(c) Damages. -

The court may assess as damages in a civil action under this section the sum of the actual damages suffered by the plaintiff and any profits made by the violator as a result of the violation, but in no case shall a person entitled to recover receive less than the sum of

$1,000. If the violation is willful or intentional, the court may assess punitive damages. In the case of a successful action to enforce liability under this section, the court may assess the costs of the action, together with reasonable attorney fees determined by the court.

(d) Administrative Discipline. If a court or appropriate department or agency determines that the United States or any of its departments or agencies has violated any provision of this chapter, and the court or appropriate department or agency finds that the circumstances surrounding the violation raise serious questions about whether or not an officer or employee of the United States acted willfully or intentionally with respect to the violation, the department or agency shall, upon receipt of a true and correct copy of the decision and findings of the court or appropriate department or agency promptly initiate a proceeding to determine whether disciplinary action against the officer or employee is warranted. If the head of the department or agency involved determines that disciplinary action is not warranted, he or she shall notify the Inspector General with jurisdiction over the department or agency concerned and shall provide the Inspector General with the reasons for such determination.

(e) Defense. - A good faith reliance on -

(1) a court warrant or order, a grand jury subpoena, a legislative authorization, or a statutory authorization (including a request of a governmental entity under section 2703(f) of this title);

(2) a request of an investigative or law enforcement officer under section 2518(7) of this title; or

(3) a good faith determination that section 2511(3), section 2702(b)(9), or section 2702(c)(7) of this title permitted the conduct complained of;

is a complete defense to any civil or criminal action brought under this chapter or any other law.

(f) Limitation. - A civil action under this section may not be commenced later than two years after the date upon which the claimant first discovered or had a reasonable opportunity to discover the violation.

(g) Improper disclosure. Any willful disclosure of a "record", as that term is defined in section 552a(a) of title 5, United States Code, obtained by an investigative or law enforcement officer, or a governmental entity, pursuant to section 2703 of this title, or from a device installed pursuant to section 3123 or 3125 of this title, that is not a disclosure made in the proper performance of the official functions of the officer or governmental entity making the disclosure, is a violation of this chapter. This provision shall not apply to information previously lawfully disclosed (prior to the commencement of any civil or administrative proceeding under this chapter) to the public by a Federal, State, or local governmental entity or by the plaintiff in a civil action under this chapter.

Sec. 2708. Exclusivity of remedies

The remedies and sanctions described in this chapter are the only judicial remedies and sanctions for nonconstitutional violations of this chapter.

Sec. 2709. Counterintelligence access to telephone toll and transactional records

(a) Duty to Provide.-A wire or electronic communication service provider shall comply with a request for subscriber information and toll billing records information, or electronic communication transactional records in its custody or possession made by the Director of the Federal Bureau of Investigation under subsection (b) of this section.

(b) Required Certification.-The Director of the Federal Bureau of Investigation, or his designee in a position not lower than Deputy Assistant Director at Bureau headquarters or a Special Agent in Charge in a Bureau field office designated by the Director, may, using a term that specifically identifies a person, entity, telephone number, or account as the basis for a request-

(1) request the name, address, length of service, and local and long distance toll billing records of a person or entity if the Director (or his designee) certifies in writing to the wire or electronic communication service provider to which the request is made that the name, address, length of service, and toll billing records sought are relevant to an authorized investigation to protect against international terrorism or clandestine intelligence activities, provided that such an investigation of a United States person is not conducted solely on the basis of activities protected by the first amendment to the Constitution of the United States; and

(2) request the name, address, and length of service of a person or entity if the Director (or his designee) certifies in writing to the wire or electronic communication service provider to which the request is made that the information sought is relevant to an authorized investigation to protect against international terrorism or clandestine intelligence activities, provided that such an investigation of a United States person is not conducted solely upon the basis of activities protected by the first amendment to the Constitution of the United States.

(c) Prohibition of Certain Disclosure.-

(1) Prohibition.-

(A) In general.-If a certification is issued under subparagraph (B) and notice of the right to judicial review under subsection (d) is provided, no wire or electronic communication service provider that receives a request under subsection (b), or officer, employee, or agent thereof, shall disclose to any person that the Federal Bureau of Investigation has sought or obtained access to information or records under this section.

(B) Certification.-The requirements of subparagraph (A) shall apply if the Director of the Federal Bureau of Investigation, or a designee of the Director whose rank shall be no lower than Deputy Assistant Director at Bureau headquarters or a Special Agent in Charge of a Bureau field office, certifies that the absence of a prohibition of disclosure under this subsection may result in-

(i) a danger to the national security of the United States;

(ii) interference with a criminal, counterterrorism, or counterintelligence investigation;

(iii) interference with diplomatic relations; or

(iv) danger to the life or physical safety of any person.

(2) Exception.-

(A) In general.-A wire or electronic communication service provider that receives a request under subsection (b), or officer, employee, or agent thereof, may disclose information otherwise subject to any applicable nondisclosure requirement to-

(i) those persons to whom disclosure is necessary in order to comply with the request;

(ii) an attorney in order to obtain legal advice or assistance regarding the request; or

(iii) other persons as permitted by the Director of the Federal Bureau of Investigation or the designee of the Director.

(B) Application.-A person to whom disclosure is made under subparagraph (A) shall be subject to the nondisclosure requirements applicable to a person to whom a request is issued under subsection (b) in the same manner as the person to whom the request is issued.

(C) Notice.-Any recipient that discloses to a person described in subparagraph (A) information otherwise subject to a nondisclosure requirement shall notify the person of the applicable nondisclosure requirement.

(D) Identification of disclosure recipients.-At the request of the Director of the Federal Bureau of Investigation or the designee of the Director, any person making or intending to make a disclosure under clause (i) or (iii) of subparagraph (A) shall identify to the Director or such designee the person to whom such disclosure will be made or to whom such disclosure was made prior to the request.

(d) Judicial Review.-

(1) In general.-A request under subsection (b) or a nondisclosure requirement imposed in connection with such request under subsection (c) shall be subject to judicial review under section 3511.

(2) Notice.-A request under subsection (b) shall include notice of the availability of judicial review described in paragraph (1).

(e) Dissemination by Bureau.-The Federal Bureau of Investigation may disseminate information and records obtained under this section only as provided in guidelines approved by the Attorney General for foreign intelligence collection and foreign counterintelligence investigations conducted by the Federal Bureau of Investigation, and, with respect to dissemination to an agency of the United States, only if such information is clearly relevant to the authorized responsibilities of such agency.

(f) Requirement That Certain Congressional Bodies Be Informed.-On a semiannual basis the Director of the Federal Bureau of Investigation shall fully inform the Permanent Select Committee on Intelligence of the House of Representatives and the Select Committee on Intelligence of the Senate, and the Committee on the Judiciary of the House of Representatives and the Committee on the Judiciary of the Senate, concerning all requests made under subsection (b) of this section.

(g) Libraries.-A library (as that term is defined in section 213(1) of the Library Services and Technology Act (20 U.S.C. 9122(1)), the services of which include access to the Internet, books, journals, magazines, newspapers, or other similar forms of communication in print or digitally by patrons for their use, review, examination, or circulation, is not a wire or electronic communication service provider for purposes of this section, unless the library is providing the services defined in section 2510(15) ("electronic communication service") of this title.

Sec. 2710. Wrongful disclosure of video tape rental or sale records

(a) Definitions.-For purposes of this section-

(1) the term "consumer" means any renter, purchaser, or subscriber of goods or services from a video tape service provider;

(2) the term "ordinary course of business" means only debt collection activities, order fulfillment, request processing, and the transfer of ownership;

(3) the term "personally identifiable information" includes information which identifies a person as having requested or obtained specific video materials or services from a video tape service provider; and

(4) the term "video tape service provider" means any person, engaged in the business, in or affecting interstate or foreign commerce, of rental, sale, or delivery of prerecorded video cassette tapes or similar audio visual materials, or any person or other entity to whom a disclosure is made under subparagraph (D) or (E) of subsection (b)(2), but only with respect to the information contained in the disclosure.

(b) Video Tape Rental and Sale Records.-

(1) A video tape service provider who knowingly discloses, to any person, personally identifiable information concerning any consumer of such provider shall be liable to the aggrieved person for the relief provided in subsection (d).

(2) A video tape service provider may disclose personally identifiable information concerning any consumer-

(A) to the consumer;

(B) to any person with the informed, written consent (including through an electronic means using the Internet) of the consumer that-

    (i) is in a form distinct and separate from any form setting forth other legal or financial obligations of the consumer;

    (ii) at the election of the consumer-

    (I) is given at the time the disclosure is sought; or

    (II) is given in advance for a set period of time, not to exceed 2 years or until consent is withdrawn by the consumer, whichever is sooner; and

    (iii) the video tape service provider has provided an opportunity, in a clear and conspicuous manner, for the consumer to withdraw on a case-by-case basis or to withdraw from ongoing disclosures, at the consumer's election;

(C) to a law enforcement agency pursuant to a warrant issued under the Federal Rules of Criminal Procedure, an equivalent State warrant, a grand jury subpoena, or a court order;

(D) to any person if the disclosure is solely of the names and addresses of consumers and if-

    (i) the video tape service provider has provided the consumer with the opportunity, in a clear and conspicuous manner, to prohibit such disclosure; and

    (ii) the disclosure does not identify the title, description, or subject matter of any video tapes or other audio visual material; however, the subject matter of such materials may be disclosed if the disclosure is for the exclusive use of marketing goods and services directly to the consumer;

(E) to any person if the disclosure is incident to the ordinary course of business of the video tape service provider; or

(F) pursuant to a court order, in a civil proceeding upon a showing of compelling need for the information that cannot be accommodated by any other means, if-

    (i) the consumer is given reasonable notice, by the person seeking the disclosure, of the court proceeding relevant to the issuance of the court order; and

    (ii) the consumer is afforded the opportunity to appear and contest the claim of the person seeking the disclosure.

If an order is granted pursuant to subparagraph (C) or (F), the court shall impose appropriate safeguards against unauthorized disclosure.

(3) Court orders authorizing disclosure under subparagraph (C) shall issue only with prior notice to the consumer and only if the law enforcement agency shows that there is probable cause to believe that the records or other information sought are relevant to a legitimate law enforcement inquiry. In the case of a State government authority, such a court order shall not issue if prohibited by the law of such State. A

court issuing an order pursuant to this section, on a motion made promptly by the video tape service provider, may quash or modify such order if the information or records requested are unreasonably voluminous in nature or if compliance with such order otherwise would cause an unreasonable burden on such provider.

(c) Civil Action.-

(1) Any person aggrieved by any act of a person in violation of this section may bring a civil action in a United States district court.

(2) The court may award-

(A) actual damages but not less than liquidated damages in an amount of $2,500;

(B) punitive damages;

(C) reasonable attorneys' fees and other litigation costs reasonably incurred; and

(D) such other preliminary and equitable relief as the court determines to be appropriate.

(3) No action may be brought under this subsection unless such action is begun within 2 years from the date of the act complained of or the date of discovery.

(4) No liability shall result from lawful disclosure permitted by this section.

(d) Personally Identifiable Information.-Personally identifiable information obtained in any manner other than as provided in this section shall not be received in evidence in any trial, hearing, arbitration, or other proceeding in or before any court, grand jury, department, officer, agency, regulatory body, legislative committee, or other authority of the United States, a State, or a political subdivision of a State.

(e) Destruction of Old Records.-A person subject to this section shall destroy personally identifiable information as soon as practicable, but no later than one year from the date the information is no longer necessary for the purpose for which it was collected and there are no pending requests or orders for access to such information under subsection (b)(2) or (c)(2) or pursuant to a court order.

(f) Preemption.-The provisions of this section preempt only the provisions of State or local law that require disclosure prohibited by this section.

Sec. 2711. Definitions for chapter

As used in this chapter-

(1) the terms defined in section 2510 of this title have, respectively, the definitions given such terms in that section;

(2) the term "remote computing service" means the provision to the public of computer storage or processing services by means of an electronic communications system;

(3) the term "court of competent jurisdiction" includes-

(A) any district court of the United States (including a magistrate judge of such a court) or any United States court of appeals that-

(i) has jurisdiction over the offense being investigated;

(ii) is in or for a district in which the provider of a wire or electronic communication service is located or in which the wire or electronic communications, records, or other information are stored; or

(iii) is acting on a request for foreign assistance pursuant to section 3512 of this title;

(B) a court of general criminal jurisdiction of a State authorized by the law of that State to issue search warrants; or

(C) a court-martial or other proceeding under chapter 47 of title 10 (the Uniform Code of Military Justice) to which a military judge has been detailed; and

(4) the term "governmental entity" means a department or agency of the United States or any State or political subdivision thereof.

Sec. 2712. Civil actions against the United States

(a) In general.—Any person who is aggrieved by any willful violation of this chapter or of chapter 119 of this title or of sections 106(a), 305(a), or 405(a) of the Foreign Intelligence Surveillance Act of 1978 (50 U.S.C. 1801 et seq.) may commence an action in United States District Court against the United States to recover money damages. In any such action, if a person who is aggrieved successfully establishes such a violation of this chapter or of chapter 119 of this title or of the above specific provisions of title 50, the Court may assess as damages—

(1) actual damages, but not less than $10,000, whichever amount is greater; and

(2) litigation costs, reasonably incurred.

(b) Procedures.—

(1) Any action against the United States under this section may be commenced only after a claim is presented to the appropriate department or agency under the procedures of the Federal Tort Claims Act, as set forth in title 28, United States Code.

(2) Any action against the United States under this section shall be forever barred unless it is presented in writing to the appropriate Federal agency within 2 years after such claim accrues or unless action is begun within 6 months after the date of mailing, by certified or registered mail, of notice of final denial of the claim by the agency to which it was presented. The claim shall accrue on the date upon which the claimant first has a reasonable opportunity to discover the violation.

(3) Any action under this section shall be tried to the court without a jury.

(4) Notwithstanding any other provision of law, the procedures set forth in section 106(f), 305(g), or 405(f) of the Foreign Intelligence Surveillance Act of 1978 (50 U.S.C. 1801 et seq.) shall be the exclusive means by which materials governed by those sections may be reviewed.

(5) An amount equal to any award against the United States under this section shall be reimbursed by the department or agency concerned to the fund described in

section 1304 of title 31, United States Code, out of any appropriation, fund, or other account (excluding any part of such appropriation, fund, or account that is available for the enforcement of any Federal law) that is available for the operating expenses of the department or agency concerned.

(c) Administrative discipline.—If a court or appropriate department or agency determines that the United States or any of its departments or agencies has violated any provision of this chapter, and the court or appropriate department or agency finds that the circumstances surrounding the violation raise serious questions about whether or not an officer or employee of the United States acted willfully or intentionally with respect to the violation, the department or agency shall, upon receipt of a true and correct copy of the decision and findings of the court or appropriate department or agency promptly initiate a proceeding to determine whether disciplinary action against the officer or employee is warranted. If the head of the department or agency involved determines that disciplinary action is not warranted, he or she shall notify the Inspector General with jurisdiction over the department or agency concerned and shall provide the Inspector General with the reasons for such determination.

(d) Exclusive remedy.—Any action against the United States under this subsection shall be the exclusive remedy against the United States for any claims within the purview of this section.

(e) Stay of proceedings.—

(1) Upon the motion of the United States, the court shall stay any action commenced under this section if the court determines that civil discovery will adversely affect the ability of the Government to conduct a related investigation or the prosecution of a related criminal case. Such a stay shall toll the limitations periods of paragraph (2) of subsection (b).

(2) In this subsection, the terms "related criminal case" and "related investigation" mean an actual prosecution or investigation in progress at the time at which the request for the stay or any subsequent motion to lift the stay is made. In determining whether an investigation or a criminal case is related to an action commenced under this section, the court shall consider the degree of similarity between the parties, witnesses, facts, and circumstances involved in the 2 proceedings, without requiring that any one or more factors be identical.

(3) In requesting a stay under paragraph (1), the Government may, in appropriate cases, submit evidence ex parte in order to avoid disclosing any matter that may adversely affect a related investigation or a related criminal case. If the Government makes such an ex parte submission, the plaintiff shall be given an opportunity to make a submission to the court, not ex parte, and the court may, in its discretion, request further information from either party.

United States
Electronic Communications Privacy Act

Sec. 2713. General prohibition on pen register and trap and trace device use; exception

A provider of electronic communication service or remote computing service shall comply with the obligations of this chapter to preserve, backup, or disclose the contents of a wire or electronic communication and any record or other information pertaining to a customer or subscriber within such provider's possession, custody, or control, regardless of whether such communication, record, or other information is located within or outside of the United States.

Sec. 3121. General prohibition on pen register and trap and trace device use; exception

(a) In General. - Except as provided in this section, no person may install or use a pen register or a trap and trace device without first obtaining a court order under section 3123 of this title or under the Foreign Intelligence Surveillance Act of 1978 (50 U.S.C. 1801 et seq.) or an order from a foreign government that is subject to an executive agreement that the Attorney General has determined and certified to Congress satisfies section 2523.

(b) Exception. - The prohibition of subsection (a) does not apply with respect to the use of a pen register or a trap and trace device by a provider of electronic or wire communication service -

(1) relating to the operation, maintenance, and testing of a wire or electronic communication service or to the protection of the rights or property of such provider, or to the protection of users of that service from abuse of service or unlawful use of service; or

(2) to record the fact that a wire or electronic communication was initiated or completed in order to protect such provider, another provider furnishing service toward the completion of the wire communication, or a user of that service, from fraudulent, unlawful or abusive use of service; or (3) where the consent of the user of that service has been obtained.

(c) Limitation. - A government agency authorized to install and use a pen register or trap and trace device under this chapter or under State law shall use technology reasonably available to it that restricts the recording or decoding of electronic or other impulses to the dialing, routing, addressing, and signaling information utilized in the processing and transmitting of wire or electronic communications so as not to include the contents of any wire or electronic communications.

(d) Penalty. - Whoever knowingly violates subsection (a) shall be fined under this title or imprisoned not more than one year, or both.

Sec. 3122. Application for an order for a pen register or a trap and trace device

(a) Application. -

(1) An attorney for the Government may make application for an order or an extension of an order under section 3123 of this title authorizing or approving the

installation and use of a pen register or a trap and trace device under this chapter, in writing under oath or equivalent affirmation, to a court of competent jurisdiction.

(2) Unless prohibited by State law, a State investigative or law enforcement officer may make application for an order or an extension of an order under section 3123 of this title authorizing or approving the installation and use of a pen register or a trap and trace device under this chapter, in writing under oath or equivalent affirmation, to a court of competent jurisdiction of such State.

(b) Contents of Application. - An application under subsection (a) of this section shall include -

(1) the identity of the attorney for the Government or the State law enforcement or investigative officer making the application and the identity of the law enforcement agency conducting the investigation; and

(2) a certification by the applicant that the information likely to be obtained is relevant to an ongoing criminal investigation being conducted by that agency.

Sec. 3123. Issuance of an order for a pen register or a trap and trace device

(a) In general.

(1) Attorney for the Government. Upon an application made under section 3122(a)(1), the court shall enter an ex parte order authorizing the installation and use of a pen register or trap and trace device anywhere within the United States, if the court finds that the attorney for the Government has certified to the court that the information likely to be obtained by such installation and use is relevant to an ongoing criminal investigation. The order, upon service of that order, shall apply to any person or entity providing wire or electronic communication service in the United States whose assistance may facilitate the execution of the order. Whenever such an order is served on any person or entity not specifically named in the order, upon request of such person or entity, the attorney for the Government or law enforcement or investigative officer that is serving the order shall provide written or electronic certification that the order applies to the person or entity being served.

(2) State investigative or law enforcement officer. Upon an application made under section 3122(a)(2), the court shall enter an ex parte order authorizing the installation and use of a pen register or trap and trace device within the jurisdiction of the court, if the court finds that the State law enforcement or investigative officer has certified to the court that the information likely to be obtained by such installation and use is relevant to an ongoing criminal investigation.

(3) (A) Where the law enforcement agency implementing an ex parte order under this subsection seeks to do so by installing and using its own pen register or trap and trace device on a packet-switched data network of a provider of electronic communication service to the public, the agency shall ensure that a record will be maintained which will identify--

(i) any officer or officers who installed the device and any officer or officers who accessed the device to obtain information from the network;

(ii) the date and time the device was installed, the date and time the device was uninstalled, and the date, time, and duration of each time the device is accessed to obtain information;

(iii) the configuration of the device at the time of its installation and any subsequent modification thereof; and

(iv) any information which has been collected by the device.

To the extent that the pen register or trap and trace device can be set automatically to record this information electronically, the record shall be maintained electronically throughout the installation and use of such device.

(B) The record maintained under subparagraph (A) shall be provided ex parte and under seal to the court which entered the ex parte order authorizing the installation and use of the device within 30 days after termination of the order (including any extensions thereof).

(b) Contents of order. An order issued under this section--

    (1) shall specify--

        (A) the identity, if known, of the person to whom is leased or in whose name is listed the telephone line or other facility to which the pen register or trap and trace device is to be attached or applied;

        (B) the identity, if known, of the person who is the subject of the criminal investigation;

        (C) the attributes of the communications to which the order applies, including the number or other identifier and, if known, the location of the telephone line or other facility to which the pen register or trap and trace device is to be attached or applied, and, in the case of an order authorizing installation and use of a trap and trace device under subsection (a)(2), the geographic limits of the order; and

        (D) a statement of the offense to which the information likely to be obtained by the pen register or trap and trace device relates; and

    (2) shall direct, upon the request of the applicant, the furnishing of information, facilities, and technical assistance necessary to accomplish the installation of the pen register or trap and trace device under section 3124 of this title.

(c) Time period and extensions.

    (1) An order issued under this section shall authorize the installation and use of a pen register or a trap and trace device for a period not to exceed sixty days.

    (2) Extensions of such an order may be granted, but only upon an application for an order under section 3122 of this title and upon the judicial finding required by subsection (a) of this section. The period of extension shall be for a period not to exceed sixty days.

(d) Nondisclosure of existence of pen register or a trap and trace device. An order authorizing or approving the installation and use of a pen register or a trap and trace device shall direct that--

(1) the order be sealed until otherwise ordered by the court; and

(2) the person owning or leasing the line or other facility to which the pen register or a trap and trace device is attached, or applied, or who is obligated by the order to provide assistance to the applicant, not disclose the existence of the pen register or trap and trace device or the existence of the investigation to the listed subscriber, or to any other person, unless or until otherwise ordered by the court.

Sec. 3124. Assistance in installation and use of a pen register or a trap and trace device

(a) Pen Registers. - Upon the request of an attorney for the Government or an officer of a law enforcement agency authorized to install and use a pen register under this chapter, a provider of wire or electronic communication service, landlord, custodian, or other person shall furnish such investigative or law enforcement officer forthwith all information, facilities, and technical assistance necessary to accomplish the installation of the pen register unobtrusively and with a minimum of interference with the services that the person so ordered by the court accords the party with respect to whom the installation and use is to take place, if such assistance is directed by a court order as provided in section 3123(b)(2) of this title.

(b) Trap and Trace Device. - Upon the request of an attorney for the Government or an officer of a law enforcement agency authorized to receive the results of a trap and trace device under this chapter, a provider of a wire or electronic communication service, landlord, custodian, or other person shall install such device forthwith on the appropriate line or other facility and shall furnish such investigative or law enforcement officer all additional information, facilities and technical assistance including installation and operation of the device unobtrusively and with a minimum of interference with the services that the person so ordered by the court accords the party with respect to whom the installation and use is to take place, if such installation and assistance is directed by a court order as provided in section 3123(b)(2) of this title. Unless otherwise ordered by the court, the results of the trap and trace device shall be furnished, pursuant to section 3123(b) or section 3125 of this title, to the officer of a law enforcement agency, designated in the court order, at reasonable intervals during regular business hours for the duration of the order.

(c) Compensation. - A provider of a wire or electronic communication service, landlord, custodian, or other person who furnishes facilities or technical assistance pursuant to this section shall be reasonably compensated for such reasonable expenses incurred in providing such facilities and assistance.

(d) No Cause of Action Against a Provider Disclosing Information Under This Chapter. - No cause of action shall lie in any court against any provider of a wire or electronic communication service, its officers, employees, agents, or other specified persons for providing information, facilities, or assistance in accordance with a court order under this chapter, request pursuant to section 3125 of this title, or an order from a foreign government that is subject to an executive agreement that the Attorney General has determined and certified to Congress satisfies section 2523..

(e) Defense. - A good faith reliance on a court order under this chapter, a request pursuant to section 3125 of this title, a legislative authorization, a statutory authorization, or a good faith determination that the conduct complained of was permitted by an order from a foreign government that is subject to executive agreement that the Attorney General has determined and certified to Congress satisfies section 2523, is a complete defense against any civil or criminal action brought under this chapter or any other law.

(f) Communications Assistance Enforcement Orders. - Pursuant to section 2522, an order may be issued to enforce the assistance capability and capacity requirements under the Communications Assistance for Law Enforcement Act.

Sec. 3125. Emergency pen register and trap and trace device installation

(a) Notwithstanding any other provision of this chapter, any investigative or law enforcement officer, specially designated by the Attorney General, the Deputy Attorney General, the Associate Attorney General, any Assistant Attorney General, any acting Assistant Attorney General, or any Deputy Assistant Attorney General, or by the principal prosecuting attorney of any State or subdivision thereof acting pursuant to a statute of that State, who reasonably determines that -

(1) an emergency situation exists that involves -

(A) immediate danger of death or serious bodily injury to any person;

(B) conspiratorial activities characteristic of organized crime;

(C) an immediate threat to a national security interest; or

(D) an ongoing attack on a protected computer (as defined in section 1030) that constitutes a crime punishable by a term of imprisonment greater than one year;

that requires the installation and use of a pen register or a trap and trace device before an order authorizing such installation and use can, with due diligence, be obtained, and

(2) there are grounds upon which an order could be entered under this chapter to authorize such installation and use; may have installed and use a pen register or trap and trace device if, within forty-eight hours after the installation has occurred, or begins to occur, an order approving the installation or use is issued in accordance with section 3123 of this title.

(b) In the absence of an authorizing order, such use shall immediately terminate when the information sought is obtained, when the application for the order is denied or when forty-eight hours have lapsed since the installation of the pen register or trap and trace device, whichever is earlier.

(c) The knowing installation or use by any investigative or law enforcement officer of a pen register or trap and trace device pursuant to subsection (a) without application for the authorizing order within forty-eight hours of the installation shall constitute a violation of this chapter.

(d) A provider of a wire or electronic service, landlord, custodian, or other person who furnished facilities or technical assistance pursuant to this section shall be reasonably compensated for such reasonable expenses incurred in providing such facilities and assistance.

Sec. 3126. Reports concerning pen registers and trap and trace devices

The Attorney General shall annually report to Congress on the number of pen register orders and orders for trap and trace devices applied for by law enforcement agencies of the Department of Justice, which report shall include information concerning--

(1) the period of interceptions authorized by the order, and the number and duration of any extensions of the order;

(2) the offense specified in the order or application, or extension of an order;

(3) the number of investigations involved;

(4) the number and nature of the facilities affected; and

(5) the identity, including district, of the applying investigative or law enforcement agency making the application and the person authorizing the order.

Sec. 3127. Definitions for chapter

As used in this chapter-

(1) the terms "wire communication", "electronic communication", "electronic communication service", and "contents" have the meanings set forth for such terms in section 2510 of this title;

(2) the term "court of competent jurisdiction" means-

(A) any district court of the United States (including a magistrate judge of such a court) or any United States court of appeals that-

(i) has jurisdiction over the offense being investigated;

(ii) is in or for a district in which the provider of a wire or electronic communication service is located;

(iii) is in or for a district in which a landlord, custodian, or other person subject to subsections (a) or (b) of section 3124 of this title is located; or

(iv) is acting on a request for foreign assistance pursuant to section 3512 of this title; or

(B) a court of general criminal jurisdiction of a State authorized by the law of that State to enter orders authorizing the use of a pen register or a trap and trace device;

(3) the term "pen register" means a device or process which records or decodes dialing, routing, addressing, or signaling information transmitted by an instrument or facility from which a wire or electronic communication is transmitted, provided, however, that such information shall not include the contents of any communication, but such term does not include any device or process used by a provider or customer of a wire or electronic communication service for billing, or recording as an incident to billing, for communications services provided by such provider or any device or process used by a provider or customer of a wire communication service for cost accounting or other like purposes in the ordinary course of its business;

(4) the term "trap and trace device" means a device or process which captures the incoming electronic or other impulses which identify the originating number or other dialing, routing, addressing, and signaling information reasonably likely to identify the source of a wire or electronic communication, provided, however, that such information shall not include the contents of any communication;

(5) the term "attorney for the Government" has the meaning given such term for the purposes of the Federal Rules of Criminal Procedure; and

(6) the term "State" means a State, the District of Columbia, Puerto Rico, and any other possession or territory of the United States.

47 U.S.C. Sec. 1001. Definitions

For purposes of this subchapter -

(1) The terms defined in section 2510 of title 18 have, respectively, the meanings stated in that section.

(2) The term "call-identifying information" means dialing or signaling information that identifies the origin, direction, destination, or termination of each communication generated or received by a subscriber by means of any equipment, facility, or service of a telecommunications carrier.

(3) The term "Commission" means the Federal Communications Commission.

(4) The term "electronic messaging services" means software-based services that enable the sharing of data, images, sound, writing, or other information among computing devices controlled by the senders or recipients of the messages.

(5) The term "government" means the government of the United States and any agency or instrumentality thereof, the District of Columbia, any commonwealth, territory, or possession of the United States, and any State or political subdivision thereof authorized by law to conduct electronic surveillance.

(6) The term "information services" –

(A) means the offering of a capability for generating, acquiring, storing, transforming, processing, retrieving, utilizing, or making available information via telecommunications; and (B) includes -

(i) a service that permits a customer to retrieve stored information from, or file information for storage in, information storage facilities;

(ii) electronic publishing; and

(iii) electronic messaging services; but

(C) does not include any capability for a telecommunications carrier's internal management, control, or operation of its telecommunications network.

(7) The term "telecommunications support services" means a product, software, or service used by a telecommunications carrier for the internal signaling or switching functions of its telecommunications network.

(8) The term "telecommunications carrier" -

(A) means a person or entity engaged in the transmission or switching of wire or electronic communications as a common carrier for hire; and

(B) includes -

(i) a person or entity engaged in providing commercial mobile service (as defined in section 332(d) of this title); or

(ii) a person or entity engaged in providing wire or electronic communication switching or transmission service to the extent that the Commission finds that such service is a replacement for a substantial portion of the local telephone exchange service and that it is in the public interest to deem such a person or entity to be a telecommunications carrier for purposes of this subchapter; but

(C) does not include -

(i) persons or entities insofar as they are engaged in providing information services; and

(ii) any class or category of telecommunications carriers that the Commission exempts by rule after consultation with the Attorney General.

Sec. 1002. Assistance capability requirements

(a) Capability requirements

Except as provided in subsections (b), (c), and (d) of this section and sections 1007(a) and 1008(b) and (d) of this title, a telecommunications carrier shall ensure that its equipment, facilities, or services that provide a customer or subscriber with the ability to originate, terminate, or direct communications are capable of -

(1) expeditiously isolating and enabling the government, pursuant to a court order or other lawful authorization, to intercept, to the exclusion of any other communications, all wire and electronic communications carried by the carrier within a service area to or from equipment, facilities, or services of a subscriber of

such carrier concurrently with their transmission to or from the subscriber's equipment, facility, or service, or at such later time as may be acceptable to the government;

(2) expeditiously isolating and enabling the government, pursuant to a court order or other lawful authorization, to access call-identifying information that is reasonably available to the carrier -

(A) before, during, or immediately after the transmission of a wire or electronic communication (or at such later time as may be acceptable to the government); and

(B) in a manner that allows it to be associated with the communication to which it pertains, except that, with regard to information acquired solely pursuant to the authority for pen registers and trap and trace devices (as defined in section 3127 of title 18), such call-identifying information shall not include any information that may disclose the physical location of the subscriber (except to the extent that the location may be determined from the telephone number);

(3) delivering intercepted communications and call-identifying information to the government, pursuant to a court order or other lawful authorization, in a format such that they may be transmitted by means of equipment, facilities, or services procured by the government to a location other than the premises of the carrier; and

(4) facilitating authorized communications interceptions and access to call-identifying information unobtrusively and with a minimum of interference with any subscriber's telecommunications service and in a manner that protects -

(A) the privacy and security of communications and call-identifying information not authorized to be intercepted; and

(B) information regarding the government's interception of communications and access to call-identifying information.

(b) Limitations

(1) Design of features and systems configurations

This subchapter does not authorize any law enforcement agency or officer -

(A) to require any specific design of equipment, facilities, services, features, or system configurations to be adopted by any provider of a wire or electronic communication service, any manufacturer of telecommunications equipment, or any provider of telecommunications support services; or

(B) to prohibit the adoption of any equipment, facility, service, or feature by any provider of a wire or electronic communication service, any manufacturer of telecommunications equipment, or any provider of telecommunications support services.

(2) Information services; private networks and interconnection services and facilities The requirements of subsection (a) of this section do not apply to -

(A) information services; or

(B) equipment, facilities, or services that support the transport or switching of communications for private networks or for the sole purpose of interconnecting telecommunications carriers.

(3) Encryption

A telecommunications carrier shall not be responsible for decrypting, or ensuring the government's ability to decrypt, any communication encrypted by a subscriber or customer, unless the encryption was provided by the carrier and the carrier possesses the information necessary to decrypt the communication.

(c) Emergency or exigent circumstances

In emergency or exigent circumstances (including those described in sections 2518(7) or (11)(b) and 3125 of title 18 and section 1805(e) of title 50), a carrier at its discretion may comply with subsection (a)(3) of this section by allowing monitoring at its premises if that is the only means of accomplishing the interception or access.

(d) Mobile service assistance requirements

A telecommunications carrier that is a provider of commercial mobile service (as defined in section 332(d) of this title) offering a feature or service that allows subscribers to redirect, hand off, or assign their wire or electronic communications to another service area or another service provider or to utilize facilities in another service area or of another service provider shall ensure that, when the carrier that had been providing assistance for the interception of wire or electronic communications or access to call-identifying information pursuant to a court order or lawful authorization no longer has access to the content of such communications or call-identifying information within the service area in which interception has been occurring as a result of the subscriber's use of such a feature or service, information is made available to the government (before, during, or immediately after the transfer of such communications) identifying the provider of a wire or electronic communication service that has acquired access to the communications.

Sec. 1003. Notices of capacity requirements

(a) Notices of maximum and actual capacity requirements

(1) In general

Not later than 1 year after October 25, 1994, after consulting with State and local law enforcement agencies, telecommunications carriers, providers of telecommunications support services, and manufacturers of telecommunications equipment, and after notice and comment, the Attorney General shall publish in the Federal Register and provide to appropriate telecommunications industry associations and standard-setting organizations -

(A) notice of the actual number of communication interceptions, pen registers, and trap and trace devices, representing a portion of the maximum capacity set forth under subparagraph (B), that the Attorney General estimates that government agencies authorized to conduct electronic surveillance may conduct and use simultaneously by the date that is 4 years after October 25, 1994; and

(B) notice of the maximum capacity required to accommodate all of the communication interceptions, pen registers, and trap and trace devices that the Attorney General estimates that government agencies authorized to conduct electronic surveillance may conduct and use simultaneously after the date that is 4 years after October 25, 1994.

(2) Basis of notices

The notices issued under paragraph (1) -

(A) may be based upon the type of equipment, type of service, number of subscribers, type or size or[1] carrier, nature of service area, or any other measure; and

(B) shall identify, to the maximum extent practicable, the capacity require at specific geographic locations.

(b) Compliance with Capacity Notices

(1) Initial capacity

Within 3 years after the publication by the Attorney General of a notice of capacity requirements or within 4 years after October 25, 1994, whichever is longer, a telecommunications carrier shall, subject to subsection (e) of this section, ensure that its systems are capable of -

(A) accommodating simultaneously the number of interceptions, pen registers, and trap and trace devices set forth in the notice under subsection (a)(1)(A) of this section; and

(B) expanding to the maximum capacity set forth in the notice under subsection (a)(1)(B) of this section.

(2) Expansion to maximum capacity

After the date described in paragraph (1), a telecommunications carrier shall, subject to subsection (e) of this section, ensure that it can accommodate expeditiously any increase in the actual number of communication interceptions, pen registers, and trap and trace devices that authorized agencies may seek to conduct and use, up to the maximum capacity requirement set forth in the notice under subsection (a)(1)(B) of this section.

(c) Notices of increased maximum capacity requirements

(1) Notice

The Attorney General shall periodically publish in the Federal Register, after notice and comment, notice of any necessary increases in the maximum capacity requirement set forth in the notice under subsection (a)(1)(B) of this section.

(2) Compliance

---

[1] So in original. Probably should be "of".

Within 3 years after notice of increased maximum capacity requirements is published under paragraph (1), or within such longer time period as the Attorney General may specify, a telecommunications carrier shall, subject to subsection (e) of this section, ensure that its systems are capable of expanding to the increased maximum capacity set forth in the notice.

(d) Carrier statement

Within 180 days after the publication by the Attorney General of a notice of capacity requirements pursuant to subsection (a) or (c) of this section, a telecommunications carrier shall submit to the Attorney General a statement identifying any of its systems or services that do not have the capacity to accommodate simultaneously the number of interceptions, pen registers, and trap and trace devices set forth in the notice under such subsection.

(e) Reimbursement required for compliance

The Attorney General shall review the statements submitted under subsection (d) of this section and may, subject to the availability of appropriations, agree to reimburse a telecommunications carrier for costs directly associated with modifications to attain such capacity requirement that are determined to be reasonable in accordance with section 1008(e) of this title. Until the Attorney General agrees to reimburse such carrier for such modification, such carrier shall be considered to be in compliance with the capacity notices under subsection (a) or (c) of this section.

Sec. 1004. Systems security and integrity

A telecommunications carrier shall ensure that any interception of communications or access to call-identifying information effected within its switching premises can be activated only in accordance with a court order or other lawful authorization and with the affirmative intervention of an individual officer or employee of the carrier acting in accordance with regulations prescribed by the Commission.

Sec. 1005. Cooperation of equipment manufacturers and providers of telecommunications support services

(a) Consultation

A telecommunications carrier shall consult, as necessary, in a timely fashion with manufacturers of its telecommunications transmission and switching equipment and its providers of telecommunications support services for the purpose of ensuring that current and planned equipment, facilities, and services comply with the capability requirements of section 1002 of this title and the capacity requirements identified by the Attorney General under section 1003 of this title.

(b) Cooperation

Subject to sections 1003(e), 1007(a), and 1008(b) and (d) of this title, a manufacturer of telecommunications transmission or switching equipment and a provider of telecommunications support services shall, on a reasonably timely basis and at a reasonable charge, make available to the telecommunications carriers using its equipment, facilities, or services such features or modifications as are necessary to permit such carriers to comply with the capability requirements of section 1002 of this title and the capacity requirements identified by the Attorney General under section 1003 of this title.

Sec. 1006. Technical requirements and standards; extension of compliance date

(a) Safe harbor

(1) Consultation

To ensure the efficient and industry-wide implementation of the assistance capability requirements under section 1002 of this title, the Attorney General, in coordination with other Federal, State, and local law enforcement agencies, shall consult with appropriate associations and standard-setting organizations of the telecommunications industry, with representatives of users of telecommunications equipment, facilities, and services, and with State utility commissions.

(2) Compliance under accepted standards

A telecommunications carrier shall be found to be in compliance with the assistance capability requirements under section 1002 of this title, and a manufacturer of telecommunications transmission or switching equipment or a provider of telecommunications support services shall be found to be in compliance with section 1005 of this title, if the carrier, manufacturer, or support service provider is in compliance with publicly available technical requirements or standards adopted by an industry association or standard-setting organization, or by the Commission under subsection (b) of this section, to meet the requirements of section 1002 of this title.

(3) Absence of standards

The absence of technical requirements or standards for implementing the assistance capability requirements of section 1002 of this title shall not -

(A) preclude a telecommunications carrier, manufacturer, or telecommunications support services provider from deploying a technology or service; or

(B) relieve a carrier, manufacturer, or telecommunications support services provider of the obligations imposed by section 1002 or 1005 of this title, as applicable.

(b) Commission authority

If industry associations or standard-setting organizations fail to issue technical requirements or standards or if a Government agency or any other person believes that such requirements or standards are deficient, the agency or person may petition the Commission to establish, by rule, technical requirements or standards that - (1) meet the assistance capability requirements of section 1002 of this title by cost-effective methods;

(2) protect the privacy and security of communications not authorized to be intercepted;

(3) minimize the cost of such compliance on residential ratepayers;

(4) serve the policy of the United States to encourage the provision of new technologies and services to the public; and

(5) provide a reasonable time and conditions for compliance with and the transition to any new standard, including defining the obligations of telecommunications carriers under section 1002 of this title during any transition period.

(c) Extension of compliance date for equipment, facilities, and services

(1) Petition

A telecommunications carrier proposing to install or deploy, or having installed or deployed, any equipment, facility, or service prior to the effective date of section 1002 of this title may petition the Commission for 1 or more extensions of the deadline for complying with the assistance capability requirements under section 1002 of this title.

(2) Grounds for extension

The Commission may, after consultation with the Attorney General, grant an extension under this subsection, if the Commission determines that compliance with the assistance capability requirements under section 1002 of this title is not reasonably achievable through application of technology available within the compliance period.

(3) Length of extension

An extension under this subsection shall extend for no longer than the earlier of -

(A) the date determined by the Commission as necessary for the carrier to comply with the assistance capability requirements under section 1002 of this title; or

(B) the date that is 2 years after the date on which the extension is granted.

(4) Applicability of extension

An extension under this subsection shall apply to only that part of the carrier's business on which the new equipment, facility, or service is used.

Sec. 1007. Enforcement orders

(a) Grounds for issuance

A court shall issue an order enforcing this subchapter under section 2522 of title 18 only if the court finds that -

(1) alternative technologies or capabilities or the facilities of another carrier are not reasonably available to law enforcement for implementing the interception of communications or access to call-identifying information; and

(2) compliance with the requirements of this subchapter is reasonably achievable through the application of available technology to the equipment, facility, or service at issue or would have been reasonably achievable if timely action had been taken.

(b) Time for compliance

Upon issuing an order enforcing this subchapter, the court shall specify a reasonable time and conditions for complying with its order, considering the good faith efforts to comply in a timely manner, any effect on the carrier's, manufacturer's, or service provider's ability to continue to do business, the degree of culpability or delay in undertaking efforts to comply, and such other matters as justice may require.

(c) Limitations

An order enforcing this subchapter may not -

(1) require a telecommunications carrier to meet the Government's [1] demand for interception of communications and acquisition of call-identifying information to any extent in excess of the capacity for which the Attorney General has agreed to reimburse such carrier;

(2) require any telecommunications carrier to comply with assistance capability requirement [2] of section 1002 of this title if the Commission has determined (pursuant to section 1008(b)(1) of this title) that compliance is not reasonably achievable, unless the Attorney General has agreed (pursuant to section 1008(b)(2) of this title) to pay the costs described in section 1008(b)(2)(A) of this title; or

(3) require a telecommunications carrier to modify, for the purpose of complying with the assistance capability requirements of section 1002 of this title, any equipment, facility, or service deployed on or before January 1, 1995, unless -

(A) the Attorney General has agreed to pay the telecommunications carrier for all reasonable costs directly associated with modifications necessary to bring the equipment, facility, or service into compliance with those requirements; or

(B) the equipment, facility, or service has been replaced or significantly upgraded or otherwise undergoes major modification.

Sec. 1008. Payment of costs of telecommunications carriers to comply with capability requirements

(a) Equipment, facilities, and services deployed on or before January 1, 1995 The Attorney General may, subject to the availability of appropriations, agree to pay telecommunications carriers for all reasonable costs directly associated with the modifications performed by carriers in connection with equipment, facilities, and services installed or deployed on or before January 1, 1995, to establish the capabilities necessary to comply with section 1002 of this title.

(b) Equipment, facilities, and services deployed after January 1, 1995

(1) Determinations of reasonably achievable

The Commission, on petition from a telecommunications carrier or any other interested person, and after notice to the Attorney General, shall determine whether compliance with the assistance capability requirements of section 1002 of this title is reasonably achievable with respect to any equipment, facility, or service installed or deployed after January 1, 1995. The Commission shall make such determination within 1 year after the date such petition is filed. In making such determination, the Commission shall determine whether compliance would impose significant difficulty or expense on the carrier or on the users of the carrier's systems and shall consider the following factors:

(A) The effect on public safety and national security.

(B) The effect on rates for basic residential telephone service.

(C) The need to protect the privacy and security of communications not authorized to be intercepted.

(D) The need to achieve the capability assistance requirements of section 1002 of this title by cost-effective methods.

(E) The effect on the nature and cost of the equipment, facility, or service at issue.

(F) The effect on the operation of the equipment, facility, or service at issue.

(G) The policy of the United States to encourage the provision of new technologies and services to the public. (H) The financial resources of the telecommunications carrier.

(I) The effect on competition in the provision of telecommunications services.

(J) The extent to which the design and development of the equipment, facility, or service was initiated before January 1, 1995.

(K) Such other factors as the Commission determines are appropriate.

(2) Compensation

If compliance with the assistance capability requirements of section 1002 of this title is not reasonably achievable with respect to equipment, facilities, or services deployed after January 1, 1995 -

(A) the Attorney General, on application of a telecommunications carrier, may agree, subject to the availability of appropriations, to pay the telecommunications carrier for the additional reasonable costs of making compliance with such assistance capability requirements reasonably achievable; and

(B) if the Attorney General does not agree to pay such costs, the telecommunications carrier shall be deemed to be in compliance with such capability requirements.

(c) Allocation of funds for payment

The Attorney General shall allocate funds appropriated to carry out this subchapter in accordance with law enforcement priorities determined by the Attorney General.

(d) Failure to make payment with respect to equipment, facilities, and services deployed on or before January 1, 1995 If a carrier has requested payment in accordance with procedures promulgated pursuant to subsection (e) of this section, and the Attorney General has not agreed to pay the telecommunications carrier for all reasonable costs directly associated with modifications necessary to bring any equipment, facility, or service deployed on or before January 1, 1995, into compliance with the assistance capability requirements of section 1002 of this title, such equipment, facility, or service shall be considered to be in compliance with the assistance capability requirements of section 1002 of this title until the equipment, facility, or service is replaced or significantly upgraded or otherwise undergoes major modification.

(e) Cost control regulations

(1) In general

The Attorney General shall, after notice and comment, establish regulations necessary to effectuate timely and cost-efficient payment to telecommunications carriers under this subchapter, under chapters 119 and 121 of title 18, and under the Foreign Intelligence Surveillance Act of 1978 (50 U.S.C. 1801 et seq.).

(2) Contents of regulations

The Attorney General, after consultation with the Commission, shall prescribe regulations for purposes of determining reasonable costs under this subchapter. Such regulations shall seek to minimize the cost to the Federal Government and shall -

(A) permit recovery from the Federal Government of -

(i) the direct costs of developing the modifications described in subsection (a) of this section, of providing the capabilities requested under subsection (b)(2) of this section, or of providing the capacities requested under section 1003(e) of this title, but only to the extent that such costs have not been recovered from any other governmental or nongovernmental entity;

(ii) the costs of training personnel in the use of such capabilities or capacities; and

(iii) the direct costs of deploying or installing such capabilities or capacities;

(B) in the case of any modification that may be used for any purpose other than lawfully authorized electronic surveillance by a law enforcement agency of a government, permit recovery of only the incremental cost of making the modification suitable for such law enforcement purposes; and

(C) maintain the confidentiality of trade secrets.

(3) Submission of claims

Such regulations shall require any telecommunications carrier that the Attorney General has agreed to pay for modifications pursuant to this section and that has installed or deployed such modification to submit to the Attorney General a claim for payment that contains or is accompanied by such information as the Attorney General may require.

Sec. 1009. Authorization of appropriations

There are authorized to be appropriated to carry out this subchapter a total of $500,000,000 for fiscal years 1995, 1996, 1997, and 1998. Such sums are authorized to remain available until expended.

Sec. 1010. Reports

(a) Reports by Attorney General

(1) In general

On or before November 30, 1995, and on or before November 30 of each year thereafter, the Attorney General shall submit to Congress and make available to the public a report on the amounts paid during the preceding fiscal year to telecommunications carriers under sections 1003(e) and 1008 of this title.

(2) Contents

A report under paragraph (1) shall include -

(A) a detailed accounting of the amounts paid to each carrier and the equipment, facility, or service for which the amounts were paid; and

(B) projections of the amounts expected to be paid in the current fiscal year, the carriers to which payment is expected to be made, and the equipment, facilities, or services for which payment is expected to be made.

(b) Reports by Comptroller General and Inspector General

(1) On or before April 1, 1996, the Comptroller General of the United States, and every two years thereafter, the Inspector General of the Department of Justice, shall submit to the Congress a report, after consultation with the Attorney General and the telecommunications industry -

(A) describing the type of equipment, facilities, and services that have been brought into compliance under this subchapter; and

(B) reflecting its analysis of the reasonableness and cost-effectiveness of the payments made by the Attorney General to telecommunications carriers for modifications necessary to ensure compliance with this subchapter.

(2) Compliance cost estimates. - A report under paragraph (1) shall include findings and conclusions on the costs to be incurred by telecommunications carriers to comply with the assistance capability requirements of section 1002 of this title after the effective date of such section 1002 of this title, including projections of the amounts expected to be incurred and a description of the equipment, facilities, or services for which they are expected to be incurred.

Sec. 1021. Department of Justice Telecommunications Carrier Compliance Fund

(a) Establishment of Fund

There is hereby established in the United States Treasury a fund to be known as the Department of Justice Telecommunications Carrier Compliance Fund (hereafter referred to as "the Fund"), which shall be available without fiscal year limitation to the Attorney General for making payments to telecommunications carriers, equipment manufacturers, and providers of telecommunications support services pursuant to section 1008 of this title.

(b) Deposits to Fund

Notwithstanding any other provision of law, any agency of the United States with law enforcement or intelligence responsibilities may deposit as offsetting collections to the Fund any unobligated balances that are available until expended, upon compliance with any Congressional notification requirements for reprogrammings of funds applicable to the appropriation from which the deposit is to be made.

(c) Termination

(1) The Attorney General may terminate the Fund at such time as the Attorney General determines that the Fund is no longer necessary.

(2) Any balance in the Fund at the time of its termination shall be deposited in the General Fund of the Treasury.

(3) A decision of the Attorney General to terminate the Fund shall not be subject to judicial review.

(d) Availability of funds for expenditure

Funds shall not be available for obligation unless an implementation plan as set forth in subsection (e) of this section is submitted to each member of the Committees on the Judiciary and Appropriations of both the House of Representatives and the Senate and the Congress does not by law block or prevent the obligation of such funds. Such funds shall be treated as a reprogramming of funds under section 605 of the Department of Commerce, Justice, and State, the Judiciary, and Related Agencies Appropriations Act, 1997, and shall not be available for obligation or expenditure except in compliance with the procedures set forth in that section and this section.

(e) Implementation plan

The implementation plan shall include:

(1) the law enforcement assistance capability requirements and an explanation of law enforcement's recommended interface;

(2) the proposed actual and maximum capacity requirements for the number of simultaneous law enforcement communications intercepts, pen registers, and trap and trace devices that authorized law enforcement agencies may seek to conduct, set forth on a county-by-county basis for wireline services and on a market service area basis for wireless services, and the historical baseline of electronic surveillance activity upon which such capacity requirements are based;

(3) a prioritized list of carrier equipment, facilities, and services deployed on or before January 1, 1995, to be modified by carriers at the request of law enforcement based on its investigative needs;

(4) a projected reimbursement plan that estimates the cost for the coming fiscal year and for each fiscal year thereafter, based on the prioritization of law enforcement needs as outlined in (3),[1] of modification by carriers of equipment, facilities and services, installed on or before January 1, 1995.

---

[1] So in original. Probably should be "paragraph (3),".

(f) Annual report to Congress

The Attorney General shall submit to the Congress each year a report specifically detailing all deposits and expenditures made pursuant to subchapter I of this chapter in each fiscal year. This report shall be submitted to each member of the Committees on the Judiciary and Appropriations of both the House of Representatives and the Senate, and to the Speaker and minority leader of the House of Representatives and to the majority and minority leaders of the Senate, no later than 60 days after the end of each fiscal year.

VIDEO PRIVACY PROTECTION ACT
(1988)

Summary

The Video Privacy Protection Act of 1988 amends the Federal criminal code to prohibit the disclosure of video rental records containing personally identifiable information. The Act permits the disclosure of such information: (1) to the consumer; (2) with the written consent of the consumer (3) pursuant to a Federal criminal warrant, an equivalent State warrant, a grand jury subpoena, or a court order under specified guidelines; (4) to any person if such disclosure is solely the names and addresses of consumers and the consumer has had the opportunity to prohibit such disclosure; (5) to any person if such disclosure is incident to the ordinary course of business of the video tape service provider; or (6) pursuant to a civil court order.

The Act permits any person who is aggrieved by a violation of this Act to bring a civil action for damages. It establishes a two-year statute of limitations for such actions. It states that any such information unlawfully obtained may not be used in any court proceeding. It further requires the destruction of personally identifiable records within a specified period of time. The Act was amended in 2012 to modify the procedures for obtaining consent and for revoking consent.

References

Public Law 100-618. Codified as amended at 18 U.S.C. § 2710.
[https://www.law.cornell.edu/uscode/text/18/2710]

EPIC, Video Privacy Protection Act
[https://www.epic.org/privacy/vppa/]

18 U.S.C. § 2710. Wrongful disclosure of video tape rental or sale records

(a) Definitions. - For purposes of this section -

(1) the term "consumer" means any renter, purchaser, or subscriber of goods or services from a video tape service provider;

(2) the term "ordinary course of business" means only debt collection activities, order fulfillment, request processing, and the transfer of ownership;

(3) the term "personally identifiable information" includes information which identifies a person as having requested or obtained specific video materials or services from a video tape service provider; and

(4) the term "video tape service provider" means any person, engaged in the business, in or affecting interstate or foreign commerce, of rental, sale, or delivery of prerecorded video cassette tapes or similar audio visual materials, or any person or other entity to whom a disclosure is made under subparagraph (D) or (E) of

subsection (b)(2), but only with respect to the information contained in the disclosure.

(b) Video Tape Rental and Sale Records. -

(1) A video tape service provider who knowingly discloses, to any person, personally identifiable information concerning any consumer of such provider shall be liable to the aggrieved person for the relief provided in subsection (d).

(2) A video tape service provider may disclose personally identifiable information concerning any consumer-

(A) to the consumer;

(B) to any person with the informed, written consent (including through an electronic means using the Internet) of the consumer that-

(i) is in a form distinct and separate from any form setting forth other legal or financial obligations of the consumer;

(ii) at the election of the consumer-

(I) is given at the time the disclosure is sought; or

(II) is given in advance for a set period of time, not to exceed 2 years or until consent is withdrawn by the consumer, whichever is sooner; and

(iii) the video tape service provider has provided an opportunity, in a clear and conspicuous manner, for the consumer to withdraw on a case-by-case basis or to withdraw from ongoing disclosures, at the consumer's election;

(C) to a law enforcement agency pursuant to a warrant issued under the Federal Rules of Criminal Procedure, an equivalent State warrant, a grand jury subpoena, or a court order;

(D) to any person if the disclosure is solely of the names and addresses of consumers and if-

(i) the video tape service provider has provided the consumer with the opportunity, in a clear and conspicuous manner, to prohibit such disclosure; and

(ii) the disclosure does not identify the title, description, or subject matter of any video tapes or other audio visual material; however, the subject matter of such materials may be disclosed if the disclosure is for the exclusive use of marketing goods and services directly to the consumer;

(E) to any person if the disclosure is incident to the ordinary course of business of the video tape service provider; or

(F) pursuant to a court order, in a civil proceeding upon a showing of compelling need for the information that cannot be accommodated by any other means, if-

(i) the consumer is given reasonable notice, by the person seeking the disclosure, of the court proceeding relevant to the issuance of the court order; and

(ii) the consumer is afforded the opportunity to appear and contest the claim of the person seeking the disclosure.

If an order is granted pursuant to subparagraph (C) or (F), the court shall impose appropriate safeguards against unauthorized disclosure.

(3) Court orders authorizing disclosure under subparagraph (C) shall issue only with prior notice to the consumer and only if the law enforcement agency shows that there is probable cause to believe that the records or other information sought are relevant to a legitimate law enforcement inquiry. In the case of a State government authority, such a court order shall not issue if prohibited by the law of such State. A court issuing an order pursuant to this section, on a motion made promptly by the video tape service provider, may quash or modify such order if the information or records requested are unreasonably voluminous in nature or if compliance with such order otherwise would cause an unreasonable burden on such provider.

(c) Civil Action. -

(1) Any person aggrieved by any act of a person in violation of this section may bring a civil action in a United States district court.

(2) The court may award-

(A) actual damages but not less than liquidated damages in an amount of $2,500;

(B) punitive damages;

(C) reasonable attorneys' fees and other litigation costs reasonably incurred; and

(D) such other preliminary and equitable relief as the court determines to be appropriate.

(3) No action may be brought under this subsection unless such action is begun within 2 years from the date of the act complained of or the date of discovery.

(4) No liability shall result from lawful disclosure permitted by this section.

(d) Personally Identifiable Information. - Personally identifiable information obtained in any manner other than as provided in this section shall not be received in evidence in any trial, hearing, arbitration, or other proceeding in or before any court, grand jury, department, officer, agency, regulatory body, legislative committee, or other authority of the United States, a State, or a political subdivision of a State.

(e) Destruction of Old Records. - A person subject to this section shall destroy personally identifiable information as soon as practicable, but no later than one year from the date the information is no longer necessary for the purpose for which it was collected and there are no pending requests or orders for access to such information under subsection (b)(2) or (c)(2) or pursuant to a court order.

(f) Preemption. - The provisions of this section preempt only the provisions of State or local law that require disclosure prohibited by this section.

EMPLOYEE POLYGRAPH PROTECTION
ACT (1988)

Summary

The Employee Polygraph Protection Act of 1988 prohibits any employer from: (1) requiring or suggesting that an employee or prospective employee take a lie detector test; (2) using lie detector test results; or (3) taking employment action against an employee or prospective employee who refuses to take a lie detector test or institutes or testifies in a proceeding under or related to this Act. The Act requires the Secretary to Labor (the Secretary) to prepare notices setting forth such prohibitions, and requires employers to post such notices.

The Act provides civil penalties for violations of this Act, and grants the Secretary authority to restrain violations of the Act. It allows employees and prospective employees to bring civil actions against any employer who violates its provisions.

The Act exempts from coverage under this Act: (1) Federal, State, and local governments; (2) certain Federal contractors; (3) tests conducted pursuant to the performance of intelligence or counterintelligence functions or Federal security clearances; (4) certain security personnel and other security services; and (5) employers who are authorized to manufacture, distribute, or dispense controlled substances. It provides a limited exemption under which an employer may request certain employees to submit to a polygraph test if the test is administered in connection with an ongoing investigation involving economic loss or injury to the employer's business, including theft, embezzlement, misappropriation, or an act of unlawful industrial espionage or sabotage. The Act specifies reporting requirements of the employer under such circumstances. It further declares that such limited exemption does not apply if an employee is discharged, dismissed, disciplined, or discriminated against in any manner on the basis of the results of one or more polygraph tests or the refusal to take a polygraph test, without additional supporting evidence.

The Act sets forth the rights of an examinee during a pretest phase, the actual testing phase, and the post-test phase. It specifies the qualification of an examiner. It prohibits the disclosure of information obtained from a polygraph test, except as provided by the Act.

References

Public Law 100-347. Codified at 29 U.S.C. § 2001 et seq.
[https://www.law.cornell.edu/uscode/text/29/2001]

Conference report, House Report 100-659 (May 26, 1988)

EPIC, Polygraph Testing
[http://www.epic.org/privacy/polygraph/]

United States
Employee Polygraph Protection Act

29 U.S.C. Sec. 2001. Definitions

As used in this chapter:

(1) Commerce

The term "commerce" has the meaning provided by section 203(b) of this title.

(2) Employer

The term "employer" includes any person acting directly or indirectly in the interest of an employer in relation to an employee or prospective employee.

(3) Lie detector

The term "lie detector" includes a polygraph, deceptograph, voice stress analyzer, psychological stress evaluator, or any other similar device (whether mechanical or electrical) that is used, or the results of which are used, for the purpose of rendering a diagnostic opinion regarding the honesty or dishonesty of an individual.

(4) Polygraph

The term "polygraph" means an instrument that -

(A) records continuously, visually, permanently, and simultaneously changes in cardiovascular, respiratory, and electrodermal patterns as minimum instrumentation standards; and

(B) is used, or the results of which are used, for the

purpose of rendering a diagnostic opinion regarding the honesty or dishonesty of an individual.

(5) Secretary

The term "Secretary" means the Secretary of Labor.

Sec. 2002. Prohibitions on lie detector use

Except as provided in sections 2006 and 2007 of this title, it shall be unlawful for any employer engaged in or affecting commerce or in the production of goods for commerce -

(1) directly or indirectly, to require, request, suggest, or cause any employee or prospective employee to take or submit to any lie detector test;

(2) to use, accept, refer to, or inquire concerning the results of any lie detector test of any employee or prospective employee;

(3) to discharge, discipline, discriminate against in any manner, or deny employment or promotion to, or threaten to take any such action against -

(A) any employee or prospective employee who refuses, declines, or fails to take or submit to any lie detector test, or

(B) any employee or prospective employee on the basis of the results of any lie detector test; or

(4) to discharge, discipline, discriminate against in any manner, or deny employment or promotion to, or threaten to take any such action against, any employee or prospective employee because -

(A) such employee or prospective employee has filed any complaint or instituted or caused to be instituted any proceeding under or related to this chapter,

(B) such employee or prospective employee has testified or is about to testify in any such proceeding, or

(C) of the exercise by such employee or prospective employee, on behalf of such employee or another person, of any right afforded by this chapter.

Sec. 2003. Notice of protection

The Secretary shall prepare, have printed, and distribute a notice setting forth excerpts from, or summaries of, the pertinent provisions of this chapter. Each employer shall post and maintain such notice in conspicuous places on its premises where notices to employees and applicants to employment are customarily posted.

Sec. 2004. Authority of Secretary

(a) In general

The Secretary shall -

(1) issue such rules and regulations as may be necessary or appropriate to carry out this chapter;

(2) cooperate with regional, State, local, and other agencies, and cooperate with and furnish technical assistance to employers, labor organizations, and employment agencies to aid in effectuating the purposes of this chapter; and

(3) make investigations and inspections and require the keeping of records necessary or appropriate for the administration of this chapter.

(b) Subpoena authority

For the purpose of any hearing or investigation under this chapter, the Secretary shall have the authority contained in sections 49 and 50 of title 15.

Sec. 2005. Enforcement provisions

(a) Civil penalties

(1) In general

Subject to paragraph (2), any employer who violates any provision of this chapter may be assessed a civil penalty of not more than $10,000.

(2) Determination of amount

In determining the amount of any penalty under paragraph (1), the Secretary shall take into account the previous record of the person in terms of compliance with this chapter and the gravity of the violation.

(3) Collection

Any civil penalty assessed under this subsection shall be collected in the same manner as is required by subsections (b) through (e) of section 1853 of this title with respect to civil penalties assessed under subsection (a) of such section.

(b) Injunctive actions by Secretary

The Secretary may bring an action under this section to restrain violations of this chapter. The Solicitor of Labor may appear for and represent the Secretary in any litigation brought under this chapter. In any action brought under this section, the district courts of the United States shall have jurisdiction, for cause shown, to issue temporary or permanent restraining orders and injunctions to require compliance with this chapter, including such legal or equitable relief incident thereto as may be appropriate, including, but not limited to, employment, reinstatement, promotion, and the payment of lost wages and benefits.

(c) Private civil actions

(1) Liability

An employer who violates this chapter shall be liable to the employee or prospective employee affected by such violation. Such employer shall be liable for such legal or equitable relief as may be appropriate, including, but not limited to, employment, reinstatement, promotion, and the payment of lost wages and benefits.

(2) Court

An action to recover the liability prescribed in paragraph (1) may be maintained against the employer in any Federal or State court of competent jurisdiction by an employee or prospective employee for or on behalf of such employee, prospective employee, and other employees or prospective employees similarly situated. No such action may be commenced more than 3 years after the date of the alleged violation.

(3) Costs

The court, in its discretion, may allow the prevailing party (other than the United States) reasonable costs, including attorney's fees.

(d) Waiver of rights prohibited

The rights and procedures provided by this chapter may not be waived by contract or otherwise, unless such waiver is part of a written settlement agreed to and signed by the parties to the pending action or complaint under this chapter.

Sec. 2006. Exemptions

(a) No application to governmental employers

This chapter shall not apply with respect to the United States Government, any State or local government, or any political subdivision of a State or local government.

(b) National defense and security exemption

(1) National defense

Nothing in this chapter shall be construed to prohibit the administration, by the Federal Government, in the performance of any counterintelligence function, of any lie detector test to-

(A) any expert or consultant under contract to the Department of Defense or any employee of any contractor of such Department; or

(B) any expert or consultant under contract with the Department of Energy in connection with the atomic energy defense activities of such Department or any employee of any contractor of such Department in connection with such activities.

(2) Security

Nothing in this chapter shall be construed to prohibit the administration, by the Federal Government, in the performance of any intelligence or counterintelligence function, of any lie detector test to-

(A)(i) any individual employed by, assigned to, or detailed to, the National Security Agency, the Defense Intelligence Agency, the National Geospatial-Intelligence Agency, or the Central Intelligence Agency,

(ii) any expert or consultant under contract to any such agency,

(iii) any employee of a contractor to any such agency,

(iv) any individual applying for a position in any such agency, or

(v) any individual assigned to a space where sensitive cryptologic information is produced, processed, or stored for any such agency; or

(B) any expert, or consultant (or employee of such expert or consultant) under contract with any Federal Government department, agency, or program whose duties involve access to information that has been classified at the level of top secret or designated as being within a special access program under section 4.2(a) of Executive Order 12356 (or a successor Executive order).

(c) FBI contractors exemption

Nothing in this chapter shall be construed to prohibit the administration, by the Federal Government, in the performance of any counterintelligence function, of any lie detector test to an employee of a contractor of the Federal Bureau of Investigation of the Department of Justice who is engaged in the performance of any work under the contract with such Bureau.

(d) Limited exemption for ongoing investigations

Subject to sections 2007 and 2009 of this title, this chapter shall not prohibit an employer from requesting an employee to submit to a polygraph test if-

(1) the test is administered in connection with an ongoing investigation involving economic loss or injury to the employer's business, such as theft, embezzlement, misappropriation, or an act of unlawful industrial espionage or sabotage;

(2) the employee had access to the property that is the subject of the investigation;

(3) the employer has a reasonable suspicion that the employee was involved in the incident or activity under investigation; and

(4) the employer executes a statement, provided to the examinee before the test, that-

(A) sets forth with particularity the specific incident or activity being investigated and the basis for testing particular employees,

(B) is signed by a person (other than a polygraph examiner) authorized to legally bind the employer,

(C) is retained by the employer for at least 3 years, and

(D) contains at a minimum-

(i) an identification of the specific economic loss or injury to the business of the employer,

(ii) a statement indicating that the employee had access to the property that is the subject of the investigation, and

(iii) a statement describing the basis of the employer's reasonable suspicion that the employee was involved in the incident or activity under investigation.

(e) Exemption for security services

(1) In general

Subject to paragraph (2) and sections 2007 and 2009 of this title, this chapter shall not prohibit the use of polygraph tests on prospective employees by any private employer whose primary business purpose consists of providing armored car personnel, personnel engaged in the design, installation, and maintenance of security alarm systems, or other uniformed or plainclothes security personnel and whose function includes protection of-

(A) facilities, materials, or operations having a significant impact on the health or safety of any State or political subdivision thereof, or the national security of the United States, as determined under rules and regulations issued by the Secretary within 90 days after June 27, 1988, including-

(i) facilities engaged in the production, transmission, or distribution of electric or nuclear power,

(ii) public water supply facilities,

(iii) shipments or storage of radioactive or other toxic waste materials, and

(iv) public transportation, or

(B) currency, negotiable securities, precious commodities or instruments, or proprietary information.

(2) Access

The exemption provided under this subsection shall not apply if the test is administered to a prospective employee who would not be employed to protect facilities, materials, operations, or assets referred to in paragraph (1).

(f) Exemption for drug security, drug theft, or drug diversion investigations

(1) In general

Subject to paragraph (2) and sections 2007 and 2009 of this title, this chapter shall not prohibit the use of a polygraph test by any employer authorized to manufacture, distribute, or dispense a controlled substance listed in schedule I, II, III, or IV of section 812 of title 21.

(2) Access

The exemption provided under this subsection shall apply-

(A) if the test is administered to a prospective employee who would have direct access to the manufacture, storage, distribution, or sale of any such controlled substance; or

(B) in the case of a test administered to a current employee, if-

(i) the test is administered in connection with an ongoing investigation of criminal or other misconduct involving, or potentially involving, loss or injury to the manufacture, distribution, or dispensing of any such controlled substance by such employer, and

(ii) the employee had access to the person or property that is the subject of the investigation.

Sec. 2007. Restrictions on use of exemptions

(a) Test as basis for adverse employment action

(1) Under ongoing investigations exemption

Except as provided in paragraph (2), the exemption under subsection (d) of section 2006 of this title shall not apply if an employee is discharged, disciplined, denied employment or promotion, or otherwise discriminated against in any manner on the basis of the analysis of a polygraph test chart or the refusal to take a polygraph test, without additional supporting evidence. The evidence required by such subsection may serve as additional supporting evidence.

(2) Under other exemptions

In the case of an exemption described in subsection (e) or (f) of such section, the exemption shall not apply if the results of an analysis of a polygraph test chart are used, or the refusal to take a polygraph test is used, as the sole basis upon which an adverse employment action described in paragraph (1) is taken against an employee or prospective employee.

(b) Rights of examinee

The exemptions provided under subsections (d), (e), and (f) of section 2006 of this title shall not apply unless the requirements described in the following paragraphs are met:

(1) All phases

Throughout all phases of the test -

(A) the examinee shall be permitted to terminate the test at any time;

(B) the examinee is not asked questions in a manner designed to degrade, or needlessly intrude on, such examinee;

(C) the examinee is not asked any question concerning -

(i) religious beliefs or affiliations,

(ii) beliefs or opinions regarding racial matters,

(iii) political beliefs or affiliations,

(iv) any matter relating to sexual behavior; and

(v) beliefs, affiliations, opinions, or lawful activities regarding unions or labor organizations; and

(D) the examiner does not conduct the test if there is sufficient written evidence by a physician that the examinee is suffering from a medical or psychological condition or undergoing treatment that might cause abnormal responses during the actual testing phase.

(2) Pretest phase

During the pretest phase, the prospective examinee -

(A) is provided with reasonable written notice of the date, time, and location of the test, and of such examinee's right to obtain and consult with legal counsel or an employee representative before each phase of the test;

(B) is informed in writing of the nature and characteristics of the tests and of the instruments involved;

(C) is informed, in writing -

(i) whether the testing area contains a two-way mirror, a camera, or any other device through which the test can be observed,

(ii) whether any other device, including any device for recording or monitoring the test, will be used, or

(iii) that the employer or the examinee may (with mutual knowledge) make a recording of the test;

(D) is read and signs a written notice informing such examinee -

(i) that the examinee cannot be required to take the test as a condition of employment,

(ii) that any statement made during the test may constitute additional supporting evidence for the purposes of an adverse employment action described in subsection (a) of this section,

(iii) of the limitations imposed under this section,

(iv) of the legal rights and remedies available to the examinee if the polygraph test is not conducted in accordance with this chapter, and

(v) of the legal rights and remedies of the employer under this chapter (including the rights of the employer under section 2008(c)(2) of this title); and

(E) is provided an opportunity to review all questions to be asked during the test and is informed of the right to terminate the test at any time.

(3) Actual testing phase

During the actual testing phase, the examiner does not ask such examinee any question relevant during the test that was not presented in writing for review to such examinee before the test.

(4) Post-test phase

Before any adverse employment action, the employer shall -

(A) further interview the examinee on the basis of the results of the test; and

(B) provide the examinee with -

(i) a written copy of any opinion or conclusion rendered as a result of the test, and

(ii) a copy of the questions asked during the test along with the corresponding charted responses.

(5) Maximum number and minimum duration of tests The examiner shall not conduct and complete more than five polygraph tests on a calendar day on which the test is given, and shall not conduct any such test for less than a 90-minute duration.

(c) Qualifications and requirements of examiners

The exemptions provided under subsections (d), (e), and (f) of section 2006 of this title shall not apply unless the individual who conducts the polygraph test satisfies the requirements under the following paragraphs:

(1) Qualifications

The examiner -

(A) has a valid and current license granted by licensing and regulatory authorities in the State in which the test is to be conducted, if so required by the State; and

(B) maintains a minimum of a $50,000 bond or an equivalent amount of professional liability coverage.

(2) Requirements

The examiner -

(A) renders any opinion or conclusion regarding the test -

(i) in writing and solely on the basis of an analysis of polygraph test charts,

(ii) that does not contain information other than admissions, information, case facts, and interpretation of the charts relevant to the purpose and stated objectives of the test, and

(iii) that does not include any recommendation concerning the employment of the examinee; and

(B) maintains all opinions, reports, charts, written questions, lists, and other records relating to the test for a minimum period of 3 years after administration of the test.

Sec. 2008. Disclosure of information

(a) In general

A person, other than the examinee, may not disclose information obtained during a polygraph test, except as provided in this section.

(b) Permitted disclosures

A polygraph examiner may disclose information acquired from a polygraph test only to -

> (1) the examinee or any other person specifically designated in writing by the examinee;
>
> (2) the employer that requested the test; or
>
> (3) any court, governmental agency, arbitrator, or mediator, in accordance with due process of law, pursuant to an order from a court of competent jurisdiction.

(c) Disclosure by employer

An employer (other than an employer described in subsection (a), (b), or (c) of section 2006 of this title) for whom a polygraph test is conducted may disclose information from the test only to -

> (1) a person in accordance with subsection (b) of this section; or
>
> (2) a governmental agency, but only insofar as the disclosed information is an admission of criminal conduct.

Sec. 2009. Effect on other law and agreements

Except as provided in subsections (a), (b), and (c) of section 2006 of this title, this chapter shall not preempt any provision of any State or local law or of any negotiated collective bargaining agreement that prohibits lie detector tests or is more restrictive with respect to lie detector tests than any provision of this chapter.

TELEPHONE CONSUMER PROTECTION ACT (1991)

Summary

The Telephone Consumer Protection Act of 1991 (TCPA) amended the Communications Act of 1934 to prohibit any person within the United States from using an automatic telephone dialing system to make a call to any emergency telephone line or to any telephone number for which the called party is charged for the call without the consent of the called party, with specified exceptions. The Act also prohibited the use of a telephone facsimile machine, computer, or other device to send an unsolicited advertisement to a FAX machine. The Act also directs the Federal Communications Commission (FCC) to issue regulations to implement these requirements, and authorizes private actions and the recovery of damages with respect to violations of such requirements.

The Act further directs the FCC to initiate a rulemaking proceeding concerning the need to protect residential telephone subscribers' privacy rights to avoid receiving telephone solicitations to which they object and issue regulations to implement methods and procedures for protecting such privacy rights without the imposition of any additional charge to telephone subscribers. It states that such regulations may require the establishment and operation of a single national database to compile a list of telephone numbers of residential subscribers who object to receiving such solicitations, or to receiving certain classes or categories of solicitations, and to make the compiled list available for purchase. The Act authorizes private actions and the recovery of damages with respect to violations of such privacy rights.

The Act makes it unlawful for any person within the United States to initiate any communication using a FAX that does not comply with certain technical and procedural standards or to use a computer or other electronic device to send any message via FAX unless such person clearly marks on the document the date and time it is sent and identifies the entity sending the message and the telephone number of the sending machine or entity.

The Act permits states to bring civil actions to enjoin calls to residents in violation of the Act and to recover monetary damages. It grants U.S. district courts exclusive jurisdiction over such actions. It prohibits a State, whenever the FCC has instituted a civil action for violation of this Act, from bringing an action against any defendant named in the FCC's complaint.

In 2002, the Federal Trade Commission, followed by the FCC, issued rules to implement a national do-not-call registry which will be fully operational in October 2003. Additionally, the FCC issued new rules regulating unsolicited commercial faxes in order to curb the practices of "fax broadcasters," companies that send massive amounts of fax advertising to individuals. The new rules, which do not take effect until 2005, require the acquisition of written consent from the recipient before individuals can transmit unsolicited commercial faxes.

References

Public Law 102-243. Codified at 47 U.S.C. § 227

United States
Telephone Consumer Protection Act

[https://www.law.cornell.edu/uscode/text/47/227]

EPIC, Telephone Consumer Protection Act (TCPA)
[https://www.epic.org/privacy/telemarketing/]

Congressional Statement of Findings

Section 2 of Pub. L. 102-243 provided that: "The Congress finds that:

"(1) The use of the telephone to market goods and services to the home and other businesses is now pervasive due to the increased use of cost-effective telemarketing techniques.

"(2) Over 30,000 businesses actively telemarket goods and services to business and residential customers.

"(3) More than 300,000 solicitors call more than 18,000,000 Americans every day.

"(4) Total United States sales generated through telemarketing amounted to $435,000,000,000 in 1990, a more than four-fold increase since 1984.

"(5) Unrestricted telemarketing, however, can be an intrusive invasion of privacy and, when an emergency or medical assistance telephone line is seized, a risk to public safety.

"(6) Many consumers are outraged over the proliferation of intrusive, nuisance calls to their homes from telemarketers.

"(7) Over half the States now have statutes restricting various uses of the telephone for marketing, but telemarketers can evade their prohibitions through interstate operations; therefore, Federal law is needed to control residential telemarketing practices.

"(8) The Constitution does not prohibit restrictions on commercial telemarketing solicitations.

"(9) Individuals' privacy rights, public safety interests, and commercial freedoms of speech and trade must be balanced in a way that protects the privacy of individuals and permits legitimate telemarketing practices.

"(10) Evidence compiled by the Congress indicates that residential telephone subscribers consider automated or prerecorded telephone calls, regardless of the content or the initiator of the message, to be a nuisance and an invasion of privacy.

"(11) Technologies that might allow consumers to avoid receiving such calls are not universally available, are costly, are unlikely to be enforced, or place an inordinate burden on the consumer.

"(12) Banning such automated or prerecorded telephone calls to the home, except when the receiving party consents to receiving the call or when such calls are necessary in an emergency situation affecting the health and safety of the consumer, is the only effective means of protecting telephone consumers from this nuisance and privacy invasion.

"(13) While the evidence presented to the Congress indicates that automated or prerecorded calls are a nuisance and an invasion of privacy, regardless of the type of call, the Federal Communications Commission should have the flexibility to design different rules for those types of automated or prerecorded calls that it finds are not considered a nuisance or invasion of privacy, or for noncommercial calls, consistent with the free speech protections embodied in the First Amendment of the Constitution.

"(14) Businesses also have complained to the Congress and the Federal Communications Commission that automated or prerecorded telephone calls are a nuisance, are an invasion of privacy, and interfere with interstate commerce.

"(15) The Federal Communications Commission should consider adopting reasonable restrictions on automated or prerecorded calls to businesses as well as to the home, consistent with the constitutional protections of free speech."

47 U.S.C. Sec. 227. Restrictions on use of telephone equipment

(a) Definitions

As used in this section-

(1) The term "automatic telephone dialing system" means equipment which has the capacity-

(A) to store or produce telephone numbers to be called, using a random or sequential number generator; and

(B) to dial such numbers.

(2) The term "established business relationship", for purposes only of subsection (b)(1)(C)(i), shall have the meaning given the term in section 64.1200 of title 47, Code of Federal Regulations, as in effect on January 1, 2003, except that-

(A) such term shall include a relationship between a person or entity and a business subscriber subject to the same terms applicable under such section to a relationship between a person or entity and a residential subscriber; and

(B) an established business relationship shall be subject to any time limitation established pursuant to paragraph (2)(G)).[1]

(3) The term "telephone facsimile machine" means equipment which has the capacity (A) to transcribe text or images, or both, from paper into an electronic signal and to transmit that signal over a regular telephone line, or (B) to transcribe text or images (or both) from an electronic signal received over a regular telephone line onto paper.

(4) The term "telephone solicitation" means the initiation of a telephone call or message for the purpose of encouraging the purchase or rental of, or investment in, property, goods, or services, which is transmitted to any person, but such term does not include a call or message (A) to any person with that person's prior express invitation or permission, (B) to any person with whom the caller has an established business relationship, or (C) by a tax exempt nonprofit organization.

(5) The term "unsolicited advertisement" means any material advertising the commercial availability or quality of any property, goods, or services which is transmitted to any person without that person's prior express invitation or permission, in writing or otherwise.

(b) Restrictions on use of automated telephone equipment

United States
Telephone Consumer Protection Act

(1) Prohibitions

It shall be unlawful for any person within the United States, or any person outside the United States if the recipient is within the United States-

(A) to make any call (other than a call made for emergency purposes or made with the prior express consent of the called party) using any automatic telephone dialing system or an artificial or prerecorded voice-

(i) to any emergency telephone line (including any "911" line and any emergency line of a hospital, medical physician or service office, health care facility, poison control center, or fire protection or law enforcement agency);

(ii) to the telephone line of any guest room or patient room of a hospital, health care facility, elderly home, or similar establishment; or

(iii) to any telephone number assigned to a paging service, cellular telephone service, specialized mobile radio service, or other radio common carrier service, or any service for which the called party is charged for the call, unless such call is made solely to collect a debt owed to or guaranteed by the United States;

(B) to initiate any telephone call to any residential telephone line using an artificial or prerecorded voice to deliver a message without the prior express consent of the called party, unless the call is initiated for emergency purposes, is made solely pursuant to the collection of a debt owed to or guaranteed by the United States, or is exempted by rule or order by the Commission under paragraph (2)(B);

(C) to use any telephone facsimile machine, computer, or other device to send, to a telephone facsimile machine, an unsolicited advertisement, unless-

(i) the unsolicited advertisement is from a sender with an established business relationship with the recipient;

(ii) the sender obtained the number of the telephone facsimile machine through-

(I) the voluntary communication of such number, within the context of such established business relationship, from the recipient of the unsolicited advertisement, or

(II) a directory, advertisement, or site on the Internet to which the recipient voluntarily agreed to make available its facsimile number for public distribution, except that this clause shall not apply in the case of an unsolicited advertisement that is sent based on an established business relationship with the recipient that was in existence before July 9, 2005, if the sender possessed the facsimile machine number of the recipient before July 9, 2005; and

(iii) the unsolicited advertisement contains a notice meeting the requirements under paragraph (2)(D),

except that the exception under clauses (i) and (ii) shall not apply with respect to an unsolicited advertisement sent to a telephone facsimile machine by a sender to whom a request has been made not to send future unsolicited advertisements to such telephone facsimile machine that complies with the requirements under paragraph (2)(E); or

(D) to use an automatic telephone dialing system in such a way that two or more telephone lines of a multi-line business are engaged simultaneously.

(2) Regulations; exemptions and other provisions

The Commission shall prescribe regulations to implement the requirements of this subsection. In implementing the requirements of this subsection, the Commission-

(A) shall consider prescribing regulations to allow businesses to avoid receiving calls made using an artificial or prerecorded voice to which they have not given their prior express consent;

(B) may, by rule or order, exempt from the requirements of paragraph (1)(B) of this subsection, subject to such conditions as the Commission may prescribe-

(i) calls that are not made for a commercial purpose; and

(ii) such classes or categories of calls made for commercial purposes as the Commission determines-

(I) will not adversely affect the privacy rights that this section is intended to protect; and

(II) do not include the transmission of any unsolicited advertisement;

(C) may, by rule or order, exempt from the requirements of paragraph (1)(A)(iii) of this subsection calls to a telephone number assigned to a cellular telephone service that are not charged to the called party, subject to such conditions as the Commission may prescribe as necessary in the interest of the privacy rights this section is intended to protect;

(D) shall provide that a notice contained in an unsolicited advertisement complies with the requirements under this subparagraph only if-

(i) the notice is clear and conspicuous and on the first page of the unsolicited advertisement;

(ii) the notice states that the recipient may make a request to the sender of the unsolicited advertisement not to send any future unsolicited advertisements to a telephone facsimile machine or machines and that failure to comply, within the shortest reasonable time, as determined by the Commission, with such a request meeting the requirements under subparagraph (E) is unlawful;

(iii) the notice sets forth the requirements for a request under subparagraph (E);

(iv) the notice includes-

(I) a domestic contact telephone and facsimile machine number for the recipient to transmit such a request to the sender; and

(II) a cost-free mechanism for a recipient to transmit a request pursuant to such notice to the sender of the unsolicited advertisement; the Commission shall by rule require the sender to provide such a mechanism and may, in the discretion of the Commission and subject to such conditions as the Commission may prescribe, exempt certain classes of small business senders, but only if the Commission determines that the costs to such class are unduly burdensome given the revenues generated by such small businesses;

(v) the telephone and facsimile machine numbers and the cost-free mechanism set forth pursuant to clause (iv) permit an individual or business to make such a request at any time on any day of the week; and

(vi) the notice complies with the requirements of subsection (d);

(E) shall provide, by rule, that a request not to send future unsolicited advertisements to a telephone facsimile machine complies with the requirements under this subparagraph only if-

(i) the request identifies the telephone number or numbers of the telephone facsimile machine or machines to which the request relates;

(ii) the request is made to the telephone or facsimile number of the sender of such an unsolicited advertisement provided pursuant to subparagraph (D)(iv) or by any other method of communication as determined by the Commission; and

(iii) the person making the request has not, subsequent to such request, provided express invitation or permission to the sender, in writing or otherwise, to send such advertisements to such person at such telephone facsimile machine;

(F) may, in the discretion of the Commission and subject to such conditions as the Commission may prescribe, allow professional or trade associations that are tax-exempt nonprofit organizations to send unsolicited advertisements to their members in furtherance of the association's tax-exempt purpose that do not contain the notice required by paragraph (1)(C)(iii), except that the Commission may take action under this subparagraph only-

(i) by regulation issued after public notice and opportunity for public comment; and

(ii) if the Commission determines that such notice required by paragraph (1)(C)(iii) is not necessary to protect the ability of the members of such associations to stop such associations from sending any future unsolicited advertisements;

(G)(i) may, consistent with clause (ii), limit the duration of the existence of an established business relationship, however, before establishing any such limits, the Commission shall-

(I) determine whether the existence of the exception under paragraph (1)(C) relating to an established business relationship has resulted in a significant number of complaints to the Commission regarding the sending of unsolicited advertisements to telephone facsimile machines;

(II) determine whether a significant number of any such complaints involve unsolicited advertisements that were sent on the basis of an established business relationship that was longer in duration than the Commission believes is consistent with the reasonable expectations of consumers;

(III) evaluate the costs to senders of demonstrating the existence of an established business relationship within a specified period of time and the benefits to recipients of establishing a limitation on such established business relationship; and

(IV) determine whether with respect to small businesses, the costs would not be unduly burdensome; and

(ii) may not commence a proceeding to determine whether to limit the duration of the existence of an established business relationship before the expiration of the 3-month period that begins on July 9, 2005; and

(H) may restrict or limit the number and duration of calls made to a telephone number assigned to a cellular telephone service to collect a debt owed to or guaranteed by the United States.

(3) Private right of action

A person or entity may, if otherwise permitted by the laws or rules of court of a State, bring in an appropriate court of that State-

(A) an action based on a violation of this subsection or the regulations prescribed under this subsection to enjoin such violation,

(B) an action to recover for actual monetary loss from such a violation, or to receive $500 in damages for each such violation, whichever is greater, or

(C) both such actions.

If the court finds that the defendant willfully or knowingly violated this subsection or the regulations prescribed under this subsection, the court may, in its discretion, increase the amount of the award to an amount equal to not more than 3 times the amount available under subparagraph (B) of this paragraph.

(c) Protection of subscriber privacy rights

(1) Rulemaking proceeding required

Within 120 days after December 20, 1991, the Commission shall initiate a rulemaking proceeding concerning the need to protect residential telephone subscribers' privacy rights to avoid receiving telephone solicitations to which they object. The proceeding shall-

(A) compare and evaluate alternative methods and procedures (including the use of electronic databases, telephone network technologies, special directory markings, industry-based or company-specific "do not call" systems, and any other alternatives, individually or in combination) for their effectiveness in protecting such privacy rights, and in terms of their cost and other advantages and disadvantages;

(B) evaluate the categories of public and private entities that would have the capacity to establish and administer such methods and procedures;

(C) consider whether different methods and procedures may apply for local telephone solicitations, such as local telephone solicitations of small businesses or holders of second class mail permits;

(D) consider whether there is a need for additional Commission authority to further restrict telephone solicitations, including those calls exempted under subsection (a)(3) of this section, and, if such a finding is made and supported by the record, propose specific restrictions to the Congress; and

(E) develop proposed regulations to implement the methods and procedures that the Commission determines are most effective and efficient to accomplish the purposes of this section.

(2) Regulations

Not later than 9 months after December 20, 1991, the Commission shall conclude the rulemaking proceeding initiated under paragraph (1) and shall prescribe regulations to implement methods and procedures for protecting the privacy rights described in such paragraph in an efficient, effective, and economic manner and without the imposition of any additional charge to telephone subscribers.

(3) Use of database permitted

The regulations required by paragraph (2) may require the establishment and operation of a single national database to compile a list of telephone numbers of residential subscribers who object to receiving telephone solicitations, and to make that compiled list and parts thereof available for purchase. If the Commission determines to require such a database, such regulations shall-

(A) specify a method by which the Commission will select an entity to administer such database;

(B) require each common carrier providing telephone exchange service, in accordance with regulations prescribed by the Commission, to inform subscribers for telephone exchange service of the opportunity to provide notification, in accordance with regulations established under this paragraph, that such subscriber objects to receiving telephone solicitations;

(C) specify the methods by which each telephone subscriber shall be informed, by the common carrier that provides local exchange service to that subscriber, of (i) the subscriber's right to give or revoke a notification of an objection under subparagraph (A), and (ii) the methods by which such right may be exercised by the subscriber;

(D) specify the methods by which such objections shall be collected and added to the database;

(E) prohibit any residential subscriber from being charged for giving or revoking such notification or for being included in a database compiled under this section;

(F) prohibit any person from making or transmitting a telephone solicitation to the telephone number of any subscriber included in such database;

(G) specify (i) the methods by which any person desiring to make or transmit telephone solicitations will obtain access to the database, by area code or local exchange prefix, as required to avoid calling the telephone numbers of subscribers included in such database; and (ii) the costs to be recovered from such persons;

(H) specify the methods for recovering, from persons accessing such database, the costs involved in identifying, collecting, updating, disseminating, and selling, and other activities relating to, the operations of the database that are incurred by the entities carrying out those activities;

(I) specify the frequency with which such database will be updated and specify the method by which such updating will take effect for purposes of compliance with the regulations prescribed under this subsection;

(J) be designed to enable States to use the database mechanism selected by the Commission for purposes of administering or enforcing State law;

(K) prohibit the use of such database for any purpose other than compliance with the requirements of this section and any such State law and specify methods for protection of the privacy rights of persons whose numbers are included in such database; and

(L) require each common carrier providing services to any person for the purpose of making telephone solicitations to notify such person of the requirements of this section and the regulations thereunder.

(4) Considerations required for use of database method

If the Commission determines to require the database mechanism described in paragraph (3), the Commission shall-

(A) in developing procedures for gaining access to the database, consider the different needs of telemarketers conducting business on a national, regional, State, or local level;

(B) develop a fee schedule or price structure for recouping the cost of such database that recognizes such differences and-

(i) reflect the relative costs of providing a national, regional, State, or local list of phone numbers of subscribers who object to receiving telephone solicitations;

(ii) reflect the relative costs of providing such lists on paper or electronic media; and

(iii) not place an unreasonable financial burden on small businesses; and

(C) consider (i) whether the needs of telemarketers operating on a local basis could be met through special markings of area white pages directories, and (ii) if such directories are needed as an adjunct to database lists prepared by area code and local exchange prefix.

(5) Private right of action

A person who has received more than one telephone call within any 12-month period by or on behalf of the same entity in violation of the regulations prescribed under this subsection may, if otherwise permitted by the laws or rules of court of a State bring in an appropriate court of that State-

(A) an action based on a violation of the regulations prescribed under this subsection to enjoin such violation,

(B) an action to recover for actual monetary loss from such a violation, or to receive up to $500 in damages for each such violation, whichever is greater, or

(C) both such actions.

It shall be an affirmative defense in any action brought under this paragraph that the defendant has established and implemented, with due care, reasonable practices and procedures to effectively prevent telephone solicitations in violation of the regulations prescribed under this subsection. If the court finds that the defendant willfully or knowingly violated the regulations prescribed under this subsection, the court may, in its discretion, increase the amount of the award to an amount equal to not more than 3 times the amount available under subparagraph (B) of this paragraph.

(6) Relation to subsection (b)

The provisions of this subsection shall not be construed to permit a communication prohibited by subsection (b).

(d) Technical and procedural standards

(1) Prohibition

It shall be unlawful for any person within the United States-

(A) to initiate any communication using a telephone facsimile machine, or to make any telephone call using any automatic telephone dialing system, that does not comply with the technical and procedural standards prescribed under this subsection, or to use any telephone facsimile machine or automatic telephone dialing system in a manner that does not comply with such standards; or

(B) to use a computer or other electronic device to send any message via a telephone facsimile machine unless such person clearly marks, in a margin at the top or bottom of each transmitted page of the message or on the first page of the transmission, the date and time it is sent and an identification of the business, other entity, or individual sending the message and the telephone number of the sending machine or of such business, other entity, or individual.

(2) Telephone facsimile machines

The Commission shall revise the regulations setting technical and procedural standards for telephone facsimile machines to require that any such machine which is manufactured after one year after December 20, 1991, clearly marks, in a margin at the top or bottom of each transmitted page or on the first page of each transmission, the date and time sent, an identification of the business, other entity, or individual sending the message, and the telephone number of the sending machine or of such business, other entity, or individual.

(3) Artificial or prerecorded voice systems

The Commission shall prescribe technical and procedural standards for systems that are used to transmit any artificial or prerecorded voice message via telephone. Such standards shall require that-

(A) all artificial or prerecorded telephone messages (i) shall, at the beginning of the message, state clearly the identity of the business, individual, or other entity initiating the call, and (ii) shall, during or after the message, state clearly the telephone number or address of such business, other entity, or individual; and

(B) any such system will automatically release the called party's line within 5 seconds of the time notification is transmitted to the system that the called party has hung up, to allow the called party's line to be used to make or receive other calls.

(e) Prohibition on provision of inaccurate caller identification information

(1) In general

It shall be unlawful for any person within the United States, in connection with any telecommunications service or IP-enabled voice service, to cause any caller identification service to knowingly transmit misleading or inaccurate caller identification information with the intent to defraud, cause harm, or wrongfully obtain anything of value, unless such transmission is exempted pursuant to paragraph (3)(B).

(2) Protection for blocking caller identification information

Nothing in this subsection may be construed to prevent or restrict any person from blocking the capability of any caller identification service to transmit caller identification information.

(3) Regulations

(A) In general

Not later than 6 months after December 22, 2010, the Commission shall prescribe regulations to implement this subsection.

(B) Content of regulations

(i) In general

The regulations required under subparagraph (A) shall include such exemptions from the prohibition under paragraph (1) as the Commission determines is appropriate.

(ii) Specific exemption for law enforcement agencies or court orders

The regulations required under subparagraph (A) shall exempt from the prohibition under paragraph (1) transmissions in connection with-

(I) any authorized activity of a law enforcement agency; or

(II) a court order that specifically authorizes the use of caller identification manipulation.

(4) Repealed. Pub. L. 115–141, div. P, title IV, §402(i)(3), Mar. 23, 2018, 132 Stat. 1089

(5) Penalties

(A) Civil forfeiture

(i) In general

Any person that is determined by the Commission, in accordance with paragraphs (3) and (4) of section 503(b) of this title, to have violated this subsection shall be liable to the United States for a forfeiture penalty. A forfeiture penalty under this paragraph shall be in addition to any other penalty provided for by this chapter. The amount of the forfeiture penalty determined under this paragraph shall not exceed $10,000 for each violation, or 3 times that amount for each day of a continuing violation, except that the amount assessed for any continuing violation shall not exceed a total of $1,000,000 for any single act or failure to act.

(ii) Recovery

Any forfeiture penalty determined under clause (i) shall be recoverable pursuant to section 504(a) of this title.

(iii) Procedure

No forfeiture liability shall be determined under clause (i) against any person unless such person receives the notice required by section 503(b)(3) of this title or section 503(b)(4) of this title.

(iv) 2-year statute of limitations

No forfeiture penalty shall be determined or imposed against any person under clause (i) if the violation charged occurred more than 2 years prior to the date of issuance of the required notice or notice or apparent liability.

(B) Criminal fine

Any person who willfully and knowingly violates this subsection shall upon conviction thereof be fined not more than $10,000 for each violation, or 3 times that amount for each day of a continuing violation, in lieu of the fine provided by section 501 of this title for such a violation. This subparagraph does not supersede the provisions of section 501 of this title relating to imprisonment or the imposition of a penalty of both fine and imprisonment.

(6) Enforcement by States

(A) In general

The chief legal officer of a State, or any other State officer authorized by law to bring actions on behalf of the residents of a State, may bring a civil action, as parens patriae, on behalf of the residents of that State in an appropriate district court of the United States to enforce this subsection or to impose the civil penalties for violation of this subsection, whenever the chief legal officer or other State officer has reason to believe that the interests of the residents of the State have been or are being threatened or adversely affected by a violation of this subsection or a regulation under this subsection.

(B) Notice

The chief legal officer or other State officer shall serve written notice on the Commission of any civil action under subparagraph (A) prior to initiating such civil action. The notice shall include a copy of the complaint to be filed to initiate such civil action, except that if it is not feasible for the State to provide such prior notice, the State shall provide such notice immediately upon instituting such civil action.

(C) Authority to intervene

Upon receiving the notice required by subparagraph (B), the Commission shall have the right-

    (i) to intervene in the action;

    (ii) upon so intervening, to be heard on all matters arising therein; and

    (iii) to file petitions for appeal.

(D) Construction

For purposes of bringing any civil action under subparagraph (A), nothing in this paragraph shall prevent the chief legal officer or other State officer from exercising the powers conferred on that officer by the laws of such State to conduct investigations or to administer oaths or affirmations or to compel the attendance of witnesses or the production of documentary and other evidence.

(E) Venue; service or process

    (i) Venue

An action brought under subparagraph (A) shall be brought in a district court of the United States that meets applicable requirements relating to venue under section 1391 of title 28.

    (ii) Service of process

In an action brought under subparagraph (A)-

        (I) process may be served without regard to the territorial limits of the district or of the State in which the action is instituted; and

        (II) a person who participated in an alleged violation that is being litigated in the civil action may be joined in the civil action without regard to the residence of the person.

(7) Effect on other laws

This subsection does not prohibit any lawfully authorized investigative, protective, or intelligence activity of a law enforcement agency of the United States, a State, or a political subdivision of a State, or of an intelligence agency of the United States.

(8) Definitions

For purposes of this subsection:

    (A) Caller identification information

The term "caller identification information" means information provided by a caller identification service regarding the telephone number of, or other information regarding the origination of, a call made using a telecommunications service or IP-enabled voice service.

    (B) Caller identification service

The term "caller identification service" means any service or device designed to provide the user of the service or device with the telephone number of, or other information regarding the origination of, a call made using a telecommunications service or IP-enabled voice service. Such term includes automatic number identification services.

    (C) IP-enabled voice service

The term "IP-enabled voice service" has the meaning given that term by section 9.3 of the Commission's regulations (47 C.F.R. 9.3), as those regulations may be amended by the Commission from time to time.

(9) Limitation

Notwithstanding any other provision of this section, subsection (f) shall not apply to this subsection or to the regulations under this subsection.

(f) Effect on State law

(1) State law not preempted

Except for the standards prescribed under subsection (d) and subject to paragraph (2) of this subsection, nothing in this section or in the regulations prescribed under this section shall preempt any State law that imposes more restrictive intrastate requirements or regulations on, or which prohibits-

(A) the use of telephone facsimile machines or other electronic devices to send unsolicited advertisements;

(B) the use of automatic telephone dialing systems;

(C) the use of artificial or prerecorded voice messages; or

(D) the making of telephone solicitations.

(2) State use of databases

If, pursuant to subsection (c)(3), the Commission requires the establishment of a single national database of telephone numbers of subscribers who object to receiving telephone solicitations, a State or local authority may not, in its regulation of telephone solicitations, require the use of any database, list, or listing system that does not include the part of such single national database that relates to such State.

(g) Actions by States

(1) Authority of States

Whenever the attorney general of a State, or an official or agency designated by a State, has reason to believe that any person has engaged or is engaging in a pattern or practice of telephone calls or other transmissions to residents of that State in violation of this section or the regulations prescribed under this section, the State may bring a civil action on behalf of its residents to enjoin such calls, an action to recover for actual monetary loss or receive $500 in damages for each violation, or both such actions. If the court finds the defendant willfully or knowingly violated such regulations, the court may, in its discretion, increase the amount of the award to an amount equal to not more than 3 times the amount available under the preceding sentence.

(2) Exclusive jurisdiction of Federal courts

The district courts of the United States, the United States courts of any territory, and the District Court of the United States for the District of Columbia shall have exclusive jurisdiction over all civil actions brought under this subsection. Upon proper application, such courts shall also have jurisdiction to issue writs of mandamus, or orders affording like relief, commanding the defendant to comply with the provisions of this section or regulations prescribed under this section, including the requirement that the defendant take such action as is necessary to remove the danger of such violation. Upon a proper showing, a permanent or temporary injunction or restraining order shall be granted without bond.

(3) Rights of Commission

The State shall serve prior written notice of any such civil action upon the Commission and provide the Commission with a copy of its complaint, except in any case where such prior notice is not feasible, in which case the State shall serve such notice immediately upon instituting such action. The Commission shall have the right (A) to intervene in the action, (B) upon so intervening, to be heard on all matters arising therein, and (C) to file petitions for appeal.

(4) Venue; service of process

Any civil action brought under this subsection in a district court of the United States may be brought in the district wherein the defendant is found or is an inhabitant or transacts business or wherein the violation occurred or is occurring, and process in such cases may be served in any district in which the defendant is an inhabitant or where the defendant may be found.

(5) Investigatory powers

For purposes of bringing any civil action under this subsection, nothing in this section shall prevent the attorney general of a State, or an official or agency designated by a State, from exercising the powers conferred on the attorney general or such official by the laws of such State to conduct investigations or to administer oaths or affirmations or to compel the attendance of witnesses or the production of documentary and other evidence.

(6) Effect on State court proceedings

Nothing contained in this subsection shall be construed to prohibit an authorized State official from proceeding in State court on the basis of an alleged violation of any general civil or criminal statute of such State.

(7) Limitation

Whenever the Commission has instituted a civil action for violation of regulations prescribed under this section, no State may, during the pendency of such action instituted by the Commission, subsequently institute a civil action against any defendant named in the Commission's complaint for any violation as alleged in the Commission's complaint.

(8) "Attorney general" defined

As used in this subsection, the term "attorney general" means the chief legal officer of a State.

(h) Junk fax enforcement report

The Commission shall submit an annual report to Congress regarding the enforcement during the past year of the provisions of this section relating to sending of unsolicited advertisements to telephone facsimile machines, which report shall include-

(1) the number of complaints received by the Commission during such year alleging that a consumer received an unsolicited advertisement via telephone facsimile machine in violation of the Commission's rules;

(2) the number of citations issued by the Commission pursuant to section 503 of this title during the year to enforce any law, regulation, or policy relating to sending of unsolicited advertisements to telephone facsimile machines;

(3) the number of notices of apparent liability issued by the Commission pursuant to section 503 of this title during the year to enforce any law, regulation, or policy relating to sending of unsolicited advertisements to telephone facsimile machines;

(4) for each notice referred to in paragraph (3)-

    (A) the amount of the proposed forfeiture penalty involved;

    (B) the person to whom the notice was issued;

    (C) the length of time between the date on which the complaint was filed and the date on which the notice was issued; and

    (D) the status of the proceeding;

(5) the number of final orders imposing forfeiture penalties issued pursuant to section 503 of this title during the year to enforce any law, regulation, or policy relating to sending of unsolicited advertisements to telephone facsimile machines;

(6) for each forfeiture order referred to in paragraph (5)-

    (A) the amount of the penalty imposed by the order;

    (B) the person to whom the order was issued;

    (C) whether the forfeiture penalty has been paid; and

    (D) the amount paid;

(7) for each case in which a person has failed to pay a forfeiture penalty imposed by such a final order, whether the Commission referred such matter for recovery of the penalty; and

(8) for each case in which the Commission referred such an order for recovery-

    (A) the number of days from the date the Commission issued such order to the date of such referral;

    (B) whether an action has been commenced to recover the penalty, and if so, the number of days from the date the Commission referred such order for recovery to the date of such commencement; and

    (C) whether the recovery action resulted in collection of any amount, and if so, the amount collected.

DRIVER'S PRIVACY PROTECTION ACT
(1994)

Summary

The Driver's Privacy Protection Act requires all States to protect the privacy of personal information contained in an individual's motor vehicle record. This information includes the driver's name, address, phone number, Social Security Number, driver identification number, photograph, height, weight, gender, age, certain medical or disability information, and in some states, fingerprints. It does not include information concerning a driver's traffic violations, license status, or accidents.

The Act has a number of exceptions. A driver's personal information may be obtained from the department of motor vehicles for any federal, state or local agency use in carrying out its functions; for any federal, state or local legal proceeding if the proceeding involves a motor vehicle; for automobile and driver safety purposes, such as conducting recall of motor vehicles; and for use in marketing activities if the individual has been given an opportunity to "opt-out." The Act imposes criminal fines for non-compliance and grants individuals a private right of action including actual and punitive damages as well as attorney's fees and litigation costs.

In 1999 Congress amended the law to give drivers additional privacy protections. The amendment requires State DMVs to obtain a driver's express consent before releasing any personal information, regardless of whether the request is made for a particular individual's information or in bulk for marketing purposes. Previously, such information would be released if the individual had failed to opt out of the disclosure.

In 2000 the Supreme Court upheld the constitutionality of the Drivers Privacy Protection Act following a challenge by the state of South Carolina which alleged that the Act violated principles of federalism. The Court held that the Act is a proper exercise of Congress' authority to regulate interstate commerce under the Commerce Clause.

References

Public Law 103-322. Codified as amended at 18 U.S.C. § 2721 et seq.
[https://www.law.cornell.edu/uscode/text/18/2721]

Condon v. Reno, 528 U.S. 141 (2000)
[https://www.law.cornell.edu/supct/html/98-1464.ZO.html]

EPIC, The Drivers Privacy Protection Act and the Privacy of Your State Motor Vehicle Record
[https://www.epic.org/privacy/drivers/]

United States
Driver's Privacy Protection Act

18 U.S.C. § 2721. Prohibition on release and use of certain personal information from State motor vehicle records

(a) In General. – A State department of motor vehicles, and any officer, employee, or contractor thereof, shall not knowingly disclose or otherwise make available to any person or entity:

    (1) personal information, as defined in 18 U.S.C. 2725(3), about any individual obtained by the department in connection with a motor vehicle record, except as provided in subsection (b) of this section; or

    (2) highly restricted personal information, as defined in 18 U.S.C. 2725(4), about any individual obtained by the department in connection with a motor vehicle record, without the express consent of the person to whom such information applies, except uses permitted in subsections (b)(1), (b)(4), (b)(6) and (b)(9): Provided, that subsection (a)(2) shall not in any way affect the use of organ donation information on an individual's license or affect the administration of organ donation initiatives in the States.

(b) Permissible Uses. - Personal information referred to in subsection (a) shall be disclosed for use in connection with matters of motor vehicle or driver safety and theft, motor vehicle emissions, motor vehicle product alterations, recalls, or advisories, performance monitoring of motor vehicles and dealers by motor vehicle manufacturers, and removal of non-owner records from the original owner records of motor vehicle manufacturers to carry out the purposes of the Automobile Information Disclosure Act, the Motor Vehicle Information and Cost Saving Act, the National Traffic and Motor Vehicle Safety Act of 1966, the Anti-Car Theft Act of 1992, and the Clean Air Act, and, subject to subsection (a)(2), may be disclosed as follows:

    (1) For use by any government agency, including any court or law enforcement agency, in carrying out its functions, or any private person or entity acting on behalf of a Federal, State, or local agency in carrying out its functions.

    (2) For use in connection with matters of motor vehicle or driver safety and theft; motor vehicle emissions; motor vehicle product alterations, recalls, or advisories; performance monitoring of motor vehicles, motor vehicle parts and dealers; motor vehicle market research activities, including survey research; and removal of non-owner records from the original owner records of motor vehicle manufacturers.

    (3) For use in the normal course of business by a legitimate business or its agents, employees, or contractors, but only -

        (A) to verify the accuracy of personal information submitted by the individual to the business or its agents, employees, or contractors; and

        (B) if such information as so submitted is not correct or is no longer correct, to obtain the correct information, but only for the purposes of preventing fraud by, pursuing legal remedies against, or recovering on a debt or security interest against, the individual.

(4) For use in connection with any civil, criminal, administrative, or arbitral proceeding in any Federal, State, or local court or agency or before any self-regulatory body, including the service of process, investigation in anticipation of litigation, and the execution or enforcement of judgments and orders, or pursuant to an order of a Federal, State, or local court.

(5) For use in research activities, and for use in producing statistical reports, so long as the personal information is not published, redisclosed, or used to contact individuals.

(6) For use by any insurer or insurance support organization, or by a self-insured entity, or its agents, employees, or contractors, in connection with claims investigation activities, antifraud activities, rating or underwriting.

(7) For use in providing notice to the owners of towed or impounded vehicles.

(8) For use by any licensed private investigative agency or licensed security service for any purpose permitted under this subsection.

(9) For use by an employer or its agent or insurer to obtain or verify information relating to a holder of a commercial driver's license that is required under the Commercial Motor Vehicle Safety Act of 1986 (49 U.S.C. App. 2710 et seq.)

(10) For use in connection with the operation of private toll transportation facilities.

(11) For any other use in response to requests for individual motor vehicle records if the State has obtained the express consent of the person to whom such personal information pertains.

(12) For bulk distribution for surveys, marketing or solicitations if the State has obtained the express consent of the person to whom such personal information pertains.

(13) For use by any requester, if the requester demonstrates it has obtained the written consent of the individual to whom the information pertains.

(14) For any other use specifically authorized under the law of the State that holds the record, if such use is related to the operation of a motor vehicle or public safety.

(c) Resale or Redisclosure. - An authorized recipient of personal information (except a recipient under subsection (b)(11) or (12)) may resell or redisclose the information only for a use permitted under subsection (b) (but not for uses under subsection (b)(11) or (12)). An authorized recipient under subsection (b)(11) may resell or redisclose personal information for any purpose. An authorized recipient under subsection (b)(12) may resell or redisclose personal information pursuant to subsection (b)(12). Any authorized recipient (except a recipient under subsection (b)(11)) that resells or rediscloses personal information covered by this title must keep for a period of 5 years records identifying each person or entity that receives information and the permitted purpose for which the information will be used and must make such records available to the motor vehicle department upon request.

(d) Waiver Procedures. - A State motor vehicle department may establish and carry out procedures under which the department or its agents, upon receiving a request for personal information that does not fall within one of the exceptions in subsection (b), may mail a copy of the request to the individual about whom the information was requested, informing such individual of the request, together with a statement to the effect that the information will not be released unless the individual waives such individual's right to privacy under this section.

(e) Prohibition on Conditions. - No State may condition or burden in any way the issuance of an individual's motor vehicle record as defined in 18 U.S.C. 2725(1) to obtain express consent. Nothing in this paragraph shall be construed to prohibit a State from charging an administrative fee for issuance of a motor vehicle record.

Sec. 2722. Additional unlawful acts

(a) Procurement for Unlawful Purpose. - It shall be unlawful for any person knowingly to obtain or disclose personal information, from a motor vehicle record, for any use not permitted under section 2721(b) of this title.

(b) False Representation. - It shall be unlawful for any person to make false representation to obtain any personal information from an individual's motor vehicle record.

Sec. 2723. Penalties

(a) Criminal Fine. - A person who knowingly violates this chapter shall be fined under this title.

(b) Violations by State Department of Motor Vehicles. - Any State department of motor vehicles that has a policy or practice of substantial noncompliance with this chapter shall be subject to a civil penalty imposed by the Attorney General of not more than $5,000 a day for each day of substantial noncompliance.

Sec. 2724. Civil action

(a) Cause of Action. - A person who knowingly obtains, discloses or uses personal information, from a motor vehicle record, for a purpose not permitted under this chapter shall be liable to the individual to whom the information pertains, who may bring a civil action in a United States district court.

(b) Remedies. - The court may award - (1) actual damages, but not less than liquidated damages in the amount of $2,500; (2) punitive damages upon proof of willful or reckless disregard of the law; (3) reasonable attorneys' fees and other litigation costs reasonably incurred; and (4) such other preliminary and equitable relief as the court determines to be appropriate.

Sec. 2725. Definitions

In this chapter -

(1) "motor vehicle record" means any record that pertains to a motor vehicle operator's permit, motor vehicle title, motor vehicle registration, or identification card issued by a department of motor vehicles;

(2) "person" means an individual, organization or entity, but does not include a State or agency thereof;

(3) "personal information" means information that identifies an individual, including an individual's photograph, social security number, driver identification number, name, address (but not the 5-digit zip code), telephone number, and medical or disability information, but does not include information on vehicular accidents, driving violations, and driver's status.

(4) "highly restricted personal information" means an individual's photograph or image, social security number, medical or disability information; and

(5) "express consent" means consent in writing, including consent conveyed electronically that bears an electronic signature as defined in section 106(5) of Public Law 106-229.

TELECOMMUNICATIONS ACT (1996)
[EXCERPT]

Summary

The Telecommunications Act of 1996 amends the 1934 Communications Act. Section 222 of the Act provides that telecommunications carriers must protect the confidentiality of Consumer Proprietary Network Information (CPNI). CPNI includes calling patterns, billing records, unlisted telephone numbers and home addresses of service subscribers. The Act further provides that carriers receiving CPNI in connection with providing services can use the information only for that purpose and not for their own marketing purposes. Moreover, the Act allows carriers to use, disclose, and permit access to individually identifiable CPNI only when directed by the consumer or in connection with providing services for the consumer.

In 1998 the Federal Communications Commission issued a Second Report and Order and Further Notice of Proposed Rulemaking, which interpreted and implemented Section 222 of the Telecommunications Act of 1996. The FCC's Order adopted an opt-in approach, requiring carriers to obtain express approval before disclosing a customer's CPNI. However, in 1999 a federal appeals court vacated the FCC's Order, holding that the regulations of the FCC violated the First Amendment.

In 1999 the Congress enacted the Wireless Communications and Public Safety Act which promoted the use of 9-1-1, the universal emergency assistance number, and established certain privacy safeguards to limit the use of call location information to the delivery of emergency services and to further limit the use of wireless location information to those circumstances where the customer has provided "express prior authorization."

References

> Public Law 104-104. Codified as amended at 47 U.S.C. §222 et seq.
> [https://www.law.cornell.edu/uscode/text/47/222]

> "In the Matter of Implementation of the Telecommunications Act of 1996: Telecommunications Carriers' Use of Customer Proprietary Network Information and Other Customer Information," adopted May 21, 1998
> [https://transition.fcc.gov/Bureaus/Common_Carrier/Orders/1998/da980971.pdf]

47 U.S.C. Sec. 222. Privacy of customer information

(a) In general

Every telecommunications carrier has a duty to protect the confidentiality of proprietary information of, and relating to, other telecommunication carriers, equipment manufacturers, and customers, including telecommunication carriers reselling telecommunications services provided by a telecommunications carrier.

(b) Confidentiality of carrier information

A telecommunications carrier that receives or obtains proprietary information from another carrier for purposes of providing any telecommunications service shall use such information only for such purpose, and shall not use such information for its own marketing efforts.

(c) Confidentiality of customer proprietary network information

(1) Privacy requirements for telecommunications carriers

Except as required by law or with the approval of the customer, a telecommunications carrier that receives or obtains customer proprietary network information by virtue of its provision of a telecommunications service shall only use, disclose, or permit access to individually identifiable customer proprietary network information in its provision of (A) the telecommunications service from which such information is derived, or (B) services necessary to, or used in, the provision of such telecommunications service, including the publishing of directories.

(2) Disclosure on request by customers

A telecommunications carrier shall disclose customer proprietary network information, upon affirmative written request by the customer, to any person designated by the customer.

(3) Aggregate customer information

A telecommunications carrier that receives or obtains customer proprietary network information by virtue of its provision of a telecommunications service may use, disclose, or permit access to aggregate customer information other than for the purposes described in paragraph (1). A local exchange carrier may use, disclose, or permit access to aggregate customer information other than for purposes described in paragraph (1) only if it provides such aggregate information to other carriers or persons on reasonable and nondiscriminatory terms and conditions upon reasonable request therefor.

(d) Exceptions

Nothing in this section prohibits a telecommunications carrier from using, disclosing, or permitting access to customer proprietary network information obtained from its customers, either directly or indirectly through its agents-

(1) to initiate, render, bill, and collect for telecommunications services;

(2) to protect the rights or property of the carrier, or to protect users of those services and other carriers from fraudulent, abusive, or unlawful use of, or subscription to, such services;

(3) to provide any inbound telemarketing, referral, or administrative services to the customer for the duration of the call, if such call was initiated by the customer and the customer approves of the use of such information to provide such service; and

(4) to provide call location information concerning the user of a commercial mobile service (as such term is defined in section 332(d) of this title) or the user of an IP-enabled voice service (as such term is defined in section 615b of this title)-

(A) to a public safety answering point, emergency medical service provider or emergency dispatch provider, public safety, fire service, or law enforcement official, or hospital emergency or trauma care facility, in order to respond to the user's call for emergency services;

(B) to inform the user's legal guardian or members of the user's immediate family of the user's location in an emergency situation that involves the risk of death or serious physical harm; or

(C) to providers of information or database management services solely for purposes of assisting in the delivery of emergency services in response to an emergency.

(e) Subscriber list information

Notwithstanding subsections (b), (c), and (d), a telecommunications carrier that provides telephone exchange service shall provide subscriber list information gathered in its capacity as a provider of such service on a timely and unbundled basis, under nondiscriminatory and reasonable rates, terms, and conditions, to any person upon request for the purpose of publishing directories in any format.

(f) Authority to use location information

For purposes of subsection (c)(1), without the express prior authorization of the customer, a customer shall not be considered to have approved the use or disclosure of or access to-

(1) call location information concerning the user of a commercial mobile service (as such term is defined in section 332(d) of this title) or the user of an IP-enabled voice service (as such term is defined in section 615b of this title), other than in accordance with subsection (d)(4); or

(2) automatic crash notification information to any person other than for use in the operation of an automatic crash notification system.

(g) Subscriber listed and unlisted information for emergency services

Notwithstanding subsections (b), (c), and (d), a telecommunications carrier that provides telephone exchange service or a provider of IP-enabled voice service (as such term is defined in section 615b of this title) shall provide information described in subsection (i)(3)(A) (including information pertaining to subscribers whose information is unlisted or unpublished) that is in its possession or control (including information pertaining to subscribers of other carriers) on a timely and unbundled basis, under nondiscriminatory and reasonable rates, terms, and conditions to providers of emergency services, and providers of emergency support services, solely for purposes of delivering or assisting in the delivery of emergency services.

(h) Definitions

As used in this section:

(1) Customer proprietary network information

The term "customer proprietary network information" means-

(A) information that relates to the quantity, technical configuration, type, destination, location, and amount of use of a telecommunications service subscribed to by any customer of a telecommunications carrier, and that is made available to the carrier by the customer solely by virtue of the carrier-customer relationship; and

(B) information contained in the bills pertaining to telephone exchange service or telephone toll service received by a customer of a carrier; except that such term does not include subscriber list information.

(2) Aggregate information

The term "aggregate customer information" means collective data that relates to a group or category of services or customers, from which individual customer identities and characteristics have been removed.

(3) Subscriber list information

The term "subscriber list information" means any information-

(A) identifying the listed names of subscribers of a carrier and such subscribers' telephone numbers, addresses, or primary advertising classifications (as such classifications are assigned at the time of the establishment of such service), or any combination of such listed names, numbers, addresses, or classifications; and

(B) that the carrier or an affiliate has published, caused to be published, or accepted for publication in any directory format.

(4) Public safety answering point

The term "public safety answering point" means a facility that has been designated to receive emergency calls and route them to emergency service personnel.

(5) Emergency services

The term "emergency services" means 9–1–1 emergency services and emergency notification services.

(6) Emergency notification services

The term "emergency notification services" means services that notify the public of an emergency.

(7) Emergency support services

The term "emergency support services" means information or data base management services used in support of emergency services.

CHILDREN'S ONLINE PRIVACY
PROTECTION ACT (1998)

Summary

The Children's Online Privacy Protection Act of 1998 prohibits an operator of a website or online service directed to children, or any operator having actual knowledge that it is doing so, from collecting personal information from a child in a manner that violates regulations required under this title which are designed to protect such children from unlawful and deceptive practices in the collection of personal information. The Act provides an exception for information disclosed to a child's parent.

The Act directs the Federal Trade Commission (FTC) to prescribe regulations requiring such operators to follow specified procedures in connection with the collection and use of personal information from children, including: (1) obtaining verifiable parental consent for the collection, use, or disclosure of such information; and (2) requiring such operators to establish and maintain procedures to protect the confidentiality, security, and integrity of collected information. It provides exceptions to the parental consent requirement. The Act allows an operator to satisfy such regulatory requirements by following a set of FTC-approved self-regulatory guidelines established by appropriate online representatives. The Act directs the FTC to provide incentives for such self-regulation.

The Act authorizes the States to enforce such regulations by bringing actions on behalf of its residents, requiring the appropriate attorney general to first notify the FTC of such action. It authorizes the FTC to intervene in any such action, and it provides for enforcement through the Federal Trade Commission Act. It also directs the FTC to review and report to the Congress on implementation.

References

Public Law 105-27. Codified at 15 U.S.C. § 6501 et seq.
[https://www.law.cornell.edu/uscode/text/15/6501]

EPIC, Children's Online Privacy Protection Act (COPPA)
[https://www.epic.org/privacy/kids/]

15 U.S.C. § 6501. Definitions

In this title:

(1) Child. The term "child" means an individual under the age of 13.

(2) Operator. The term "operator"–

(A) means any person who operates a website located on the Internet or an online service and who collects or maintains personal information from or about the users of or visitors to such website or online service, or on whose behalf such information is collected or maintained, where such website or online service is operated for commercial purposes, including any person offering products or services for sale through that website or online service, involving commerce–

(i) among the several States or with 1 or more foreign nations;

(ii) in any territory of the United States or in the District of Columbia, or between any such territory and–

(I) another such territory; or

(II) any State or foreign nation; or

(iii) between the District of Columbia and any State, territory, or foreign nation; but

(B) does not include any nonprofit entity that would otherwise be exempt from coverage under section 5 of the Federal Trade Commission Act.

(3) Commission. The term "Commission" means the Federal Trade Commission.

(4) Disclosure. The term "disclosure" means, with respect to personal information–

(A) the release of personal information collected from a child in identifiable form by an operator for any purpose, except where such information is provided to a person other than the operator who provides support for the internal operations of the website and does not disclose or use that information for any other purpose; and

(B) making personal information collected from a child by a website or online service directed to children or with actual knowledge that such information was collected from a child, publicly available in identifiable form, by any means including by a public posting, through the Internet, or through–

(i) a home page of a website;

(ii) a pen pal service;

(iii) an electronic mail service;

(iv) a message board; or

(v) a chat room.

(5) Federal agency. The term "Federal agency" means an agency, as that term is defined in section 551(1) of title 5, United States Code.

(6) Internet. The term "Internet" means collectively the myriad of computer and telecommunications facilities, including equipment and operating software, which comprise the interconnected world-wide network of networks that employ the Transmission Control Protocol/Internet Protocol, or any predecessor or successor protocols to such protocol, to communicate information of all kinds by wire or radio.

(7) Parent. The term "parent" includes a legal guardian.

(8) Personal information. The term "personal information" means individually identifiable information about an individual collected online, including–

(A) a first and last name;

(B) a home or other physical address including street name and name of a city or town;

(C) an e-mail address;

(D) a telephone number;

(E) a Social Security number;

(F) any other identifier that the Commission determines permits the physical or online contacting of a specific individual; or

(G) information concerning the child or the parents of that child that the website collects online from the child and combines with an identifier described in this paragraph.

(9) Verifiable parental consent. The term "verifiable parental consent" means any reasonable effort (taking into consideration available technology), including a request for authorization for future collection, use, and disclosure described in the notice, to ensure that a parent of a child receives notice of the operator's personal information collection, use, and disclosure practices, and authorizes the collection, use, and disclosure, as applicable, of personal information and the subsequent use of that information before that information is collected from that child.

(10) Website or online service directed to children.

(A) In general. The term "website or online service directed to children" means–

(i) a commercial website or online service that is targeted to children; or

(ii) that portion of a commercial website or online service that is targeted to children.

(B) Limitation. A commercial website or online service, or a portion of a commercial website or online service, shall not be deemed directed to children solely for referring or linking to a commercial website or online service directed to children by using information location tools, including a directory, index, reference, pointer, or hypertext link.

(11) Person. The term "person" means any individual, partnership, corporation, trust, estate, cooperative, association, or other entity.

(12) Online contact information. The term "online contact information" means an e-mail address or another substantially similar identifier that permits direct contact with a person online.

§ 6502. Regulation of unfair and deceptive acts and practices in connection with the collection and use of personal information from and about children on the Internet

(a) Acts prohibited

(1) In general. It is unlawful for an operator of a website or online service directed to children, or any operator that has actual knowledge that it is collecting personal information from a child, to collect personal information from a child in a manner that violates the regulations prescribed under subsection (b).

(2) Disclosure to parent protected. Notwithstanding paragraph (1), neither an operator of such a website or online service nor the operator's agent shall be held to be liable under any Federal or State law for any disclosure made in good faith and following reasonable procedures in responding to a request for disclosure of personal information under subsection (b)(1)(B)(iii) to the parent of a child.

(b) Regulations

(1) In general. Not later than 1 year after the date of the enactment of this Act, the Commission shall promulgate under section 553 of title 5, United States Code, regulations that–

(A) require the operator of any website or online service directed to children that collects personal information from children or the operator of a website or online service that has actual knowledge that it is collecting personal information from a child–

(i) to provide notice on the website of what information is collected from children by the operator, how the operator uses such information, and the operator's disclosure practices for such information; and

(ii) to obtain verifiable parental consent for the collection, use, or disclosure of personal information from children;

(B) require the operator to provide, upon request of a parent under this subparagraph whose child has provided personal information to that website or online service, upon proper identification of that parent, to such parent–

(i) a description of the specific types of personal information collected from the child by that operator;

(ii) the opportunity at any time to refuse to permit the operator's further use or maintenance in retrievable form, or future online collection, of personal information from that child; and

(iii) notwithstanding any other provision of law, a means that is reasonable under the circumstances for the parent to obtain any personal information collected from that child;

(C) prohibit conditioning a child's participation in a game, the offering of a prize, or another activity on the child disclosing more personal information than is reasonably necessary to participate in such activity; and

(D) require the operator of such a website or online service to establish and maintain reasonable procedures to protect the confidentiality, security, and integrity of personal information collected from children.

(2) When consent not required. The regulations shall provide that verifiable parental consent under paragraph (1)(A)(ii) is not required in the case of–

(A) online contact information collected from a child that is used only to respond directly on a one-time basis to a specific request from the child and is not used to recontact the child and is not maintained in retrievable form by the operator;

(B) a request for the name or online contact information of a parent or child that is used for the sole purpose of obtaining parental consent or providing notice under this section and where such information is not maintained in retrievable form by the operator if parental consent is not obtained after a reasonable time;

(C) online contact information collected from a child that is used only to respond more than once directly to a specific request from the child and is not used to recontact the child beyond the scope of that request–

(i) if, before any additional response after the initial response to the child, the operator uses reasonable efforts to provide a parent notice of the online contact information collected from the child, the purposes for which it is to be used, and an opportunity for the parent to request that the operator make no further use of the information and that it not be maintained in retrievable form; or

(ii) without notice to the parent in such circumstances as the Commission may determine are appropriate, taking into consideration the benefits to the child of access to information and services, and risks to the security and privacy of the child, in regulations promulgated under this subsection;

(D) the name of the child and online contact information (to the extent reasonably necessary to protect the safety of a child participant on the site)–

(i) used only for the purpose of protecting such safety;

(ii) not used to recontact the child or for any other purpose; and

(iii) not disclosed on the site,

if the operator uses reasonable efforts to provide a parent notice of the name and online contact information collected from the child, the purposes for which it is to be used, and an opportunity for the parent to request that the operator make no further use of the information and that it not be maintained in retrievable form; or

(E) the collection, use, or dissemination of such information by the operator of such a website or online service necessary–

(i) to protect the security or integrity of its website;

(ii) to take precautions against liability;

(iii) to respond to judicial process; or

(iv) to the extent permitted under other provisions of law, to provide information to law enforcement agencies or for an investigation on a matter related to public safety.

(3) Termination of service. The regulations shall permit the operator of a website or an online service to terminate service provided to a child whose parent has refused, under the regulations prescribed under paragraph (1)(B)(ii), to permit the operator's further use or maintenance in retrievable form, or future online collection, of personal information from that child.

(c) Enforcement. Subject to sections 1304 and 1306, a violation of a regulation prescribed under subsection (a) shall be treated as a violation of a rule defining an unfair or deceptive act or practice prescribed under section 18(a)(1)(B) of the Federal Trade Commission Act *(15 U.S.C. 57a(a)(1)(B))*.

(d) Inconsistent State law. No State or local government may impose any liability for commercial activities or actions by operators in interstate or foreign commerce in connection with an activity or action described in this title that is inconsistent with the treatment of those activities or actions under this section.

§ 6503. Safe harbors

(a) Guidelines. An operator may satisfy the requirements of regulations issued under section 1303(b) by following a set of self-regulatory guidelines, issued by representatives of the marketing or online industries, or by other persons, approved under subsection (b).

(b) Incentives

(1) Self-regulatory incentives. In prescribing regulations under section 1303, the Commission shall provide incentives for self-regulation by operators to implement the protections afforded children under the regulatory requirements described in subsection (b) of that section.

(2) Deemed compliance. Such incentives shall include provisions for ensuring that a person will be deemed to be in compliance with the requirements of the regulations under section 1303 if that person complies with guidelines that, after notice and comment, are approved by the Commission upon making a determination that the guidelines meet the requirements of the regulations issued under section 1303.

(3) Expedited response to requests. The Commission shall act upon requests for safe harbor treatment within 180 days of the filing of the request, and shall set forth in writing its conclusions with regard to such requests.

(c) Appeals. Final action by the Commission on a request for approval of guidelines, or the failure to act within 180 days on a request for approval of guidelines, submitted under subsection (b) may be appealed to a district court of the United States of appropriate jurisdiction as provided for in section 706 of title 5, United States Code.

§ 6504. Actions by States

(a) In general

(1) Civil actions. In any case in which the attorney general of a State has reason to believe that an interest of the residents of that State has been or is threatened or adversely affected by the engagement of any person in a practice that violates any regulation of the Commission prescribed under section 1303(b), the State, as parens patriae, may bring a civil action on behalf of the residents of the State in a district court of the United States of appropriate jurisdiction to–

(A) enjoin that practice;

(B) enforce compliance with the regulation;

(C) obtain damage, restitution, or other compensation on behalf of residents of the State; or

(D) obtain such other relief as the court may consider to be appropriate.

(2) Notice

(A) In general. Before filing an action under paragraph (1), the attorney general of the State involved shall provide to the Commission–

(i) written notice of that action; and

(ii) a copy of the complaint for that action.

(B) Exemption

(i) In general. Subparagraph (A) shall not apply with respect to the filing of an action by an attorney general of a State under this subsection, if the attorney general determines that it is not feasible to provide the notice described in that subparagraph before the filing of the action.

(ii) Notification. In an action described in clause (i), the attorney general of a State shall provide notice and a copy of the complaint to the Commission at the same time as the attorney general files the action.

(b) Intervention

(1) In general. On receiving notice under subsection (a)(2), the Commission shall have the right to intervene in the action that is the subject of the notice.

(2) Effect of intervention. If the Commission intervenes in an action under subsection (a), it shall have the right–

(A) to be heard with respect to any matter that arises in that action; and

(B) to file a petition for appeal.

(3) Amicus curiae. Upon application to the court, a person whose self-regulatory guidelines have been approved by the Commission and are relied upon as a defense by any defendant to a proceeding under this section may file amicus curiae in that proceeding.

(c) Construction. For purposes of bringing any civil action under subsection (a), nothing in this title shall be construed to prevent an attorney general of a State from exercising the powers conferred on the attorney general by the laws of that State to–

(1) conduct investigations;

(2) administer oaths or affirmations; or

(3) compel the attendance of witnesses or the production of documentary and other evidence.

(d) Actions by the Commission. In any case in which an action is instituted by or on behalf of the Commission for violation of any regulation prescribed under section 1303, no State may, during the pendency of that action, institute an action under subsection (a) against any defendant named in the complaint in that action for violation of that regulation.

(e) Venue; service of process.

(1) Venue. Any action brought under subsection (a) may be brought in the district court of the United States that meets applicable requirements relating to venue under section 1391 of title 28, United States Code.

(2) Service of process. In an action brought under subsection (a), process may be served in any district in which the defendant–

(A) is an inhabitant; or

(B) may be found.

§ 6505. Administration and applicability of Act

(a) In general. Except as otherwise provided, this title shall be enforced by the Commission under the Federal Trade Commission Act *(15 U.S.C. 41* et seq.).

(b) Provisions. Compliance with the requirements imposed under this title shall be enforced under–

(1) section 8 of the Federal Deposit Insurance Act *(12 U.S.C. 1818),* in the case of–

(A) national banks, and Federal branches and Federal agencies of foreign banks, by the Office of the Comptroller of the Currency;

(B) member banks of the Federal Reserve System (other than national banks), branches and agencies of foreign banks (other than Federal branches, Federal agencies, and insured State branches of foreign banks), commercial lending companies owned or controlled by foreign banks, and organizations operating under section 25 or 25(a) of the Federal Reserve Act *(12 U.S.C. 601* et seq. and 611 et seq.), by the Board; and

(C) banks insured by the Federal Deposit Insurance Corporation (other than members of the Federal Reserve System) and insured State branches of foreign banks, by the Board of Directors of the Federal Deposit Insurance Corporation;

(2) section 8 of the Federal Deposit Insurance Act *(12 U.S.C. 1818),* by the Director of the Office of Thrift Supervision, in the case of a savings association the deposits of which are insured by the Federal Deposit Insurance Corporation;

(3) the Federal Credit Union Act *(12 U.S.C. 1751* et seq.) by the National Credit Union Administration Board with respect to any Federal credit union;

(4) part A of subtitle VII of title 49, United States Code, by the Secretary of Transportation with respect to any air carrier or foreign air carrier subject to that part;

(5) the Packers and Stockyards Act, 1921 *(7 U.S.C. 181* et seq.) (except as provided in section 406 of that Act *(7 U.S.C. 226, 227)),* by the Secretary of Agriculture with respect to any activities subject to that Act; and

(6) the Farm Credit Act of 1971 *(12 U.S.C. 2001* et seq.) by the Farm Credit Administration with respect to any Federal land bank, Federal land bank association, Federal intermediate credit bank, or production credit association.

(c) Exercise of certain powers. For the purpose of the exercise by any agency referred to in subsection (a) of its powers under any Act referred to in that subsection, a violation of any requirement imposed under this title shall be deemed to be a violation of a requirement imposed under that Act. In addition to its powers under any provision of law specifically referred to in subsection (a), each of the agencies referred to in that subsection may exercise, for the purpose of enforcing compliance with any requirement imposed under this title, any other authority conferred on it by law.

(d) Actions by the Commission. The Commission shall prevent any person from violating a rule of the Commission under section 1303 in the same manner, by the same means, and with the same jurisdiction, powers, and duties as though all applicable terms and provisions of the Federal Trade Commission Act *(15 U.S.C. 41* et seq.) were incorporated into and made a part of this title. Any entity that violates such rule shall be subject to the penalties and entitled to the privileges and immunities provided in the Federal Trade Commission Act in the same manner, by the same means, and with the same jurisdiction, power, and duties as though all applicable terms and provisions of the Federal Trade Commission Act were incorporated into and made a part of this title.

(e) Effect on other laws. Nothing contained in the Act shall be construed to limit the authority of the Commission under any other provisions of law.

§ 6506. Review

Not later than 5 years after the effective date of the regulations initially issued under section 6502 of this title, the Commission shall -

> (1) review the implementation of this chapter, including the effect of the implementation of this chapter on practices relating to the collection and disclosure of information relating to children, children's ability to obtain access to information of their choice online, and on the availability of websites directed to children; and
> (2) prepare and submit to Congress a report on the results of the review under paragraph (1).

IDENTITY THEFT AND ASSUMPTION
DETERRENCE ACT (1998)

Summary

Congress passed the Identity Theft and Assumption Deterrence Act in 1998 to address the increasing problem of identity theft. The Act specifically made it a federal crime to "knowingly transfer or use, without lawful authority, a means of identification of another person with the intent to commit, or to aid or abet, any unlawful activity that constitutes a violation of federal law, or that constitutes a felony under any applicable state or local law."

References

Public Law 97-398. Codified as amended at 18 U.S.C. § 1028.
[https://www.law.cornell.edu/uscode/text/18/1028]

§1028. Fraud and related activity in connection with identification documents, authentication features, and information

(a) Whoever, in a circumstance described in subsection (c) of this section-

(1) knowingly and without lawful authority produces an identification document, authentication feature, or a false identification document;

(2) knowingly transfers an identification document, authentication feature, or a false identification document knowing that such document or feature was stolen or produced without lawful authority;

(3) knowingly possesses with intent to use unlawfully or transfer unlawfully five or more identification documents (other than those issued lawfully for the use of the possessor), authentication features, or false identification documents;

(4) knowingly possesses an identification document (other than one issued lawfully for the use of the possessor), authentication feature, or a false identification document, with the intent such document or feature be used to defraud the United States;

(5) knowingly produces, transfers, or possesses a document-making implement or authentication feature with the intent such document-making implement or authentication feature will be used in the production of a false identification document or another document-making implement or authentication feature which will be so used;

(6) knowingly possesses an identification document or authentication feature that is or appears to be an identification document or authentication feature of the United States or a sponsoring entity of an event designated as a special event of national

significance which is stolen or produced without lawful authority knowing that such document or feature was stolen or produced without such authority;

(7) knowingly transfers, possesses, or uses, without lawful authority, a means of identification of another person with the intent to commit, or to aid or abet, or in connection with, any unlawful activity that constitutes a violation of Federal law, or that constitutes a felony under any applicable State or local law; or

(8) knowingly traffics in false or actual authentication features for use in false identification documents, document-making implements, or means of identification; shall be punished as provided in subsection (b) of this section.

(b) The punishment for an offense under subsection (a) of this section is-

(1) except as provided in paragraphs (3) and (4), a fine under this title or imprisonment for not more than 15 years, or both, if the offense is-

(A) the production or transfer of an identification document, authentication feature, or false identification document that is or appears to be-

(i) an identification document or authentication feature issued by or under the authority of the United States; or

(ii) a birth certificate, or a driver's license or personal identification card;

(B) the production or transfer of more than five identification documents, authentication features, or false identification documents;

(C) an offense under paragraph (5) of such subsection; or

(D) an offense under paragraph (7) of such subsection that involves the transfer, possession, or use of 1 or more means of identification if, as a result of the offense, any individual committing the offense obtains anything of value aggregating $1,000 or more during any 1-year period;

(2) except as provided in paragraphs (3) and (4), a fine under this title or imprisonment for not more than 5 years, or both, if the offense is-

(A) any other production, transfer, or use of a means of identification, an identification document, authentication feature, or a false identification document; or

(B) an offense under paragraph (3) or (7) of such subsection;

(3) a fine under this title or imprisonment for not more than 20 years, or both, if the offense is committed-

(A) to facilitate a drug trafficking crime (as defined in section 929(a)(2));

(B) in connection with a crime of violence (as defined in section 924(c)(3)); or

(C) after a prior conviction under this section becomes final;

(4) a fine under this title or imprisonment for not more than 30 years, or both, if the offense is committed to facilitate an act of domestic terrorism (as defined under section 2331(5) of this title) or an act of international terrorism (as defined in section 2331(1) of this title);

(5) in the case of any offense under subsection (a), forfeiture to the United States of any personal property used or intended to be used to commit the offense; and

(6) a fine under this title or imprisonment for not more than one year, or both, in any other case.

(c) The circumstance referred to in subsection (a) of this section is that-

(1) the identification document, authentication feature, or false identification document is or appears to be issued by or under the authority of the United States or a sponsoring entity of an event designated as a special event of national significance or the document-making implement is designed or suited for making such an identification document, authentication feature, or false identification document;

(2) the offense is an offense under subsection (a)(4) of this section; or

(3) either-

(A) the production, transfer, possession, or use prohibited by this section is in or affects interstate or foreign commerce, including the transfer of a document by electronic means; or

(B) the means of identification, identification document, false identification document, or document-making implement is transported in the mail in the course of the production, transfer, possession, or use prohibited by this section.

(d) In this section and section 1028A-

(1) the term "authentication feature" means any hologram, watermark, certification, symbol, code, image, sequence of numbers or letters, or other feature that either individually or in combination with another feature is used by the issuing authority on an identification document, document-making implement, or means of identification to determine if the document is counterfeit, altered, or otherwise falsified;

(2) the term "document-making implement" means any implement, impression, template, computer file, computer disc, electronic device, or computer hardware or software, that is specifically configured or primarily used for making an identification document, a false identification document, or another document-making implement;

(3) the term "identification document" means a document made or issued by or under the authority of the United States Government, a State, political subdivision of a State, a sponsoring entity of an event designated as a special event of national significance, a foreign government, political subdivision of a foreign government, an international governmental or an international quasi-governmental organization which, when completed with information concerning a particular individual, is of a type intended or commonly accepted for the purpose of identification of individuals;

(4) the term "false identification document" means a document of a type intended or commonly accepted for the purposes of identification of individuals that-

    (A) is not issued by or under the authority of a governmental entity or was issued under the authority of a governmental entity but was subsequently altered for purposes of deceit; and

    (B) appears to be issued by or under the authority of the United States Government, a State, a political subdivision of a State, a sponsoring entity of an event designated by the President as a special event of national significance, a foreign government, a political subdivision of a foreign government, or an international governmental or quasi-governmental organization;

(5) the term "false authentication feature" means an authentication feature that-

    (A) is genuine in origin, but, without the authorization of the issuing authority, has been tampered with or altered for purposes of deceit;

    (B) is genuine, but has been distributed, or is intended for distribution, without the authorization of the issuing authority and not in connection with a lawfully made identification document, document-making implement, or means of identification to which such authentication feature is intended to be affixed or embedded by the respective issuing authority; or

    (C) appears to be genuine, but is not;

(6) the term "issuing authority"-

    (A) means any governmental entity or agency that is authorized to issue identification documents, means of identification, or authentication features; and

    (B) includes the United States Government, a State, a political subdivision of a State, a sponsoring entity of an event designated by the President as a special event of national significance, a foreign government, a political subdivision of a foreign government, or an international government or quasi-governmental organization;

(7) the term "means of identification" means any name or number that may be used, alone or in conjunction with any other information, to identify a specific individual, including any-

    (A) name, social security number, date of birth, official State or government issued driver's license or identification number, alien registration number, government passport number, employer or taxpayer identification number;

    (B) unique biometric data, such as fingerprint, voice print, retina or iris image, or other unique physical representation;

    (C) unique electronic identification number, address, or routing code; or

    (D) telecommunication identifying information or access device (as defined in section 1029(e));

(8) the term "personal identification card" means an identification document issued by a State or local government solely for the purpose of identification;

(9) the term "produce" includes alter, authenticate, or assemble;

(10) the term "transfer" includes selecting an identification document, false identification document, or document-making implement and placing or directing the placement of such identification document, false identification document, or document-making implement on an online location where it is available to others;

(11) the term "State" includes any State of the United States, the District of Columbia, the Commonwealth of Puerto Rico, and any other commonwealth, possession, or territory of the United States; and

(12) the term "traffic" means-

(A) to transport, transfer, or otherwise dispose of, to another, as consideration for anything of value; or

(B) to make or obtain control of with intent to so transport, transfer, or otherwise dispose of.

(e) This section does not prohibit any lawfully authorized investigative, protective, or intelligence activity of a law enforcement agency of the United States, a State, or a political subdivision of a State, or of an intelligence agency of the United States, or any activity authorized under chapter 224 of this title.

(f) Attempt and Conspiracy.-Any person who attempts or conspires to commit any offense under this section shall be subject to the same penalties as those prescribed for the offense, the commission of which was the object of the attempt or conspiracy.

(g) Forfeiture Procedures.-The forfeiture of property under this section, including any seizure and disposition of the property and any related judicial or administrative proceeding, shall be governed by the provisions of section 413 (other than subsection (d) of that section) of the Comprehensive Drug Abuse Prevention and Control Act of 1970 (21 U.S.C. 853).

(h) Forfeiture; Disposition.-In the circumstance in which any person is convicted of a violation of subsection (a), the court shall order, in addition to the penalty prescribed, the forfeiture and destruction or other disposition of all illicit authentication features, identification documents, document-making implements, or means of identification.

(i) Rule of Construction.-For purpose of subsection (a)(7), a single identification document or false identification document that contains 1 or more means of identification shall be construed to be 1 means of identification.

United States
Financial Services Modernization Act

FINANCIAL SERVICES
MODERNIZATION ACT (1999)
[EXCERPTS]

Summary

The Financial Services Modernization Act (also known as the Gramm-Leach-Bliley Act or GLBA) is regarded as the most sweeping legislation affecting banks and other financial institutions since the Depression. The passage of GLBA permits banks, insurance companies, and brokerage firms to operate as one entity, transforming them into a "financial supermarket" and enabling them to offer a wider range of products and services.

The consolidation of these financial institutions, however, has great implications for consumer privacy rights. It enables financial institutions to share consumer information with their affiliates (other commonly owned companies) for sales and promotional purposes. Hence, to regulate the disclosure of consumer data amongst affiliates, GLBA requires financial institutions to give consumers a privacy policy notice informing them of the kind of information it collects about the individual and how it uses that information. It also requires financial institutions to give consumers the right to opt-out or prevent the sale of personal data to third parties. Moreover, GLBA requires financial institutions to develop policies to prevent fraudulent access to confidential financial information. July 1, 2001 is the deadline for financial institutions to comply with the notice requirements.

Although GLBA prohibits financial institutions from disclosing nonpublic information, such as an individual's account number or access code to a third party non-affiliated company (an outside company), it does not prevent these institutions from selling publicly available information, that is information the financial institution reasonably believes is lawfully made available to the general public, to a non-affiliated telemarketer. Thus, if the consumer does not opt-out, the institution is free to sell, lease or otherwise disclose almost anything in its files about the consumer, including medical information, to non-affiliates.

Under GLBA the consumer has no private right of action if a financial institution violates GLBA privacy requirements. However, the consumer can complain to one of the seven federal agencies that have jurisdiction and enforcement authority over financial institutions under GLBA. Once a complaint is made the enforcing agency will investigate the complaint and may bring a court action or an administrative case against the company. However, the agency cannot represent or give legal advice to the complaining party.

Seven federal agencies enforce the privacy provisions of the GLBA. They include the Federal Deposit Insurance Corporation (FDIC), the Federal Reserve, the Office of Thrift Supervision, the Office of Comptroller of the Currency (OCC), the National Credit Union Administration (NCUA), the Securities and Exchange Commission (SEC) and the Federal Trade Commission (FTC).

References

Public Law, 106-102. Codified as amended at 16 U.S.C. §6801 et seq.
[https://www.law.cornell.edu/uscode/text/15/6801

Senate Report, 106-44, Financial Services Modernization Act of 1999
[https://www.congress.gov/congressional-report/106th-congress/senate-report/44/1]

House Report, 106-434, Gramm-Leach-Bliley Act of 1999
[https://www.congress.gov/congressional-report/106th-congress/house-report/434/1]

L. Richard Fischer, *The Law of Financial Privacy* (A.S. Pratt & Sons 2000)

EPIC, Financial Services Modernization Act
[https://www.epic.org/privacy/glba/]

§ 6801. Protection of nonpublic personal information

(a) Privacy obligation policy

It is the policy of the Congress that each financial institution has an affirmative and continuing obligation to respect the privacy of its customers and to protect the security and confidentiality of those customers' nonpublic personal information.

(b) Financial institutions safeguards

In furtherance of the policy in subsection (a), each agency or authority described in section 6805(a) of this title, other than the Bureau of Consumer Financial Protection, shall establish appropriate standards for the financial institutions subject to their jurisdiction relating to administrative, technical, and physical safeguards-

(1) to insure the security and confidentiality of customer records and information;

(2) to protect against any anticipated threats or hazards to the security or integrity of such records; and

(3) to protect against unauthorized access to or use of such records or information which could result in substantial harm or inconvenience to any customer.

§ 6802. Obligations with respect to disclosures of personal information

(a) Notice requirements

Except as otherwise provided in this subchapter, a financial institution may not, directly or through any affiliate, disclose to a nonaffiliated third party any nonpublic personal information, unless such financial institution provides or has provided to the consumer a notice that complies with section 6803 of this title.

(b) Opt out

(1) In general

A financial institution may not disclose nonpublic personal information to a nonaffiliated third party unless-

(A) such financial institution clearly and conspicuously discloses to the consumer, in writing or in electronic form or other form permitted by the regulations prescribed under section 6804 of this title, that such information may be disclosed to such third party;

(B) the consumer is given the opportunity, before the time that such information is initially disclosed, to direct that such information not be disclosed to such third party; and

(C) the consumer is given an explanation of how the consumer can exercise that nondisclosure option.

(2) Exception

This subsection shall not prevent a financial institution from providing nonpublic personal information to a nonaffiliated third party to perform services for or functions on behalf of the financial institution, including marketing of the financial institution's own products or services, or financial products or services offered pursuant to joint agreements between two or more financial institutions that comply with the requirements imposed by the regulations prescribed under section 6804 of this title, if the financial institution fully discloses the providing of such information and enters into a contractual agreement with the third party that requires the third party to maintain the confidentiality of such information.

(c) Limits on reuse of information

Except as otherwise provided in this subchapter, a nonaffiliated third party that receives from a financial institution nonpublic personal information under this section shall not, directly or through an affiliate of such receiving third party, disclose such information to any other person that is a nonaffiliated third party of both the financial institution and such receiving third party, unless such disclosure would be lawful if made directly to such other person by the financial institution.

(d) Limitations on the sharing of account number information for marketing purposes

A financial institution shall not disclose, other than to a consumer reporting agency, an account number or similar form of access number or access code for a credit card account, deposit account, or transaction account of a consumer to any nonaffiliated third party for use in telemarketing, direct mail marketing, or other marketing through electronic mail to the consumer.

(e) General exceptions

Subsections (a) and (b) shall not prohibit the disclosure of nonpublic personal information-

(1) as necessary to effect, administer, or enforce a transaction requested or authorized by the consumer, or in connection with-

(A) servicing or processing a financial product or service requested or authorized by the consumer;

(B) maintaining or servicing the consumer's account with the financial institution, or with another entity as part of a private label credit card program or other extension of credit on behalf of such entity; or

(C) a proposed or actual securitization, secondary market sale (including sales of servicing rights), or similar transaction related to a transaction of the consumer;

(2) with the consent or at the direction of the consumer;

(3)(A) to protect the confidentiality or security of the financial institution's records pertaining to the consumer, the service or product, or the transaction therein; (B) to protect against or prevent actual or potential fraud, unauthorized transactions, claims, or other liability; (C) for required institutional risk control, or for resolving customer disputes or inquiries; (D) to persons holding a legal or beneficial interest relating to the consumer; or (E) to persons acting in a fiduciary or representative capacity on behalf of the consumer;

(4) to provide information to insurance rate advisory organizations, guaranty funds or agencies, applicable rating agencies of the financial institution, persons assessing the institution's compliance with industry standards, and the institution's attorneys, accountants, and auditors;

(5) to the extent specifically permitted or required under other provisions of law and in accordance with the Right to Financial Privacy Act of 1978 [12 U.S.C. 3401 et seq.], to law enforcement agencies (including the Bureau of Consumer Financial Protection a Federal functional regulator, the Secretary of the Treasury with respect to subchapter II of chapter 53 of title 31, and chapter 2 of title I of Public Law 91–508 (12 U.S.C. 1951–1959), a State insurance authority, or the Federal Trade Commission), self-regulatory organizations, or for an investigation on a matter related to public safety;

(6)(A) to a consumer reporting agency in accordance with the Fair Credit Reporting Act [15 U.S.C. 1681 et seq.], or (B) from a consumer report reported by a consumer reporting agency;

(7) in connection with a proposed or actual sale, merger, transfer, or exchange of all or a portion of a business or operating unit if the disclosure of nonpublic personal information concerns solely consumers of such business or unit; or

(8) to comply with Federal, State, or local laws, rules, and other applicable legal requirements; to comply with a properly authorized civil, criminal, or regulatory investigation or subpoena or summons by Federal, State, or local authorities; or to respond to judicial process or government regulatory authorities having jurisdiction over the financial institution for examination, compliance, or other purposes as authorized by law.

United States
Financial Services Modernization Act

§ 6803. Disclosure of institution privacy policy
(a) Disclosure required

At the time of establishing a customer relationship with a consumer and not less than annually during the continuation of such relationship, a financial institution shall provide a clear and conspicuous disclosure to such consumer, in writing or in electronic form or other form permitted by the regulations prescribed under section 6804 of this title, of such financial institution's policies and practices with respect to-

> (1) disclosing nonpublic personal information to affiliates and nonaffiliated third parties, consistent with section 6802 of this title, including the categories of information that may be disclosed;

> (2) disclosing nonpublic personal information of persons who have ceased to be customers of the financial institution; and

> (3) protecting the nonpublic personal information of consumers.

(b) Regulations

Disclosures required by subsection (a) shall be made in accordance with the regulations prescribed under section 6804 of this title.

(c) Information to be included

The disclosure required by subsection (a) shall include-

> (1) the policies and practices of the institution with respect to disclosing nonpublic personal information to nonaffiliated third parties, other than agents of the institution, consistent with section 6802 of this title, and including-

>> (A) the categories of persons to whom the information is or may be disclosed, other than the persons to whom the information may be provided pursuant to section 6802(e) of this title; and

>> (B) the policies and practices of the institution with respect to disclosing of nonpublic personal information of persons who have ceased to be customers of the financial institution;

> (2) the categories of nonpublic personal information that are collected by the financial institution;

> (3) the policies that the institution maintains to protect the confidentiality and security of nonpublic personal information in accordance with section 6801 of this title; and

> (4) the disclosures required, if any, under section 1681a(d)(2)(A)(iii) of this title.

(d) Exemption for certified public accountants

> (1) In general

The disclosure requirements of subsection (a) do not apply to any person, to the extent that the person is-

>> (A) a certified public accountant;

>> (B) certified or licensed for such purpose by a State; and

>> (C) subject to any provision of law, rule, or regulation issued by a legislative or regulatory body of the State, including rules of professional conduct or

ethics, that prohibits disclosure of nonpublic personal information without the knowing and expressed consent of the consumer.

(2) Limitation

Nothing in this subsection shall be construed to exempt or otherwise exclude any financial institution that is affiliated or becomes affiliated with a certified public accountant described in paragraph (1) from any provision of this section.

(3) Definitions

For purposes of this subsection, the term "State" means any State or territory of the United States, the District of Columbia, Puerto Rico, Guam, American Samoa, the Trust Territory of the Pacific Islands, the Virgin Islands, or the Northern Mariana Islands.

(e) Model forms

(1) In general

The agencies referred to in section 6804(a)(1) of this title shall jointly develop a model form which may be used, at the option of the financial institution, for the provision of disclosures under this section.

(2) Format

A model form developed under paragraph (1) shall-

(A) be comprehensible to consumers, with a clear format and design;

(B) provide for clear and conspicuous disclosures;

(C) enable consumers easily to identify the sharing practices of a financial institution and to compare privacy practices among financial institutions; and

(D) be succinct, and use an easily readable type font.

(3) Timing

A model form required to be developed by this subsection shall be issued in proposed form for public comment not later than 180 days after October 13, 2006.

(4) Safe harbor

Any financial institution that elects to provide the model form developed by the agencies under this subsection shall be deemed to be in compliance with the disclosures required under this section.

(f) Exception to annual notice requirement

A financial institution that-

(1) provides nonpublic personal information only in accordance with the provisions of subsection (b)(2) or (e) of section 6802 of this title or regulations prescribed under section 6804(b) of this title, and

(2) has not changed its policies and practices with regard to disclosing nonpublic personal information from the policies and practices that were disclosed in the most recent disclosure sent to consumers in accordance with this section,

shall not be required to provide an annual disclosure under this section until such time as the financial institution fails to comply with any criteria described in paragraph (1) or (2).

United States
Financial Services Modernization Act

§ 6804. Rulemaking

(a) Regulatory authority

(1) Rulemaking

(A) In general

Except as provided in subparagraph (C), the Bureau of Consumer Financial Protection and the Securities and Exchange Commission shall have authority to prescribe such regulations as may be necessary to carry out the purposes of this subchapter with respect to financial institutions and other persons subject to their respective jurisdiction under section 6805 of this title (and notwithstanding subtitle B of the Consumer Financial Protection Act of 2010 [12 U.S.C. 5511 et seq.]), except that the Bureau of Consumer Financial Protection shall not have authority to prescribe regulations with respect to the standards under section 6801 of this title.

(B) CFTC

The Commodity Futures Trading Commission shall have authority to prescribe such regulations as may be necessary to carry out the purposes of this subchapter with respect to financial institutions and other persons subject to the jurisdiction of the Commodity Futures Trading Commission under section 7b–2 of title 7.

(C) Federal Trade Commission authority

Notwithstanding the authority of the Bureau of Consumer Financial Protection under subparagraph (A), the Federal Trade Commission shall have authority to prescribe such regulations as may be necessary to carry out the purposes of this subchapter with respect to any financial institution that is a person described in section 1029(a) of the Consumer Financial Protection Act of 2010 [12 U.S.C. 5519(a)].

(D) Rule of construction

Nothing in this paragraph shall be construed to alter, affect, or otherwise limit the authority of a State insurance authority to adopt regulations to carry out this subchapter.

(2) Coordination, consistency, and comparability

Each of the agencies authorized under paragraph (1) to prescribe regulations shall consult and coordinate with the other such agencies and, as appropriate, and with representatives of State insurance authorities designated by the National Association of Insurance Commissioners, for the purpose of assuring, to the extent possible, that the regulations prescribed by each such agency are consistent and comparable with the regulations prescribed by the other such agencies.

(3) Procedures and deadline

Such regulations shall be prescribed in accordance with applicable requirements of title 5.

(b) Authority to grant exceptions

The regulations prescribed under subsection (a) may include such additional exceptions to subsections (a) through (d) of section 6802 of this title as are deemed consistent with the purposes of this subchapter.

§ 6805. Enforcement

(a) In general

Subject to subtitle B of the Consumer Financial Protection Act of 2010 [12 U.S.C. 5511 et seq.], this subchapter and the regulations prescribed thereunder shall be enforced by the Bureau of Consumer Financial Protection, the Federal functional regulators, the State insurance authorities, and the Federal Trade Commission with respect to financial institutions and other persons subject to their jurisdiction under applicable law, as follows:

(1) Under section 1818 of title 12, by the appropriate Federal banking agency, as defined in section 1813(q) of title 12, in the case of-

(A) national banks, Federal branches and Federal agencies of foreign banks, and any subsidiaries of such entities (except brokers, dealers, persons providing insurance, investment companies, and investment advisers);

(B) member banks of the Federal Reserve System (other than national banks), branches and agencies of foreign banks (other than Federal branches, Federal agencies, and insured State branches of foreign banks), commercial lending companies owned or controlled by foreign banks, organizations operating under section 25 or 25A of the Federal Reserve Act [12 U.S.C. 601 et seq., 611 et seq.], and bank holding companies and their nonbank subsidiaries or affiliates (except brokers, dealers, persons providing insurance, investment companies, and investment advisers);

(C) banks insured by the Federal Deposit Insurance Corporation (other than members of the Federal Reserve System), insured State branches of foreign banks, and any subsidiaries of such entities (except brokers, dealers, persons providing insurance, investment companies, and investment advisers); and

(D) savings associations the deposits of which are insured by the Federal Deposit Insurance Corporation, and any subsidiaries of such savings associations (except brokers, dealers, persons providing insurance, investment companies, and investment advisers).

(2) Under the Federal Credit Union Act [12 U.S.C. 1751 et seq.], by the Board of the National Credit Union Administration with respect to any federally insured credit union, and any subsidiaries of such an entity.

(3) Under the Securities Exchange Act of 1934 [15 U.S.C. 78a et seq.], by the Securities and Exchange Commission with respect to any broker or dealer.

(4) Under the Investment Company Act of 1940 [15 U.S.C. 80a–1 et seq.], by the Securities and Exchange Commission with respect to investment companies.

(5) Under the Investment Advisers Act of 1940 [15 U.S.C. 80b–1 et seq.], by the Securities and Exchange Commission with respect to investment advisers registered with the Commission under such Act.

(6) Under State insurance law, in the case of any person engaged in providing insurance, by the applicable State insurance authority of the State in which the person is domiciled, subject to section 6701 of this title.

(7) Under the Federal Trade Commission Act [15 U.S.C. 41 et seq.], by the Federal Trade Commission for any other financial institution or other person that is not subject to the jurisdiction of any agency or authority under paragraphs (1) through (6) of this subsection.

(8) Under subtitle E of the Consumer Financial Protection Act of 2010 [12 U.S.C. 5561 et seq.], by the Bureau of Consumer Financial Protection, in the case of any financial institution and other covered person or service provider that is subject to the jurisdiction of the Bureau and any person subject to this subchapter, but not with respect to the standards under section 6801 of this title.

(b) Enforcement of section 6801

(1) In general

Except as provided in paragraph (2), the agencies and authorities described in subsection (a), other than the Bureau of Consumer Financial Protection, shall implement the standards prescribed under section 6801(b) of this title in the same manner, to the extent practicable, as standards prescribed pursuant to section 1831p–1(a) of title 12 are implemented pursuant to such section.

(2) Exception

The agencies and authorities described in paragraphs (3), (4), (5), (6), and (7) of subsection (a) shall implement the standards prescribed under section 6801(b) of this title by rule with respect to the financial institutions and other persons subject to their respective jurisdictions under subsection (a).

(c) Absence of State action

If a State insurance authority fails to adopt regulations to carry out this subchapter, such State shall not be eligible to override, pursuant to section 1831x(g)(2)(B)(iii) of title 12, the insurance customer protection regulations prescribed by a Federal banking agency under section 1831x(a) of title 12.

(d) Definitions

The terms used in subsection (a)(1) that are not defined in this subchapter or otherwise defined in section 1813(s) of title 12 shall have the same meaning as given in section 3101 of title 12.

§ 6806. Relation to other provisions

Except for the amendments made by subsections (a) and (b), nothing in this chapter shall be construed to modify, limit, or supersede the operation of the Fair Credit Reporting Act [15 U.S.C. 1681 et seq.], and no inference shall be drawn on the basis of the provisions of this chapter regarding whether information is transaction or experience information under section 603 of such Act [15 U.S.C. 1681a].

§ 6807. Relation to State laws

(a) In general

This subchapter and the amendments made by this subchapter shall not be construed as superseding, altering, or affecting any statute, regulation, order, or interpretation in effect in any State, except to the extent that such statute, regulation, order, or interpretation is inconsistent with the provisions of this subchapter, and then only to the extent of the inconsistency.

(b) Greater protection under State law

For purposes of this section, a State statute, regulation, order, or interpretation is not inconsistent with the provisions of this subchapter if the protection such statute, regulation, order, or interpretation affords any person is greater than the protection provided under this subchapter and the amendments made by this subchapter, as determined by the Bureau of Consumer Financial Protection, after consultation with the agency or authority with jurisdiction under section 6805(a) of this title of either the person that initiated the complaint or that is the subject of the complaint, on its own motion or upon the petition of any interested party.

§ 6808. Study of information sharing among financial affiliates

(a) In general

The Secretary of the Treasury, in conjunction with the Federal functional regulators and the Federal Trade Commission, shall conduct a study of information sharing practices among financial institutions and their affiliates. Such study shall include-

(1) the purposes for the sharing of confidential customer information with affiliates or with nonaffiliated third parties;

(2) the extent and adequacy of security protections for such information;

(3) the potential risks for customer privacy of such sharing of information;

(4) the potential benefits for financial institutions and affiliates of such sharing of information;

(5) the potential benefits for customers of such sharing of information;

(6) the adequacy of existing laws to protect customer privacy;

(7) the adequacy of financial institution privacy policy and privacy rights disclosure under existing law;

(8) the feasibility of different approaches, including opt-out and opt-in, to permit customers to direct that confidential information not be shared with affiliates and nonaffiliated third parties; and

(9) the feasibility of restricting sharing of information for specific uses or of permitting customers to direct the uses for which information may be shared.

(b) Consultation

The Secretary shall consult with representatives of State insurance authorities designated by the National Association of Insurance Commissioners, and also with financial services industry, consumer organizations and privacy groups, and other representatives of the general public, in formulating and conducting the study required by subsection (a).

(c) Report

On or before January 1, 2002, the Secretary shall submit a report to the Congress containing the findings and conclusions of the study required under subsection (a), together with such recommendations for legislative or administrative action as may be appropriate.

§ 6809. Definitions

As used in this subchapter:

(1) Federal banking agency

The term "Federal banking agency" has the same meaning as given in section 1813 of title 12.

(2) Federal functional regulator

The term "Federal functional regulator" means-

(A) the Board of Governors of the Federal Reserve System;

(B) the Office of the Comptroller of the Currency;

(C) the Board of Directors of the Federal Deposit Insurance Corporation;

(D) the Director of the Office of Thrift Supervision;

(E) the National Credit Union Administration Board; and

(F) the Securities and Exchange Commission.

(3) Financial institution

(A) In general

The term "financial institution" means any institution the business of which is engaging in financial activities as described in section 1843(k) of title 12.

(B) Persons subject to CFTC regulation

Notwithstanding subparagraph (A), the term "financial institution" does not include any person or entity with respect to any financial activity that is subject to the jurisdiction of the Commodity Futures Trading Commission under the Commodity Exchange Act [7 U.S.C. 1 et seq.].

(C) Farm credit institutions

Notwithstanding subparagraph (A), the term "financial institution" does not include the Federal Agricultural Mortgage Corporation or any entity chartered and operating under the Farm Credit Act of 1971 [12 U.S.C. 2001 et seq.].

(D) Other secondary market institutions

Notwithstanding subparagraph (A), the term "financial institution" does not include institutions chartered by Congress specifically to engage in transactions described in section 6802(e)(1)(C) of this title, as long as such institutions do not sell or transfer nonpublic personal information to a nonaffiliated third party.

(4) Nonpublic personal information

(A) The term "nonpublic personal information" means personally identifiable financial information-

(i) provided by a consumer to a financial institution;

(ii) resulting from any transaction with the consumer or any service performed for the consumer; or

(iii) otherwise obtained by the financial institution.

(B) Such term does not include publicly available information, as such term is defined by the regulations prescribed under section 6804 of this title.

(C) Notwithstanding subparagraph (B), such term-

(i) shall include any list, description, or other grouping of consumers (and publicly available information pertaining to them) that is derived using any nonpublic personal information other than publicly available information; but

(ii) shall not include any list, description, or other grouping of consumers (and publicly available information pertaining to them) that is derived without using any nonpublic personal information.

(5) Nonaffiliated third party

The term "nonaffiliated third party" means any entity that is not an affiliate of, or related by common ownership or affiliated by corporate control with, the financial institution, but does not include a joint employee of such institution.

(6) Affiliate

The term "affiliate" means any company that controls, is controlled by, or is under common control with another company.

(7) Necessary to effect, administer, or enforce

The term "as necessary to effect, administer, or enforce the transaction" means-

(A) the disclosure is required, or is a usual, appropriate, or acceptable method, to carry out the transaction or the product or service business of which the transaction is a part, and record or service or maintain the consumer's account in the ordinary course of providing the financial service or financial product, or to administer or service benefits or claims relating to the transaction or the product or service business of which it is a part, and includes-

(i) providing the consumer or the consumer's agent or broker with a confirmation, statement, or other record of the transaction, or information on the status or value of the financial service or financial product; and

(ii) the accrual or recognition of incentives or bonuses associated with the transaction that are provided by the financial institution or any other party;

(B) the disclosure is required, or is one of the lawful or appropriate methods, to enforce the rights of the financial institution or of other persons engaged in carrying out the financial transaction, or providing the product or service;

(C) the disclosure is required, or is a usual, appropriate, or acceptable method, for insurance underwriting at the consumer's request or for reinsurance purposes, or for any of the following purposes as they relate to a consumer's insurance: Account administration, reporting, investigating, or preventing fraud or material misrepresentation, processing premium payments, processing insurance claims, administering insurance benefits (including utilization review activities), participating in research projects, or as otherwise required or specifically permitted by Federal or State law; or

(D) the disclosure is required, or is a usual, appropriate or acceptable method, in connection with-

(i) the authorization, settlement, billing, processing, clearing, transferring, reconciling, or collection of amounts charged, debited, or otherwise paid using a debit, credit or other payment card, check, or account number, or by other payment means;

(ii) the transfer of receivables, accounts or interests therein; or

(iii) the audit of debit, credit or other payment information.

(8) State insurance authority

The term "State insurance authority" means, in the case of any person engaged in providing insurance, the State insurance authority of the State in which the person is domiciled.

(9) Consumer

The term "consumer" means an individual who obtains, from a financial institution, financial products or services which are to be used primarily for personal, family, or household purposes, and also means the legal representative of such an individual.

(10) Joint agreement

The term "joint agreement" means a formal written contract pursuant to which two or more financial institutions jointly offer, endorse, or sponsor a financial product or service, and as may be further defined in the regulations prescribed under section 6804 of this title.

(11) Customer relationship

The term "time of establishing a customer relationship" shall be defined by the regulations prescribed under section 6804 of this title, and shall, in the case of a financial institution engaged in extending credit directly to consumers to finance purchases of goods or services, mean the time of establishing the credit relationship with the consumer.

Subtitle B--Fraudulent Access to Financial Information

§ 6821. Privacy protection for customer information of financial institutions

(a) Prohibition on obtaining customer information by false pretenses

It shall be a violation of this subchapter for any person to obtain or attempt to obtain, or cause to be disclosed or attempt to cause to be disclosed to any person, customer information of a financial institution relating to another person-

(1) by making a false, fictitious, or fraudulent statement or representation to an officer, employee, or agent of a financial institution;

(2) by making a false, fictitious, or fraudulent statement or representation to a customer of a financial institution; or

(3) by providing any document to an officer, employee, or agent of a financial institution, knowing that the document is forged, counterfeit, lost, or stolen, was fraudulently obtained, or contains a false, fictitious, or fraudulent statement or representation.

(b) Prohibition on solicitation of a person to obtain customer information from financial institution under false pretenses

It shall be a violation of this subchapter to request a person to obtain customer information of a financial institution, knowing that the person will obtain, or attempt to obtain, the information from the institution in any manner described in subsection (a).

(c) Nonapplicability to law enforcement agencies

No provision of this section shall be construed so as to prevent any action by a law enforcement agency, or any officer, employee, or agent of such agency, to obtain customer information of a financial institution in connection with the performance of the official duties of the agency.

(d) Nonapplicability to financial institutions in certain cases

No provision of this section shall be construed so as to prevent any financial institution, or any officer, employee, or agent of a financial institution, from obtaining customer information of such financial institution in the course of-

(1) testing the security procedures or systems of such institution for maintaining the confidentiality of customer information;

(2) investigating allegations of misconduct or negligence on the part of any officer, employee, or agent of the financial institution; or

(3) recovering customer information of the financial institution which was obtained or received by another person in any manner described in subsection (a) or (b).

(e) Nonapplicability to insurance institutions for investigation of insurance fraud

No provision of this section shall be construed so as to prevent any insurance institution, or any officer, employee, or agency of an insurance institution, from obtaining information as part of an insurance investigation into criminal activity, fraud, material misrepresentation, or material nondisclosure that is authorized for such institution under State law, regulation, interpretation, or order.

(f) Nonapplicability to certain types of customer information of financial institutions

No provision of this section shall be construed so as to prevent any person from obtaining customer information of a financial institution that otherwise is available as a public record filed pursuant to the securities laws (as defined in section 78c(a)(47) of this title).

(g) Nonapplicability to collection of child support judgments

No provision of this section shall be construed to prevent any State-licensed private investigator, or any officer, employee, or agent of such private investigator, from obtaining customer information of a financial institution, to the extent reasonably necessary to collect child support from a person adjudged to have been delinquent in his or her obligations by a Federal or State court, and to the extent that such action by a State-licensed private investigator is not unlawful under any other Federal or State law or regulation, and has been authorized by an order or judgment of a court of competent jurisdiction.

§ 6822. Administrative enforcement

(a) Enforcement by Federal Trade Commission

Except as provided in subsection (b), compliance with this subchapter shall be enforced by the Federal Trade Commission in the same manner and with the same power and authority as the Commission has under the Fair Debt Collection Practices Act [15 U.S.C. 1692 et seq.] to enforce compliance with such Act.

(b) Enforcement by other agencies in certain cases

(1) In general

Compliance with this subchapter shall be enforced under-

(A) section 8 of the Federal Deposit Insurance Act [12 U.S.C. 1818], in the case of-

(i) national banks, and Federal branches and Federal agencies of foreign banks, by the Office of the Comptroller of the Currency;

(ii) member banks of the Federal Reserve System (other than national banks), branches and agencies of foreign banks (other than Federal branches, Federal agencies, and insured State branches of foreign banks), commercial lending companies owned or controlled by foreign banks, and organizations operating under section 25 or 25A of the Federal Reserve Act [12 U.S.C. 601 et seq., 611 et seq.], by the Board;

(iii) banks insured by the Federal Deposit Insurance Corporation (other than members of the Federal Reserve System and national nonmember banks) and insured State branches of foreign banks, by the Board of Directors of the Federal Deposit Insurance Corporation; and

(iv) savings associations the deposits of which are insured by the Federal Deposit Insurance Corporation, by the Director of the Office of Thrift Supervision; and

(B) the Federal Credit Union Act [12 U.S.C. 1751 et seq.], by the Administrator of the National Credit Union Administration with respect to any Federal credit union.

(2) Violations of this subchapter treated as violations of other laws

For the purpose of the exercise by any agency referred to in paragraph (1) of its powers under any Act referred to in that paragraph, a violation of this subchapter shall be deemed to be a violation of a requirement imposed under that Act. In addition to its powers under any provision of law specifically referred to in paragraph (1), each of the agencies referred to in that paragraph may exercise, for the purpose of enforcing compliance with this subchapter, any other authority conferred on such agency by law.

§ 6823. Criminal penalty

(a) In general

Whoever knowingly and intentionally violates, or knowingly and intentionally attempts to violate, section 6821 of this title shall be fined in accordance with title 18 or imprisoned for not more than 5 years, or both.

(b) Enhanced penalty for aggravated cases

Whoever violates, or attempts to violate, section 6821 of this title while violating another law of the United States or as part of a pattern of any illegal activity involving more than $100,000 in a 12-month period shall be fined twice the amount provided in subsection (b)(3) or (c)(3) (as the case may be) of section 3571 of title 18, imprisoned for not more than 10 years, or both.

§ 6824. Relation to State laws

(a) In general

This subchapter shall not be construed as superseding, altering, or affecting the statutes, regulations, orders, or interpretations in effect in any State, except to the extent that such statutes, regulations, orders, or interpretations are inconsistent with the provisions of this subchapter, and then only to the extent of the inconsistency.

(b) Greater protection under State law

For purposes of this section, a State statute, regulation, order, or interpretation is not inconsistent with the provisions of this subchapter if the protection such statute, regulation, order, or interpretation affords any person is greater than the protection provided under this subchapter as determined by the Federal Trade Commission, after consultation with the agency or authority with jurisdiction under section 6822 of this title of either the person that initiated the complaint or that is the subject of the complaint, on its own motion or upon the petition of any interested party.

§ 6825. Agency guidance

In furtherance of the objectives of this subchapter, each Federal banking agency (as defined in section 1813(z) of title 12), the National Credit Union Administration, and the Securities and Exchange Commission or self-regulatory organizations, as appropriate, shall review regulations and guidelines applicable to financial institutions under their respective jurisdictions and shall prescribe such revisions to such regulations and guidelines as may be necessary to ensure that such financial institutions have policies, procedures, and controls in place to prevent the unauthorized disclosure of customer financial information and to deter and detect activities proscribed under section 6821 of this title.

§ 6826. Reports

(a) Report to the Congress

Before the end of the 18-month period beginning on November 12, 1999, the Comptroller General, in consultation with the Federal Trade Commission, Federal banking agencies, the National Credit Union Administration, the Securities and Exchange Commission, appropriate Federal law enforcement agencies, and appropriate State insurance regulators, shall submit to the Congress a report on the following:

(1) The efficacy and adequacy of the remedies provided in this subchapter in addressing attempts to obtain financial information by fraudulent means or by false pretenses.

(2) Any recommendations for additional legislative or regulatory action to address threats to the privacy of financial information created by attempts to obtain information by fraudulent means or false pretenses.

(b) Annual report by administering agencies

The Federal Trade Commission and the Attorney General shall submit to Congress an annual report on number and disposition of all enforcement actions taken pursuant to this subchapter.

§ 6827. Definitions

For purposes of this subchapter, the following definitions shall apply:

(1) Customer

The term "customer" means, with respect to a financial institution, any person (or authorized representative of a person) to whom the financial institution provides a product or service, including that of acting as a fiduciary.

(2) Customer information of a financial institution

The term "customer information of a financial institution" means any information maintained by or for a financial institution which is derived from the relationship between the financial institution and a customer of the financial institution and is identified with the customer.

(3) Document

The term "document" means any information in any form.

(4) Financial institution

(A) In general

The term "financial institution" means any institution engaged in the business of providing financial services to customers who maintain a credit, deposit, trust, or other financial account or relationship with the institution.

(B) Certain financial institutions specifically included

The term "financial institution" includes any depository institution (as defined in section 461(b)(1)(A) of title 12), any broker or dealer, any investment adviser or investment company, any insurance company, any loan or finance company, any credit card issuer or operator of a credit card system, and any consumer reporting agency that compiles and maintains files on consumers on a nationwide basis (as defined in section 1681a(p) of this title).

(C) Securities institutions

For purposes of subparagraph (B)-

(i) the terms "broker" and "dealer" have the same meanings as given in section 78c of this title;

(ii) the term "investment adviser" has the same meaning as given in section 80b–2(a)(11) of this title; and

(iii) the term "investment company" has the same meaning as given in section 80a–3 of this title.

(D) Certain persons and entities specifically excluded

The term "financial institution" does not include any person or entity with respect to any financial activity that is subject to the jurisdiction of the Commodity Futures Trading Commission under the Commodity Exchange Act [7 U.S.C. 1 et seq.] and does not include the Federal Agricultural Mortgage Corporation or any entity chartered and operating under the Farm Credit Act of 1971 [12 U.S.C. 2001 et seq.].

(E) Further definition by regulation

The Federal Trade Commission, after consultation with Federal banking agencies and the Securities and Exchange Commission, may prescribe regulations clarifying or describing the types of institutions which shall be treated as financial institutions for purposes of this subchapter.

NO CHILD LEFT BEHIND ACT (2001)
[EXCERPT]

Summary

Congress passed the No Child Left Behind Act in December 2001, making significant amendments to the General Education Provisions Act to protect students' privacy. The amendments require educational agencies to give parents annual notice of and access to certain surveys and examinations administered students. Notice is required for student surveys that are performed for marketing purposes, for surveys that collect sensitive information, and for non-emergency invasive physical examinations. Sensitive information includes political and religious beliefs of the student or parent, sexual behavior, mental health information, income, and anti-social or illegal behavior.

Educational agencies must allow parents or adult students to opt-out of surveys administered for marketing purposes and of non-emergency invasive physical examinations. Some marketing activities, such as book clubs, military and college recruitment, and student "recognition" awards, are not subject to the opt-out requirement. Prior consent must be obtained before an educational agency administers a mandatory survey that collects sensitive information. Stricter state laws are not preempted by the privacy amendments.

References

> Public Law 107-110. Codified as amended at 20 U.S.C. § 1232h
> [https://www.law.cornell.edu/uscode/text/20/1232h]
>
> EPIC, EPIC Student Privacy Project
> [https://www.epic.org/privacy/student/]

20 U.S.C. § 1232h

> (a) Inspection of instructional materials by parents or guardians
> All instructional materials, including teacher's manuals, films, tapes, or other supplementary material which will be used in connection with any survey, analysis, or evaluation as part of any applicable program shall be available for inspection by the parents or guardians of the children.
> (b) Limits on survey, analysis, or evaluations
> No student shall be required, as part of any applicable program, to submit to a survey, analysis, or evaluation that reveals information concerning-
>> (1) political affiliations or beliefs of the student or the student's parent;
>> (2) mental or psychological problems of the student or the student's family;
>> (3) sex behavior or attitudes;
>> (4) illegal, anti-social, self-incriminating, or demeaning behavior;

(5) critical appraisals of other individuals with whom respondents have close family relationships;

(6) legally recognized privileged or analogous relationships, such as those of lawyers, physicians, and ministers;

(7) religious practices, affiliations, or beliefs of the student or student's parent; or

(8) income (other than that required by law to determine eligibility for participation in a program or for receiving financial assistance under such program), without the prior consent of the student (if the student is an adult or emancipated minor), or in the case of an unemancipated minor, without the prior written consent of the parent.

(c) Development of local policies concerning student privacy, parental access to information, and administration of certain physical examinations to minors

(1) Development and adoption of local policies

Except as provided in subsections (a) and (b), a local educational agency that receives funds under any applicable program shall develop and adopt policies, in consultation with parents, regarding the following:

(A)(i) The right of a parent of a student to inspect, upon the request of the parent, a survey created by a third party before the survey is administered or distributed by a school to a student; and

(ii) any applicable procedures for granting a request by a parent for reasonable access to such survey within a reasonable period of time after the request is received.

(B) Arrangements to protect student privacy that are provided by the agency in the event of the administration or distribution of a survey to a student containing one or more of the following items (including the right of a parent of a student to inspect, upon the request of the parent, any survey containing one or more of such items):

(i) Political affiliations or beliefs of the student or the student's parent.

(ii) Mental or psychological problems of the student or the student's family.

(iii) Sex behavior or attitudes.

(iv) Illegal, anti-social, self-incriminating, or demeaning behavior.

(v) Critical appraisals of other individuals with whom respondents have close family relationships.

(vi) Legally recognized privileged or analogous relationships, such as those of lawyers, physicians, and ministers.

(vii) Religious practices, affiliations, or beliefs of the student or the student's parent.

(viii) Income (other than that required by law to determine eligibility for participation in a program or for receiving financial assistance under such program).

(C)(i) The right of a parent of a student to inspect, upon the request of the parent, any instructional material used as part of the educational curriculum for the student; and

(ii) any applicable procedures for granting a request by a parent for reasonable access to instructional material within a reasonable period of time after the request is received.

(D) The administration of physical examinations or screenings that the school or agency may administer to a student.

(E) The collection, disclosure, or use of personal information collected from students for the purpose of marketing or for selling that information (or otherwise providing that information to others for that purpose), including arrangements to protect student privacy that are provided by the agency in the event of such collection, disclosure, or use.

(F)(i) The right of a parent of a student to inspect, upon the request of the parent, any instrument used in the collection of personal information under subparagraph (E) before the instrument is administered or distributed to a student; and

(ii) any applicable procedures for granting a request by a parent for reasonable access to such instrument within a reasonable period of time after the request is received.

(2) Parental notification

(A) Notification of policies

The policies developed by a local educational agency under paragraph (1) shall provide for reasonable notice of the adoption or continued use of such policies directly to the parents of students enrolled in schools served by that agency. At a minimum, the agency shall-

(i) provide such notice at least annually, at the beginning of the school year, and within a reasonable period of time after any substantive change in such policies; and

(ii) offer an opportunity for the parent (and for purposes of an activity described in subparagraph (C)(i), in the case of a student of an appropriate age, the student) to opt the student out of participation in an activity described in subparagraph (C).

(B) Notification of specific events

The local educational agency shall directly notify the parent of a student, at least annually at the beginning of the school year, of the specific or approximate dates during the school year when activities described in subparagraph (C) are scheduled, or expected to be scheduled.

(C) Activities requiring notification

The following activities require notification under this paragraph:

(i) Activities involving the collection, disclosure, or use of personal information collected from students for the purpose of marketing or for selling that information (or otherwise providing that information to others for that purpose).

(ii) The administration of any survey containing one or more items described in clauses (i) through (viii) of paragraph (1)(B).

(iii) Any nonemergency, invasive physical examination or screening that is-

   (I) required as a condition of attendance;

   (II) administered by the school and scheduled by the school in advance; and

   (III) not necessary to protect the immediate health and safety of the student, or of other students.

(3) Existing policies

A local educational agency need not develop and adopt new policies if the State educational agency or local educational agency has in place, on January 8, 2002, policies covering the requirements of paragraph (1). The agency shall provide reasonable notice of such existing policies to parents and guardians of students, in accordance with paragraph (2).

(4) Exceptions

   (A) Educational products or services

   Paragraph (1)(E) does not apply to the collection, disclosure, or use of personal information collected from students for the exclusive purpose of developing, evaluating, or providing educational products or services for, or to, students or educational institutions, such as the following:

   (i) College or other postsecondary education recruitment, or military recruitment.

   (ii) Book clubs, magazines, and programs providing access to low-cost literary products.

   (iii) Curriculum and instructional materials used by elementary schools and secondary schools.

   (iv) Tests and assessments used by elementary schools and secondary schools to provide cognitive, evaluative, diagnostic, clinical, aptitude, or achievement information about students (or to generate other statistically useful data for the purpose of securing such tests and assessments) and the subsequent analysis and public release of the aggregate data from such tests and assessments.

   (v) The sale by students of products or services to raise funds for school-related or education-related activities.

   (vi) Student recognition programs.

   (B) State law exception

The provisions of this subsection-

(i) shall not be construed to preempt applicable provisions of State law that require parental notification; and

(ii) do not apply to any physical examination or screening that is permitted or required by an applicable State law, including physical examinations or screenings that are permitted without parental notification.

(5) General provisions

(A) Rules of construction

(i) This section does not supersede section 1232g of this title.

(ii) Paragraph (1)(D) does not apply to a survey administered to a student in accordance with the Individuals with Disabilities Education Act (20 U.S.C. 1400 et seq.).

(B) Student rights

The rights provided to parents under this section transfer to the student when the student turns 18 years old, or is an emancipated minor (under an applicable State law) at any age.

(C) Information activities

The Secretary shall annually inform each State educational agency and each local educational agency of the educational agency's obligations under this section and section 1232g of this title.

(D) Funding

A State educational agency or local educational agency may use funds provided under part A of title IV of the Elementary and Secondary Education Act of 1965 [20 U.S.C. 7101 et seq.] to enhance parental involvement in areas affecting the in-school privacy of students.

(6) Definitions

As used in this subsection:

(A) Instructional material

The term "instructional material" means instructional content that is provided to a student, regardless of its format, including printed or representational materials, audio-visual materials, and materials in electronic or digital formats (such as materials accessible through the Internet). The term does not include academic tests or academic assessments.

(B) Invasive physical examination

The term "invasive physical examination" means any medical examination that involves the exposure of private body parts, or any act during such examination that includes incision, insertion, or injection into the body, but does not include a hearing, vision, or scoliosis screening.

(C) Local educational agency

The term "local educational agency" means an elementary school, secondary school, school district, or local board of education that is the recipient of funds under an applicable program, but does not include a postsecondary institution.

(D) Parent

The term "parent" includes a legal guardian or other person standing in loco parentis (such as a grandparent or stepparent with whom the child lives, or a person who is legally responsible for the welfare of the child).

(E) Personal information

The term "personal information" means individually identifiable information including-

(i) a student or parent's first and last name;

(ii) a home or other physical address (including street name and the name of the city or town);

(iii) a telephone number; or

(iv) a Social Security identification number.

(F) Student

The term "student" means any elementary school or secondary school student.

(G) Survey

The term "survey" includes an evaluation.

(d) Notice

Educational agencies and institutions shall give parents and students effective notice of their rights under this section.

(e) Enforcement

The Secretary shall take such action as the Secretary determines appropriate to enforce this section, except that action to terminate assistance provided under an applicable program shall be taken only if the Secretary determines that-

(1) there has been a failure to comply with such section; and

(2) compliance with such section cannot be secured by voluntary means.

(f) Office and review board

The Secretary shall establish or designate an office and review board within the Department of Education to investigate, process, review, and adjudicate violations of the rights established under this section.

US HOMELAND SECURITY ACT (2002)
[EXCERPTS]

Summary

Congress passed the Department of Homeland Security Act in 2002, combining 22 agencies for the purpose of securing the United States from threats. Four provisions of the bill are excerpted here. First, the Act broadly exempts "critical infrastructure information" voluntarily submitted to the Department of Homeland Security from the Freedom of Information Act. Critical infrastructure information relates to the operation of systems such as the national power grid and telecommunications networks. Once disclosed to the government, the information could not be used against the company in civil litigation, and government agents who disclose the information would be subject to criminal penalties and fines. Second, the Act creates a privacy officer for the Department charged with the responsibility of compliance with the Privacy Act, with formulating privacy impact assessments for rules proposed by the Department, and with preparing an annual report to Congress. Third, the Act prohibits all federal agencies from implementing the Terrorism Information and Prevention System (TIPS). TIPS was a program that encouraged individuals to report the suspicious behaviors of others. Fourth, the Act prohibits the new agency from developing a national identification system or card. The Act also makes certaiu changes to the Electronic Communications Privacy Act (ECPA). Those changes increased prison sentences for computer crimes, lowered burdens for law enforcement access to communications data, and expanded law enforcement authority to use pen register and trap and trace devices. The changes have been incorporated in the ECPA section.

References

Public Law 107-296. Codified as amended at 6 U.S.C. § 671 et seq.
[https://www.law.cornell.edu/uscode/text/6/671]

§ 671 Definitions

In this part:

(1) Agency

The term "agency" has the meaning given it in section 551 of title 5.

(2) Covered Federal agency

The term "covered Federal agency" means the Department of Homeland Security.

(3) Critical infrastructure information

The term "critical infrastructure information" means information not customarily in the public domain and related to the security of critical infrastructure or protected systems-

(A) actual, potential, or threatened interference with, attack on, compromise of, or incapacitation of critical infrastructure or protected systems by either physical or computer-based attack or other similar conduct (including the misuse of or unauthorized access to all types of communications and data transmission systems) that violates Federal, State, or local law, harms interstate commerce of the United States, or threatens public health or safety;

(B) the ability of any critical infrastructure or protected system to resist such interference, compromise, or incapacitation, including any planned or past assessment, projection, or estimate of the vulnerability of critical infrastructure or a protected system, including security testing, risk evaluation thereto, risk management planning, or risk audit; or

(C) any planned or past operational problem or solution regarding critical infrastructure or protected systems, including repair, recovery, reconstruction, insurance, or continuity, to the extent it is related to such interference, compromise, or incapacitation.

(4) Critical infrastructure protection program

The term "critical infrastructure protection program" means any component or bureau of a covered Federal agency that has been designated by the President or any agency head to receive critical infrastructure information.

(5) Information Sharing and Analysis Organization

The term "Information Sharing and Analysis Organization" means any formal or informal entity or collaboration created or employed by public or private sector organizations, for purposes of-

(A) gathering and analyzing critical infrastructure information, including information related to cybersecurity risks and incidents, in order to better understand security problems and interdependencies related to critical infrastructure, including cybersecurity risks and incidents, and protected systems, so as to ensure the availability, integrity, and reliability thereof;

(B) communicating or disclosing critical infrastructure information, including cybersecurity risks and incidents, to help prevent, detect, mitigate, or recover from the effects of a interference, compromise, or an incapacitation problem related to critical infrastructure, including cybersecurity risks and incidents, or protected systems; and

(C) voluntarily disseminating critical infrastructure information, including cybersecurity risks and incidents, to its members, State, local, and Federal Governments, or any other entities that may be of assistance in carrying out the purposes specified in subparagraphs (A) and (B).

(6) Protected system

The term "protected system"-

(A) means any service, physical or computer-based system, process, or procedure that directly or indirectly affects the viability of a facility of critical infrastructure; and

(B) includes any physical or computer-based system, including a computer, computer system, computer or communications network, or any component hardware or element thereof, software program, processing instructions, or information or data in transmission or storage therein, irrespective of the medium of transmission or storage.

(7) Voluntary

(A) In general

The term "voluntary", in the case of any submittal of critical infrastructure information to a covered Federal agency, means the submittal thereof in the absence of such agency's exercise of legal authority to compel access to or submission of such information and may be accomplished by a single entity or an Information Sharing and Analysis Organization on behalf of itself or its members.

(B) Exclusions

The term "voluntary"-

(i) in the case of any action brought under the securities laws as is defined in section 78c(a)(47) of title 15-

(I) does not include information or statements contained in any documents or materials filed with the Securities and Exchange Commission, or with Federal banking regulators, pursuant to section 78l(i) of title 15; and

(II) with respect to the submittal of critical infrastructure information, does not include any disclosure or writing that when made accompanied the solicitation of an offer or a sale of securities; and

(ii) does not include information or statements submitted or relied upon as a basis for making licensing or permitting determinations, or during regulatory proceedings.

(8) Cybersecurity risk; incident

The terms "cybersecurity risk" and "incident" have the meanings given those terms in section 148 of this title.

§ 672. Designation of critical infrastructure protection program

A critical infrastructure protection program may be designated as such by one of the following:

(1) The President.

(2) The Secretary of Homeland Security.

§ 673. Protection of voluntarily shared critical infrastructure information

(a) Protection

(1) In general

Notwithstanding any other provision of law, critical infrastructure information (including the identity of the submitting person or entity) that is voluntarily submitted to a covered Federal agency for use by that agency regarding the security of critical infrastructure and protected systems, analysis, warning, interdependency study, recovery, reconstitution, or other informational purpose, when accompanied by an express statement specified in paragraph (2)-

(A) shall be exempt from disclosure under section 552 of title 5 (commonly referred to as the Freedom of Information Act);

(B) shall not be subject to any agency rules or judicial doctrine regarding ex parte communications with a decision making official;

(C) shall not, without the written consent of the person or entity submitting such information, be used directly by such agency, any other Federal, State, or local authority, or any third party, in any civil action arising under Federal or State law if such information is submitted in good faith;

(D) shall not, without the written consent of the person or entity submitting such information, be used or disclosed by any officer or employee of the United States for purposes other than the purposes of this part, except-

(i) in furtherance of an investigation or the prosecution of a criminal act; or

(ii) when disclosure of the information would be-

(I) to either House of Congress, or to the extent of matter within its jurisdiction, any committee or subcommittee thereof, any joint committee thereof or subcommittee of any such joint committee; or

(II) to the Comptroller General, or any authorized representative of the Comptroller General, in the course of the performance of the duties of the Government Accountability Office.

(E) shall not, if provided to a State or local government or government agency-

(i) be made available pursuant to any State or local law requiring disclosure of information or records;

(ii) otherwise be disclosed or distributed to any party by said State or local government or government agency without the written consent of the person or entity submitting such information; or

(iii) be used other than for the purpose of protecting critical infrastructure or protected systems, or in furtherance of an investigation or the prosecution of a criminal act; and

(F) does not constitute a waiver of any applicable privilege or protection provided under law, such as trade secret protection.

(2) Express statement

For purposes of paragraph (1), the term "express statement", with respect to information or records, means-

(A) in the case of written information or records, a written marking on the information or records substantially similar to the following: "This information is voluntarily submitted to the Federal Government in expectation of protection from disclosure as provided by the provisions of the Critical Infrastructure Information Act of 2002."; or

(B) in the case of oral information, a similar written statement submitted within a reasonable period following the oral communication.

(b) Limitation

No communication of critical infrastructure information to a covered Federal agency made pursuant to this part shall be considered to be an action subject to the requirements of the Federal Advisory Committee Act.

(c) Independently obtained information

Nothing in this section shall be construed to limit or otherwise affect the ability of a State, local, or Federal Government entity, agency, or authority, or any third party, under applicable law, to obtain critical infrastructure information in a manner not covered by subsection (a), including any information lawfully and properly disclosed generally or broadly to the public and to use such information in any manner permitted by law. For purposes of this section a permissible use of independently obtained information includes the disclosure of such information under section 2302(b)(8) of title 5.

(d) Treatment of voluntary submittal of information

The voluntary submittal to the Government of information or records that are protected from disclosure by this part shall not be construed to constitute compliance with any requirement to submit such information to a Federal agency under any other provision of law.

(e) Procedures

(1) In general

The Secretary of the Department of Homeland Security shall, in consultation with appropriate representatives of the National Security Council and the Office of Science and Technology Policy, establish uniform procedures for the receipt, care, and storage by Federal agencies of critical infrastructure information that is voluntarily submitted to the Government. The procedures shall be established not later than 90 days after November 25, 2002.

(2) Elements

The procedures established under paragraph (1) shall include mechanisms regarding-

(A) the acknowledgement of receipt by Federal agencies of critical infrastructure information that is voluntarily submitted to the Government;

(B) the maintenance of the identification of such information as voluntarily submitted to the Government for purposes of and subject to the provisions of this part;

(C) the care and storage of such information; and

(D) the protection and maintenance of the confidentiality of such information so as to permit the sharing of such information within the Federal Government and with State and local governments, and the issuance of notices and warnings related to the protection of critical infrastructure and protected systems, in such manner as to protect from public disclosure the identity of the submitting person or entity, or information that is proprietary, business sensitive, relates specifically to the submitting person or entity, and is otherwise not appropriately in the public domain.

(f) Penalties

Whoever, being an officer or employee of the United States or of any department or agency thereof, knowingly publishes, divulges, discloses, or makes known in any manner or to any extent not authorized by law, any critical infrastructure information protected from disclosure by this part coming to him in the course of this employment or official duties or by reason of any examination or investigation made by, or return, report, or record made to or filed with, such department or agency or officer or employee thereof, shall be fined under title 18, imprisoned not more than 1 year, or both, and shall be removed from office or employment.

(g) Authority to issue warnings

The Federal Government may provide advisories, alerts, and warnings to relevant companies, targeted sectors, other governmental entities, or the general public regarding potential threats to critical infrastructure as appropriate. In issuing a warning, the Federal Government shall take appropriate actions to protect from disclosure-

(1) the source of any voluntarily submitted critical infrastructure information that forms the basis for the warning; or

(2) information that is proprietary, business sensitive, relates specifically to the submitting person or entity, or is otherwise not appropriately in the public domain.

(h) Authority to delegate

The President may delegate authority to a critical infrastructure protection program, designated under section 132 of this title, to enter into a voluntary agreement to promote critical infrastructure security, including with any Information Sharing and Analysis Organization, or a plan of action as otherwise defined in section 4558 of title 50.

§ 674. No private right of action

Nothing in this subtitle may be construed to create a private right of action for enforcement of any provision of this Act.

§ 142. Privacy officer

(a) Appointment and responsibilities

The Secretary shall appoint a senior official in the Department, who shall report directly to the Secretary, to assume primary responsibility for privacy policy, including-

(1) assuring that the use of technologies sustain, and do not erode, privacy protections relating to the use, collection, and disclosure of personal information;

(2) assuring that personal information contained in Privacy Act systems of records is handled in full compliance with fair information practices as set out in the Privacy Act of 1974 [5 U.S.C. 552a];

(3) evaluating legislative and regulatory proposals involving collection, use, and disclosure of personal information by the Federal Government;

(4) conducting a privacy impact assessment of proposed rules of the Department or that of the Department on the privacy of personal information, including the type of personal information collected and the number of people affected;

(5) coordinating with the Officer for Civil Rights and Civil Liberties to ensure that-

(A) programs, policies, and procedures involving civil rights, civil liberties, and privacy considerations are addressed in an integrated and comprehensive manner; and

(B) Congress receives appropriate reports on such programs, policies, and procedures; and

(6) preparing a report to Congress on an annual basis on activities of the Department that affect privacy, including complaints of privacy violations, implementation of the Privacy Act of 1974 [5 U.S.C. 552a], internal controls, and other matters.

(b) Authority to investigate

(1) In general

The senior official appointed under subsection (a) may-

(A) have access to all records, reports, audits, reviews, documents, papers, recommendations, and other materials available to the Department that relate to programs and operations with respect to the responsibilities of the senior official under this section;

(B) make such investigations and reports relating to the administration of the programs and operations of the Department as are, in the senior official's judgment, necessary or desirable;

(C) subject to the approval of the Secretary, require by subpoena the production, by any person other than a Federal agency, of all information, documents, reports, answers, records, accounts, papers, and other data and documentary evidence necessary to performance of the responsibilities of the senior official under this section; and

(D) administer to or take from any person an oath, affirmation, or affidavit, whenever necessary to performance of the responsibilities of the senior official under this section.

(2) Enforcement of subpoenas

Any subpoena issued under paragraph (1)(C) shall, in the case of contumacy or refusal to obey, be enforceable by order of any appropriate United States district court.

(3) Effect of oaths

Any oath, affirmation, or affidavit administered or taken under paragraph (1)(D) by or before an employee of the Privacy Office designated for that purpose by the senior official appointed under subsection (a) shall have the same force and effect as if administered or taken by or before an officer having a seal of office.

(c) Supervision and coordination

(1) In general

The senior official appointed under subsection (a) shall-

(A) report to, and be under the general supervision of, the Secretary; and

(B) coordinate activities with the Inspector General of the Department in order to avoid duplication of effort.

(2) Coordination with the Inspector General

(A) In general

Except as provided in subparagraph (B), the senior official appointed under subsection (a) may investigate any matter relating to possible violations or abuse concerning the administration of any program or operation of the Department relevant to the purposes under this section.

(B) Coordination

(i) Referral

Before initiating any investigation described under subparagraph (A), the senior official shall refer the matter and all related complaints, allegations, and information to the Inspector General of the Department.

(ii) Determinations and notifications by the Inspector General

(I) In general

Not later than 30 days after the receipt of a matter referred under clause (i), the Inspector General shall-

(aa) make a determination regarding whether the Inspector General intends to initiate an audit or investigation of the matter referred under clause (i); and

(bb) notify the senior official of that determination.

(II) Investigation not initiated

If the Inspector General notifies the senior official under subclause (I)(bb) that the Inspector General intended to initiate an audit or investigation, but does not initiate that audit or investigation within 90 days after providing that notification, the Inspector General shall further notify the senior official that an audit or investigation was not initiated. The further notification under this subclause shall be made not later than 3 days after the end of that 90-day period.

(iii) Investigation by senior official

The senior official may investigate a matter referred under clause (i) if-

(I) the Inspector General notifies the senior official under clause (ii)(I)(bb) that the Inspector General does not intend to initiate an audit or investigation relating to that matter; or

(II) the Inspector General provides a further notification under clause (ii)(II) relating to that matter.

(iv) Privacy training

Any employee of the Office of Inspector General who audits or investigates any matter referred under clause (i) shall be required to receive adequate training on privacy laws, rules, and regulations, to be provided by an entity approved by the Inspector General in consultation with the senior official appointed under subsection (a).

(d) Notification to Congress on removal

If the Secretary removes the senior official appointed under subsection (a) or transfers that senior official to another position or location within the Department, the Secretary shall-

(1) promptly submit a written notification of the removal or transfer to Houses of Congress; and

(2) include in any such notification the reasons for the removal or transfer.

(e) Reports by senior official to Congress

The senior official appointed under subsection (a) shall-

(1) submit reports directly to the Congress regarding performance of the responsibilities of the senior official under this section, without any prior comment or amendment by the Secretary, Deputy Secretary, or any other officer or employee of the Department or the Office of Management and Budget; and

(2) inform the Committee on Homeland Security and Governmental Affairs of the Senate and the Committee on Homeland Security of the House of Representatives not later than-

(A) 30 days after the Secretary disapproves the senior official's request for a subpoena under subsection (b)(1)(C) or the Secretary substantively modifies the requested subpoena; or

(B) 45 days after the senior official's request for a subpoena under subsection (b)(1)(C), if that subpoena has not either been approved or disapproved by the Secretary.

§ 460. Prohibition of the Terrorism Information and Prevention System

Any and all activities of the Federal Government to implement the proposed component program of the Citizen Corps known as Operation TIPS (Terrorism Information and Prevention System) are hereby prohibited.

§ 554. National identification system not authorized

Nothing in this Act shall be construed to authorize the development of a national identification system or card.

US E-GOVERNMENT ACT (2002)
[EXCERPT]

Summary

Enacted in December 2002, the E-Government Act was intended to make federal agencies more accessible to the public by electronic means. Among other things, the Act created an Office of Electronic Government within the Office of Management and Budget, and requires that regulatory proceedings and other material appear on agency web sites.

The Act also requires agencies to perform Privacy Impact Assessments (PIAs) whenever procuring an information system, or initiating a new collection of personal information. The PIA must include a description of what information is collected, the purpose for the collection, how the information will be shared, intended uses of the information, and security measures for protecting the information. Assessments must be provided to the Office of Management and Budget and made public where possible.

References

Public Law 107-347. Codified at 44 U.S.C. § 3501 note.
[https://www.law.cornell.edu/uscode/text/44/3501]

44 U.S.C. § 3501 Note. Sec. 208. Privacy provisions.

(a) Purpose. The purpose of this section is to ensure sufficient protections for the privacy of personal information as agencies implement citizen-centered electronic Government.

(b) Privacy impact assessments.

(1) Responsibilities of agencies.

(A) In general. An agency shall take actions described under subparagraph (B) before--

(i) developing or procuring information technology that collects, maintains, or disseminates information that is in an identifiable form; or

(ii) initiating a new collection of information that--

(I) will be collected, maintained, or disseminated using information technology; and

(II) includes any information in an identifiable form permitting the physical or online contacting of a specific individual, if identical questions have been posed to, or identical reporting requirements imposed on, 10 or more persons, other than agencies, instrumentalities, or employees of the Federal Government.

(B) Agency activities. To the extent required under subparagraph (A), each agency shall--

(i) conduct a privacy impact assessment;

(ii) ensure the review of the privacy impact assessment by the Chief Information Officer, or equivalent official, as determined by the head of the agency; and

(iii) if practicable, after completion of the review under clause (ii), make the privacy impact assessment publicly available through the website of the agency, publication in the Federal Register, or other means.

(C) Sensitive information. Subparagraph (B)(iii) may be modified or waived for security reasons, or to protect classified, sensitive, or private information contained in an assessment.

(D) Copy to Director. Agencies shall provide the Director with a copy of the privacy impact assessment for each system for which funding is requested.

(2) Contents of a privacy impact assessment.

(A) In general. The Director shall issue guidance to agencies specifying the required contents of a privacy impact assessment.

(B) Guidance. The guidance shall--

(i) ensure that a privacy impact assessment is commensurate with the size of the information system being assessed, the sensitivity of information that is in an identifiable form in that system, and the risk of harm from unauthorized release of that information; and

(ii) require that a privacy impact assessment address--

(I) what information is to be collected;

(II) why the information is being collected;

(III) the intended use of the agency of the information;

(IV) with whom the information will be shared;

(V) what notice or opportunities for consent would be provided to individuals regarding what information is collected and how that information is shared;

(VI) how the information will be secured; and

(VII) whether a system of records is being created under section 552a of title 5, United States Code, (commonly referred to as the "Privacy Act").

(3) Responsibilities of the Director. The Director shall--

(A) develop policies and guidelines for agencies on the conduct of privacy impact assessments;

(B) oversee the implementation of the privacy impact assessment process throughout the Government; and

(C) require agencies to conduct privacy impact assessments of existing information systems or ongoing collections of information that is in an identifiable form as the Director determines appropriate.

(c) Privacy protections on agency websites.

(1) Privacy policies on websites.

(A) Guidelines for notices. The Director shall develop guidance for privacy notices on agency websites used by the public.

(B) Contents. The guidance shall require that a privacy notice address, consistent with section 552a of title 5, United States Code--

(i) what information is to be collected;

(ii) why the information is being collected;

(iii) the intended use of the agency of the information;

(iv) with whom the information will be shared;

(v) what notice or opportunities for consent would be provided to individuals regarding what information is collected and how that information is shared;

(vi) how the information will be secured; and

(vii) the rights of the individual under section 552a of title 5, United States Code (commonly referred to as the "Privacy Act"), and other laws relevant to the protection of the privacy of an individual.

(2) Privacy policies in machine-readable formats. The Director shall issue guidance requiring agencies to translate privacy policies into a standardized machine-readable format.

(d) Definition. In this section, the term "identifiable form" means any representation of information that permits the identity of an individual to whom the information applies to be reasonably inferred by either direct or indirect means.

United States
Do-Not-Call Implementation Act

DO-NOT-CALL IMPLEMENTATION ACT
(2003)

Summary

In 2002, the Federal Trade Commission proposed the creation of a national "do-not-call" registry. The rule establishes a presumption that telemarketers may not contact people on the list, unless the telemarketer has either express written authorization or an existing business relationship with the person.

The regulation has been challenged in court several times. On September 23, 2003, a federal district judge held that the registry exceeded the scope of the FTC's statutory authority. Within a week, Congress ratified the list by statute. Telemarketers have also challenged the statute as an unconstitutional restriction on speech; courts have generally rejected that argument on the grounds that the privacy interests of the people on the list outweigh the telemarketers' right to commercial speech.

There are three main pieces of law that make up the Do-Not-Call registry. The FTC's regulation, 16 C.F.R. 310.4(b)(iii)(B), establishes the registry itself and the related prohibitions on telemarketing. Public Law 108-10 authorizes the FTC to collect fees to operate the registry and requires the FTC to report on the progress of the registry. Public Law 108-82, discussed in the previous paragraph, granted statutory authority to the FTC to operate the registry.

References

> Public Law 108-10 & 108-82, Codified at as amended at 15 U.S.C. § 6151 et seq.
> [https://www.law.cornell.edu/uscode/text/15/6151]

> 16 C.F.R. 310.4(b)(iii)(B).
> [https://www.law.cornell.edu/cfr/text/16/310.4]

> FTC's Do-Not-Call Registry
> [https://donotcall.gov/]

16 C.F.R. § 310.4

> . . . .
> (b) Pattern of calls.
>> (1) It is an abusive telemarketing act or practice and a violation of this Rule for a telemarketer to engage in, or for a seller to cause a telemarketer to engage in, the following conduct:
>> . . . .
>>> (iii) Initiating any outbound telephone call to a person when:

(A) That person previously has stated that he or she does not wish to receive an outbound telephone call made by or on behalf of the seller whose goods or services are being offered or made on behalf of the charitable organization for which a charitable contribution is being solicited; or

(B) That person's telephone number is on the "do-not-call" registry, maintained by the Commission, of persons who do not wish to receive outbound telephone calls to induce the purchase of goods or services unless the seller or telemarketer:

(1) Can demonstrate that the seller has obtained the express agreement, in writing, of such person to place calls to that person. Such written agreement shall clearly evidence such person's authorization that calls made by or on behalf of a specific party may be placed to that person, and shall include the telephone number to which the calls may be placed and the signature [FN] of that person; or

(2) Can demonstrate that the seller has an established business relationship with such person, and that person has not stated that he or she does not wish to receive outbound telephone calls under paragraph (b)(1)(iii)(A) of this section. . . .

[FN: For purposes of this Rule, the term "signature" shall include an electronic or digital form of signature, to the extent that such form of signature is recognized as a valid signature under applicable federal law or state contract law.]

Public Law 108-10

§ 1. Short Title.

This Act may be cited as the "Do-Not-Call Implementation Act".

§ 2. Telemarketing Sales Rule; Do-Not-Call Registry Fees.

The Federal Trade Commission may promulgate regulations establishing fees sufficient to implement and enforce the provisions relating to the "do-not-call" registry of the Telemarketing Sales Rule (16 CFR 310.4(b)(1)(iii)), promulgated under the Telemarketing and Consumer Fraud and Abuse Prevention Act (15 U.S.C. 6101 et seq.). Such regulations shall be promulgated in accordance with section 553 of title 5, United States Code. Fees may be collected pursuant to this section for fiscal years 2003 through 2007, and shall be deposited and credited as offsetting collections to the account, Federal Trade Commission--Salaries and Expenses, and shall remain available until expended. No amounts shall be collected as fees pursuant to this section for such fiscal years except to the extent provided in advance in appropriations Acts. Such amounts shall be available for expenditure only to offset the costs of activities and services related to the implementation and enforcement of the Telemarketing Sales Rule, and other activities resulting from such implementation and enforcement.

§ 3. Federal Communications Commission Do-Not-Call Regulations.

Not later than 180 days after the date of enactment of this Act, the Federal Communications Commission shall issue a final rule pursuant to the rulemaking proceeding that it began on September 18, 2002, under the Telephone Consumer Protection Act (47 U.S.C. 227 et seq.). In issuing such rule, the Federal Communications Commission shall consult and coordinate with the Federal Trade Commission to maximize consistency with the rule promulgated by the Federal Trade Commission (16 CFR 310.4(b)).

§ 4. Reporting Requirements.

(a) Report on Regulatory Coordination.--Within 45 days after the promulgation of a final rule by the Federal Communications Commission as required by section 3, the Federal Trade Commission and the Federal Communications Commission shall each transmit to the Committee on Energy and Commerce of the House of Representatives and the Committee on Commerce, Science, and Transportation of the Senate a report which shall include--

    (1) an analysis of the telemarketing rules promulgated by both the Federal Trade Commission and the Federal Communications Commission;

    (2) any inconsistencies between the rules promulgated by each such Commission and the effect of any such inconsistencies on consumers, and persons paying for access to the registry; and

    (3) proposals to remedy any such inconsistencies.

(b) Annual Report.--For each of fiscal years 2003 through 2007, the Federal Trade Commission and the Federal Communications Commission shall each transmit an annual report to the Committee on Energy and Commerce of the House of Representatives and the Committee on Commerce, Science, and Transportation of the Senate a report which shall include--

    (1) an analysis of the effectiveness of the "do-not-call" registry as a national registry;

    (2) the number of consumers who have placed their telephone numbers on the registry;

    (3) the number of persons paying fees for access to the registry and the amount of such fees;

    (4) an analysis of the progress of coordinating the operation and enforcement of the "do-not-call" registry with similar registries established and maintained by the various States;

    (5) an analysis of the progress of coordinating the operation and enforcement of the "do-not-call" registry with the enforcement activities of the Federal

Communications Commission pursuant to the Telephone Consumer Protection Act (47 U.S.C. 227 et seq.); and

(6) a review of the enforcement proceedings under the Telemarketing Sales Rule (16 CFR 310), in the case of the Federal Trade Commission, and under the Telephone Consumer Protection Act (47 U.S.C. 227 et seq.), in the case of the Federal Communications Commission.

United States
Do-Not-Call Implementation Act

VIDEO VOYEURISM PREVENTION ACT
(2004)

Summary

The Video Voyeurism Prevention Act of 2004 was passed in response to the growing popularity of miniature spy cameras. The Act is very limited in scope: it only covers voyeuristic acts performed on federal lands such as federal parks.

References

> Public Law 108-495. Codified at 18 U.S.C. § 1801.
> [https://www.law.cornell.edu/uscode/text/18/1801]

18 U.S.C. § 1801. Video voyeurism

(a) Whoever, in the special maritime and territorial jurisdiction of the United States, has the intent to capture an image of a private area of an individual without their consent, and knowingly does so under circumstances in which the individual has a reasonable expectation of privacy, shall be fined under this title or imprisoned not more than one year, or both.

(b) In this section--

(1) the term "capture", with respect to an image, means to videotape, photograph, film, record by any means, or broadcast;

(2) the term "broadcast" means to electronically transmit a visual image with the intent that it be viewed by a person or persons;

(3) the term "a private area of the individual" means the naked or undergarment clad genitals, pubic area, buttocks, or female breast of that individual;

(4) the term "female breast" means any portion of the female breast below the top of the areola; and

(5) the term "under circumstances in which that individual has a reasonable expectation of privacy" means--

(A) circumstances in which a reasonable person would believe that he or she could disrobe in privacy, without being concerned that an image of a private area of the individual was being captured; or

(B) circumstances in which a reasonable person would believe that a private area of the individual would not be visible to the public, regardless of whether that person is in a public or private place.

(c) This section does not prohibit any lawful law enforcement, correctional, or intelligence activity.

IDENTITY THEFT PENALTY ENHANCEMENT ACT (2004)

Summary

The Identity Theft Penalty Enhancement Act of 2004 strengthens the criminal punishments for identity theft. The Act creates a five-year sentence for identity theft committed in relation to terrorism and a two-year sentence for identity theft committed in relation to felonies such as fraud and immigration violations. The Act also prohibits judicial alteration of these sentences or conversion to probation.

References

> Public Law No. 108-275. Codified as amended at 18 U.S.C. § 1028A, § 641.
> [https://www.law.cornell.edu/uscode/text/18/1028]

18 U.S.C. § 1028A. Aggravated identity theft

(a) Offenses.--

(1) In general.--Whoever, during and in relation to any felony violation enumerated in subsection (c), knowingly transfers, possesses, or uses, without lawful authority, a means of identification of another person shall, in addition to the punishment provided for such felony, be sentenced to a term of imprisonment of 2 years.

(2) Terrorism offense.--Whoever, during and in relation to any felony violation enumerated in section 2332b(g)(5)(B), knowingly transfers, possesses, or uses, without lawful authority, a means of identification of another person or a false identification document shall, in addition to the punishment provided for such felony, be sentenced to a term of imprisonment of 5 years.

(b) Consecutive Sentence.--Notwithstanding any other provision of law--

(1) a court shall not place on probation any person convicted of a violation of this section;

(2) except as provided in paragraph (4), no term of imprisonment imposed on a person under this section shall run concurrently with any other term of imprisonment imposed on the person under any other provision of law, including any term of imprisonment imposed for the felony during which the means of identification was transferred, possessed, or used;

(3) in determining any term of imprisonment to be imposed for the felony during which the means of identification was transferred, possessed, or used, a court shall not in any way reduce the term to be imposed for such crime so as to compensate for, or otherwise take into account, any separate term of imprisonment imposed or to be imposed for a violation of this section; and

(4) a term of imprisonment imposed on a person for a violation of this section may, in the discretion of the court, run concurrently, in whole or in part, only with another

term of imprisonment that is imposed by the court at the same time on that person for an additional violation of this section, provided that such discretion shall be exercised in accordance with any applicable guidelines and policy statements issued by the Sentencing Commission pursuant to section 994 of title 28.

(c) Definition.--For purposes of this section, the term "felony violation enumerated in subsection (c)" means any offense that is a felony violation of--

(1) section 641 (relating to theft of public money, property, or rewards), section 656 (relating to theft, embezzlement, or misapplication by bank officer or employee), or section 664 (relating to theft from employee benefit plans);

(2) section 911 (relating to false personation of citizenship);

(3) section 922(a)(6) (relating to false statements in connection with the acquisition of a firearm);

(4) any provision contained in this chapter (relating to fraud and false statements), other than this section or section 1028(a)(7);

(5) any provision contained in chapter 63 (relating to mail, bank, and wire fraud);

(6) any provision contained in chapter 69 (relating to nationality and citizenship);

(7) any provision contained in chapter 75 (relating to passports and visas);

(8) section 523 of the Gramm-Leach-Bliley Act (15 U.S.C. 6823) (relating to obtaining customer information by false pretenses);

(9) section 243 or 266 of the Immigration and Nationality Act (8 U.S.C. 1253 and 1306) (relating to willfully failing to leave the United States after deportation and creating a counterfeit alien registration card);

(10) any provision contained in chapter 8 of title II of the Immigration and Nationality Act (8 U.S.C. 1321 et seq.) (relating to various immigration offenses); or

(11) section 208, 811, 1107(b), 1128B(a), or 1632 of the Social Security Act (42 U.S.C. 408, 1011, 1307(b), 1320a-7b(a), and 1383a) (relating to false statements relating to programs under the Act).

. . .

18 U.S.C. § 641. Public money, property or records

Whoever embezzles, steals, purloins, or knowingly converts to his use or the use of another, or without authority, sells, conveys or disposes of any record, voucher, money, or thing of value of the United States or of any department or agency thereof, or any property made or being made under contract for the United States or any department or agency thereof; or

Whoever receives, conceals, or retains the same with intent to convert it to his use or gain, knowing it to have been embezzled, stolen, purloined or converted—

Shall be fined under this title or imprisoned not more than ten years, or both; but if the value of such property <in the aggregate, combining amounts from all the counts for which the

defendant is convicted in a single case,> does not exceed the sum of $1,000, he shall be fined under this title or imprisoned not more than one year, or both.

The word "value" means face, par, or market value, or cost price, either wholesale or retail, whichever is greater.

United States
HITECH Act

HEALTH INFORMATION TECHNOLOGY FOR CLINICAL AND ECONOMIC HEALTH (HITECH) ACT (2009) [EXCERPT]

Summary

The Health Information Technology for Economic and Clinical Health (HITECH) Act was passed in 2009 and sought to promote and expand the adoption of health information technology. The HITECH Act requires entities covered by the Health Insurance Portability and Accountability Act (HIPAA) to report data breaches to affected individuals and to the U.S. Department of Health and Human Services. The Act also sets restrictions on the sale or disclosure of patient health information, and establishes rules on how regulated entities must account for such disclosures.

Reference

> Public Law 111–5. Codified as amended at 42 U.S.C. § 300jj et seq., § 17901 et seq.
> [https://www.law.cornell.edu/uscode/text/42/300jj]
> [https://www.law.cornell.edu/uscode/text/42/17901]

42 U.S.C. § 17932. Notification in the case of breach

(a) In general

A covered entity that accesses, maintains, retains, modifies, records, stores, destroys, or otherwise holds, uses, or discloses unsecured protected health information (as defined in subsection (h)(1)) shall, in the case of a breach of such information that is discovered by the covered entity, notify each individual whose unsecured protected health information has been, or is reasonably believed by the covered entity to have been, accessed, acquired, or disclosed as a result of such breach.

(b) Notification of covered entity by business associate

A business associate of a covered entity that accesses, maintains, retains, modifies, records, stores, destroys, or otherwise holds, uses, or discloses unsecured protected health information shall, following the discovery of a breach of such information, notify the covered entity of such breach. Such notice shall include the identification of each individual whose unsecured protected health information has been, or is reasonably believed by the business associate to have been, accessed, acquired, or disclosed during such breach.

(c) Breaches treated as discovered

For purposes of this section, a breach shall be treated as discovered by a covered entity or by a business associate as of the first day on which such breach is known to such entity or associate, respectively, (including any person, other than the individual committing the breach, that is an employee, officer, or other agent of such entity or associate, respectively) or should reasonably have been known to such entity or associate (or person) to have occurred.

(d) Timeliness of notification

(1) In general

Subject to subsection (g), all notifications required under this section shall be made without unreasonable delay and in no case later than 60 calendar days after the discovery of a breach by the covered entity involved (or business associate involved in the case of a notification required under subsection (b)).

(2) Burden of proof

The covered entity involved (or business associate involved in the case of a notification required under subsection (b)), shall have the burden of demonstrating that all notifications were made as required under this part, including evidence demonstrating the necessity of any delay.

(e) Methods of notice

(1) Individual notice

Notice required under this section to be provided to an individual, with respect to a breach, shall be provided promptly and in the following form:

(A) Written notification by first-class mail to the individual (or the next of kin of the individual if the individual is deceased) at the last known address of the individual or the next of kin, respectively, or, if specified as a preference by the individual, by electronic mail. The notification may be provided in one or more mailings as information is available.

(B) In the case in which there is insufficient, or out-of-date contact information (including a phone number, email address, or any other form of appropriate communication) that precludes direct written (or, if specified by the individual under subparagraph (A), electronic) notification to the individual, a substitute form of notice shall be provided, including, in the case that there are 10 or more individuals for which there is insufficient or out-of-date contact information, a conspicuous posting for a period determined by the Secretary on the home page of the Web site of the covered entity involved or notice in major print or broadcast media, including major media in geographic areas where the individuals affected by the breach likely reside. Such a notice in media or web posting will include a toll-free phone number where an individual can learn whether or not the individual's unsecured protected health information is possibly included in the breach.

(C) In any case deemed by the covered entity involved to require urgency because of possible imminent misuse of unsecured protected health information, the covered entity, in addition to notice provided under subparagraph (A), may provide information to individuals by telephone or other means, as appropriate.

(2) Media notice

Notice shall be provided to prominent media outlets serving a State or jurisdiction, following the discovery of a breach described in subsection (a), if the unsecured protected health information of more than 500 residents of such State or jurisdiction is, or is reasonably believed to have been, accessed, acquired, or disclosed during such breach.

(3) Notice to Secretary

Notice shall be provided to the Secretary by covered entities of unsecured protected health information that has been acquired or disclosed in a breach. If the breach was with respect to 500 or more individuals than such notice must be provided immediately. If the breach was with respect to less than 500 individuals, the covered entity may maintain a log of any such breach occurring and annually submit such a log to the Secretary documenting such breaches occurring during the year involved.

(4) Posting on HHS public website

The Secretary shall make available to the public on the Internet website of the Department of Health and Human Services a list that identifies each covered entity involved in a breach described in subsection (a) in which the unsecured protected health information of more than 500 individuals is acquired or disclosed.

(f) Content of notification

Regardless of the method by which notice is provided to individuals under this section, notice of a breach shall include, to the extent possible, the following:

(1) A brief description of what happened, including the date of the breach and the date of the discovery of the breach, if known.

(2) A description of the types of unsecured protected health information that were involved in the breach (such as full name, Social Security number, date of birth, home address, account number, or disability code).

(3) The steps individuals should take to protect themselves from potential harm resulting from the breach.

(4) A brief description of what the covered entity involved is doing to investigate the breach, to mitigate losses, and to protect against any further breaches.

(5) Contact procedures for individuals to ask questions or learn additional information, which shall include a toll-free telephone number, an e-mail address, Web site, or postal address.

(g) Delay of notification authorized for law enforcement purposes

If a law enforcement official determines that a notification, notice, or posting required under this section would impede a criminal investigation or cause damage to national security, such notification, notice, or posting shall be delayed in the same manner as provided under section 164.528(a)(2) of title 45, Code of Federal Regulations, in the case of a disclosure covered under such section.

(h) Unsecured protected health information

(1) Definition

(A) In general

Subject to subparagraph (B), for purposes of this section, the term "unsecured protected health information" means protected health information that is not secured through the use of a technology or methodology specified by the Secretary in the guidance issued under paragraph (2).

(B) Exception in case timely guidance not issued

In the case that the Secretary does not issue guidance under paragraph (2) by the date specified in such paragraph, for purposes of this section, the term "unsecured protected health information" shall mean protected health information that is not secured by a technology standard that renders protected health information unusable, unreadable, or indecipherable to unauthorized individuals and is developed or endorsed by a standards developing organization that is accredited by the American National Standards Institute.

(2) Guidance

For purposes of paragraph (1) and section 17937(f)(3) of this title, not later than the date that is 60 days after February 17, 2009, the Secretary shall, after consultation with stakeholders, issue (and annually update) guidance specifying the technologies and methodologies that render protected health information unusable, unreadable, or indecipherable to unauthorized individuals, including the use of standards developed under section 300jj–12(b)(2)(B)(vi) of this title, as added by section 13101 of this Act.

(i) Report to Congress on breaches

(1) In general

Not later than 12 months after February 17, 2009, and annually thereafter, the Secretary shall prepare and submit to the Committee on Finance and the Committee on Health, Education, Labor, and Pensions of the Senate and the Committee on Ways and Means and the Committee on Energy and Commerce of the House of Representatives a report containing the information described in paragraph (2) regarding breaches for which notice was provided to the Secretary under subsection (e)(3).

(2) Information

The information described in this paragraph regarding breaches specified in paragraph (1) shall include-

(A) the number and nature of such breaches; and

(B) actions taken in response to such breaches.

(j) Regulations; effective date

To carry out this section, the Secretary of Health and Human Services shall promulgate interim final regulations by not later than the date that is 180 days after February 17, 2009. The provisions of this section shall apply to breaches that are discovered on or after the date that is 30 days after the date of publication of such interim final regulations.

. . .

§17934. Application of privacy provisions and penalties to business associates of covered entities

(a) Application of contract requirements

In the case of a business associate of a covered entity that obtains or creates protected health information pursuant to a written contract (or other written arrangement) described in section 164.502(e)(2) of title 45, Code of Federal Regulations, with such covered entity, the business associate may use and disclose such protected health information only if such use or disclosure, respectively, is in compliance with each applicable requirement of section 164.504(e) of such title. The additional requirements of this subchapter that relate to privacy and that are made applicable with respect to covered entities shall also be applicable to such a business associate and shall be incorporated into the business associate agreement between the business associate and the covered entity.

(b) Application of knowledge elements associated with contracts

Section 164.504(e)(1)(ii) of title 45, Code of Federal Regulations, shall apply to a business associate described in subsection (a), with respect to compliance with such subsection, in the same manner that such section applies to a covered entity, with respect to compliance with the standards in sections 164.502(e) and 164.504(e) of such title, except that in applying such section 164.504(e)(1)(ii) each reference to the business associate, with respect to a contract, shall be treated as a reference to the covered entity involved in such contract.

(c) Application of civil and criminal penalties

In the case of a business associate that violates any provision of subsection (a) or (b), the provisions of sections 1176 and 1177 of the Social Security Act (42 U.S.C. 1320d–5, 1320d–6) shall apply to the business associate with respect to such violation in the same manner as such provisions apply to a person who violates a provision of part C of title XI of such Act [42 U.S.C. 1320d et seq.].

§17935. Restrictions on certain disclosures and sales of health information; accounting of certain protected health information disclosures; access to certain information in electronic format

(a) Requested restrictions on certain disclosures of health information

In the case that an individual requests under paragraph (a)(1)(i)(A) of section 164.522 of title 45, Code of Federal Regulations, that a covered entity restrict the disclosure of the protected health information of the individual, notwithstanding paragraph (a)(1)(ii) of such section, the covered entity must comply with the requested restriction if-

> (1) except as otherwise required by law, the disclosure is to a health plan for purposes of carrying out payment or health care operations (and is not for purposes of carrying out treatment); and

(2) the protected health information pertains solely to a health care item or service for which the health care provider involved has been paid out of pocket in full.

(b) Disclosures required to be limited to the limited data set or the minimum necessary

(1) In general

(A) In general

Subject to subparagraph (B), a covered entity shall be treated as being in compliance with section 164.502(b)(1) of title 45, Code of Federal Regulations, with respect to the use, disclosure, or request of protected health information described in such section, only if the covered entity limits such protected health information, to the extent practicable, to the limited data set (as defined in section 164.514(e)(2) of such title) or, if needed by such entity, to the minimum necessary to accomplish the intended purpose of such use, disclosure, or request, respectively.

(B) Guidance

Not later than 18 months after February 17, 2009, the Secretary shall issue guidance on what constitutes "minimum necessary" for purposes of subpart E of part 164 of title 45, Code of Federal Regulation.[1] In issuing such guidance the Secretary shall take into consideration the guidance under section 17953(c) of this title and the information necessary to improve patient outcomes and to detect, prevent, and manage chronic disease.

(C) Sunset

Subparagraph (A) shall not apply on and after the effective date on which the Secretary issues the guidance under subparagraph (B).

(2) Determination of minimum necessary

For purposes of paragraph (1), in the case of the disclosure of protected health information, the covered entity or business associate disclosing such information shall determine what constitutes the minimum necessary to accomplish the intended purpose of such disclosure.

(3) Application of exceptions

The exceptions described in section 164.502(b)(2) of title 45, Code of Federal Regulations, shall apply to the requirement under paragraph (1) as of the effective date described in section 13423 [2] in the same manner that such exceptions apply to section 164.502(b)(1) of such title before such date.

(4) Rule of construction

Nothing in this subsection shall be construed as affecting the use, disclosure, or request of protected health information that has been de-identified.

(c) Accounting of certain protected health information disclosures required if covered entity uses electronic health record

(1) In general

In applying section 164.528 of title 45, Code of Federal Regulations, in the case that a covered entity uses or maintains an electronic health record with respect to protected health information-

(A) the exception under paragraph (a)(1)(i) of such section shall not apply to disclosures through an electronic health record made by such entity of such information; and

(B) an individual shall have a right to receive an accounting of disclosures described in such paragraph of such information made by such covered entity during only the three years prior to the date on which the accounting is requested.

(2) Regulations

The Secretary shall promulgate regulations on what information shall be collected about each disclosure referred to in paragraph (1), not later than 6 months after the date on which the Secretary adopts standards on accounting for disclosure described in the section 300jj–12(b)(2)(B)(iv) of this title, as added by section 13101. Such regulations shall only require such information to be collected through an electronic health record in a manner that takes into account the interests of the individuals in learning the circumstances under which their protected health information is being disclosed and takes into account the administrative burden of accounting for such disclosures.

(3) Process

In response to an[4] request from an individual for an accounting, a covered entity shall elect to provide either an-

(A) accounting, as specified under paragraph (1), for disclosures of protected health information that are made by such covered entity and by a business associate acting on behalf of the covered entity; or

(B) accounting, as specified under paragraph (1), for disclosures that are made by such covered entity and provide a list of all business associates acting on behalf of the covered entity, including contact information for such associates (such as mailing address, phone, and email address).

A business associate included on a list under subparagraph (B) shall provide an accounting of disclosures (as required under paragraph (1) for a covered entity) made by the business associate upon a request made by an individual directly to the business associate for such an accounting.

(4) Effective date

(A) Current users of electronic records

In the case of a covered entity insofar as it acquired an electronic health record as of January 1, 2009, paragraph (1) shall apply to disclosures, with respect to protected health information, made by the covered entity from such a record on and after January 1, 2014.

(B) Others

In the case of a covered entity insofar as it acquires an electronic health record after January 1, 2009, paragraph (1) shall apply to disclosures, with respect to protected health information, made by the covered entity from such record on and after the later of the following:

(i) January 1, 2011; or

(ii) the date that it acquires an electronic health record.

(C) Later date

The Secretary may set an effective date that is later that [5] the date specified under subparagraph (A) or (B) if the Secretary determines that such later date is necessary, but in no case may the date specified under-

(i) subparagraph (A) be later than 2016; or

(ii) subparagraph (B) be later than 2013.

(d) Prohibition on sale of electronic health records or protected health information

(1) In general

Except as provided in paragraph (2), a covered entity or business associate shall not directly or indirectly receive remuneration in exchange for any protected health information of an individual unless the covered entity obtained from the individual, in accordance with section 164.508 of title 45, Code of Federal Regulations, a valid authorization that includes, in accordance with such section, a specification of whether the protected health information can be further exchanged for remuneration by the entity receiving protected health information of that individual.

(2) Exceptions

Paragraph (1) shall not apply in the following cases:

(A) The purpose of the exchange is for public health activities (as described in section 164.512(b) of title 45, Code of Federal Regulations).

(B) The purpose of the exchange is for research (as described in sections 164.501 and 164.512(i) of title 45, Code of Federal Regulations) and the price charged reflects the costs of preparation and transmittal of the data for such purpose.

(C) The purpose of the exchange is for the treatment of the individual, subject to any regulation that the Secretary may promulgate to prevent protected health information from inappropriate access, use, or disclosure.

(D) The purpose of the exchange is the health care operation specifically described in subparagraph (iv) of paragraph (6) of the definition of healthcare operations in section 164.501 of title 45, Code of Federal Regulations.

(E) The purpose of the exchange is for remuneration that is provided by a covered entity to a business associate for activities involving the exchange of protected health information that the business associate undertakes on behalf of and at the specific request of the covered entity pursuant to a business associate agreement.

(F) The purpose of the exchange is to provide an individual with a copy of the individual's protected health information pursuant to section 164.524 of title 45, Code of Federal Regulations.

(G) The purpose of the exchange is otherwise determined by the Secretary in regulations to be similarly necessary and appropriate as the exceptions provided in subparagraphs (A) through (F).

(3) Regulations

Not later than 18 months after February 17, 2009, the Secretary shall promulgate regulations to carry out this subsection. In promulgating such regulations, the Secretary-

(A) shall evaluate the impact of restricting the exception described in paragraph (2)(A) to require that the price charged for the purposes described in such paragraph reflects the costs of the preparation and transmittal of the data for such purpose, on research or public health activities, including those conducted by or for the use of the Food and Drug Administration; and

(B) may further restrict the exception described in paragraph (2)(A) to require that the price charged for the purposes described in such paragraph reflects the costs of the preparation and transmittal of the data for such purpose, if the Secretary finds that such further restriction will not impede such research or public health activities.

(4) Effective date

Paragraph (1) shall apply to exchanges occurring on or after the date that is 6 months after the date of the promulgation of final regulations implementing this subsection.

(e) Access to certain information in electronic format

In applying section 164.524 of title 45, Code of Federal Regulations, in the case that a covered entity uses or maintains an electronic health record with respect to protected health information of an individual-

(1) the individual shall have a right to obtain from such covered entity a copy of such information in an electronic format and, if the individual chooses, to direct the covered entity to transmit such copy directly to an entity or person designated by the individual, provided that any such choice is clear, conspicuous, and specific;

(2) if the individual makes a request to a business associate for access to, or a copy of, protected health information about the individual, or if an individual makes a request to a business associate to grant such access to, or transmit such copy directly to, a person or entity designated by the individual, a business associate may provide the individual with such access or copy, which may be in an electronic form, or grant or transmit such access or copy to such person or entity designated by the individual; and

(3) notwithstanding paragraph (c)(4) of such section, any fee that the covered entity may impose for providing such individual with a copy of such information (or a summary or explanation of such information) if such copy (or summary or explanation) is in an electronic form shall not be greater than the entity's labor costs in responding to the request for the copy (or summary or explanation).

. . .

§17937. Temporary breach notification requirement for vendors of personal health records and other non-HIPAA covered entities

(a) In general

In accordance with subsection (c), each vendor of personal health records, following the discovery of a breach of security of unsecured PHR identifiable health information that is in a personal health record maintained or offered by such vendor, and each entity described in clause (ii), (iii), or (iv) of section 17953(b)(1)(A) of this title, following the discovery of a breach of security of such information that is obtained through a product or service provided by such entity, shall-

> (1) notify each individual who is a citizen or resident of the United States whose unsecured PHR identifiable health information was acquired by an unauthorized person as a result of such a breach of security; and

> (2) notify the Federal Trade Commission.

(b) Notification by third party service providers

A third party service provider that provides services to a vendor of personal health records or to an entity described in clause (ii), (iii).1 or (iv) of section 17953(b)(1)(A) of this title in connection with the offering or maintenance of a personal health record or a related product or service and that accesses, maintains, retains, modifies, records, stores, destroys, or otherwise holds, uses, or discloses unsecured PHR identifiable health information in such a record as a result of such services shall, following the discovery of a breach of security of such information, notify such vendor or entity, respectively, of such breach. Such notice shall include the identification of each individual whose unsecured PHR identifiable health information has been, or is reasonably believed to have been, accessed, acquired, or disclosed during such breach.

(c) Application of requirements for timeliness, method, and content of notifications

Subsections (c), (d), (e), and (f) of section 17932 of this title shall apply to a notification required under subsection (a) and a vendor of personal health records, an entity described in subsection (a) and a third party service provider described in subsection (b), with respect to a breach of security under subsection (a) of unsecured PHR identifiable health information in such records maintained or offered by such vendor, in a manner specified by the Federal Trade Commission.

(d) Notification of the Secretary

Upon receipt of a notification of a breach of security under subsection (a)(2), the Federal Trade Commission shall notify the Secretary of such breach.

(e) Enforcement

A violation of subsection (a) or (b) shall be treated as an unfair and deceptive act or practice in violation of a regulation under section 57a(a)(1)(B) of title 15 regarding unfair or deceptive acts or practices.

(f) Definitions

For purposes of this section:

> (1) Breach of security

The term "breach of security" means, with respect to unsecured PHR identifiable health information of an individual in a personal health record, acquisition of such information without the authorization of the individual.

(2) PHR identifiable health information

The term "PHR identifiable health information" means individually identifiable health information, as defined in section 1320d(6) of this title, and includes, with respect to an individual, information-

(A) that is provided by or on behalf of the individual; and

(B) that identifies the individual or with respect to which there is a reasonable basis to believe that the information can be used to identify the individual.

(3) Unsecured PHR identifiable health information

(A) In general

Subject to subparagraph (B), the term "unsecured PHR identifiable health information" means PHR identifiable health information that is not protected through the use of a technology or methodology specified by the Secretary in the guidance issued under section 17932(h)(2) of this title.

(B) Exception in case timely guidance not issued

In the case that the Secretary does not issue guidance under section 17932(h)(2) of this title by the date specified in such section, for purposes of this section, the term "unsecured PHR identifiable health information" shall mean PHR identifiable health information that is not secured by a technology standard that renders protected health information unusable, unreadable, or indecipherable to unauthorized individuals and that is developed or endorsed by a standards developing organization that is accredited by the American National Standards Institute.

(g) Regulations; effective date; sunset

(1) Regulations; effective date

To carry out this section, the Federal Trade Commission shall promulgate interim final regulations by not later than the date that is 180 days after February 17, 2009. The provisions of this section shall apply to breaches of security that are discovered on or after the date that is 30 days after the date of publication of such interim final regulations.

(2) Sunset

If Congress enacts new legislation establishing requirements for notification in the case of a breach of security, that apply to entities that are not covered entities or business associates, the provisions of this section shall not apply to breaches of security discovered on or after the effective date of regulations implementing such legislation.

. . .

§17939. Improved enforcement

(a) In general

(1) Omitted

(2) Enforcement under Social Security Act

Any violation by a covered entity under this subchapter is subject to enforcement and penalties under section 1176 and 1177 of the Social Security Act [42 U.S.C. 1320d–5, 1320d–6].

(b) Effective date; regulations

(1) The amendments made by subsection (a) shall apply to penalties imposed on or after the date that is 24 months after February 17, 2009.

(2) Not later than 18 months after February 17, 2009, the Secretary of Health and Human Services shall promulgate regulations to implement such amendments.

(c) Distribution of certain civil monetary penalties collected

(1) In general

Subject to the regulation promulgated pursuant to paragraph (3), any civil monetary penalty or monetary settlement collected with respect to an offense punishable under this subchapter or section 1176 of the Social Security Act (42 U.S.C. 1320d–5) insofar as such section relates to privacy or security shall be transferred to the Office for Civil Rights of the Department of Health and Human Services to be used for purposes of enforcing the provisions of this subchapter and subparts C and E of part 164 of title 45, Code of Federal Regulations, as such provisions are in effect as of February 17, 2009.

(2) GAO report

Not later than 18 months after February 17, 2009, the Comptroller General shall submit to the Secretary a report including recommendations for a methodology under which an individual who is harmed by an act that constitutes an offense referred to in paragraph (1) may receive a percentage of any civil monetary penalty or monetary settlement collected with respect to such offense.

(3) Establishment of methodology to distribute percentage of CMPS collected to harmed individuals

Not later than 3 years after February 17, 2009, the Secretary shall establish by regulation and based on the recommendations submitted under paragraph (2), a methodology under which an individual who is harmed by an act that constitutes an offense referred to in paragraph (1) may receive a percentage of any civil monetary penalty or monetary settlement collected with respect to such offense.

(4) Application of methodology

The methodology under paragraph (3) shall be applied with respect to civil monetary penalties or monetary settlements imposed on or after the effective date of the regulation.

(d) Tiered increase in amount of civil monetary penalties

(1) to (3) Omitted

(4) Effective date

The amendments made by this subsection shall apply to violations occurring after February 17, 2009.

(e) Enforcement through State attorneys general

(1), (2) Omitted

(3) Effective date

The amendments made by this subsection shall apply to violations occurring after February 17, 2009.

International Privacy Law

UNIVERSAL DECLARATION OF HUMAN RIGHTS (1948)

Summary

On December 10, 1948 the General Assembly of the United Nations adopted and proclaimed the Universal Declaration of Human Rights. The Declaration sets forth a comprehensive list of the rights to which all people are entitled. Because nations initially resisted the creation of a legally binding instrument defining these human rights and fundamental freedoms, the Universal Declaration of Human Rights at its inception was viewed by the nations as a non-binding agreement, without the force of law. However, with passage of time, the UDHR has acquired the force of law through its incorporation into national laws, and because its language and ideas have been included in subsequent, binding treaties on human rights.

Article 12 of the Universal Declaration recognizes the right to privacy. It states: "No one shall be subjected to arbitrary interference with his privacy, family, home or correspondence, nor to attacks upon his honour and reputation. Everyone has the right to the protection of the law against such interference or attacks." Article 12 was the first statement of privacy as a basic human right that ought to be recognized by all nations.

The privacy right envisioned by the Declaration is a universal right that seeks to safeguard the individual across a wide range of activities, including family life, physical residence, and correspondence. The privacy right is coupled with a right to freedom from attacks upon honor and reputation, thereby linking the idea of privacy with human dignity. It is also worth noting that the second sentence of Article 12 imposes a duty upon states to establish rights in law to protect citizens against arbitrary interference with privacy.

Many subsequent international agreements have recognized the right to privacy outlined in Article 12. Article 17 of the International Covenant on Civil and Political Rights adopts the language verbatim. The European Convention on Human Rights, the U.N. Convention on the Rights of the Child, and the American Convention on Human Rights also incorporate a right to privacy based on Article 12.

References

United Nations, Universal Declaration of Human Rights
[http://www.un.org/en/universal-declaration-human-rights/index.html]

UN, Office of the High Commission for Human Rights
[http://www.ohchr.org/EN/Pages/Home.aspx]

International
Universal Declaration of Human Rights

ADOPTED BY THE UNITED NATIONS GENERAL ASSEMBLY 10 DECEMBER 1948

Whereas recognition of the inherent dignity and of the equal and inalienable rights of all members of the human family is the foundation of freedom, justice and peace in the world,

Whereas disregard and contempt for human rights have resulted in barbarous acts which have outraged the conscience of mankind, and the advent of a world in which human beings shall enjoy freedom of speech and belief and freedom from fear and want has been proclaimed as the highest aspiration of the common people,

Whereas it is essential, if man is not to be compelled to have recourse, as a last resort, to rebellion against tyranny and oppression, that human rights should be protected by the rule of law,

Whereas it is essential to promote the development of friendly relations between nations,

Whereas the peoples of the United Nations have in the Charter reaffirmed their faith in fundamental human rights, in the dignity and worth of the human person and in the equal rights of men and women and have determined to promote social progress and better standards of life in larger freedom,

Whereas Member States have pledged themselves to achieve, in co-operation with the United Nations, the promotion of universal respect for and observance of human rights and fundamental freedoms,

Whereas a common understanding of these rights and freedoms is of the greatest importance for the full realisation of this pledge,

Now, Therefore, THE GENERAL ASSEMBLY proclaims THIS UNIVERSAL DECLARATION OF HUMAN RIGHTS as a common standard of achievement for all peoples and all nations, to the end that every individual and every organ of society, keeping this Declaration constantly in mind, shall strive by teaching and education to promote respect for these rights and freedoms and by progressive measures, national and international, to secure their universal and effective recognition and observance, both among the peoples of the Member States themselves and among the peoples of territories under their jurisdiction.

ARTICLE 1. All human beings are born free and equal in dignity and rights. They are endowed with reason and conscience and should act towards one another in a spirit of brotherhood.

ARTICLE 2. Everyone is entitled to all the rights and freedoms set forth in this Declaration, without distinction of any kind, such as race, colour, sex, language, religion, political or other opinion, national or social origin, property, birth or other status.

Furthermore, no distinction shall be made on the basis of the political, jurisdictional or international status of the country or territory to which a person belongs, whether it be independent, trust, non-self-governing or under any other limitation of sovereignty.

ARTICLE 3. Everyone has the right to life, liberty and security of person.

ARTICLE 4. No one shall be held in slavery or servitude; slavery and the slave trade shall be prohibited in all their forms.

ARTICLE 5. No one shall be subjected to torture or to cruel, inhuman or degrading treatment or punishment.

ARTICLE 6. Everyone has the right to recognition everywhere as a person before the law.

ARTICLE 7. All are equal before the law and are entitled without any discrimination to equal protection of the law. All are entitled to equal protection against any discrimination in violation of this Declaration and against any incitement to such discrimination.

ARTICLE 8. Everyone has the right to an effective remedy by the competent national tribunals for acts violating the fundamental rights granted him by the constitution or by law.

ARTICLE 9. No one shall be subjected to arbitrary arrest, detention or exile.

ARTICLE 10. Everyone is entitled in full equality to a fair and public hearing by an independent and impartial tribunal, in the determination of his rights and obligations and of any criminal charge against him.

ARTICLE 11. (1) Everyone charged with a penal offence has the right to be presumed innocent until proved guilty according to law in a public trial at which he has had all the guarantees necessary for his defence. (2) No one shall be held guilty of any penal offence on account of any act or omission which did not constitute a penal offence, under national or international law, at the time when it was committed. Nor shall a heavier penalty be imposed than the one that was applicable at the time the penal offence was committed.

ARTICLE 12. No one shall be subjected to arbitrary interference with his privacy, family, home or correspondence, nor to attacks upon his honour and reputation. Everyone has the right to the protection of the law against such interference or attacks.

ARTICLE 13. (1) Everyone has the right to freedom of movement and residence within the borders of each State. (2) Everyone has the right to leave any country, including his own, and to return to his country.

ARTICLE 14. (1) Everyone has the right to seek and to enjoy in other countries asylum from persecution. (2) This right may not be invoked in the case of prosecutions genuinely arising from non-political crimes or from acts contrary to the purposes and principles of the United Nations.

ARTICLE 15. (1) Everyone has the right to a nationality. (2) No one shall be arbitrarily deprived of his nationality nor denied the right to change his nationality.

ARTICLE 16. (1) Men and women of full age, without any limitation due to race, nationality or religion, have the right to marry and to found a family. They are entitled to equal rights as to marriage, during marriage and at its dissolution. (2) Marriage shall be entered into only with the free and full consent of the intending spouses. (3) The family is the natural and fundamental group unit of society and is entitled to protection by society and the State.

ARTICLE 17. (1) Everyone has the right to own property alone as well as in association with others. (2) No one shall be arbitrarily deprived of his property.

ARTICLE 18. Everyone has the right to freedom of thought, conscience and religion; this right includes freedom to change his religion or belief, and freedom, either alone or in community with others and in public or private, to manifest his religion or belief in teaching, practice, worship and observance.

ARTICLE 19. Everyone has the right to freedom of opinion and expression; this right includes freedom to hold opinions without interference and to seek, receive and impart information and ideas through any media and regardless of frontiers.

ARTICLE 20. (1) Everyone has the right to freedom of peaceful assembly and association. (2) No one may be compelled to belong to an association.

ARTICLE 21. (1) Everyone has the right to take part in the government of his country, directly or through chosen representatives. (2) Everyone has the right of equal access to public service in his country. (3) The will of the people shall be the basis of the authority of government; this will shall be expressed in periodic and genuine elections which shall be held by universal and equal suffrage and shall be held by secret vote or by equivalent free voting procedures.

ARTICLE 22. Everyone, as a member of society, has the right to social security and is entitled to realisation, through national effort and international co-operation and in accordance with the organisation and resources of each State, of the economic, social and cultural rights indispensable for his dignity and the free development of his personality.

ARTICLE 23. (1) Everyone has the right to work, to free choice of employment, to just and favourable conditions of work and to protection against unemployment. (2) Everyone, without any discrimination, has the right to equal pay for equal work. (3) Everyone has the right to just and favourable remuneration ensuring for himself and his family an existence worthy of human dignity, and supplemented, if necessary, by other means of social protection. (4) Everyone has the right to form and to join trade unions for the protection of his interests.

ARTICLE 24. Everyone has the right to rest and leisure, including reasonable limitation of working hours and periodic holidays with pay.

ARTICLE 25. (1) Everyone has the right to a standard of living adequate for the health and well-being of himself and of his family, including food, clothing, housing and medical care and necessary social services, and the right to security in the event of unemployment, sickness, disability, widowhood, old age and other lack of livelihood in circumstances beyond his control. (2) Motherhood and childhood are entitled to special care and assistance. All children, whether born in or out of wedlock, shall enjoy the same social protection.

ARTICLE 26. (1) Everyone has the right to education. Education shall be free, at least in the elementary and fundamental stages. Elementary education shall be compulsory. Technical and professional education shall be made generally available and higher education shall be equally accessible to all on the basis of merit. (2) Education shall be directed to the full development of the human personality and to the strengthening of respect for human rights and fundamental freedoms. It shall promote understanding, tolerance and friendship among all nations, racial or religious groups, and shall further the activities of the United Nations for the maintenance of peace. (3) Parents have a prior right to choose the kind of education that shall be given their children.

ARTICLE 27. (1) Everyone has the right to freely participate in the cultural life of the community, to enjoy the arts and to share in scientific advancement and its benefits. (2) Everyone has the right to the protection of the moral and material interests resulting from any scientific, literary or artistic production of which he is the author.

ARTICLE 28. Everyone is entitled to a social and international order in which the rights and freedoms set forth in this Declaration can be fully realised.

ARTICLE 29. (1) Everyone has duties to the community in which alone the free and full development of is personality is possible. (2) In the exercise of his rights and freedoms, everyone shall be subject only to such limitations as are determined by law solely for the purpose of securing due recognition and respect for the rights and freedoms of others and of meeting the just requirements of morality, public order and the general welfare in a democratic society. (3) These rights and freedoms may in no case be exercised contrary to the purposes and principles of the United Nations.

ARTICLE 30. Nothing in this Declaration may be interpreted as implying for any State, group or person any right to engage in any activity or to perform any act aimed at the destruction of any of the rights and freedoms set forth herein.

International
Council of Europe Convention on Human Rights

COUNCIL OF EUROPE CONVENTION FOR THE PROTECTION OF HUMAN RIGHTS AND FUNDAMENTAL FREEDOMS (1950) [EXCERPT]

Summary

The Council of Europe Convention for the Protection of Human Rights was adopted shortly after the Universal Declaration of Human Rights of the United Nations. Article 8 in the Council of Europe Convention addresses the right to respect for private and family life.

References

Council of Europe, Legal Affairs, Treaty Office
[http://www.coe.int/en/web/conventions/]
[http://www.coe.int/en/web/conventions/full-list/-/conventions/treaty/005]

* * *

Article 8 – Right to respect for private and family life

1. Everyone has the right to respect for his private and family life, his home and his correspondence.

2. There shall be no interference by a public authority with the exercise of this right except such as is in accordance with the law and is necessary in a democratic society in the interests of national security, public safety or the economic well-being of the country, for the prevention of disorder or crime, for the protection of health or morals, or for the protection of the rights and freedoms of others.

* * *

CHARTER OF FUNDAMENTAL RIGHTS
OF THE EUROPEAN UNION (2000)
[EXCERPT]

Reference

Charter of Fundamental Rights
[http://eur-lex.europa.eu/legal-content/EN/TXT/?uri=CELEX:12012P/TXT]

The European Parliament, the Council and the Commission solemnly proclaim the text below as the Charter of fundamental rights of the European Union.

Done at Nice on the seventh day of December in the year two thousand.

C 364/8 Official Journal of the European Communities 18.12.2000

Incorporated into a Treaty establishing a Constitution for Europe in 2004
C 310/41 Official Journal of the European Communities 16.12.2004

* * *

Article 7 - Respect for private and family life

Everyone has the right to respect for his or her private and family life, home and communications.

Article 8 - Protection of personal data

1. Everyone has the right to the protection of personal data concerning him or her.
2. Such data must be processed fairly for specified purposes and on the basis of the consent of the person concerned or some other legitimate basis laid down by law. Everyone has the right of access to data which has been collected concerning him or her, and the right to have it rectified.
3. Compliance with these rules shall be subject to control by an independent authority.

* * *

OECD PRIVACY GUIDELINES (2013)

Summary

On September 23, 1980, the Organization for Economic Cooperation and Development, a group of leading industrial countries concerned with global economic and democratic development, issued guidelines for privacy protection in the transfer of personal information across national borders. These are the Guidelines on the Protection of Privacy and Transborder Flows of Personal Data. On July 11, 2013 those guidelines were updated for the first time to reflect decades of change in the digital environment, building off the original foundation of eight key principles.

First is the principle of collection limitation. This principle states that there should be limits to the collection of personal data; any such data collected should be obtained by lawful means and with the consent of the data subject, where appropriate. Second is the principle of data quality. This principle embodies the notion that collected data should be relevant to a specific purpose, and be accurate, complete, and up-to-date. Third is the principle of purpose specification; that is, the purpose for collecting data should be settled at the outset. The fourth principle, use limitation, works in tandem with the third. It states that the use of personal data ought be limited to specified purposes, and that data acquired for one purpose ought not be used for others. The fifth principle is security: data must be collected and stored in a way reasonably calculated to prevent its loss, theft, or modification. The sixth principle is openness. There should be a general position of transparency with respect to the practices of handling data. The seventh principle is individual participation: individual should have the right to access, confirm, and demand correction of their personal data. The eighth and last principle is accountability. Those in charge of handling data should be responsible for complying with the principles of the privacy guidelines.

In developing the guidelines, the OECD worked closely with the Council of Europe , which was at that time drafting its own Convention on Privacy. Examination of both the Guidelines and the Convention will show that they have much in common, as well as pointing to the general concern for individual privacy protection that arose in the late 1970s. Since the Guidelines' release, many OECD countries have enacted laws to implement them. In 1985, OECD extended the guidelines to cover transborder data flow. Although the OECD Guidelines are nonbinding on signatories, the eight privacy principles have had a significant impact on the development of privacy law around the globe. The 2013 update included strategies for implementation and international co-operation.

Today, the full OECD document includes six chapters. Chapter one, included below, is the text of the 2013 guidelines themselves. Chapters two through six are explanatory memoranda, background, and guidelines on cross-border privacy law enforcement co-operation. The full six chapters are located at:

> http://www.oecd.org/internet/ieconomy/oecdguidelinesontheprotectionofprivacyandt ransborderflowsofpersonaldata.htm

References

> OECD, Guidelines on the Protection of Privacy and Transborder Flows of Personal Data (2013)
> [http://www.oecd.org/internet/ieconomy/oecdguidelinesontheprotectionofprivacyand transborderflowsofpersonaldata.htm]
> OECD, Guidelines on the Protection of Privacy and Transborder Flows of Personal Data (1980)
> [http://www.oecd.org/internet/ieconomy/oecdguidelinesontheprotectionofprivacyand transborderflowsofpersonaldata.htm]
> OECD, Declaration on Transborder Data Flows (1985)
> [http://www.oecd.org/internet/ieconomy/declarationontransborderdataflows.htm]
> OECD, Ministerial Declaration on the Protection of Privacy on Global Networks (1998)
> [http://acts.oecd.org/Instruments/ShowInstrumentView.aspx?InstrumentID=109&]

Chapter 1.

RECOMMENDATION OF THE COUNCIL CONCERNING GUIDELINES GOVERNING THE PROTECTION OF PRIVACY AND TRANSBORDER FLOWS OF PERSONAL DATA (2013)

THE COUNCIL,

HAVING REGARD to Article 5(b) of the Convention on the Organisation for Economic Co-operation and Development of 14th December, 1960;

HAVING REGARD to the Ministerial Declaration on the Protection of Privacy on Global Networks [Annex 1 to C(98)177]; the Recommenda- tion of the Council concerning Guidelines for the Security of Information Systems and Networks [C(2002)131/FINAL], the Recommendation of the Council on Cross-border Co-operation in the Enforcement of Laws Protecting Privacy [C(2007)67], the Declaration for the Future of the Internet Economy (The Seoul Declaration) [C(2008)99], the Recommenda- tion of the Council on Principles for Internet Policy Making [C(2011)154], the Recommendation of the Council on the Protection of Children Online [C(2011)155] and the Recommendation of the Council on Regulatory Policy and Governance [C(2012)37];

RECOGNISING that Member countries have a common interest in promoting and protecting the fundamental values of privacy, individual liberties and the global free flow of information; RECOGNISING that more extensive and innovative uses of personal data bring greater economic and social benefits, but also increase privacy risks;

International
OECD Privacy Guidelines

RECOGNISING that the continuous flows of personal data across global networks amplify the need for improved interoperability among privacy frameworks as well as strengthened cross-border co-operation among privacy enforcement authorities;

RECOGNISING the importance of risk assessment in the development of policies and safeguards to protect privacy;

RECOGNISING the challenges to the security of personal data in an open, interconnected environment in which personal data is increasingly a valuable asset;

DETERMINED to further advance the free flow of information between Member countries and to avoid the creation of unjustified obstacles to the development of economic and social relations among them;

On the proposal of the Committee for Information, Computer and Communications Policy:

I. RECOMMENDS that Member countries
- Demonstrate leadership and commitment to the protection of privacy and free flow of information at the highest levels of government;
- Implement the Guidelines contained in the Annex to this Recommendation, and of which they form an integral part, through processes that include all relevant stakeholders;
- Disseminate this Recommendation throughout the public and private sectors;

II. INVITES non-Members to adhere to this Recommendation and to collaborate with Member countries in its implementation across borders.

III. INSTRUCTS the Committee for Information, Computer and Communication Policy to monitor the implementation of this Recommendation, review that information, and report to the Council within five years of its adoption and thereafter as appropriate.

This Recommendation revises the Recommendation of the Council concerning Guidelines Governing the Protection of Privacy and Transborder Flows of Personal Data of 23 September 1980 [C(80)58/FINAL].

ANNEX
GUIDELINES GOVERNING THE PROTECTION OF PRIVACY AND TRANSBORDER
FLOWS OF PERSONAL DATA

PART ONE. GENERAL

Definitions

1. For the purposes of these Guidelines:

(a) "Data controller" means a party who, according to domestic law, is competent to decide about the contents and use of personal data regardless of whether or not such data are collected, stored, processed or disseminated by that party or by an agent on its behalf.

(b) "Personal data" means any information relating to an identified or identifiable individual (data subject).

(c) "Laws protecting privacy" means national laws or regulations, the enforcement of which has the effect of protecting personal data consistent with these Guidelines.

(d) "Privacy enforcement authority" means any public body, as determined by each Member country, that is responsible for enforcing laws protecting privacy, and that has powers to conduct investigations or pursue enforcement proceedings.

(e) "Transborder flows of personal data" means movements of personal data across national borders.

Scope of Guidelines

2. These Guidelines apply to personal data, whether in the public or private sectors, which, because of the manner in which they are processed, or because of their nature or the context in which they are used, pose a danger to privacy and individual liberties.

3. These Guidelines should not be interpreted:

(a) as preventing the application of different protective measures to different categories of personal data, depending upon their nature and the context in which they are collected, stored, processed or disseminated; or

(b) in a manner which unduly limits the freedom of expression.

4. Exceptions to the Guidelines, including those relating to national sovereignty, national security and public policy ("ordre public"), should be:

(a) as few as possible, and

(b) made known to the public.

5. In the particular case of federal countries the observance of these Guidelines may be affected by the division of powers in the federation.

6. These Guidelines should be regarded as minimum standards which can be supplemented by additional measures for the protection of privacy and individual liberties, which may impact transborder flows of personal data.

PART TWO. BASIC PRINCIPLES OF NATIONAL APPLICATION

Collection Limitation Principle

7. There should be limits to the collection of personal data and any such data should be obtained by lawful and fair means and, where appropriate, with the knowledge or consent of the data subject.

Data Quality Principle

8. Personal data should be relevant to the purposes for which they are to be used, and, to the extent necessary for those purposes, should be accurate, complete and kept up-to-date.

Purpose Specification Principle

9. The purposes for which personal data are collected should be specified not later than at the time of data collection and the subsequent use limited to the fulfillment of those purposes or such others as are not incompatible with those purposes and as are specified on each occasion of change of purpose.

Use Limitation Principle

10. Personal data should not be disclosed, made available or otherwise used for purposes other than those specified in accordance with Paragraph 9 except: (a) with the consent of the data subject; or (b) by the authority of law.

Security Safeguards Principle

11. Personal data should be protected by reasonable security safeguards against such risks as loss or unauthorised access, destruction, use, modification or disclosure of data.

Openness Principle

12. There should be a general policy of openness about developments, practices and policies with respect to personal data. Means should be readily available of establishing the existence and nature of personal data, and the main purposes of their use, as well as the identity and usual residence of the data controller.

Individual Participation Principle

13. An individual should have the right:

(a) to obtain from a data controller, or otherwise, confirmation of whether or not the data controller has data relating to him;

(b) to have communicated to him, data relating to him (i) within a reasonable time; (ii) at a charge, if any, that is not excessive; (iii) in a reasonable manner; and (iv) in a form that is readily intelligible to him;

(c) to be given reasons if a request made under subparagraphs (a) and (b) is denied, and to be able to challenge such denial; and

(d) to challenge data relating to him and, if the challenge is successful, to have the data erased, rectified, completed or amended.

Accountability Principle

14. A data controller should be accountable for complying with measures which give effect to the principles stated above.

PART THREE. IMPLEMENTING ACCOUNTABILITY

15. A data controller should:
> (a) Have in place a privacy management programme that:
>> i. gives effect to these Guidelines for all personal data under its control;
>> ii. is tailored to the structure, scale, volume and sensitivity of its operations;
>> iii. provides for appropriate safeguards based on privacy risk assessment;
>> iv. is integrated into its governance structure and establishes internal oversight mechanisms;
>> v. includes plans for responding to inquiries and incidents;
>> vi. is updated in light of ongoing monitoring and periodic assessment;
>
> (b) Be prepared to demonstrate its privacy management programme as appropriate, in particular at the request of a competent privacy enforcement authority or another entity responsible for promoting adherence to a code of conduct or similar arrangement giving binding effect to these Guidelines; and
>
> (c) Provide notice, as appropriate, to privacy enforcement authorities or other relevant authorities where there has been a significant security breach affecting personal data. Where the breach is likely to adversely affect data subjects, a data controller should notify affected data subjects.

PART FOUR. BASIC PRINCIPLES OF INTERNATIONAL APPLICATION: FREE FLOW AND LEGITIMATE RESTRICTIONS

16. A data controller remains accountable for personal data under its control without regard to the location of the data.

17. A Member country should refrain from restricting transborder flows of personal data between itself and another country where (a) the other country substantially observes these Guidelines or (b) sufficient safeguards exist, including effective enforcement mechanisms and appropriate measures put in place by the data controller, to ensure a continuing level of protection consistent with these Guidelines.

18. Any restrictions to transborder flows of personal data should be proportionate to the risks presented, taking into account the sensitivity of the data, and the purpose and context of the processing.

PART FIVE. NATIONAL IMPLEMENTATION

19. In implementing these Guidelines, Member countries should:
    (a) develop national privacy strategies that reflect a co-ordinated approach across governmental bodies;
    (b) adopt laws protecting privacy;
    (c) establish and maintain privacy enforcement authorities with the governance, resources and technical expertise necessary to exercise their powers effectively and to make decisions on an objective, impartial and consistent basis;
    (d) encourage and support self-regulation, whether in the form of codes of conduct or otherwise;
    (e) provide for reasonable means for individuals to exercise their rights;
    (f) provide for adequate sanctions and remedies in case of failures to comply with laws protecting privacy;
    (g) consider the adoption of complementary measures, including education and awareness raising, skills development, and the promotion of technical measures which help to protect privacy;
    (h) consider the role of actors other than data controllers, in a manner appropriate to their individual role; and
    (i) ensure that there is no unfair discrimination against data subjects.

PART SIX. INTERNATIONAL CO-OPERATION AND INTEROPERABILITY

20. Member countries should take appropriate measures to facilitate cross- border privacy law enforcement co-operation, in particular by enhancing information sharing among privacy enforcement authorities.

21. Member countries should encourage and support the development of international arrangements that promote interoperability among privacy frameworks that give practical effect to these Guidelines.

22. Member countries should encourage the development of internationally comparable metrics to inform the policy making process related to privacy and transborder flows of personal data.

23. Member countries should make public the details of their observance of these Guidelines.

COUNCIL OF EUROPE CONVENTION
ON PRIVACY (2018)

Summary

The Council of Europe concluded the Convention for the Protection of Individuals with Regard to Automatic Processing of Personal Data in 1981, and it entered into force in 1985. The Council negotiated the Convention in response to the rapid rise of automated data processing, and advances in computer technology that were allowing more and more records to be stored and transferred digitally. The Council also noted that there was a lack of rules generally applicable across Europe for dealing with the legal issues that might arise from computerized data transfer.

The convention's point of departure is that certain rights of the individual may have to be protected vis-à-vis the free flow of information regardless of frontiers, the latter principle being enshrined in international and European instruments on human rights. To this end, the convention consists of three main parts: substantive law provisions in the form of basic principles; special rules on transborder data flows; and mechanisms for mutual assistance and consultation between the Parties.

The Council of Europe worked closely with the OECD in drafting the Convention. The result is that both privacy frameworks are similar.

In 2018, the Council adopted an amending protocol which modernizes the Convention. The 2018 Convention preserves and strengthens the original principles. It contains new principles to address emerging technologies and global data flows, as well as to strengthen implementation.

References

Council of Europe, Legal Affairs, Treaty Office, Convention No. 108 (2018)
[http://search.coe.int/cm/Pages/result_details.aspx?ObjectId=09000016807c65bf]

MODERNISED CONVENTION FOR THE PROTECTION OF INDIVIDUALS
WITH REGARD TO THE PROCESSING OF PERSONAL DATA (2018)

The Member States of the Council of Europe, signatory hereto,
Considering that the aim of he Council of Europe is to achieve greater unity between its members, based in particular on respect for the rule of law, as well as human rights and fundamental freedoms;

Considering that it is necessary to secure the human dignity and protection of the human rights and fundamental freedoms of every individual and, given the diversification, intensification and globalisation of data processing and personal data flows, personal autonomy based on a person's right to control of his or her personal data and the processing of such data;

Recalling that the right to protection of personal data is to be considered in respect of its role in society and that it has to be reconciled with other human rights and fundamental freedoms, including freedom of expression;

Considering that this Convention permits account to be taken, in the implementation of the rules laid down therein, of the principle of the right of access to official documents;

Recognising that it is necessary to promote at the global level the fundamental values of respect for privacy and protection of personal data, thereby contributing to the free flow of information between people;

Recognising the interest of a reinforcement of international co-operation between the Parties to the Convention,

Have agreed as follows:

CHAPTER I – GENERAL PROVISIONS

Article 1: Object and purpose

The purpose of this convention is to protect every individual, whatever his or her nationality or residence, with regard to th processing of their personal data, thereby contributing to respect for his or her human rights and fundamental freedoms, and in particular the right to privacy.

Article 2: Definitions

For the purposes of this convention:

a. "personal data" means any information relating to an identifiedor identifiable individual ("data subject");

b. "data processing" means any operation or set of operations performed on personal data, such as the collection, storage, preservation, alteration, retrieval, disclosure, making available, erasure, or destruction of, or the carrying out of logical and/or arithmetical operations on such data;

c. where automated processing is not used, data processing means an operation or set of operations performed upon personal data within a structured set of such data which are accessible or retrievable according to specific criteria;

International
Council of Europe Convention on Privacy

d. "controller" means the natural or legal person, public authority, agency or any other body which alone or jointly with others has decision-making power with respect to data processing;

e. "recipient" means a natural or legal person, public authority, service, agency or any other body to whom data are disclosed or made available;

f. "processor" means a natural or legal person, public authority, service, agency or any other body which processes personal data on behalf of the controller.

Article 3: Scope

1. Each Party undertakes to apply this Convention to data processing subject to its jurisdiction in the public and private sectors, thereby securing every individual's right to protection of his or her personal data .

2. This Convention shall not apply to data processing carried out by an individual in the course of purely personal or household activities:

CHAPTER II - BASIC PRINCIPLES FOR DATA PROTECTION

Article 4: Duties of the Parties

1. Each Party shall take the necessary measures in its law to give effect to the provisions of this Convention and secure their effective application.

2. These measures shall be taken by each party and shall have come into force by the time of ratification or of accession to this Convention.

3. Each Party undertakes:

a. to allow the Convention Committee provided for in Chapter VI to evaluate the effectiveness of the measures it has taken in its law to give effect to the provisions of this Convention; and

b. to contribute actively to this evaluation process.

Article 5: Legitimacy of data processing and quality of data

1. Data processing shall be proportionate in relation to the legitimate purpose pursued and reflect at all stages of the processing a fair balance between all interests concerned, whether public or private, and the rights and freedoms at stake.

2. Each Party shall provide that data processing can be carried out on the basis of the free, specific, informed and unambiguous consent of the data subject or of some other legitimate basis laid down by law.

3. Personal data undergoing processing shall be processed lawfully.

4. Personal data undergoing processing shall be:

a. processed fairly and in a transparent manner;

b. collected for explicit, specified and legitimate purposes and not processed in a way incompatible with those purposes; further processing for archiving purposes in the public interest, scientific or historical research purposes or statistical purposes is, subject to appropriate safeguards, compatible with those purposes;

c. adequate, relevant and not excessive in relation to the purposes for which they are processed;

d. accurate and, where necessary, kept up to date

e. preserved in a form which permits identification of the data subjects for no longer than is necessary for the purposes for which those data are processed.

Article 6: Special categories of data

1. The processing of:

- genetic data;

- personal data relating to offences, criminal proceedings and convictions, and related security measures;

- biometric data uniquely identifying a person;

- personal data for the information they reveal relating to racial or ethnic origin, political opinions, trade-union membership, religious or other beliefs, health or sexual life, shall only be allowed where appropriate safeguards are enshrined in law, complementing those of this Convention.

2. Such safeguards shall guard against the risks that the processing of sensitive data may present for the interests, rights and fundamental freedoms of the data subject, notably a risk of discrimination.

Article 7: Data security

1. Each Party shall provide that the controller, and, where applicable the processor, take appropriate security measures against risks such as accidental or unauthorised access to, destruction, loss, use, modification or disclosure of personal data.

2. Each Party shall provide that the controller notifies, without delay, at least the competent supervisory authority within the meaning of Article 15 of this Convention, of those data

breaches which may seriously interfere with the rights and fundamental freedoms of data subjects.

Article 8: Transparency of Processing

1. Each Party shall provide that the controller informs the data subjects of:

a. his or her identity and habitual residence or establishment;

b. the legal basis and the purposes of the intended processing;

c. the categories of personal data processed;

d. the recipients or categories of recipients of the personal data, if any; and

e. the means of exercising the rights set out in Article 9, as well as any necessary additional information in order to ensure fair and transparent processing of the personal data.

2. Paragraph 1 shall not apply where the data subject already has the relevant information.

3. Where the personal data are not collected from the data subjects, the controller shall not be required to provide such information where the processing is expressly prescribed by law or this proves to be impossible or involves disproportionate efforts.

Article 9: Rights of the data subject

1. Every individual shall have a right:

a. not to be subject to a decision significantly affecting him or her based solely on an automated processing of data without having his or her views taken into consideration;

b. to obtain, on request, at reasonable intervals and without excessive delay or expense, confirmation of the processing of personal data relating to him or her, the communication in an intelligible form of the data processed, all available information on their origin, on the preservation period as well as any other information that the controller is required to provide in order to ensure the transparency of processing in accordance with Article 8, paragraph 1;

c. to obtain, on request, knowledge of the reasoning underlying data processing where the results of such processing are applied to him or her;

d. to object at any time, on grounds relating to his or her situation, to the processing of personal data concerning him or her unless the controller demonstrates legitimate grounds for the processing which override his or her interests or rights and fundamental freedoms;

e. to obtain, on request, free of charge and without excessive delay, rectification or erasure, as the case may be, of such data if these are being, or have been, processed contrary to the provisions of this Convention;

f. to have a remedy under Article 12 where his or her rights under this Convention have been violated;

g. to benefit, whatever his or her nationality or residence, from the assistance of a supervisory authority within the meaning of Article 15, in exercising his or her rights under this Convention.

2. Paragraph 1.a shall not apply if the decision is authorised by a law to which the controller is subject and which also lays down suitable measures to safeguard the data subject's rights, freedoms and legitimate interests.

Article 10: Additional obligations

1. Each Party shall provide that controllers and, where applicable, processors, take all appropriate measures to comply with the obligations of this Convention and be able to demonstrate, subject to the domestic legislation adopted in accordance with Article 11, paragraph 3, in particular to the competent supervisory authority provided for in Article 15, that the data processing under their control is in compliance with the provisions of this Convention.

2. Each Party shall provide that controllers and, where applicable, processors, examine the likely impact of intended data processing on the rights and fundamental freedoms of data subjects prior to the commencement of such processing, and shall design the data processing in such a manner as to prevent or minimise the risk of interference with those rights and fundamental freedoms.

3. Each Party shall provide that controllers, and, where applicable, processors, implement technical and organisational measures which take into account the implications of the right to the protection of personal data at all stages of the data processing.

4. Each Party may, having regard to the risks arising for the interests, rights and fundamental freedoms of the data subjects, adapt the application of the provisions of paragraphs 1, 2 and 3 in the law giving effect to the provisions of this Convention, according to the nature and volume

of the data, the nature, scope and purpose of the processing and, where appropriate, the size of the controller or processor.

Article 11: Exceptions and restrictions

1. No exception to the provisions set out in this Chapter shall be allowed except to the provisions of Article 5 paragraph 4, Article 7 paragraph 2, Article 8 paragraph 1 and Article 9, when such an exception is provided for by law, respects the essence of the fundamental rights and freedoms and constitutes a necessary and proportionate measure in a democratic society for:

a. the protection of national security, defense, public safety, important economic and financial interests of the State, the impartiality and independence of the judiciary or the prevention, investigation and prosecution of criminal offences and the execution of criminal penalties, and other essential objectives of general public interest;

b. the protection of the data subject or the rights and fundamental freedoms of others, notably freedom of expression.

2. Restrictions on the exercise of the provisions specified in Articles 8 and 9 may be provided for by law with respect to data processing for archiving purposes in the public interest, scientific or historical research purposes or statistical purposes when there is no recognisable risk of infringement of the rights and fundamental freedoms of data subjects.

3. In addition to the exceptions allowed for in paragraph 1 of this article, with reference to processing activities for national security and defense purposes, each Party may provide, by law and only to the extent that it constitutes a necessary and proportionate measure in a

democratic society to fulfill such aim, exceptions to Article 4 paragraph 3, Article 14 paragraphs 5 and 6 and Article 15, paragraph 2, litterae a, b, c and d.

This is without prejudice to the requirement that processing activities for national security and defense purposes are subject to independent and effective review and supervision under the domestic legislation of the respective Party.

Article 12: Sanctions and remedies

Each Party undertakes to establish appropriate judicial and non-judicial sanctions and remedies for violations of the provisions of this Convention.

Article 13: Extended protection

None of the provisions of this chapter shall be interpreted as limiting or otherwise affectingthe possibility for a Party to grant data subjects of wider measure of protection than that stipulated in this convention.

CHAPTER III – TRANSBORDER DATA FLOWS OF PERSONAL DATA

Article 14: Transborder flows of personal data

1. A Party shall not, for the sole purpose of the protection of personal data, prohibit or subject to special authorisation the transfer of such data to a recipient who is subject to the jurisdiction of another Party to the Convention. Such a Party may, however, do so if there is a real and serious risk that the transfer to another Party, or from that other Party to a non-Party, would lead to circumventing the provisions of the Convention. A Party may also do so, if bound by

harmonised rules of protection shared by States belonging to a regional international organisation.

2. When the recipient is subject to the jurisdiction of a State or international organisation which is not Party to this Convention, the transfer of personal data may only take place where an appropriate level of protection based on the provisions of this Convention is secured.

3. An appropriate level of protection can be secured by:

a. the law of that State or international organisation, including the applicable international treaties or agreements; or

b. ad hoc or approved standardised safeguards provided by legally-binding and enforceable instruments adopted and implemented by the persons involved in the transfer and further processing.

4. Notwithstanding the provisions of the previous paragraphs, each Party may provide that the transfer of personal data may take place if:

a. the data subject has given explicit, specific and free consent, after being informed of risks arising in the absence of appropriate safeguards; or

b. the specific interests of the data subject require it in the particular case; or

c. prevailing legitimate interests, in particular important public interests, are provided for by law and such transfer constitutes a necessary and proportionate measure in a democratic society; or

d. it constitutes a necessary and proportionate measure in a democratic society for freedom of expression.

5. Each Party shall provide that the competent supervisory authority within the meaning of Article 15 of this Convention is provided with all relevant information concerning the transfers of data referred to in paragraph 3.b and, upon request, paragraphs 4.b and 4.c.

6. Each Party shall also provide that the supervisory authority is entitled to request that the person who transfers data demonstrates the effectiveness of the safeguards or the existence of prevailing legitimate interests and that the supervisory authority may, in order to protect the

rights and fundamental freedoms of data subjects, prohibit such transfers, suspend them or subject them to condition.

CHAPTER IV – SUPERVISORY AUTHORITIES

Article 15: Supervisory authorities

1 Each Party shall provide for one or more authorities to be responsible for ensuring compliance with the provisions of this Convention.

2 To this end, such authorities:

a. shall have powers of investigation and intervention;

b. shall perform the functions relating to transfers of data provided for under Article 14, notably the approval of standardised safeguards;

c. shall have powers to issue decisions with respect to violations of the provisions of this Convention and may, in particular, impose administrative sanctions;

d. shall have the power to engage in legal proceedings or to bring to the attention of the competent judicial authorities violations of the provisions of this Convention;

e. shall promote:

i. public awareness of their functions and powers as well as their activities;

ii. public awareness of the rights of data subjects and the exercise of such rights;

iii. awareness of controllers and processors of their responsibilities under this Convention;

specific attention shall be given to the data protection rights of children and other vulnerable individuals.

3. The competent supervisory authorities shall be consulted on proposals for any legislative or administrative measures which provide for the processing of personal data.

4. Each competent supervisory authority shall deal with requests and complaints lodged by data subjects concerning their data protection rights and shall keep data subjects informed of progress.

5. The supervisory authorities shall act with complete independence and impartiality in performing their duties and exercising their powers and in doing so shall neither seek nor accept instructions.

6. Each Party shall ensure that the supervisory authorities are provided with the resources necessary for the effective performance of their functions and exercise of their powers.

7. Each supervisory authority shall prepare and publish a periodical report outlining its activities.

8. Members and staff of the supervisory authorities shall be bound by obligations of confidentiality with regard to confidential information to which they have access, or have had access to, in the performance of their duties and exercise of their powers.

9. Decisions of the supervisory authorities may be subject to appeal through the courts.

10. The supervisory authorities shall not be competent with respect to processing carried out by bodies when acting in their judicial capacity.

CHAPTER V – CO-OPERATION AND MUTUAL ASSISTANCE

Article 16: Designation of supervisory authorities

1. The Parties agree to co-operate and render each other mutual assistance in order to implement this Convention.

2. For that purpose:

a. each Party shall designate one or more supervisory authorities within the meaning of Article 15 of this Convention, the name and address of each of which it shall communicate to the Secretary General of the Council of Europe;

b. each Party which has designated more than one supervisory authority shall specify the competence of each authority in its communication referred to in the previous littera.

Article 17: Forms of co-operation

1. The supervisory authorities shall co-operate with one another to the extent necessary for the performance of their duties and exercise of their powers, in particular by:

a. providing mutual assistance by exchanging relevant and useful information and co-operating with each other under the condition that, as regards the protection of personal data, all the rules and safeguards of this Convention are complied with;

b. co-ordinating their investigations or interventions, or conducting joint actions;

c. providing information and documentation on their law and administrative practice relating to data protection.

2. The information referred to in paragraph 1 shall not include personal data undergoing processing unless such data are essential for co-operation, or where the data subject concerned has given explicit, specific, free and informed consent to its provision.

3. In order to organise their co-operation and to perform the duties set out in the preceding paragraphs, the supervisory authorities of the Parties shall form a network.

Article 18: Assistance to data subjects

1. Each Party shall assist any data subject, whatever his or her nationality or residence, to exercise his or her rights under Article 9 of this Convention.

2. Where a data subject resides on the territory of another Party, he or she shall be given the option of submitting the request through the intermediary of the supervisory authority designated by that Party.

3. The request for assistance shall contain all the necessary particulars, relating inter alia to:

a. the name, address and any other relevant particulars identifying the data subject making the request;

b. the processing to which the request pertains, or its controller;

c. the purpose of the request.

Article 19: Safeguards

1. A supervisory authority which has received information from another supervisory authority, either accompanying a request or in reply to its own request, shall not use that information for purposes other than those specified in the request.

2. In no case may a supervisory authority be allowed to make a request on behalf of a data subject of its own accord and without the express approval of the data subject concerned.

Article 20: Refusal of requests

A supervisory authority to which a request is addressed under Article 17 of this Convention may not refuse to comply with it unless:

a. the request is not compatible with its powers;

b. the request does not comply with the provisions of this Convention;

c. compliance with the request would be incompatible with the sovereignty, national security or public order of the Party by which it was designated, or with the rights and fundamental freedoms of individuals under the jurisdiction of that Party.

Article 21: Costs and procedures

1. Co-operation and mutual assistance which the Parties render each other under Article 17 and assistance they render to data subjects under Articles 9 and 18 shall not give rise to the payment of any costs or fees other than those incurred for experts and interpreters. The latter costs or fees shall be borne by the Party making the request.

2. The data subject may not be charged costs or fees in connection with the steps taken on his or her behalf in the territory of another Party other than those lawfully payable by residents of that Party.

3. Other details concerning the co-operation and assistance, relating in particular to the forms and procedures and the languages to be used, shall be established directly between the Parties concerned.

CHAPTER VI – Convention Committee

Article 22: Composition of the committee

1. A Convention Committee shall be set up after the entry into force of this Convention.

2. Each Party shall appoint a representative to the committee and a deputy representative. Any member State of the Council of Europe which is not a Party to the Convention shall have the right to be represented on the committee by an observer.

3. The Convention Committee may, by a decision taken by a majority of two-thirds of the representatives of the Parties, invite an observer to be represented at its meetings.

4. Any Party which is not a member of the Council of Europe shall contribute to the funding of the activities of the Convention Committee according to the modalities established by the Committee of Ministers in agreement with that Party.

Article 23: Functions of the committee

The Convention Committee:

a. may make recommendations with a view to facilitating or improving the application of the Convention;

b. may make proposals for amendment of this Convention in accordance with Article 25;

c. shall formulate its opinion on any proposal for amendment of this Convention which is referred to it in accordance with Article 25, paragraph 3;

d. may express an opinion on any question concerning the interpretation or application of this Convention;

e. shall prepare, before any new accession to the Convention, an opinion for the Committee of Ministers relating to the level of personal data protection of the candidate for accession and, where necessary, recommend measures to take to reach compliance with the provisions of this Convention;

f. may, at the request of a State or an international organisation, evaluate whether the level of personal data protection the former provides is in compliance with the provisions of this Convention and, where necessary, recommend measures to be taken to reach such compliance;

g. may develop or approve models of standardised safeguards referred to in Article 14;

h. shall review the implementation of this Convention by the Parties and recommend measures to be taken in the case where a Party is not in compliance with this Convention;

i. shall facilitate, where necessary, the friendly settlement of all difficulties related to the application of this Convention.

CHAPTER VII– AMENDMENTS

Article 25. Amendments

1. Amendments to this Convention may be proposed by a Party, the Committee of Ministers of the Council of Europe or the Convention Committee.

2. Any proposal for amendment shall be communicated by the Secretary General of the Council of Europe to the Parties to this Convention, to the other member States of the Council of Europe,

to the European Union and to every non-member State or international organisation which has been invited to accede to this Convention in accordance with the provisions of Article 28.

3. Moreover, any amendment proposed by a Party or the Committee of Ministers shall be communicated to the Convention Committee, which shall submit to the Committee of Ministers its opinion on that proposed amendment.

4. The Committee of Ministers shall consider the proposed amendment and any opinion submitted by the Convention Committee and may approve the amendment.

5. The text of any amendment approved by the Committee of Ministers in accordance with paragraph 4 of this article shall be forwarded to the Parties for acceptance.

6. Any amendment approved in accordance with paragraph 4 of this article shall come into force on the thirtieth day after all Parties have informed the Secretary General of their acceptance thereof.

7. Moreover, the Committee of Ministers may, after consulting the Convention Committee, decide unanimously that a particular amendment shall enter into force at the expiration of a period of three years from the date on which it has been opened to acceptance, unless a Party notifies the Secretary General of the Council of Europe of an objection to its entry into force. If such an objection is notified, the amendment shall enter into force on the first day of the month following the date on which the Party to this Convention which has notified the objection has deposited its instrument of acceptance with the Secretary General of the Council of Europe

CHAPTER VIII – FINAL CLAUSES

Article 26: Entry into force

1. This convention shall be open for signature by the member States of the Council of Europe and by the European Union. It is subject to ratification, acceptance or approval. Instruments of ratification, acceptance or approval shall be deposited with the Secretary General of the Council of Europe.

2. This convention shall enter into force on the first day of the month following the expiration of a period of three months after the date on which five member States of the Council of Europe have expressed their consent to be bound by the convention in accordance with the provisions of the preceding paragraph.

3. In respect of any Party which subsequently expresses its consent to be bound by it, the convention shall enter into force on the first day of the month following the expiration of a period of three months after the date of the deposit of the instrument of ratification, acceptance or approval.

Article 27: Accession by non-member States or international organisations

1. After the entry into force of this Convention, the Committee of Ministers of the Council of Europe may, after consulting the Parties to this Convention and obtaining their unanimous agreement, and in light of the opinion prepared by the Convention Committee in accordance

with Article 23.e, invite any State not a member of the Council of Europe or an international organisation to accede to this Convention by a decision taken by the majority provided for in Article 20.d of the Statute of the Council of Europe and by the unanimous vote of the representatives of the Contracting States entitled to sit on the Committee of Ministers.

2. In respect of any State or international organisation acceding to this Convention according to paragraph 1 above, the Convention shall enter into force on the first day of the month following the expiration of a period of three months after the date of deposit of the instrument of accession with the Secretary General of the Council of Europe.

Article 28: Territorial clause

1. Any State, the European Union or other international organisation may, at the time of signature or when depositing its instrument of ratification, acceptance, approval or accession, specify the territory or territories to which this convention shall apply.

2. Any State, the European Union or other international organization, may at any later date, by a declaration addressed to the Secretary General of the Council of Europe, extend the application of this convention to any other territory specified in the declaration. In respect of such territory the convention shall enter into force on the first day of the month following the expiration of a period of three months after the date of receipt of such declaration by the Secretary General.

3. Any declaration made under the two preceding paragraphs may, in respect of any territory specified in such declaration, be withdrawn by a notification addressed to the Secretary General.

The withdrawal shall become effective on the first day of the month following the expiration of a period of six months after the date of receipt of such notification by the Secretary General.

Article 29: Reservations

No reservation may be made in respect of the provisions of this convention.

Article 30: Denunciation

1. Any Party may at any time denounce this convention by means of a notification addressed to the Secretary General of the Council of Europe.

2. Such denunciation shall become effective on the first day of the month following the expiration of a period of six months after the date of receipt of the notification by the Secretary General.

Article 31: Notifications

The Secretary General of the Council of Europe shall notify the member States of the Council and any Party which has acceded to this convention of

a. any signature;

b. the deposit of any instrument of ratification, acceptance, approval or accession

c. any date of entry into force of this convention in accordance with Articles 26, 27 and 28;

d. any other act, notification or communication relating to this convention.

In witness whereof the undersigned, being duly authorised thereto, have signed this Convention.

Appendix to the Protocol: Elements for the Rules of Procedure of the Convention Committee

1. Each Party has a right to vote and shall have one vote.

2. A two-thirds majority of representatives of the Parties shall constitute a quorum for the meetings of the Convention Committee. In case the amending Protocol to the Convention enters into force in accordance with its Article 37 (2) before its entry into force in respect of all Contracting States to the Convention, the quorum for the meetings of the Convention Committee shall be no less than 34 Parties to the Protocol.

3. The decisions under Article 23 shall be taken by a four-fifths majority. The decisions pursuant to Article 23 *littera h* shall be taken by a four-fifths majority, including a majority of the votes of States Parties not members of a regional integration organisation that is a Party to the Convention.

4. Where the Convention Committee takes decisions pursuant to Article 23 *littera h*, the Party concerned by the review shall not vote. Whenever such a decision concerns a matter falling

within the competence of a regional integration organisation, neither the organisation nor its member States shall vote.

5. Decisions concerning procedural issues shall be taken by a simple majority.

6. Regional integration organisations, in matters within their competence, may exercise their right to vote in the Convention Committee, with a number of votes equal to the number of their member States that are Parties to the Convention. Such an organisation shall not exercise its right to vote if any of its member States exercises its right.

7. In case of vote, all Parties must be informed of the subject and time for the vote, as well as whether the vote will be exercised by the Parties individually or by a regional integration organisation on behalf of its member States.

8. The Convention Committee may further amend its rules of procedure by a two-thirds majority, except for the voting arrangements which may only be amended by unanimous vote of the Parties and to which Article 25 of the Convention applies.

EU GENERAL DATA PROTECTION
REGULATION (2016)

Summary

The General Data Protection Regulation is a comprehensive legal framework for the processing of personal information. It was adopted on April 27, 2016 and will enter into force on May 25, 2018. The regulation will replace the EU Data Protection Directive of 1995. The regulation is directly applicable to the Members States and does not require transposition by means of national law. The aim of the Regulation is to provide a harmonized legal framework for data protection while strengthening enforcement and establishing new privacy rights for data breaches, transparency, data portability, and erasure.

References

Regulation (EU) 2016/679 of the European Parliament and of the Council of 27 April 2016 on the protection of natural persons with regard to the processing of personal data and on the free movement of such data, and repealing Directive 95/46/EC (General Data Protection Regulation)

[http://eur-lex.europa.eu/eli/reg/2016/679/oj]

European Data Protection Supervisor Opinions

[https://secure.edps.europa.eu/EDPSWEB/edps/cache/bypass/Consultation/Opinions C]

Article 29 Working Party Statement on 2016 Action Plan for the Implementation of the GDPR

[http://ec.europa.eu/justice/data-protection/article-29/documentation/opinion-recommendation/files/2016/wp236_en.pdf]

European Commission – Data Protection

[http://ec.europa.eu/justice/data-protection/index_en.htm]

European Commission – Fact Sheet – Data protection reform

[http://europa.eu/rapid/press-release_MEMO-15-6385_en.htm]

CHAPTER I: General provisions

Article 1: Subject-matter and objectives

1. This Regulation lays down rules relating to the protection of natural persons with regard to the processing of personal data and rules relating to the free movement of personal data.

2. This Regulation protects fundamental rights and freedoms of natural persons and in particular their right to the protection of personal data.

3. The free movement of personal data within the Union shall be neither restricted nor prohibited for reasons connected with the protection of natural persons with regard to the processing of personal data.

Article 2: Material scope

1. This Regulation applies to the processing of personal data wholly or partly by automated means and to the processing other than by automated means of personal data which form part of a filing system or are intended to form part of a filing system.

2. This Regulation does not apply to the processing of personal data:

> (a) in the course of an activity which falls outside the scope of Union law;

> (b) by the Member States when carrying out activities which fall within the scope of Chapter 2 of Title V of the TEU;

> (c) by a natural person in the course of a purely personal or household activity;

> (d) by competent authorities for the purposes of the prevention, investigation, detection or prosecution of criminal offences or the execution of criminal penalties, including the safeguarding against and the prevention of threats to public security.

3. For the processing of personal data by the Union institutions, bodies, offices and agencies, Regulation (EC) No 45/2001 applies. Regulation (EC) No 45/2001 and other Union legal acts applicable to such processing of personal data shall be adapted to the principles and rules of this Regulation in accordance with Article 98.

4. This Regulation shall be without prejudice to the application of Directive 2000/31/EC, in particular of the liability rules of intermediary service providers in Articles 12 to 15 of that Directive.

Article 3: Territorial scope

1. This Regulation applies to the processing of personal data in the context of the activities of an establishment of a controller or a processor in the Union, regardless of whether the processing takes place in the Union or not.

2. This Regulation applies to the processing of personal data of data subjects who are in the Union by a controller or processor not established in the Union, where the processing activities are related to:

> (a) the offering of goods or services, irrespective of whether a payment of the data subject is required, to such data subjects in the Union; or

> (b) the monitoring of their behaviour as far as their behaviour takes place within the Union.

3. This Regulation applies to the processing of personal data by a controller not established in the Union, but in a place where Member State law applies by virtue of public international law.

Article 4: Definitions

For the purposes of this Regulation:

(1) 'personal data' means any information relating to an identified or identifiable natural person ('data subject'); an identifiable natural person is one who can be identified, directly or indirectly, in particular by reference to an identifier such as a name, an identification number, location data, an online identifier or to one or more factors specific to the physical, physiological, genetic, mental, economic, cultural or social identity of that natural person;

(2) 'processing' means any operation or set of operations which is performed on personal data or on sets of personal data, whether or not by automated means, such as collection, recording, organisation, structuring, storage, adaptation or alteration, retrieval, consultation, use, disclosure by transmission, dissemination or otherwise making available, alignment or combination, restriction, erasure or destruction;

(3) 'restriction of processing' means the marking of stored personal data with the aim of limiting their processing in the future;

(4) 'profiling' means any form of automated processing of personal data consisting of the use of personal data to evaluate certain personal aspects relating to a natural person, in particular to analyse or predict aspects concerning that natural person's performance at work, economic situation, health, personal preferences, interests, reliability, behaviour, location or movements;

(5) 'pseudonymisation' means the processing of personal data in such a manner that the personal data can no longer be attributed to a specific data subject without the use of additional information, provided that such additional information is kept separately and is subject to technical and organisational measures to ensure that the personal data are not attributed to an identified or identifiable natural person;

(6) 'filing system' means any structured set of personal data which are accessible according to specific criteria, whether centralised, decentralised or dispersed on a functional or geographical basis;

(7) 'controller' means the natural or legal person, public authority, agency or other body which, alone or jointly with others, determines the purposes and means of the processing of personal data; where the purposes and means of such processing are determined by Union or Member State law, the controller or the specific criteria for its nomination may be provided for by Union or Member State law;

(8) 'processor' means a natural or legal person, public authority, agency or other body which processes personal data on behalf of the controller;

(9) 'recipient' means a natural or legal person, public authority, agency or another body, to which the personal data are disclosed, whether a third party or not. However, public authorities which may receive personal data in the framework of a particular inquiry in accordance with Union or Member State law shall not be regarded as recipients; the

processing of those data by those public authorities shall be in compliance with the applicable data protection rules according to the purposes of the processing;

(10) 'third party' means a natural or legal person, public authority, agency or body other than the data subject, controller, processor and persons who, under the direct authority of the controller or processor, are authorised to process personal data;

(11) 'consent' of the data subject means any freely given, specific, informed and unambiguous indication of the data subject's wishes by which he or she, by a statement or by a clear affirmative action, signifies agreement to the processing of personal data relating to him or her;

(12) 'personal data breach' means a breach of security leading to the accidental or unlawful destruction, loss, alteration, unauthorised disclosure of, or access to, personal data transmitted, stored or otherwise processed;

(13) 'genetic data' means personal data relating to the inherited or acquired genetic characteristics of a natural person which give unique information about the physiology or the health of that natural person and which result, in particular, from an analysis of a biological sample from the natural person in question;

(14) 'biometric data' means personal data resulting from specific technical processing relating to the physical, physiological or behavioural characteristics of a natural person, which allow or confirm the unique identification of that natural person, such as facial images or dactyloscopic data;

(15) 'data concerning health' means personal data related to the physical or mental health of a natural person, including the provision of health care services, which reveal information about his or her health status;

(16) 'main establishment' means:

(a) as regards a controller with establishments in more than one Member State, the place of its central administration in the Union, unless the decisions on the purposes and means of the processing of personal data are taken in another establishment of the controller in the Union and the latter establishment has the power to have such decisions implemented, in which case the establishment having taken such decisions is to be considered to be the main establishment;

(b) as regards a processor with establishments in more than one Member State, the place of its central administration in the Union, or, if the processor has no central administration in the Union, the establishment of the processor in the Union where the main processing activities in the context of the activities of an establishment of the processor take place to the extent that the processor is subject to specific obligations under this Regulation;

(17) 'representative' means a natural or legal person established in the Union who, designated by the controller or processor in writing pursuant to Article 27, represents the controller or processor with regard to their respective obligations under this Regulation;

(18) 'enterprise' means a natural or legal person engaged in an economic activity, irrespective of its legal form, including partnerships or associations regularly engaged in an economic activity;

(19) 'group of undertakings' means a controlling undertaking and its controlled undertakings;

(20) 'binding corporate rules' means personal data protection policies which are adhered to by a controller or processor established on the territory of a Member State for transfers or a set of transfers of personal data to a controller or processor in one or more third countries within a group of undertakings, or group of enterprises engaged in a joint economic activity;

(21) 'supervisory authority' means an independent public authority which is established by a Member State pursuant to Article 51;

(22) 'supervisory authority concerned' means a supervisory authority which is concerned by the processing of personal data because:

(a) the controller or processor is established on the territory of the Member State of that supervisory authority;

(b) data subjects residing in the Member State of that supervisory authority are substantially affected or likely to be substantially affected by the processing; or

(c) a complaint has been lodged with that supervisory authority;

(23) 'cross-border processing' means either:

(a) processing of personal data which takes place in the context of the activities of establishments in more than one Member State of a controller or processor in the Union where the controller or processor is established in more than one Member State; or

(b) processing of personal data which takes place in the context of the activities of a single establishment of a controller or processor in the Union but which substantially affects or is likely to substantially affect data subjects in more than one Member State.

(24) 'relevant and reasoned objection' means an objection to a draft decision as to whether there is an infringement of this Regulation, or whether envisaged action in relation to the controller or processor complies with this Regulation, which clearly demonstrates the significance of the risks posed by the draft decision as regards the fundamental rights and freedoms of data subjects and, where applicable, the free flow of personal data within the Union;

(25) 'information society service' means a service as defined in point (b) of Article 1(1) of Directive (EU) 2015/1535 of the European Parliament and of the Council (19);

(26) 'international organisation' means an organisation and its subordinate bodies governed by public international law, or any other body which is set up by, or on the basis of, an agreement between two or more countries.

International
European Union General Data Protection Regulation

CHAPTER II: Principles

Article 5: Principles relating to processing of personal data

1. Personal data shall be:

> (a) processed lawfully, fairly and in a transparent manner in relation to the data subject ('lawfulness, fairness and transparency');

> (b) collected for specified, explicit and legitimate purposes and not further processed in a manner that is incompatible with those purposes; further processing for archiving purposes in the public interest, scientific or historical research purposes or statistical purposes shall, in accordance with Article 89(1), not be considered to be incompatible with the initial purposes ('purpose limitation');

> (c) adequate, relevant and limited to what is necessary in relation to the purposes for which they are processed ('data minimisation');

> (d) accurate and, where necessary, kept up to date; every reasonable step must be taken to ensure that personal data that are inaccurate, having regard to the purposes for which they are processed, are erased or rectified without delay ('accuracy');

> (e) kept in a form which permits identification of data subjects for no longer than is necessary for the purposes for which the personal data are processed; personal data may be stored for longer periods insofar as the personal data will be processed solely for archiving purposes in the public interest, scientific or historical research purposes or statistical purposes in accordance with Article 89(1) subject to implementation of the appropriate technical and organisational measures required by this Regulation in order to safeguard the rights and freedoms of the data subject ('storage limitation');

> (f) processed in a manner that ensures appropriate security of the personal data, including protection against unauthorised or unlawful processing and against accidental loss, destruction or damage, using appropriate technical or organisational measures ('integrity and confidentiality').

2. The controller shall be responsible for, and be able to demonstrate compliance with, paragraph 1 ('accountability').

Article 6: Lawfulness of processing

1. Processing shall be lawful only if and to the extent that at least one of the following applies:

> (a) the data subject has given consent to the processing of his or her personal data for one or more specific purposes;

> (b) processing is necessary for the performance of a contract to which the data subject is party or in order to take steps at the request of the data subject prior to entering into a contract;

> (c) processing is necessary for compliance with a legal obligation to which the controller is subject;

(d) processing is necessary in order to protect the vital interests of the data subject or of another natural person;

(e) processing is necessary for the performance of a task carried out in the public interest or in the exercise of official authority vested in the controller;

(f) processing is necessary for the purposes of the legitimate interests pursued by the controller or by a third party, except where such interests are overridden by the interests or fundamental rights and freedoms of the data subject which require protection of personal data, in particular where the data subject is a child.

Point (f) of the first subparagraph shall not apply to processing carried out by public authorities in the performance of their tasks.

2. Member States may maintain or introduce more specific provisions to adapt the application of the rules of this Regulation with regard to processing for compliance with points (c) and (e) of paragraph 1 by determining more precisely specific requirements for the processing and other measures to ensure lawful and fair processing including for other specific processing situations as provided for in Chapter IX.

3. The basis for the processing referred to in point (c) and (e) of paragraph 1 shall be laid down by:

(a) Union law; or

(b) Member State law to which the controller is subject.

The purpose of the processing shall be determined in that legal basis or, as regards the processing referred to in point (e) of paragraph 1, shall be necessary for the performance of a task carried out in the public interest or in the exercise of official authority vested in the controller. That legal basis may contain specific provisions to adapt the application of rules of this Regulation, inter alia: the general conditions governing the lawfulness of processing by the controller; the types of data which are subject to the processing; the data subjects concerned; the entities to, and the purposes for which, the personal data may be disclosed; the purpose limitation; storage periods; and processing operations and processing procedures, including measures to ensure lawful and fair processing such as those for other specific processing situations as provided for in Chapter IX. The Union or the Member State law shall meet an objective of public interest and be proportionate to the legitimate aim pursued.

4. Where the processing for a purpose other than that for which the personal data have been collected is not based on the data subject's consent or on a Union or Member State law which constitutes a necessary and proportionate measure in a democratic society to safeguard the objectives referred to in Article 23(1), the controller shall, in order to ascertain whether processing for another purpose is compatible with the purpose for which the personal data are initially collected, take into account, inter alia:

(a) any link between the purposes for which the personal data have been collected and the purposes of the intended further processing;

(b) the context in which the personal data have been collected, in particular regarding the relationship between data subjects and the controller;

(c) the nature of the personal data, in particular whether special categories of personal data are processed, pursuant to Article 9, or whether personal data related to criminal convictions and offences are processed, pursuant to Article 10;

(d) the possible consequences of the intended further processing for data subjects;

(e) the existence of appropriate safeguards, which may include encryption or pseudonymisation.

Article 7: Conditions for consent

1. Where processing is based on consent, the controller shall be able to demonstrate that the data subject has consented to processing of his or her personal data.

2. If the data subject's consent is given in the context of a written declaration which also concerns other matters, the request for consent shall be presented in a manner which is clearly distinguishable from the other matters, in an intelligible and easily accessible form, using clear and plain language. Any part of such a declaration which constitutes an infringement of this Regulation shall not be binding.

3. The data subject shall have the right to withdraw his or her consent at any time. The withdrawal of consent shall not affect the lawfulness of processing based on consent before its withdrawal. Prior to giving consent, the data subject shall be informed thereof. It shall be as easy to withdraw as to give consent.

4. When assessing whether consent is freely given, utmost account shall be taken of whether, inter alia, the performance of a contract, including the provision of a service, is conditional on consent to the processing of personal data that is not necessary for the performance of that contract.

Article 8: Conditions applicable to child's consent in relation to information society services

1. Where point (a) of Article 6(1) applies, in relation to the offer of information society services directly to a child, the processing of the personal data of a child shall be lawful where the child is at least 16 years old. Where the child is below the age of 16 years, such processing shall be lawful only if and to the extent that consent is given or authorised by the holder of parental responsibility over the child.

Member States may provide by law for a lower age for those purposes provided that such lower age is not below 13 years.

2. The controller shall make reasonable efforts to verify in such cases that consent is given or authorised by the holder of parental responsibility over the child, taking into consideration available technology.

3. Paragraph 1 shall not affect the general contract law of Member States such as the rules on the validity, formation or effect of a contract in relation to a child.

Article 9: Processing of special categories of personal data

1. Processing of personal data revealing racial or ethnic origin, political opinions, religious or philosophical beliefs, or trade union membership, and the processing of genetic data, biometric data for the purpose of uniquely identifying a natural person, data concerning health or data concerning a natural person's sex life or sexual orientation shall be prohibited.

2. Paragraph 1 shall not apply if one of the following applies:

    (a) the data subject has given explicit consent to the processing of those personal data for one or more specified purposes, except where Union or Member State law provide that the prohibition referred to in paragraph 1 may not be lifted by the data subject;

    (b) processing is necessary for the purposes of carrying out the obligations and exercising specific rights of the controller or of the data subject in the field of employment and social security and social protection law in so far as it is authorised by Union or Member State law or a collective agreement pursuant to Member State law providing for appropriate safeguards for the fundamental rights and the interests of the data subject;

    (c) processing is necessary to protect the vital interests of the data subject or of another natural person where the data subject is physically or legally incapable of giving consent;

    (d) processing is carried out in the course of its legitimate activities with appropriate safeguards by a foundation, association or any other not-for-profit body with a political, philosophical, religious or trade union aim and on condition that the processing relates solely to the members or to former members of the body or to persons who have regular contact with it in connection with its purposes and that the personal data are not disclosed outside that body without the consent of the data subjects;

    (e) processing relates to personal data which are manifestly made public by the data subject;

    (f) processing is necessary for the establishment, exercise or defence of legal claims or whenever courts are acting in their judicial capacity;

    (g) processing is necessary for reasons of substantial public interest, on the basis of Union or Member State law which shall be proportionate to the aim pursued, respect the essence of the right to data protection and provide for suitable and specific measures to safeguard the fundamental rights and the interests of the data subject;

    (h) processing is necessary for the purposes of preventive or occupational medicine, for the assessment of the working capacity of the employee, medical diagnosis, the provision of health or social care or treatment or the management of health or social care systems and services on the basis of Union or Member State law or pursuant to contract with a health professional and subject to the conditions and safeguards referred to in paragraph 3;

    (i) processing is necessary for reasons of public interest in the area of public health, such as protecting against serious cross-border threats to health or ensuring high standards of quality and safety of health care and of medicinal products or medical devices, on the basis of Union or Member State law which provides for suitable and specific measures to safeguard the rights and freedoms of the data subject, in particular professional secrecy;

(j) processing is necessary for archiving purposes in the public interest, scientific or historical research purposes or statistical purposes in accordance with Article 89(1) based on Union or Member State law which shall be proportionate to the aim pursued, respect the essence of the right to data protection and provide for suitable and specific measures to safeguard the fundamental rights and the interests of the data subject.

3. Personal data referred to in paragraph 1 may be processed for the purposes referred to in point (h) of paragraph 2 when those data are processed by or under the responsibility of a professional subject to the obligation of professional secrecy under Union or Member State law or rules established by national competent bodies or by another person also subject to an obligation of secrecy under Union or Member State law or rules established by national competent bodies.

4. Member States may maintain or introduce further conditions, including limitations, with regard to the processing of genetic data, biometric data or data concerning health.

Article 10: Processing of personal data relating to criminal convictions and offences

Processing of personal data relating to criminal convictions and offences or related security measures based on Article 6(1) shall be carried out only under the control of official authority or when the processing is authorised by Union or Member State law providing for appropriate safeguards for the rights and freedoms of data subjects. Any comprehensive register of criminal convictions shall be kept only under the control of official authority.

Article 11: Processing which does not require identification

1. If the purposes for which a controller processes personal data do not or do no longer require the identification of a data subject by the controller, the controller shall not be obliged to maintain, acquire or process additional information in order to identify the data subject for the sole purpose of complying with this Regulation.

2. Where, in cases referred to in paragraph 1 of this Article, the controller is able to demonstrate that it is not in a position to identify the data subject, the controller shall inform the data subject accordingly, if possible. In such cases, Articles 15 to 20 shall not apply except where the data subject, for the purpose of exercising his or her rights under those articles, provides additional information enabling his or her identification.

CHAPTER III: Rights of the data subject

Section 1: Transparency and modalities

Article 12: Transparent information, communication and modalities for the exercise of the rights of the data subject

1.   The controller shall take appropriate measures to provide any information referred to in Articles 13 and 14 and any communication under Articles 15 to 22 and 34 relating to processing to the data subject in a concise, transparent, intelligible and easily accessible form, using clear and plain language, in particular for any information addressed specifically to a child. The information shall be provided in writing, or by other means, including, where appropriate, by electronic means. When requested by the data subject, the information may be provided orally, provided that the identity of the data subject is proven by other means.

2.   The controller shall facilitate the exercise of data subject rights under Articles 15 to 22. In the cases referred to in Article 11(2), the controller shall not refuse to act on the request of the data subject for exercising his or her rights under Articles 15 to 22, unless the controller demonstrates that it is not in a position to identify the data subject.

3.   The controller shall provide information on action taken on a request under Articles 15 to 22 to the data subject without undue delay and in any event within one month of receipt of the request. That period may be extended by two further months where necessary, taking into account the complexity and number of the requests. The controller shall inform the data subject of any such extension within one month of receipt of the request, together with the reasons for the delay. Where the data subject makes the request by electronic form means, the information shall be provided by electronic means where possible, unless otherwise requested by the data subject.

4.   If the controller does not take action on the request of the data subject, the controller shall inform the data subject without delay and at the latest within one month of receipt of the request of the reasons for not taking action and on the possibility of lodging a complaint with a supervisory authority and seeking a judicial remedy.

5.   Information provided under Articles 13 and 14 and any communication and any actions taken under Articles 15 to 22 and 34 shall be provided free of charge. Where requests from a data subject are manifestly unfounded or excessive, in particular because of their repetitive character, the controller may either:

> (a) charge a reasonable fee taking into account the administrative costs of providing the information or communication or taking the action requested; or

> (b) refuse to act on the request.

The controller shall bear the burden of demonstrating the manifestly unfounded or excessive character of the request.

6.   Without prejudice to Article 11, where the controller has reasonable doubts concerning the identity of the natural person making the request referred to in Articles 15 to 21, the controller may request the provision of additional information necessary to confirm the identity of the data subject.

7.   The information to be provided to data subjects pursuant to Articles 13 and 14 may be provided in combination with standardised icons in order to give in an easily visible, intelligible

and clearly legible manner a meaningful overview of the intended processing. Where the icons are presented electronically they shall be machine-readable.

8. The Commission shall be empowered to adopt delegated acts in accordance with Article 92 for the purpose of determining the information to be presented by the icons and the procedures for providing standardised icons.

Section 2: Information and access to personal data

Article 13: Information to be provided where personal data are collected from the data subject

1. Where personal data relating to a data subject are collected from the data subject, the controller shall, at the time when personal data are obtained, provide the data subject with all of the following information:

> (a) the identity and the contact details of the controller and, where applicable, of the controller's representative;

> (b) the contact details of the data protection officer, where applicable;

> (c) the purposes of the processing for which the personal data are intended as well as the legal basis for the processing;

> (d) where the processing is based on point (f) of Article 6(1), the legitimate interests pursued by the controller or by a third party;

> (e) the recipients or categories of recipients of the personal data, if any;

> (f) where applicable, the fact that the controller intends to transfer personal data to a third country or international organisation and the existence or absence of an adequacy decision by the Commission, or in the case of transfers referred to in Article 46 or 47, or the second subparagraph of Article 49(1), reference to the appropriate or suitable safeguards and the means by which to obtain a copy of them or where they have been made available.

2. In addition to the information referred to in paragraph 1, the controller shall, at the time when personal data are obtained, provide the data subject with the following further information necessary to ensure fair and transparent processing:

> (a) the period for which the personal data will be stored, or if that is not possible, the criteria used to determine that period;

> (b) the existence of the right to request from the controller access to and rectification or erasure of personal data or restriction of processing concerning the data subject or to object to processing as well as the right to data portability;

> (c) where the processing is based on point (a) of Article 6(1) or point (a) of Article 9(2), the existence of the right to withdraw consent at any time, without affecting the lawfulness of processing based on consent before its withdrawal;

> (d) the right to lodge a complaint with a supervisory authority;

(e) whether the provision of personal data is a statutory or contractual requirement, or a requirement necessary to enter into a contract, as well as whether the data subject is obliged to provide the personal data and of the possible consequences of failure to provide such data;

(f) the existence of automated decision-making, including profiling, referred to in Article 22(1) and (4) and, at least in those cases, meaningful information about the logic involved, as well as the significance and the envisaged consequences of such processing for the data subject.

3.   Where the controller intends to further process the personal data for a purpose other than that for which the personal data were collected, the controller shall provide the data subject prior to that further processing with information on that other purpose and with any relevant further information as referred to in paragraph 2.

4.   Paragraphs 1, 2 and 3 shall not apply where and insofar as the data subject already has the information.

Article 14: Information to be provided where personal data have not been obtained from the data subject

1.   Where personal data have not been obtained from the data subject, the controller shall provide the data subject with the following information:

(a) the identity and the contact details of the controller and, where applicable, of the controller's representative;

(b) the contact details of the data protection officer, where applicable;

(c) the purposes of the processing for which the personal data are intended as well as the legal basis for the processing;

(d) the categories of personal data concerned;

(e) the recipients or categories of recipients of the personal data, if any;

(f) where applicable, that the controller intends to transfer personal data to a recipient in a third country or international organisation and the existence or absence of an adequacy decision by the Commission, or in the case of transfers referred to in Article 46 or 47, or the second subparagraph of Article 49(1), reference to the appropriate or suitable safeguards and the means to obtain a copy of them or where they have been made available.

2.   In addition to the information referred to in paragraph 1, the controller shall provide the data subject with the following information necessary to ensure fair and transparent processing in respect of the data subject:

(a) the period for which the personal data will be stored, or if that is not possible, the criteria used to determine that period;

(b) where the processing is based on point (f) of Article 6(1), the legitimate interests pursued by the controller or by a third party;

(c) the existence of the right to request from the controller access to and rectification or erasure of personal data or restriction of processing concerning the data subject and to object to processing as well as the right to data portability;

(d) where processing is based on point (a) of Article 6(1) or point (a) of Article 9(2), the existence of the right to withdraw consent at any time, without affecting the lawfulness of processing based on consent before its withdrawal;

(e) the right to lodge a complaint with a supervisory authority;

(f) from which source the personal data originate, and if applicable, whether it came from publicly accessible sources;

(g) the existence of automated decision-making, including profiling, referred to in Article 22(1) and (4) and, at least in those cases, meaningful information about the logic involved, as well as the significance and the envisaged consequences of such processing for the data subject.

3. The controller shall provide the information referred to in paragraphs 1 and 2:

(a) within a reasonable period after obtaining the personal data, but at the latest within one month, having regard to the specific circumstances in which the personal data are processed;

(b) if the personal data are to be used for communication with the data subject, at the latest at the time of the first communication to that data subject; or

(c) if a disclosure to another recipient is envisaged, at the latest when the personal data are first disclosed.

4. Where the controller intends to further process the personal data for a purpose other than that for which the personal data were obtained, the controller shall provide the data subject prior to that further processing with information on that other purpose and with any relevant further information as referred to in paragraph 2.

5. Paragraphs 1 to 4 shall not apply where and insofar as:

(a) the data subject already has the information;

(b) the provision of such information proves impossible or would involve a disproportionate effort, in particular for processing for archiving purposes in the public interest, scientific or historical research purposes or statistical purposes, subject to the conditions and safeguards referred to in Article 89(1) or in so far as the obligation referred to in paragraph 1 of this Article is likely to render impossible or seriously impair the achievement of the objectives of that processing. In such cases the controller shall take appropriate measures to protect the data subject's rights and freedoms and legitimate interests, including making the information publicly available;

(c) obtaining or disclosure is expressly laid down by Union or Member State law to which the controller is subject and which provides appropriate measures to protect the data subject's legitimate interests; or

(d) where the personal data must remain confidential subject to an obligation of professional secrecy regulated by Union or Member State law, including a statutory obligation of secrecy.

Article 15: Right of access by the data subject

1. The data subject shall have the right to obtain from the controller confirmation as to whether or not personal data concerning him or her are being processed, and, where that is the case, access to the personal data and the following information:

(a) the purposes of the processing;

(b) the categories of personal data concerned;

(c) the recipients or categories of recipient to whom the personal data have been or will be disclosed, in particular recipients in third countries or international organisations;

(d) where possible, the envisaged period for which the personal data will be stored, or, if not possible, the criteria used to determine that period;

(e) the existence of the right to request from the controller rectification or erasure of personal data or restriction of processing of personal data concerning the data subject or to object to such processing;

(f) the right to lodge a complaint with a supervisory authority;

(g) where the personal data are not collected from the data subject, any available information as to their source;

(h) the existence of automated decision-making, including profiling, referred to in Article 22(1) and (4) and, at least in those cases, meaningful information about the logic involved, as well as the significance and the envisaged consequences of such processing for the data subject.

2. Where personal data are transferred to a third country or to an international organisation, the data subject shall have the right to be informed of the appropriate safeguards pursuant to Article 46 relating to the transfer.

3. The controller shall provide a copy of the personal data undergoing processing. For any further copies requested by the data subject, the controller may charge a reasonable fee based on administrative costs. Where the data subject makes the request by electronic means, and unless otherwise requested by the data subject, the information shall be provided in a commonly used electronic form.

4. The right to obtain a copy referred to in paragraph 3 shall not adversely affect the rights and freedoms of others.

Section 3: Rectification and erasure

International
European Union General Data Protection Regulation

Article 16: Right to rectification

The data subject shall have the right to obtain from the controller without undue delay the rectification of inaccurate personal data concerning him or her. Taking into account the purposes of the processing, the data subject shall have the right to have incomplete personal data completed, including by means of providing a supplementary statement.

Article 17: Right to erasure ('right to be forgotten')

1. The data subject shall have the right to obtain from the controller the erasure of personal data concerning him or her without undue delay and the controller shall have the obligation to erase personal data without undue delay where one of the following grounds applies:

    (a) the personal data are no longer necessary in relation to the purposes for which they were collected or otherwise processed;

    (b) the data subject withdraws consent on which the processing is based according to point (a) of Article 6(1), or point (a) of Article 9(2), and where there is no other legal ground for the processing;

    (c) the data subject objects to the processing pursuant to Article 21(1) and there are no overriding legitimate grounds for the processing, or the data subject objects to the processing pursuant to Article 21(2);

    (d) the personal data have been unlawfully processed;

    (e) the personal data have to be erased for compliance with a legal obligation in Union or Member State law to which the controller is subject;

    (f) the personal data have been collected in relation to the offer of information society services referred to in Article 8(1).

2. Where the controller has made the personal data public and is obliged pursuant to paragraph 1 to erase the personal data, the controller, taking account of available technology and the cost of implementation, shall take reasonable steps, including technical measures, to inform controllers which are processing the personal data that the data subject has requested the erasure by such controllers of any links to, or copy or replication of, those personal data.

3. Paragraphs 1 and 2 shall not apply to the extent that processing is necessary:

    (a) for exercising the right of freedom of expression and information;

    (b) for compliance with a legal obligation which requires processing by Union or Member State law to which the controller is subject or for the performance of a task carried out in the public interest or in the exercise of official authority vested in the controller;

    (c) for reasons of public interest in the area of public health in accordance with points (h) and (i) of Article 9(2) as well as Article 9(3);

    (d) for archiving purposes in the public interest, scientific or historical research purposes or statistical purposes in accordance with Article 89(1) in so far as the right referred to in paragraph 1 is likely to render impossible or seriously impair the achievement of the objectives of that processing; or

(e) for the establishment, exercise or defence of legal claims.

Article 18: Right to restriction of processing

1. The data subject shall have the right to obtain from the controller restriction of processing where one of the following applies:

(a) the accuracy of the personal data is contested by the data subject, for a period enabling the controller to verify the accuracy of the personal data;

(b) the processing is unlawful and the data subject opposes the erasure of the personal data and requests the restriction of their use instead;

(c) the controller no longer needs the personal data for the purposes of the processing, but they are required by the data subject for the establishment, exercise or defence of legal claims;

(d) the data subject has objected to processing pursuant to Article 21(1) pending the verification whether the legitimate grounds of the controller override those of the data subject.

2. Where processing has been restricted under paragraph 1, such personal data shall, with the exception of storage, only be processed with the data subject's consent or for the establishment, exercise or defence of legal claims or for the protection of the rights of another natural or legal person or for reasons of important public interest of the Union or of a Member State.

3. A data subject who has obtained restriction of processing pursuant to paragraph 1 shall be informed by the controller before the restriction of processing is lifted.

Article 19: Notification obligation regarding rectification or erasure of personal data or restriction of processing

The controller shall communicate any rectification or erasure of personal data or restriction of processing carried out in accordance with Article 16, Article 17(1) and Article 18 to each recipient to whom the personal data have been disclosed, unless this proves impossible or involves disproportionate effort. The controller shall inform the data subject about those recipients if the data subject requests it.

Article 20: Right to data portability

1. The data subject shall have the right to receive the personal data concerning him or her, which he or she has provided to a controller, in a structured, commonly used and machine-readable format and have the right to transmit those data to another controller without hindrance from the controller to which the personal data have been provided, where:

(a) the processing is based on consent pursuant to point (a) of Article 6(1) or point (a) of Article 9(2) or on a contract pursuant to point (b) of Article 6(1); and

(b) the processing is carried out by automated means.

2. In exercising his or her right to data portability pursuant to paragraph 1, the data subject shall have the right to have the personal data transmitted directly from one controller to another, where technically feasible.

3. The exercise of the right referred to in paragraph 1 of this Article shall be without prejudice to Article 17. That right shall not apply to processing necessary for the performance of a task carried out in the public interest or in the exercise of official authority vested in the controller.

4. The right referred to in paragraph 1 shall not adversely affect the rights and freedoms of others.

Section 4: Right to object and automated individual decision-making

Article 21: Right to object

1. The data subject shall have the right to object, on grounds relating to his or her particular situation, at any time to processing of personal data concerning him or her which is based on point (e) or (f) of Article 6(1), including profiling based on those provisions. The controller shall no longer process the personal data unless the controller demonstrates compelling legitimate grounds for the processing which override the interests, rights and freedoms of the data subject or for the establishment, exercise or defence of legal claims.

2. Where personal data are processed for direct marketing purposes, the data subject shall have the right to object at any time to processing of personal data concerning him or her for such marketing, which includes profiling to the extent that it is related to such direct marketing.

3. Where the data subject objects to processing for direct marketing purposes, the personal data shall no longer be processed for such purposes.

4. At the latest at the time of the first communication with the data subject, the right referred to in paragraphs 1 and 2 shall be explicitly brought to the attention of the data subject and shall be presented clearly and separately from any other information.

5. In the context of the use of information society services, and notwithstanding Directive 2002/58/EC, the data subject may exercise his or her right to object by automated means using technical specifications.

6. Where personal data are processed for scientific or historical research purposes or statistical purposes pursuant to Article 89(1), the data subject, on grounds relating to his or her particular situation, shall have the right to object to processing of personal data concerning him or her, unless the processing is necessary for the performance of a task carried out for reasons of public interest.

Article 22: Automated individual decision-making, including profiling

1. The data subject shall have the right not to be subject to a decision based solely on automated processing, including profiling, which produces legal effects concerning him or her or similarly significantly affects him or her.

2. Paragraph 1 shall not apply if the decision:

> (a) is necessary for entering into, or performance of, a contract between the data subject and a data controller;

(b) is authorised by Union or Member State law to which the controller is subject and which also lays down suitable measures to safeguard the data subject's rights and freedoms and legitimate interests; or

(c) is based on the data subject's explicit consent.

3. In the cases referred to in points (a) and (c) of paragraph 2, the data controller shall implement suitable measures to safeguard the data subject's rights and freedoms and legitimate interests, at least the right to obtain human intervention on the part of the controller, to express his or her point of view and to contest the decision.

4. Decisions referred to in paragraph 2 shall not be based on special categories of personal data referred to in Article 9(1), unless point (a) or (g) of Article 9(2) applies and suitable measures to safeguard the data subject's rights and freedoms and legitimate interests are in place.

Section 5: Restrictions

Article 23: Restrictions

1. Union or Member State law to which the data controller or processor is subject may restrict by way of a legislative measure the scope of the obligations and rights provided for in Articles 12 to 22 and Article 34, as well as Article 5 in so far as its provisions correspond to the rights and obligations provided for in Articles 12 to 22, when such a restriction respects the essence of the fundamental rights and freedoms and is a necessary and proportionate measure in a democratic society to safeguard:

(a) national security;

(b) defence;

(c) public security;

(d) the prevention, investigation, detection or prosecution of criminal offences or the execution of criminal penalties, including the safeguarding against and the prevention of threats to public security;

(e) other important objectives of general public interest of the Union or of a Member State, in particular an important economic or financial interest of the Union or of a Member State, including monetary, budgetary and taxation a matters, public health and social security;

(f) the protection of judicial independence and judicial proceedings;

(g) the prevention, investigation, detection and prosecution of breaches of ethics for regulated professions;

(h) a monitoring, inspection or regulatory function connected, even occasionally, to the exercise of official authority in the cases referred to in points (a) to (e) and (g);

(i) the protection of the data subject or the rights and freedoms of others;

(j) the enforcement of civil law claims.

2.   In particular, any legislative measure referred to in paragraph 1 shall contain specific provisions at least, where relevant, as to:

(a) the purposes of the processing or categories of processing;

(b) the categories of personal data;

(c) the scope of the restrictions introduced;

(d) the safeguards to prevent abuse or unlawful access or transfer;

(e) the specification of the controller or categories of controllers;

(f) the storage periods and the applicable safeguards taking into account the nature, scope and purposes of the processing or categories of processing;

(g) the risks to the rights and freedoms of data subjects; and

(h) the right of data subjects to be informed about the restriction, unless that may be prejudicial to the purpose of the restriction.

CHAPTER IV: Controller and processor

Section 1: General obligations

Article 24: Responsibility of the controller

1.   Taking into account the nature, scope, context and purposes of processing as well as the risks of varying likelihood and severity for the rights and freedoms of natural persons, the controller shall implement appropriate technical and organisational measures to ensure and to be able to demonstrate that processing is performed in accordance with this Regulation. Those measures shall be reviewed and updated where necessary.

2.   Where proportionate in relation to processing activities, the measures referred to in paragraph 1 shall include the implementation of appropriate data protection policies by the controller.

3.   Adherence to approved codes of conduct as referred to in Article 40 or approved certification mechanisms as referred to in Article 42 may be used as an element by which to demonstrate compliance with the obligations of the controller.

Article 25: Data protection by design and by default

1.   Taking into account the state of the art, the cost of implementation and the nature, scope, context and purposes of processing as well as the risks of varying likelihood and severity for rights and freedoms of natural persons posed by the processing, the controller shall, both at the time of the determination of the means for processing and at the time of the processing itself, implement appropriate technical and organisational measures, such as pseudonymisation, which are designed to implement data-protection principles, such as data minimisation, in an effective manner and to integrate the necessary safeguards into the processing in order to meet the requirements of this Regulation and protect the rights of data subjects.

2.   The controller shall implement appropriate technical and organisational measures for ensuring that, by default, only personal data which are necessary for each specific purpose of the processing are processed. That obligation applies to the amount of personal data collected, the extent of their processing, the period of their storage and their accessibility. In particular, such measures shall ensure that by default personal data are not made accessible without the individual's intervention to an indefinite number of natural persons.

3.   An approved certification mechanism pursuant to Article 42 may be used as an element to demonstrate compliance with the requirements set out in paragraphs 1 and 2 of this Article.

Article 26: Joint controllers

1.   Where two or more controllers jointly determine the purposes and means of processing, they shall be joint controllers. They shall in a transparent manner determine their respective responsibilities for compliance with the obligations under this Regulation, in particular as regards the exercising of the rights of the data subject and their respective duties to provide the information referred to in Articles 13 and 14, by means of an arrangement between them unless, and in so far as, the respective responsibilities of the controllers are determined by Union or Member State law to which the controllers are subject. The arrangement may designate a contact point for data subjects.

2.   The arrangement referred to in paragraph 1 shall duly reflect the respective roles and relationships of the joint controllers vis-à-vis the data subjects. The essence of the arrangement shall be made available to the data subject.

3.   Irrespective of the terms of the arrangement referred to in paragraph 1, the data subject may exercise his or her rights under this Regulation in respect of and against each of the controllers.

Article 27: Representatives of controllers or processors not established in the Union

1.   Where Article 3(2) applies, the controller or the processor shall designate in writing a representative in the Union.

2.   The obligation laid down in paragraph 1 of this Article shall not apply to:

  (a) processing which is occasional, does not include, on a large scale, processing of special categories of data as referred to in Article 9(1) or processing of personal data relating to criminal convictions and offences referred to in Article 10, and is unlikely to result in a risk to the rights and freedoms of natural persons, taking into account the nature, context, scope and purposes of the processing; or

  (b) a public authority or body.

3.   The representative shall be established in one of the Member States where the data subjects, whose personal data are processed in relation to the offering of goods or services to them, or whose behaviour is monitored, are.

4.   The representative shall be mandated by the controller or processor to be addressed in addition to or instead of the controller or the processor by, in particular, supervisory authorities

and data subjects, on all issues related to processing, for the purposes of ensuring compliance with this Regulation.

5. The designation of a representative by the controller or processor shall be without prejudice to legal actions which could be initiated against the controller or the processor themselves.

Article 28: Processor

1. Where processing is to be carried out on behalf of a controller, the controller shall use only processors providing sufficient guarantees to implement appropriate technical and organisational measures in such a manner that processing will meet the requirements of this Regulation and ensure the protection of the rights of the data subject.

2. The processor shall not engage another processor without prior specific or general written authorisation of the controller. In the case of general written authorisation, the processor shall inform the controller of any intended changes concerning the addition or replacement of other processors, thereby giving the controller the opportunity to object to such changes.

3. Processing by a processor shall be governed by a contract or other legal act under Union or Member State law, that is binding on the processor with regard to the controller and that sets out the subject-matter and duration of the processing, the nature and purpose of the processing, the type of personal data and categories of data subjects and the obligations and rights of the controller. That contract or other legal act shall stipulate, in particular, that the processor:

(a) processes the personal data only on documented instructions from the controller, including with regard to transfers of personal data to a third country or an international organisation, unless required to do so by Union or Member State law to which the processor is subject; in such a case, the processor shall inform the controller of that legal requirement before processing, unless that law prohibits such information on important grounds of public interest;

(b) ensures that persons authorised to process the personal data have committed themselves to confidentiality or are under an appropriate statutory obligation of confidentiality;

(c) takes all measures required pursuant to Article 32;

(d) respects the conditions referred to in paragraphs 2 and 4 for engaging another processor;

(e) taking into account the nature of the processing, assists the controller by appropriate technical and organisational measures, insofar as this is possible, for the fulfilment of the controller's obligation to respond to requests for exercising the data subject's rights laid down in Chapter III;

(f) assists the controller in ensuring compliance with the obligations pursuant to Articles 32 to 36 taking into account the nature of processing and the information available to the processor;

(g) at the choice of the controller, deletes or returns all the personal data to the controller after the end of the provision of services relating to processing, and deletes existing copies unless Union or Member State law requires storage of the personal data;

(h) makes available to the controller all information necessary to demonstrate compliance with the obligations laid down in this Article and allow for and contribute to audits, including inspections, conducted by the controller or another auditor mandated by the controller.

With regard to point (h) of the first subparagraph, the processor shall immediately inform the controller if, in its opinion, an instruction infringes this Regulation or other Union or Member State data protection provisions.

4.   Where a processor engages another processor for carrying out specific processing activities on behalf of the controller, the same data protection obligations as set out in the contract or other legal act between the controller and the processor as referred to in paragraph 3 shall be imposed on that other processor by way of a contract or other legal act under Union or Member State law, in particular providing sufficient guarantees to implement appropriate technical and organisational measures in such a manner that the processing will meet the requirements of this Regulation. Where that other processor fails to fulfil its data protection obligations, the initial processor shall remain fully liable to the controller for the performance of that other processor's obligations.

5.   Adherence of a processor to an approved code of conduct as referred to in Article 40 or an approved certification mechanism as referred to in Article 42 may be used as an element by which to demonstrate sufficient guarantees as referred to in paragraphs 1 and 4 of this Article.

6.   Without prejudice to an individual contract between the controller and the processor, the contract or the other legal act referred to in paragraphs 3 and 4 of this Article may be based, in whole or in part, on standard contractual clauses referred to in paragraphs 7 and 8 of this Article, including when they are part of a certification granted to the controller or processor pursuant to Articles 42 and 43.

7.   The Commission may lay down standard contractual clauses for the matters referred to in paragraph 3 and 4 of this Article and in accordance with the examination procedure referred to in Article 93(2).

8.   A supervisory authority may adopt standard contractual clauses for the matters referred to in paragraph 3 and 4 of this Article and in accordance with the consistency mechanism referred to in Article 63.

9.   The contract or the other legal act referred to in paragraphs 3 and 4 shall be in writing, including in electronic form.

10.   Without prejudice to Articles 82, 83 and 84, if a processor infringes this Regulation by determining the purposes and means of processing, the processor shall be considered to be a controller in respect of that processing.

Article 29: Processing under the authority of the controller or processor

The processor and any person acting under the authority of the controller or of the processor, who has access to personal data, shall not process those data except on instructions from the controller, unless required to do so by Union or Member State law.

Article 30: Records of processing activities

1. Each controller and, where applicable, the controller's representative, shall maintain a record of processing activities under its responsibility. That record shall contain all of the following information:

> (a) the name and contact details of the controller and, where applicable, the joint controller, the controller's representative and the data protection officer;

> (b) the purposes of the processing;

> (c) a description of the categories of data subjects and of the categories of personal data;

> (d) the categories of recipients to whom the personal data have been or will be disclosed including recipients in third countries or international organisations;

> (e) where applicable, transfers of personal data to a third country or an international organisation, including the identification of that third country or international organisation and, in the case of transfers referred to in the second subparagraph of Article 49(1), the documentation of suitable safeguards;

> (f) where possible, the envisaged time limits for erasure of the different categories of data;

> (g) where possible, a general description of the technical and organisational security measures referred to in Article 32(1).

2. Each processor and, where applicable, the processor's representative shall maintain a record of all categories of processing activities carried out on behalf of a controller, containing:

> (a) the name and contact details of the processor or processors and of each controller on behalf of which the processor is acting, and, where applicable, of the controller's or the processor's representative, and the data protection officer;

> (b) the categories of processing carried out on behalf of each controller;

> (c) where applicable, transfers of personal data to a third country or an international organisation, including the identification of that third country or international organisation and, in the case of transfers referred to in the second subparagraph of Article 49(1), the documentation of suitable safeguards;

> (d) where possible, a general description of the technical and organisational security measures referred to in Article 32(1).

3. The records referred to in paragraphs 1 and 2 shall be in writing, including in electronic form.

4.   The controller or the processor and, where applicable, the controller's or the processor's representative, shall make the record available to the supervisory authority on request.

5.   The obligations referred to in paragraphs 1 and 2 shall not apply to an enterprise or an organisation employing fewer than 250 persons unless the processing it carries out is likely to result in a risk to the rights and freedoms of data subjects, the processing is not occasional, or the processing includes special categories of data as referred to in Article 9(1) or personal data relating to criminal convictions and offences referred to in Article 10.

Article 31: Cooperation with the supervisory authority

The controller and the processor and, where applicable, their representatives, shall cooperate, on request, with the supervisory authority in the performance of its tasks.

Section 2: Security of personal data

Article 32: Security of processing

1.   Taking into account the state of the art, the costs of implementation and the nature, scope, context and purposes of processing as well as the risk of varying likelihood and severity for the rights and freedoms of natural persons, the controller and the processor shall implement appropriate technical and organisational measures to ensure a level of security appropriate to the risk, including inter alia as appropriate:

(a) the pseudonymisation and encryption of personal data;

(b) the ability to ensure the ongoing confidentiality, integrity, availability and resilience of processing systems and services;

(c) the ability to restore the availability and access to personal data in a timely manner in the event of a physical or technical incident;

(d) a process for regularly testing, assessing and evaluating the effectiveness of technical and organisational measures for ensuring the security of the processing.

2.   In assessing the appropriate level of security account shall be taken in particular of the risks that are presented by processing, in particular from accidental or unlawful destruction, loss, alteration, unauthorised disclosure of, or access to personal data transmitted, stored or otherwise processed.

3.   Adherence to an approved code of conduct as referred to in Article 40 or an approved certification mechanism as referred to in Article 42 may be used as an element by which to demonstrate compliance with the requirements set out in paragraph 1 of this Article.

4.   The controller and processor shall take steps to ensure that any natural person acting under the authority of the controller or the processor who has access to personal data does not process them except on instructions from the controller, unless he or she is required to do so by Union or Member State law.

International
European Union General Data Protection Regulation

Article 33: Notification of a personal data breach to the supervisory authority

1. In the case of a personal data breach, the controller shall without undue delay and, where feasible, not later than 72 hours after having become aware of it, notify the personal data breach to the supervisory authority competent in accordance with Article 55, unless the personal data breach is unlikely to result in a risk to the rights and freedoms of natural persons. Where the notification to the supervisory authority is not made within 72 hours, it shall be accompanied by reasons for the delay.

2. The processor shall notify the controller without undue delay after becoming aware of a personal data breach.

3. The notification referred to in paragraph 1 shall at least:

   (a) describe the nature of the personal data breach including where possible, the categories and approximate number of data subjects concerned and the categories and approximate number of personal data records concerned;

   (b) communicate the name and contact details of the data protection officer or other contact point where more information can be obtained;

   (c) describe the likely consequences of the personal data breach;

   (d) describe the measures taken or proposed to be taken by the controller to address the personal data breach, including, where appropriate, measures to mitigate its possible adverse effects.

4. Where, and in so far as, it is not possible to provide the information at the same time, the information may be provided in phases without undue further delay.

5. The controller shall document any personal data breaches, comprising the facts relating to the personal data breach, its effects and the remedial action taken. That documentation shall enable the supervisory authority to verify compliance with this Article.

Article 34: Communication of a personal data breach to the data subject

1. When the personal data breach is likely to result in a high risk to the rights and freedoms of natural persons, the controller shall communicate the personal data breach to the data subject without undue delay.

2. The communication to the data subject referred to in paragraph 1 of this Article shall describe in clear and plain language the nature of the personal data breach and contain at least the information and measures referred to in points (b), (c) and (d) of Article 33(3).

3. The communication to the data subject referred to in paragraph 1 shall not be required if any of the following conditions are met:

   (a) the controller has implemented appropriate technical and organisational protection measures, and those measures were applied to the personal data affected by the personal data breach, in particular those that render the personal data unintelligible to any person who is not authorised to access it, such as encryption;

(b) the controller has taken subsequent measures which ensure that the high risk to the rights and freedoms of data subjects referred to in paragraph 1 is no longer likely to materialise;

(c) it would involve disproportionate effort. In such a case, there shall instead be a public communication or similar measure whereby the data subjects are informed in an equally effective manner.

4. If the controller has not already communicated the personal data breach to the data subject, the supervisory authority, having considered the likelihood of the personal data breach resulting in a high risk, may require it to do so or may decide that any of the conditions referred to in paragraph 3 are met.

Section 3: Data protection impact assessment and prior consultation

Article 35: Data protection impact assessment

1. Where a type of processing in particular using new technologies, and taking into account the nature, scope, context and purposes of the processing, is likely to result in a high risk to the rights and freedoms of natural persons, the controller shall, prior to the processing, carry out an assessment of the impact of the envisaged processing operations on the protection of personal data. A single assessment may address a set of similar processing operations that present similar high risks.

2. The controller shall seek the advice of the data protection officer, where designated, when carrying out a data protection impact assessment.

3. A data protection impact assessment referred to in paragraph 1 shall in particular be required in the case of:

(a) a systematic and extensive evaluation of personal aspects relating to natural persons which is based on automated processing, including profiling, and on which decisions are based that produce legal effects concerning the natural person or similarly significantly affect the natural person;

(b) processing on a large scale of special categories of data referred to in Article 9(1), or of personal data relating to criminal convictions and offences referred to in Article 10; or

(c) a systematic monitoring of a publicly accessible area on a large scale.

4. The supervisory authority shall establish and make public a list of the kind of processing operations which are subject to the requirement for a data protection impact assessment pursuant to paragraph 1. The supervisory authority shall communicate those lists to the Board referred to in Article 68.

5. The supervisory authority may also establish and make public a list of the kind of processing operations for which no data protection impact assessment is required. The supervisory authority shall communicate those lists to the Board.

6. Prior to the adoption of the lists referred to in paragraphs 4 and 5, the competent supervisory authority shall apply the consistency mechanism referred to in Article 63 where such lists involve processing activities which are related to the offering of goods or services to data subjects or to the monitoring of their behaviour in several Member States, or may substantially affect the free movement of personal data within the Union.

7. The assessment shall contain at least:

(a) a systematic description of the envisaged processing operations and the purposes of the processing, including, where applicable, the legitimate interest pursued by the controller;

(b) an assessment of the necessity and proportionality of the processing operations in relation to the purposes;

(c) an assessment of the risks to the rights and freedoms of data subjects referred to in paragraph 1; and

(d) the measures envisaged to address the risks, including safeguards, security measures and mechanisms to ensure the protection of personal data and to demonstrate compliance with this Regulation taking into account the rights and legitimate interests of data subjects and other persons concerned.

8. Compliance with approved codes of conduct referred to in Article 40 by the relevant controllers or processors shall be taken into due account in assessing the impact of the processing operations performed by such controllers or processors, in particular for the purposes of a data protection impact assessment.

9. Where appropriate, the controller shall seek the views of data subjects or their representatives on the intended processing, without prejudice to the protection of commercial or public interests or the security of processing operations.

10. Where processing pursuant to point (c) or (e) of Article 6(1) has a legal basis in Union law or in the law of the Member State to which the controller is subject, that law regulates the specific processing operation or set of operations in question, and a data protection impact assessment has already been carried out as part of a general impact assessment in the context of the adoption of that legal basis, paragraphs 1 to 7 shall not apply unless Member States deem it to be necessary to carry out such an assessment prior to processing activities.

11. Where necessary, the controller shall carry out a review to assess if processing is performed in accordance with the data protection impact assessment at least when there is a change of the risk represented by processing operations.

Article 36: Prior consultation

1. The controller shall consult the supervisory authority prior to processing where a data protection impact assessment under Article 35 indicates that the processing would result in a high risk in the absence of measures taken by the controller to mitigate the risk.

2. Where the supervisory authority is of the opinion that the intended processing referred to in paragraph 1 would infringe this Regulation, in particular where the controller has insufficiently

identified or mitigated the risk, the supervisory authority shall, within period of up to eight weeks of receipt of the request for consultation, provide written advice to the controller and, where applicable to the processor, and may use any of its powers referred to in Article 58. That period may be extended by six weeks, taking into account the complexity of the intended processing. The supervisory authority shall inform the controller and, where applicable, the processor, of any such extension within one month of receipt of the request for consultation together with the reasons for the delay. Those periods may be suspended until the supervisory authority has obtained information it has requested for the purposes of the consultation.

3.   When consulting the supervisory authority pursuant to paragraph 1, the controller shall provide the supervisory authority with:

(a) where applicable, the respective responsibilities of the controller, joint controllers and processors involved in the processing, in particular for processing within a group of undertakings;

(b) the purposes and means of the intended processing;

(c) the measures and safeguards provided to protect the rights and freedoms of data subjects pursuant to this Regulation;

(d) where applicable, the contact details of the data protection officer;

(e) the data protection impact assessment provided for in Article 35; and

(f) any other information requested by the supervisory authority.

4.   Member States shall consult the supervisory authority during the preparation of a proposal for a legislative measure to be adopted by a national parliament, or of a regulatory measure based on such a legislative measure, which relates to processing.

5.   Notwithstanding paragraph 1, Member State law may require controllers to consult with, and obtain prior authorisation from, the supervisory authority in relation to processing by a controller for the performance of a task carried out by the controller in the public interest, including processing in relation to social protection and public health.

Section 4: Data protection officer

Article 37: Designation of the data protection officer

1. The controller and the processor shall designate a data protection officer in any case where:

(a) the processing is carried out by a public authority or body, except for courts acting in their judicial capacity;

(b) the core activities of the controller or the processor consist of processing operations which, by virtue of their nature, their scope and/or their purposes, require regular and systematic monitoring of data subjects on a large scale; or

(c) the core activities of the controller or the processor consist of processing on a large scale of special categories of data pursuant to Article 9 and personal data relating to criminal convictions and offences referred to in Article 10.

2. A group of undertakings may appoint a single data protection officer provided that a data protection officer is easily accessible from each establishment.

3. Where the controller or the processor is a public authority or body, a single data protection officer may be designated for several such authorities or bodies, taking account of their organisational structure and size.

4. In cases other than those referred to in paragraph 1, the controller or processor or associations and other bodies representing categories of controllers or processors may or, where required by Union or Member State law shall, designate a data protection officer. The data protection officer may act for such associations and other bodies representing controllers or processors.

5. The data protection officer shall be designated on the basis of professional qualities and, in particular, expert knowledge of data protection law and practices and the ability to fulfil the tasks referred to in Article 39.

6. The data protection officer may be a staff member of the controller or processor, or fulfil the tasks on the basis of a service contract.

7. The controller or the processor shall publish the contact details of the data protection officer and communicate them to the supervisory authority.

Article 38: Position of the data protection officer

1. The controller and the processor shall ensure that the data protection officer is involved, properly and in a timely manner, in all issues which relate to the protection of personal data.

2. The controller and processor shall support the data protection officer in performing the tasks referred to in Article 39 by providing resources necessary to carry out those tasks and access to personal data and processing operations, and to maintain his or her expert knowledge.

3. The controller and processor shall ensure that the data protection officer does not receive any instructions regarding the exercise of those tasks. He or she shall not be dismissed or penalised by the controller or the processor for performing his tasks. The data protection officer shall directly report to the highest management level of the controller or the processor.

4. Data subjects may contact the data protection officer with regard to all issues related to processing of their personal data and to the exercise of their rights under this Regulation.

5. The data protection officer shall be bound by secrecy or confidentiality concerning the performance of his or her tasks, in accordance with Union or Member State law.

6. The data protection officer may fulfil other tasks and duties. The controller or processor shall ensure that any such tasks and duties do not result in a conflict of interests.

Article 39: Tasks of the data protection officer

1. The data protection officer shall have at least the following tasks:

> (a) to inform and advise the controller or the processor and the employees who carry out processing of their obligations pursuant to this Regulation and to other Union or Member State data protection provisions;

(b) to monitor compliance with this Regulation, with other Union or Member State data protection provisions and with the policies of the controller or processor in relation to the protection of personal data, including the assignment of responsibilities, awareness-raising and training of staff involved in processing operations, and the related audits;

(c) to provide advice where requested as regards the data protection impact assessment and monitor its performance pursuant to Article 35;

(d) to cooperate with the supervisory authority;

(e) to act as the contact point for the supervisory authority on issues relating to processing, including the prior consultation referred to in Article 36, and to consult, where appropriate, with regard to any other matter.

2.   The data protection officer shall in the performance of his or her tasks have due regard to the risk associated with processing operations, taking into account the nature, scope, context and purposes of processing.

Section 5: Codes of conduct and certification

Article 40: Codes of conduct

1.   The Member States, the supervisory authorities, the Board and the Commission shall encourage the drawing up of codes of conduct intended to contribute to the proper application of this Regulation, taking account of the specific features of the various processing sectors and the specific needs of micro, small and medium-sized enterprises.

2.   Associations and other bodies representing categories of controllers or processors may prepare codes of conduct, or amend or extend such codes, for the purpose of specifying the application of this Regulation, such as with regard to:

(a) fair and transparent processing;

(b) the legitimate interests pursued by controllers in specific contexts;

(c) the collection of personal data;

(d) the pseudonymisation of personal data;

(e) the information provided to the public and to data subjects;

(f) the exercise of the rights of data subjects;

(g) the information provided to, and the protection of, children, and the manner in which the consent of the holders of parental responsibility over children is to be obtained;

(h) the measures and procedures referred to in Articles 24 and 25 and the measures to ensure security of processing referred to in Article 32;

(i) the notification of personal data breaches to supervisory authorities and the communication of such personal data breaches to data subjects;

(j) the transfer of personal data to third countries or international organisations; or

(k) out-of-court proceedings and other dispute resolution procedures for resolving disputes between controllers and data subjects with regard to processing, without prejudice to the rights of data subjects pursuant to Articles 77 and 79.

3. In addition to adherence by controllers or processors subject to this Regulation, codes of conduct approved pursuant to paragraph 5 of this Article and having general validity pursuant to paragraph 9 of this Article may also be adhered to by controllers or processors that are not subject to this Regulation pursuant to Article 3 in order to provide appropriate safeguards within the framework of personal data transfers to third countries or international organisations under the terms referred to in point (e) of Article 46(2). Such controllers or processors shall make binding and enforceable commitments, via contractual or other legally binding instruments, to apply those appropriate safeguards including with regard to the rights of data subjects.

4. A code of conduct referred to in paragraph 2 of this Article shall contain mechanisms which enable the body referred to in Article 41(1) to carry out the mandatory monitoring of compliance with its provisions by the controllers or processors which undertake to apply it, without prejudice to the tasks and powers of supervisory authorities competent pursuant to Article 55 or 56.

5. Associations and other bodies referred to in paragraph 2 of this Article which intend to prepare a code of conduct or to amend or extend an existing code shall submit the draft code, amendment or extension to the supervisory authority which is competent pursuant to Article 55. The supervisory authority shall provide an opinion on whether the draft code, amendment or extension complies with this Regulation and shall approve that draft code, amendment or extension if it finds that it provides sufficient appropriate safeguards.

6. Where the draft code, or amendment or extension is approved in accordance with paragraph 5, and where the code of conduct concerned does not relate to processing activities in several Member States, the supervisory authority shall register and publish the code.

7. Where a draft code of conduct relates to processing activities in several Member States, the supervisory authority which is competent pursuant to Article 55 shall, before approving the draft code, amendment or extension, submit it in the procedure referred to in Article 63 to the Board which shall provide an opinion on whether the draft code, amendment or extension complies with this Regulation or, in the situation referred to in paragraph 3 of this Article, provides appropriate safeguards.

8. Where the opinion referred to in paragraph 7 confirms that the draft code, amendment or extension complies with this Regulation, or, in the situation referred to in paragraph 3, provides appropriate safeguards, the Board shall submit its opinion to the Commission.

9. The Commission may, by way of implementing acts, decide that the approved code of conduct, amendment or extension submitted to it pursuant to paragraph 8 of this Article have general validity within the Union. Those implementing acts shall be adopted in accordance with the examination procedure set out in Article 93(2).

10. The Commission shall ensure appropriate publicity for the approved codes which have been decided as having general validity in accordance with paragraph 9.

11. The Board shall collate all approved codes of conduct, amendments and extensions in a register and shall make them publicly available by way of appropriate means.

Article 41: Monitoring of approved codes of conduct

1. Without prejudice to the tasks and powers of the competent supervisory authority under Articles 57 and 58, the monitoring of compliance with a code of conduct pursuant to Article 40 may be carried out by a body which has an appropriate level of expertise in relation to the subject-matter of the code and is accredited for that purpose by the competent supervisory authority.

2. A body as referred to in paragraph 1 may be accredited to monitor compliance with a code of conduct where that body has:

(a) demonstrated its independence and expertise in relation to the subject-matter of the code to the satisfaction of the competent supervisory authority;

(b) established procedures which allow it to assess the eligibility of controllers and processors concerned to apply the code, to monitor their compliance with its provisions and to periodically review its operation;

(c) established procedures and structures to handle complaints about infringements of the code or the manner in which the code has been, or is being, implemented by a controller or processor, and to make those procedures and structures transparent to data subjects and the public; and

(d) demonstrated to the satisfaction of the competent supervisory authority that its tasks and duties do not result in a conflict of interests.

3. The competent supervisory authority shall submit the draft criteria for accreditation of a body as referred to in paragraph 1 of this Article to the Board pursuant to the consistency mechanism referred to in Article 63.

4. Without prejudice to the tasks and powers of the competent supervisory authority and the provisions of Chapter VIII, a body as referred to in paragraph 1 of this Article shall, subject to appropriate safeguards, take appropriate action in cases of infringement of the code by a controller or processor, including suspension or exclusion of the controller or processor concerned from the code. It shall inform the competent supervisory authority of such actions and the reasons for taking them.

5. The competent supervisory authority shall revoke the accreditation of a body as referred to in paragraph 1 if the conditions for accreditation are not, or are no longer, met or where actions taken by the body infringe this Regulation.

6. This Article shall not apply to processing carried out by public authorities and bodies.

Article 42: Certification

1. The Member States, the supervisory authorities, the Board and the Commission shall encourage, in particular at Union level, the establishment of data protection certification mechanisms and of data protection seals and marks, for the purpose of demonstrating

compliance with this Regulation of processing operations by controllers and processors. The specific needs of micro, small and medium-sized enterprises shall be taken into account.

2.   In addition to adherence by controllers or processors subject to this Regulation, data protection certification mechanisms, seals or marks approved pursuant to paragraph 5 of this Article may be established for the purpose of demonstrating the existence of appropriate safeguards provided by controllers or processors that are not subject to this Regulation pursuant to Article 3 within the framework of personal data transfers to third countries or international organisations under the terms referred to in point (f) of Article 46(2). Such controllers or processors shall make binding and enforceable commitments, via contractual or other legally binding instruments, to apply those appropriate safeguards, including with regard to the rights of data subjects.

3. The certification shall be voluntary and available via a process that is transparent.

4.   A certification pursuant to this Article does not reduce the responsibility of the controller or the processor for compliance with this Regulation and is without prejudice to the tasks and powers of the supervisory authorities which are competent pursuant to Article 55 or 56.

5. A certification pursuant to this Article shall be issued by the certification bodies referred to in Article 43 or by the competent supervisory authority, on the basis of criteria approved by that competent supervisory authority pursuant to Article 58(3) or by the Board pursuant to Article 63. Where the criteria are approved by the Board, this may result in a common certification, the European Data Protection Seal.

6.   The controller or processor which submits its processing to the certification mechanism shall provide the certification body referred to in Article 43, or where applicable, the competent supervisory authority, with all information and access to its processing activities which are necessary to conduct the certification procedure.

7. Certification shall be issued to a controller or processor for a maximum period of three years and may be renewed, under the same conditions, provided that the relevant requirements continue to be met. Certification shall be withdrawn, as applicable, by the certification bodies referred to in Article 43 or by the competent supervisory authority where the requirements for the certification are not or are no longer met.

8. The Board shall collate all certification mechanisms and data protection seals and marks in a register and shall make them publicly available by any appropriate means.

Article 43: Certification bodies

1.   Without prejudice to the tasks and powers of the competent supervisory authority under Articles 57 and 58, certification bodies which have an appropriate level of expertise in relation to data protection shall, after informing the supervisory authority in order to allow it to exercise its powers pursuant to point (h) of Article 58(2) where necessary, issue and renew certification. Member States shall ensure that those certification bodies are accredited by one or both of the following:

   (a) the supervisory authority which is competent pursuant to Article 55 or 56;

(b) the national accreditation body named in accordance with Regulation (EC) No 765/2008 of the European Parliament and of the Council (20) in accordance with EN-ISO/IEC 17065/2012 and with the additional requirements established by the supervisory authority which is competent pursuant to Article 55 or 56.

2. Certification bodies referred to in paragraph 1 shall be accredited in accordance with that paragraph only where they have:

(a) demonstrated their independence and expertise in relation to the subject-matter of the certification to the satisfaction of the competent supervisory authority;

(b) undertaken to respect the criteria referred to in Article 42(5) and approved by the supervisory authority which is competent pursuant to Article 55 or 56 or by the Board pursuant to Article 63;

(c) established procedures for the issuing, periodic review and withdrawal of data protection certification, seals and marks;

(d) established procedures and structures to handle complaints about infringements of the certification or the manner in which the certification has been, or is being, implemented by the controller or processor, and to make those procedures and structures transparent to data subjects and the public; and

(e) demonstrated, to the satisfaction of the competent supervisory authority, that their tasks and duties do not result in a conflict of interests.

3. The accreditation of certification bodies as referred to in paragraphs 1 and 2 of this Article shall take place on the basis of criteria approved by the supervisory authority which is competent pursuant to Article 55 or 56 or by the Board pursuant to Article 63. In the case of accreditation pursuant to point (b) of paragraph 1 of this Article, those requirements shall complement those envisaged in Regulation (EC) No 765/2008 and the technical rules that describe the methods and procedures of the certification bodies.

4. The certification bodies referred to in paragraph 1 shall be responsible for the proper assessment leading to the certification or the withdrawal of such certification without prejudice to the responsibility of the controller or processor for compliance with this Regulation. The accreditation shall be issued for a maximum period of five years and may be renewed on the same conditions provided that the certification body meets the requirements set out in this Article.

5. The certification bodies referred to in paragraph 1 shall provide the competent supervisory authorities with the reasons for granting or withdrawing the requested certification.

6. The requirements referred to in paragraph 3 of this Article and the criteria referred to in Article 42(5) shall be made public by the supervisory authority in an easily accessible form. The supervisory authorities shall also transmit those requirements and criteria to the Board. The Board shall collate all certification mechanisms and data protection seals in a register and shall make them publicly available by any appropriate means.

7. Without prejudice to Chapter VIII, the competent supervisory authority or the national accreditation body shall revoke an accreditation of a certification body pursuant to paragraph 1

of this Article where the conditions for the accreditation are not, or are no longer, met or where actions taken by a certification body infringe this Regulation.

8. The Commission shall be empowered to adopt delegated acts in accordance with Article 92 for the purpose of specifying the requirements to be taken into account for the data protection certification mechanisms referred to in Article 42(1).

9.   The Commission may adopt implementing acts laying down technical standards for certification mechanisms and data protection seals and marks, and mechanisms to promote and recognise those certification mechanisms, seals and marks. Those implementing acts shall be adopted in accordance with the examination procedure referred to in Article 93(2).

CHAPTER V: Transfers of personal data to third countries or international organisations

Article 44: General principle for transfers

Any transfer of personal data which are undergoing processing or are intended for processing after transfer to a third country or to an international organisation shall take place only if, subject to the other provisions of this Regulation, the conditions laid down in this Chapter are complied with by the controller and processor, including for onward transfers of personal data from the third country or an international organisation to another third country or to another international organisation. All provisions in this Chapter shall be applied in order to ensure that the level of protection of natural persons guaranteed by this Regulation is not undermined.

Article 45: Transfers on the basis of an adequacy decision

1. A transfer of personal data to a third country or an international organisation may take place where the Commission has decided that the third country, a territory or one or more specified sectors within that third country, or the international organisation in question ensures an adequate level of protection. Such a transfer shall not require any specific authorisation.

2. When assessing the adequacy of the level of protection, the Commission shall, in particular, take account of the following elements:

(a) the rule of law, respect for human rights and fundamental freedoms, relevant legislation, both general and sectoral, including concerning public security, defence, national security and criminal law and the access of public authorities to personal data, as well as the implementation of such legislation, data protection rules, professional rules and security measures, including rules for the onward transfer of personal data to another third country or international organisation which are complied with in that country or international organisation, case-law, as well as effective and enforceable data subject rights and effective administrative and judicial redress for the data subjects whose personal data are being transferred;

(b) the existence and effective functioning of one or more independent supervisory authorities in the third country or to which an international organisation is subject, with responsibility for ensuring and enforcing compliance with the data protection rules, including adequate enforcement powers, for assisting and advising the data subjects in exercising their rights and for cooperation with the supervisory authorities of the Member States; and

(c) the international commitments the third country or international organisation concerned has entered into, or other obligations arising from legally binding conventions or instruments as well as from its participation in multilateral or regional systems, in particular in relation to the protection of personal data.

3.   The Commission, after assessing the adequacy of the level of protection, may decide, by means of implementing act, that a third country, a territory or one or more specified sectors within a third country, or an international organisation ensures an adequate level of protection within the meaning of paragraph 2 of this Article. The implementing act shall provide for a mechanism for a periodic review, at least every four years, which shall take into account all relevant developments in the third country or international organisation. The implementing act shall specify its territorial and sectoral application and, where applicable, identify the supervisory authority or authorities referred to in point (b) of paragraph 2 of this Article. The implementing act shall be adopted in accordance with the examination procedure referred to in Article 93(2).

4.   The Commission shall, on an ongoing basis, monitor developments in third countries and international organisations that could affect the functioning of decisions adopted pursuant to paragraph 3 of this Article and decisions adopted on the basis of Article 25(6) of Directive 95/46/EC.

5.   The Commission shall, where available information reveals, in particular following the review referred to in paragraph 3 of this Article, that a third country, a territory or one or more specified sectors within a third country, or an international organisation no longer ensures an adequate level of protection within the meaning of paragraph 2 of this Article, to the extent necessary, repeal, amend or suspend the decision referred to in paragraph 3 of this Article by means of implementing acts without retro-active effect. Those implementing acts shall be adopted in accordance with the examination procedure referred to in Article 93(2).

On duly justified imperative grounds of urgency, the Commission shall adopt immediately applicable implementing acts in accordance with the procedure referred to in Article 93(3).

6.   The Commission shall enter into consultations with the third country or international organisation with a view to remedying the situation giving rise to the decision made pursuant to paragraph 5.

7.   A decision pursuant to paragraph 5 of this Article is without prejudice to transfers of personal data to the third country, a territory or one or more specified sectors within that third country, or the international organisation in question pursuant to Articles 46 to 49.

8.   The Commission shall publish in the Official Journal of the European Union and on its website a list of the third countries, territories and specified sectors within a third country and international organisations for which it has decided that an adequate level of protection is or is no longer ensured.

9. Decisions adopted by the Commission on the basis of Article 25(6) of Directive 95/46/EC shall remain in force until amended, replaced or repealed by a Commission Decision adopted in accordance with paragraph 3 or 5 of this Article.

Article 46: Transfers subject to appropriate safeguards

1. In the absence of a decision pursuant to Article 45(3), a controller or processor may transfer personal data to a third country or an international organisation only if the controller or processor has provided appropriate safeguards, and on condition that enforceable data subject rights and effective legal remedies for data subjects are available.

2. The appropriate safeguards referred to in paragraph 1 may be provided for, without requiring any specific authorisation from a supervisory authority, by:

(a) a legally binding and enforceable instrument between public authorities or bodies;

(b) binding corporate rules in accordance with Article 47;

(c) standard data protection clauses adopted by the Commission in accordance with the examination procedure referred to in Article 93(2);

(d) standard data protection clauses adopted by a supervisory authority and approved by the Commission pursuant to the examination procedure referred to in Article 93(2);

(e) an approved code of conduct pursuant to Article 40 together with binding and enforceable commitments of the controller or processor in the third country to apply the appropriate safeguards, including as regards data subjects' rights; or

(f) an approved certification mechanism pursuant to Article 42 together with binding and enforceable commitments of the controller or processor in the third country to apply the appropriate safeguards, including as regards data subjects' rights.

3. Subject to the authorisation from the competent supervisory authority, the appropriate safeguards referred to in paragraph 1 may also be provided for, in particular, by:

(a) contractual clauses between the controller or processor and the controller, processor or the recipient of the personal data in the third country or international organisation; or

(b) provisions to be inserted into administrative arrangements between public authorities or bodies which include enforceable and effective data subject rights.

4. The supervisory authority shall apply the consistency mechanism referred to in Article 63 in the cases referred to in paragraph 3 of this Article.

5. Authorisations by a Member State or supervisory authority on the basis of Article 26(2) of Directive 95/46/EC shall remain valid until amended, replaced or repealed, if necessary, by that supervisory authority. Decisions adopted by the Commission on the basis of Article 26(4) of Directive 95/46/EC shall remain in force until amended, replaced or repealed, if necessary, by a Commission Decision adopted in accordance with paragraph 2 of this Article.

Article 47: Binding corporate rules

1. The competent supervisory authority shall approve binding corporate rules in accordance with the consistency mechanism set out in Article 63, provided that they:

> (a) are legally binding and apply to and are enforced by every member concerned of the group of undertakings, or group of enterprises engaged in a joint economic activity, including their employees;

> (b) expressly confer enforceable rights on data subjects with regard to the processing of their personal data; and

> (c) fulfil the requirements laid down in paragraph 2.

2. The binding corporate rules referred to in paragraph 1 shall specify at least:

> (a) the structure and contact details of the group of undertakings, or group of enterprises engaged in a joint economic activity and of each of its members;

> (b) the data transfers or set of transfers, including the categories of personal data, the type of processing and its purposes, the type of data subjects affected and the identification of the third country or countries in question;

> (c) their legally binding nature, both internally and externally;

> (d) the application of the general data protection principles, in particular purpose limitation, data minimisation, limited storage periods, data quality, data protection by design and by default, legal basis for processing, processing of special categories of personal data, measures to ensure data security, and the requirements in respect of onward transfers to bodies not bound by the binding corporate rules;

> (e) the rights of data subjects in regard to processing and the means to exercise those rights, including the right not to be subject to decisions based solely on automated processing, including profiling in accordance with Article 22, the right to lodge a complaint with the competent supervisory authority and before the competent courts of the Member States in accordance with Article 79, and to obtain redress and, where appropriate, compensation for a breach of the binding corporate rules;

> (f) the acceptance by the controller or processor established on the territory of a Member State of liability for any breaches of the binding corporate rules by any member concerned not established in the Union; the controller or the processor shall be exempt from that liability, in whole or in part, only if it proves that that member is not responsible for the event giving rise to the damage;

> (g) how the information on the binding corporate rules, in particular on the provisions referred to in points (d), (e) and (f) of this paragraph is provided to the data subjects in addition to Articles 13 and 14;

> (h) the tasks of any data protection officer designated in accordance with Article 37 or any other person or entity in charge of the monitoring compliance with the binding corporate rules within the group of undertakings, or group of enterprises engaged in a joint economic activity, as well as monitoring training and complaint-handling;

> (i) the complaint procedures;

(j) the mechanisms within the group of undertakings, or group of enterprises engaged in a joint economic activity for ensuring the verification of compliance with the binding corporate rules. Such mechanisms shall include data protection audits and methods for ensuring corrective actions to protect the rights of the data subject. Results of such verification should be communicated to the person or entity referred to in point (h) and to the board of the controlling undertaking of a group of undertakings, or of the group of enterprises engaged in a joint economic activity, and should be available upon request to the competent supervisory authority;

(k) the mechanisms for reporting and recording changes to the rules and reporting those changes to the supervisory authority;

(l) the cooperation mechanism with the supervisory authority to ensure compliance by any member of the group of undertakings, or group of enterprises engaged in a joint economic activity, in particular by making available to the supervisory authority the results of verifications of the measures referred to in point (j);

(m) the mechanisms for reporting to the competent supervisory authority any legal requirements to which a member of the group of undertakings, or group of enterprises engaged in a joint economic activity is subject in a third country which are likely to have a substantial adverse effect on the guarantees provided by the binding corporate rules; and

(n) the appropriate data protection training to personnel having permanent or regular access to personal data.

3. The Commission may specify the format and procedures for the exchange of information between controllers, processors and supervisory authorities for binding corporate rules within the meaning of this Article. Those implementing acts shall be adopted in accordance with the examination procedure set out in Article 93(2).

Article 48: Transfers or disclosures not authorised by Union law

Any judgment of a court or tribunal and any decision of an administrative authority of a third country requiring a controller or processor to transfer or disclose personal data may only be recognised or enforceable in any manner if based on an international agreement, such as a mutual legal assistance treaty, in force between the requesting third country and the Union or a Member State, without prejudice to other grounds for transfer pursuant to this Chapter.

Article 49: Derogations for specific situations

1. In the absence of an adequacy decision pursuant to Article 45(3), or of appropriate safeguards pursuant to Article 46, including binding corporate rules, a transfer or a set of transfers of personal data to a third country or an international organisation shall take place only on one of the following conditions:

(a) the data subject has explicitly consented to the proposed transfer, after having been informed of the possible risks of such transfers for the data subject due to the absence of an adequacy decision and appropriate safeguards;

(b) the transfer is necessary for the performance of a contract between the data subject and the controller or the implementation of pre-contractual measures taken at the data subject's request;

(c) the transfer is necessary for the conclusion or performance of a contract concluded in the interest of the data subject between the controller and another natural or legal person;

(d) the transfer is necessary for important reasons of public interest;

(e) the transfer is necessary for the establishment, exercise or defence of legal claims;

(f) the transfer is necessary in order to protect the vital interests of the data subject or of other persons, where the data subject is physically or legally incapable of giving consent;

(g) the transfer is made from a register which according to Union or Member State law is intended to provide information to the public and which is open to consultation either by the public in general or by any person who can demonstrate a legitimate interest, but only to the extent that the conditions laid down by Union or Member State law for consultation are fulfilled in the particular case.

Where a transfer could not be based on a provision in Article 45 or 46, including the provisions on binding corporate rules, and none of the derogations for a specific situation referred to in the first subparagraph of this paragraph is applicable, a transfer to a third country or an international organisation may take place only if the transfer is not repetitive, concerns only a limited number of data subjects, is necessary for the purposes of compelling legitimate interests pursued by the controller which are not overridden by the interests or rights and freedoms of the data subject, and the controller has assessed all the circumstances surrounding the data transfer and has on the basis of that assessment provided suitable safeguards with regard to the protection of personal data. The controller shall inform the supervisory authority of the transfer. The controller shall, in addition to providing the information referred to in Articles 13 and 14, inform the data subject of the transfer and on the compelling legitimate interests pursued.

2.   A transfer pursuant to point (g) of the first subparagraph of paragraph 1 shall not involve the entirety of the personal data or entire categories of the personal data contained in the register. Where the register is intended for consultation by persons having a legitimate interest, the transfer shall be made only at the request of those persons or if they are to be the recipients.

3.   Points (a), (b) and (c) of the first subparagraph of paragraph 1 and the second subparagraph thereof shall not apply to activities carried out by public authorities in the exercise of their public powers.

4.   The public interest referred to in point (d) of the first subparagraph of paragraph 1 shall be recognised in Union law or in the law of the Member State to which the controller is subject.

5.   In the absence of an adequacy decision, Union or Member State law may, for important reasons of public interest, expressly set limits to the transfer of specific categories of personal data to a third country or an international organisation. Member States shall notify such provisions to the Commission.

6. The controller or processor shall document the assessment as well as the suitable safeguards referred to in the second subparagraph of paragraph 1 of this Article in the records referred to in Article 30.

Article 50: International cooperation for the protection of personal data

In relation to third countries and international organisations, the Commission and supervisory authorities shall take appropriate steps to:

(a) develop international cooperation mechanisms to facilitate the effective enforcement of legislation for the protection of personal data;

(b) provide international mutual assistance in the enforcement of legislation for the protection of personal data, including through notification, complaint referral, investigative assistance and information exchange, subject to appropriate safeguards for the protection of personal data and other fundamental rights and freedoms;

(c) engage relevant stakeholders in discussion and activities aimed at furthering international cooperation in the enforcement of legislation for the protection of personal data;

(d) promote the exchange and documentation of personal data protection legislation and practice, including on jurisdictional conflicts with third countries.

CHAPTER VI: Independent supervisory authorities

Section 1: Independent status

Article 51: Supervisory authority

1. Each Member State shall provide for one or more independent public authorities to be responsible for monitoring the application of this Regulation, in order to protect the fundamental rights and freedoms of natural persons in relation to processing and to facilitate the free flow of personal data within the Union ('supervisory authority').

2. Each supervisory authority shall contribute to the consistent application of this Regulation throughout the Union. For that purpose, the supervisory authorities shall cooperate with each other and the Commission in accordance with Chapter VII.

3. Where more than one supervisory authority is established in a Member State, that Member State shall designate the supervisory authority which is to represent those authorities in the Board and shall set out the mechanism to ensure compliance by the other authorities with the rules relating to the consistency mechanism referred to in Article 63.

4. Each Member State shall notify to the Commission the provisions of its law which it adopts pursuant to this Chapter, by 25 May 2018 and, without delay, any subsequent amendment affecting them.

Article 52: Independence

1.   Each supervisory authority shall act with complete independence in performing its tasks and exercising its powers in accordance with this Regulation.

2.   The member or members of each supervisory authority shall, in the performance of their tasks and exercise of their powers in accordance with this Regulation, remain free from external influence, whether direct or indirect, and shall neither seek nor take instructions from anybody.

3.   Member or members of each supervisory authority shall refrain from any action incompatible with their duties and shall not, during their term of office, engage in any incompatible occupation, whether gainful or not.

4.   Each Member State shall ensure that each supervisory authority is provided with the human, technical and financial resources, premises and infrastructure necessary for the effective performance of its tasks and exercise of its powers, including those to be carried out in the context of mutual assistance, cooperation and participation in the Board.

5.   Each Member State shall ensure that each supervisory authority chooses and has its own staff which shall be subject to the exclusive direction of the member or members of the supervisory authority concerned.

6.   Each Member State shall ensure that each supervisory authority is subject to financial control which does not affect its independence and that it has separate, public annual budgets, which may be part of the overall state or national budget.

Article 53: General conditions for the members of the supervisory authority

1.   Member States shall provide for each member of their supervisory authorities to be appointed by means of a transparent procedure by:

their parliament;

their government;

their head of State; or

an independent body entrusted with the appointment under Member State law.

2.   Each member shall have the qualifications, experience and skills, in particular in the area of the protection of personal data, required to perform its duties and exercise its powers.

3.   The duties of a member shall end in the event of the expiry of the term of office, resignation or compulsory retirement, in accordance with the law of the Member State concerned.

4.   A member shall be dismissed only in cases of serious misconduct or if the member no longer fulfils the conditions required for the performance of the duties.

Article 54: Rules on the establishment of the supervisory authority

1.   Each Member State shall provide by law for all of the following:

(a) the establishment of each supervisory authority;

(b) the qualifications and eligibility conditions required to be appointed as member of each supervisory authority;

(c) the rules and procedures for the appointment of the member or members of each supervisory authority;

(d) the duration of the term of the member or members of each supervisory authority of no less than four years, except for the first appointment after 24 May 2016, part of which may take place for a shorter period where that is necessary to protect the independence of the supervisory authority by means of a staggered appointment procedure;

(e) whether and, if so, for how many terms the member or members of each supervisory authority is eligible for reappointment;

(f) the conditions governing the obligations of the member or members and staff of each supervisory authority, prohibitions on actions, occupations and benefits incompatible therewith during and after the term of office and rules governing the cessation of employment.

2. The member or members and the staff of each supervisory authority shall, in accordance with Union or Member State law, be subject to a duty of professional secrecy both during and after their term of office, with regard to any confidential information which has come to their knowledge in the course of the performance of their tasks or exercise of their powers. During their term of office, that duty of professional secrecy shall in particular apply to reporting by natural persons of infringements of this Regulation.

Section 2: Competence, tasks and powers

Article 55: Competence

1. Each supervisory authority shall be competent for the performance of the tasks assigned to and the exercise of the powers conferred on it in accordance with this Regulation on the territory of its own Member State.

2. Where processing is carried out by public authorities or private bodies acting on the basis of point (c) or (e) of Article 6(1), the supervisory authority of the Member State concerned shall be competent. In such cases Article 56 does not apply.

3. Supervisory authorities shall not be competent to supervise processing operations of courts acting in their judicial capacity.

Article 56: Competence of the lead supervisory authority

1. Without prejudice to Article 55, the supervisory authority of the main establishment or of the single establishment of the controller or processor shall be competent to act as lead supervisory authority for the cross-border processing carried out by that controller or processor in accordance with the procedure provided in Article 60.

2. By derogation from paragraph 1, each supervisory authority shall be competent to handle a complaint lodged with it or a possible infringement of this Regulation, if the subject matter relates only to an establishment in its Member State or substantially affects data subjects only in its Member State.

3. In the cases referred to in paragraph 2 of this Article, the supervisory authority shall inform the lead supervisory authority without delay on that matter. Within a period of three weeks after being informed the lead supervisory authority shall decide whether or not it will handle the case in accordance with the procedure provided in Article 60, taking into account whether or not there is an establishment of the controller or processor in the Member State of which the supervisory authority informed it.

4. Where the lead supervisory authority decides to handle the case, the procedure provided in Article 60 shall apply. The supervisory authority which informed the lead supervisory authority may submit to the lead supervisory authority a draft for a decision. The lead supervisory authority shall take utmost account of that draft when preparing the draft decision referred to in Article 60(3).

5. Where the lead supervisory authority decides not to handle the case, the supervisory authority which informed the lead supervisory authority shall handle it according to Articles 61 and 62.

6. The lead supervisory authority shall be the sole interlocutor of the controller or processor for the cross-border processing carried out by that controller or processor.

Article 57: Tasks

1. Without prejudice to other tasks set out under this Regulation, each supervisory authority shall on its territory:

(a) monitor and enforce the application of this Regulation;

(b) promote public awareness and understanding of the risks, rules, safeguards and rights in relation to processing. Activities addressed specifically to children shall receive specific attention;

(c) advise, in accordance with Member State law, the national parliament, the government, and other institutions and bodies on legislative and administrative measures relating to the protection of natural persons' rights and freedoms with regard to processing;

(d) promote the awareness of controllers and processors of their obligations under this Regulation;

(e) upon request, provide information to any data subject concerning the exercise of their rights under this Regulation and, if appropriate, cooperate with the supervisory authorities in other Member States to that end;

(f) handle complaints lodged by a data subject, or by a body, organisation or association in accordance with Article 80, and investigate, to the extent appropriate, the subject matter of the complaint and inform the complainant of the progress and the outcome of the investigation within a reasonable period, in particular if further investigation or coordination with another supervisory authority is necessary;

(g) cooperate with, including sharing information and provide mutual assistance to, other supervisory authorities with a view to ensuring the consistency of application and enforcement of this Regulation;

(h) conduct investigations on the application of this Regulation, including on the basis of information received from another supervisory authority or other public authority;

(i) monitor relevant developments, insofar as they have an impact on the protection of personal data, in particular the development of information and communication technologies and commercial practices;

(j) adopt standard contractual clauses referred to in Article 28(8) and in point (d) of Article 46(2);

(k) establish and maintain a list in relation to the requirement for data protection impact assessment pursuant to Article 35(4);

(l) give advice on the processing operations referred to in Article 36(2);

(m) encourage the drawing up of codes of conduct pursuant to Article 40(1) and provide an opinion and approve such codes of conduct which provide sufficient safeguards, pursuant to Article 40(5);

(n) encourage the establishment of data protection certification mechanisms and of data protection seals and marks pursuant to Article 42(1), and approve the criteria of certification pursuant to Article 42(5);

(o) where applicable, carry out a periodic review of certifications issued in accordance with Article 42(7);

(p) draft and publish the criteria for accreditation of a body for monitoring codes of conduct pursuant to Article 41 and of a certification body pursuant to Article 43;

(q) conduct the accreditation of a body for monitoring codes of conduct pursuant to Article 41 and of a certification body pursuant to Article 43;

(r) authorise contractual clauses and provisions referred to in Article 46(3);

(s) approve binding corporate rules pursuant to Article 47;

(t) contribute to the activities of the Board;

(u) keep internal records of infringements of this Regulation and of measures taken in accordance with Article 58(2); and

(v) fulfil any other tasks related to the protection of personal data.

2. Each supervisory authority shall facilitate the submission of complaints referred to in point (f) of paragraph 1 by measures such as a complaint submission form which can also be completed electronically, without excluding other means of communication.

3. The performance of the tasks of each supervisory authority shall be free of charge for the data subject and, where applicable, for the data protection officer.

4. Where requests are manifestly unfounded or excessive, in particular because of their repetitive character, the supervisory authority may charge a reasonable fee based on

administrative costs, or refuse to act on the request. The supervisory authority shall bear the burden of demonstrating the manifestly unfounded or excessive character of the request.

Article 58: Powers

1. Each supervisory authority shall have all of the following investigative powers:

    (a) to order the controller and the processor, and, where applicable, the controller's or the processor's representative to provide any information it requires for the performance of its tasks;

    (b) to carry out investigations in the form of data protection audits;

    (c) to carry out a review on certifications issued pursuant to Article 42(7);

    (d) to notify the controller or the processor of an alleged infringement of this Regulation;

    (e) to obtain, from the controller and the processor, access to all personal data and to all information necessary for the performance of its tasks;

    (f) to obtain access to any premises of the controller and the processor, including to any data processing equipment and means, in accordance with Union or Member State procedural law.

2. Each supervisory authority shall have all of the following corrective powers:

    (a) to issue warnings to a controller or processor that intended processing operations are likely to infringe provisions of this Regulation;

    (b) to issue reprimands to a controller or a processor where processing operations have infringed provisions of this Regulation;

    (c) to order the controller or the processor to comply with the data subject's requests to exercise his or her rights pursuant to this Regulation;

    (d) to order the controller or processor to bring processing operations into compliance with the provisions of this Regulation, where appropriate, in a specified manner and within a specified period;

    (e) to order the controller to communicate a personal data breach to the data subject;

    (f) to impose a temporary or definitive limitation including a ban on processing;

    (g) to order the rectification or erasure of personal data or restriction of processing pursuant to Articles 16, 17 and 18 and the notification of such actions to recipients to whom the personal data have been disclosed pursuant to Article 17(2) and Article 19;

    (h) to withdraw a certification or to order the certification body to withdraw a certification issued pursuant to Articles 42 and 43, or to order the certification body not to issue certification if the requirements for the certification are not or are no longer met;

    (i) to impose an administrative fine pursuant to Article 83, in addition to, or instead of measures referred to in this paragraph, depending on the circumstances of each individual case;

    (j) to order the suspension of data flows to a recipient in a third country or to an international organisation.

3.   Each supervisory authority shall have all of the following authorisation and advisory powers:

> (a) to advise the controller in accordance with the prior consultation procedure referred to in Article 36;

> (b) to issue, on its own initiative or on request, opinions to the national parliament, the Member State government or, in accordance with Member State law, to other institutions and bodies as well as to the public on any issue related to the protection of personal data;

> (c) to authorise processing referred to in Article 36(5), if the law of the Member State requires such prior authorisation;

> (d) to issue an opinion and approve draft codes of conduct pursuant to Article 40(5);

> (e) to accredit certification bodies pursuant to Article 43;

> (f) to issue certifications and approve criteria of certification in accordance with Article 42(5);

> (g) to adopt standard data protection clauses referred to in Article 28(8) and in point (d) of Article 46(2);

> (h) to authorise contractual clauses referred to in point (a) of Article 46(3);

> (i) to authorise administrative arrangements referred to in point (b) of Article 46(3);

> (j) to approve binding corporate rules pursuant to Article 47.

4.   The exercise of the powers conferred on the supervisory authority pursuant to this Article shall be subject to appropriate safeguards, including effective judicial remedy and due process, set out in Union and Member State law in accordance with the Charter.

5.   Each Member State shall provide by law that its supervisory authority shall have the power to bring infringements of this Regulation to the attention of the judicial authorities and where appropriate, to commence or engage otherwise in legal proceedings, in order to enforce the provisions of this Regulation.

6.   Each Member State may provide by law that its supervisory authority shall have additional powers to those referred to in paragraphs 1, 2 and 3. The exercise of those powers shall not impair the effective operation of Chapter VII.

Article 59: Activity reports

Each supervisory authority shall draw up an annual report on its activities, which may include a list of types of infringement notified and types of measures taken in accordance with Article 58(2). Those reports shall be transmitted to the national parliament, the government and other authorities as designated by Member State law. They shall be made available to the public, to the Commission and to the Board.

CHAPTER VII: Cooperation and consistency

Section 1: Cooperation

Article 60: Cooperation between the lead supervisory authority and the other supervisory authorities concerned

1. The lead supervisory authority shall cooperate with the other supervisory authorities concerned in accordance with this Article in an endeavour to reach consensus. The lead supervisory authority and the supervisory authorities concerned shall exchange all relevant information with each other.

2. The lead supervisory authority may request at any time other supervisory authorities concerned to provide mutual assistance pursuant to Article 61 and may conduct joint operations pursuant to Article 62, in particular for carrying out investigations or for monitoring the implementation of a measure concerning a controller or processor established in another Member State.

3. The lead supervisory authority shall, without delay, communicate the relevant information on the matter to the other supervisory authorities concerned. It shall without delay submit a draft decision to the other supervisory authorities concerned for their opinion and take due account of their views.

4. Where any of the other supervisory authorities concerned within a period of four weeks after having been consulted in accordance with paragraph 3 of this Article, expresses a relevant and reasoned objection to the draft decision, the lead supervisory authority shall, if it does not follow the relevant and reasoned objection or is of the opinion that the objection is not relevant or reasoned, submit the matter to the consistency mechanism referred to in Article 63.

5. Where the lead supervisory authority intends to follow the relevant and reasoned objection made, it shall submit to the other supervisory authorities concerned a revised draft decision for their opinion. That revised draft decision shall be subject to the procedure referred to in paragraph 4 within a period of two weeks.

6. Where none of the other supervisory authorities concerned has objected to the draft decision submitted by the lead supervisory authority within the period referred to in paragraphs 4 and 5, the lead supervisory authority and the supervisory authorities concerned shall be deemed to be in agreement with that draft decision and shall be bound by it.

7. The lead supervisory authority shall adopt and notify the decision to the main establishment or single establishment of the controller or processor, as the case may be and inform the other supervisory authorities concerned and the Board of the decision in question, including a summary of the relevant facts and grounds. The supervisory authority with which a complaint has been lodged shall inform the complainant on the decision.

8. By derogation from paragraph 7, where a complaint is dismissed or rejected, the supervisory authority with which the complaint was lodged shall adopt the decision and notify it to the complainant and shall inform the controller thereof.

9. Where the lead supervisory authority and the supervisory authorities concerned agree to dismiss or reject parts of a complaint and to act on other parts of that complaint, a separate decision shall be adopted for each of those parts of the matter. The lead supervisory authority

shall adopt the decision for the part concerning actions in relation to the controller, shall notify it to the main establishment or single establishment of the controller or processor on the territory of its Member State and shall inform the complainant thereof, while the supervisory authority of the complainant shall adopt the decision for the part concerning dismissal or rejection of that complaint, and shall notify it to that complainant and shall inform the controller or processor thereof.

10. After being notified of the decision of the lead supervisory authority pursuant to paragraphs 7 and 9, the controller or processor shall take the necessary measures to ensure compliance with the decision as regards processing activities in the context of all its establishments in the Union. The controller or processor shall notify the measures taken for complying with the decision to the lead supervisory authority, which shall inform the other supervisory authorities concerned.

11. Where, in exceptional circumstances, a supervisory authority concerned has reasons to consider that there is an urgent need to act in order to protect the interests of data subjects, the urgency procedure referred to in Article 66 shall apply.

12. The lead supervisory authority and the other supervisory authorities concerned shall supply the information required under this Article to each other by electronic means, using a standardised format.

Article 61: Mutual assistance

1. Supervisory authorities shall provide each other with relevant information and mutual assistance in order to implement and apply this Regulation in a consistent manner, and shall put in place measures for effective cooperation with one another. Mutual assistance shall cover, in particular, information requests and supervisory measures, such as requests to carry out prior authorisations and consultations, inspections and investigations.

2. Each supervisory authority shall take all appropriate measures required to reply to a request of another supervisory authority without undue delay and no later than one month after receiving the request. Such measures may include, in particular, the transmission of relevant information on the conduct of an investigation.

3. Requests for assistance shall contain all the necessary information, including the purpose of and reasons for the request. Information exchanged shall be used only for the purpose for which it was requested.

4. The requested supervisory authority shall not refuse to comply with the request unless:

(a) it is not competent for the subject-matter of the request or for the measures it is requested to execute; or

(b) compliance with the request would infringe this Regulation or Union or Member State law to which the supervisory authority receiving the request is subject.

5. The requested supervisory authority shall inform the requesting supervisory authority of the results or, as the case may be, of the progress of the measures taken in order to respond to the request. The requested supervisory authority shall provide reasons for any refusal to comply with a request pursuant to paragraph 4.

6. Requested supervisory authorities shall, as a rule, supply the information requested by other supervisory authorities by electronic means, using a standardised format.

7. Requested supervisory authorities shall not charge a fee for any action taken by them pursuant to a request for mutual assistance. Supervisory authorities may agree on rules to indemnify each other for specific expenditure arising from the provision of mutual assistance in exceptional circumstances.

8. Where a supervisory authority does not provide the information referred to in paragraph 5 of this Article within one month of receiving the request of another supervisory authority, the requesting supervisory authority may adopt a provisional measure on the territory of its Member State in accordance with Article 55(1). In that case, the urgent need to act under Article 66(1) shall be presumed to be met and require an urgent binding decision from the Board pursuant to Article 66(2).

9. The Commission may, by means of implementing acts, specify the format and procedures for mutual assistance referred to in this Article and the arrangements for the exchange of information by electronic means between supervisory authorities, and between supervisory authorities and the Board, in particular the standardised format referred to in paragraph 6 of this Article. Those implementing acts shall be adopted in accordance with the examination procedure referred to in Article 93(2).

Article 62: Joint operations of supervisory authorities

1. The supervisory authorities shall, where appropriate, conduct joint operations including joint investigations and joint enforcement measures in which members or staff of the supervisory authorities of other Member States are involved.

2. Where the controller or processor has establishments in several Member States or where a significant number of data subjects in more than one Member State are likely to be substantially affected by processing operations, a supervisory authority of each of those Member States shall have the right to participate in joint operations. The supervisory authority which is competent pursuant to Article 56(1) or (4) shall invite the supervisory authority of each of those Member States to take part in the joint operations and shall respond without delay to the request of a supervisory authority to participate.

3. A supervisory authority may, in accordance with Member State law, and with the seconding supervisory authority's authorisation, confer powers, including investigative powers on the seconding supervisory authority's members or staff involved in joint operations or, in so far as the law of the Member State of the host supervisory authority permits, allow the seconding supervisory authority's members or staff to exercise their investigative powers in accordance with the law of the Member State of the seconding supervisory authority. Such investigative powers may be exercised only under the guidance and in the presence of members or staff of the host supervisory authority. The seconding supervisory authority's members or staff shall be subject to the Member State law of the host supervisory authority.

4. Where, in accordance with paragraph 1, staff of a seconding supervisory authority operate in another Member State, the Member State of the host supervisory authority shall assume

responsibility for their actions, including liability, for any damage caused by them during their operations, in accordance with the law of the Member State in whose territory they are operating.

5. The Member State in whose territory the damage was caused shall make good such damage under the conditions applicable to damage caused by its own staff. The Member State of the seconding supervisory authority whose staff has caused damage to any person in the territory of another Member State shall reimburse that other Member State in full any sums it has paid to the persons entitled on their behalf.

6. Without prejudice to the exercise of its rights vis-à-vis third parties and with the exception of paragraph 5, each Member State shall refrain, in the case provided for in paragraph 1, from requesting reimbursement from another Member State in relation to damage referred to in paragraph 4.

7. Where a joint operation is intended and a supervisory authority does not, within one month, comply with the obligation laid down in the second sentence of paragraph 2 of this Article, the other supervisory authorities may adopt a provisional measure on the territory of its Member State in accordance with Article 55. In that case, the urgent need to act under Article 66(1) shall be presumed to be met and require an opinion or an urgent binding decision from the Board pursuant to Article 66(2).

Section 2: Consistency

Article 63: Consistency mechanism

In order to contribute to the consistent application of this Regulation throughout the Union, the supervisory authorities shall cooperate with each other and, where relevant, with the Commission, through the consistency mechanism as set out in this Section.

Article 64: Opinion of the Board

1. The Board shall issue an opinion where a competent supervisory authority intends to adopt any of the measures below. To that end, the competent supervisory authority shall communicate the draft decision to the Board, when it:

> (a) aims to adopt a list of the processing operations subject to the requirement for a data protection impact assessment pursuant to Article 35(4);
>
> (b) concerns a matter pursuant to Article 40(7) whether a draft code of conduct or an amendment or extension to a code of conduct complies with this Regulation;
>
> (c) aims to approve the criteria for accreditation of a body pursuant to Article 41(3) or a certification body pursuant to Article 43(3);
>
> (d) aims to determine standard data protection clauses referred to in point (d) of Article 46(2) and in Article 28(8);
>
> (e) aims to authorise contractual clauses referred to in point (a) of Article 46(3); or
>
> (f) aims to approve binding corporate rules within the meaning of Article 47.

2. Any supervisory authority, the Chair of the Board or the Commission may request that any matter of general application or producing effects in more than one Member State be examined by the Board with a view to obtaining an opinion, in particular where a competent supervisory authority does not comply with the obligations for mutual assistance in accordance with Article 61 or for joint operations in accordance with Article 62.

3. In the cases referred to in paragraphs 1 and 2, the Board shall issue an opinion on the matter submitted to it provided that it has not already issued an opinion on the same matter. That opinion shall be adopted within eight weeks by simple majority of the members of the Board. That period may be extended by a further six weeks, taking into account the complexity of the subject matter. Regarding the draft decision referred to in paragraph 1 circulated to the members of the Board in accordance with paragraph 5, a member which has not objected within a reasonable period indicated by the Chair, shall be deemed to be in agreement with the draft decision.

4. Supervisory authorities and the Commission shall, without undue delay, communicate by electronic means to the Board, using a standardised format any relevant information, including as the case may be a summary of the facts, the draft decision, the grounds which make the enactment of such measure necessary, and the views of other supervisory authorities concerned.

5. The Chair of the Board shall, without undue, delay inform by electronic means:

(a) the members of the Board and the Commission of any relevant information which has been communicated to it using a standardised format. The secretariat of the Board shall, where necessary, provide translations of relevant information; and

(b) the supervisory authority referred to, as the case may be, in paragraphs 1 and 2, and the Commission of the opinion and make it public.

6. The competent supervisory authority shall not adopt its draft decision referred to in paragraph 1 within the period referred to in paragraph 3.

7. The supervisory authority referred to in paragraph 1 shall take utmost account of the opinion of the Board and shall, within two weeks after receiving the opinion, communicate to the Chair of the Board by electronic means whether it will maintain or amend its draft decision and, if any, the amended draft decision, using a standardised format.

8. Where the supervisory authority concerned informs the Chair of the Board within the period referred to in paragraph 7 of this Article that it does not intend to follow the opinion of the Board, in whole or in part, providing the relevant grounds, Article 65(1) shall apply.

Article 65: Dispute resolution by the Board

1. In order to ensure the correct and consistent application of this Regulation in individual cases, the Board shall adopt a binding decision in the following cases:

(a) where, in a case referred to in Article 60(4), a supervisory authority concerned has raised a relevant and reasoned objection to a draft decision of the lead authority or the lead authority has rejected such an objection as being not relevant or reasoned. The binding decision shall concern all the matters which are the subject of the relevant and reasoned objection, in particular whether there is an infringement of this Regulation;

(b) where there are conflicting views on which of the supervisory authorities concerned is competent for the main establishment;

(c) where a competent supervisory authority does not request the opinion of the Board in the cases referred to in Article 64(1), or does not follow the opinion of the Board issued under Article 64. In that case, any supervisory authority concerned or the Commission may communicate the matter to the Board.

2. The decision referred to in paragraph 1 shall be adopted within one month from the referral of the subject-matter by a two-thirds majority of the members of the Board. That period may be extended by a further month on account of the complexity of the subject-matter. The decision referred to in paragraph 1 shall be reasoned and addressed to the lead supervisory authority and all the supervisory authorities concerned and binding on them.

3. Where the Board has been unable to adopt a decision within the periods referred to in paragraph 2, it shall adopt its decision within two weeks following the expiration of the second month referred to in paragraph 2 by a simple majority of the members of the Board. Where the members of the Board are split, the decision shall by adopted by the vote of its Chair.

4. The supervisory authorities concerned shall not adopt a decision on the subject matter submitted to the Board under paragraph 1 during the periods referred to in paragraphs 2 and 3.

5. The Chair of the Board shall notify, without undue delay, the decision referred to in paragraph 1 to the supervisory authorities concerned. It shall inform the Commission thereof. The decision shall be published on the website of the Board without delay after the supervisory authority has notified the final decision referred to in paragraph 6.

6. The lead supervisory authority or, as the case may be, the supervisory authority with which the complaint has been lodged shall adopt its final decision on the basis of the decision referred to in paragraph 1 of this Article, without undue delay and at the latest by one month after the Board has notified its decision. The lead supervisory authority or, as the case may be, the supervisory authority with which the complaint has been lodged, shall inform the Board of the date when its final decision is notified respectively to the controller or the processor and to the data subject. The final decision of the supervisory authorities concerned shall be adopted under the terms of Article 60(7), (8) and (9). The final decision shall refer to the decision referred to in paragraph 1 of this Article and shall specify that the decision referred to in that paragraph will be published on the website of the Board in accordance with paragraph 5 of this Article. The final decision shall attach the decision referred to in paragraph 1 of this Article.

Article 66: Urgency procedure

1. In exceptional circumstances, where a supervisory authority concerned considers that there is an urgent need to act in order to protect the rights and freedoms of data subjects, it may, by way of derogation from the consistency mechanism referred to in Articles 63, 64 and 65 or the procedure referred to in Article 60, immediately adopt provisional measures intended to produce legal effects on its own territory with a specified period of validity which shall not

exceed three months. The supervisory authority shall, without delay, communicate those measures and the reasons for adopting them to the other supervisory authorities concerned, to the Board and to the Commission.

2. Where a supervisory authority has taken a measure pursuant to paragraph 1 and considers that final measures need urgently be adopted, it may request an urgent opinion or an urgent binding decision from the Board, giving reasons for requesting such opinion or decision.

3. Any supervisory authority may request an urgent opinion or an urgent binding decision, as the case may be, from the Board where a competent supervisory authority has not taken an appropriate measure in a situation where there is an urgent need to act, in order to protect the rights and freedoms of data subjects, giving reasons for requesting such opinion or decision, including for the urgent need to act.

4. By derogation from Article 64(3) and Article 65(2), an urgent opinion or an urgent binding decision referred to in paragraphs 2 and 3 of this Article shall be adopted within two weeks by simple majority of the members of the Board.

Article 67: Exchange of information

The Commission may adopt implementing acts of general scope in order to specify the arrangements for the exchange of information by electronic means between supervisory authorities, and between supervisory authorities and the Board, in particular the standardised format referred to in Article 64.

Those implementing acts shall be adopted in accordance with the examination procedure referred to in Article 93(2).

Section 3: European data protection board

Article 68: European Data Protection Board

1. The European Data Protection Board (the 'Board') is hereby established as a body of the Union and shall have legal personality.

2. The Board shall be represented by its Chair.

3. The Board shall be composed of the head of one supervisory authority of each Member State and of the European Data Protection Supervisor, or their respective representatives.

4. Where in a Member State more than one supervisory authority is responsible for monitoring the application of the provisions pursuant to this Regulation, a joint representative shall be appointed in accordance with that Member State's law.

5. The Commission shall have the right to participate in the activities and meetings of the Board without voting right. The Commission shall designate a representative. The Chair of the Board shall communicate to the Commission the activities of the Board.

6. In the cases referred to in Article 65, the European Data Protection Supervisor shall have voting rights only on decisions which concern principles and rules applicable to the Union

institutions, bodies, offices and agencies which correspond in substance to those of this Regulation.

Article 69: Independence

1. The Board shall act independently when performing its tasks or exercising its powers pursuant to Articles 70 and 71.

2. Without prejudice to requests by the Commission referred to in point (b) of Article 70(1) and in Article 70(2), the Board shall, in the performance of its tasks or the exercise of its powers, neither seek nor take instructions from anybody.

Article 70: Tasks of the Board

1. The Board shall ensure the consistent application of this Regulation. To that end, the Board shall, on its own initiative or, where relevant, at the request of the Commission, in particular:

(a) monitor and ensure the correct application of this Regulation in the cases provided for in Articles 64 and 65 without prejudice to the tasks of national supervisory authorities;

(b) advise the Commission on any issue related to the protection of personal data in the Union, including on any proposed amendment of this Regulation;

(c) advise the Commission on the format and procedures for the exchange of information between controllers, processors and supervisory authorities for binding corporate rules;

(d) issue guidelines, recommendations, and best practices on procedures for erasing links, copies or replications of personal data from publicly available communication services as referred to in Article 17(2);

(e) examine, on its own initiative, on request of one of its members or on request of the Commission, any question covering the application of this Regulation and issue guidelines, recommendations and best practices in order to encourage consistent application of this Regulation;

(f) issue guidelines, recommendations and best practices in accordance with point (e) of this paragraph for further specifying the criteria and conditions for decisions based on profiling pursuant to Article 22(2);

(g) issue guidelines, recommendations and best practices in accordance with point (e) of this paragraph for establishing the personal data breaches and determining the undue delay referred to in Article 33(1) and (2) and for the particular circumstances in which a controller or a processor is required to notify the personal data breach;

(h) issue guidelines, recommendations and best practices in accordance with point (e) of this paragraph as to the circumstances in which a personal data breach is likely to result in a high risk to the rights and freedoms of the natural persons referred to in Article 34(1).

(i) issue guidelines, recommendations and best practices in accordance with point (e) of this paragraph for the purpose of further specifying the criteria and requirements for personal data transfers based on binding corporate rules adhered to by controllers and binding corporate rules adhered to by processors and on further necessary requirements to ensure the protection of personal data of the data subjects concerned referred to in Article 47;

(j) issue guidelines, recommendations and best practices in accordance with point (e) of this paragraph for the purpose of further specifying the criteria and requirements for the personal data transfers on the basis of Article 49(1);

(k) draw up guidelines for supervisory authorities concerning the application of measures referred to in Article 58(1), (2) and (3) and the setting of administrative fines pursuant to Article 83;

(l) review the practical application of the guidelines, recommendations and best practices referred to in points (e) and (f);

(m) issue guidelines, recommendations and best practices in accordance with point (e) of this paragraph for establishing common procedures for reporting by natural persons of infringements of this Regulation pursuant to Article 54(2);

(n) encourage the drawing-up of codes of conduct and the establishment of data protection certification mechanisms and data protection seals and marks pursuant to Articles 40 and 42;

(o) carry out the accreditation of certification bodies and its periodic review pursuant to Article 43 and maintain a public register of accredited bodies pursuant to Article 43(6) and of the accredited controllers or processors established in third countries pursuant to Article 42(7);

(p) specify the requirements referred to in Article 43(3) with a view to the accreditation of certification bodies under Article 42;

(q) provide the Commission with an opinion on the certification requirements referred to in Article 43(8);

(r) provide the Commission with an opinion on the icons referred to in Article 12(7);

(s) provide the Commission with an opinion for the assessment of the adequacy of the level of protection in a third country or international organisation, including for the assessment whether a third country, a territory or one or more specified sectors within that third country, or an international organisation no longer ensures an adequate level of protection. To that end, the Commission shall provide the Board with all necessary documentation, including correspondence with the government of the third country, with regard to that third country, territory or specified sector, or with the international organisation.

(t) issue opinions on draft decisions of supervisory authorities pursuant to the consistency mechanism referred to in Article 64(1), on matters submitted pursuant to Article 64(2) and to issue binding decisions pursuant to Article 65, including in cases referred to in Article 66;

(u) promote the cooperation and the effective bilateral and multilateral exchange of information and best practices between the supervisory authorities;

(v) promote common training programmes and facilitate personnel exchanges between the supervisory authorities and, where appropriate, with the supervisory authorities of third countries or with international organisations;

(w) promote the exchange of knowledge and documentation on data protection legislation and practice with data protection supervisory authorities worldwide.

(x) issue opinions on codes of conduct drawn up at Union level pursuant to Article 40(9); and

(y) maintain a publicly accessible electronic register of decisions taken by supervisory authorities and courts on issues handled in the consistency mechanism.

2.   Where the Commission requests advice from the Board, it may indicate a time limit, taking into account the urgency of the matter.

3.   The Board shall forward its opinions, guidelines, recommendations, and best practices to the Commission and to the committee referred to in Article 93 and make them public.

4.   The Board shall, where appropriate, consult interested parties and give them the opportunity to comment within a reasonable period. The Board shall, without prejudice to Article 76, make the results of the consultation procedure publicly available.

Article 71: Reports

1.   The Board shall draw up an annual report regarding the protection of natural persons with regard to processing in the Union and, where relevant, in third countries and international organisations. The report shall be made public and be transmitted to the European Parliament, to the Council and to the Commission.

2.   The annual report shall include a review of the practical application of the guidelines, recommendations and best practices referred to in point (l) of Article 70(1) as well as of the binding decisions referred to in Article 65.

Article 72: Procedure

1.   The Board shall take decisions by a simple majority of its members, unless otherwise provided for in this Regulation.

2.   The Board shall adopt its own rules of procedure by a two-thirds majority of its members and organise its own operational arrangements.

Article 73: Chair

1.   The Board shall elect a chair and two deputy chairs from amongst its members by simple majority.

2.   The term of office of the Chair and of the deputy chairs shall be five years and be renewable once.

Article 74: Tasks of the Chair

1. The Chair shall have the following tasks:

> (a) to convene the meetings of the Board and prepare its agenda;
>
> (b) to notify decisions adopted by the Board pursuant to Article 65 to the lead supervisory authority and the supervisory authorities concerned;
>
> (c) to ensure the timely performance of the tasks of the Board, in particular in relation to the consistency mechanism referred to in Article 63.

2. The Board shall lay down the allocation of tasks between the Chair and the deputy chairs in its rules of procedure.

Article 75: Secretariat

1. The Board shall have a secretariat, which shall be provided by the European Data Protection Supervisor.

2. The secretariat shall perform its tasks exclusively under the instructions of the Chair of the Board.

3. The staff of the European Data Protection Supervisor involved in carrying out the tasks conferred on the Board by this Regulation shall be subject to separate reporting lines from the staff involved in carrying out tasks conferred on the European Data Protection Supervisor.

4. Where appropriate, the Board and the European Data Protection Supervisor shall establish and publish a Memorandum of Understanding implementing this Article, determining the terms of their cooperation, and applicable to the staff of the European Data Protection Supervisor involved in carrying out the tasks conferred on the Board by this Regulation.

5. The secretariat shall provide analytical, administrative and logistical support to the Board.

6. The secretariat shall be responsible in particular for:

> (a) the day-to-day business of the Board;
>
> (b) communication between the members of the Board, its Chair and the Commission;
>
> (c) communication with other institutions and the public;
>
> (d) the use of electronic means for the internal and external communication;
>
> (e) the translation of relevant information;
>
> (f) the preparation and follow-up of the meetings of the Board;
>
> (g) the preparation, drafting and publication of opinions, decisions on the settlement of disputes between supervisory authorities and other texts adopted by the Board.

Article 76: Confidentiality

1. The discussions of the Board shall be confidential where the Board deems it necessary, as provided for in its rules of procedure.

2.   Access to documents submitted to members of the Board, experts and representatives of third parties shall be governed by Regulation (EC) No 1049/2001 of the European Parliament and of the Council (21).

CHAPTER VIII: Remedies, liability and penalties

Article 77: Right to lodge a complaint with a supervisory authority

1.   Without prejudice to any other administrative or judicial remedy, every data subject shall have the right to lodge a complaint with a supervisory authority, in particular in the Member State of his or her habitual residence, place of work or place of the alleged infringement if the data subject considers that the processing of personal data relating to him or her infringes this Regulation.

2.   The supervisory authority with which the complaint has been lodged shall inform the complainant on the progress and the outcome of the complaint including the possibility of a judicial remedy pursuant to Article 78.

Article 78: Right to an effective judicial remedy against a supervisory authority

1.   Without prejudice to any other administrative or non-judicial remedy, each natural or legal person shall have the right to an effective judicial remedy against a legally binding decision of a supervisory authority concerning them.

2.   Without prejudice to any other administrative or non-judicial remedy, each data subject shall have the right to a an effective judicial remedy where the supervisory authority which is competent pursuant to Articles 55 and 56 does not handle a complaint or does not inform the data subject within three months on the progress or outcome of the complaint lodged pursuant to Article 77.

3.   Proceedings against a supervisory authority shall be brought before the courts of the Member State where the supervisory authority is established.

4.   Where proceedings are brought against a decision of a supervisory authority which was preceded by an opinion or a decision of the Board in the consistency mechanism, the supervisory authority shall forward that opinion or decision to the court.

Article 79: Right to an effective judicial remedy against a controller or processor

1.   Without prejudice to any available administrative or non-judicial remedy, including the right to lodge a complaint with a supervisory authority pursuant to Article 77, each data subject shall have the right to an effective judicial remedy where he or she considers that his or her rights under this Regulation have been infringed as a result of the processing of his or her personal data in non-compliance with this Regulation.

2.   Proceedings against a controller or a processor shall be brought before the courts of the Member State where the controller or processor has an establishment. Alternatively, such

proceedings may be brought before the courts of the Member State where the data subject has his or her habitual residence, unless the controller or processor is a public authority of a Member State acting in the exercise of its public powers.

Article 80: Representation of data subjects

1. The data subject shall have the right to mandate a not-for-profit body, organisation or association which has been properly constituted in accordance with the law of a Member State, has statutory objectives which are in the public interest, and is active in the field of the protection of data subjects' rights and freedoms with regard to the protection of their personal data to lodge the complaint on his or her behalf, to exercise the rights referred to in Articles 77, 78 and 79 on his or her behalf, and to exercise the right to receive compensation referred to in Article 82 on his or her behalf where provided for by Member State law.

2. Member States may provide that any body, organisation or association referred to in paragraph 1 of this Article, independently of a data subject's mandate, has the right to lodge, in that Member State, a complaint with the supervisory authority which is competent pursuant to Article 77 and to exercise the rights referred to in Articles 78 and 79 if it considers that the rights of a data subject under this Regulation have been infringed as a result of the processing.

Article 81: Suspension of proceedings

1. Where a competent court of a Member State has information on proceedings, concerning the same subject matter as regards processing by the same controller or processor, that are pending in a court in another Member State, it shall contact that court in the other Member State to confirm the existence of such proceedings.

2. Where proceedings concerning the same subject matter as regards processing of the same controller or processor are pending in a court in another Member State, any competent court other than the court first seized may suspend its proceedings.

3. Where those proceedings are pending at first instance, any court other than the court first seized may also, on the application of one of the parties, decline jurisdiction if the court first seized has jurisdiction over the actions in question and its law permits the consolidation thereof.

Article 82: Right to compensation and liability

1. Any person who has suffered material or non-material damage as a result of an infringement of this Regulation shall have the right to receive compensation from the controller or processor for the damage suffered.

2. Any controller involved in processing shall be liable for the damage caused by processing which infringes this Regulation. A processor shall be liable for the damage caused by processing only where it has not complied with obligations of this Regulation specifically directed to processors or where it has acted outside or contrary to lawful instructions of the controller.

3. A controller or processor shall be exempt from liability under paragraph 2 if it proves that it is not in any way responsible for the event giving rise to the damage.

4. Where more than one controller or processor, or both a controller and a processor, are involved in the same processing and where they are, under paragraphs 2 and 3, responsible for any damage caused by processing, each controller or processor shall be held liable for the entire damage in order to ensure effective compensation of the data subject.

5. Where a controller or processor has, in accordance with paragraph 4, paid full compensation for the damage suffered, that controller or processor shall be entitled to claim back from the other controllers or processors involved in the same processing that part of the compensation corresponding to their part of responsibility for the damage, in accordance with the conditions set out in paragraph 2.

6. Court proceedings for exercising the right to receive compensation shall be brought before the courts competent under the law of the Member State referred to in Article 79(2).

Article 83: General conditions for imposing administrative fines

1. Each supervisory authority shall ensure that the imposition of administrative fines pursuant to this Article in respect of infringements of this Regulation referred to in paragraphs 4, 5 and 6 shall in each individual case be effective, proportionate and dissuasive.

2. Administrative fines shall, depending on the circumstances of each individual case, be imposed in addition to, or instead of, measures referred to in points (a) to (h) and (j) of Article 58(2). When deciding whether to impose an administrative fine and deciding on the amount of the administrative fine in each individual case due regard shall be given to the following:

    (a) the nature, gravity and duration of the infringement taking into account the nature scope or purpose of the processing concerned as well as the number of data subjects affected and the level of damage suffered by them;

    (b) the intentional or negligent character of the infringement;

    (c) any action taken by the controller or processor to mitigate the damage suffered by data subjects;

    (d) the degree of responsibility of the controller or processor taking into account technical and organisational measures implemented by them pursuant to Articles 25 and 32;

    (e) any relevant previous infringements by the controller or processor;

    (f) the degree of cooperation with the supervisory authority, in order to remedy the infringement and mitigate the possible adverse effects of the infringement;

    (g) the categories of personal data affected by the infringement;

    (h) the manner in which the infringement became known to the supervisory authority, in particular whether, and if so to what extent, the controller or processor notified the infringement;

(i) where measures referred to in Article 58(2) have previously been ordered against the controller or processor concerned with regard to the same subject-matter, compliance with those measures;

(j) adherence to approved codes of conduct pursuant to Article 40 or approved certification mechanisms pursuant to Article 42; and

(k) any other aggravating or mitigating factor applicable to the circumstances of the case, such as financial benefits gained, or losses avoided, directly or indirectly, from the infringement.

3. If a controller or processor intentionally or negligently, for the same or linked processing operations, infringes several provisions of this Regulation, the total amount of the administrative fine shall not exceed the amount specified for the gravest infringement.

4. Infringements of the following provisions shall, in accordance with paragraph 2, be subject to administrative fines up to 10 000 000 EUR, or in the case of an undertaking, up to 2 % of the total worldwide annual turnover of the preceding financial year, whichever is higher:

(a) the obligations of the controller and the processor pursuant to Articles 8, 11, 25 to 39 and 42 and 43;

(b) the obligations of the certification body pursuant to Articles 42 and 43;

(c) the obligations of the monitoring body pursuant to Article 41(4).

5. Infringements of the following provisions shall, in accordance with paragraph 2, be subject to administrative fines up to 20 000 000 EUR, or in the case of an undertaking, up to 4 % of the total worldwide annual turnover of the preceding financial year, whichever is higher:

(a) the basic principles for processing, including conditions for consent, pursuant to Articles 5, 6, 7 and 9;

(b) the data subjects' rights pursuant to Articles 12 to 22;

(c) the transfers of personal data to a recipient in a third country or an international organisation pursuant to Articles 44 to 49;

(d) any obligations pursuant to Member State law adopted under Chapter IX;

(e) non-compliance with an order or a temporary or definitive limitation on processing or the suspension of data flows by the supervisory authority pursuant to Article 58(2) or failure to provide access in violation of Article 58(1).

6. Non-compliance with an order by the supervisory authority as referred to in Article 58(2) shall, in accordance with paragraph 2 of this Article, be subject to administrative fines up to 20 000 000 EUR, or in the case of an undertaking, up to 4 % of the total worldwide annual turnover of the preceding financial year, whichever is higher.

7. Without prejudice to the corrective powers of supervisory authorities pursuant to Article 58(2), each Member State may lay down the rules on whether and to what extent administrative fines may be imposed on public authorities and bodies established in that Member State.

8. The exercise by the supervisory authority of its powers under this Article shall be subject to appropriate procedural safeguards in accordance with Union and Member State law, including effective judicial remedy and due process.

9. Where the legal system of the Member State does not provide for administrative fines, this Article may be applied in such a manner that the fine is initiated by the competent supervisory authority and imposed by competent national courts, while ensuring that those legal remedies are effective and have an equivalent effect to the administrative fines imposed by supervisory authorities. In any event, the fines imposed shall be effective, proportionate and dissuasive. Those Member States shall notify to the Commission the provisions of their laws which they adopt pursuant to this paragraph by 25 May 2018 and, without delay, any subsequent amendment law or amendment affecting them.

Article 84: Penalties

1. Member States shall lay down the rules on other penalties applicable to infringements of this Regulation in particular for infringements which are not subject to administrative fines pursuant to Article 83, and shall take all measures necessary to ensure that they are implemented. Such penalties shall be effective, proportionate and dissuasive.

2. Each Member State shall notify to the Commission the provisions of its law which it adopts pursuant to paragraph 1, by 25 May 2018 and, without delay, any subsequent amendment affecting them.

CHAPTER IX: Provisions relating to specific processing situations

Article 85: Processing and freedom of expression and information

1. Member States shall by law reconcile the right to the protection of personal data pursuant to this Regulation with the right to freedom of expression and information, including processing for journalistic purposes and the purposes of academic, artistic or literary expression.

2. For processing carried out for journalistic purposes or the purpose of academic artistic or literary expression, Member States shall provide for exemptions or derogations from Chapter II (principles), Chapter III (rights of the data subject), Chapter IV (controller and processor), Chapter V (transfer of personal data to third countries or international organisations), Chapter VI (independent supervisory authorities), Chapter VII (cooperation and consistency) and Chapter IX (specific data processing situations) if they are necessary to reconcile the right to the protection of personal data with the freedom of expression and information.

3. Each Member State shall notify to the Commission the provisions of its law which it has adopted pursuant to paragraph 2 and, without delay, any subsequent amendment law or amendment affecting them.

Article 86: Processing and public access to official documents

Personal data in official documents held by a public authority or a public body or a private body for the performance of a task carried out in the public interest may be disclosed by the authority or body in accordance with Union or Member State law to which the public authority or body is subject in order to reconcile public access to official documents with the right to the protection of personal data pursuant to this Regulation.

Article 87: Processing of the national identification number

Member States may further determine the specific conditions for the processing of a national identification number or any other identifier of general application. In that case the national identification number or any other identifier of general application shall be used only under appropriate safeguards for the rights and freedoms of the data subject pursuant to this Regulation.

Article 88: Processing in the context of employment

1. Member States may, by law or by collective agreements, provide for more specific rules to ensure the protection of the rights and freedoms in respect of the processing of employees' personal data in the employment context, in particular for the purposes of the recruitment, the performance of the contract of employment, including discharge of obligations laid down by law or by collective agreements, management, planning and organisation of work, equality and diversity in the workplace, health and safety at work, protection of employer's or customer's property and for the purposes of the exercise and enjoyment, on an individual or collective basis, of rights and benefits related to employment, and for the purpose of the termination of the employment relationship.

2. Those rules shall include suitable and specific measures to safeguard the data subject's human dignity, legitimate interests and fundamental rights, with particular regard to the transparency of processing, the transfer of personal data within a group of undertakings, or a group of enterprises engaged in a joint economic activity and monitoring systems at the work place.

3. Each Member State shall notify to the Commission those provisions of its law which it adopts pursuant to paragraph 1, by 25 May 2018 and, without delay, any subsequent amendment affecting them.

Article 89: Safeguards and derogations relating to processing for archiving purposes in the public interest, scientific or historical research purposes or statistical purposes

1. Processing for archiving purposes in the public interest, scientific or historical research purposes or statistical purposes, shall be subject to appropriate safeguards, in accordance with this Regulation, for the rights and freedoms of the data subject. Those safeguards shall ensure that technical and organisational measures are in place in particular in order to ensure respect for the principle of data minimisation. Those measures may include pseudonymisation provided that those purposes can be fulfilled in that manner. Where those purposes can be fulfilled by further processing which does not permit or no longer permits the identification of data subjects, those purposes shall be fulfilled in that manner.

2. Where personal data are processed for scientific or historical research purposes or statistical purposes, Union or Member State law may provide for derogations from the rights referred to in Articles 15, 16, 18 and 21 subject to the conditions and safeguards referred to in paragraph 1 of this Article in so far as such rights are likely to render impossible or seriously impair the achievement of the specific purposes, and such derogations are necessary for the fulfilment of those purposes.

3. Where personal data are processed for archiving purposes in the public interest, Union or Member State law may provide for derogations from the rights referred to in Articles 15, 16, 18, 19, 20 and 21 subject to the conditions and safeguards referred to in paragraph 1 of this Article in so far as such rights are likely to render impossible or seriously impair the achievement of the specific purposes, and such derogations are necessary for the fulfilment of those purposes.

4. Where processing referred to in paragraphs 2 and 3 serves at the same time another purpose, the derogations shall apply only to processing for the purposes referred to in those paragraphs.

Article 90: Obligations of secrecy

1. Member States may adopt specific rules to set out the powers of the supervisory authorities laid down in points (e) and (f) of Article 58(1) in relation to controllers or processors that are subject, under Union or Member State law or rules established by national competent bodies, to an obligation of professional secrecy or other equivalent obligations of secrecy where this is necessary and proportionate to reconcile the right of the protection of personal data with the obligation of secrecy. Those rules shall apply only with regard to personal data which the controller or processor has received as a result of or has obtained in an activity covered by that obligation of secrecy.

2. Each Member State shall notify to the Commission the rules adopted pursuant to paragraph 1, by 25 May 2018 and, without delay, any subsequent amendment affecting them.

Article 91: Existing data protection rules of churches and religious associations

1. Where in a Member State, churches and religious associations or communities apply, at the time of entry into force of this Regulation, comprehensive rules relating to the protection of natural persons with regard to processing, such rules may continue to apply, provided that they are brought into line with this Regulation.

2. Churches and religious associations which apply comprehensive rules in accordance with paragraph 1 of this Article shall be subject to the supervision of an independent supervisory authority, which may be specific, provided that it fulfils the conditions laid down in Chapter VI of this Regulation.

CHAPTER X: Delegated acts and implementing acts

Article 92: Exercise of the delegation

1. The power to adopt delegated acts is conferred on the Commission subject to the conditions laid down in this Article.

2. The delegation of power referred to in Article 12(8) and Article 43(8) shall be conferred on the Commission for an indeterminate period of time from 24 May 2016.

3. The delegation of power referred to in Article 12(8) and Article 43(8) may be revoked at any time by the European Parliament or by the Council. A decision of revocation shall put an end to the delegation of power specified in that decision. It shall take effect the day following that of its publication in the Official Journal of the European Union or at a later date specified therein. It shall not affect the validity of any delegated acts already in force.

4. As soon as it adopts a delegated act, the Commission shall notify it simultaneously to the European Parliament and to the Council.

5. A delegated act adopted pursuant to Article 12(8) and Article 43(8) shall enter into force only if no objection has been expressed by either the European Parliament or the Council within a period of three months of notification of that act to the European Parliament and the Council or if, before the expiry of that period, the European Parliament and the Council have both informed the Commission that they will not object. That period shall be extended by three months at the initiative of the European Parliament or of the Council.

Article 93: Committee procedure

1. The Commission shall be assisted by a committee. That committee shall be a committee within the meaning of Regulation (EU) No 182/2011.

2. Where reference is made to this paragraph, Article 5 of Regulation (EU) No 182/2011 shall apply.

3. Where reference is made to this paragraph, Article 8 of Regulation (EU) No 182/2011, in conjunction with Article 5 thereof, shall apply.

CHAPTER XI: Final provisions

Article 94: Repeal of Directive 95/46/EC

1. Directive 95/46/EC is repealed with effect from 25 May 2018.

2. References to the repealed Directive shall be construed as references to this Regulation. References to the Working Party on the Protection of Individuals with regard to the Processing of Personal Data established by Article 29 of Directive 95/46/EC shall be construed as references to the European Data Protection Board established by this Regulation.

Article 95: Relationship with Directive 2002/58/EC

This Regulation shall not impose additional obligations on natural or legal persons in relation to processing in connection with the provision of publicly available electronic communications services in public communication networks in the Union in relation to matters for which they are subject to specific obligations with the same objective set out in Directive 2002/58/EC.

Article 96: Relationship with previously concluded Agreements

International agreements involving the transfer of personal data to third countries or international organisations which were concluded by Member States prior to 24 May 2016, and which comply with Union law as applicable prior to that date, shall remain in force until amended, replaced or revoked.

Article 97: Commission reports

1. By 25 May 2020 and every four years thereafter, the Commission shall submit a report on the evaluation and review of this Regulation to the European Parliament and to the Council. The reports shall be made public.

2. In the context of the evaluations and reviews referred to in paragraph 1, the Commission shall examine, in particular, the application and functioning of:

> (a) Chapter V on the transfer of personal data to third countries or international organisations with particular regard to decisions adopted pursuant to Article 45(3) of this Regulation and decisions adopted on the basis of Article 25(6) of Directive 95/46/EC;

> (b) Chapter VII on cooperation and consistency.

3. For the purpose of paragraph 1, the Commission may request information from Member States and supervisory authorities.

4. In carrying out the evaluations and reviews referred to in paragraphs 1 and 2, the Commission shall take into account the positions and findings of the European Parliament, of the Council, and of other relevant bodies or sources.

5. The Commission shall, if necessary, submit appropriate proposals to amend this Regulation, in particular taking into account of developments in information technology and in the light of the state of progress in the information society.

Article 98: Review of other Union legal acts on data protection

The Commission shall, if appropriate, submit legislative proposals with a view to amending other Union legal acts on the protection of personal data, in order to ensure uniform and consistent protection of natural persons with regard to processing. This shall in particular concern the rules relating to the protection of natural persons with regard to processing by Union institutions, bodies, offices and agencies and on the free movement of such data.

Article 99: Entry into force and application

1. This Regulation shall enter into force on the twentieth day following that of its publication in the Official Journal of the European Union.

2. It shall apply from 25 May 2018.

OECD CRYPTOGRAPHY GUIDELINES
(1997)

Summary

The unprecedented growth of communication networks and associated technologies for privacy and security created a need for an international policy framework to harmonize national policies and promote techniques to safeguard communication networks . In 1997 the OECD, an international body of 29 countries, adopted the Guidelines for Cryptography Policy. The Guidelines are a non-binding agreement identifying the policy goals that countries should implement when drawing up cryptography policies at the national and international levels.

The Guidelines set out eight principles for cryptography policy: (i) Cryptographic methods should be trustworthy in order to generate confidence in the use of information and communications systems; (ii) Users should have a right to choose any cryptographic method, subject to applicable law; (iii) Cryptographic methods should be developed in response to the needs, demands and responsibilities of individuals, businesses and governments; (iv) Technical standards, criteria and protocols for cryptographic methods should be developed and promulgated at the national and international level; (v) The fundamental rights of individuals to privacy, including secrecy of communications and protection of personal data, should be respected in national cryptography policies and in the implementation and use of cryptographic methods; (vi) National cryptography policies may allow lawful access to plain-text, or cryptographic keys, of encrypted data. These policies must respect the other principles contained in the guidelines to the greatest extent possible; (vii) Whether established by contract or legislation, the liability of individuals and entities that offer cryptographic services or hold or access cryptographic keys should be clearly stated; (viii) Governments should co-operate to co-ordinate cryptography policies. As part of this effort, governments should remove, or avoid creating in the name of cryptography policy, unjustified obstacles to trade.

During deliberations a proposal for the adoption of key escrow techniques that would enable routine law enforcement access to computer communications was put forward. The OECD member countries firmly rejected the recommendation. Reasons given disfavoring the proposal were that key escrow would undermine trust and could not be included in a nation-wide card system. In the end, member states adopted the OECD Guidelines as a coordinated effort to facilitate the smooth development of an efficient secure information infrastructure and to address issues of privacy, law enforcement, national security, technology development and commerce.

References

OECD, Guidelines for Cryptography Policy
[http://www.oecd.org/internet/ieconomy/guidelinesforcryptographypolicy.htm]

International
OECD Cryptography Guidelines

OECD, *Report on Background and Issues of Cryptography Policy* (1997)
[http://www.oecd.org/internet/ieconomy/reportonbackgroundandissuesofcryptograph
ypolicy.htm]

EPIC, *Cryptography & Liberty 2000: An International Survey of Encryption Policy*,
(EPIC 2000)
[https://www2.epic.org/reports/crypto2000/]

RECOMMENDATION OF THE COUNCIL CONCERNING GUIDELINES FOR
CRYPTOGRAPHY POLICY
27 March 1997

THE COUNCIL, HAVING REGARD TO:
* the Convention on the Organisation for Economic Co-operation and Development of
14 December 1960, in particular, articles 1 b), 1 c), 3 a) and 5 b) thereof;
* the Recommendation of the Council concerning Guidelines Governing the Protection
of Privacy and Transborder Flows of Personal Data of 23 September 1980
[C(80)58(Final)];
* the Declaration on Transborder Data Flows adopted by the Governments of OECD
Member countries on 11 April 1985 [Annex to C(85)139];
* the Recommendation of the Council concerning Guidelines for the Security of
Information Systems of 26-27 November 1992 [C(92)188/FINAL];
* the Directive [95/46/EC] of the European Parliament and of the Council of the
European Union of 24 October 1995 on the protection of individuals with regard to the
processing of personal data and on the free movement of such data;
* the Wassenaar Arrangement on Export Controls for Conventional Arms and Dual-use
Goods and Technologies agreed on 13 July 1996;
* the Regulation [(EC) 3381/94] and the Decision [94/942/PESC] of the Council of the
European Union of 19 December 1994 concerning the control of the export of dual-use
goods;
* and the Recommendation [R(95)13] of the Council of Europe of 11 September 1995
concerning problems of criminal procedural law connected with information technology;

CONSIDERING:
* that national and global information infrastructures are developing rapidly to provide
a seamless network for world-wide communications and access to data;
* that this emerging information and communications network is likely to have an
important impact on economic development and world trade;
* that the users of information technology must have trust in the security of information
and communications infrastructures, networks and systems; in the confidentiality,

integrity, and availability of data on them; and in the ability to prove the origin and receipt of data;

* that data is increasingly vulnerable to sophisticated threats to its security, and ensuring the security of data through legal, procedural and technical means is fundamentally important in order for national and international information infrastructures to reach their full potential;

RECOGNISING:

* that, as cryptography can be an effective tool for the secure use of information technology by ensuring confidentiality, integrity and availability of data and by providing authentication and

non-repudiation mechanisms for that data, it is an important component of secure information and communications networks and systems;

* that cryptography has a variety of applications related to the protection of privacy, intellectual property, business and financial information, public safety and national security, and the operation of electronic commerce, including secure anonymous payments and transactions;

* that the failure to utilise cryptographic methods can adversely affect the protection of privacy, intellectual property, business and financial information, public safety and national security and the

operation of electronic commerce because data and communications may be inadequately protected from unauthorised access, alteration, and improper use, and, therefore, users may not trust information and communications systems, networks and infrastructures;

* that the use of cryptography to ensure integrity of data, including authentication and non-repudiation mechanisms, is distinct from its use to ensure confidentiality of data, and that each of these uses presents different issues;

1. that the quality of information protection afforded by cryptography depends not only on the selected technical means, but also on good managerial, organisational and operational procedures;

AND FURTHER RECOGNISING:

* that governments have wide-ranging responsibilities, several of which are specifically implicated in the use of cryptography, including protection of privacy and facilitating information and communications systems security; encouraging economic well-being by, in part, promoting commerce; maintaining public safety; and enabling the enforcement of laws and the protection of national security;

* that although there are legitimate governmental, commercial and individual needs and uses for cryptography, it may also be used by individuals or entities for illegal activities, which can affect public safety, national security, the enforcement of laws, business

interests, consumer interests or privacy; therefore governments, together with industry and the general public, are challenged to develop balanced policies;

* that due to the inherently global nature of information and communications networks, implementation of incompatible national policies will not meet the needs of individuals, business and governments and may create obstacles to economic co-operation and development; and, therefore, national policies may require international co-ordination;

* that this Recommendation of the Council does not affect the sovereign rights of national governments and that the Guidelines contained in the Annex to this Recommendation are always subject to the requirements of national law;

On the proposal of the Committee for Information, Computer and Communications Policy;

RECOMMENDS THAT MEMBER COUNTRIES:

1. establish new, or amend existing, policies, methods, measures, practices and procedures to reflect and take into account the Principles concerning cryptography policy set forth in the Guidelines contained in the Annex to this Recommendation (hereinafter "the Guidelines"), which is an integral part hereof; in so doing, also take into account the Recommendation of the Council concerning Guidelines Governing the Protection of Privacy and Transborder Flows of Personal Data of 23 September 1980 [C(80)58(Final)] and the Recommendation of the Council concerning Guidelines for the Security of Information Systems of 26-27 November 1992 [C(92)188/FINAL];

2. consult, co-ordinate and co-operate at the national and international level in the implementation of the Guidelines;

3. act on the need for practical and operational solutions in the area of international cryptography policy by using the Guidelines as a basis for agreements on specific issues related to international cryptography policy;

4. disseminate the Guidelines throughout the public and private sectors to promote awareness of the issues and policies related to cryptography;

5. remove, or avoid creating in the name of cryptography policy, unjustified obstacles to international trade and the development of information and communications networks;

6. state clearly and make publicly available, any national controls imposed by governments relating to the use of cryptography;

7. review the Guidelines at least every five years, with a view to improving international co-operation on issues relating to cryptography policy.

ANNEX

GUIDELINES FOR CRYPTOGRAPHY POLICY

I. AIMS

The Guidelines are intended:

* to promote the use of cryptography:
* to foster confidence in information and communication infrastructures, networks and systems and the manner in which they are used;
* to help ensure the security of data, and to protect privacy, in national and global information and communications infrastructures, networks and systems;
* to promote this use of cryptography without unduly jeopardising public safety, law enforcement, and national security;
* to raise awareness of the need for compatible cryptography policies and laws, as well as the need for interoperable, portable and mobile cryptographic methods in national and global information and communications networks;
* to assist decision-makers in the public and private sectors in developing and implementing coherent national and international policies, methods, measures, practices and procedures for the effective use of cryptography;
* to promote co-operation between the public and private sectors in the development and implementation of national and international cryptography policies, methods, measures, practices and procedures;
* to facilitate international trade by promoting cost-effective, interoperable, portable and mobile cryptographic systems;
* to promote international co-operation among governments, business and research communities, and standards-making bodies in achieving co-ordinated use of cryptographic methods.

II. SCOPE

The Guidelines are primarily aimed at governments, in terms of the policy recommendations herein, but with anticipation that they will be widely read and followed by both the private and public sectors.

It is recognised that governments have separable and distinct responsibilities for the protection of information which requires security in the national interest; the Guidelines are not intended for application in these matters.

III. DEFINITIONS

For the purposes of the Guidelines:
* "Authentication" means a function for establishing the validity of a claimed identity of a user, device or another entity in an information or communications system.
* "Availability" means the property that data, information, and information and communications systems are accessible and usable on a timely basis in the required manner.
* "Confidentiality" means the property that data or information is not made available or disclosed to unauthorised individuals, entities, or processes.

* "Cryptography" means the discipline which embodies principles, means, and methods for the transformation of data in order to hide its information content, establish its authenticity, prevent its undetected modification, prevent its repudiation, and/or prevent its unauthorised use.

* "Cryptographic key" means a parameter used with a cryptographic algorithm to transform, validate, authenticate, encrypt or decrypt data.

* "Cryptographic methods" means cryptographic techniques, services, systems, products and key management systems.

* "Data" means the representation of information in a manner suitable for communication, interpretation, storage, or processing.

* "Decryption" means the inverse function of encryption.

* "Encryption" means the transformation of data by the use of cryptography to produce unintelligible data (encrypted data) to ensure its confidentiality.

* "Integrity" means the property that data or information has not been modified or altered in an unauthorised manner.

* "Interoperability" of cryptographic methods means the technical ability of multiple cryptographic methods to function together.

* "Key management system" means a system for generation, storage, distribution, revocation, deletion, archiving, certification or application of cryptographic keys.

* "Keyholder" means an individual or entity in possession or control of cryptographic keys. A keyholder is not necessarily a user of the key.

* "Law enforcement" or "enforcement of laws" refers to the enforcement of all laws, without regard to subject matter.

* "Lawful access" means access by third party individuals or entities, including governments, to plaintext, or cryptographic keys, of encrypted data, in accordance with law.

* "Mobility" of cryptographic methods only means the technical ability to function in multiple countries or information and communications infrastructures.

* "Non-repudiation" means a property achieved through cryptographic methods, which prevents an individual or entity from denying having performed a particular action related to data (such as mechanisms for non-rejection of authority (origin); for proof of obligation, intent, or commitment; or for proof of ownership).

* "Personal data" means any information relating to an identified or identifiable individual.

* "Plaintext" means intelligible data.

* "Portability" of cryptographic methods means the technical ability to be adapted and function in multiple systems.

IV. INTEGRATION

The principles in Section V of this Annex, each of which addresses an important policy concern, are interdependent and should be implemented as a whole so as to balance the various interests at stake. No principle should be implemented in isolation from the rest.

V. PRINCIPLES

1. TRUST IN CRYPTOGRAPHIC METHODS

CRYPTOGRAPHIC METHODS SHOULD BE TRUSTWORTHY IN ORDER TO GENERATE CONFIDENCE IN THE USE OF INFORMATION AND COMMUNICATIONS SYSTEMS.

Market forces should serve to build trust in reliable systems, and government regulation, licensing, and use of cryptographic methods may also encourage user trust. Evaluation of cryptographic methods, especially against market-accepted criteria, could also generate user trust.

In the interests of user trust, a contract dealing with the use of a key management system should indicate the jurisdiction whose laws apply to that system.

2. CHOICE OF CRYPTOGRAPHIC METHODS

USERS SHOULD HAVE A RIGHT TO CHOOSE ANY CRYPTOGRAPHIC METHOD, SUBJECT TO APPLICABLE LAW.

Users should have access to cryptography that meets their needs, so that they can trust in the security of information and communications systems, and the confidentiality and integrity of data on those systems. Individuals or entities who own, control, access, use or store data may have a responsibility to protect the confidentiality and integrity of such data, and may therefore be responsible for using appropriate cryptographic methods. It is expected that a variety of cryptographic methods may be needed to fulfil different data security requirements. Users of cryptography should be free, subject to applicable law, to determine the type and level of data security needed, and to select and implement appropriate cryptographic methods, including a key management system that suits their needs.

In order to protect an identified public interest, such as the protection of personal data or electronic commerce, governments may implement policies requiring cryptographic methods to achieve a sufficient level of protection.

Government controls on cryptographic methods should be no more than are essential to the discharge of government responsibilities and should respect user choice to the greatest extent possible. This principle should not be interpreted as implying that governments should initiate legislation which limits user choice.

3. MARKET DRIVEN DEVELOPMENT OF CRYPTOGRAPHIC METHODS

CRYPTOGRAPHIC METHODS SHOULD BE DEVELOPED IN RESPONSE TO THE NEEDS, DEMANDS AND RESPONSIBILITIES OF INDIVIDUALS, BUSINESSES AND GOVERNMENTS.

The development and provision of cryptographic methods should be determined by the market in an open and competitive environment. Such an approach would best ensure that solutions keep pace with changing technology, the demands of users and evolving threats to information and communications systems security. The development of international technical standards, criteria and protocols related to cryptographic methods should also be market driven. Governments should encourage and co-operate with business and the research community in the development of cryptographic methods.

4. STANDARDS FOR CRYPTOGRAPHIC METHODS

TECHNICAL STANDARDS, CRITERIA AND PROTOCOLS FOR CRYPTOGRAPHIC METHODS SHOULD BE DEVELOPED AND PROMULGATED AT THE NATIONAL AND INTERNATIONAL LEVEL.

In response to the needs of the market, internationally-recognised standards-making bodies, governments, business and other relevant experts should share information and collaborate to develop and promulgate interoperable technical standards, criteria and protocols for cryptographic methods. National standards for cryptographic methods, if any, should be consistent with international standards to facilitate global interoperability, portability and mobility. Mechanisms to evaluate conformity to such technical standards, criteria and protocols for interoperability, portability and mobility of cryptographic methods should be developed. To the extent that testing of conformity to, or evaluation of, standards may occur, the broad acceptance of such results should be encouraged.

5. PROTECTION OF PRIVACY AND PERSONAL DATA

THE FUNDAMENTAL RIGHTS OF INDIVIDUALS TO PRIVACY, INCLUDING SECRECY OF COMMUNICATIONS AND PROTECTION OF PERSONAL DATA, SHOULD BE RESPECTED IN NATIONAL CRYPTOGRAPHY POLICIES AND IN THE IMPLEMENTATION AND USE OF CRYPTOGRAPHIC METHODS.

Cryptographic methods can be a valuable tool for the protection of privacy, including both the confidentiality of data and communications and the protection of the identity of individuals. Cryptographic methods also offer new opportunities to minimise the collection of personal data, by enabling secure but anonymous payments, transactions and interactions. At the same time, cryptographic methods to ensure the integrity of data in electronic transactions raise privacy implications. These implications, which include the collection of personal data and the creation of systems for personal identification, should be considered and explained, and, where appropriate, privacy safeguards should be established.

The OECD Guidelines for the Protection of Privacy and Transborder Flows of Personal Data provide general guidance concerning the collection and management of personal information, and should be applied in concert with relevant national law when implementing cryptographic methods.

6. LAWFUL ACCESS

NATIONAL CRYPTOGRAPHY POLICIES MAY ALLOW LAWFUL ACCESS TO PLAINTEXT, OR CRYPTOGRAPHIC KEYS, OF ENCRYPTED DATA. THESE POLICIES MUST RESPECT THE OTHER PRINCIPLES CONTAINED IN THE GUIDELINES TO THE GREATEST EXTENT POSSIBLE.

If considering policies on cryptographic methods that provide for lawful access, governments should carefully weigh the benefits, including the benefits for public safety, law enforcement and national security, as well as the risks of misuse, the additional expense of any supporting infrastructure, the prospects of technical failure, and other costs. This principle should not be interpreted as implying that governments should, or should not, initiate legislation that would allow lawful access.

Where access to the plaintext, or cryptographic keys, of encrypted data is requested under lawful process, the individual or entity requesting access must have a legal right to possession of the plaintext, and once obtained the data must only be used for lawful purposes. The process through which lawful access is obtained should be recorded, so that the disclosure of the cryptographic keys or the data can be audited or reviewed in accordance with national law. Where lawful access is requested and obtained, such access should be granted within designated time limits appropriate to the circumstances. The conditions of lawful access should be stated clearly and published in a way that they are easily available to users, keyholders and providers of cryptographic methods.

Key management systems could provide a basis for a possible solution which could balance the interest of users and law enforcement authorities; these techniques could also be used to recover data, when keys are lost. Processes for lawful access to cryptographic keys must recognise the distinction between keys which are used to protect confidentiality and keys which are used for other purposes only. A cryptographic key that provides for identity or integrity only (as distinct from a cryptographic key that verifies identity or integrity only) should not be made available without the consent of the individual or entity in lawful possession of that key.

7. LIABILITY

WHETHER ESTABLISHED BY CONTRACT OR LEGISLATION, THE LIABILITY OF INDIVIDUALS AND ENTITIES THAT OFFER CRYPTOGRAPHIC SERVICES OR HOLD OR ACCESS CRYPTOGRAPHIC KEYS SHOULD BE CLEARLY STATED.

The liability of any individual or entity, including a government entity, that offers cryptographic services or holds or has access to cryptographic keys, should be made clear by contract or where appropriate by national legislation or international agreement. The liability of users for misuse of their own keys should also be made clear. A keyholder should not be held liable for providing cryptographic keys or plaintext of encrypted data in accordance with lawful access. The party that obtains lawful access should be liable for misuse of cryptographic keys or plaintext that it has obtained.

8. INTERNATIONAL CO-OPERATION

GOVERNMENTS SHOULD CO-OPERATE TO CO-ORDINATE CRYPTOGRAPHY POLICIES. AS PART OF THIS EFFORT, GOVERNMENTS SHOULD REMOVE, OR AVOID CREATING IN THE NAME OF CRYPTOGRAPHY POLICY, UNJUSTIFIED OBSTACLES TO TRADE.

In order to promote the broad international acceptance of cryptography and enable the full potential of the national and global information and communications networks, cryptography policies adopted by a country should be co-ordinated as much as possible with similar policies of other countries. To that end, the Guidelines should be used for national policy formulation.

If developed, national key management systems must, where appropriate, allow for international use of cryptography.

Lawful access across national borders may be achieved through bilateral and multilateral co-operation and agreement.

No government should impede the free flow of encrypted data passing through its jurisdiction merely on the basis of cryptography policy. In order to promote international trade, governments should avoid developing cryptography policies and practices which create unjustified obstacles to global electronic commerce. Governments should avoid creating unjustified obstacles to international availability of cryptographic methods.

GENERAL AGREEMENT ON TRADE IN SERVICES (1994) [EXCERPT]

Reference

> WTO | Legal Texts – The WTO Agreements
> [http://www.wto.org/english/docs_e/legal_e/final_e.htm]

Article XIV General Exceptions

Subject to the requirement that such measures are not applied in a manner which would constitute a means of arbitrary or unjustifiable discrimination between countries where like conditions prevail, or a disguised restriction on trade in services, nothing in this Agreement shall be construed to prevent the adoption or enforcement by any Member of measures:

(a) necessary to protect public morals or to maintain public order;[1]

(b) necessary to protect human, animal or plant life or health;

(c) necessary to secure compliance with laws or regulations which are not inconsistent with the provisions of this Agreement including those relating to:

(i) the prevention of deceptive and fraudulent practices or to deal with the effects of a default on services contracts;

(ii) the protection of the privacy of individuals in relation to the processing and dissemination of personal data and the protection of confidentiality of individual records and accounts;

(iii) safety;

(d) inconsistent with Article XVII, provided that the difference in treatment is aimed at ensuring the equitable or effective [2]imposition or collection of direct taxes in respect of services or service suppliers of other Members;

---

[1] The public order exception may be invoked only where a genuine and sufficiently serious threat is posed to one of the fundamental interests of society.

[2] Measures that are aimed at ensuring the equitable or effective imposition or collection of direct taxes include measures taken by a Member under its taxation system which:

(i) apply to non-resident service suppliers in recognition of the fact that the tax obligation of non-residents is determined with respect to taxable items sourced or located in the Member's territory; or

(ii) apply to non-residents in order to ensure the imposition or collection of taxes in the Member's territory; or

(iii) apply to non-residents or residents in order to prevent the avoidance or evasion of taxes, including compliance measures; or

(iv) apply to consumers of services supplied in or from the territory of another Member in order to ensure the imposition or collection of taxes on such consumers derived from sources in the Member's territory; or

(v) distinguish service suppliers subject to tax on worldwide taxable items from other service suppliers, in recognition of the difference in the nature of the tax base between them; or

(e) inconsistent with Article II, provided that the difference in treatment is the result of an agreement on the avoidance of double taxation or provisions on the avoidance of double taxation in any other international agreement or arrangement by which the Member is bound.

(vi) determine, allocate or apportion income, profit, gain, loss, deduction or credit of resident persons or branches, or between related persons or branches of the same person, in order to safeguard the Member's tax base.

Tax terms or concepts in paragraph (d) of Article XIV and in this footnote are determined according to tax definitions and concepts, or equivalent or similar definitions and concepts, under the domestic law of the Member taking the measure.

EUROPEAN UNION DIRECTIVE ON PRIVACY AND ELECTRONIC COMMUNICATIONS (2002)

Reference

The European Union: Official Journal of the European Communities 31.7.2002 L 201/44
[http://eur-lex.europa.eu/legal-content/EN/TXT/HTML/?uri=CELEX:32002L0058&from=EN]

DIRECTIVE 2002/58/EC OF THE EUROPEAN PARLIAMENT
AND OF THE COUNCIL
of 12 July 2002
concerning the processing of personal data and the protection of
privacy in the electronic communications sector
(Directive on privacy and electronic communications)

THE EUROPEAN PARLIAMENT AND THE COUNCIL OF THE EUROPEAN UNION,

Having regard to the Treaty establishing the European Community, and in particular Article 95 thereof,

Having regard to the proposal from the Commission[1],

Having regard to the opinion of the Economic and Social Committee[2],

Having consulted the Committee of the Regions,

Acting in accordance with the procedure laid down in Article 251 of the Treaty (3),

Whereas:

(1) Directive 95/46/EC of the European Parliament and of the Council of 24 October 1995 on the protection of individuals with regard to the processing of personal data and on the free movement of such data (4) requires Member States to ensure the rights and freedoms of natural persons with regard to the processing of personal data, and in particular their right to privacy, in order to ensure the free flow of personal data in the Community.

(2) This Directive seeks to respect the fundamental rights and observes the principles recognised in particular by the Charter of fundamental rights of the European Union. In particular, this Directive seeks to ensure full respect for the rights set out in Articles 7 and 8 of that Charter.

(3) Confidentiality of communications is guaranteed in accordance with the international instruments relating to human rights, in particular the European Convention for the Protection of Human Rights and Fundamental Freedoms, and the constitutions of the Member States.

(4) Directive 97/66/EC of the European Parliament and of the Council of 15 December 1997 concerning the processing of personal data and the protection of privacy in the telecommunications

---

[1] (1) OJ L 178, 17.7.2000, p. 1.

[2] (2) OJ L 91, 7.4.1999, p.10.

sector (5) translated the principles set out in Directive 95/46/EC into specific rules for the telecommunications sector. Directive 97/66/EC has to be adapted to developments in the markets and technologies for electronic communications services in order to provide an equal level of protection of personal data and privacy for users of publicly available electronic communications services, regardless of the technologies used. That Directive should therefore be repealed and replaced by this Directive.

(5) New advanced digital technologies are currently being introduced in public communications networks in the Community, which give rise to specific requirements concerning the protection of personal data and privacy of the user. The development of the information society is characterised by the introduction of new electronic communications services. Access to digital mobile networks has become available and affordable for a large public. These digital networks have large capacities and possibilities for processing personal data. The successful cross-border development of these services is partly dependent on the confidence of users that their privacy will not be at risk.

(6) The Internet is overturning traditional market structures by providing a common, global infrastructure for the delivery of a wide range of electronic communications services. Publicly available electronic communications services over the Internet open new possibilities for users but also new risks for their personal data and privacy.

(7) In the case of public communications networks, specific legal, regulatory and technical provisions should be made in order to protect fundamental rights and freedoms of natural persons and legitimate interests of legal persons, in particular with regard to the increasing capacity for automated storage and processing of data relating to subscribers and users.

(8) Legal, regulatory and technical provisions adopted by the Member States concerning the protection of personal data, privacy and the legitimate interest of legal persons, in the electronic communication sector, should be harmonised in order to avoid obstacles to the internal market for electronic communication in accordance with Article 14 of the Treaty. Harmonisation should be limited to requirements necessary to guarantee that the promotion and development of new electronic communications services and networks between Member States are not hindered. 31.7.2002 L 201/37 Official Journal of the European Communities EN (1) OJ C 365 E, 19.12.2000, p. 223. (2) OJ C 123, 25.4.2001, p. 53. (3) Opinion of the European Parliament of 13 November 2001 (not yet published in the Official Journal), Council Common Position of 28 January 2002 (OJ C 113 E, 14.5.2002, p. 39) and Decision of the European Parliament of 30 May 2002 (not yet published in the Official Journal). Council Decision of 25 June 2002. (4) OJ L 281, 23.11.1995, p. 31. (5) OJ L 24, 30.1.1998, p. 1.

(9) The Member States, providers and users concerned, together with the competent Community bodies, should cooperate in introducing and developing the relevant technologies where this is necessary to apply the guarantees provided for by this Directive and taking particular account of the objectives of minimising the processing of personal data and of using anonymous or pseudonymous data where possible.

(10) In the electronic communications sector, Directive 95/ 46/EC applies in particular to all matters concerning protection of fundamental rights and freedoms, which are not specifically covered by

the provisions of this Directive, including the obligations on the controller and the rights of individuals. Directive 95/46/EC applies to non-public communications services.

(11) Like Directive 95/46/EC, this Directive does not address issues of protection of fundamental rights and freedoms related to activities which are not governed by Community law. Therefore it does not alter the existing balance between the individual's right to privacy and the possibility for Member States to take the measures referred to in Article 15(1) of this Directive, necessary for the protection of public security, defence, State security (including the economic well-being of the State when the activities relate to State security matters) and the enforcement of criminal law. Consequently, this Directive does not affect the ability of Member States to carry out lawful interception of electronic communications, or take other measures, if necessary for any of these purposes and in accordance with the European Convention for the Protection of Human Rights and Fundamental Freedoms, as interpreted by the rulings of the European Court of Human Rights. Such measures must be appropriate, strictly proportionate to the intended purpose and necessary within a democratic society and should be subject to adequate safeguards in accordance with the European Convention for the Protection of Human Rights and Fundamental Freedoms.

(12) Subscribers to a publicly available electronic communications service may be natural or legal persons. By supplementing Directive 95/46/EC, this Directive is aimed at protecting the fundamental rights of natural persons and particularly their right to privacy, as well as the legitimate interests of legal persons. This Directive does not entail an obligation for Member States to extend the application of Directive 95/46/EC to the protection of the legitimate interests of legal persons, which is ensured within the framework of the applicable Community and national legislation.

(13) The contractual relation between a subscriber and a service provider may entail a periodic or a one-off payment for the service provided or to be provided. Prepaid cards are also considered as a contract.

(14) Location data may refer to the latitude, longitude and altitude of the user's terminal equipment, to the direction of travel, to the level of accuracy of the location information, to the identification of the network cell in which the terminal equipment is located at a certain point in time and to the time the location information was recorded.

(15) A communication may include any naming, numbering or addressing information provided by the sender of a communication or the user of a connection to carry out the communication. Traffic data may include any translation of this information by the network over which the communication is transmitted for the purpose of carrying out the transmission. Traffic data may, inter alia, consist of data referring to the routing, duration, time or volume of a communication, to the protocol used, to the location of the terminal equipment of the sender or recipient, to the network on which the communication originates or terminates, to the beginning, end or duration of a connection. They may also consist of the format in which the communication is conveyed by the network.

(16) Information that is part of a broadcasting service provided over a public communications network is intended for a potentially unlimited audience and does not constitute a communication in the sense of this Directive. However, in cases where the individual subscriber or user receiving

such information can be identified, for example with video-on-demand services, the information conveyed is covered within the meaning of a communication for the purposes of this Directive.

(17) For the purposes of this Directive, consent of a user or subscriber, regardless of whether the latter is a natural or a legal person, should have the same meaning as the data subject's consent as defined and further specified in Directive 95/46/EC. Consent may be given by any appropriate method enabling a freely given specific and informed indication of the user's wishes, including by ticking a box when visiting an Internet website.

(18) Value added services may, for example, consist of advice on least expensive tariff packages, route guidance, traffic information, weather forecasts and tourist information.

(19) The application of certain requirements relating to presentation and restriction of calling and connected line identification and to automatic call forwarding to subscriber lines connected to analogue exchanges should not be made mandatory in specific cases where such application would prove to be technically impossible or would require a disproportionate economic effort. It is important for interested parties to be informed of such cases and the Member States should therefore notify them to the Commission.

(20) Service providers should take appropriate measures to safeguard the security of their services, if necessary in conjunction with the provider of the network, and inform subscribers of any special risks of a breach of the security of the network. Such risks may especially occur for electronic communications services over an open network such as the Internet or analogue mobile telephony. It is particularly important for subscribers and users of such services to be fully informed by their service provider of the existing security risks which lie outside the scope of possible remedies by the service provider. Service providers who offer publicly available electronic communications services over the Internet should inform users and subscribers of measures they can take to protect the security of their communications for instance by using specific types of software or encryption technologies. The requirement to inform subscribers of particular security risks does not discharge a service provider from the obligation to take, at its own costs, appropriate and immediate measures to remedy any new, unforeseen security risks and restore the normal security level of the service. The provision of information about security risks to the subscriber should be free of charge except for any nominal costs which the subscriber may incur while receiving or collecting the information, for instance by downloading an electronic mail message. Security is appraised in the light of Article 17 of Directive 95/46/EC.

(21) Measures should be taken to prevent unauthorised access to communications in order to protect the confidentiality of communications, including both the contents and any data related to such communications, by means of public communications networks and publicly available electronic communications services. National legislation in some Member States only prohibits intentional unauthorised access to communications.

(22) The prohibition of storage of communications and the related traffic data by persons other than the users or without their consent is not intended to prohibit any automatic, intermediate and transient storage of this information in so far as this takes place for the sole purpose of carrying out the transmission in the electronic communications network and provided that the information is not

stored for any period longer than is necessary for the transmission and for traffic management purposes, and that during the period of storage the confidentiality remains guaranteed. Where this is necessary for making more efficient the onward transmission of any publicly accessible information to other recipients of the service upon their request, this Directive should not prevent such information from being further stored, provided that this information would in any case be accessible to the public without restriction and that any data referring to the individual subscribers or users requesting such information are erased.

(23) Confidentiality of communications should also be ensured in the course of lawful business practice. Where necessary and legally authorised, communications can be recorded for the purpose of providing evidence of a commercial transaction. Directive 95/46/EC applies to such processing. Parties to the communications should be informed prior to the recording about the recording, its purpose and the duration of its storage. The recorded communication should be erased as soon as possible and in any case at the latest by the end of the period during which the transaction can be lawfully challenged.

(24) Terminal equipment of users of electronic communications networks and any information stored on such equipment are part of the private sphere of the users requiring protection under the European Convention for the Protection of Human Rights and Fundamental Freedoms. So-called spyware, web bugs, hidden identifiers and other similar devices can enter the user's terminal without their knowledge in order to gain access to information, to store hidden information or to trace the activities of the user and may seriously intrude upon the privacy of these users. The use of such devices should be allowed only for legitimate purposes, with the knowledge of the users concerned.

(25) However, such devices, for instance so-called 'cookies', can be a legitimate and useful tool, for example, in analysing the effectiveness of website design and advertising, and in verifying the identity of users engaged in on-line transactions. Where such devices, for instance cookies, are intended for a legitimate purpose, such as to facilitate the provision of information society services, their use should be allowed on condition that users are provided with clear and precise information in accordance with Directive 95/46/EC about the purposes of cookies or similar devices so as to ensure that users are made aware of information being placed on the terminal equipment they are using. Users should have the opportunity to refuse to have a cookie or similar device stored on their terminal equipment. This is particularly important where users other than the original user have access to the terminal equipment and thereby to any data containing privacy-sensitive information stored on such equipment. Information and the right to refuse may be offered once for the use of various devices to be installed on the user's terminal equipment during the same connection and also covering any further use that may be made of those devices during subsequent connections. The methods for giving information, offering a right to refuse or requesting consent should be made as userfriendly as possible. Access to specific website content may still be made conditional on the well-informed acceptance of a cookie or similar device, if it is used for a legitimate purpose.

(26) The data relating to subscribers processed within electronic communications networks to establish connections and to transmit information contain information on the private life of natural

persons and concern the right to respect for their correspondence or concern the legitimate interests of legal persons. Such data may only be stored to the extent that is necessary for the provision of the service for the purpose of billing and for interconnection payments, and for a limited time. Any further processing of such data which the provider of the publicly available electronic communications services may want to perform, for the marketing of electronic communications services or for the provision of value added services, may only be allowed if the subscriber has agreed to this on the basis of accurate and full information given by the provider of the publicly available electronic communications services about the types of further processing it intends to perform and about the subscriber's right not to give or to withdraw his/her consent to such processing. Traffic data used for marketing communications services or for the provision of value added services should also be erased or made anonymous after the provision of the service. Service providers should always keep subscribers informed of the types of data they are processing and the purposes and duration for which this is done.

(27) The exact moment of the completion of the transmission of a communication, after which traffic data should be erased except for billing purposes, may depend on the type of electronic communications service that is provided. For instance for a voice telephony call the transmission will be completed as soon as either of the users terminates the connection. For electronic mail the transmission is completed as soon as the addressee collects the message, typically from the server of his service provider.

(28) The obligation to erase traffic data or to make such data anonymous when it is no longer needed for the purpose of the transmission of a communication does not conflict with such procedures on the Internet as the caching in the domain name system of IP addresses or the caching of IP addresses to physical address bindings or the use of log-in information to control the right of access to networks or services.

(29) The service provider may process traffic data relating to subscribers and users where necessary in individual cases in order to detect technical failure or errors in the transmission of communications. Traffic data necessary for billing purposes may also be processed by the provider in order to detect and stop fraud consisting of unpaid use of the electronic communications service.

(30) Systems for the provision of electronic communications networks and services should be designed to limit the amount of personal data necessary to a strict minimum. Any activities related to the provision of the electronic communications service that go beyond the transmission of a communication and the billing thereof should be based on aggregated, traffic data that cannot be related to subscribers or users. Where such activities cannot be based on aggregated data, they should be considered as value added services for which the consent of the subscriber is required.

(31) Whether the consent to be obtained for the processing of personal data with a view to providing a particular value added service should be that of the user or of the subscriber, will depend on the data to be processed and on the type of service to be provided and on whether it is technically, procedurally and contractually possible to distinguish the individual using an electronic communications service from the legal or natural person having subscribed to it.

(32) Where the provider of an electronic communications service or of a value added service subcontracts the processing of personal data necessary for the provision of these services to another entity, such subcontracting and subsequent data processing should be in full compliance with the requirements regarding controllers and processors of personal data as set out in Directive 95/46/EC. Where the provision of a value added service requires that traffic or location data are forwarded from an electronic communications service provider to a provider of value added services, the subscribers or users to whom the data are related should also be fully informed of this forwarding before giving their consent for the processing of the data.

(33) The introduction of itemised bills has improved the possibilities for the subscriber to check the accuracy of the fees charged by the service provider but, at the same time, it may jeopardise the privacy of the users of publicly available electronic communications services. Therefore, in order to preserve the privacy of the user, Member States should encourage the development of electronic communication service options such as alternative payment facilities which allow anonymous or strictly private access to publicly available electronic communications services, for example calling cards and facilities for payment by credit card. To the same end, Member States may ask the operators to offer their subscribers a different type of detailed bill in which a certain number of digits of the called number have been deleted.

(34) It is necessary, as regards calling line identification, to protect the right of the calling party to withhold the presentation of the identification of the line from which the call is being made and the right of the called party to reject calls from unidentified lines. There is justification for overriding the elimination of calling line identification presentation in specific cases. Certain subscribers, in particular help lines and similar organisations, have an interest in guaranteeing the anonymity of their callers. It is necessary, as regards connected line identification, to protect the right and the legitimate interest of the called party to withhold the presentation of the identification of the line to which the calling party is actually connected, in particular in the case of forwarded calls. The providers of publicly available electronic communications services should inform their subscribers of the existence of calling and connected line identification in the network and of all services which are offered on the basis of calling and connected line identification as well as the privacy options which are available. This will allow the subscribers to make an informed choice about the privacy facilities they may want to use. The privacy options which are offered on a per-line basis do not necessarily have to be available as an automatic network service but may be obtainable through a simple request to the provider of the publicly available electronic communications service.

(35) In digital mobile networks, location data giving the geographic position of the terminal equipment of the mobile user are processed to enable the transmission of communications. Such data are traffic data covered by Article 6 of this Directive. However, in addition, digital mobile networks may have the capacity to process location data which are more precise than is necessary for the transmission of communications and which are used for the provision of value added services such as services providing individualised traffic information and guidance to drivers. The processing of such data for value added services should only be allowed where subscribers have

given their consent. Even in cases where subscribers have given their consent, they should have a simple means to temporarily deny the processing of location data, free of charge.

(36) Member States may restrict the users' and subscribers' rights to privacy with regard to calling line identification where this is necessary to trace nuisance calls and with regard to calling line identification and location data where this is necessary to allow emergency services to carry out their tasks as effectively as possible. For these purposes, Member States may adopt specific provisions to entitle providers of electronic communications services to provide access to calling line identification and location data without the prior consent of the users or subscribers concerned.

(37) Safeguards should be provided for subscribers against the nuisance which may be caused by automatic call forwarding by others. Moreover, in such cases, it must be possible for subscribers to stop the forwarded calls being passed on to their terminals by simple request to the provider of the publicly available electronic communications service.

(38) Directories of subscribers to electronic communications services are widely distributed and public. The right to privacy of natural persons and the legitimate interest of legal persons require that subscribers are able to determine whether their personal data are published in a directory and if so, which. Providers of public directories should inform the subscribers to be included in such directories of the purposes of the directory and of any particular usage which may be made of electronic versions of public directories especially through search functions embedded in the software, such as reverse search functions enabling users of the directory to discover the name and address of the subscriber on the basis of a telephone number only.

(39) The obligation to inform subscribers of the purpose(s) of public directories in which their personal data are to be included should be imposed on the party collecting the data for such inclusion. Where the data may be transmitted to one or more third parties, the subscriber should be informed of this possibility and of the recipient or the categories of possible recipients. Any transmission should be subject to the condition that the data may not be used for other purposes than those for which they were collected. If the party collecting the data from the subscriber or any third party to whom the data have been transmitted wishes to use the data for an additional purpose, the renewed consent of the subscriber is to be obtained either by the initial party collecting the data or by the third party to whom the data have been transmitted.

(40) Safeguards should be provided for subscribers against intrusion of their privacy by unsolicited communications for direct marketing purposes in particular by means of automated calling machines, telefaxes, and e-mails, including SMS messages. These forms of unsolicited commercial communications may on the one hand be relatively easy and cheap to send and on the other may impose a burden and/or cost on the recipient. Moreover, in some cases their volume may also cause difficulties for electronic communications networks and terminal equipment. For such forms of unsolicited communications for direct marketing, it is justified to require that prior explicit consent of the recipients is obtained before such communications are addressed to them. The single market requires a harmonised approach to ensure simple, Community-wide rules for businesses and users.

(41) Within the context of an existing customer relationship, it is reasonable to allow the use of electronic contact details for the offering of similar products or services, but only by the same

company that has obtained the electronic contact details in accordance with Directive 95/46/EC. When electronic contact details are obtained, the customer should be informed about their further use for direct marketing in a clear and distinct manner, and be given the opportunity to refuse such usage. This opportunity should continue to be offered with each subsequent direct marketing message, free of charge, except for any costs for the transmission of this refusal.

(42) Other forms of direct marketing that are more costly for the sender and impose no financial costs on subscribers and users, such as person-to-person voice telephony calls, may justify the maintenance of a system giving subscribers or users the possibility to indicate that they do not want to receive such calls. Nevertheless, in order not to decrease existing levels of privacy protection, Member States should be entitled to uphold national systems, only allowing such calls to subscribers and users who have given their prior consent.

(43) To facilitate effective enforcement of Community rules on unsolicited messages for direct marketing, it is necessary to prohibit the use of false identities or false return addresses or numbers while sending unsolicited messages for direct marketing purposes.

(44) Certain electronic mail systems allow subscribers to view the sender and subject line of an electronic mail, and also to delete the message, without having to download the rest of the electronic mail's content or any attachments, thereby reducing costs which could arise from downloading unsolicited electronic mails or attachments. These arrangements may continue to be useful in certain cases as an additional tool to the general obligations established in this Directive.

(45) This Directive is without prejudice to the arrangements which Member States make to protect the legitimate interests of legal persons with regard to unsolicited communications for direct marketing purposes. Where Member States establish an opt-out register for such communications to legal persons, mostly business users, the provisions of Article 7 of Directive 2000/31/EC of the European Parliament and of the Council of 8 June 2000 on certain legal aspects of information society services, in particular electronic commerce, in the internal market (Directive on electronic commerce) (1) are fully applicable.

(46) The functionalities for the provision of electronic communications services may be integrated in the network or in any part of the terminal equipment of the user, including the software. The protection of the personal data and the privacy of the user of publicly available electronic communications services should be independent of the configuration of the various components necessary to provide the service and of the distribution of the necessary functionalities between these components. Directive 95/46/EC covers any form of processing of personal data regardless of the technology used. The existence of specific rules for electronic communications services alongside general rules for other components necessary for the provision of such services may not facilitate the protection of personal data and privacy in a technologically neutral way. It may therefore be necessary to adopt measures requiring manufacturers of certain types of equipment used for electronic communications services to construct their product in such a way as to incorporate safeguards to ensure that the personal data and privacy of the user and subscriber are protected. The adoption of such measures in accordance with Directive 1999/5/EC of the European Parliament and of the Council of 9 March 1999 on radio equipment and telecommunications

terminal equipment and the mutual recognition of their conformity (2) will ensure that the introduction of technical features of electronic communication equipment including software for data protection purposes is harmonised in order to be compatible with the implementation of the internal market.

(47) Where the rights of the users and subscribers are not respected, national legislation should provide for judicial remedies. Penalties should be imposed on any person, whether governed by private or public law, who fails to comply with the national measures taken under this Directive.

(48) It is useful, in the field of application of this Directive, to draw on the experience of the Working Party on the Protection of Individuals with regard to the Processing of Personal Data composed of representatives of the supervisory authorities of the Member States, set up by Article 29 of Directive 95/46/EC.

(49) To facilitate compliance with the provisions of this Directive, certain specific arrangements are needed for processing of data already under way on the date that national implementing legislation pursuant to this Directive enters into force,

HAVE ADOPTED THIS DIRECTIVE:

Article 1 - Scope and aim

1. This Directive harmonises the provisions of the Member States required to ensure an equivalent level of protection of fundamental rights and freedoms, and in particular the right to privacy, with respect to the processing of personal data in the electronic communication sector and to ensure the free movement of such data and of electronic communication equipment and services in the Community.

2. The provisions of this Directive particularise and complement Directive 95/46/EC for the purposes mentioned in paragraph 1. Moreover, they provide for protection of the legitimate interests of subscribers who are legal persons. 3. This Directive shall not apply to activities which fall outside the scope of the Treaty establishing the European Community, such as those covered by Titles V and VI of the Treaty on European Union, and in any case to activities concerning public security, defence, State security (including the economic well-being of the State when the activities relate to State security matters) and the activities of the State in areas of criminal law.

Article 2 - Definitions

Save as otherwise provided, the definitions in Directive 95/46/ EC and in Directive 2002/21/EC of the European Parliament and of the Council of 7 March 2002 on a common regulatory framework for electronic communications networks and services (Framework Directive) (1) shall apply. The following definitions shall also apply:

(a) 'user' means any natural person using a publicly available electronic communications service, for private or business purposes, without necessarily having subscribed to this service;

(b) 'traffic data' means any data processed for the purpose of the conveyance of a communication on an electronic communications network or for the billing thereof;

(c) 'location data' means any data processed in an electronic communications network, indicating the geographic position of the terminal equipment of a user of a publicly available electronic communications service;

(d) 'communication' means any information exchanged or conveyed between a finite number of parties by means of a publicly available electronic communications service. This does not include any information conveyed as part of a broadcasting service to the public over an electronic communications network except to the extent that the information can be related to the identifiable subscriber or user receiving the information;

(e) 'call' means a connection established by means of a publicly available telephone service allowing two-way communication in real time;

(f) 'consent' by a user or subscriber corresponds to the data subject's consent in Directive 95/46/EC;

(g) 'value added service' means any service which requires the processing of traffic data or location data other than traffic data beyond what is necessary for the transmission of a communication or the billing thereof;

(h) 'electronic mail' means any text, voice, sound or image message sent over a public communications network which can be stored in the network or in the recipient's terminal equipment until it is collected by the recipient.

Article 3 - Services concerned

1. This Directive shall apply to the processing of personal data in connection with the provision of publicly available electronic communications services in public communications networks in the Community. 2. Articles 8, 10 and 11 shall apply to subscriber lines connected to digital exchanges and, where technically possible and if it does not require a disproportionate economic effort, to subscriber lines connected to analogue exchanges. 3. Cases where it would be technically impossible or require a disproportionate economic effort to fulfil the requirements of Articles 8, 10 and 11 shall be notified to the Commission by the Member States.

Article 4 - Security

1. The provider of a publicly available electronic communications service must take appropriate technical and organisational measures to safeguard security of its services, if necessary in conjunction with the provider of the public communications network with respect to network security. Having regard to the state of the art and the cost of their implementation, these measures shall ensure a level of security appropriate to the risk presented. 2. In case of a particular risk of a breach of the security of the network, the provider of a publicly available electronic communications service must inform the subscribers concerning such risk and, where the risk lies outside the scope of the measures to be taken by the service provider, of any possible remedies, including an indication of the likely costs involved.

International
EU Directive on Privacy and Electronic Communications

Article 5 - Confidentiality of the communications

1. Member States shall ensure the confidentiality of communications and the related traffic data by means of a public communications network and publicly available electronic communications services, through national legislation. In particular, they shall prohibit listening, tapping, storage or other kinds of interception or surveillance of communications and the related traffic data by persons other than users, without the consent of the users concerned, except when legally authorised to do so in accordance with Article 15(1). This paragraph shall not prevent technical storage which is necessary for the conveyance of a communication without prejudice to the principle of confidentiality.

2. Paragraph 1 shall not affect any legally authorised recording of communications and the related traffic data when carried out in the course of lawful business practice for the purpose of providing evidence of a commercial transaction or of any other business communication.

3. Member States shall ensure that the use of electronic communications networks to store information or to gain access to information stored in the terminal equipment of a subscriber or user is only allowed on condition that the subscriber or user concerned is provided with clear and comprehensive information in accordance with Directive 95/ 46/EC, inter alia about the purposes of the processing, and is offered the right to refuse such processing by the data controller. This shall not prevent any technical storage or access for the sole purpose of carrying out or facilitating the transmission of a communication over an electronic communications network, or as strictly necessary in order to provide an information society service explicitly requested by the subscriber or user.

Article 6 - Traffic data

1. Traffic data relating to subscribers and users processed and stored by the provider of a public communications network or publicly available electronic communications service must be erased or made anonymous when it is no longer needed for the purpose of the transmission of a communication without prejudice to paragraphs 2, 3 and 5 of this Article and Article 15(1).

2. Traffic data necessary for the purposes of subscriber billing and interconnection payments may be processed. Such processing is permissible only up to the end of the period during which the bill may lawfully be challenged or payment pursued.

3. For the purpose of marketing electronic communications services or for the provision of value added services, the provider of a publicly available electronic communications service may process the data referred to in paragraph 1 to the extent and for the duration necessary for such services or marketing, if the subscriber or user to whom the data relate has given his/her consent. Users or subscribers shall be given the possibility to withdraw their consent for the processing of traffic data at any time.

4. The service provider must inform the subscriber or user of the types of traffic data which are processed and of the duration of such processing for the purposes mentioned in paragraph 2 and, prior to obtaining consent, for the purposes mentioned in paragraph 3.

5. Processing of traffic data, in accordance with paragraphs 1, 2, 3 and 4, must be restricted to persons acting under the authority of providers of the public communications networks and publicly available electronic communications services handling billing or traffic management, customer enquiries, fraud detection, marketing electronic communications services or providing a value added service, and must be restricted to what is necessary for the purposes of such activities.

6. Paragraphs 1, 2, 3 and 5 shall apply without prejudice to the possibility for competent bodies to be informed of traffic data in conformity with applicable legislation with a view to settling disputes, in particular interconnection or billing disputes.

Article 7 - Itemised billing

1. Subscribers shall have the right to receive non-itemised bills.

2. Member States shall apply national provisions in order to reconcile the rights of subscribers receiving itemised bills with the right to privacy of calling users and called subscribers, for example by ensuring that sufficient alternative privacy enhancing methods of communications or payments are available to such users and subscribers.

Article 8 - Presentation and restriction of calling and connected line identification

1. Where presentation of calling line identification is offered, the service provider must offer the calling user the possibility, using a simple means and free of charge, of preventing the presentation of the calling line identification on a per-call basis. The calling subscriber must have this possibility on a per-line basis.

2. Where presentation of calling line identification is offered, the service provider must offer the called subscriber the possibility, using a simple means and free of charge for reasonable use of this function, of preventing the presentation of the calling line identification of incoming calls.

3. Where presentation of calling line identification is offered and where the calling line identification is presented prior to the call being established, the service provider must offer the called subscriber the possibility, using a simple means, of rejecting incoming calls where the presentation of the calling line identification has been prevented by the calling user or subscriber.

4. Where presentation of connected line identification is offered, the service provider must offer the called subscriber the possibility, using a simple means and free of charge, of preventing the presentation of the connected line identification to the calling user.

5. Paragraph 1 shall also apply with regard to calls to third countries originating in the Community. Paragraphs 2, 3 and 4 shall also apply to incoming calls originating in third countries.

6. Member States shall ensure that where presentation of calling and/or connected line identification is offered, the providers of publicly available electronic communications services inform the public thereof and of the possibilities set out in paragraphs 1, 2, 3 and 4.

Article 9 - Location data other than traffic data

1. Where location data other than traffic data, relating to users or subscribers of public communications networks or publicly available electronic communications services, can be

processed, such data may only be processed when they are made anonymous, or with the consent of the users or subscribers to the extent and for the duration necessary for the provision of a value added service. The service provider must inform the users or subscribers, prior to obtaining their consent, of the type of location data other than traffic data which will be processed, of the purposes and duration of the processing and whether the data will be transmitted to a third party for the purpose of providing the value added service. Users or subscribers shall be given the possibility to withdraw their consent for the processing of location data other than traffic data at any time.

2. Where consent of the users or subscribers has been obtained for the processing of location data other than traffic data, the user or subscriber must continue to have the possibility, using a simple means and free of charge, of temporarily refusing the processing of such data for each connection to the network or for each transmission of a communication.

3. Processing of location data other than traffic data in accordance with paragraphs 1 and 2 must be restricted to persons acting under the authority of the provider of the public communications network or publicly available communications service or of the third party providing the value added service, and must be restricted to what is necessary for the purposes of providing the value added service.

Article 10 - Exceptions

Member States shall ensure that there are transparent procedures governing the way in which a provider of a public communications network and/or a publicly available electronic communications service may override:

(a) the elimination of the presentation of calling line identification, on a temporary basis, upon application of a subscriber requesting the tracing of malicious or nuisance calls. In this case, in accordance with national law, the data containing the identification of the calling subscriber will be stored and be made available by the provider of a public communications network and/or publicly available electronic communications service;

(b) the elimination of the presentation of calling line identification and the temporary denial or absence of consent of a subscriber or user for the processing of location data, on a per-line basis for organisations dealing with emergency calls and recognised as such by a Member State, including law enforcement agencies, ambulance services and fire brigades, for the purpose of responding to such calls.

Article 11 - Automatic call forwarding

Member States shall ensure that any subscriber has the possibility, using a simple means and free of charge, of stopping automatic call forwarding by a third party to the subscriber's terminal.

Article 12 - Directories of subscribers

1. Member States shall ensure that subscribers are informed, free of charge and before they are included in the directory, about the purpose(s) of a printed or electronic directory of subscribers available to the public or obtainable through directory enquiry services, in which their personal data

can be included and of any further usage possibilities based on search functions embedded in electronic versions of the directory.

2. Member States shall ensure that subscribers are given the opportunity to determine whether their personal data are included in a public directory, and if so, which, to the extent that such data are relevant for the purpose of the directory as determined by the provider of the directory, and to verify, correct or withdraw such data. Not being included in a public subscriber directory, verifying, correcting or withdrawing personal data from it shall be free of charge.

3. Member States may require that for any purpose of a public directory other than the search of contact details of persons on the basis of their name and, where necessary, a minimum of other identifiers, additional consent be asked of the subscribers.

4. Paragraphs 1 and 2 shall apply to subscribers who are natural persons. Member States shall also ensure, in the framework of Community law and applicable national legislation, that the legitimate interests of subscribers other than natural persons with regard to their entry in public directories are sufficiently protected.

Article 13 - Unsolicited communications

1. The use of automated calling systems without human intervention (automatic calling machines), facsimile machines (fax) or electronic mail for the purposes of direct marketing may only be allowed in respect of subscribers who have given their prior consent.

2. Notwithstanding paragraph 1, where a natural or legal person obtains from its customers their electronic contact details for electronic mail, in the context of the sale of a product or a service, in accordance with Directive 95/46/EC, the same natural or legal person may use these electronic contact details for direct marketing of its own similar products or services provided that customers clearly and distinctly are given the opportunity to object, free of charge and in an easy manner, to such use of electronic contact details when they are collected and on the occasion of each message in case the customer has not initially refused such use.

3. Member States shall take appropriate measures to ensure that, free of charge, unsolicited communications for purposes of direct marketing, in cases other than those referred to in paragraphs 1 and 2, are not allowed either without the consent of the subscribers concerned or in respect of subscribers who do not wish to receive these communications, the choice between these options to be determined by national legislation.

4. In any event, the practice of sending electronic mail for purposes of direct marketing disguising or concealing the identity of the sender on whose behalf the communication is made, or without a valid address to which the recipient may send a request that such communications cease, shall be prohibited.

5. Paragraphs 1 and 3 shall apply to subscribers who are natural persons. Member States shall also ensure, in the framework of Community law and applicable national legislation, that the legitimate interests of subscribers other than natural persons with regard to unsolicited communications are sufficiently protected.

International
EU Directive on Privacy and Electronic Communications

Article 14 - Technical features and standardisation

1. In implementing the provisions of this Directive, Member States shall ensure, subject to paragraphs 2 and 3, that no mandatory requirements for specific technical features are imposed on terminal or other electronic communication equipment which could impede the placing of equipment on the market and the free circulation of such equipment in and between Member States.
2. Where provisions of this Directive can be implemented only by requiring specific technical features in electronic communications networks, Member States shall inform the Commission in accordance with the procedure provided for by Directive 98/34/EC of the European Parliament and of the Council of 22 June 1998 laying down a procedure for the provision of information in the field of technical standards and regulations and of rules on information society services (1).
3. Where required, measures may be adopted to ensure that terminal equipment is constructed in a way that is compatible with the right of users to protect and control the use of their personal data, in accordance with Directive 1999/5/EC and Council Decision 87/95/EEC of 22 December 1986 on standardisation in the field of information technology and communications (2).

Article 15 - Application of certain provisions of Directive 95/46/EC

1. Member States may adopt legislative measures to restrict the scope of the rights and obligations provided for in Article 5, Article 6, Article 8(1), (2), (3) and (4), and Article 9 of this Directive when such restriction constitutes a necessary, appropriate and proportionate measure within a democratic society to safeguard national security (i.e. State security), defence, public security, and the prevention, investigation, detection and prosecution of criminal offences or of unauthorised use of the electronic communication system, as referred to in Article 13(1) of Directive 95/46/EC. To this end, Member States may, inter alia, adopt legislative measures providing for the retention of data for a limited period justified on the grounds laid down in this paragraph. All the measures referred to in this paragraph shall be in accordance with the general principles of Community law, including those referred to in Article 6(1) and (2) of the Treaty on European Union.
2. The provisions of Chapter III on judicial remedies, liability and sanctions of Directive 95/46/EC shall apply with regard to national provisions adopted pursuant to this Directive and with regard to the individual rights derived from this Directive.
3. The Working Party on the Protection of Individuals with regard to the Processing of Personal Data instituted by Article 29 of Directive 95/46/EC shall also carry out the tasks laid down in Article 30 of that Directive with regard to matters covered by this Directive, namely the protection of fundamental rights and freedoms and of legitimate interests in the electronic communications sector.

Article 16 - Transitional arrangements

1. Article 12 shall not apply to editions of directories already produced or placed on the market in printed or off-line electronic form before the national provisions adopted pursuant to this Directive enter into force.

2. Where the personal data of subscribers to fixed or mobile public voice telephony services have been included in a public subscriber directory in conformity with the provisions of Directive 95/46/EC and of Article 11 of Directive 97/66/EC before the national provisions adopted in pursuance of this Directive enter into force, the personal data of such subscribers may remain included in this public directory in its printed or electronic versions, including versions with reverse search functions, unless subscribers indicate otherwise, after having received complete information about purposes and options in accordance with Article 12 of this Directive.

(1) OJ L 204, 21.7.1998, p. 37. Directive as amended by Directive 98/ 48/EC (OJ L 217, 5.8.1998, p. 18).

(2) OJ L 36, 7.2.1987, p. 31.

Article 17 - Transposition

1. Before 31 October 2003 Member States shall bring into force the provisions necessary to comply with this Directive. They shall forthwith inform the Commission thereof.

Decision as last amended by the 1994 Act of Accession. When Member States adopt those provisions, they shall contain a reference to this Directive or be accompanied by such a reference on the occasion of their official publication. The methods of making such reference shall be laid down by the Member States.

2. Member States shall communicate to the Commission the text of the provisions of national law which they adopt in the field governed by this Directive and of any subsequent amendments to those provisions.

Article 18 - Review

The Commission shall submit to the European Parliament and the Council, not later than three years after the date referred to in Article 17(1), a report on the application of this Directive and its impact on economic operators and consumers, in particular as regards the provisions on unsolicited communications, taking into account the international environment. For this purpose, the Commission may request information from the Member States, which shall be supplied without undue delay. Where appropriate, the Commission shall submit proposals to amend this Directive, taking account of the results of that report, any changes in the sector and any other proposal it may deem necessary in order to improve the effectiveness of this Directive.

Article 19 – Repeal

Directive 97/66/EC is hereby repealed with effect from the date referred to in Article 17(1). References made to the repealed Directive shall be construed as being made to this Directive.

Article 20 - Entry into force

This Directive shall enter into force on the day of its publication in the Official Journal of the European Communities.

Article 21 - Addressees

This Directive is addressed to the Member States.

Done at Brussels, 12 July 2002.

For the European Parliament

The President

P. COX

For the Council

The President

T. PEDERSEN

CAIRO DECLARATION OF HUMAN RIGHTS IN ISLAM [EXCERPT]

References

Organization of Islamic Cooperation, Cairo Declaration on Human Rights in Islam [http://www.oic-oci.org/english/article/human.htm]

The Member States of the Organization of the Islamic Conference,

Reaffirming the civilizing and historical role of the Islamic Ummah which God made the best nation that has given mankind a universal and well-balanced civilization in which harmony is established between this life and the hereafter and knowledge is combined with faith; and the role that this Ummah should play to guide a humanity confused by competing trends and ideologies and to provide solutions to the chronic problems of this materialistic civilization.

Wishing to contribute to the efforts of mankind to assert human rights, to protect man from exploitation and persecution, and to affirm his freedom and right to a dignified life in accordance with the Islamic Shari'ah

Convinced that mankind which has reached an advanced stage in materialistic science is still, and shall remain, in dire need of faith to support its civilization and of a self motivating force to guard its rights;

Believing that fundamental rights and universal freedoms in Islam are an integral part of the Islamic religion and that no one as a matter of principle has the right to suspend them in whole or in part or violate or ignore them in as much as they are binding divine commandments, which are contained in the Revealed Books of God and were sent through the last of His Prophets to complete the preceding divine messages thereby making their observance an act of worship and their neglect or violation an abominable sin, and accordingly every person is individually responsible - and the Ummah collectively responsible - for their safeguard.

Proceeding from the above-mentioned principles,

Declare the following:

ARTICLE 18:

(a) Everyone shall have the right to live in security for himself, his religion, his dependents, his honor and his property.

(b) Everyone shall have the right to privacy in the conduct of his private affairs, in his home, among his family, with regard to his property and his relationships. It is not permitted to spy on him, to place him under surveillance or to besmirch his good name. The State shall protect him from arbitrary interference.

(c) A private residence is inviolable in all cases. It will not be entered without permission from its inhabitants or in any unlawful manner, nor shall it be demolished or confiscated and its dwellers evicted.

DECLARATION OF PRINCIPLES ON FREEDOM OF EXPRESSION IN AFRICA [EXCERPT]

References

> African Commission on Human and Peoples' Rights, Resolution on the Adoption of the Declaration of Principles on Freedom of Expression in Africa [http://www.achpr.org/sessions/32nd/resolutions/62/]

Preamble

Reaffirming the fundamental importance of freedom of expression as an individual human right, as a cornerstone of democracy and as a means of ensuring respect for all human rights and freedoms;

Reaffirming Article 9 of the African Charter on Human and Peoples' Rights;

Desiring to promote the free flow of information and ideas and greater respect for freedom of expression;

Convinced that respect for freedom of expression, as well as the right of access to information held by public bodies and companies, will lead to greater public transparency and accountability, as well as to good governance and the strengthening of democracy;

Convinced that laws and customs that repress freedom of expression are a disservice to society; Recalling that freedom of expression is a fundamental human right guaranteed by the African Charter on Human and Peoples' Rights, the Universal Declaration of Human Rights and the International Covenant on Civil and Political Rights, as well as other international documents and national constitutions;

Considering the key role of the media and other means of communication in ensuring full respect for freedom of expression, in promoting the free flow of information and ideas, in assisting people to make informed decisions and in facilitating and strengthening democracy; Aware of the particular importance of the broadcast media in Africa, given its capacity to reach a wide audience due to the comparatively low cost of receiving transmissions and its ability to overcome barriers of illiteracy;

Noting that oral traditions, which are rooted in African cultures, lend themselves particularly well to radio broadcasting;

International
Declaration of Principles on Freedom of Expression in Africa

Noting the important contribution that can be made to the realisation of the right to freedom of expression by new information and communication technologies;

Mindful of the evolving human rights and human development environment in Africa, especially in light of the adoption of the Protocol to the African Charter on Human and Peoples' Rights on the establishment of an African Court on Human and Peoples' Rights, the principles of the Constitutive Act of the African Union, 2000, as well as the significance of the human rights and good governance provisions in the New Partnership for Africa's Development (NEPAD); and

Recognising the need to ensure the right to freedom of expression in Africa, the African Commission on Human and Peoples' Rights declares that:

* * *

IV. Freedom of Information

1. Public bodies hold information not for themselves but as custodians of the public good and everyone has a right to access this information, subject only to clearly defined rules established by law.

2. The right to information shall be guaranteed by law in accordance with the following principles:

> everyone has the right to access information held by public bodies;
> everyone has the right to access information held by private bodies which is necessary for the exercise or protection of any right;
> any refusal to disclose information shall be subject to appeal to an independent body and/or the courts;
> public bodies shall be required, even in the absence of a request, actively to publish important information of significant public interest;
> no one shall be subject to any sanction for releasing in good faith information on wrongdoing, or that which would disclose a serious threat to health, safety or the environment save where the imposition of sanctions serves a legitimate interest and is necessary in a democratic society; and
> secrecy laws shall be amended as necessary to comply with freedom of information principles.

3. Everyone has the right to access and update or otherwise correct their personal information, whether it is held by public or by private bodies.

* * *

STANDARDS FOR PERSONAL DATA
PROTECTION FOR IBERO-AMERICAN
STATES (2017) [EXCERPT]

References

> Standards for Personal Data Protection for Ibero-American States (June 20, 2017)
> [https://iapp.org/media/pdf/resource_center/Ibero-Am_standards.pdf]

The Ibero-American States:

(1) Considering that the protection of individuals regarding treatment of their personal data is a fundamental right that is acknowledged at the highest level in most of the Constitutions of the Ibero-American States, under personal data protection law, or habeas data, and that in some cases it has been defined in court cases by its Courts or Constitutional Courts.

(2) Determining that the right to the protection of personal data has been conceptualized in some Ibero-American countries, by legal provisions and by court cases, as a right of a different nature than the right to private and family life, to intimacy, to honor, to a good name, and other similar rights that collectively guarantee the free development of an individual's personality, until it becomes an autonomous right, with its own characteristics and dynamics, which purpose is to safeguard the power of disposition and control that any individual has with regard to the information that concerns him, basically regarding the use of information and communication technology, which are increasingly relevant in every aspect of daily life.

(3) Assuming that safeguarding the right of the individuals with respect to the treatment of their personal data is compatible with the purpose of guaranteeing and protecting other rights, which are acknowledged as indivisible and interdependent among each other, and that require protection in order to safeguard individuals, in their wider scope, against illegal or arbitrary intrusions, and even those resulting from the treatment of personal data. The foregoing does not prevent applying the right to the protection of personal data to legal entities, in compliance with the provisions of the internal law of the Ibero-American States.

(4) Remembering that the Ibero-American Data Protection Network emerged in connection with the agreement reached in the Ibero-American Data Protection Conference, held in La Antigua, Guatemala, from June 1 to 6, 2003, with 14 Ibero-American countries in attendance. This initiative had, since the beginning, a political support reflected in the Final Declaration of the XIII Ibero-American Summit of Heads of State and Government, held in Santa Cruz de la Sierra, Bolivia, on November 14 and 15, 2003, aware of the nature of personal data protection as a fundamental right.

International
Standards for Personal Data Protection
for Ibero-American States

(5) Taking into consideration the on the occasion of the Resolution taken in the XXV Ibero-American Summit of Heads of State and Government, which was held in Cartagena de Indias, Colombia on October 28 and 29, 2016, it was reaffirmed that the adoption, preparation and promotion of different manuals, programs, initiatives and projects would strengthen the management and effect of cooperation actions among Ibero-American countries.

(6) Assuming that the Ibero-American Network is formed in a permanent forum for the exchange of information, open to all member countries of the Ibero-American Community, and that it allows the involvement of the public, private and social sectors, with the purpose of promoting the necessary regulatory developments in order to guarantee an advanced regulation of the right to the protection of personal data in a democratic and global context;

(7) Remembering that on the occasion of the meeting held in Santa Cruz de la Sierra, Bolivia, on May 3 to 5, 2006, the document called Guidelines for the Harmonization of Data Protection in the Ibero-American Community was prepared, which establishes a set of provisions which purpose is to contribute to the preparation of the regulatory initiatives for data protection that may arise in the Ibero-American Community, establishing them- selves as a reference for the development of these Standards.

(8) Taking into consideration that the European Union has adopted a new regulatory framework on the matter, with the purpose of modernizing its provisions and guaran- teeing greater soundness and consistency in the effective protection of the fundamental right to personal data protection in the European Union, and with the purpose of gene- rating trust in society in general and, in turn, to facilitate the development of a digital economy, both in its internal market as in its global relations, this regulatory framework is positioned as a benchmark for the preparation of the national laws for data protection in Ibero-America.

(9) Acknowledging that there is a lack of harmonization in the Ibero-American States regarding the acknowledgment, adoption, definition and development of the figures, principles, rights and procedures that provide the contents of the right to personal data protection in their national laws, which without any doubt, is currently preventing these countries from facing the new challenges for the protection of this right, resulting from the ongoing and rapid technological evolution and globalization in various fields.

(10) Becoming a pressing fact within the framework of constant technological innovation, the adoption of regulatory instruments that guarantee, on the one hand, the protection of the individuals regarding the treatment of their personal data, that is currently the base for the development, strengthening and exchange of goods and services in a global and digital economy, over which the economies of the Ibero-American states are built.

(11) Agreeing that in order to guarantee a high level of protection of the rights and freedoms of the individuals, we require in turn, among other matters, a uniform and high level of

protection of the individuals regarding their personal information, which answers to current needs and demands in a global context, with the purpose of not raising barriers against free circulation of personal data in the Ibero-American States, and, therefore, favoring commercial activities in the region, as well as other economic regions.

(12) Accepting that with the purpose of widening and strengthening the regime of the protection of individuals regarding the treatment of their personal data, it is imperative to establish a balance among the interests of all the actors in the public, private and social sector and the holders involved, including the establishment of exceptions due to public interest matters that are reasonable and compatible with rights and freedoms, in order to prevent incurring in unjustified or disproportionate restrictions or limitations, that are not consistent with the purposes of democratic societies.

(13) Being aware of the potential risks that could result within the sphere of the individuals, due to the treatment of their personal data on a large scale, by public and private bodies, and specifically, taking into consideration the particular vulnerability of girls, boys and adolescents, who demand appropriate and sufficient protection guarantees, preserving in this way their best interest, the free development of their personality, their safety and other values that are subject to the highest protection by the Ibero-American States.

(14) Agreeing that technological development facilitates the treatment of new categories of personal data that represent specific risks, specially the inappropriate use thereof; therefore, it is highly relevant to achieve a minimum consensus regarding the categories of personal data considered sensitive or especially protected, as well as the rules for their treatment, taking into consideration that the consequences and negative interference that could result from the inappropriate use of these type of personal data can generate unfair or discriminatory conditions for individuals.

(15) Admitting that not all the Ibero-American States have laws on the matter, a situation that can affect the safeguarding and treatment of personal information, if we take into consideration the accelerated use of information technology that facilitates and allows massive communication of personal data in an immediate and almost unlimited way;

(16) Establishing that the laws on protection of personal data in the Ibero-American States must adopt the references contained in these Standards, in order to have a harmonized regulatory framework that offers a level of protection to individuals, regarding the treatment of their personal data and, in turn, guaranteeing the commercial and economic development of the zone;

(17) Admitting that currently the legal bases that legitimize every public or private body in order to treat the personal data in their possession are holder's consent; compliance with a

legal provision; compliance with a court order, a founded and motivated resolution or mandate from a competent public authority; the exercise of the powers of public authorities; the acknowledgment or defense of holder's rights before a competent public authority; the execution of an agreement or pre-agreement in which holder is a part; compliance with a legal obligation applicable to the person responsible; the protection of holder's or another individual's vital interests; the legitimate interest of the public or private body; or due to reasons of public interest;

(18) Emphasizing the need to treat personal data under the same standards and homogeneous rules offered to holders of the same protection guarantees in the Ibero-American States, by establishing a mandatory catalog of principles, that responds to the current national and international standards on the matter, as well as the demands of an effective exercise and respect of this fundamental right.

(19) Acknowledging that with the purpose of effectively guaranteeing the right to the protection of personal data, it is necessary to adopt a regulatory framework that acknowledges any individual, in his capacity as holder of his personal data, the possibility of exercising, by general rule, in a without any charge, and exceptionally with an additional cost, due to reproduction, shipping, certification or others, the rights of access, correction, cancellation, opposition and portability, even in the context of the treatment of personal data performed by search engines in the Internet; these rights supplement the necessary conditions for holders to fully exercise their right to information self-determination.

(20) Highlighting the importance and fundamental role that service providers that treat personal data in the name and on behalf of the person responsible, including those that provide computer services in the cloud and other matters, which leads the Ibero-American States to adopt, in a global world, a regime that allows them to regulate this type of services, with the purpose of establishing a series of guarantees for the protection of the personal data, that they have and treat due to their commission, without releasing the person responsible from its duties and responsibilities before holders and control authorities.

(21) Considering that the development of new information and communication technologies, as well as the services developed within the context of a digital economy, are contributing to the continuous growth of the trans-border flow of personal data within the framework of a global society, the obligation to establish a minimum base that facilitates and allows those responsible and those in charge, in their capacity as exporters, the performance of international transfers of personal data, fully respecting holders' rights, is unavoidable.

(22) Taking into consideration that it is possible, through the Internet, to access and collect information available in any country, as well as to treat it, such as collecting in- formation from millions of people without being physically established there, a circum- stance that

should not be a factor that prevents the effective protection of the rights and freedoms of individuals in the cyberspace.

(23) Acknowledging the importance of adopting preventive measures that allow the person responsible to proactively respond to the possible problems related to the adoption of binding self-regulation schemes or certification systems on the matter; appointing a personal data protection officer; preparing impact assessments on the protection of personal data and privacy by default and by design, among others, which is essential within the field of information and communication technology.

(24) Admitting the compelling need for each Ibero-American State to have an independent and impartial control authority, which decisions can only be appealed by judicial control, free of any external influence, with supervision and investigation powers on personal data protection, and in charge of supervising compliance with national legislation on the matter, which must be granted sufficient human and material resources in order to guarantee the exercise of its powers and the effective performance of its functions;

(25) Acknowledging that the Ibero-American States are bound to adopt a regime that guarantees holders a series of mechanisms and procedures in order to submit their claims before the control authority, when they consider that their right to the protection of personal data has been violated, as well as to be compensated when they have suffered damages and lost profits as a consequence of the violation of their right;

(26) Emphasizing the importance of establishing a minimum base for international cooperation between the Latin American control authorities, and between them and those of third party countries, with the purpose of encouraging and facilitating the application of the legislation on the matter, and an effective protection of the holders.

They have agreed to adopt these Standards as a maximum priority in the Ibero-American Community in order for them to contribute, in the capacity as orienting guidelines, to the issuance of regulatory initiatives for the protection of personal data in the region of the countries that do not have these laws yet, or if applicable, to serve as reference for the modernization and update of the existing legislations, encouraging the adoption of a harmonized regulatory framework that offers an appropriate level of protection to the individuals, regarding the treatment of their personal data and guaranteeing, in turn, the commercial and economic development of the regions, under the following...

* * *

MADRID DECLARATION

References

Madrid Declaration
[http://thepublicvoice.org/madrid-declaration/]

3 November 2009

Affirming that privacy is a fundamental human right set out in the Universal Declaration of Human Rights, the International Covenant on Civil and Political Rights, and other human rights instruments and national constitutions;

Reminding the EU member countries of their obligations to enforce the provisions of the 1995 Data Protection Directive and the 2002 Electronic Communications Directive;

Reminding the other OECD member countries of their obligations to uphold the principles set out in the 1980 OECD Privacy Guidelines;

Reminding all countries of their obligations to safeguard the civil rights of their citizens and residents under the provisions of their national constitutions and laws, as well as international human rights law;

Anticipating the entry into force of provisions strengthening the Constitutional rights to privacy and data protection in the European Union;

Noting with alarm the dramatic expansion of secret and unaccountable surveillance, as well as the growing collaboration between governments and vendors of surveillance technology that establish new forms of social control;

Further noting that new strategies to pursue copyright and unlawful content investigations pose substantial threats to communications privacy, intellectual freedom, and due process of law;

Further noting the growing consolidation of Internet-based services, and the fact that some corporations are acquiring vast amounts of personal data without independent oversight;

Warning that privacy law and privacy institutions have failed to take full account of new surveillance practices, including behavioral targeting, databases of DNA and other biometric identifiers, the fusion of data between the public and private sectors, and the particular risks to vulnerable groups, including children, migrants, and minorities;

Warning that the failure to safeguard privacy jeopardizes associated freedoms, including freedom of expression, freedom of assembly, freedom of access to information, non-discrimination, and ultimately the stability of constitutional democracies;

Civil Society takes the occasion of the 31st annual meeting of the International Conference of Privacy and Data Protection Commissioners to:

(1) Reaffirm support for a global framework of Fair Information Practices that places obligations on those who collect and process personal information and gives rights to those whose personal information is collected;

(2) Reaffirm support for independent data protection authorities that make determinations, in the context of a legal framework, transparently and without commercial advantage or political influence;

(3) Reaffirm support for genuine Privacy Enhancing Techniques that minimize or eliminate the collection of personally identifiable information and for meaningful Privacy Impact Assessments that require compliance with privacy standards;

(4) Urge countries that have not ratified Council of Europe Convention 108 together with the Protocol of 2001 to do so as expeditiously as possible;

(5) Urge countries that have not yet established a comprehensive framework for privacy protection and an independent data protection authority to do so as expeditiously as possible;

(6) Urge those countries that have established legal frameworks for privacy protection to ensure effective implementation and enforcement, and to cooperate at the international and regional level;

(7) Urge countries to ensure that individuals are promptly notified when their personal information is improperly disclosed or used in a manner inconsistent with its collection;

(8) Recommend comprehensive research into the adequacy of techniques that deidentify; data to determine whether in practice such methods safeguard privacy and anonymity;

(9) Call for a moratorium on the development or implementation of new systems of mass surveillance, including facial recognition, whole body imaging, biometric identifiers, and embedded RFID tags, subject to a full and transparent evaluation by independent authorities and democratic debate; and

(10) Call for the establishment of a new international framework for privacy protection, with the full participation of civil society, that is based on the rule of law, respect for fundamental human rights, and support for democratic institutions.

Recent Developments

EU-US "PRIVACY SHIELD"

Summary

The "Privacy Shield" is a quasi-legal framework for EU-US data flows that emerged after the Court of Justice of the European Union ruled in 2015 that the Safe Harbor arrangement failed to provide adequate protection for transborder data flows. The basis of the "shield" is a series of representation made by the US government in late 2015 and early 2016 regarding the protection afforded to data that is transferred to the United States, Prior to finalization, substantial opinions were prepared by privacy agencies, including the European Data Protection Supervisor and the Article 29 Working Party.

References

EU-U.S. Privacy Shield Framework
[https://www.privacyshield.gov/EU-US-Framework]

EPIC – Privacy Shield EU-U.S. Data Transfer Agreement
[https://epic.org/privacy/intl/privacy-shield/]

European Commission, Privacy Shield Draft Adequacy Decision
[http://ec.europa.eu/justice/data-protection/files/privacy-shield-adequacy-decision_en.pdf]

European Data Protection Supervisor, Opinion on the EU-U.S. Privacy Shield (May 30, 2016)
[https://secure.edps.europa.eu/EDPSWEB/webdav/site/mySite/shared/Documents/Consultation/Opinions/2016/16-05-30_Privacy_Shield_EN.pdf]

European Commission, Press Release - Restoring trust in transatlantic data flows through strong safeguards: European Commission presents EU-U.S. Privacy Shield (Feb. 29, 2016)
[http://europa.eu/rapid/press-release_IP-16-433_en.htm]

U.S. Department of Commerce, EU-U.S. Privacy Shield (Feb. 2, 2016)
[https://www.commerce.gov/news/fact-sheets/2016/02/eu-us-privacy-shield]

I. OVERVIEW

Recent Developments
EU-US "Privacy Shield"

1. While the United States and the European Union share the goal of enhancing privacy protection, the United States takes a different approach to privacy from that taken by the European Union. The United States uses a sectoral approach that relies on a mix of legislation, regulation, and self-regulation. Given those differences and to provide organizations in the United States with a reliable mechanism for personal data transfers to the United States from the European Union while ensuring that EU data subjects continue to benefit from effective safeguards and protection as required by European legislation with respect to the processing of their personal data when they have been transferred to non-EU countries, the Department of Commerce is issuing these Privacy Shield Principles, including the Supplemental Principles (collectively "the Principles") under its statutory authority to foster, promote, and develop international commerce (15 U.S.C. § 1512). The Principles were developed in consultation with the European Commission, and with industry and other stakeholders, to facilitate trade and commerce between the United States and European Union. They are intended for use solely by organizations in the United States receiving personal data from the European Union for the purpose of qualifying for the Privacy Shield and thus benefitting from the European Commission's adequacy decision. The Principles do not affect the application of national provisions implementing Directive 95/46/EC ("the Directive") that apply to the processing of personal data in the Member States. Nor do the Principles limit privacy obligations that otherwise apply under U.S. law.

2. In order to rely on the Privacy Shield to effectuate transfers of personal data from the EU, an organization must self-certify its adherence to the Principles to the Department of Commerce (or its designee) ("the Department"). While decisions by organizations to thus enter the Privacy Shield are entirely voluntary, effective compliance is compulsory: organizations that self-certify to the Department and publicly declare their commitment to adhere to the Principles must comply fully with the Principles. In order to enter the Privacy Shield, an organization must (a) be subject to the investigatory and enforcement powers of the Federal Trade Commission (the "FTC"), the Department of Transportation or another statutory body that will effectively ensure compliance with the Principles (other U.S. statutory bodies recognized by the EU may be included as an annex in the future); (b) publicly declare its commitment to comply with the Principles; (c) publicly disclose its privacy policies in line with these Principles; and (d) fully implement them. An organization's failure to comply is enforceable under Section 5 of the Federal Trade Commission Act prohibiting unfair and deceptive acts in or affecting commerce (15 U.S.C. § 45(a)) or other laws or regulations prohibiting such acts.

3. The Department of Commerce will maintain and make available to the public an authoritative list of U.S. organizations that have self-certified to the Department and declared their commitment to adhere to the Principles ("the Privacy Shield List"). Privacy Shield benefits are assured from the date that the Department places the organization on the Privacy Shield List. The Department will remove an organization from the Privacy Shield List if it

voluntarily withdraws from the Privacy Shield or if it fails to complete its annual re-certification to the Department. An organization's removal from the Privacy Shield List means it may no longer benefit from the European Commission's adequacy decision to receive personal information from the EU. The organization must continue to apply the Principles to the personal information it received while it participated in the Privacy Shield, and affirm to the Department on an annual basis its commitment to do so, for as long as it retains such information; otherwise, the organization must return or delete the information or provide "adequate" protection for the information by another authorized means. The Department will also remove from the Privacy Shield List those organizations that have persistently failed to comply with the Principles; these organizations do not qualify for Privacy Shield benefits and must return or delete the personal information they received under the Privacy Shield.

4. The Department will also maintain and make available to the public an authoritative record of U.S. organizations that had previously self-certified to the Department, but that have been removed from the Privacy Shield List. The Department will provide a clear warning that these organizations are not participants in the Privacy Shield; that removal from the Privacy Shield List means that such organizations cannot claim to be Privacy Shield compliant and must avoid any statements or misleading practices implying that they participate in the Privacy Shield; and that such organizations are no longer entitled to benefit from the European Commission's adequacy decision that would enable those organizations to receive personal information from the EU. An organization that continues to claim participation in the Privacy Shield or makes other Privacy Shield-related misrepresentations after it has been removed from the Privacy Shield List may be subject to enforcement action by the FTC, the Department of Transportation, or other enforcement authorities.

5. Adherence to these Principles may be limited: (a) to the extent necessary to meet national security, public interest, or law enforcement requirements; (b) by statute, government regulation, or case law that creates conflicting obligations or explicit authorizations, provided that, in exercising any such authorization, an organization can demonstrate that its non-compliance with the Principles is limited to the extent necessary to meet the overriding legitimate interests furthered by such authorization; or (c) if the effect of the Directive or Member State law is to allow exceptions or derogations, provided such exceptions or derogations are applied in comparable contexts. Consistent with the goal of enhancing privacy protection, organizations should strive to implement these Principles fully and transparently, including indicating in their privacy policies where exceptions to the Principles permitted by (b) above will apply on a regular basis. For the same reason, where the option is allowable under the Principles and/or U.S. law, organizations are expected to opt for the higher protection where possible.

6.   Organizations are obligated to apply the Principles to all personal data transferred in reliance on the Privacy Shield after they enter the Privacy Shield. An organization that chooses to extend Privacy Shield benefits to human resources personal information transferred from the EU for use in the context of an employment relationship must indicate this when it self-certifies to the Department and conform to the requirements set forth in the Supplemental Principle on Self-Certification.

7.   U.S. law will apply to questions of interpretation and compliance with the Principles and relevant privacy policies by Privacy Shield organizations, except where such organizations have committed to cooperate with European data protection authorities ("DPAs"). Unless otherwise stated, all provisions of the Principles apply where they are relevant.

8.   Definitions:
    a.   "Personal data" and "personal information" are data about an identified or identifiable individual that are within the scope of the Directive, received by an organization in the United States from the European Union, and recorded in any form.
    b.   "Processing" of personal data means any operation or set of operations which is performed upon personal data, whether or not by automated means, such as collection, recording, organization, storage, adaptation or alteration, retrieval, consultation, use, disclosure or dissemination, and erasure or destruction.
    c.   "Controller" means a person or organization which, alone or jointly with others, determines the purposes and means of the processing of personal data.

9.   The effective date of the Principles is the date of final approval of the European Commission's adequacy determination.

II. PRINCIPLES

1. Notice

    a.   An organization must inform individuals about:
        i.   its participation in the Privacy Shield and provide a link to, or the web address for, the Privacy Shield List,
        ii.   the types of personal data collected and, where applicable, the entities or subsidiaries of the organization also adhering to the Principles,
        iii.   its commitment to subject to the Principles all personal data received from the EU in reliance on the Privacy Shield,
        iv.   the purposes for which it collects and uses personal information about them,
        v.   how to contact the organization with any inquiries or complaints, including any relevant establishment in the EU that can respond to such inquiries or complaints,
        vi.   the type or identity of third parties to which it discloses personal information, and the purposes for which it does so,

vii.   the right of individuals to access their personal data,

viii.   the choices and means the organization offers individuals for limiting the use and disclosure of their personal data,

ix.   the independent dispute resolution body designated to address complaints and provide appropriate recourse free of charge to the individual, and whether it is: (1) the panel established by DPAs, (2) an alternative dispute resolution provider based in the EU, or (3) an alternative dispute resolution provider based in the United States,

x.   being subject to the investigatory and enforcement powers of the FTC, the Department of Transportation or any other U.S. authorized statutory body,

xi.   the possibility, under certain conditions, for the individual to invoke binding arbitration,

xii.   the requirement to disclose personal information in response to lawful requests by public authorities, including to meet national security or law enforcement requirements, and

xiii.   its liability in cases of onward transfers to third parties.

b.   This notice must be provided in clear and conspicuous language when individuals are first asked to provide personal information to the organization or as soon thereafter as is practicable, but in any event before the organization uses such information for a purpose other than that for which it was originally collected or processed by the transferring organization or discloses it for the first time to a third party.

2. Choice

a.   An organization must offer individuals the opportunity to choose (opt out) whether their personal information is (i) to be disclosed to a third party or (ii) to be used for a purpose that is materially different from the purpose(s) for which it was originally collected or subsequently authorized by the individuals. Individuals must be provided with clear, conspicuous, and readily available mechanisms to exercise choice.

b.   By derogation to the previous paragraph, it is not necessary to provide choice when disclosure is made to a third party that is acting as an agent to perform task(s) on behalf of and under the instructions of the organization. However, an organization shall always enter into a contract with the agent.

c.   For sensitive information (i.e., personal information specifying medical or health conditions, racial or ethnic origin, political opinions, religious or philosophical beliefs, trade union membership or information specifying the sex life of the individual), organizations must obtain affirmative express consent (opt in) from individuals if such information is to be (i) disclosed to a third party or (ii) used for a purpose other than those for which it was originally collected or subsequently authorized by the individuals through the exercise of opt-in choice. In addition, an organization should treat as sensitive any personal information received from a third party where the third party identifies and treats it as sensitive.

3. Accountability for Onward Transfer

a.   To transfer personal information to a third party acting as a controller, organizations must comply with the Notice and Choice Principles. Organizations must also enter into a contract with the third-party controller that provides that such data may only be processed for limited and specified purposes consistent with the consent provided by the individual and that the recipient will provide the same level of protection as the Principles and will notify the organization if it makes a determination that it can no longer meet this obligation. The contract shall provide that when such a determination is made the third party controller ceases processing or takes other reasonable and appropriate steps to remediate.

b.   To transfer personal data to a third party acting as an agent, organizations must: (i) transfer such data only for limited and specified purposes; (ii) ascertain that the agent is obligated to provide at least the same level of privacy protection as is required by the Principles; (iii) take reasonable and appropriate steps to ensure that the agent effectively processes the personal information transferred in a manner consistent with the organization's obligations under the Principles; (iv) require the agent to notify the organization if it makes a determination that it can no longer meet its obligation to provide the same level of protection as is required by the Principles; (v) upon notice, including under (iv), take reasonable and appropriate steps to stop and remediate unauthorized processing; and (vi) provide a summary or a representative copy of the relevant privacy provisions of its contract with that agent to the Department upon request.

4. Security

a.   Organizations creating, maintaining, using or disseminating personal information must take reasonable and appropriate measures to protect it from loss, misuse and unauthorized access, disclosure, alteration and destruction, taking into due account the risks involved in the processing and the nature of the personal data.

5. Data Integrity and Purpose Limitation

a.   Consistent with the Principles, personal information must be limited to the information that is relevant for the purposes of processing.[3] An organization may not process personal information in a way that is incompatible with the purposes for which it has been collected or subsequently authorized by the individual. To the extent necessary for those purposes, an organization must take reasonable steps to ensure that personal data is reliable for its intended use, accurate, complete, and current. An organization must adhere to the Principles for as long as it retains such information.

b.   Information may be retained in a form identifying or making identifiable[4] the individual only for as long as it serves a purpose of processing within the meaning of 5a. This obligation does not prevent organizations from processing personal information for longer periods for the time and to the extent such processing reasonably serves the purposes of archiving in the public interest, journalism, literature and art, scientific or historical research, and statistical analysis. In these cases, such processing shall be subject to the other Principles and provisions of the Framework. Organizations should take reasonable and appropriate measures in complying with this provision.

6. Access

a. Individuals must have access to personal information about them that an organization holds and be able to correct, amend, or delete that information where it is inaccurate, or has been processed in violation of the Principles, except where the burden or expense of providing access would be disproportionate to the risks to the individual's privacy in the case in question, or where the rights of persons other than the individual would be violated.

7. Recourse, Enforcement and Liability

a.   Effective privacy protection must include robust mechanisms for assuring compliance with the Principles, recourse for individuals who are affected by non-

---

[3] Depending on the circumstances, examples of compatible processing purposes may include those that reasonably serve customer relations, compliance and legal considerations, auditing, security and fraud prevention, preserving or defending the organization's legal rights, or other purposes consistent with the expectations of a reasonable person given the context of the collection.

[4] In this context, if, given the means of identification reasonably likely to be used (considering, among other things, the costs of and the amount of time required for identification and the available technology at the time of the processing) and the form in which the data is retained, an individual could reasonably be identified by the organization, or a third party if it would have access to the data, then the individual is "identifiable."

compliance with the Principles, and consequences for the organization when the Principles are not followed. At a minimum such mechanisms must include:

    i.   readily available independent recourse mechanisms by which each individual's complaints and disputes are investigated and expeditiously resolved at no cost to the individual and by reference to the Principles, and damages awarded where the applicable law or private-sector initiatives so provide;

    ii.   follow-up procedures for verifying that the attestations and assertions organizations make about their privacy practices are true and that privacy practices have been implemented as presented and, in particular, with regard to cases of non-compliance; and

    iii.   obligations to remedy problems arising out of failure to comply with the Principles by organizations announcing their adherence to them and consequences for such organizations. Sanctions must be sufficiently rigorous to ensure compliance by organizations.

b.   Organizations and their selected independent recourse mechanisms will respond promptly to inquiries and requests by the Department for information relating to the Privacy Shield. All organizations must respond expeditiously to complaints regarding compliance with the Principles referred by EU Member State authorities through the Department. Organizations that have chosen to cooperate with DPAs, including organizations that process human resources data, must respond directly to such authorities with regard to the investigation and resolution of complaints.

c.   Organizations are obligated to arbitrate claims and follow the terms as set forth in Annex I, provided that an individual has invoked binding arbitration by delivering notice to the organization at issue and following the procedures and subject to conditions set forth in Annex I.

d. In the context of an onward transfer, a Privacy Shield organization has responsibility for the processing of personal information it receives under the Privacy Shield and subsequently transfers to a third party acting as an agent on its behalf. The Privacy Shield organization shall remain liable under the Principles if its agent processes such personal information in a manner inconsistent with the Principles, unless the organization proves that it is not responsible for the event giving rise to the damage.

e.   When an organization becomes subject to an FTC or court order based on non-compliance, the organization shall make public any relevant Privacy Shield-related sections of any compliance or assessment report submitted to the FTC, to the extent consistent with confidentiality requirements. The Department has established a dedicated point of contact for DPAs for any problems of compliance by Privacy Shield organizations. The FTC will give priority consideration to referrals of non-compliance with the Principles from the Department and EU Member State authorities, and will exchange information regarding referrals with the referring state authorities on a timely basis, subject to existing confidentiality restrictions.

CALIFORNIA CONSUMER PRIVACY
ACT (2018)

Summary

In 2018, the State of California enacted the California Consumer Privacy Act (CCPA). The Act established Californians' right to know what data about them is being collected, whether their information is sold or disclosed and to whom, to limit the sale, and more. The Act also allowed individuals to delete their data, established opt-in consent for children, provided for enforcement by the Attorney General, and created a private right of action for data breaches. In October 2018, the period for amendment of the CCPA, built into the law, ended. The final step in implementing the law is the promulgation of additional regulations by the California Attorney General.

References

California Consumer Privacy Act, Cal. Civ. Code §§ 1798.100−1798.198

California Attorney General, Proposed Text of Regulations (DRAFT), [https://oag.ca.gov/sites/all/files/agweb/pdfs/privacy/ccpa-proposed-regs.pdf]

1798.100.

(a) A consumer shall have the right to request that a business that collects a consumer's personal information disclose to that consumer the categories and specific pieces of personal information the business has collected.

(b) A business that collects a consumer's personal information shall, at or before the point of collection, inform consumers as to the categories of personal information to be collected and the purposes for which the categories of personal information shall be used. A business shall not collect additional categories of personal information or use personal information collected for additional purposes without providing the consumer with notice consistent with this section.

(c) A business shall provide the information specified in sub- division (a) to a consumer only upon receipt of a verifiable consumer request.

(d) A business that receives a verifiable consumer request from a consumer to access personal information shall promptly take steps to disclose and deliver, free of charge to the consumer, the personal information required by this section. The information may be delivered by mail or electronically, and if provided electronically, the information shall be in a portable and, to the extent technically feasible, readily useable format that allows the consumer to transmit this information to another entity without hindrance. A business may provide personal information to a consumer at any time, but shall not be required to provide personal information to a consumer more than twice in a 12-month period.

(e) This section shall not require a business to retain any personal information collected for a single, one-time trans- action, if such information is not sold or retained by the business or to reidentify or otherwise link information that is not maintained in a manner that would be considered personal information.

1798.105.

(a) A consumer shall have the right to request that a business delete any personal information about the consumer which the business has collected from the consumer.

(b) A business that collects personal information about consumers shall disclose, pursuant to Section 1798.130, the consumer's rights to request the deletion of the consumer's personal information.

(c) A business that receives a verifiable consumer request from a consumer to delete the consumer's personal information pursuant to subdivision (a) of this section shall delete the consumer's personal information from its records and direct any service providers to delete the consumer's personal information from their records.

(d) A business or a service provider shall not be required to comply with a consumer's request to delete the consumer's personal information if it is necessary for the business or service provider to maintain the consumer's personal information in order to:

(1) Complete the transaction for which the personal in- formation was collected, fulfill the terms of a written warranty or product recall conducted in accordance with federal law, provide a good or service requested by the consumer, or reasonably anticipated within the context of a business' ongoing business relationship with the consumer, or otherwise perform a contract between the business and the consumer.

(2) Detect security incidents, protect against malicious, deceptive, fraudulent, or illegal activity; or prosecute those responsible for that activity.

(3) Debug to identify and repair errors that impair existing intended functionality.

(4) Exercise free speech, ensure the right of another consumer to exercise that consumer's right of free speech, or exercise another right provided for by law.

(5) Comply with the California Electronic Communications Privacy Act pursuant to Chapter 3.6 (commencing with Section 1546) of Title 12 of Part 2 of the Penal Code.

(6) Engage in public or peer-reviewed scientific, historical, or statistical research in the public interest that adheres to all other applicable ethics and privacy laws, when the business' deletion of the information is likely to render impossible or seriously impair the achievement of

such research, if the consumer has provided informed consent.

(7) To enable solely internal uses that are reasonably aligned with the expectations of the consumer based on the consumer's relationship with the business.

(8) Comply with a legal obligation.

(9) Otherwise use the consumer's personal information, internally, in a lawful manner that is compatible with the context in which the consumer provided the information.

Recent Developments
California Consumer Privacy Act

1798.110.

(a) A consumer shall have the right to request that a business that collects personal information about the consumer disclose to the consumer the following:

(1) The categories of personal information it has collected about consumers.

(2) The categories of sources from which the personal information is collected.

(3) The business or commercial purpose for collecting or selling personal information.

(4) The categories of third parties with whom the business shares personal information.

(5) That a consumer has the right to request the specific pieces of personal information it has collected about that consumer.

(b) A business that collects personal information about a consumer shall disclose to the consumer, pursuant to paragraph (3) of subdivision (a) of Section 1798.130, the information specified in subdivision (a) upon receipt of a verifiable consumer request from the consumer.

(c) A business that collects personal information about consumers shall disclose, pursuant to subparagraph (B) of paragraph (5) of subdivision (a) of Section 1798.130:

(1) The categories of personal information it has collected about that consumer.

(2) The categories of sources from which the personal information is collected.

(3) The business or commercial purpose for collecting or selling personal information.

(4) The categories of third parties with whom the business shares personal information.

(5) The specific pieces of personal information the business has collected about that consumer.

(d) This section does not require a business to do the following:

(1) Retain any personal information about a consumer collected for a single one-time transaction if, in the ordinary course of business, that information about the consumer is not retained.

(2) Reidentify or otherwise link any data that, in the ordinary course of business, is not maintained in a manner that would be considered personal information.

1798.115.

(a) A consumer shall have the right to request that a business that sells the consumer's personal information, or that dis- closes it for a business purpose, disclose to that consumer:

(1) The categories of personal information that the business collected about the consumer.

(2) The categories of personal information that the business sold about the consumer and the categories of third parties to whom the personal information was sold, by category or categories of personal information for each category of third parties to whom the person- al information was sold.

(3) The categories of personal information that the business disclosed about the consumer for a business purpose.

(b) A business that sells personal information about a consumer, or that discloses a consumer's personal information for a business purpose, shall disclose, pursuant to paragraph (4) of subdivision (a) of Section 1798.130, the information specified in subdivision (a) to the consumer upon receipt of a verifiable consumer request from the consumer.

(c) A business that sells consumers' personal information, or that discloses consumers' personal information for a business purpose, shall disclose, pursuant to subparagraph (C) of paragraph (5) of subdivision (a) of Section 1798.130:

(1) The category or categories of consumers' personal information it has sold, or if the business has not sold consumers' personal information, it shall dis- close that fact.

(2) The category or categories of consumers' personal information it has disclosed for a business purpose, or if the business has not disclosed the consumers' personal information for a business purpose, it shall disclose that fact.

(d) A third party shall not sell personal information about a consumer that has been sold to the third party by a busi- ness unless the consumer has received explicit notice and is provided an opportunity to exercise the right to opt out pursuant to Section 1798.120.

1798.120.

(a) A consumer shall have the right, at any time, to direct a business that sells personal information about the consumer to third parties not to sell the consumer's personal information. This right may be referred to as the right to opt out.

(b) A business that sells consumers' personal information to third parties shall provide notice to consumers, pursuant to subdivision (a) of Section 1798.135, that this information may be sold and that consumers have the right to opt out of the sale of their personal information.

(c) Notwithstanding subdivision(a), a business shall not sell the personal information of consumers if the business has actual knowledge that the consumer is less than 16 years of age, unless the consumer, in the case of consumers at least 13 years of age and less than 16 years of age, or the consumer's parent or guardian, in the case of consumers who are less than 13 years of age, has affirmatively authorized the sale of the consumer's personal information. A business that willfully disregards the consumer's age shall be deemed to have had actual knowledge of the consumer's age. This right may be referred to as the "right to opt in."

(d) A business that has received direction from a consumer not to sell the consumer's personal information or, in the case of a minor consumer's personal information has not received consent to sell the minor consumer's personal information shall be prohibited, pursuant to paragraph (4) of subdivision (a) of Section 1798.135, from selling the consumer's personal information after its receipt of the consumer's direction, unless the consumer subsequently provides express authorization for the sale of the consumer's personal information.

1798.125.

(a)

(1) A business shall not discriminate against a consumer because the consumer exercised any of the consumer's rights under this title, including, but not limited to, by:

(A) Denying goods or services to the consumer.

(B) Charging different prices or rates for goods or services, including through the use of discounts or other benefits or imposing penalties.

(C) Providing a different level or quality of goods or services to the consumer.

(D) Suggesting that the consumer will receive a different price or rate for goods or services or a different level or quality of goods or services.

(2) Nothing in this subdivision prohibits a business from charging a consumer a different price or rate, or from providing a different level or quality of goods or ser- vices to the consumer, if that difference is reasonably related to the value provided to the business by the consumer's data.

(b)

(1) A business may offer financial incentives, including payments to consumers as compensation, for the collection of personal information, the sale of personal information, or the deletion of personal information. A business may also offer a different price, rate, level, or quality of goods or services to the consumer if that price or difference is directly related to the value pro- vided to the business by the consumer's data.

(2) A business that offers any financial incentives pursuant this subdivision shall notify consumers of the financial incentives pursuant to Section 1798.130.

(3) A business may enter a consumer into a financial incentive program only if the consumer gives the business prior opt-in consent pursuant to Section 1798.130 that clearly describes the material terms of the financial incentive program, and which may be revoked by the consumer at any time.

(4) A business shall not use financial incentive practices that are unjust, unreasonable, coercive, or usurious in nature.

1798.130.

(a) In order to comply with Sections 1798.100, 1798.105, 1798.110, 1798.115, and 1798.125, a business shall, in a form that is reasonably accessible to consumers:

(1)(A) Make available to consumers two or more designated methods for submitting requests for information required to be disclosed pursuant to Sections 1798.110 and

1798.115, including, at a minimum, a toll-free telephone number, and if the business maintains an Internet Web site, a Web site address.

(1)(B) If the business maintains an internet website, make the internet website available to consumers to submit requests for information required to be dis- closed pursuant to Sections 1798.110 and 1798.115.

(2) Disclose and deliver the required information to a consumer free of charge within 45 days of receiving a verifiable consumer request from the consumer. The business shall promptly take steps to determine whether the request is a verifiable consumer request, but this shall not extend the business' duty to disclose and deliver the information within 45 days of receipt of the consumer's request. The time period to provide the required information may be extended once by an additional 45 days when reasonably necessary, provid- ed the consumer is provided notice of the extension within the first 45-day period. The disclosure shall cov- er the 12-month period preceding the business' receipt of the verifiable consumer request and shall be made in writing and delivered through the consumer's ac- count with the business, if the consumer maintains an account with the business, or by mail or electronically at the consumer's option if the consumer does not maintain an account with the business, in a readily use- able format that allows the consumer to transmit this information from one entity to another entity without hindrance. The business may require authentication of the consumer that is reasonable in light of the nature of the personal information requested, but shall not require the consumer to create an account with the business in order to make a verifiable consumer re- quest. If the consumer maintains an account with the business, the business may require the consumer to submit the request through that account.

(3) For purposes of subdivision (b) of Section 1798.110:

    (A) To identify the consumer, associate the information provided by the consumer in the verifiable consumer request to any personal information previously collected by the business about the consumer.

    (B) Identify by category or categories the personal information collected about the consumer in the preceding 12 months by reference to the enumerated category or categories in subdivision (c) that most closely describes the personal information collected.

(4) For purposes of subdivision (b) of Section 1798.115:

    (A) Identify the consumer and associate the information provided by the consumer in the verifiable consumer request to any personal information previously collected by the business about the consumer.

    (B) Identify by category or categories the personal information of the consumer that the business sold in the preceding 12 months by reference to the enumerated category in subdivision (c) that most closely describes the personal information, and provide the categories of third parties to whom the consumer's personal information was sold in the preceding 12 months by reference to the enumerated category or categories in subdivision (c) that most closely describes the personal information sold. The business shall disclose the information in a list that is separate from a list generated for the purposes of subparagraph (C).

(C) Identify by category or categories the personal information of the consumer that the business disclosed for a business purpose in the preceding 12 months by reference to the enumerated category or categories in subdivision (c) that most closely describes the personal information, and provide the categories of third parties to whom the consumer's personal information was disclosed for a business purpose in the preceding 12 months by reference to the enumerated category or categories in subdivision (c) that most closely describes the personal information disclosed. The business shall disclose the information in a list that is separate from a list generated for the purposes of subparagraph (B).

(5) Disclose the following information in its online privacy policy or policies if the business has an online privacy policy or policies and in any California-specific description of consumers' privacy rights, or if the business does not maintain those policies, on its internet web- site, and update that information at least once every 12 months:

(A) A description of a consumer's rights pursuant to Sections 1798.100, 1798.105, 1798.110, 1798.115, and 1798.125 and one or more designated methods for submitting requests.

(B) For purposes of subdivision (c) of Section 1798.110, a list of the categories of personal information it has collected about consumers in the preceding 12 months by reference to the enumerated category or categories in subdivision (c) that most closely describe the personal information collected.

(C) For purposes of paragraphs (1) and (2) of subdivision (c) of Section 1798.115, two separate lists:

(i) A list of the categories of personal information it has sold about consumers in the preceding 12 months by reference to the enumerated category or categories in subdivision (c) that most closely describe the personal information sold, or if the business has not sold consumers' personal information in the preceding 12 months, the business shall disclose that fact.

(ii) A list of the categories of personal information it has disclosed about consumers for a business purpose in the preceding 12 months by reference to the enumerated category in subdivision (c) that most closely describe the personal information disclosed, or if the business has not disclosed consumers' personal information for a business purpose in the preceding 12 months, the business shall disclose that fact.

(6) Ensure that all individuals responsible for handling consumer inquiries about the business' privacy practices or the business' compliance with this title are informed of all requirements in Sections 1798.100, 1798.105, 1798.110, 1798.115, and 1798.125, and this section, and how to direct consumers to exercise their rights under those sections.

(7) Use any personal information collected from the consumer in connection with the business' verification of the consumer's request solely for the purposes of verification.

(b) A business is not obligated to provide the information required by Sections 1798.110 and 1798.115 to the same consumer more than twice in a 12-month period.

(c) The categories of personal information required to be dis- closed pursuant to Sections 1798.110 and 1798.115 shall follow the definition of personal information in Section 1798.140.

1798.135.

(a) A business that is required to comply with Section 1798.120 shall, in a form that is reasonably accessible to consumers:

(1) Provide a clear and conspicuous link on the business's Internet homepage, titled "Do Not Sell My Personal Information," to an Internet Web page that enables a consumer, or a person authorized by the consumer, to opt out of the sale of the consumer's personal information. A business shall not require a consumer to create an account in order to direct the business not to sell the consumer's personal information.

(2) Include a description of a consumer's rights pursuant to Section 1798.120, along with a separate link to the "Do Not Sell My Personal Information" Internet Web page in:

(A) Its online privacy policy or policies if the business has an online privacy policy or policies.

(B) Any California-specific description of consumers' privacy rights.

(3) Ensure that all individuals responsible for handling consumer inquiries about the business's privacy practices or the business's compliance with this title are informed of all requirements in Section 1798.120 and this section and how to direct consumers to exercise their rights under those sections.

(4) For consumers who exercise their right to opt out of the sale of their personal information, refrain from selling personal information collected by the business about the consumer.

(5) For a consumer who has opted-out of the sale of the consumer's personal information, respect the consumer's decision to opt-out for at least 12 months before

requesting that the consumer authorize the sale of the consumer's personal information.

(6) Use any personal information collected from the consumer in connection with the submission of the consumer's opt-out request solely for the purposes of complying with the opt-out request.

(b) Nothing in this title shall be construed to require a business to comply with the title by including the required links and text on the homepage that the business makes available to the public generally, if the business maintains a separate and additional homepage that is dedicated to California consumers and that includes the required links and text, and the business takes reasonable steps to ensure that California consumers are directed to the homepage for California consumers and not the homepage made available to the public generally.

(c) A consumer may authorize another person solely to opt- out of the sale of the consumer's personal information on the consumer's behalf, and a business shall comply with an opt-out request received from a person authorized by the consumer to act on the consumer's behalf, pursuant to regulations adopted by the Attorney General.

1798.140.

For purposes of this title:

(a) "Aggregate consumer information" means information that relates to a group or category of consumers, from which individual consumer identities have been removed, that is not linked or reasonably linkable to any consumer or household, including via a device. "Aggregate consumer information" does not mean one or more individual consumer records that have been deidentified.

(b) "Biometric information" means an individual's physiological, biological, or behavioral characteristics, including an individual's deoxyribonucleic acid (DNA), that can be used, singly or in combination with each other or with other identifying data, to establish individual identity. Biometric information includes, but is not limited to, imagery of the iris, retina, fingerprint, face, hand, palm, vein patterns, and voice recordings, from which an identifier template, such as a faceprint, a minutiae template, or a voiceprint, can be extracted, and keystroke patterns or rhythms, gait pat- terns or rhythms, and sleep, health, or exercise data that contain identifying information.

(c) "Business" means:

(1) A sole proprietorship, partnership, limited liability company, corporation, association, or other legal entity that is organized or operated for the profit or financial benefit of its shareholders or other owners that collects consumers' personal information or on the behalf of which that information is collected and that alone, or jointly with others, determines the purposes and means of the processing of consumers' personal information, that does business in the State of California, and that satisfies one or more of the following thresholds:

(A) Has annual gross revenues in excess of twenty-five million dollars ($25,000,000), as adjusted pursu ant to paragraph (5) of subdivision (a) of Section 1798.185.

(B) Alone or in combination, annually buys, receives for the business's commercial purposes, sells, or shares for commercial purposes, alone or in combi- nation, the personal information of 50,000 or more consumers, households, or devices.

(C) Derives 50 percent or more of its annual revenues from selling consumers' personal information.

(2) Any entity that controls or is controlled by a business as defined in paragraph (1) and that shares common branding with the business. "Control" or "controlled" means ownership of, or the power to vote, more than 50 percent of the outstanding shares of any class of voting security of a business; control in any manner over the election of a majority of the directors, or of individuals exercising similar functions; or the power to exercise a controlling influence over the management of a company. "Common branding" means a shared name, servicemark, or trademark.

(d) "Business purpose" means the use of personal information for the business's or a service provider's operational purposes, or other notified purposes, provided that the use of personal information shall be reasonably necessary and proportionate to achieve the operational purpose for which the personal information was collected or processed or for another operational purpose that is compatible with the context in which the personal information was collect- ed. Business purposes are:

(1) Auditing related to a current interaction with the consumer and concurrent transactions, including, but not limited to, counting ad impressions to unique visitors, verifying positioning and quality of ad impressions, and auditing compliance with this specification and other standards.

(2) Detecting security incidents, protecting against malicious, deceptive, fraudulent, or illegal activity, and prosecuting those responsible for that activity.

(3) Debugging to identify and repair errors that impair existing intended functionality.

(4) Short-term, transient use, provided that the personal information is not disclosed to another third party and is not used to build a profile about a consumer or other- wise alter an individual consumer's experience outside the current interaction, including, but not limited to, the contextual customization of ads shown as part of the same interaction.

(5) Performing services on behalf of the business or service provider, including maintaining or servicing accounts, providing customer service, processing or fulfilling orders and transactions, verifying customer information, processing payments, providing financing, providing advertising or marketing services,

providing analytic services, or providing similar services on behalf of the business or service provider.

(6) Undertaking internal research for technological development and demonstration.

(7) Undertaking activities to verify or maintain the quality or safety of a service or device that is owned, manufactured, manufactured for, or controlled by the business, and to improve, upgrade, or enhance the service or device that is owned, manufactured, manufactured for, or controlled by the business.

(e) "Collects," "collected," or "collection" means buying, renting, gathering, obtaining, receiving, or accessing any personal information pertaining to a consumer by any means. This includes receiving information from the consumer, either actively or passively, or by observing the consumer's behavior.

(f) "Commercial purposes" means to advance a person's commercial or economic interests, such as by inducing another person to buy, rent, lease, join, subscribe to, pro- vide, or exchange products, goods, property, information, or services, or enabling or effecting, directly or indirectly, a commercial transaction. "Commercial purposes" do not include for the purpose of engaging in speech that state or federal courts have recognized as noncommercial speech, including political speech and journalism.

(g) "Consumer" means a natural person who is a California resident, as defined in Section 17014 of Title 18 of the California Code of Regulations, as that section read on September 1, 2017, however identified, including by any unique identifier.

(h) "Deidentified" means information that cannot reasonably identify, relate to, describe, be capable of being associated with, or be linked, directly or indirectly, to a particular consumer, provided that a business that uses deidentified information:

(1) Has implemented technical safeguards that prohibit reidentification of the consumer to whom the information may pertain.

(2) Has implemented business processes that specifically prohibit reidentification of the information.

(3) Has implemented business processes to prevent inadvertent release of deidentified information.

(4) Makes no attempt to reidentify the information.

(i) "Designated methods for submitting requests" means a mailing address, email address, internet web page, internet web portal, toll-free telephone number, or other applicable contact information, whereby consumers may submit a request or direction under this title, and any new, consumer-friendly means of contacting a business, as approved by the Attorney General pursuant to Section 1798.185.

(j) "Device" means any physical object that is capable of connecting to the internet, directly or indirectly, or to another device.

(k) "Health insurance information" means a consumer's insurance policy number or subscriber identification number, any unique identifier used by a health insurer to identify the consumer, or any information in the consumer's application and claims history, including any appeals records, if the information is linked or reasonably linkable to a consumer or household, including via a device, by a business or service provider.

(l) "Homepage" means the introductory page of an internet website and any internet web page where personal information is collected. In the case of an online service, such as a mobile application, homepage means the application's platform page or download page, a link within the application, such as from the application configuration, "About," "Information," or settings page, and any other location that allows consumers to review the notice required by subdivision (a) of Section 1798.135, including, but not limited to, before downloading the application.

(m) "Infer" or "inference" means the derivation of information, data, assumptions, or conclusions from facts, evidence, or another source of information or data.

(n) "Person" means an individual, proprietorship, firm, partnership, joint venture, syndicate, business trust, company, corporation, limited liability company, association, commit- tee, and any other organization or group of persons acting in concert.

(o)

(1) "Personal information" means information that identifies, relates to, describes, is reasonably capable of being associated with, or could reasonably be linked, directly or indirectly, with a particular consumer or household. Personal information includes, but is not limited to, the following if it identifies, relates to, de- scribes, is reasonably capable of being associated with, or could be reasonably linked, directly or indirectly, with a particular consumer or household:

(A) Identifiers such as a real name, alias, postal ad- dress, unique personal identifier, online identifier, internet protocol address, email address, account name, social security number, driver's license num- ber, passport number, or other similar identifiers.

(B) Any categories of personal information de- scribed in subdivision (e) of Section 1798.80.

(C) Characteristics of protected classifications under California or federal law.

(D) Commercial information, including records of personal property, products or services purchased, obtained, or considered, or other purchasing or consuming histories or tendencies.

(E) Biometric information.

(F) Internet or other electronic network activity information, including, but not limited to, browsing history, search history, and information regarding a consumer's interaction with an internet website, application, or advertisement.

(G) Geolocation data.

(H) Audio, electronic, visual, thermal, olfactory, or similar information.

(I) Professional or employment-related information.

(J) Education information, defined as information that is not publicly available personally identifiable information as defined in the Family Educational Rights and Privacy Act (20 U.S.C. Sec. 1232g; 34 C.F.R. Part 99).

(K) Inferences drawn from any of the information identified in this subdivision to create a profile about a consumer reflecting the consumer's preferences, characteristics, psychological trends, predispositions, behavior, attitudes, intelligence, abilities, and aptitudes.

(2) "Personal information" does not include publicly available information. For purposes of this paragraph, "publicly available" means information that is lawfully made available from federal, state, or local government records. "Publicly available" does not mean biometric information collected by a business about a consumer without the consumer's knowledge.

(3) "Personal information" does not include consumer information that is deidentified or aggregate consumer information.

(p) "Probabilistic identifier" means the identification of a consumer or a device to a degree of certainty of more probable than not based on any categories of personal information included in, or similar to, the categories enumerated in the definition of personal information.

(q) "Processing" means any operation or set of operations that are performed on personal data or on sets of personal data, whether or not by automated means.

(r) "Pseudonymize" or "Pseudonymization" means the processing of personal information in a manner that renders the personal information no longer attributable to a specific consumer without the use of additional information, provided that the additional information is kept separately and is subject to technical and organizational measures to ensure that the personal information is not attributed to an identified or identifiable consumer.

(s) "Research" means scientific, systematic study and observation, including basic research or applied research that is in the public interest and that adheres to all other applicable ethics and privacy laws or studies conducted in the public interest in the area of public health. Research with personal information that may have been collected from a consumer in the course of the consumer's interactions with a business's service or device for other purposes shall be:

(1) Compatible with the business purpose for which the personal information was collected.

(2) Subsequently pseudonymized and deidentified, or deidentified and in the aggregate, such that the information cannot reasonably identify, relate to, describe, be capable of being associated with, or be linked, directly or indirectly, to a particular consumer.

(3) Made subject to technical safeguards that prohibit reidentification of the consumer to whom the information may pertain.

(4) Subject to business processes that specifically prohibit reidentification of the information.

(5) Made subject to business processes to prevent inadvertent release of deidentified information.

(6) Protected from any reidentification attempts.

(7) Used solely for research purposes that are compatible with the context in which the personal information was collected.

(8) Not be used for any commercial purpose.

(9) Subjected by the business conducting the research to additional security controls that limit access to the research data to only those individuals in a business as are necessary to carry out the research purpose.

(t)

(1) "Sell," "selling," "sale," or "sold," means selling, renting, releasing, disclosing, disseminating, making available, transferring, or otherwise communicating orally, in writing, or by electronic or other means, a consumer's personal information by the business to another business or a third party for monetary or other valuable consideration.

(2) For purposes of this title, a business does not sell personal information when:

(A) A consumer uses or directs the business to intentionally disclose personal information or uses the business to intentionally interact with a third party, provided the third party does not also sell the personal information, unless that disclosure would be consistent with the provisions of this title. An intentional interaction occurs when the consumer intends to interact with the third party, via one or more deliberate interactions. Hovering over, muting, pausing, or closing a given piece of content does not constitute a consumer's intent to interact with a third party.

(B) The business uses or shares an identifier for a consumer who has opted out of the sale of the consumer's personal information for the purposes of alerting third parties that the consumer has opted out of the sale of the consumer's personal information.

(C) The business uses or shares with a service provider personal information of a consumer that is necessary to perform a business purpose if both of the following conditions are met:

(i) The business has provided notice of that information being used or shared in its terms and conditions consistent with Section 1798.135.

(ii) The service provider does not further collect, sell, or use the personal information of the consumer except as necessary to perform the business purpose.

(D) The business transfers to a third party the personal information of a consumer as an asset that is part of a merger, acquisition, bankruptcy, or other transaction in which the third party assumes control of all or part of the business, provided that information is used or shared consistently with Sections 1798.110 and 1798.115. If a third party materially alters how it uses or shares the personal information of a consumer in a manner that is materially inconsistent with the promises made at the time of collection, it shall provide prior notice of the new or changed practice to the consumer. The notice shall be sufficiently prominent and robust to ensure that existing consumers can easily exercise their choices consistently with Section 1798.120. This subparagraph does not authorize a business to make material, retroactive privacy policy changes or make other changes in their privacy policy in a manner that would violate the Unfair and Deceptive Practices Act (Chapter 5 (commencing with Section 17200) of Part 2 of Division 7 of the Business and Professions Code).

(u) "Service" or "services" means work, labor, and services, including services furnished in connection with the sale or repair of goods.

(v) "Service provider" means a sole proprietorship, partner- ship, limited liability company, corporation, association, or other legal entity that is organized or operated for the profit or financial benefit of its shareholders or other owners, that processes information on behalf of a business and to which the business discloses a consumer's personal information for a business purpose pursuant to a written contract, provided that the contract prohibits the entity receiving the information from retaining, using, or disclosing the personal information for any purpose other than for the specific purpose of performing the services specified in the contract for the business, or as otherwise permitted by this title, including retaining, using, or dis- closing the personal information for a commercial purpose other than providing the services specified in the contract with the business.

(w) "Third party" means a person who is not any of the following:

(1) The business that collects personal information from consumers under this title.

(2)

(A) A person to whom the business discloses a consumer's personal information for a business purpose pursuant to a written contract, provided that the contract:

(i) Prohibits the person receiving the personal information from:

(I) Selling the personal information.

(II) Retaining, using, or disclosing the personal information for any purpose other than for the specific purpose of performing the services specified in the contract, including retaining, using, or disclosing the personal information for a commercial purpose other than providing the services specified in the contract

> > (III) Retaining, using, or disclosing the information outside of the direct business relation- ship between the person and the business.
>
> > (ii) Includes a certification made by the person receiving the personal information that the person understands the restrictions in subparagraph (A) and will comply with them.
>
> (B) A person covered by this paragraph that violates any of the restrictions set forth in this title shall be liable for the violations. A business that discloses personal information to a person covered by this paragraph in compliance with this paragraph shall not be liable under this title if the person receiving the personal information uses it in violation of the restrictions set forth in this title, provided that, at the time of disclosing the personal information, the business does not have actual knowledge, or rea- son to believe, that the person intends to commit such a violation.

(x) "Unique identifier" or "Unique personal identifier" means a persistent identifier that can be used to recognize a consumer, a family, or a device that is linked to a consumer or family, over time and across different services, including, but not limited to, a device identifier; an Internet Protocol address; cookies, beacons, pixel tags, mobile ad identifiers, or similar technology; customer number, unique pseudonym, or user alias; telephone numbers, or other forms of persistent or probabilistic identifiers that can be used to identify a particular consumer or device. For purposes of this subdivision, "family" means a custodial parent or guardian and any minor children over which the parent or guardian has custody.

(y) "Verifiable consumer request" means a request that is made by a consumer, by a consumer on behalf of the consumer's minor child, or by a natural person or a person registered with the Secretary of State, authorized by the consumer to act on the consumer's behalf, and that the business can reasonably verify, pursuant to regulations ad- opted by the Attorney General pursuant to paragraph (7) of subdivision (a) of Section 1798.185 to be the consumer about whom the business has collected personal information. A business is not obligated to provide information to the consumer pursuant to Sections 1798.100, 1798.105, 1798.110, and 1798.115 if the business cannot verify, pursuant to this subdivision and regulations adopted by the Attorney General pursuant to paragraph (7) of subdivision (a) of Section 1798.185, that the consumer making the request is the consumer about whom the business has collected information or is a person authorized by the consumer to act on such consumer's behalf.

1798.145.

> (a) The obligations imposed on businesses by this title shall not restrict a business' ability to:
>
> > (1) Comply with federal, state, or local laws.
>
> > (2) Comply with a civil, criminal, or regulatory inquiry, investigation, subpoena, or summons by federal, state, or local authorities.

(3) Cooperate with law enforcement agencies concerning conduct or activity that the business, service provider, or third party reasonably and in good faith believes may violate federal, state, or local law.

(4) Exercise or defend legal claims.

(5) Collect, use, retain, sell, or disclose consumer information that is deidentified or in the aggregate consumer information.

(6) Collect or sell a consumer's personal information if every aspect of that commercial conduct takes place wholly outside of California. For purposes of this title, commercial conduct takes place wholly outside of California if the business collected that information while the consumer was outside of California, no part of the sale of the consumer's personal information occurred in California, and no personal information collected while the consumer was in California is sold. This paragraph shall not permit a business from storing, including on a device, personal information about a consumer when the consumer is in California and then collecting that personal information when the consumer and stored personal information is outside of California.

(b) The obligations imposed on businesses by Sections 1798.110 to 1798.135, inclusive, shall not apply where compliance by the business with the title would violate an evidentiary privilege under California law and shall not prevent a business from providing the personal information of a consumer to a person covered by an evidentiary privilege under California law as part of a privileged communication.

(c)

(1) This title shall not apply to any of the following:

(A) Medical information governed by the Confidentiality of Medical Information Act (Part 2.6 (commencing with Section 56) of Division 1) or protected health information

that is collected by a covered entity or business associate governed by the privacy, security, and breach notification rules issued by the United States Department of Health and Hu- man Services, Parts 160 and 164 of Title 45 of the Code of Federal Regulations, established pursuant to the Health Insurance Portability and Account- ability Act of 1996 (Public Law 104-191) and the Health Information Technology for Economic and Clinical Health Act (Public Law 111-5)

(B) A provider of health care governed by the Confidentiality of Medical Information Act (Part 2.6 (commencing with Section 56) of Division 1) or a covered entity governed by the privacy, security, and breach notification rules issued by the United States Department of Health and Human Services, Parts 160 and 164 of Title 45 of the Code of Federal Regulations, established pursuant to the Health Insurance Portability and Accountability Act of 1996 (Public Law 104-191), to the extent the provider or covered entity maintains patient information in the same manner as medical information or protected health information as described in subparagraph (A) of this section.

(C) Information collected as part of a clinical trial subject to the Federal Policy for the Protection of Human Subjects, also known as the Common Rule, pursuant to good clinical practice guidelines issued by the International Council for Harmonisation or pursuant to human subject protection requirements of the United States Food and Drug Administration.

(2) For purposes of this subdivision, the definitions of "medical information" and "provider of health care" in Section 56.05 shall apply and the definitions of "business associate," "covered entity," and "protected health information" in Section 160.103 of Title 45 of the Code of Federal Regulations shall apply.

(d)

(1) This title shall not apply to an activity involving the collection, maintenance, disclosure, sale, communication, or use of any personal information bearing on a consumer's credit worthiness, credit standing, credit capacity, character, general reputation, personal characteristics, or mode of living by a consumer reporting agency, as defined in subdivision (f) of Section 1681a of Title 15 of the United States Code, by a furnisher of information, as set forth in Section 1681s-2 of Title 15 of the United States Code, who provides information for use in a consumer report, as defined in subdivision (d) of Section 1681a of Title 15 of the United States Code, and by a user of a consumer report as set forth in Section 1681b of Title 15 of the United States Code.

(2) Paragraph (1) shall apply only to the extent that such activity involving the collection, maintenance, disclosure, sale, communication, or use of such information by that agency, furnisher, or user is subject to regulation under the Fair Credit Reporting Act, section 1681 et seq., Title 15 of the United States Code and the information is not used, communicated, disclosed, or sold except as authorized by the Fair Credit Reporting Act.

(3) This subdivision shall not apply to Section 1798.150.

(e) This title shall not apply to personal information collected, processed, sold, or disclosed pursuant to the federal Gramm-Leach-Bliley Act (Public Law 106-102), and implementing regulations, or the California Financial Information Privacy Act (Division 1.4 (commencing with Section 4050) of the Financial Code). This subdivision shall not apply to Section 1798.150.

(f) This title shall not apply to personal information collected, processed, sold, or disclosed pursuant to the Driver's Privacy Protection Act of 1994 (18 U.S.C. Sec. 2721 et seq.). This subdivision shall not apply to Section 1798.150.

(g)

(1) Section 1798.120 shall not apply to vehicle information or ownership information retained or shared between a new motor vehicle dealer, as defined in Section 426 of the Vehicle Code, and the vehicle's manufacturer, as defined in Section 672 of the Vehicle Code, if the vehicle or ownership information is shared for the purpose of effectuating, or in anticipation of effectuating, a vehicle repair covered by a vehicle warranty or a recall conducted pursuant to Sections 30118 to 30120, inclusive, of Title 49 of the United States Code, provided that the new motor vehicle dealer or vehicle manufacturer with which that vehicle information or ownership information is shared does not sell, share, or use that information for any other purpose.

(2) For purposes of this subdivision:

(A) "Vehicle information" means the vehicle information number, make, model, year, and odometer reading.

(B) "Ownership information" means the name or names of the registered owner or owners and the contact information for the owner or owners.

(h)

(1) This title shall not apply to any of the following:

(A) Personal information that is collected by a business about a natural person in the course of the natural person acting as a job applicant to, an employee of, owner of, director of, officer of, medical staff mem- ber of, or contractor of that business to the extent that the natural person's personal information is collected and used by the business solely within the context of the natural person's role or former role as a job applicant to, an employee of, owner of, director of, officer of, medical staff member of, or a contractor of that business.

(B) Personal information that is collected by a business that is emergency contact information of the natural person acting as a job applicant to, an employee of, owner of, director of, officer of, medical staff member of, or contractor of that business to the extent that the personal information is collected and used solely within the context of having an emergency contact on file.

(C) Personal information that is necessary for the business to retain to administer benefits for an- other natural person relating to the natural person acting as a job applicant to, an employee of, owner of, director of, officer of, medical staff member of, or contractor of that business to the extent that the personal information is collected and used solely within the context of administering those benefits.

(2) For purposes of this subdivision:

(A) "Contractor" means a natural person who provides any service to a business pursuant to a written contract.

(B) "Director" means a natural person designated in the articles of incorporation as such or elected by the incorporators and natural persons designated, elected, or appointed by any other name or title to act as directors, and their successors.

(C) "Medical staff member" means a licensed physician and surgeon, dentist, or podiatrist, licensed pursuant to Division 2 (commencing with Section 500) of the Business and Professions Code and a clinical psychologist as defined in Section 1316.5 of the Health and Safety Code.

(D) "Officer" means a natural person elected or ap- pointed by the board of directors to manage the daily operations of a corporation, such as a chief executive officer, president, secretary, or treasurer.

(E) "Owner" means a natural person who meets one of the following:

(i) Has ownership of, or the power to vote, more than 50 percent of the outstanding shares of any class of voting security of a business.

(ii) Has control in any manner over the election of a majority of the directors or of individuals exercising similar functions.

(iii) Has the power to exercise a controlling influence over the management of a company.

(3) This subdivision shall not apply to subdivision (b) of Section 1798.100 or Section 1798.150.

(4) This subdivision shall become inoperative on January 1, 2021.

(i) Notwithstanding a business' obligations to respond to and honor consumer rights requests pursuant to this title:

(1) A time period for a business to respond to any verified consumer request may be extended by up to 90 additional days where necessary, taking into account the complexity and number of the requests. The business shall inform the consumer of any such extension within 45 days of receipt of the request, together with the reasons for the delay.

(2) If the business does not take action on the request of the consumer, the business shall inform the consumer, without delay and at the latest within the time period permitted of response by this section, of the reasons for not taking action and any rights the consumer may have to appeal the decision to the business.

(3) If requests from a consumer are manifestly unfound- ed or excessive, in particular because of their repetitive character, a business may either charge a reasonable fee, taking into account the administrative costs of providing the information or communication or taking the action requested, or refuse to act on the request and notify the consumer of the reason for refusing the request. The business shall bear the burden of demonstrating that any verified consumer request is manifestly unfounded or excessive.

(j) A business that discloses personal information to a service provider shall not be liable under this title if the service provider receiving the personal information uses it in violation of the restrictions set forth in the title, pro- vided that, at the time of disclosing the personal information, the business does not have actual knowledge, or reason to believe, that the service provider intends to commit such a violation. A service provider shall likewise not be liable under this title for the obligations of a business for which it provides services as set forth in this title.

(k) This title shall not be construed to require a business to collect personal information that it would not otherwise collect in the ordinary course of its business, retain personal information for longer than it would otherwise retain such information in the ordinary course of its business, or reidentify or otherwise link information that is not maintained in a manner that would be considered personal information.

(l) The rights afforded to consumers and the obligations imposed on the business in this title shall not adversely affect the rights and freedoms of other consumers.

(m) The rights afforded to consumers and the obligations imposed on any business under this title shall not apply to the extent that they infringe on the noncommercial activities of a person or entity described in subdivision (b) of Section 2 of Article I of the California Constitution.

(n)

> (1) The obligations imposed on businesses by Sections 1798.100, 1798.105, 1798.110, 1798.115, 1798.130, and 1798.135 shall not apply to personal information reflecting a written or verbal communication or a trans- action between the business and the consumer, where the consumer is a natural person who is acting as an employee, owner, director, officer, or contractor of a company, partnership, sole proprietorship, non-profit, or government agency and whose communications or transaction with the business occur solely within the context of the business conducting due diligence regarding, or providing or receiving a product or service to or from such company, partnership, sole proprietor- ship, non-profit, or government agency.
>
> (2) For purposes of this subdivision:
>
> > (A) "Contractor" means a natural person who provides any service to a business pursuant to a written contract.
> >
> > (B) "Director" means a natural person designated in the articles of incorporation as such or elected by the incorporators and natural persons designated, elected, or appointed by any other name or title to act as directors, and their successors.
> >
> > (C) "Officer" means a natural person elected or ap- pointed by the board of directors to manage the daily operations of a corporation, such as a chief executive officer, president, secretary, or treasurer.
> >
> > (D) "Owner" means a natural person who meets one of the following:

(i) Has ownership of, or the power to vote, more than 50 percent of the outstanding shares of any class of voting security of a business.

(ii) Has control in any manner over the election of a majority of the directors or of individuals exercising similar functions.

(iii) Has the power to exercise a controlling influence over the management of a company.

(3) This subdivision shall become inoperative on January 1, 2021.

1798.150.

(a)

(1) Any consumer whose nonencrypted and nonredacted personal information, as defined in subparagraph (A) of paragraph (1) of subdivision (d) of Section 1798.81.5, is subject to an unauthorized access and exfiltration, theft, or disclosure as a result of the business's violation of the duty to implement and maintain reasonable security procedures and practices appropriate to the nature of the information to protect the personal information may institute a civil action for any of the following:

(A) To recover damages in an amount not less than one hundred dollars ($100) and not greater than seven hundred and fifty ($750) per consumer per incident or actual damages, whichever is greater.

(B) Injunctive or declaratory relief.

(C) Any other relief the court deems proper.

(2) In assessing the amount of statutory damages, the court shall consider any one or more of the relevant circumstances presented by any of the parties to the case, including, but not limited to, the nature and seriousness of the misconduct, the number of violations, the persistence of the misconduct, the length of time over which the misconduct occurred, the willfulness of the defendant's misconduct, and the defendant's assets, liabilities, and net worth.

(b) Actions pursuant to this section may be brought by a consumer if prior to initiating any action against a business for statutory damages on an individual or class-wide basis, a consumer provides a business 30 days' written notice identifying the specific provisions of this title the consumer alleges have been or are being violated. In the event a cure is possible, if within the 30 days the business actually cures the noticed violation and provides the consumer an express written statement that the violations have been cured and that no further violations shall occur, no action for individual statutory damages or class-wide statutory damages may be initiated against the business. No notice shall be required prior to an individual consumer initiating an action solely for actual pecuniary damages suffered as a result of the alleged violations of this title. If a business continues to violate this title in breach of the express written statement provided to the consumer under this section, the consumer may initiate an action against the business to enforce the written statement and may pursue statutory damages for each breach of the express written statement, as well as any other violation of the title that postdates the written statement.

(c) The cause of action established by this section shall apply only to violations as defined in subdivision (a) and shall not be based on violations of any other section of this title. Nothing in this title shall be interpreted to serve as the basis for a private right of action under any other law. This shall not be construed to relieve any party from any duties or obligations imposed under other law or the United States or California Constitution.

1798.155.

(a) Any business or third party may seek the opinion of the Attorney General for guidance on how to comply with the provisions of this title.

(b) A business shall be in violation of this title if it fails to cure any alleged violation within 30 days after being notified of alleged noncompliance. Any business, service provider, or other person that violates this title shall be subject to an injunction and liable for a civil penalty of not more than two thousand five hundred dollars ($2,500) for each violation or seven thousand five hundred dollars ($7,500) for each intentional violation, which shall be assessed and recovered in a civil action brought in the name of the people of the State of California by the Attorney General. The civil penalties provided for in this section shall be exclusively assessed and recovered in a civil action brought in the name of the people of the State of California by the Attorney General.

(c) Any civil penalty assessed for a violation of this title, and the proceeds of any settlement of an action brought pursuant to subdivision (b), shall be deposited in the Consumer Privacy Fund, created within the General Fund pursuant to subdivision (a) of Section 1798.160 with the intent to fully offset any costs incurred by the state courts and the Attorney General in connection with this title.

1798.160.

(a) A special fund to be known as the "Consumer Privacy Fund" is hereby created within the General Fund in the State Treasury, and is available upon appropriation by the Legislature to offset any costs incurred by the state courts in connection with actions brought to enforce this title and any costs incurred by the Attorney General in carrying out the Attorney General's duties under this title.

(b) Funds transferred to the Consumer Privacy Fund shall be used exclusively to offset any costs incurred by the state courts and the Attorney General in connection with this title. These funds shall not be subject to appropriation or transfer by the Legislature for any other purpose, unless the Director of Finance determines that the funds are in excess of the funding needed to fully offset the costs incurred by the state courts and the Attorney General in connection with this title, in which case the Legislature may appropriate excess funds for other purposes.

1798.175.

This title is intended to further the constitutional right of privacy and to supplement existing laws relating to consumers' personal information, including, but not limited to, Chapter 22 (commencing with Section 22575) of Division 8 of the Business and Professions Code and Title 1.81 (commencing with Section 1798.80). The provisions of this title are not limited to information collected electronically or over the Internet, but apply to the collection and sale of all personal information collected by a business from consumers. Wherever possible, law relating to consumers' personal information should be construed to harmonize with the provisions of this title, but in the event of a conflict between other laws and the provisions of this title, the provisions of the law that afford the greatest protection for the right of privacy for consumers shall control.

1798.180.

This title is a matter of statewide concern and supersedes and preempts all rules, regulations, codes, ordinances, and other laws adopted by a city, county, city and county, municipality, or local agency regarding the collection and sale of consumers' personal information by a business.

1798.185.

(a) On or before July 1, 2020, the Attorney General shall solicit broad public participation and adopt regulations to further the purposes of this title, including, but not limited to, the following areas:

(1) Updating as needed additional categories of personal information to those enumerated in subdivision (c) of Section 1798.130 and subdivision (o) of Section 1798.140 in order to address changes in technology, data collection practices, obstacles to implementation, and privacy concerns.

(2) Updating as needed the definition of unique identifiers to address changes in technology, data collection, obstacles to implementation, and privacy concerns, and additional categories to the definition of designated methods for submitting requests to facilitate a consumer's ability to obtain information from a business pursuant to Section 1798.130.

(3) Establishing any exceptions necessary to comply with state or federal law, including, but not limited to, those relating to trade secrets and intellectual property rights, within one year of passage of this title and as needed thereafter.

(4) Establishing rules and procedures for the following:

(A) To facilitate and govern the submission of a re- quest by a consumer to opt out of the sale of personal information pursuant to Section 1798.120.

(B) To govern business compliance with a consumer's opt-out request.

(C) For the development and use of a recognizable and uniform opt-out logo or button by all businesses to promote consumer awareness of the opportunity to opt-out of the sale of personal information.

(5) Adjusting the monetary threshold in subparagraph (A) of paragraph (1) of subdivision (c) of Section 1798.140 in January of every odd-numbered year to reflect any increase in the Consumer Price Index.

(6) Establishing rules, procedures, and any exceptions necessary to ensure that the notices and information that businesses are required to provide pursuant to this title are provided in a manner that may be easily understood by the average consumer, are accessible to consumers with disabilities, and are available in the language primarily used to interact with the consumer, including establishing rules and guidelines regarding financial incentive offerings, within one year of passage of this title and as needed thereafter.

(7) Establishing rules and procedures to further the purposes of Sections 1798.110 and 1798.115 and to facilitate a consumer's or the consumer's authorized agent's ability to obtain information pursuant to Section 1798.130, with the goal of minimizing the administrative burden on consumers, taking into account available technology, security concerns, and the burden on the business, to govern a business's determination that a request for information received from a consumer is a verifiable consumer request, including treating a request submitted through a password-protected account maintained by the consumer with the business while the consumer is logged into the account as a verifiable consumer request

and providing a mechanism for a consumer who does not maintain an account with the business to request information through the business's authentication of the consumer's identity, within one year of passage of this title and as needed thereafter.

(b) The Attorney General may adopt additional regulations as follows:

(1) To establish rules and procedures on how to process and comply with verifiable consumer requests for specific pieces of personal information relating to a household in order to address obstacles to implementation and privacy concerns.

(2) As necessary to further the purposes of this title.

(c) The Attorney General shall not bring an enforcement action under this title until six months after the publication of the final regulations issued pursuant to this section or July 1, 2020, whichever is sooner.

1798.190.

If a series of steps or transactions were component parts of a single transaction intended from the beginning to be taken with the intention of avoiding the reach of this title, including the disclosure of information by a business to a third party in order to avoid the definition of sell, a court shall disregard the intermediate steps or transactions for purposes of effectuating the purposes of this title.

1798.192.

Any provision of a contract or agreement of any kind that purports to waive or limit in any way a consumer's rights under this title, including, but not limited to, any right to a remedy or means of enforcement, shall be deemed contrary to public policy and shall be void and unenforceable. This section shall not prevent a consumer from declining to request information from a business, declining to opt out of a business's sale of the consumer's personal information, or authorizing a business to sell the consumer's personal information after previously opting out.

1798.194.

This title shall be liberally construed to effectuate its purposes.

1798.196.

This title is intended to supplement federal and state law, if permissible, but shall not apply if such application is preempt- ed by, or in conflict with, federal law or the United States or California Constitution.

1798.198.

(a) Subject to limitation provided in subdivision (b), and in Section 1798.199, this title shall be operative January 1, 2020.

(b) This title shall become operative only if initiative measure No. 17-0039, The Consumer Right to Privacy Act of 2018, is withdrawn from the ballot pursuant to Section 9604 of the Elections Code.

1798.199.

Notwithstanding Section 1798.198, Section 1798.180 shall be operative on the effective date of the act adding this section.

1798.99.80.

For purposes of this title:

(a) "Business" has the meaning provided in subdivision (c) of Section 1798.140.

(b) "Collect" and "collected" have the meaning provided in subdivision (e) of Section 1798.140.

(c) "Consumer" has the meaning provided in subdivision (g) of Section 1798.140.

(d) "Data broker" means a business that knowingly collects and sells to third parties the personal information of a consumer with whom the business does not have a direct relationship. "Data broker" does not include any of the following:

(1) A consumer reporting agency to the extent that it is covered by the federal Fair Credit Reporting Act (15 U.S.C. Sec. 1681 et seq.).

(2) A financial institution to the extent that it is covered by the Gramm-Leach-Bliley Act (Public Law 106-102) and implementing regulations.

(3) An entity to the extent that it is covered by the Insurance Information and Privacy Protection Act (Article 6.6 (commencing with Section 1791) of Chapter 1 of Part 2 of Division 1 of the Insurance Code).

(e) "Personal information" has the meaning provided in subdivision (o) of Section 1798.140.

(f) "Sale" or "sold" have the meaning provided in subdivision (t) of Section 1798.140.

(g) "Third party" has the meaning provided in subdivision (w) of Section 1798.140.

1798.99.82.

(a) On or before January 31 following each year in which a business meets the definition of data broker as provided in this title, the business shall register with the Attorney General pursuant to the requirements of this section.

(b) In registering with the Attorney General, as described in subdivision (a), a data broker shall do all of the following:

(1) Pay a registration fee in an amount determined by the Attorney General, not to exceed the reasonable costs of establishing and maintaining the informational internet website described in Section 1798.99.84.

(2) Provide the following information:

(A) The name of the data broker and its primary physical, email, and internet website addresses.

(B) Any additional information or explanation the data broker chooses to provide concerning its data collection practices.

(c)

(1) A data broker that fails to register as required by this section is subject to injunction and is liable for civil penalties, fees, and costs in an action brought in the name of the people of the State of California by the Attorney General as follows:

(A) A civil penalty of one hundred dollars ($100) for each day the data broker fails to register as re- quired by this section.

(B) An amount equal to the fees that were due during the period it failed to register.

(C) Expenses incurred by the Attorney General in the investigation and prosecution of the action as the court deems appropriate.

(2) Any penalties, fees, and expenses recovered in an action prosecuted under this section shall be deposited in the Consumer Privacy Fund, created within the General Fund pursuant to subdivision (a) of Section 1798.160, with the intent that they be used to fully offset costs incurred by the state courts and the Attorney General in connection with this title.

1798.99.84.

The Attorney General shall create a page on its internet web- site where the information provided by data brokers under this title shall be accessible to the public.

1798.99.88.

Nothing in this title shall be construed to supersede or interfere with the operation of the California Consumer Privacy Act of 2018 (Title 1.81.5 (commencing with Section 1798.100)).

ILLINOIS BIOMETRIC INFORMATION
PRIVACY ACT (2009)

Summary

The Illinois Biometric Information Privacy Act (BIPA) introduced safeguards on collection and dissemination of biometric data by private entities collecting. This includes a prohibition on collection of biometric data without written notice containing an explanation of the purpose and duration of collection storage and use, as well as express consent from the data subject. BIPA gained new attention with a series of pivotal court rulings in 2019. In Rosenbach v. Six Flags, the Illinois Supreme Court found that a violation of the law, without additional harm, was sufficient to bring pursue claims under the law. In Patel v. Facebook, the Ninth Circuit Court of Appeals found that individuals have Constitutional standing to bring suit when an entity violates the law, certifying a class action suit against the company for allegedly creating biometric templates of their faces without their consent.

References

740 ILCS 14/1 et seq.
[http://www.ilga.gov/legislation/ilcs/ilcs3.asp?ActID=3004&ChapterID=57]

EPIC, *Patel. v. Facebook*
[https://epic.org/amicus/bipa/patel-v-facebook/]

EPIC, *Rosenbach v. Six Flags*
[https://epic.org/amicus/bipa/rosenbach/]

(740 ILCS 14/1)

Sec. 1. Short title. This Act may be cited as the Biometric Information Privacy Act. (Source: P.A. 95-994, eff. 10-3-08.)

(740 ILCS 14/5)

Sec. 5. Legislative findings; intent. The General Assembly finds all of the following:

(a) The use of biometrics is growing in the business and security screening sectors and appears to promise streamlined financial transactions and security screenings.

(b) Major national corporations have selected the City of Chicago and other locations in this State as pilot testing sites for new applications of biometric-facilitated financial transactions, including finger-scan technologies at grocery stores, gas stations, and school cafeterias.

(c) Biometrics are unlike other unique identifiers that are used to access finances or other sensitive information. For example, social security numbers, when compromised, can be changed. Biometrics, however, are biologically unique to the individual; therefore, once compromised, the individual has no recourse, is at heightened risk for identity theft, and is likely to withdraw from biometric-facilitated transactions.

(d) An overwhelming majority of members of the public are weary of the use of biometrics when such information is tied to finances and other personal information.

(e) Despite limited State law regulating the collection, use, safeguarding, and storage of biometrics, many members of the public are deterred from partaking in biometric identifier-facilitated transactions.

(f) The full ramifications of biometric technology are not fully known.

(g) The public welfare, security, and safety will be served by regulating the collection, use, safeguarding, handling, storage, retention, and destruction of biometric identifiers and information.
(Source: P.A. 95-994, eff. 10-3-08.)

(740 ILCS 14/10)
Sec. 10. Definitions. In this Act:

"Biometric identifier" means a retina or iris scan, fingerprint, voiceprint, or scan of hand or face geometry. Biometric identifiers do not include writing samples, written signatures, photographs, human biological samples used for valid scientific testing or screening, demographic data, tattoo descriptions, or physical descriptions such as height, weight, hair color, or eye color. Biometric identifiers do not include donated organs, tissues, or parts as defined in the Illinois Anatomical Gift Act or blood or serum stored on behalf of recipients or potential recipients of living or cadaveric transplants and obtained or stored by a federally designated organ procurement agency. Biometric identifiers do not include biological materials regulated under the Genetic Information Privacy Act. Biometric identifiers do not include information captured from a patient in a health care setting or information collected, used, or stored for health care treatment, payment, or operations under the federal Health Insurance Portability and Accountability Act of 1996. Biometric identifiers do not include an X-ray, roentgen process, computed tomography, MRI, PET scan, mammography, or other image or film of the human anatomy used to diagnose, prognose, or treat an illness or other medical condition or to further validate scientific testing or screening.

"Biometric information" means any information, regardless of how it is captured, converted, stored, or shared, based on an individual's biometric identifier used to identify an individual. Biometric information does not include information derived from items or procedures excluded under the definition of biometric identifiers.

"Confidential and sensitive information" means personal information that can be used to uniquely identify an individual or an individual's account or property. Examples of confidential and sensitive information include, but are not limited to, a genetic marker, genetic testing information, a unique identifier number to locate an account or property, an account number, a PIN number, a pass code, a driver's license number, or a social security number.

"Private entity" means any individual, partnership, corporation, limited liability company, association, or other group, however organized. A private entity does not include a State or local government agency. A private entity does not include any court of Illinois, a clerk of the court, or a judge or justice thereof.

"Written release" means informed written consent or, in the context of employment, a release executed by an employee as a condition of employment.
(Source: P.A. 95-994, eff. 10-3-08.)

(740 ILCS 14/15)
Sec. 15. Retention; collection; disclosure; destruction.

(a) A private entity in possession of biometric identifiers or biometric information must develop a written policy, made available to the public, establishing a retention schedule and guidelines for permanently destroying biometric identifiers and biometric information when the initial purpose for collecting or obtaining such identifiers or information has been satisfied or within 3 years of the individual's last interaction with the private entity, whichever occurs first. Absent a valid warrant or subpoena issued by a court of competent jurisdiction, a private entity in possession of biometric identifiers or biometric information must comply with its established retention schedule and destruction guidelines.

(b) No private entity may collect, capture, purchase, receive through trade, or otherwise obtain a person's or a customer's biometric identifier or biometric information, unless it first:

(1) informs the subject or the subject's legally

authorized representative in writing that a biometric identifier or biometric information is being collected or stored;

(2) informs the subject or the subject's legally

authorized representative in writing of the specific purpose and length of term for which a biometric identifier or biometric information is being collected, stored, and used; and

(3) receives a written release executed by the

subject of the biometric identifier or biometric information or the subject's legally authorized representative.

(c) No private entity in possession of a biometric identifier or biometric information may sell, lease, trade, or otherwise profit from a person's or a customer's biometric identifier or biometric information.

(d) No private entity in possession of a biometric identifier or biometric information may disclose, redisclose, or otherwise disseminate a person's or a customer's biometric identifier or biometric information unless:

(1) the subject of the biometric identifier or

biometric information or the subject's legally authorized representative consents to the disclosure or redisclosure;

(2) the disclosure or redisclosure completes a

financial transaction requested or authorized by the subject of the biometric identifier or the biometric information or the subject's legally authorized representative;

(3) the disclosure or redisclosure is required by

State or federal law or municipal ordinance; or

(4) the disclosure is required pursuant to a valid

warrant or subpoena issued by a court of competent jurisdiction.

(e) A private entity in possession of a biometric identifier or biometric information shall:

(1) store, transmit, and protect from disclosure all

biometric identifiers and biometric information using the reasonable standard of care within the private entity's industry; and

(2) store, transmit, and protect from disclosure all

biometric identifiers and biometric information in a manner that is the same as or more protective than the manner in which the private entity stores, transmits, and protects other confidential and sensitive information.

(Source: P.A. 95-994, eff. 10-3-08.)

(740 ILCS 14/20)

Sec. 20. Right of action. Any person aggrieved by a violation of this Act shall have a right of action in a State circuit court or as a supplemental claim in federal district court against an offending party. A prevailing party may recover for each violation:

(1) against a private entity that negligently

violates a provision of this Act, liquidated damages of $1,000 or actual damages, whichever is greater;

(2) against a private entity that intentionally or

recklessly violates a provision of this Act, liquidated damages of $5,000 or actual damages, whichever is greater;

(3) reasonable attorneys' fees and costs, including

expert witness fees and other litigation expenses; and

(4) other relief, including an injunction, as the

State or federal court may deem appropriate.

(Source: P.A. 95-994, eff. 10-3-08.)

(740 ILCS 14/25)

Sec. 25. Construction.

(a) Nothing in this Act shall be construed to impact the admission or discovery of biometric identifiers and biometric information in any action of any kind in any court, or before any tribunal, board, agency, or person.

(b) Nothing in this Act shall be construed to conflict with the X-Ray Retention Act, the federal Health Insurance Portability and Accountability Act of 1996 and the rules promulgated under either Act.

(c) Nothing in this Act shall be deemed to apply in any manner to a financial institution or an affiliate of a financial institution that is subject to Title V of the federal Gramm-Leach-Bliley Act of 1999 and the rules promulgated thereunder.

(d) Nothing in this Act shall be construed to conflict with the Private Detective, Private Alarm, Private Security, Fingerprint Vendor, and Locksmith Act of 2004 and the rules promulgated thereunder.

(e) Nothing in this Act shall be construed to apply to a contractor, subcontractor, or agent of a State agency or local unit of government when working for that State agency or local unit of government.

(Source: P.A. 95-994, eff. 10-3-08.)

(740 ILCS 14/30)
Sec. 30. (Repealed).
(Source: P.A. 95-994, eff. 10-3-08. Repealed internally, eff. 1-1-09.)

(740 ILCS 14/99)
Sec. 99. Effective date. This Act takes effect upon becoming law.
(Source: P.A. 95-994, eff. 10-3-08.)

CYBERSECURITY LAW OF THE PEOPLE'S REPUBLIC OF CHINA (2016)

Summary

China's Cybersecurity Law has been the subject of significant controversy since it was passed 2016. The law includes requirements for the private sector to secure networks, obligations to store data in China, and enhanced cyber monitoring authority for the government. However, the law is also the first national Chinese law to address the protection of personal data. The law been the basis of numerous guidelines published by elements of the PRC government beginning in 2018 - such as the Guideline for Internet Personal Information Security Protection - making it the centerpiece of Chinese privacy law.

References

Zhonghua Renmin Gongheguo Wanglao Anquan Fa [Cybersecurity Law] (promulgated by the Standing Comm. Nat'l People's Cong., Nov. 7, 2016, effective June 1, 2017)

[http://www.npc.gov.cn/npc/xinwen /2016-11/07/content_2001605.htm]

Rogier Creemers, Paul Triolo, and Graham Webster, Translation: Cybersecurity Law of the People's Republic of China (Effective June 1, 2017),

[https://iapp.org/resources/article/cybersecurity-law-of-the-peoples-republic-of-china-english-translation/]

Table of Contents

Chapter I: General Provisions

Article 1: This Law is formulated in order to: ensure cybersecurity; safeguard cyberspace sovereignty and national security, and social and public interests; protect the lawful rights and interests of citizens, legal persons, and other organizations; and promote the healthy development of the informatization of the economy and society.

Recent Developments
Cybersecurity Law of the People's Republic of China

Article 2: This Law is applicable to the construction, operation, maintenance, and use of networks, as well as to cybersecurity supervision and management within the mainland territory of the People's Republic of China.

Article 3: The State persists in equally stressing cybersecurity and informatization development, and abides by the principles of active use, scientific development, management in accordance with law, and ensuring security. The State advances the construction of network infrastructure and interconnectivity, encourages the innovation and application of network technology, supports the cultivation of qualified cybersecurity personnel, establishes a complete system to safeguard cybersecurity, and raises capacity to protect cybersecurity.

Article 4: The State formulates and continuously improves cybersecurity strategy, clarifies the fundamental requirements and primary goals of ensuring cybersecurity, and puts forward cybersecurity policies, work tasks, and procedures for key sectors.

Article 5: The State takes measures for monitoring, preventing, and handling cybersecurity risks and threats arising both within and without the mainland territory of the People's Republic of China. The State protects critical information infrastructure against attacks, intrusions, interference, and destruction; the State punishes unlawful and criminal cyber activities in accordance with the law, preserving the security and order of cyberspace.

Article 6: The State advocates sincere, honest, healthy and civilized online conduct; it promotes the dissemination of core socialist values, adopts measures to raise the entire society's awareness and level of cybersecurity, and formulates a good environment for the entire society to jointly participate in advancing cybersecurity.

Article 7: The State actively carries out international exchanges and cooperation in the areas of cyberspace governance, research and development of network technologies, formulation of standards, attacking cybercrime and illegality, and other such areas; it promotes constructing a peaceful, secure, open, and cooperative cyberspace, and establishing a multilateral, democratic, and transparent Internet governance system.

Article 8: State cybersecurity and informatization departments are responsible for comprehensively planning and coordinating cybersecurity efforts and related supervision and management efforts. The State Council departments for telecommunications, public security, and other relevant organs, are responsible for cybersecurity protection, supervision, and management efforts within the scope of their responsibilities, in accordance with the provisions of this Law and relevant laws and administrative regulations.

Cybersecurity protection, supervision, and management duties for relevant departments in people's governments at the county level or above will be determined by relevant national regulations.

Article 9: Network operators carrying out business and service activities must follow laws and administrative regulations, respect social morality, abide by commercial ethics, be honest and credible, perform obligations to protect cybersecurity, accept supervision from the government and public, and bear social responsibility.

Article 10: The construction and operation of networks, or the provision of services through networks, shall be done: in accordance with the provisions of laws and administrative regulations, and with the mandatory requirements of national standards; adopting technical measures and other necessary measures to safeguard cybersecurity and operational stability; effectively responding to cybersecurity incidents; preventing cybercrimes and unlawful activity; and preserving the integrity, secrecy, and usability of online data.

Article 11: Relevant Internet industry organizations, according to their Articles of Association, shall strengthen industry self-discipline, formulate cybersecurity norms of behavior, guide their members in strengthening cybersecurity protection according to the law, raise the level of cybersecurity protection, and stimulate the healthy development of the industry.

Article 12: The State protects the rights of citizens, legal persons, and other organizations to use networks in accordance with the law; it promotes widespread network access, raises the level of network services, provides secure and convenient network services to society, and guarantees the lawful, orderly, and free circulation of network information.

Any person and organization using networks shall abide by the Constitution and laws, observe public order, and respect social morality; they must not endanger cybersecurity, and must not use the Internet to engage in activities endangering national security, national honor, and national interests; they must not incite subversion of national sovereignty, overturn the socialist system, incite separatism, break national unity, advocate terrorism or extremism, advocate ethnic hatred and ethnic discrimination, disseminate violent, obscene, or sexual information, create or disseminate false information to disrupt the economic or social order, or information that infringes on the reputation, privacy, intellectual property or other lawful rights and interests of others, and other such acts.

Article 13: The State encourages research and development of network products and services conducive to the healthy upbringing of minors; the State will lawfully punish the use of networks to engage in activities that endanger the psychological and physical well-being of minors; and the State will provide a safe and healthy network environment for minors.

Article 14: All individuals and organizations have the right to report conduct endangering cybersecurity to cybersecurity and informatization, telecommunications, public security, and other departments. Departments receiving reports shall promptly process them in accordance with law; where matters do not fall within the responsibilities of that department, they shall promptly transfer them to the department empowered to handle them.

Relevant departments shall preserve the confidentiality of the informants' information and protect the lawful rights and interests of informants.

Chapter II: The Support and Promotion of Cybersecurity

Article 15: The State establishes and improves a system of cybersecurity standards. State Council standardization administrative departments and other relevant State Council departments, on the basis of their individual responsibilities, shall organize the formulation and timely revision of relevant national and industry standards for cybersecurity management, as well as for the security of network products, services, and operations.

The State supports enterprises, research institutions, schools of higher learning, and network-related industry organizations to participate in the formulation of national and industry standards for cybersecurity.

Article 16: The State Council and people's governments of provinces, autonomous regions, and directly-governed municipalities shall: do comprehensive planning; expand investment; support key cybersecurity technology industries and programs; support cybersecurity technology research and development, application, and popularization; promote secure and trustworthy network products and services; protect intellectual property rights for network technologies; and support research and development institutions, schools of higher learning, etc., to participate in State cybersecurity technology innovation programs.

Article 17: The State advances the establishment of socialized service systems for cybersecurity, encouraging relevant enterprises and institutions to carry out cybersecurity certifications, testing, risk assessment, and other such security services.

Article 18: The State encourages the development of network data security protection and utilization technologies, advancing the opening of public data resources, and promoting technical innovation and economic and social development.

The State supports innovative methods of cybersecurity management, utilizing new network technologies to enhance the level of cybersecurity protection.

Article 19: All levels of people's governments and their relevant departments shall organize and carry out regular cybersecurity publicity and education, and guide and stimulate relevant units in properly carrying out cybersecurity publicity and education work.
The mass media shall conduct targeted cybersecurity publicity and education aimed at the public.

Article 20: The State supports enterprises and education or training institutions, such as schools of higher learning and vocational schools, in carrying out cybersecurity-related education and training, and it employs multiple methods to cultivate qualified personnel in cybersecurity and promote the interaction of cybersecurity professionals.

Chapter III: Network Operations Security

Section 1: Ordinary Provisions

Article 21: The State implements a cybersecurity multi-level protection system [MLPS]. Network operators shall perform the following security protection duties according to the requirements of the cybersecurity multi-level protection system to ensure the network is free from interference, damage, or unauthorized access, and to prevent network data leaks, theft, or falsification:

(1) Formulate internal security management systems and operating rules, determine persons who are responsible for cybersecurity, and implement cybersecurity protection responsibility;

(2) Adopt technical measures to prevent computer viruses, cyber attacks, network intrusions, and other actions endangering cybersecurity;

(3) Adopt technical measures for monitoring and recording network operational statuses and cybersecurity incidents, and follow provisions to store network logs for at least six months;

(4) Adopt measures such as data classification, backup of important data, and encryption;

(5) Other obligations provided by law or administrative regulations.

Article 22: Network products and services shall comply with the relevant national and mandatory requirements. Providers of network products and services must not install malicious programs; when discovering that their products and services have security flaws or vulnerabilities, they shall immediately adopt remedial measures, and follow provisions to promptly inform users and report to the competent departments.

Providers of network products and services shall provide security maintenance for their products and services, and they must not terminate the provision of security maintenance during the time limits or period agreed on with clients.

If a network product or service has the function of collecting user information, its provider shall clearly indicate this and obtain consent from the user; and if this involves a user's personal information, the provider shall also comply with the provisions of this law and relevant laws and administrative regulations on the protection of personal information.

Article 23: Critical network equipment and specialized cybersecurity products shall follow national standards and mandatory requirements, and be security certified by a qualified establishment or meet the requirements of a security inspection, before being sold or provided. The state cybersecurity and informatization departments, together with the relevant departments of the State Council, will formulate and release a catalog of critical network equipment and specialized cybersecurity products, and promote reciprocal recognition of security certifications and security inspection results to avoid duplicative certifications and inspections.

Recent Developments
Cybersecurity Law of the People's Republic of China

Article 24: Network operators handling network access and domain name registration services for users, handling stationary or mobile phone network access, or providing users with information publication or instant messaging services, shall require users to provide real identity information when signing agreements with users or confirming the provision of services. Where users do not provide real identity information, network operators must not provide them with relevant services.

The State implements a network identity credibility strategy and supports research and development of secure and convenient electronic identity authentication technologies, promoting reciprocal acceptance among different electronic identity authentication methods.

Article 25: Network operators shall formulate emergency response plans for cybersecurity incidents and promptly address system vulnerabilities, computer viruses, cyber attacks, network intrusions, and other such cybersecurity risks. When cybersecurity incidents occur, network operators should immediately initiate an emergency response plan, adopt corresponding remedial measures, and report to the relevant competent departments in accordance with relevant provisions.

Article 26: Those carrying out cybersecurity certification, testing, risk assessment, or other such activities—or publicly publishing cybersecurity information such as system vulnerabilities, computer viruses, network attacks, or network incursions—shall comply with relevant national provisions.

Article 27: Individuals and organizations must not engage in illegal intrusion into the networks of other parties, disrupt the normal functioning of the networks of other parties, or steal network data or engage in other activities endangering cybersecurity; they must not provide programs, or tools specially used in network intrusions, that disrupt normal network functions and protection measures, steal network data, or engage in other acts endangering cybersecurity; and where they clearly are aware that others will engage in actions that endanger cybersecurity, they must not provide help such as technical support, advertisement and promotion, or payment of expenses.

Article 28: Network operators shall provide technical support and assistance to public security organs and national security organs that are safeguarding national security and investigating criminal activities in accordance with the law.

Article 29: The State supports cooperation between network operators in areas such as the gathering, analysis, reporting, and emergency handling of cybersecurity information, increasing the security safeguarding capacity of network operators.

Relevant industrial organizations are to establish and complete mechanisms for standardization and coordination of cybersecurity for their industry, strengthen their analysis and assessment of cybersecurity, and periodically conduct risk warnings, support, and coordination for members in responding to cybersecurity risks.

Article 30: Information obtained by cybersecurity and informatization departments and relevant departments performing cybersecurity protection duties can only be used as necessary for the protection of cybersecurity, and must not be used in other ways.

Section 2: Operations Security for Critical Information Infrastructure

Article 31: The State implements key protection on the basis of the cybersecurity multi-level protection system for public communication and information services, power, traffic, water resources, finance, public service, e-government, and other critical information infrastructure which—if destroyed, suffering a loss of function, or experiencing leakage of data—might seriously endanger national security, national welfare, the people's livelihood, or the public interest. The State Council will formulate the specific scope and security protection measures for critical information infrastructure.

The State encourages operators of networks outside the [designated] critical information infrastructure systems to voluntarily participate in the critical information infrastructure protection system.

Article 32: In accordance with the duties and division of labor provided by the State Council, departments responsible for security protection work for critical information infrastructure are to separately compile and organize security implementation plans for their industry's or sector's critical information infrastructure, and to guide and supervise security protection efforts for critical information infrastructure operations.

Article 33: Those constructing critical information infrastructure shall ensure that it has the capability to support business stability and sustained operations, and ensure the synchronous planning, synchronous establishment, and synchronous application of security technical measures.

Article 34: In addition to the provisions of Article 21 of this Law, critical information infrastructure operators shall also perform the following security protection duties:

(1) Set up specialized security management bodies and persons responsible for security management, and conduct security background checks on those responsible persons and personnel in critical positions;

(2) Periodically conduct cybersecurity education, technical training, and skills evaluations for employees;

(3) Conduct disaster recovery backups of important systems and databases;

(4) Formulate emergency response plans for cybersecurity incidents, and periodically organize drills;

(5) Other duties provided by law or administrative regulations.

Article 35: Critical information infrastructure operators purchasing network products and services that might impact national security shall undergo a national security review organized by the State cybersecurity and informatization departments and relevant departments of the State Council.

Article 36: Critical information infrastructure operators purchasing network products and services shall follow relevant provisions and sign a security and confidentiality agreement with the provider, clarifying duties and responsibilities for security and confidentiality.

Article 37: Critical information infrastructure operators that gather or produce personal information or important data during operations within the mainland territory of the People's Republic of China, shall store it within mainland China. Where due to business requirements it is truly necessary to provide it outside the mainland, they shall follow the measures jointly formulated by the State cybersecurity and informatization departments and the relevant departments of the State Council to conduct a security assessment; where laws and administrative regulations provide otherwise, follow those provisions.

Article 38: At least once a year, critical information infrastructure operators shall conduct an inspection and assessment of their networks' security and risks that might exist, either on their own or through retaining a cybersecurity services organization; CII operators should submit a cybersecurity report on the circumstances of the inspection and assessment as well as improvement measures, to be sent to the relevant department responsible for critical information infrastructure security protection efforts.

Article 39: State cybersecurity and informatization departments shall coordinate relevant departments in employing the following measures for critical information infrastructure security protection:

(1) Conduct spot testing of critical information infrastructure security risks, put forward improvement measures, and when necessary they can retain a cybersecurity services organization to conduct testing and assessment of cybersecurity risks;

(2) Periodically organize critical information infrastructure operators to conduct emergency cybersecurity response drills, increasing the level, coordination, and capacity of responses to cybersecurity incidents.

(3) Promote cybersecurity information sharing among relevant departments, critical information infrastructure operators, and also relevant research institutions and cybersecurity services organizations.

(4) Provide technical support and assistance for cybersecurity emergency management and recovery, etc.

Chapter IV: Network Information Security

Article 40: Network operators shall strictly maintain the confidentiality of user information they collect, and establish and complete user information protection systems.

Article 41: Network operators collecting and using personal information shall abide by the principles of legality, propriety, and necessity; they shall publish rules for collection and use, explicitly stating the purposes, means, and scope for collecting or using information, and obtain the consent of the persons whose data is gathered.

Network operators must not gather personal information unrelated to the services they provide; must not violate the provisions of laws, administrative regulations or agreements between the parties to gather or use personal information; and shall follow the provisions of laws, administrative regulations, and agreements with users to process personal information they have stored.

Article 42: Network operators must not disclose, tamper with, or destroy personal information they gather; and, absent the consent of the person whose information was collected, must not provide personal information to others. However, this is the case with the exception that information can be provided if after processing there is no way to identify a specific individual, and the identity cannot be recovered.

Network operators shall adopt technical measures and other necessary measures to ensure the security of personal information they gather and to prevent personal information from leaking, being destroyed, or lost. When the leak, destruction, or loss of personal information occurs, or might have occured, remedial measures shall be immediately taken, and provisions followed to promptly inform users and to make a report to the competent departments in accordance with regulations.

Article 43: Where individuals discover that network operators have violated the provisions of laws, administrative regulations, or agreements between the parties to gather or use their personal information, they have the right to demand the network operators delete their personal information; where discovering that personal information gathered or stored by network operators has errors, they have the right to demand the network operators make corrections. Network operators shall employ measures for deletions and corrections.

Article 44: Individuals or organizations must not steal or use other illegal methods to acquire personal information, and must not unlawfully sell or unlawfully provide others with personal information.

Article 45: Departments lawfully having cybersecurity supervision and management duties, and their staffs, must keep strictly confidential personal information, private information, and commercial secrets that they learn of in performing their duties, and they must not leak, sell, or unlawfully provide it to others.

Recent Developments
Cybersecurity Law of the People's Republic of China

Article 46: All individuals and organizations shall be responsible for their use of websites and must not establish websites or communications groups for use in perpetrating fraud, imparting criminal methods, the creation or sale of prohibited or controlled items, or other unlawful activities, and websites must not be exploited to publish information related to perpetrating fraud, the creation or sale of prohibited or controlled items, or other unlawful activities.

Article 47: Network operators shall strengthen management of information published by users and, upon discovering information that the law or administrative regulations prohibits the publication or transmission of, they shall immediately stop transmission of that information, employ handling measures such as deleting the information, prevent the information from spreading, save relevant records, and report to the relevant competent departments.

Article 48: Electronic information sent, or application software provided by any individual or organization, must not install malicious programs, and must not contain information that laws and administrative regulations prohibit the publication or transmission of.

Electronic information distribution service providers, and application software download service providers, shall perform security management duties; where they know that their users have engaged in conduct provided for in the preceding paragraph, they shall: employ measures such as stopping provision of services and removal of information or malicious programs; store relevant records; and report to the relevant competent departments.

Article 49: Network operators shall establish network information security complaint and reporting systems, publicly disclose information such as the methods for making complaints or reports, and promptly accept and handle complaints and reports relevant to network information security.

Network operators shall cooperate with cybersecurity and informatization departments and relevant departments in conducting implementation of supervision and inspections in accordance with the law.

Article 50: State cybersecurity and informatization departments and relevant departments will perform network information security supervision and management responsibilities in accordance with law; and where they discover the publication or transmission of information which is prohibited by laws or administrative regulations, shall request that network operators stop transmission, employ disposition measures such as deletion, and store relevant records; for information described above that comes from outside the mainland People's Republic of China, they shall notify the relevant organization to adopt technical measures and other necessary measures to block transmission.

Chapter V: Monitoring, Early Warning, and Emergency Response

Article 51: The State will establish a cybersecurity monitoring, early warning, and information communication system. The State cybersecurity and informatization departments shall do overall coordination of relevant departments to strengthen collection, analysis, and reporting efforts for cybersecurity information, and follow regulations for the unified release of cybersecurity monitoring and early warning information.

Article 52: Departments responsible for critical information infrastructure security protection efforts shall establish and complete cybersecurity monitoring, early warning, and information reporting systems for their respective industry or sector, and report cybersecurity monitoring and early warning information in accordance with regulations.

Article 53: State cybersecurity and informatization departments will coordinate with relevant departments to establish and complete mechanisms for cybersecurity risk assessment and emergency response efforts, formulate cybersecurity incident emergency response plans, and periodically organize drills.

Departments responsible for critical information infrastructure security protection efforts shall formulate cybersecurity incident emergency response plans for their respective industry or sector, and periodically organize drills.

Cybersecurity incident emergency response plans shall rank cybersecurity incidents on the basis of factors such as the degree of damage after the incident occurs and the scope of impact, and provide corresponding emergency response handling measures.

Article 54: When the risk of cybersecurity incidents increases, the relevant departments of people's governments at the provincial level and above shall follow the scope of authority and procedures provided, and employ the following measures on the basis of the characteristics of the cybersecurity risk and the damage it might cause:

(1) Require that relevant departments, institutions, and personnel promptly gather and report relevant information, and strengthen monitoring of the occurrence of cybersecurity risks;

(2) Organize relevant departments, institutions, and specialist personnel to conduct analysis and assessment of information on the cybersecurity risk, and predict the likelihood of incident occurrence, the scope of impact, and the level of damage;

(3) Issue cybersecurity risk warnings to the public, and publish measures for avoiding or reducing damage.

Article 55: When a cybersecurity incident occurs, the cybersecurity incident emergency response plan shall be immediately initiated, an evaluation and assessment of the cybersecurity incident shall be conducted, network operators shall be requested to adopt technical and other necessary measures, potential security risks shall be removed, the threat shall be prevented from expanding, and warnings relevant to the public shall be promptly published.

Article 56: Where, while performing cybersecurity supervision and management duties, relevant departments of people's governments at the provincial level or above discover that networks have a relatively large security risk or the occurrence of a security incident, they may call in the legal representative or responsible party for the operator of that network to conduct interviews in accordance with the scope of authority and procedures provided. Network operators shall follow requirements to employ procedures, make corrections, and eliminate hidden dangers.

Article 57: Where sudden emergencies or production security accidents occur as a result of cybersecurity incidents, they shall be handled in accordance with the provisions the "Emergency Response Law of the People's Republic of China," the "Production Safety Law of the People's Republic of China," and other relevant laws and administrative regulations.

Article 58: To fulfill the need to protect national security and the social public order, and to respond to the requirements of major security incidents within the society, it is possible, as stipulated or approved by the State Council, to take temporary measures regarding network communications in a specially designated region, such as limiting such communications.

Chapter VI: Legal Responsibility

Article 59: Where network operators do not perform cybersecurity protection duties provided for in Articles 21 and 25 of this Law, the competent departments will order corrections and give warnings; where corrections are refused or it leads to harm to cybersecurity or other such consequences, a fine of between RMB 10,000 and 100,000 shall be levied; and the directly responsible management personnel shall be fined between RMB 5,000 and 50,000.

Where critical information infrastructure operators do not perform cybersecurity protection duties as provided for in Articles 33, 34, 36, and 38 of this Law, the competent departments will order corrections and give warnings; where corrections are refused or it leads to harm to cybersecurity or other such consequences, a fine of between RMB 100,000 and 1,000,000 shall be levied; and the directly responsible management personnel shall be fined between RMB 10,000 and 100,000.

Article 60: Where Article 22 Paragraphs 1 or 2 or Article 48 Paragraph 1 of this Law are violated by any of the following conduct, the relevant competent departments shall order corrections and give warnings; where corrections are refused or it causes harm to cybersecurity or other consequences, a fine of between RMB 50,000 and 500,000 shall be levied; and the persons who are directly in charge shall be fined between RMB 10,000 and 100,000:

(1) Installing malicious programs;

(2) Failure to immediately take remedial measures for security flaws or vulnerabilities that exist in products or services, or not informing users and reporting to the competent departments in accordance with regulations;

(3) Unauthorized ending of the provision of security maintenance for their products or services.

Article 61: Network operators violating Article 24 Paragraph 1 of this Law in failing to require users to provide real identity information or providing relevant services to users who do not provide real identity information, are ordered to make corrections by the relevant competent department; where corrections are refused or the circumstances are serious, a fine of between RMB 50,000 and 500,000 shall be levied, and the relevant competent department may order a temporary suspension of operations, a suspension of business for corrections, closing down of websites, cancellation of relevant operations permits, or cancellation of business licenses; persons who are directly in charge and other directly responsible personnel shall be fined between RMB 10,000 and 100,000.

Article 62: Where Article 26 of this Law is violated in carrying out cybersecurity certifications, testing, or risk assessments, or publishing cybersecurity information such as system vulnerabilities, computer viruses, cyber attacks, or network incursions, corrections are to be ordered and a warning given; where corrections are refused or the circumstances are serious, a fine of between RMB 10,000 and 100,000 shall be imposed, and the relevant competent department may order a temporary suspension of operations, a suspension of business for corrections, closing down of websites, cancellation of relevant operations permits, or cancellation of business licenses; persons who are directly in charge and other directly responsible personnel shall be fined between RMB 5,000 and 50,000.

Article 63: Where Article 27 of this Law is violated in engaging in activities harming cybersecurity, or by providing specialized software or tools used in engaging in activities harming cybersecurity, or by providing others engaging in activities harming cybersecurity with assistance such as technical support, advertising and promotions, or payment of expenses, and where this does not constitute a crime, public security organizations shall confiscate unlawful gains and impose up to 5 days detention, and may levy a fine of between RMB 50,000 and 500,000; and where circumstances are serious, shall impose between 5 and 15 days detention, and may levy a fine of between 100,000 and 1,000,000 RMB.

Where units have engaged in the conduct of the preceding paragraph, public security organizations shall confiscate unlawful gains and levy a fine of between RMB 100,000 and 1,000,000, and the directly responsible persons in charge and other directly responsible personnel shall be fined in accordance with the preceding paragraph.

Where Article 27 of this Law is violated, persons who receive public security administrative sanctions must not engage in cybersecurity management or key network operations positions for 5 years; those receiving criminal punishments will be subject to a lifetime ban on engaging in work in cybersecurity management and key network operations positions.

Article 64: Network operators, and network product or service providers violating Article 22 Paragraph 3 or Articles 41-43 of this Law by infringing on personal information that is protected in accordance with law, shall be ordered to make corrections by the relevant competent department and may, either independently or concurrently, be given warnings, be subject to confiscation of unlawful gains, and/or be fined between 1 to 10 times the amount of unlawful gains; where there are no unlawful gains, the fine shall be up to RMB 1,000,000, and a fine of between RMB 10,000 and 100,000 shall be given to persons who are directly in charge and other directly responsible personnel; where the circumstances are serious, the relevant competent department may order a temporary suspension of operations, a suspension of business for corrections, closing down of websites, cancellation of relevant operations permits, or cancellation of business licenses.

Where Article 44 of this Law is violated in stealing or using other illegal means to obtain, illegally sell, or illegally provide others with personal information, and this does not constitute a crime, public security organizations shall confiscate unlawful gains and levy a fine of between 1 and 10 times the amount of unlawful gains, and where there are no unlawful gains, levy a fine of up to RMB 1,000,000.

Article 65: Where critical information infrastructure operators violate Article 35 of this Law by using network products or services that have not had security inspections or did not pass security inspections, the relevant competent department shall order the usage to stop and levy a fine in the amount of 1 to 10 times the purchase price; the persons who are directly in charge and other directly responsible personnel shall be fined between RMB 10,000 and 100,000.

Article 66: Where critical information infrastructure operators violate Article 37 of this Law by storing network data outside the mainland territory, or provide network data to those outside of the mainland territory, the relevant competent department: shall order corrective measures, provide warning, confiscate unlawful gains, and levy fines between RMB 50,000 and 500,000; and may order a temporary suspension of operations, a suspension of business for corrective measures, closing down of websites, revocation of relevant operations permits, or cancellation of business licenses. Persons who are directly in charge and other directly responsible personnel shall be fined between RMB 10,000 and 100,000.

Article 67: Where Article 46 of this Law is violated by establishing a website or communications group used for the commission of illegal or criminal activities, or the network is used to publish information related to the commission of illegal or criminal activities, but a crime has not been committed, public security organizations shall impose up to 5 days detention and may levy a fine of between RMB 10,000 and 15,000; and where circumstances are serious, they may impose between 5 and 15 days detention, and may give a fine of between 50,000 and 500,000 RMB. They may also close websites and communications groups used for illegal or criminal activities.

Where units have engaged in conduct covered by the preceding paragraph, a fine of between RMB 100,000 and 500,000 shall be levied by public security organizations, and the principal responsible managers and other directly responsible personnel shall be fined in accordance with the preceding paragraph.

Article 68: Where network operators violate Article 47 of this Law by failing to stop the transmission of information for which transmission and publication are prohibited by laws or administrative regulations, failing to employ disposition measures such as deletion or failing to preserve relevant records, the relevant competent department shall order correction, provide warning, and confiscate unlawful gains; where correction is refused or circumstances are serious, fines between RMB 100,000 and 500,000 shall be imposed, and a temporary suspension of operations, a suspension of business to conduct correction, closing down of websites, cancellation of relevant operations permits, or cancellation of business licenses may be ordered; and persons who are directly in charge and other directly responsible personnel are fined between RMB 10,000 and 100,000.

Where electronic information service providers and application software download service providers do not perform their security management duties provided for in Paragraph 2 of Article 48 of this Law, punishment shall be in accordance with the provisions of the preceding paragraph.

Article 69: Network operators violating the provisions of this Law, who exhibit any of the following conduct, will be ordered to make corrections by the relevant competent departments; where corrections are refused or the circumstances are serious, a fine of between RMB 50,000 and 500,000 shall be imposed, and directly responsible management personnel and other directly responsible personnel are to be fined between RMB 10,000 and 100,000:

(1) Not following the requirements of relevant departments to adopt disposition measures such as stopping dissemination or deleting information for which laws or administrative regulations prohibit publication or dissemination;

(2) Refusal or obstruction of the competent departments in their lawful supervision and inspection;

(3) Refusing to provide technical support and assistance to public security organs and state security organs.

Article 70: Publication or transmission of information prohibited by Article 12 Paragraph 2 of this Law or other laws or administrative regulations shall be punished in accordance with the provisions of the relevant laws and administrative regulations.

Article 71: When there is conduct violating the provisions of this Law, it shall be recorded in credit files and made public in accordance with relevant laws and administrative regulations.

Article 72: Where state organization government affairs network operators do not perform cybersecurity protection duties as provided by this Law, the organization at the level above or relevant organizations will order corrections; sanctions will be levied on the directly responsible managers and other directly responsible personnel.

Article 73: Where cybersecurity and informatization and other relevant departments violate the provisions of Article 30 of this Law by using personal information acquired while performing cybersecurity protection duties for other purposes, the directly responsible persons in charge and other directly responsible personnel shall be given sanctions.

Where cybersecurity and informatization departments and other relevant departments' personnel neglect their duties, abuse their authority, show favoritism, and it does not constitute a crime, sanctions will be imposed in accordance with law.

Article 74: Where violations of the provisions of this Law cause harm to others, civil liability is borne in accordance with law.

Where provisions of this Law are violated, constituting a violation of public order management, public order administrative sanctions will be imposed in accordance with law; where a crime is constituted, criminal responsibility will be pursued in accordance with law.

Article 75: Where foreign institutions, organizations, or individuals engage in attacks, intrusions, interference, damage, or other activities the endanger the critical information infrastructure of the People's Republic of China, and cause serious consequences, legal responsibility is to be pursued in accordance with the law; public security departments under the State Council and relevant departments may also decide to freeze institutional, organization, or individual assets or take other necessary punitive measures.

Chapter VII: Supplementary Provisions

Article 76: The language below has the following meanings in this law:

(1) "Network" [网络, also "cyber"] refers to a system comprised of computers or other information terminals and related equipment that follows certain rules and procedures for information gathering, storage, transmission, exchange, and processing.

(2) "Cybersecurity" [网络安全, also "network security"] refers to taking the necessary measures to prevent cyber attacks, intrusions, interference, destruction, and unlawful use, as well as unexpected accidents, to place networks in a state of stable and reliable operation, as well as ensuring the capacity for network data to be complete, confidential, and usable.

(3) "Network operators" [网络运营者] refers to network owners, managers, and network service providers.

(4) "Network data" [网络数据] refers to all kinds of electronic data collected, stored, transmitted, processed, and produced through networks.

(5) "Personal information" [个人信息] refers to all kinds of information, recorded electronically or through other means, that taken alone or together with other information, is sufficient to identify a natural person's identity, including but not limited to natural persons' full names, birth dates, national identification numbers, personal biometric information, addresses, telephone numbers, and so forth.

Article 77: Protection of the operational security of networks that store or process information touching on national secrets shall follow this Law and shall also uphold the provisions of laws and administrative regulations pertaining to secrecy protection.

Article 78: The security protection rules for military networks are formulated by the Central Military Commission.

Article 79: This Law shall enter into effect June 1, 2017

DECLARATION: A MORATORIUM ON FACIAL RECOGNITION TECHNOLOGY FOR MASS SURVEILLANCE

References

Declaration: A Moratorium on Facial Recognition Technology for Mass Surveillance [https://thepublicvoice.org/ban-facial-recognition/]

October 2019

We the undersigned call for a moratorium on the use of facial recognition technology that enables mass surveillance.

We recognize the increasing use of this technology for commercial services, government administration, and policing functions. But the technology has evolved from a collection of niche systems to a powerful integrated network capable of mass surveillance and political control.

Facial recognition is now deployed for human identification, behavioral assessment, and predictive analysis.

Unlike other forms of biometric technology, facial recognition is capable of scrutinizing entire urban areas, capturing the identities of tens or hundreds of thousands of people at any one time.

Facial recognition can amplify identification asymmetry as it tends to be invisible or at best, opaque.

Facial recognition can be deployed in almost every dimension of life, from banking and commerce to transportation and communications.

We acknowledge that some facial recognition techniques enable authentication for the benefit of the user. However facial recognition also enables the development of semi-autonomous processes that minimize the roles of humans in decision making.

We note with alarm recent reports about bias, coercion, and fraud in the collection of facial images and the use of facial recognition techniques. Images are collected and used with forced consent or without consent at all.

We recall that in the 2009 Madrid Declaration, civil society called for a moratorium on the development or implementation of facial recognition, subject to a full and transparent evaluation by independent authorities and through democratic debate.

There is growing awareness of the need for a moratorium. In 2019 the Swedish Data Protection Authority prohibited the use of facial recognition in schools. The state of California prohibited the use facial recognition on police-worn body cameras. Several cities in the United States have banned the use of facial recognition systems, and there is growing protest around the world.

Therefore

1. We urge countries to suspend the further deployment of facial recognition technology for mass surveillance;

2. We urge countries to review all facial recognition systems to determine whether personal data was obtained lawfully and to destroy data that was obtained unlawfully;

3. We urge countries to undertake research to assess bias, privacy and data protection, risk, and cyber vulnerability, as well as the ethical, legal, and social implications associated with the deployment of facial recognition technologies; and

4. We urge countries to establish the legal rules, technical standards, and ethical guidelines necessary to safeguard fundamental rights and comply with legal obligations before further deployment of this technology occurs.

Selected Bibliography

(available at www.epic.org/bookstore)

Hal Abelson (Author), Ken Ledeen (Author), Harry Lewis (Author), *Blown to Bits: Your Life, Liberty, and Happiness After the Digital Explosion* (Addison-Wesley Professional 2008)

Alessandro Acquisti (Editor), Stefanos Gritzalis (Editor), Costos Lambrinoudakis (Editor), Sabrina di Vimercati (Editor), *Digital Privacy: Theory, Technologies, and Practices* (Auerbach Publications 2007)

Philip E. Agre & Marc Rotenberg, *Technology and Privacy: The New Landscape* (The MIT Press 1998)

Philip E. Agre, *Computation and Human Experience (Learning in Doing: Social, Cognitive and Computational Perspectives)* (Cambridge University Press 1997)

Anita Allen & Marc Rotenberg, *Privacy Law and Society* (West 2015)

Anita Allen, *Unpopular Privacy: What Must We Hide? (Studies in Feminist Philosophy)* (Oxford University Press 2011)

Anita L. Allen, *Why Privacy Isn't Everything: Feminist Reflections on Personal Accountability (Feminist Constructions)* (Rowman & Littlefield Publishers 2003)

Ross J. Anderson, *Security Engineering: A Guide to Building Dependable Distributed Systems* (Wiley 2008)

Jack M. Balkin, *Constitutional Redemption: Political Faith in an Unjust World* (Harvard University Press 2011)

Jack M. Balkin, *Living Originalism* (Belknap Press 2011)

Jack M. Balkin (Editor), Reva B. Siegel (Editor), *The Constitution in 2020* (Oxford University Press 2009)

James Bamford, *The Shadow Factory: The NSA from 9/11 to the Eavesdropping on America* (Anchor 2009)

James Bamford, *A Pretext for War: 9/11, Iraq, and the Abuse of America's Intelligence Agencies* (Anchor 2005)

James Bamford, *Body of Secrets: Anatomy of the Ultra-Secret National Security Agency* (Anchor Books 2001)

Michael J. Bazyler & Frank M. Tuerkheimer, *Forgotten Trials of the Holocaust* (NYU Press 2014)

Ori Brafman & Rod Beckstrom, *The Starfish and the Spider* (Portfolio 2006)

Colin Bennett (Editor), Kevin Haggerty (Editor), David Lyon (Editor), Valerie Steeves (Editor), *Transparent Lives: Surveillance in Canada* (Athabasca University Press 2014)

Colin J. Bennett (Editor), Kevin Haggerty (Editor), *Security Games: Surveillance and Control at Mega-Events* (Routledge 2012)

Colin Bennett, *The Privacy Advocates: Resisting the Spread of Surveillance* (The MIT Press 2010)

Christine L. Borgman, *Big Data, Little Data, No Data: Scholarship in the Networked World* (The MIT Press 2015)

Christine L. Borgman, *Scholarship in the Digital Age: Information, Infrastructure, and the Internet* (The MIT Press 2007, 2010)

Christine L. Borgman, *From Gutenberg to the Global Information Infrastructure: Access to Information in the Networked World* (The MIT Press 2000)

danah boyd, *It's Complicated: The Social Lives of Networked Teens* (Yale University Press 2014)

David Burnham, *The Rise of the Computer State* (Random House 1983)

Ryan Calo, A. Michael Froomkin, Ian Kerr , *Robot Law* (Edward Elgar Publishing 2016)

David Chaum, *Advances in Cryptology: Proceedings of Crypto 83* (Springer 2013)

Danielle Keats Citron, *Hate Crimes in Cyberspace* (Harvard University Press 2014)

Julie Cohen, *Between Truth and Power* (Oxford University Press 2019)

Julie E. Cohen, *Configuring the Networked Self: Law, Code, and the Play of Everyday Practice* (Yale University Press 2012)

Susan Crawford, *Captive Audience: The Telecom Industry and Monopoly Power in the New Gilded Age* (Yale University Press 2014)

Simon Davies, *Privacy: A Personal Chronicle* (2019)

Whitfield Diffie & Susan Landau, *Privacy on the Line: The Politics of Wiretapping and Encryption* (The MIT Press 2010)

Laura K. Donohue, *The Future of Foreign Intelligence: Privacy and Surveillance in a Digital Age* (Oxford University Press 2016)

Privacy Resources
Selected Bibliography

Laura K. Donohue, *The Cost of Counterterrorism: Power, Politics, and Liberty* (Cambridge University Press 2008)

Cynthia Dwork & Aaron Roth, *The Algorithmic Foundations of Differential Privacy* (Now Publishers 2014)

Niels Ferguson, Bruce Schneier, & Tadayoshi Kohno, *Cryptography Engineering* (John Wiley & Sons 2010)

David H. Flaherty, *Protecting Privacy in Surveillance Societies: The Federal Republic of Germany, Sweden, France, Canada, and the United States* (The University of North Carolina Press 1989)

David H. Flaherty, *Privacy in Colonial New England 1630-1776* (Univ of Virginia Press 1972)

Mary Flanagan (Author), Helen Nissenbaum (Author), *Values at Play in Digital Games* (The MIT Press 2014)

Nancy Gertner, *In Defense of Women: Memoirs of an Unrepentant Advocate* (Beacon Press 2011)

Jack Goldsmith & Tim Wu, *Who Controls the Internet?: Illusions of a Borderless World* (Oxford University Press 2008)

Stephen Goldsmith & Susan Crawford, *The Responsive City: Engaging Communities Through Data-Smart Governance* (Jossey-Bass 2014)

Woodrow Hartzog, *Privacy's Blueprint* (Harvard University Press 2018)

Aziz Z. Huq, *Assessing Constitutional Performance* (Cambridge University Press 2016)

Aziz Z. Huq, *Unchecked And Unbalanced: Presidential Power in a Time of Terror* (New Press 2011)

Joi Ito, *Whiplash: How to Survive Our Faster Future* (Grand Central Publishing 2016)

Deborah Hurley & James Keller, *The First 100 Feet: Options for Internet and Broadband Access* (Mit Press 1999)

Jerry Kang & Alan Butler, *Communications Law and Policy* (Direct Injection Press 2016)

Pamela S. Karlan, *A Constitution for All Times (Boston Review Books)* (The MIT Press 2013)

Goodwin Liu (Author), Pamela S. Karlan (Author), Christopher H. Schroeder (Author), *Keeping Faith with the Constitution (Inalienable Rights)* (Oxford University Press 2010)

Glenn C. Loury (Author), Pamela S. Karlan (Contributor), Lo?c Wacquant (Contributor), Tommie Shelby (Contributor), *Race, Incarceration, and American Values (Boston Review Books)* (The MIT Press 2008)

Ian Kerr (Author), Carole Lucock (Author), Valerie Steeves (Author), *Lessons from the Identity Trail: Anonymity, Privacy and Identity in a Networked Society* (Oxford University Press 2009)

Ellen Condliffe Lagemann (Author), Harry Lewis (Author), *What Is College For? The Public Purpose of Higher Education* (Teachers College Press 2013)

Harry Lewis, *Excellence Without a Soul: Does Liberal Education Have a Future?* (PublicAffairs 2007)

Rebecca MacKinnon, *Consent of the Networked: The Worldwide Struggle For Internet Freedom* (Basic Books 2012)

Alice E. Marwick, *Status Update: Celebrity, Publicity, and Branding in the Social Media Age* (Yale University Press 2013)

Gary T. Marx, *Windows into the Soul: Surveillance and Society in an Age of High Technology* (University Of Chicago Press 2016)

Gary T. Marx (Author), Douglas McAdam (Author), *Collective Behavior And Social Movements: Process and Structure* (Pearson 1993)

Gary T. Marx, *Undercover: Police Surveillance in America* (University of California Press 1989)

Gary T Marx, *Protest and Prejudice: A Study of Belief in the Black Community* (Harper & Row 1969)

Gary McGraw & Edward W. Felten, *Securing Java: Getting Down to Business with Mobile Code, 2nd Edition* (Wiley 1999)

Gary McGraw & Edward W. Felten, *Java Security* (Wiley 1996)

Roger McNamee, *Zucked: Waking Up to the Facebook Catastrophe* (Penguin Press 2019)

Mary Minow, *Library's Legal Answer Book* (American Library Association 2003)

Peter G. Neumann, *Computer-Related Risks* (Addison-Wesley 1994)

Julia Lane (Editor), Victoria Stodden (Editor), Stefan Bender (Editor), Helen Nissenbaum (Editor), *Privacy, Big Data, and the Public Good: Frameworks for Engagement* (Cambridge University Press 2014)

Helen Nissenbaum, *Obfuscation: A User's Guide for Privacy and Protest* (MIT Press 2016)

Privacy Resources
Selected Bibliography

Helen Nissenbaum, *Privacy in Context: Technology, Policy, and the Integrity of Social Life* (Stanford Law Books 2009)

Cathy O'Neil, *Weapons of Math Destruction: How Big Data Increases Inequality and Threatens Democracy* (Crown 2016)

Judith O'Neill (Editor), Eli M. Noam (Editor), Darcy Gerbarg (Editor), *Broadband as a Video Platform* (Springer 2014)

Eli Noam, *Media Ownership and Concentration in America* (Oxford University Press 2009)

Eli M. Noam (Editor), Jo Groebel (Editor), Darcy Gerbarg (Editor), *Internet Television* (Routledge 2003)

Frank Pasquale, *The Black Box Society: The Secret Algorithms That Control Money and Information* (Harvard University Press 2015)

Chip Pitts, *Corporate Social Responsibility - A Legal Analysis* (LexisNexis Canada 2009)

Artemi Rallo, *The Right to Be forgotten on the Internet: Google v. Spain* (EPIC 2018)

Jeffrey Rosen, *Louis D. Brandeis: American Prophet* (Yale University Press 2016)

Jeffrey Rosen & Benjamin Wittes, *Constitution 3.0: Freedom and Technological Change* (Brookings Institution Press 2013)

Jeffrey Rosen, *The Supreme Court: The Personalities and Rivalries That Defined America* (St. Martins Griffin 2007)

Jeffrey Rosen, *The Most Democratic Branch: How the Courts Serve America* (Oxford University Press 2006)

Marc Rotenberg, *The AI Policy Sourcebook 2019* (EPIC 2019)

Marc Rotenberg, *The Mueller Report* (EPIC 2019)

Marc Rotenberg, *Privacy & Human Rights* (EPIC 2006)

Marc Rotenberg, Julia Horwitz & Jeramie Scott, *Privacy in the Modern Age: The Search for Solutions* (The New Press 2015)

Bruce Schneier & David Banisar, *The Electronic Privacy Papers: Documents on the Battle for Privacy in the Age of Surveillance* (Wiley 1997)

Bruce Schneier, *Carry On: Sound Advice from Schneier on Security* (Wiley 2013)

Bruce Schneier, *Click Here to Kill Everybody: Security and Survival in A Hyper-connected World* (W.W. Norton & Company 2018)

Bruce Schneier, *Data and Goliath: The Hidden Battles to Collect Your Data and Control Your World* (W.W. Norton & Company 2015)

Bruce Schneier, *Liars and Outliers: Enabling the Trust that Society Needs to Thrive* (Wiley 2012)

Wolfgang Schulz (Editor), Peggy Valcke (Editor), Kristina Irion (Editor), *The Independence of the Media and its Regulatory Agencies* (Intellect Ltd 2014)

Robert Ellis Smith, *Compilation of State and Federal Privacy Laws 2013* (Privacy Journal 2013)

Nadine Strossen, *HATE: Why We Should Resist It with Free Speech, Not Censorship* (Oxford University Press 2018)

Nadine Strossen, *Defending Pornography: Free Speech, Sex, and the Fight for Women's Rights* (NYU Press 2000)

Sherry Turtle, *Reclaiming Conversation: The Power of Talk in a Digital Age* (Penguin Press 2015)

Sherry Turkle, *Alone Together: Why We Expect More from Technology and Less from Each Other* (Basic Books 2012)

Sherry Turkle, Editor, *Evocative Objects Things We Think With* (The MIT Press 2011)

Sherry Turkle, Editor, *Falling for Science Objects in Mind* (The MIT Press 2011)

Willis H. Ware, *RAND and the Information Evolution: A History in Essays and Vignettes* (RAND Corporation 2008)

Tim Wu, *The Attention Merchants: The Epic Scramble to Get Inside Our Heads* (Knopf 2016)

Tim Wu, *The Curse of Bigness* (Columbia Global Reports 2018)

Tim Wu, *The Master Switch: The Rise and Fall of Information Empires* (Vintage 2011)

Shoshana Zuboff, *The Age of Surveillance Capitalism: The Fight for a Human Future at the New Frontier of Power* (PublicAffairs 2019)

Privacy Resources

PRIVACY YEAR IN REVIEW 2018-2020

<u>2018</u>

January

3rd– Presidential Advisory Commission on Election Integrity, which sought to collect state voter data on hundreds of millions of Americans, was disbanded on by President Trump. The Commission had faced an ongoing lawsuit by EPIC (*EPIC v. Commission*) over its failure to conduct and publish a Privacy Impact Assessment before collecting personal data, as required by law.

19th – President Trump signed the FISA Amendment Reauthorization Act of 2017 into law. The Act renews Section 702 of the Foreign Intelligence Surveillance Act, which permits broad surveillance of individuals outside the U.S., for six years. The Act also permits the US government to renew the controversial "about" collection program.

19th – The Court of Justice of the European Union ruled in *Schrems v. Facebook Ireland, Ltd.* that a class action brought by Max Schrem's in Austria cannot proceed against Facebook, but individual privacy claims can.

February

3th– The U.S. Securities and Exchange Commission released guidance for cybersecurity risks and incidents. The SEC stated that "in light of the increasing significance of cybersecurity incidents," it is "critical" for companies to routinely report cybersecurity threats. The Commission also emphasized that corporate officers must not trade on nonpublic information.

March

18th – Investigative reporting revealed Facebook disclosed the personal data of 50 million users without their consent to Cambridge Analytica, the controversial British data mining firm that sought to influence the 2016 presidential election. The unlawful disclosure of user records to the data mining firm likely violated a 2011 FTC Consent Order against Facebook that resulted from a sustained campaign by US privacy organizations, including EPIC.

23th – President Trump signed the Clarifying Lawful Overseas Use of Data (CLOUD) Act into law. The CLOUD Act amends U.S. law to provide U.S. law enforcement access to foreign stored data. The Act also allows U.S. officials to enter into executive agreements for foreign countries to access to U.S. stored data.

26th – The U.S. Federal Election Commission published proposed rules concerning transparency requirements for online political ads and began receiving comments from the public. The proposals aim to providing the public clear disclosure of the payor or sponsor of internet communications that contain express advocacy, solicit contributions, or are made by political committee.

30th – The U.S. State Department formally proposed to require all visa applicants submit social media identifiers to the federal government.

April

2nd – The U.S. Senate confirmed five new nominees to serve as Commissioners for the Federal Trade Commission. The five new additions bring the FTC back to full capacity.

26th – The U.S. Senate confirmed five new nominees to serve as Commissioners for the Federal Trade Commission. The five new additions bring the FTC back to full capacity.

May

10th – The White House established the "Select Committee on Artificial Intelligence" to advise the President and coordinate AI policies among executive branch agencies. The stated goals of the Committee were (1) prioritize funding for AI research and development; (2) remove barriers to AI innovation; (3) train the future American workforce; (4) achieve strategic military advantage; (5) leverage AI for government services; and (6) lead international AI negotiations. The Committee would also coordinate efforts across federal agencies to research and adopt new technologies.

14th – In *Byrd v. United States*, the Supreme Court ruled that a driver in lawful possession of a rental car has a reasonable expectation of privacy regardless of a rental car agreement.

18th – The Council of Europe updated Convention, the first international treaty for privacy and data protection. Among other changes, the amending protocol required prompt data breach notification, establishes national supervisory authorities to ensure compliance, permits transfers abroad only when personal data is sufficiently protected, and provides new user rights including algorithmic transparency.

25th – The General Data Protection Regulation (GDPR) came into effect. The Regulation was European Union's update to its comprehensive data protection law and contains provisions on algorithmic transparency, requires entities to demonstrate compliance with the GDPR for all data processing, the creation of a new European Data Protection board, and more.

June

22nd – In *Carpenter v. United States*, the U.S. Supreme Court held that the Fourth Amendment protects location records generated by mobile phones. The government had obtained more than 6 months of location records without a warrant. The Court held that "an individual maintains a legitimate expectation of privacy in the record of his physical movements as captured through" a cell phone.

28th – State of California enacted the California Consumer Privacy Act of 2018, the most comprehensive consumer privacy state law ever enacted in the U.S. The Act established Californians' right to know what data about them is being collected, whether their information is sold or disclosed and to whom, to limit the sale, and more. The Act also allowed individuals to delete their data, established opt-in consent for children, provided for enforcement by the Attorney General, and created a private right of action.

July

5th – The European Parliament passed a resolution calling for the suspension of the Privacy Shield if the U.S. does not comply in full by September 1, 2018. The resolution citied numerous privacy concerns, including the Cambridge Analytica breach, reauthorization of FISA Section 702, and passage of the CLOUD Act.

September

13th – In *Big Brother Watch v. UK*, the European Court of Human Rights ruled that the UK's surveillance regime violated the right to privacy because there were "inadequate" safeguards for selecting the data subject to surveillance and violated the right of free expression.

26th – A ruling by the Indian Supreme Court imposed new limits on Aadhar, India's national biometric identification system. The Court found the system did not violate the Indian Constitution, but struck down a sections of the law permitting private entities to demand Aadhar to verify identity and authorizing disclosure of Aadhar data for national security purposes. The state-issued number may still be required for purposes related to government funds, including filing an income tax.

26th – The U.S. National Telecommunications and Information Administration, the agency that advises the White House on telecommunications and information policy, released a proposed framework for consumer privacy. The NTIA framework outlines seven "desired outcomes" for the processing of personal data: (1) transparency, (2) control, (3) minimization, (4) security, (5) access and correction, (6) risk management, and (7) accountability.

2019

January

17th – EPIC and 16 organizations outlined a new approach to privacy protection "A Framework for Privacy Protection in the United States": (1) enact baseline federal legislation; (2) enforce fair information practices; (3) establish a data protection agency; (4) ensure robust enforcement; (5) establish algorithmic governance; (6) prohibit "take it or leave it" terms; (7) promote privacy innovation; and (8) limit government access to personal data.

22nd – The European Commission adopts the first mutual adequacy decision with Japan, allowing for free data transfer between the two regions.

February

7th – Germany's competition agency imposed restrictions on Facebook's practice of combining user data from across platforms, such as WhatsApp and Instagram, and prohibited the company from linking third-party data to specific Facebook user accounts. The agency President said, "Today data are a decisive factor in competition. In the case of Facebook they are the essential factor for establishing the company's dominant position."

8th – The U.S. Privacy and Civil Liberties Oversight Board held the first public forum since regaining a quorum.

Privacy Resources
Agencies

11th – President Trump signed the Executive Order on Maintaining American Leadership in Artificial Intelligence.

26th – European Data Protection Supervisor Giovanni Buttarelli released the 2018 EDPS annual report, featuring recent accomplishments such as the 2018 Conference on Digital Ethics, adoption of an EU-Japanese data transfer deal, and implementation of the GDPR.

27th – TikTok settled with the FTC for $5.7 million over allegations that the Chinese video app company violated the Children's Online Privacy Protection Act. The FTC complaint alleged that TikTok violated COPPA by collecting personal information from kids without parental consent.

March

5th – Reports emerge that the NSA shut down the broad based collection of call metadata under Section 215 of the Patriot Act.

April

8th – The European Commission's Expert Group on Artificial Intelligence released Guidelines for Trustworthy AI. The EU Guidelines identify seven principles for ethical AI: (1) Human agency and oversight; (2) Robustness and safety; (3) Privacy and data governance (4) Transparency; (5) Diversity, non-discrimination and fairness; (6) Societal and environmental well-being; and (7) Accountability.

May

10th – For the first time, the United Nations Human Rights Committee asked the U.S. to report about consumer privacy protections as a part of the periodic review of compliance with the International Covenant on Civil and Political Rights.

15th – The San Francisco Board of Supervisors passed a resolution to limit the use of surveillance technology by city departments. San Francisco now requires surveillance impact reports, annual audits, and review by the city controller.

22nd – The OECD announced The Principles on Artificial Intelligence, the first intergovernmental standard on AI , with the backing of 42 countries. The OECD AI principles make central "the rule of law, human rights and democratic values" and set out requirements for fairness, accountability and transparency.

June

12th – The European Union established a comprehensive set of drone rules for drone operators. The EU drone rules require the real-time broadcasting of certain data, including the drone operator registration number, the geographical position of the drone, the drone route course, and the position of the drone operator.

24th – In *Food Marketing Institute v. Argus Leader Media*, the Supreme Court narrowed public access to government documents by expanding the definition of "confidential" information. The 6-3 decision by Justice Gorsuch overturned four decades of caselaw which held that a company must show substantial competitive harm to block an open government request.

26th – The U.S. Supreme Court blocked the citizenship question from inclusion on the 2020 Census *in Department of Commerce v. New York*. The Court ruled that the Commerce Department's decision to collect citizenship data "cannot be adequately explained" by the rationale provided by the agency.

July

3rd – A coalition of consumer groups, including EPIC, wrote to Congress calling for an end to Facebook's Libra plan, a blockchain currency proposed by a Facebook and an association of companies. The groups identified "profound questions" about governance, national sovereignty, law enforcement, consumer protection, privacy, competition and systemic risk.

24th – The FTC announced a settlement with Facebook for the disclosure of 87 million users records to Cambridge Analytica, a data mining firm that sought to influence the 2016 presidential election. The settlement included a $5 billion fine, prohibits misrepresentations, requires clear disclosure and consent for data sharing that overrides user privacy settings, requires that data users deletes cannot be accessed by third parties or Facebook, and other requirements.

29th – In *Fashion ID v Verbraucherzentrale NRW*, the Court of Justice for the European Union ruled websites embedding the Facebook "like" button are jointly responsible with Facebook for compliance with Europe's data protection rules.

August

3rd – Following an investigation by a German data protection agency, Google has suspended Assistant for a three-month period. The DPA found Google was recording and transcribing private conversations for examination by Google contractors.

September

4th – The FTC announced a settlement with YouTube and parent company Google of $170 million to settle claims that they violated the Children's Online Privacy Protection Act. The settlement required the companies to have channel owners identify children's content, comply with COPPA, and notify channel owners their content may be subject to COPPA

25th – In *Google v. CNIL*, the Court of Justice for the European Union ruled Google is not required to apply Europeans' requests to de-reference search results globally. The Court also stated that national authorities, in some circumstances, could require global delisting.

October

3rd – The Court of Justice for the European Union ruled that member states may order internet providers to remove globally content found to be defamatory. In *Eva Glawischnig-Piesczek v Facebook* Ireland, the Court ruled that the e-Commerce directive does not prohibit orders to remove content from all domains globally that is identical or equivalent to content found to be defamatory.

3rd – The US and UK signed a CLOUD Act "executive agreement," permitting direct cross-border requests by law enforcement agencies to communications content.

8th – California Governor Gavin Newsom signed The Body Camera Accountability Act to ban the use of facial-recognition technology in law enforcement body cameras.

23rd – A declaration from the Public Voice called for a moratorium on the further deployment of facial recognition, gathering the support of more than 60 organizations and many leading experts in 30 countries around the world. The declaration calls on countries to (1) suspend the further deployment of facial recognition for mass surveillance; (2) review all facial recognition systems to determine whether personal data was obtained lawfully; (3) undertake research to assess bias and risk; and (4) establish legal rules, technical standards, and ethical guidelines before further deployment occurs.

November

5th – Representatives Eshoo and Lofgren introduced the Online Privacy Act, a comprehensive framework for data protection in the United States. The bill would establish a data protection agency, is based on Fair Information Practices, and includes a provision on algorithmic accountability.

7th – The International Grand Committee on Fake News and Disinformation, meeting in Dublin, Ireland agreed principles to advance the global regulation of social media.

AGENCIES

Angola

Ministro das Telecomunicações e das
Tecnologias de Informação
www.mtti.gov.ao

Argentina

Agncia Nacional de Protección de Datos
Personales
Av. Pte. Gral. Julio A. Roca 710 . Piso 2º
Ciudad Autónoma de Buenos Aires,
Argentina
5411-2821-0047
http://www.jus.gob.ar/datos-
personales.aspx/

Australia

Office of the Australian Information
Commissioner
Level 3
175 Pitt Street
Sydney NSW 2000, Australia
1300-363-992 (within Australia)
61 2 9284 9749 (outside Australia)
https://www.oaic.gov.au

Austria

Österreichische Datenschutzbehörde
Wickenburggasse 8
1080 Wien
43 1 52 152-0
dsb@dsb.gv.at

Belgium

Commission for the Protection of Privacy
Rue de la Presse 35
1000 Brussels

32 (0)2 274 48 00
commission@privacycommision.be
https://www.privacycommission.be

Bosnia and Herzegovina

Personal Data Protection Agency in
Bosnia and Herzegovina
Dubrovačka br. 6
71000 Sarajevo, Bosnia and Herzegovina
387 33 726 250
azlpinfo@azlp.ba
www.azlp.gov.ba

Brazil

Brazilian Internet Steering Committee
Av. das Nações Unidas, 11541, 7º andar
04578-000 - São Paulo – SP
55 11 5509 3511
info@cgi.br
www.cgi.br

Bulgaria

Personal Data Protection Commission
2 Professor Tsvetan Larazog
Sofia 1592, Bulgaria
02 / 91-53-518
www.cpdp.bg
kzld@cpdp.bg

Canada

Office of the Privacy Commissioner of
Canada
30, Victoria Street
Gatineau, Quebec
K1A 1H3
1-800-282-1376
819-994-5444
https://www.priv.gc.ca/en/?

Cape Verde

Comissão Nacional de Proteção de Dados
Pessoais
Avenida China
Rampa Terra Branca
Praia, Santiago
CaboVerde
238 5340390
cnpd@cnpd.cv
www.cnpd.cv

Croatia

Croatian Personal Data Protection Agency
Martićeva ulica 14
HR - 10 000 Zagreb
00385 (0)1 4609-000
azop@azop.hr
www.azop.hr

Cyprus

Office of the Commissioner for Personal
Data Protection
Iasonos str. 1,
1082 Nicosia
357 22818456
commissioner@dataprotection.gov.cy
www.dataprotection.gov.cy

Czech Republic

Office for Personal Data Protection
Pplk. Sochora 27
170 00 Praha 7, Czech Republic
420 234 665 111
https://www.uoou.cz/en

Denmark

Datatilsynet
Borgergade 28, 5.

1300 København K
45 33 19 32 00
dt@datatilsynet.dk
www.datatilsynet.dk

Estonia

Estonian Data Protection Inspectorate
19 Väike-Ameerika St.
10129 Tallinn, Estonia
372 627 4135 (international calls)
http://www.aki.ee/en

Finland

Office of Data Protection Ombudsman
Ministry of Justice
Ratapihantie 9, 6th floor
00520 Helsinki, Finland
358 29 56 16670
tietosuoja@om.fi
http://www.tietosuoja.fi/en/index.html

France

Commission Nationale de l'Informatique
et des Libertés
3 Place de Fontenoy
75007 Paris, France
Tel: +33 (0)1.53.73.22.22
www.cnil.fr

Germany

Die Bundesbeauftragte für den
Datenschutz und die Informationsfreiheit
Husarenstr. 30
53117 Bonn
+49 (0)228-997799-0
poststelle@bfdi.bund.de
http://www.bfdi.bund.de/

Privacy Resources
Agencies

Ghana

Data Protection Commission
4th Floor, Ramia House
No. E1 35/2
Kojo Thompson Road, Adabraka.
P.O.Box CT7195, Accra
233-(0)30 2222 929
info@ataprotection.org.gh
www.dataprotection.org.gh

Gibraltar

Data Protection Commissioner
Gibraltar Regulatory Authority
2nd floor
Eurotowers 4,
1 Europort Road, Gibraltar.
(350) 200 74636
info@gra.gi
www.gra.gi

Greece

Hellenic Data Protection Authority
Kifissias 1-3, 115 23
Athens, Greece
30 210 6475600
contact@dpa.gr
www.dpa.gr

Hong Kong

Privacy Commissioner for Personal Data
12/F, Sunlight Tower,
248 Queen's Road East,
Wanchai,Hong Kong
2827 2827
enquiry@pcpd.org.hk
https://www.pcpd.org.hk/

Hungary

Hungarian National Authority for Data
Protection and Freedom of Information
H-1125 Budapest
Szilágyi Erzsébet fasor 22/C.
36 (1) 391-1400
privacy@naih.hu
www.naih.hu

Iceland

Persónuvernd
Rauðarárstíg 10
105 Reykjavík , Iceland
510 9600
postur@personuvernd.is
http://www.personuvernd.is

Ireland

Data Protection Commissioner
Canal House, Station Road
Portarlington
Co. Laois, R32 AP23
353 (0761) 104 800
info@dataprotection.ie
www.dataprotection.ie

Israel

Privacy Protection Authority
Tel Aviv Government Complex, P.O.
BOX 7360, Tel-Aviv, Israel 6107202
ppa@justice.gov.il
www.gov.il/en/Departments/the_privacy_
protection_authority

Italy

Italian Data Protection Authority
Piazza di Monte Citorio
121 – 00186 Roma
39-06-6967 71
www.granteprivacy.it

Japan

Personal Info. Protection Commission
Kasumigaseki Common Gate West Tower
32nd Floor 3-2-1
Kasumigaseki, Chiyoda-ku, Tokyo,
100-0013, Japan
81-(0)3-6457-9680
www.ppc.go.jp/en/

Latvia

Data State Inspectorate
Blaumana Street 11/13-11
Riga, LV-1011
Latvia
info@dvi.gov.lv
http://www.dvi.gov.lv/en/
371 67 23 31 31

Luxembourg

National Commission for Data Protectoin
1, avenue du Rock'n'Roll
L-4361 Esch-sur-Alzette
352 26 10 60-1
cnpd.public.lu/en.html

Lithuania

The State Data Protection Inspectorate
A. Juozapavičiaus g. 6
LT-09310 Vilnius, Lithuania
271 2804 279 1445
mail ada@ada.lt
www.ada.lt

Macau

Office for Data Protection
Avenida da Praia Grande
n.º 804 , Edifício "China Plaza"
17.º andar, Macau
853 2871 6006
www.gpdp.gov.mo

Macedonia

Directorate for Personal Data Protection
Bulevar Goce Delcev 18
1000, Skopje, R.Macedonia
389 (2) 3230 635
www.dzlp.mk/en/node/46

Malaysia

Department of Personal Data Protection
Aras 6, Kompleks Kementerian
Komunikasi dan Multimedia,
Lot 4G9, Persiaran Perdana, Presint 4
Pusat Pentadbiran Kerajaan Persekutuan
62100 Putrajaya, Malaysia.
03-8000 8000
webmaster@pdp.gov.my
www.pdp.gov.my

Malta

Office of the Information and Data
Protection Commissioner
Second Floor, High Street
Sliema SLM 1549
356 2328 7100
idpc.org.mt

Mauritius

Data Protection Office
5th Floor, SICOM Tower
Wall Street
Ebène, Mauritius
Tel: +230 212 22 18
dpo@govmu.org
www.dataprotection.govmu.org

Privacy Resources
Agencies

Mexico

Instituto Nacoinal de Transparencia,
Accesso a la Información y Protección de
Datos Personales
Insurgentes Sur # 3211
Colonia Insurgentes Cuicuilco
Delegación Coyoacán, C.P. 04530
Ciudad de México.
01 800 835 43 24
www.inicio.ifai.org.mx

Monaco

Commission de Contrôle des Informations
Nominatives

12, Avenue de Fontvieille
98000 – Monaco
337 92 70 22 44
ccin@ccin.mc
www.ccin.mc

Montenegro

Agency for the Protection of Personal
Data and the Free Access to Information
Bulevar Svetog Petra Cetinjskog br. 147
382 20 634 883
azlp@t-com.me
www.azlp.me

Morocco

La Commission Nationale de contrôle de
la protection des Données à Caractère
Personnel
Angle Boulevard Annakhil et Avenue
Mehdi ben Barka, Immeuble Les Patios
3ème ètage Ha Riad – Rabat, Morocco
212 537 57 11 24
contact@cndp.ma
www.cndp.ma

Netherlands

Dutch Data Protection Authority
Autoriteit Persoonsgegevens
Postbus 93374
2509 AJ DEN HAAG
31-(0)70- 888 85 00
autoriteitpersoonsgegevens.nl

New Zealand

Office of the Privacy Commissioner
Level 8, 109 – 111 Featherston Street
Wellington 6011
(04) 474 7590
https://www.privacy.org.nz

Norway

Datatilsynet
Tollbugata 3
0152 Oslo, Norway
22 39 69 00
postkasse@datatilsynet.no
https://www.datatilsynet.no

Peru

The General Agency on Data Protection
Scipión Llona N° 350, Miraflores
Lima, Peru
511 204 8020
http://www.minjus.gob.pe/proteccion%20
datos%20personales/

Poland

Generalny Inspektor Ochrony Danych
Osobowych
ul. Stawki 2
00-193 Warsaw, Poland
22 531 03 00
http://www.giodo.gov.pl

Portugal

Comissão Nacional de Protecção de
Dados
Av. D. Carlos I, 134 - 1.°
1200-821 Lisboa
351 21 392 8400
https://www.cnpd.pt

Romania

National Supervisory Authority for
Personal Data Processing
B-dul G-ral. Gheorghe Magheru 28-30
Sector 1, postal code 010336
Bucuresti, Romania
40 318 059 211
www.dataprotection.ro

Russia

Federal Service for Supervision of
Communications, Information
Technologies and Mass Media
Build. 2, 7, Kitaigorodskiy proezd
Moscow, 109074
7 495 987 6800
www.rsoc.ru/

Serbia

Commissioner for Information of Public
Importance and Personal Data Protection
15 Bulevar Kralja Alksandra str
Belgrade 11000
381 11 3408 900
www.poverenik.rs

Singapore

Personal Data Protection Commission
10 Pasir Panjang Road
#03-01 Mapletree Business City
Singapore 117438
65 6508 7333
www.pdpc.gov.sg

Slovak Republic

Office for the Protection of Personal Data
of the Slovak Republic
Hraničná 12
820 07 Bratislava 27
Slovak Republic
421 2 32313214
statny.dozor@pdp.gov.sk
dataprotection.gov.sk

Spain

Agencia Española de Protección de datos
Calle de Jorge Juan, 6
28001 Madrid, Spain
901 100 099
www.agpd.es

Sweden

Datainspektionen
Drottninggatan 29, 5th floor
Stockholm
08-657 61 00
datainspektionen@datainspektionen.se
www.datainspektionen.se

Switzerland

Federal Data Protection and Information
Commissioner
Feldeggweg 1
CH - 3003 Berne
41 (0)58 462 43 95
www.edoeb.admin.ch

Taiwan

The Ministry of Justice
130, Sec 1 Chung Ching S. Rd,
Taipei City, ROC
886-2-21910189
www.moj.gov.tw

Privacy Resources
Agencies

United Kingdom

Information Commissioner's Office

Wycliffe House

Water Lane,Wilmslow, Cheshire

SK9 5AF

0303 123 1113

ico.org.uk

Uruguay

Unidad Reguladora y de Control de Datos
Personales

Liniers 1324, 4th floor, Montevideo,
Uruguay

2901 00 65 option 3

infourcdp@datospersonales.gub.uy

www.datospersonales.gub.uy

NATIONAL LEGISLATION

References

PrivacyExchange, Index of National Law
[http://www.privacyexchange.org/legal/nat/omni/nol.html]

Privacy International, Country Reports
[https://www.privacyinternational.org/reports]

Albania

Law on the Protection of Personal Data (No. 9887 dated 10.03.2008)
https://www.afapdp.org/wp-content/uploads/2018/05/Albanie-Loi-n°-9887-sur-la-protection-
des-donnees-personnelles-2008.pdf

Andorra

Law on the Protection of Personal Data (Law no. 15/2003)
https://www.apda.ad/system/files/1-
%20%28FR%29%20Llei%20qualificada%20de%20protecció%20de%20dades%20personals.
pdf

Angola

Data Protection Law (Law no.22/11)
http://www.mtti.gov.ao/verlegislacao.aspx?id=457

Electronic Communications and Information Society Services Law (Law no. 23/11)
http://www.mtti.gov.ao/verlegislacao.aspx?id=456

Antigua and Barbuda

Data Protection Act of 2013
http://laws.gov.ag/acts/2013/a2013-10.pdf

Argentina

Argentina Personal Data Protection Act
http://unpan1.un.org/intradoc/groups/public/documents/un-dpadm/unpan044147.pdf

Armemia

Law of the Republic of Armenia on the Protection of Personal Data
http://www.legislationline.org/download/action/download/id/5317/file/Armenia_Law_on_per
sonal_data_2002_am2012_en.pdf

Privacy Resources
National Legislation

Australia

Privacy Act 1988

https://www.legislation.gov.au/Details/C2016C00838

Austria

Data Protection Act 2018 (*Datenschutzgesetz, DSG*)
https://www.ris.bka.gv.at/Dokumente/Erv/ERV_1999_1_165/ERV_1999_1_165.pdf

Azerbaijan

Law on Personal Data

http://www.mincom.gov.az/qanunvericilik/qanunlar/

Bahamas

Data Protection Act

http://laws.bahamas.gov.bs/cms/images/LEGISLATION/PRINCIPAL/2003/2003-
0003/DataProtectionPrivacyofPersonalInformationAct_1.pdf

Bahrain

Bahrain's Personal Data Protection Law (PDPL) (Law No. (30) of 2018)

Barbados

Data Protection Act

http://unpan1.un.org/intradoc/groups/public/documents/TASF/UNPAN024631.pdf

Belarus

Law on Information, Informatisation and Information Protection of 10 November 2008 No. 455
Z

http://www.e-belarus.org/docs/informationlawdraft.html

Belgium

Act of 30 July 2018 on the protection of natural persons with regard to the processing of their
personal data

Benin

Loi n°2009-09 du 22 mai 2009 portant organisation de la protection des données à caractère
personnel
http://www.cdp.sn/sites/default/files/doc/LOI_2009_09_PROTECTION_DES_DONNEES_P
ERSONNELLES_benin.pdf

Bolivia

Ley general de Telecomunicaciones, Tecnologías de Información y Comunicación

http://www.wipo.int/edocs/lexdocs/laws/es/bo/bo052es.pdf

Bosnia and Herzegovina

Law on the Protection of Personal Data

http://www.azlp.gov.ba/propisi/Default.aspx?id=5&pageIndex=1&langTag=en-US

Brazil

General Data Protection Law of 2018

https://iapp.org/media/pdf/resource_center/Brazilian_General_Data_Protection_Law.pdf

Bulgaria

Law for the Protection of Personal Data

https://www.cpdp.bg/en/?p=element&aid=373

Burkina Faso

Loi n° 010-2004/AN Portant Protection des Données à Caractère Personnel

https://www.afapdp.org/wp-content/uploads/2012/01/Burkina-Faso-Loi-portant-protection-des-données-à-caractère-personnel-20042.pdf

Canada

The Personal Information Protection and Electronic Documents Act (2000)

http://laws-lois.justice.gc.ca/eng/acts/P-8.6/index.html

Cape Verde

Data Protection Act, law 133/V/2001

http://www.cnpd.cv/leis/DATA%20PROTECTION%20Law%20133.pdf

Chad

Law 007/PR/2015 on the Protection of Personal Data

Chile

Law for the Protection of Private Life of 1999

https://www.leychile.cl/Navegar?idNorma=141599

China

Cybersecurity Law of the People's Republic of China 2016

https://www.newamerica.org/cybersecurity-initiative/digichina/blog/translation-cybersecurity-law-peoples-republic-china/

Privacy Resources
National Legislation

Colombia

Law 1266 of 2008- Habeas Data Act

http://media.mofo.com/docs/mofoprivacy/LEY_HABEAS_DATA_ing.pdf

Costa Rica

Ley de Protección de la Persona frente al tratamiento de sus datos personales, N° 8968

http://www.archivonacional.go.cr/pdf/ley_8968_proteccion_datos_personales.pdf

Côte d'Ivoire

Loi n° 2013-450 du 19 juin 2013 relative à la protection des données à caractère personnel

http://media.mofo.com/files/PrivacyLibrary/3979/Cote-d-voire-loi_2013_450.pdf

Croatia

Croatian Law on Implementation of General Data Protection Regulation (Cro. Zakon o provedbi Opće uredbe o zaštiti podataka)

Cyprus

Protection of Physical Persons Against the Processing of Personal Data and Free Movement of such Data Law 125(I)/2018

http://www.dataprotection.gov.cy/dataprotection/dataprotection.nsf/2B53605103DCE4A4C22 5826300362211/$file/Law%20125(I)%20of%202018%20ENG%20final.pdf

Czech Republic

Act No. 101/2000 Coll., on the Protection of Personal Data and on Amendment to Some Acts

https://www.uoou.cz/en/vismo/zobraz_dok.asp?id_ktg=1107

Denmark

Danish Data Protection Act (2018)

https://www.datatilsynet.dk/media/6894/danish-data-protection-act.pdf

Dominican Republic

Ley No. 172-13, sobre Protección de Datos de Carácter Personal del 13 de diciembre de 2013

http://www.redipd.org/legislacion/common/legislacion/rep_dominicana/Ley_172_13_Protecci on_Datos_Caracter_Personal.pdf

Estonia

Personal Data Protection Act 2018

https://www.riigiteataja.ee/en/eli/523012019001/consolide

Finland

Data Protection Act of Finland (*Tietosuojalaki*)

https://www.finlex.fi/en/laki/kaannokset/2018/en20181050.pdf

France

LAW n ° 2018-493 of June 20, 2018 on to the protection of the personal data

https://www.legifrance.gouv.fr/affichTexte.do;jsessionid=985D7411D55F795FEA6B5F9C48

5F9417.tplgfr24s_3?cidTexte=JORFTEXT000037085952&dateTexte=20180621

Decree No. 2018-687 of 1 August 2018 adopted for the application of Law No. 78-17 of 6 January 1978 relating to data, files and freedoms, as amended by Law No. 2018-493 of 20 June 2018 on the protection of personal data

https://www.legifrance.gouv.fr/affichTexte.do;jsessionid=371DEAE83DB1CB49543E60B3D

E9B2EC6.tplgfr26s_2?cidTexte=JORFTEXT000037277401&dateTexte=

Gabon

Loi n°001/2011 relative à la protection des données à caractère personnel

https://www.afapdp.org/wp-content/uploads/2012/01/Gabon-Loi-relative-à-la-protection-des-

données-personnelles-du-4-mai-20112.pdf

Gambia

Information and Communications Act No. 2 of 2009

http://www.wipo.int/wipolex/en/text.jsp?file_id=238413

Georgia

Law of Georgia on Personal Data Protection

https://matsne.gov.ge/en/document/download/1561437/7/en/pdf

Germany

Federal Data Protection Act of 2017 (*Bundesdatenschutzgesetz* – 'BDSG')

https://iapp.org/media/pdf/resource_center/Eng-trans-Germany-DPL.pdf

Ghana

Data Protection Act (Act 843)

https://www.dataprotection.org.gh/sites/default/files/Data%20Protection%20Act%20%2C%2

02012%20%28Act%20843%29.pdf

Gibraltar

Data Protection Act 2004

Privacy Resources
National Legislation

http://www.gibraltarlaws.gov.gi/articles/2004-01o.pdf

Greece

Law on the Protection of Individuals with regard to the Processing of Personal Data 1997
http://www.legislationline.org/documents/action/popup/id/6961

Honduras

Anteproyecto de Ley de Protección de Datos Personales y Acción de Hábeas Data de Honduras
https://cei.iaip.gob.hn/doc/Anteproyecto%20de%20Ley%20de%20Proteccion%20de%20Dato
s%20Personales%20y%20Accion%20de%20Habeas%20Data%20de%20Honduras%20%20F
inal%2021%2001%2014.pdf

Hong Kong

Personal Data (Privacy) Ordinance
http://www.legislation.gov.hk/blis_pdf.nsf/4f0db701c6c25d4a4825755c00352e35/B4DF8B41
25C4214D482575EF000EC5FF/$FILE/CAP_486_e_b5.pdf

Hungary

Act CXII of 2011 on the Right of Informational Self-Determination and on Freedom of Information (as amended July 2018)

Iceland

Act No. 90/2018 on Data Protection and the Processing of Personal Data
https://www.althingi.is/lagas/nuna/2018090.html

India

Information Technology (Reasonable Security Practices and Procedures and Sensitive Personal Data or Information) Rules (Privacy Rules).
https://www.wipo.int/edocs/lexdocs/laws/en/in/in098en.pdf

Indonesia

Law of the Republic of Indonesia Number 11 of 2008 Concerning Electronic Information and Transactions
http://www.bu.edu/bucflp-fig/files/2012/01/Law-No.-11-Concerning-Electronic-Information-and-Transactions.pdf

Ireland

Data Protection Act (2018)
http://www.irishstatutebook.ie/eli/2018/act/7/enacted/en/html

Israel

Protection of Privacy Law (1981)

http://www.wipo.int/wipolex/en/text.jsp?file_id=347462

Italy

Legislative Decree 101/2018

https://www.gazzettaufficiale.it/atto/serie_generale/caricaDettaglioAtto/originario?atto.dataPubblicazioneGazzetta=2018-09-04&atto.codiceRedazionale=18G00129&elenco30giorni=false

Japan

Act on the Protection of Personal Information

http://www.cas.go.jp/jp/seisaku/hourei/data/APPI.pdf

Kazakhstan

Law on personal data and their protection, 21 May 2013

http://www.ilo.org/dyn/natlex/natlex4.detail?p_lang=en&p_isn=96710&p_country=KAZ&p_count=7

Kuwait

Law No. 20 of 2014 concerning Electronic Transactions

http://www.ilo.org/dyn/natlex/docs/ELECTRONIC/99810/119249/F-546024079/kuw%201172%20(1).pdf

Kyrgyzstan

Law of the Kyrgyz Republic On Personal Data

http://media.mofo.com/docs/mofoprivacy/Kyrgyz_DPLaw_EN.pdf

Latvia

Personal Data Processing Law

Liechtenstein

Data Protection Act

http://regierung.gmgnet.li/files/medienarchiv/header/235_1_12_12_2016_en.pdf

Lithuania

Law on Legal Protection of Personal Data (2018)

https://e-seimas.lrs.lt/portal/legalAct/lt/TAP/952a77b0709011e8a76a9c274644efa9

Luxembourg

Law on the organization of the National Data Protection Commission (CNPD) (2018) https://cnpd.public.lu/dam-assets/fr/legislation/droit-lux/Act-of-1-August-2018-on-the-organisation-of-the-National-Data-Protection-Commission-and-the-general-data-protection-framework.pdf

Macau
Personal Data Protection Act
http://www.gpdp.gov.mo/uploadfile/2013/1217/20131217120421182.pdf

Madagascar
LOI N° 2014 – 038 Sur la protection des données à caractère personnel
https://www.afapdp.org/wp-content/uploads/2015/01/Madagascar-L-2014-038-du-09-01-15-sur-la-protection-des-données-à-caractère-personnel.pdf

Malaysia
Personal Data Protection Act 2010
http://www.kkmm.gov.my/pdf/Personal%20Data%20Protection%20Act%202010.pdf

Mali
Loi n° 2013-015 du 21 mai 2013
https://www.afapdp.org/wp-content/uploads/2012/01/Mali-Loi-sur-la-protection-des-données-personnelles-du-21-mai-2013.pdf

Macedonia
Law on Personal Data Protection
http://www.ceecprivacy.org/pdf/Law%20on%20Personal%20Data%20Protection.pdf

Malta
Data Protection Act 2018 (Act) (Chapter 586 of the Laws of Malta)
http://www.justiceservices.gov.mt/DownloadDocument.aspx?app=lom&itemid=12839&l=1
Mauritius
Data Protection Act 2017 (DPA 2017 or Act)
https://rm.coe.int/dpa-2017-maurice/168077c5b8

Mexico
Ley Federal de Protección de Datos Personales en Posesión de los Particulares
http://www.diputados.gob.mx/LeyesBiblio/pdf/LFPDPPP.pdf

Moldova
Law on Personal Data Protection
https://pd.rkn.gov.ru/authority/p146/p164/

Monaco

Act no. 1.165 on the Protection of Personal Data

https://www.ccin.mc/legislation/lois/act-1-165-on-the-protection-of-personal-data.pdf

Montenegro

Law on Personal Data Protection 2008

https://www.afapdp.org/wp-content/uploads/2012/01/Monténégro-Personal-Data-Protection-Law-79-08-and-70-09.pdf

Netherlands

Dutch GDPR Implementation Act (*Uitvoeringswet AVG*)

New Zealand

Privacy Act

http://www.legislation.govt.nz/act/public/1993/0028/latest/DLM296639.html

Nicaragua

Ley No. 787 Ley de Protección de Datos Personales

http://www.pgr.gob.ni/PDF/Constitucional/ley%20787.pdf

Norway

Norweigan Personal Data Act (2018)

Oman

Royal Decree no. 69 of 2008 - Electronic Transactions Law

http://www.cert.gov.om/library/information/Electronic%20Transactions%20Law%20English.pdf

Paraguay

Law for the Protection of Personal Data in the Private Sector

http://www.redipd.org/legislacion/common/legislacion/paraguay/Ley_1682_de_2001.pdf

Peru

Ley N° 29733 - Ley de Protección de Datos Personales

http://www.leyes.congreso.gob.pe/Documentos/Leyes/29733.pdf

Philippines

Republic Act No. 10173 - Data Privacy Act

https://privacy.gov.ph/data-privacy-act/

Privacy Resources
National Legislation

Poland

Personal Data Protection Act of 10 May 2018

https://uodo.gov.pl/data/filemanager_pl/757.pdf

Portugal

Portuguese Data Protection Law – Law nº. 67/98

https://www.cnpd.pt/english/bin/legislation/Law6798EN.HTM

Qatar

Law No. 13 of 2016 Concerning Privacy and Protection of Personal Data

https://qatarlaw.com/wp-content/uploads/2017/05/Personal-Data-Privacy-Law-No.-13-of-2016.pdf

Romania

Law no. 190/2018 on the measures for the application of Regulation (EU) 2016/679 of the European Parliament and of the Council of 27 April 2016 on the protection of natural persons with regard to the processing of personal data and on the free movement of such data, and repealing Directive 95/46/EC

https://www.dataprotection.ro/servlet/ViewDocument?id=1520

Russia

Federal Law of 27 July 2006 N 152-FZ on Personal Data

https://pd.rkn.gov.ru/authority/p146/p164/

Saint Lucia

Data Protection Act

http://slugovprintery.com/template/files/document_for_sale/laws/3547/Act%202%20of%202015.pdf

San Marino

Law n. 70: Act on Collection, Elaboration and Use of Computerised Personal Data 1995 (reforming Law n. 27 of 1 March 1983)

São Tomé and Príncipe

Data Protection Law 2016

Senegal

Loi n° 2008-12 sur la Protection des données à caractère personnel

http://www.wipo.int/wipolex/fr/text.jsp?file_id=181186

Serbia

Data Protection Law 2018 (No. 87/2018)

Seychelles

Data Protection Act 2003 (not in force)

https://seylii.org/sc/legislation/act/2002/9

Singapore

Personal Data Protection Act 2012

https://sso.agc.gov.sg/Act/PDPA2012

Slovakia

Act No. 18/2018 Coll. on the protection of personal data and on amending and supplementing certain acts

https://dataprotection.gov.sk/uoou/en/content/english-version-act-182018-personal-data-protection-and-amending-and-supplementing-certain

Slovenia

Personal Data Protection Act

https://www.ip-rs.si/fileadmin/user_upload/doc/ZVOP-1_in_ZVOP-1a__English_/Personal_Data_Protection_Act_of_Slovenia_status_2013_final_eng.doc

South Africa

Protection of Personal Information Act 4 of 2013 (POPIA)

http://www.justice.gov.za/inforeg/docs/InfoRegSA-POPIA-act2013-004.pdf

South Korea

Personal Information Protection Act

http://koreanlii.or.kr/w/images/0/0e/KoreanDPAct2011.pdf

Spain

Spanish Data Protection Act (Organic Law 3/2018)

Sweden

Data Protection Act (2018:218)

http://www.qcert.org/sites/default/files/public/documents/swe-privacy-personal_data_act-eng-1998.pdf

Switzerland

Federal Act on Data Protection

Privacy Resources
National Legislation

https://www.admin.ch/opc/en/classified-compilation/19920153/

Taiwan
Personal Information Protection Act
http://law.moj.gov.tw/Eng/LawClass/LawAll.aspx?PCode=I0050021

Trinidad and Tobago
Data Protection Act, 2011
http://www.ttparliament.org/legislations/a2011-13.pdf

Tunisia
Organic Act n°2004-63 of July 27th 2004 on the protection of personal data
https://media2.mofo.com/documents/The+Organic+Act+2004-63.pdf

Turkey
Data Protection Law 2016

Ukraine
Law on Personal Data Protection 2010 (as amended)
https://www.legislationline.org/.../id/.../Ukraine_law_protection_personal_data_2011_en.pdf

United Kingdom
The Data Protection Act 2018
http://www.legislation.gov.uk/ukpga/2018/12/pdfs/ukpga_20180012_en.pdf

Uruguay
Ley No 18.331 Protección de Datos Personales y Acción de Habeas Data
https://www.datospersonales.gub.uy/wps/wcm/connect/urcdp/f085d1b8-0a24-4070-9dad-adc87b7595f2/18.331_con_modificaciones_de_la_19.355..pdf?MOD=AJPERES&CONVERT_TO=url&CACHEID=f085d1b8-0a24-4070-9dad-adc87b7595f2

ORGANIZATIONS

US Organizations

American Civil Liberties Union
125 Broad Street, 18th Floor
New York, New York 10004-2400
212-549-2500
http://www.aclu.org/

The American Civil Liberties Union is the United States foremost advocate of individual rights -- litigating, lobbying, and educating the public on a broad array of issues affecting individual freedom in the United States.

Brennan Center for Justice
120 Broadway. Suite 1750
New York, NY 10271
646-292-8310
brennancenter@nyu.edu
http://www.brennancenter.org/

The Brennan Center for Justice at NYU School of Law is a nonpartisan law and policy institute that seeks to improve our systems of democracy and justice. We work to hold our political institutions and laws accountable to the twin American ideals of democracy and equal justice for all. The Center's work ranges from voting rights to campaign finance reform, from ending mass incarceration to preserving Constitutional protection in the fight against terrorism.

Center for Democracy and Technology
1401 K Street NW, Suite 200
Washington, DC 20005
202-637-9800
http://www.cdt.org/

The Center for Democracy and Technology works to support laws, corporate policies, and technology tools that protect the privacy of Internet users, and advocate for stronger legal controls on government surveillance.

Center for Digital Democracy
1015 15th Street, NW, #600
Washington, DC 20005
202-986-2220

Privacy Resources
Organizations

https://www.democraticmedia.org/

The Center for Digital Democracy (CDD) serves a vitally important mission protecting the privacy and welfare of the public in the "Big Data" digitally driven marketplace. CDD's work helps nonprofits, the news media, policymakers, and concerned citizens/consumers understand and address the online business practices that increasingly influence our lives.

Center on Privacy & Technology
Georgetown Law
600 New Jersey Ave. NW
Washington, DC 20001
202-662-9000
https://www.law.georgetown.edu/academics/centers-institutes/privacy-technology/

The Center on Privacy & Technology at Georgetown Law Center is a think tank focused on privacy and surveillance law and policy.

Consumer Federation of America
1620 I Street, NW, Suite 200
Washington, DC 20006
202-387-6121
cfa@consumerfed.org
http://consumerfed.org/

The Consumer Federation of America (CFA) is an association of non-profit consumer organizations that was established in 1968 to advance the consumer interest through research, advocacy, and education. Today, nearly 300 of these groups participate in the federation and govern it through their representatives on the organization's Board of Directors.

Electronic Frontier Foundation
815 Eddy Street
San Francisco CA 94109
415-436-9333
info@eff.org
https://www.eff.org/

Founded in 1990, EFF champions user privacy, free expression, and innovation through impact litigation, policy analysis, grassroots activism, and technology development. We work to ensure that rights and freedoms are enhanced and protected as our use of technology grows.

Electronic Privacy Information Center
1519 New Hampshire Ave. NW
Washington, DC 20037
202-483-1140
info@epic.org
http://www.epic.org/

EPIC is a public interest research center in Washington, DC. EPIC was established in 1994 to focus public attention on emerging privacy and civil liberties issues and to protect privacy, freedom of expression, and democratic values in the information age.

The Identity Project
1222 Preservation Park Way, Suite 200
Oakland, CA 94612
512-208-7744
info@papersplease.org
https://papersplease.org/wp/

IDP builds public awareness about the effects of ID requirements on fundamental rights. The First Amendment rights of assembly, petition, and speech, our fundamental right to travel, and our basic rights to hold property and transact business are all affected. IDP builds public awareness about the effects of ID requirements on fundamental rights. The First Amendment rights of assembly, petition, and speech, our fundamental right to travel, and our basic rights to hold property and transact business are all affected.

National Consumers League
1701 K Street, NW, Suite 1200
Washington, DC 20006
202-835-3323
info@nclnet.org
http://www.nclnet.org/

NCL provides government, businesses, and other organizations with the consumer's perspective on concerns including child labor, privacy, food safety, and medication information. The mission of the National Consumers League is to protect and promote social and economic justice for consumers and workers in the United States and abroad.

The National Consumers League is a private, nonprofit advocacy group representing consumers on marketplace and workplace issues. We are the nation's oldest consumer organization.

Privacy Resources
Organizations

Patient Privacy Rights
1006 Mopac Circle, Suite 102
Austin, TX 78746
512-732-0033
https://patientprivacyrights.org/

PPR's purpose is to honor and empower the individual's right to privacy through personal control of health information wherever such information is collected and used. PPR works to educate, collaborate and partner with people to ensure privacy in law, policy, technology, and maximize the benefits from the use of personal health information with consent.

Privacy Rights Clearinghouse
3033 5th Ave, Suite 223
San Diego, CA 92103
619-298-3396
admin@privacyrights.org
http://www.privacyrights.org/

The Privacy Rights Clearinghouse is a nonprofit consumer information and advocacy program. It offers consumers an opportunity to learn how to protect their personal privacy and publications that provide information on a variety of informational privacy issues, as well as practical tips on safeguarding personal privacy.

World Privacy Forum
3 Monroe Parkway, Suite P #148
Lake Oswego, OR 97035
760-712-4281
info@worldprivacyforum.org
https://www.worldprivacyforum.org/

The World Privacy Forum is a nonprofit, non-partisan 501(C)(3) public interest research group. The organization is focused on conducting in-depth research, analysis, and consumer education in the area of privacy. It is the only privacy-focused public interest research group conducting independent, original, longitudinal work.

International Organizations

Access Now
P.O. Box 20429
Greeley Square Station

4 East 27th Street
New York, NY 10001-9998
888-414-0100
info@accessnow.org
https://www.accessnow.org/

Access Now defends and extends the digital rights of users at risk around the world.

BEUC
The European Consumer Organisation
Rue d'Arlon, 80 Bte 1
B - 1040 Brussels, Belgium
32 2 743 15 90
http://www.beuc.eu/

BEUC, the European Consumers' Organisation, is the Brussels based fderation of independent national consumer organisations from all the Member States of the EU and from other European countries. BEUC's job is to try to influence, in the consumer interest, the development of EU policy and to promote and defend the interests of all European consumers.

Consumers International
Head Office
24 Highbury Crescent
London N5 1RX United Kingdom
Tel 44 171 226 6663
consint@consint.org
http://www.consumersinternational.org/

A worldwide non-profit federation of consumer organisations, dedicated to the protection and promotion of consumer interests.

European Data Protection Board
Rue Montoyer 30, B-1000 Brussels, Belgium
edpb@edpb.europa.eu
https://edpb.europa.eu/edpb_en

The European Data Protection Board (EDPB) is an independent European body, which contributes to the consistent application of data protection rules throughout the European Union, and promotes cooperation between the EU's data protection authorities. The EDPB is made up of representatives of the EU member states' data protection authorities and the

Privacy Resources
Organizations

European Data Protection Supervisor (EDPS). The EDPB is established by the EU's comprehensive privacy law, the General Data Protection Regulation (GDPR).

European Data Protection Supervisor
Rue Montoyer, 30 Brussels, Belgium
https://edps.europa.eu/

The European Data Protection Supervisor (EDPS) is the independent supervisory authority at EU level with responsibility for: monitoring the processing of personal data by the EU institutions and bodies, advising on policies and legislation that affect privacy, cooperating with similar authorities to ensure consistent data protection. The EDPS is a relatively new but increasingly influential independent supervisory authority, with responsibility for monitoring the processing of personal data by the EU institutions and bodies, advising on policies and legislation that affect privacy and cooperating with similar authorities to ensure consistent data protection.

European Digital Rights Initiative (EDRi)
12 Rue Belliard
1040 Brussels, Belgium
32 2 274 25 70
brussels@edri.org
http://www.edri.org/

European Digital Rights is an association in which existing European privacy and civil rights organizations work together in informing decision makers and the public about the upcoming threats to our privacy and civil rights. European Digital Rights will focus its activities towards developments in the European Union and the Council of Europe. European Digital Rights is seated in Brussels.

Human Rights Watch
350 Fifth Ave, 34th Floor
New York, NY 10118
212-290-4700
http://www.hrw.org/

Human Rights Watch is dedicated to protecting the human rights of people around the world. Web sites includes comprehensive information about human rights campaigns around the globe.

Privacy International
62 Britton Street
London, EC1M 5UY
United Kingdom
http://www.privacyinternational.org/

Privacy International is a human rights group formed in 1990 as a watchdog on surveillance by governments and corporations. PI is based in London, UK and has an office in Washington, D.C. PI has conducted campaigns in Europe, Asia and North America to counter abuses of privacy by way of information technology such as telephone tapping, ID card systems, video surveillance, data matching, police information systems, and medical records.

Global Privacy Assembly
Secretariat: Information Commissioner's Office
Wycliffe House, Water Lane
Wilmslow SK9 5AF
United Kingdom
secretariat[at]globalprivacyassembly.org
https://globalprivacyassembly.org

The International Conference of Data Protection and Privacy Commissioners, now referred to as the "Global Privacy Assembly." first met in 1979 and has been the premier global forum for data protection authorities for over four decades. The Assembly seeks to provide leadership at international level in data protection and privacy. It does this by connecting the efforts of about 130 privacy and data protection authorities from across the globe. The website provides many important resources, including resolutions adopted by data protection officials.

International Working Group on Data Protection in Telecommunications (IWGDPT)
Chair: Berlin Commissioner
An der Urania 4 – 10
10787 Berlin
Germany
mailbox@datenschutz-berlin.de
https://www.datenschutz-berlin.de/gremien.html#BerlinGroup

Privacy Resources
Organizations

The IWGDPT (also known as the "Berlin Group") was founded in 1983 at the initiative of the Berlin Commissioner for Data Protection, who chairs the Group. The Group adopts recommendations ("Common Positions" and "Working Papers") aimed at improving the protection of privacy in telecommunications. Membership of the Group includes representatives from Data Protection Authorities and other bodies of national public administrations, international organisations and scientists from all over the world.

PUBLICATIONS

US Publications

Access Reports, Inc.
1624 Dogwood Lane
Lychnburg, VA 24503
434-384-5334
hhammitt@accessreports.com
http://www.accessreports.com/

Law360 - Cybersecurity & Privacy
Portfolio Media, Inc.
111 West 19th Street, 5th Floor
New York, NY 10011
646-783-7100
https://www.law360.com/about/cybersecurity-privacy

EPIC Alert
Electronic Privacy Information Center (EPIC)
1519 New Hampshire Ave. NW
Washington, DC 20036
202-483-1140
https://www.epic.org/alert/subscription.html

International Publications

Computer Law & Security Report
Elsevier Advanced Technology
Radarwg 29
1043 NX Amsterdam
Netherlands
http://www.journals.elsevier.com/computer-law-and-security-review/

Privacy Resources
Publications

ISPI Clips
Institute for the Study of Privacy Issues
P.O. Box 201
Crofton, British Columbia
Canada, V0R 1R0
250-246-2784
ISPI@PrivacyNews.com
http://www.ispiclips.com

European Data Protection Law Review
Lexxion Verlagsgesellschaft mbH
Güntzelstr. 63 · 10717 Berlin
0049-30-814506-0
info@lexxion.eu
https://edpl.lexxion.eu/

Privacy Laws and Business
2nd Floor Monument House
215 Marsh Road
Pinner
Middx HA5 5NE
United Kingdom
44 20 8868 9200
Info@privacylaws.co.uk
http://www.privacylaws.com

Reports

Connected Cars Workshop: The Federal Trade Commission Staff Perspective (January 2018)
 https://www.ftc.gov/reports/connected-cars-workshop-federal-trade-commission-staff-
perspective

Cross-Device Tracking (January 2017)
https://www.ftc.gov/reports/cross-device-tracking-federal-trade-commission-staff-report-
january-2017

Privacy & Data Security Update (2016)
Federal Trade Commission Report (January 2017)
https://www.ftc.gov/reports/privacy-data-security-update-2016

Big Data: A tool for Inclusion or Exclusion? Understanding the Issues
Federal Trade Commission Report (January 2016)
https://www.ftc.gov/reports/big-data-tool-inclusion-or-exclusion-understanding-issues-ftc-report

Restoring Internet Freedom: FCC-FTC Memorandum of Understanding (December 2017)
https://www.ftc.gov/policy/cooperation-agreements/restoring-internet-freedom-fcc-ftc-memorandum-understanding

Consumer Data Privacy In A Networked World: A Framework for Protecting Privacy and Innovation (Consumer Privacy Bill of Rights)
The White House (February 2012)
https://www.whitehouse.gov/sites/default/files/privacy-final.pdf

Commercial Data Privacy and Innovation in the Internet Economy: A Dynamic Policy Framework
Department of Commerce (December 2010)
https://www.ntia.doc.gov/files/ntia/publications/iptf_privacy_greenpaper_12162010.pdf

Executive Order 13800 – Strengthening the Cybersecurity of Federal Networks and Critical Infrastructure (May 11, 2017)
https://www.whitehouse.gov/presidential-actions/presidential-executive-order-strengthening-cybersecurity-federal-networks-critical-infrastructure/

Privacy and Civil Liberties Oversight Board Enabling Statute
https://www.pclob.gov/library/42USC2000ee-PCLOB_Enabling_Statute-2.pdf

Report on the Surveillance Program Operated Pursuant to Section 702 of the Foreign Intelligence Surveillance Act
Privacy and Civil Liberties Oversight Board (July 2, 2014)
https://www.pclob.gov/library/702-Report.pdf

Report on the Telephone Records Program Conducted under Section 215 of the USA PATRIOT Act and on the Operations of the Foreign Intelligence Surveillance Court
Privacy and Civil Liberties Oversight Board (January 23, 2014)
https://www.pclob.gov/library/215-Report_on_the_Telephone_Records_Program.pdf

The right to privacy in the digital age, UN Doc. A/HRC/39/29 (Aug. 3, 2018),
https://www.ohchr.org/EN/HRBodies/HRC/RegularSessions/Session39/Pages/ListReports.as

WEBSITES

General Interest

Access Reports

http://www.accessreports.com

> *A biweekly newsletter covering the Freedom of Information Act, other federal open government statutes, and information policy issues on both the legislative and administrative level. It also covers case law development on open government issues in the states. Current trends and issues in privacy are also covered.*

EPIC Online Guide to Privacy Resources

https://epic.org/privacy/privacy_resources_faq.html

> *This site contains links to printed publications, US and international privacy sites, and electronic mailing lists and newsgroups. It also contains information about upcoming privacy related conference and events.*

EPIC Privacy Issues

http://www.epic.org/privacy/

> *EPIC's Privacy Issues page contains an A to Z list of topics relating to privacy, general privacy information, and hot topics as well as new resources relating to privacy.*

EPIC Bookstore

http://www.epic.org/bookstore/

> *At the EPIC Bookstore you will find all of EPIC's past and present publications on issues such as privacy, cryptography, free speech and consumer protection. You will also find links to a wide range of other books recommended by EPIC.*

Law of Information Privacy

http://www.epic.org/misc/gulc/

> *This site contains a description of the Law of Information Privacy course taught at Georgetown University. It contains links to recent privacy cases, privacy articles, and a bibliography of books on privacy and related topics.*

Privacy International - Investigation and Research

https://www.privacyinternational.org/how-we-fight/investigation-and-research

> *The Privacy International website provides the latest news on privacy issues. It contains a educational and explanatory documents, as well as in depth reports concerning privacy laws and individual privacy issues.*

The Privacy Journal

http://www.privacyjournal.net/

> *Privacy Journal is a monthly newsletter reporting on new technology and its impact on personal privacy. The site gives tips on how to protect privacy and provides an outline of Model Privacy Policies.*

Privacy Law and Society

http://privacylawandsociety.org

> *The Third Edition of Privacy Law and Society is the most comprehensive casebook on privacy law ever produced. The companion website provides updates on recent privacy law developments.*

Privacy Rights Clearinghouse Fact Sheets

https://www.privacyrights.org/Privacy-Rights-Fact-Sheets (in English)

https://www.privacyrights.org/espanol (in Spanish)

> *The site contains fact sheets about workplace privacy, overcoming the emotional impact of identity theft, privacy in Cyberspace, online shopping tips, protecting financial privacy, and much more.*

Schneier on Security

https://www.schneier.com

> *Bruce Schneier is an internationally renowned security technologist, called a "security guru" by The Economist. His influential newsletter "Crypto-Gram" and his blog "Schneier on Security" are read by over 250,000 people.*

Government

International Conference on Privacy and Data Protection Commissioners

https://icdppc.org

> *The ICDPPC is a forum for collaboration between privacy and data protection authorities around the world.*

The European Commission – "Protection of Personal Data"

https://ec.europa.eu/info/aid-development-cooperation-fundamental-rights/your-rights-eu/know-your-rights/freedoms/protection-personal-data_en

> *Information on data protection efforts in the EU.*

Federal Trade Commission - "Privacy, Identity & Online Security"

https://www.consumer.ftc.gov/topics/privacy-identity-online-security

Privacy Resources
Websites

The FTC Privacy page educates consumers and businesses about the importance of personal information privacy. It talks about FTC efforts, what they've learned, and what consumers can do to protect the privacy of their personal information.

Federal Trade Commission - "ID Theft"
http://www.consumer.gov/idtheft/
> *The FTC's ID Theft page includes resources on what to do if you are the victim of identity theft.*

Federal Trade Commission's National Do Not Call Registry
https://www.donotcall.gov
> *If you've had your dinner interrupted one too many times, this website dedicated to eradicating telemarketers' hold over your time may be for you. The National Do Not Call Registry allows consumers to put their phone number on a "do not call" list for telemarketers.*

Organization for Economic Cooperation and Development - Internet
http://www.oecd.org/internet/
> *The OECD's Internet Policy site offers extensive list of reports released by the OECD about workshops, conferences and activities regarding e-commerce and internet communications.*

United Nations Special Rapporteur on the right to privacy
http://www.ohchr.org/EN/Issues/Privacy/SR/Pages/SRPrivacyIndex.aspx
> *Information from the UN Special Rapporteur on the right to privacy.*

Legal

EUR-Lex: European Union Law
http://eur-lex.europa.eu
> *This site provides links to European treaties, legislation, case law, and documents of interest.*

Legal Information Institute
Cornell Law School
https://www.law.cornell.edu/
> *The Legal Information Institute provides access to constitutions and codes, court opinions, and law directories.*

Library of Congress
https://www.congress.gov/

> *Congress.gov provides extensive information about legislative activities. It contains Library of Congress Web links and information about the legislative process.*